INFORMATION SYSTEMS THROUGH COBOL

SECOND EDITION

Andreas S. Philippakis
Arizona State University

Leonard J. Kazmier
Arizona State University

McGRAW-HILL BOOK COMPANY   New York St. Louis San Francisco Auckland Bogotá
Düsseldorf Johannesburg London Madrid Mexico Montreal New Delhi Panama
Paris São Paulo Singapore Sydney Tokyo Toronto

Library of Congress Cataloging in Publication Data

Philippakis, Andreas S
  Information systems through COBOL.

  Includes index.
  1. Management information systems. 2. COBOL
(Computer program language) I. Kazmier, Leonard J.,
joint author. II. Title.
T58.6.P48 1978   658.4'03 77-11612
ISBN 0-07-049791-5

    4567890 DODO   83210

This book was set in Optima by Cobb/Dunlop Publisher Services
Incorporated. The editors were Julienne V. Brown and Peter D. Nalle;
the designer was Cobb/Dunlop Publisher Services Incorporated; the
production supervisor was Milton J. Heiberg. The cover was designed
by Edward Aho.
R. R. Donnelley & Sons Company was printer and binder.

To our wives
PATRICIA
LORRAINE

CONTENTS

PREFACE

COBOL (COmmon Business Oriented Language) has been adopted as the standard programming medium for administrative applications of the computer. The language has been continuously reviewed and modified under the sponsorship of the Conference on Data Systems Language (CODASYL), a working committee composed of representatives from major language users in industry and government as well as computer manufacturers.

This book has been developed for use as a basic text for college-level courses in information systems. COBOL is used as the programming language and as the vehicle by which the systems concepts discussed in this book are implemented. Reflective of the information systems orientation of this book, primary consideration is given to the concepts of data base systems and file processing. The description of data processing equipment is given minor consideration and is included only when such discussion enhances the coverage of systems concepts. An understanding of COBOL enables the student to implement, test, and apply the systems concepts included in this book, and it is for this reason that a substantial portion of this book is devoted to the study of this language.

As compared with the previous edition of this book, the present edition has been substantially reorganized so that students will be prepared to write complete COBOL programs much earlier. The concepts of *structured programming* have been incorporated throughout the text, resulting in an improvement in the readability and self-documenting feature of COBOL programs. Coverage has been expanded in the areas of data base concepts, structured programming, modular programs and subroutines, and the Report Writer feature of COBOL. On the other hand, based on responses from users of the first edition of this book, the coverage of simulation models has been deleted. Finally, the number of applications-oriented examples and exercises has been increased throughout the book, and a case study in sequential file processing has been added as a separate chapter.

The authors express their appreciation to Peter D. Nalle and Julienne V. Brown for their very capable supervision of this project as our editors. We extend thanks to several anonymous reviewers for their comments and recommendations in respect to this revision. Finally, without the able assistance of Beverly Lindskog timely completion of the manuscript for this revision would have been difficult.

Andreas S. Philippakis
Leonard J. Kazmier

ACKNOWLEDGMENT

Management
Information Systems

INTRODUCTION

The term *management information system (MIS)* refers to the data, equipment, and computer programs that are used to develop information for managerial use. Although organizations have always had some type of information system, the concept of a management information system places particular emphasis on the availability of organizational data and the ease with which the data can be analyzed and made meaningful for managerial decision making. Thus, the key ingredient in the concept of a management information system is the transformation of *data* into *information*.

The initial applications of computers to administrative tasks as contrasted to scientific computations were directed entirely toward reducing clerical costs associated with the routine processing of data, and it was in such a context that the term *data processing* was coined. Examples of such applications are the preparation of employee payroll and the billing function in an organization. The use of computers as clerical substitutes is now thoroughly established, and indeed it is difficult to imagine functions such as payroll being done in any other way in large organizations. But with the rapid technological advances and availability of computers there developed the realization that administrative applications of computers should extend beyond routine data processing functions. Thus, the management information systems concept is a direct outgrowth from the administrative data processing functions in an organization.

The development of a computer-based management information system requires the use of a programming language. COBOL (COmmon Business Oriented Language) was developed specifically for administrative data processing applications and has now become the principal language associated with the development of management information systems. For this reason, many of the chapters in this book are devoted to developing your knowledge of COBOL, while other chapters are concerned with the applications of the language to produce administrative information. Much of the knowledge which you will acquire through your reading is relatively detailed and sometimes complex. You will find that your learning will be enhanced by answering the *Review* items at the end of each section, and that your understanding will be improved by completing the *Exercises* presented at the end of each chapter.

REVIEW

1   The early applications of computers to administrative tasks were such that such applications can be called _____ systems.

data processing

2   The continued development of computer methods to develop information relevant to managerial decision making has led to the concept of the _____ _____ system.

management information

3   The programming language which has the widest applicability for data processing tasks and the development of management information systems is _____.

COBOL

ADMINISTRATIVE VERSUS SCIENTIFIC APPLICATIONS OF COMPUTERS

Administrative applications of computers share a number of characteristics which differentiate such applications from scientific computing. Data input typically is voluminous in administrative applications, and consists of numeric and nonnumeric data records of varying lengths. For example, a sales data record would generally include the name of the customer, the date, amount of purchase, the item description, and the like. In a retail business these sales data records can easily total in the thousands per week.

The processing of administrative data is characterized by the updating of files. Business activities are complex and require large files of data in order for the data processing system to be a fairly accurate reflection of those activities. Data files constitute a symbolic model of the activities taking place in an organization. Keeping this model current is the function of file updating. Input data is processed with respect to historical files in order to update the data in the files. For example, a bank maintains a file of its checking account customers which reflects the state of the bank's checking account function. When input data is accumulated in groups and is processed periodically, we have a *batch processing* system and the data files reflect the state of the activity as of a point in time. When input data is processed as each transaction occurs, the files reflect the current state of business activity, and we have a *real-time* system. File updating requires complex logic, because files contain a variety of data and the processing logic must foresee all possibilities that can arise. For instance, a payroll system is a very complex data processing task often requiring many labor-months of effort, even though at first glance it would seem a trivial matter involving simple arithmetic.

The output of administrative data processing is characterized by the production of reports which group and summarize data by meaningful catogories which correspond to various functions.

In contrast to administrative data processing, scientific computing is typically characterized by a relatively low volume of input, small or nonexisting files, less complex processing logic but extensive arithmetic manipulations, and more limited report production needs. It should be pointed out that some scientific applications are characterized by extremely large volumes of input. For example, off-shore oil exploration instruments often generate several million data items in just one day.

In computer systems, the term *software* refers to the set of computer programs that make such systems operational. In contrast, *hardware* refers to the physical components of computer systems. With respect to software, the needs associated with administrative data processing are particularly well served by COBOL as the programming language, as indicated in the preceding section of this chapter. The counterpart languages for scientific computation are FORTRAN (FORmula TRANslation) and ALGOL (ALGOrithmic Language). With respect to hardware, administrative applications of the computer are associated with an interest in high input and output speed and the availability of mass storage. In comparison with scientific applications, computational speed is less critical because such tasks represent only a small part of the data processing objective. Although some second-generation computers were specifically oriented toward either administrative or scientific applications in terms of hardware configuration, such distinctions were abandoned during the latter part of the 1960s. ("Computer generations" are described in the last section of the following chapter.) The flexible control features of current computer systems and the broad range of peripheral equipment which can be used in these systems makes it unnecessary to design different computer systems for different applications. In this sense, modern computer systems realistically can be called general-purpose computer systems.

REVIEW

1 As contrasted to scientific computing, administrative applications of computers typically involve a [high / low] volume of input, a [high / low] storage capacity requirement, a [high / low] number of calculations, and a [high / low] volume of output.

high; high; low; high

2 When data is accumulated and processed periodically, _____ processing is involved. When input data is processed as each transaction occurs, a _____ system is involved.

batch; real-time

3 The computer programs that constitute part of a computer system are called
_____. In contrast, the physical components of a computer system are
called _____.

software; hardware

ELEMENTS OF A COMPREHENSIVE INFORMATION SYSTEM

An information system in an ongoing organization is complex by the very nature
of communications processes in general and the fact that human interaction is
involved. In this section we consider the parts, or elements, that can be studied in
order to gain an understanding of how such systems function.

FORMAL VERSUS INFORMAL INFORMATION SYSTEMS

Every management information system exists in an environment which includes
social as well as physical processes. People are dynamic, flexible, and interacting
elements in the system. In the design of an information system we are concerned with
arranging an efficient flow of data and the conversion of data into information. In just
about every case, however, the formal design is supplemented by informal communications—the informal information system.

Management theorists have observed that there is always an informal organization
with its own communication system—often called the "grapevine." The flexibility of
this informal system makes it very efficient for disseminating short, terse descriptions
of significant events, such as the appointment of a new manager, a merger in the
offing, or the possibility that the plant will be closed for a period of time. The MIS
designer should take account of the presence of the informal information system
rather than attempt to ignore it.

People like the flexibility associated with informal systems. However, formal
management information systems need to be made inflexible in the sense that a given
communication form and channel is always followed under given circumstances. For
example, in a formal system a materials order would always be processed in a
designated way. In an informal system, on the other hand, we can rely on people's
memories of given events, as indicated by the following conversation:

"Say Bob, do you remember that fellow who was asking something about prices the
other day?"

"No, when?"

"Oh, about the middle of last week. You remember, he came in just before we went
to lunch."

"Yes, I do now. What about him?"

"Was it prices on brass bolts or steel bolts that he was concerned about?"

This kind of flexibility in an interactive interpersonal environment is useful as a
supplement to a formal management information system, but it should not be used in

lieu of such a system. If customer inquiries are an important aspect of the organizational activity, such inquiries should be recorded, indexed, and filed for later retrieval. In the long run this type of formality pays off. If Bob quits or if he has a bad day, the system will not break down because of him. On the other hand, nondocumentary information can also have great value. For example, if an executive has lunch with the "right" government official, he may get more information about the likely effect of a new ruling on import restrictions than any rationally planned information system could produce within the same time framework. We simply have to realize that much information that is extremely useful evolves out of the fluid developments of everyday life.

Thus, MIS design should complement informal information systems that are in themselves effective, rather than attempt to substitute for them. Often, systems analysts devise elaborate information systems and then complain that managers are ignoring the system. It may be that the information being produced is insignificant. For one thing, the information may have already been disseminated by an informal system. For another, it may not be the appropriate type of information. The really important information currently may not be that which is included in the labor cost efficiency report, but rather whether a particular contract on which we submitted a bid has been awarded, whether a consumer group has developed enough adverse publicity to force us to modify our product design, and the like.

DATA ENTRY

In addition to the informal information system, another element that can be studied in a comprehensive system concerns the entry of data into the information system. Data may be generated within a system or outside the system. Historically, information systems have dealt almost exclusively with internal data, as exemplified by the traditional orientation of accountants. Now firms are increasingly concerned with external data. For example, a company that manufactures and sells ballpoint pens in over a hundred countries around the world should be concerned about a number of areas of marketing-oriented data, such as literacy programs, educational trends, and local distribution systems. Corporate managers have come to realize that considerable benefits accrue for those who are aware of external developments. Arranging a merger with a company that has a complementary technology may be a much more profound step in terms of corporate success than minor improvements in internal efficiency. The recent trends in government actions which affect company policy, the activity of civic and consumer groups, and the selective addition and deletion of product lines have focused attention on the importance of external information.

Of course, data entering a formal information system must be documentary—it must be recorded in some permanent form. A telephone conversation is not documentary and thus is not part of a formal information system, even though such input is important in the total system. Conceptually, we must decide what data to enter into the formal system. Obviously, we cannot enter every input. In a manufacturing plant, for example, should we collect labor data on each worker every minute, every hour, every day, or as the worker changes tasks? Similar questions could be raised about the much more complex external environment. The data that enters the system ultimately determines the type of output for that system. An old data processing acronym that describes this relationship is GIGO—garbage in, garbage out.

Given that decisions have been made at the conceptual level regarding the data to be collected, at the implementation level data entry brings us to questions of source document design, data transcription, and source data equipment. Source documents, or forms, are important in all information systems, particularly since they all include at least some manual aspects. Forms design and control is a specialty in itself. Not only do large firms have forms experts of their own, but there are also major firms that design and produce business forms as their main product.

Associated with data entry, the term *data transcription* refers to recording data in another form. Normally, we transcribe from handwritten to machine-processable form. Costs of transcription are substantial and are mostly personnel costs. Assuring accuracy and efficiency of transcription is an important area of analysis and control in data processing centers. There is a variety of source data equipment, with the keypunch being just one of the available choices. Other equipment possibilities are optical readers, direct entry keyboards, and special inscribers. Such equipment is described and discussed in Chapter 2, "Data Processing Concepts."

The systems designer needs to consider the several factors concerned with data entry so that the system receives neither too much nor too little data, the data is recorded and transcribed accurately and with minimum cost, and the reports contain information that is both timely and important.

DATA STORAGE

Data that enter an information system must be stored for future use. Data storage involves decisions about the encoding of data, assignment of data to meaningful classes, and the organization of data in the form of files.

On the conceptual level, data is stored in related groupings of *records* which constitute the files of the system. The logical relations among the records of a file are indicated by the *file organization,* and this topic is treated at length in several sections of this book. The organization of data which is stored in a system is very important in terms of the ultimate availability of data at the right time, in the right place, and in the appropriate amounts.

At the physical level, data storage involves consideration of storage media, such as punched cards, magnetic tape, and magnetic disk. The choice of physical storage media is affected by factors associated with the subsequent accessibility of the data, as well as by factors associated with the process of storage as such.

DISSEMINATION OF INFORMATION

Every information system should provide for the automatic flow of data from storage to processing, from processing back to storage, and from processing (or storage) to user. Dissemination refers to the automatic channeling of information to users. The fact that a shipment has been delayed should be channeled to the office or offices that should be apprised of this fact. Analysis of dissemination paths involves analysis of user information needs: who needs to know what, and at what point in time. This is a very important and very difficult question. Yet it must be answered. How well or how poorly it is answered will determine whether users fail to obtain required information, obtain the information they need, or are flooded with irrelevant information.

INFORMATION RETRIEVAL

The final element of a comprehensive information system which we consider is information retrieval. Information needs are not static, and they are frequently also not predictable. A dissemination system cannot be designed to provide answers to questions that have not yet been asked. Yet, an effective MIS should provide for the possibility of answering new questions. Since such questions cannot all be anticipated, it is important that the file system be such that maximum flexibility is provided for using the stored data to generate different types of information. The hierarchical structure of data associated with the use of COBOL programming makes it possible to retrieve information in a variety of ways. The concept of the hierarchical structure of data is described in Chapter 3, "Programming Concepts and the COBOL Language."

REVIEW

1   Every information system includes an informal component as well as the formal system itself. In general, the informal system should be [eliminated and replaced by the formal system / used to supplement the formal system].

used to supplement the formal system

2   The informal communication network which exists in organizations is often referred to as the _____.

grapevine

3   Data which is entered into an information system may originate within the system itself or outside the system. Traditionally, information systems have been concerned primarily with [internal / external] data.

internal

4   The acronym GIGO suggest that [good / bad] data input leads to [good / bad] information output.

bad; bad

5   The use of punched cards to record data contained on sales invoices is an example of [data transcription / data processing].

data transcription

6   The fact that data can be kept on such media as punched cards, magnetic tape, or magnetic disk for subsequent use represents the element, or process, of data _____.

storage

7   The automatic channeling of information to the places in the organization where the information is needed is referred to as the _____ of information.

dissemination

8   The final element of a comprehensive information system which we considered is concerned with designing the system so that questions which have not yet been asked can be answered when the need arises. This is concerned with the flexibility of the information [output / retrieval] system.

retrieval

MANAGEMENT INFORMATION NEEDS

In terms of managerial level, we can conceive of there being at least three distinct levels of management in large organizations: the top or corporate level, the general or executive management level, and the functional or operating management level. We use the terms "top," "general," and "functional" to distinguish these levels. Top management personnel are particularly concerned with the functions of planning and organizing for the overall firm. Furthermore, theirs is a long-run rather than a short-run viewpoint. For this reason, their information needs include awareness of the environment, including customers, the general public, and government; long-run strategy alternatives; and the evaluation of performance with respect to major ventures of the organization. The information needs of general managers include the information needed to implement higher-level strategic decisions, integrate and evaluate the performance of functional groups, and control the operations in these groups. Finally, functional managers need information on a day-by-day or at least weekly basis to determine if the specific objectives assigned to their groups as part of an overall strategic plan are being fulfilled. In this regard, there is particular emphasis on the need for information to set particular schedules and specifications and to control operations. With respect to both planning and controlling, the time horizon shortens as we move from the top level to the functional level. The top-level board of directors and administrative committee are concerned with annual objectives and with plans extending for the next decade and perhaps longer. The general managers are concerned with the performance of the various divisions and departments on perhaps a weekly, but more likely a monthly basis, with the objective being to achieve plans for the designated year. Functional managers are concerned with results on a daily or weekly basis, and in the case of first-level supervisors even on an hourly basis.

Partly because of the kind of management information which was first made available through the operation of computer information systems and partly because of the speed of data processing, the management information needs that represented the focus of computerized MIS during the late 1950s and early 1960s were largely those of functional managers. Thus, during this period of time management information systems were particularly useful for developing routine information in such areas as quality control, budgeting, and production scheduling. Figure 1-1 portrays some of the areas of information thus supplied. Note that these areas of information are concerned directly with the decision-making needs of managers. By contrast, the applications of the computer during the early 1950s were more in the nature of "clerical substitutes" in such areas as payroll and accounting systems, and thus were entirely in the category of data processing applications.

Since the mid-1970s the forms of MIS have been directed at the information needs of general managers, as indicated in Figure 1-2. Of course, this does not imply that the use of computers as a substitute for clerical effort and as a basis for developing information for functional managers has been abandoned. Rather, the focus on general management needs represents an extension in the scope of MIS. Further, it also includes greater emphasis on the use of the techniques of quantitative decision analysis in conjunction with a computerized information system. Thus, information in such areas as "inventory optimization" and "product mix" is not simply the output of data processing in the classical sense but is concerned with data analysis and the consideration of alternative strategies.

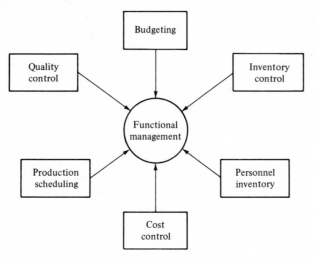

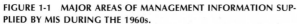

FIGURE 1-1   MAJOR AREAS OF MANAGEMENT INFORMATION SUP-
PLIED BY MIS DURING THE 1960s.

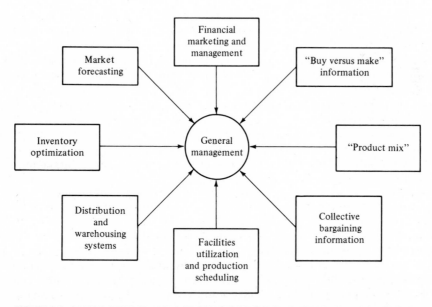

FIGURE 1-2   MAJOR AREAS OF MANAGEMENT INFORMATION SUPPLIED BY MIS SINCE THE
MID-1970s.

Given the success of current efforts to provide the kind of information relevant to the needs of general managers, the focus of MIS during the 1980s will presumably further broaden in scope to include the information needs of top managers. Such an application will include even greater emphasis on quantitative decision analysis techniques being used in conjunction with MIS. The form of such an application for long-run strategic planning can only be anticipated and vaguely discerned at this time. In any event, there is certainly no early end to the continued development of MIS for improving organizational performance.

REVIEW

1 For the purposes of our discussion we described three distinct levels of management: _____, _____, and _____.
> top (or corporate); general (or executive);
> functional (or operating)

2 Of the three groups above, the managers who are concerned with *implementing* higher-level strategic decisions and monitoring the performance of a *number* of functional groups in the organization are the _____ managers.
> general

3 Of the three groups of managers above, the managers with the shortest time horizon for planning and control purposes are the _____ managers.
> functional

4 During the 1960s the management needs satisfied by MIS were concerned largely with the needs of _____ managers. In the last decade the focus of MIS has been broadened to include the information needs of _____ managers.
> functional; general

THE STRUCTURE OF MANAGEMENT INFORMATION SYSTEMS

In this section we consider some of the structural characteristics of information systems, and hence the term *structure of MIS*. In general, an information system should be so designed that those with assigned responsibilities in the formal organization structure have the necessary information to fulfill their responsibilities.

FUNCTIONAL STRUCTURE
In the process of the development of information systems, the extension in the scope of MIS has been accompanied by increasing complexity in the structure of such a system. One of the simplest structural forms is what has been called the functional structure. Organizations include such major functions as production, marketing, finance, and personnel. In the early stages of development, management information systems tend to develop in parallel with this functional orientation. Examples are payroll systems, inventory control systems, and accounts-receivable systems.

The functional structure of an information system is desirable because it is at a low level of complexity. It has the advantage that the systems analyst and the manager can attend to one segment of operations at a time and implement the information system with respect to one function at a time. It is much easier to implement the system in respect to one function, such as accounts receivable, than it is to implement an overall system involving several functions. On the other hand, a disadvantage of the functional structure is that it results in suboptimization of the total systems design. This is a typical problem in both organizational and information systems design: The optimization with respect to the individual functions can often result in suboptimization in terms of achieving the goals of the total organization. For example, the inventory manager may strive for high inventory turnover—which means that he or she tries to keep the stock level low. On the other hand, the sales manager wants stock levels to be high so that sales are not lost because of the unavailability of merchandise. An information system designed independently for these two functions will tend to increase this type of goal conflict.

As the level of sophistication with regard to the development of information and decision systems has increased, the architecture of such systems has been refined so as to conceive of interrelated rather than independent modules. By analogy, instead of a simple structure of separate rooms, we now attempt to design an integrated structure with a unified heating and cooling system, and the like. So we move toward *integration* with its associated structural complexities. In the design of management information systems two approaches to integration have been developed: horizontal and vertical.

HORIZONTAL INTEGRATION

Horizontal integration refers to integration of data pertaining to several functions at the same organizational level. Examples are combining payroll with general personnel records or sales with finance records. Usually, horizontal integration comes about in a stepwise fashion after a functional information system has been established. It may be that certain data in the system has been used for accounting purposes, and then some managers realize that it could be used for certain marketing purposes as well— such as analyzing sales according to type of customer and determining if a seasonal purchasing pattern applies to some of the products. A frequent form of horizontal integration is to integrate on the one hand all functions concerned with *personnel,* such as payroll and skills inventories, and on the other hand to integrate all functions concerned with *materials,* such as purchasing, receiving, inventory, accounts payable, and inventory control.

VERTICAL INTEGRATION

Vertical integration refers to integration of data pertaining to different organizational levels. For example, a company that has several plants and a home office may integrate data analysis for the operating plant level onto the corporate level, so that the information system that is concerned with processing operating data is integrated with the system concerned with processing data for strategic planning and company-wide control systems. Although the concept of vertical integration is applicable to any organization with several organizational levels, it is particularly meaningful for multidivisional organizations and for companies that are "national" or "multinational" in their scope of operations.

TOTAL INTEGRATION

In terms of the current state of the development of information systems, the concept of a totally integrated system reflects a desirable direction rather than an immediately attainable objective. In theory, the decisions and activities in all parts of the organization are interrelated, and therefore all the data in the organization should be integrated both horizontally and vertically. In practice, however, the logical complexity of such a system as well as the physical storage requirements associated with such a data bank make the implementation of a totally integrated system impractical at the present time. Current implementation of the concept of integration is limited to piecemeal integration rather than total integration. Compared with management information systems of a few years ago, however, information systems today are at a relatively advanced level of integration in many companies. As computer processing and storage capabilities continue to improve and systems analysts have more experience with designing information systems, there is every reason to believe that the movement toward more integration of information systems will continue.

REVIEW

1   In terms of the architecture of a management information system, the structure which is simplest in form is the _____ structure.

functional

2   The fact that each unit of an organization strives to achieve optimum results in terms of its specific goals by the use of a functional information structure is considered to be an important [advantage / disadvantage] of such a structure.

disadvantage

3   When data pertaining to different functions at the same organizational level is integrated, such as accounting and financial planning, such a development is referred to as _____ integration.

horizontal

4   When data pertaining to functions at different organizational levels is integrated, such as plant and divisional data, such a development is referred to as _____ integration.

vertical

THE COST AND VALUE OF INFORMATION

Historically, computers have entered organizations through the door of the cost-reduction promise. Thus, it has been typically the case that computers are first used in an organization in the areas in which the cost-reduction potential is the greatest. Such functions as accounting, payroll, and billing are generally among the first to be "computerized." These functions have been prime candidates because they are high-volume, recurring data processing operations in which accuracy is required. If we conceive of *efficiency e* as being concerned with minimizing the amount of input in respect to a given amount of output, then e = output / input. The efficiency, or cost-reduction, approach has been a time-honored approach used extensively in the design of manufacturing facilities since Frederick Taylor's work in scientific management. A particular advantage of the cost-reduction approach to determining if work methods and equipment should be changed is that the effect of the change in terms of quality and cost is measurable.

In the area of installing computer equipment, however, many organizations have found that the expectation of reduced costs has not been fulfilled. While it is true that clerical costs are typically reduced following the installation of a computer system, other personnel costs enter the picture. For every $100 in monthly hardware costs it has been estimated that about $200 per month is spent on computer-related payroll costs. Observing such cost increases, one might conclude that the installation of a computer leads to a reduction in efficiency. Such a conclusion implies that while the input is often increased with the advent of such a system, the output remains the same in the equation e = output / input. But this assumption is not true, because computer systems invariably produce more information than the manual systems which they replace. And in fact, one important reason why computer-related costs usually increase after the installation of such systems is the requests for new types of information on the part of managers who become aware of the potential of such systems.

Therefore, an alternative to the efficiency and related cost-reduction concepts is needed to evaluate the contribution of computer information systems. If we acknowledge that the output as well as the input can increase in the equation e = output / input, we can address ourselves to *value creation* in addition to cost reduction. Thus relative efficiency e can be improved if the increase in new output exceeds the increase in input. But how can the value of the new information, such as information leading to better managerial control, be measured? In contrast to measuring reductions in cost, such evaluation is difficult. Yet the value of improved control, increased inventory turnaround, reduced delivery time to customers, and the like has to be assessed by the management of a firm as the basis for determining the extent and type of information system expenditures.

Conceptually, we can apply the technique of marginal analysis as developed by economists to consider the value of new information. In general, we can observe that the utility of additional outputs is not constant. Beyond some point, the marginal (additional) utility associated with further increases in output tends to diminish and perhaps even to approach a value of zero. Considering "information" to be such an output, beyond some point further addition of information may have little value. If the information system is very limited, an increase in information by a given amount may have considerable utility. However, if the information system is already well developed, the same amount of increase may be associated with a small increase in utility. In terms of marginal cost, an increase in output typically is first associated with a decrease in marginal cost because of economies of scale, and then beyond some point increases in marginal cost tend to occur as the system becomes saturated and additional capital investments or overtime work are required. The general relationship of the marginal utility of information and the marginal cost of information is represented by the graph in Figure 1-3.

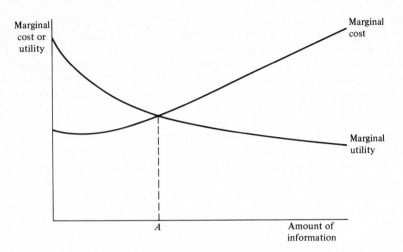

**FIGURE 1-3   MARGINAL COST AND MARGINAL UTILITY ASSOCIATED WITH INCREAS-
ING AMOUNTS OF INFORMATION.**

As indicated in Figure 1-3, up to the point A an increase in information has a marginal utility (value) which is greater than the marginal cost of producing it, while beyond point A the value of further information is less than the additional cost. In economic terms, point A, which represents the point at which the two curves intersect, is the optimum amount of information to be produced. The relationship between cost and utility can also be viewed from the standpoint of total cost and total utility, rather than marginal analysis. The graph in Figure 1-4 portrays such a relationship.

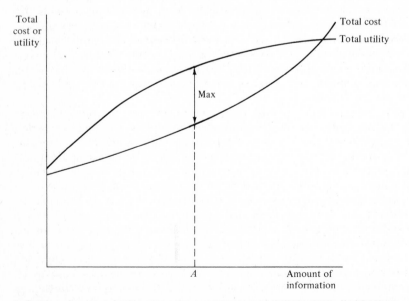

**FIGURE 1-4   TOTAL COST AND TOTAL UTILITY ASSOCIATED WITH INCREASING
AMOUNTS OF INFORMATION.**

In terms of total cost and total utility, the optimum amount of information to be produced is at the point at which the positive difference between total utility and total cost is maximized. This point is represented by point *A* in Figure 1-4. For a given analysis, this point will always correspond to the point at which the marginal cost and utility curves intersect, because it follows that the total difference between utility and cost increases up to the point at which marginal utility and cost are equal to one another.

Well, what practical value does such economic analysis have for the management of a firm with regard to the development of an information system? Can such curves be constructed to determine the "amount of information" to be produced for managerial use? Not quite, or at least not in the smoothed form illustrated (left). But we can determine several graphic points for such curves and then use these as the basis for a marginal type of analysis. For example, suppose we present a manager with the following possibilities:

FREQUENCY OF REPORT	COST
A: Daily	$10,000/year
B: Twice weekly	7,000/year
C: Weekly	5,000/year
D: Twice monthly	4,000/year

If the manager prefers *B* to *A*, such a decision implies that the marginal utility associated with daily reports as contrasted to twice-weekly reports is not worth the incremental $3,000 per year. On the other hand, if he prefers *B* to *C*, this implies that the marginal utility of twice-weekly reports as contrasted to weekly reports is at least equal to $2,000 per year. Setting up the decision problem in this way forces the manager to direct attention to the marginal utility of various amounts of information in terms of cash equivalents. Such an approach is useful in determining the development of a management information system, particularly since both value considerations and cost considerations are included.

In considering the total cost associated with producing desired information, we should recognize that some costs are one-time costs while other costs will be experienced each time that the desired information is produced. Broadly speaking, the *one-time costs* are those associated with designing the required information system and developing the programs for the system. In designing the system, a review of the existing system may be necessary, while the programs that are developed also will need to be tested and debugged. Further one-time costs are experienced at the time that an information system is first implemented. These costs include necessary training of personnel and testing of the system in an actual operational environment.

In contrast to the one-time costs, *recurring costs* are experienced each time that an established information system is used. These costs include the costs of data collection, data input, and the computer processing costs. When the decision to be made is concerned only with the frequency of a report, then only the recurring costs need to be considered. However, if new reports are being considered, then the one-time costs may be a major factor in the decision.

REVIEW

1   The application of computer methods to business data analysis has historically been based on the expectation of increasing efficiency by reducing ——————.

costs

2   The *value creation* approach to evaluating the organizational contribution of a MIS is based on the assumption that in the equation $e = $ output / input, the [input / output] increases with the introduction of a computer information system.

output

3   If marginal cost and utility analysis are used to determine the amount of information to be produced, that amount should be produced such that ——————— ——————————————————————————.

marginal cost equals marginal utility

4   If the total cost and total utility of the information to be produced are considered, that amount of information should be produced such that ——————— ——————————————————————.

the difference between total utility and total cost is maximized

5   In considering the total cost associated with desired information, the design of the information system and the development of required computer programs are —————— costs.

one-time

6   In considering the total cost associated with desired information, costs of data collection, data input, and computer processing are —————— costs.

recurring

EXERCISES

1   Differentiate the terms *data processing* and *management information systems.*

2   What are the main differences between administrative data processing and scientific computing?

3   An information system should be inflexible in terms of what is done with particular data in particular circumstances, and yet it should be flexible in terms of information retrieval. Are these two objectives compatible? Discuss.

4   Define and differentiate *data entry* and *data storage* as elements of an information system.

5   It is logical that an information system would include so-called "internal data." But what is the logic for including "external data" in such a system?

6   In the context of control systems, describe the concept of "real time" and explain why the specific definition of what constitutes "real time" depends on the process being controlled.

7   The information made available by management information systems has been extended to the general (middle) management level during the last decade, as contrasted with earlier applications as clerical substitutes and at the functional management level. What does this imply about the use of horizontal and vertical integration in such systems?

8   Why is total integration of a management information system more of a conceptual abstraction than an applicable procedure at this time?

9   Suppose that the manager of a manufacturing plant can be supplied cost information (a) by individual product or by product group; (b) in terms of an overall analysis or according to work shift (days versus nights); and (c) on a daily, twice-weekly, or weekly basis. Using any hypothetical cost figures that you wish, describe how you would use marginal analysis to help determine the specific type of report to be prepared.

10 Differentiate one-time costs from recurring costs in determining the total cost of desired information. Under what circumstances would only the one-time costs be relevant? Under what circumstances would only the recurring costs be relevant?

Data Processing Concepts

INTRODUCTION

Modern organizations are highly complex, consisting of thousands of people performing a variety of tasks in a number of locations. Without modern data processing systems the required scope and tempo of activities could not be carried out. Indeed, a close look at the functions of managers reveals that managers are, to a great extent, information processors. Blue-collar employees usually devote most of their time to actual physical work. As we go up the organizational ladder from worker to executive, we increasingly deal with people whose concern is centered around data and information, rather than physical "work." The typical executive spends considerable time studying internal reports and requesting the production of such reports.

Managers do not manage by getting a first-hand view of all the activities in a firm. They are not direct observers of all the actual sales transactions, production processes, or quality inspection functions. Managers monitor the course of business by reviewing the output of data processing systems. Therefore, a data processing system is important because it provides the reflection of the real situation in a company, and it is on the basis of this reflection that managers evaluate results and make decisions.

Parallel to every physical event in an organization there are data processing events that capture the origin of the physical event and follow it through its development to completion. For example, take the physical event of manufacturing a product. As a batch of units is placed into production, this action reduces the stock of some part to a relatively low level. As a result, a parts requisition is sent to the purchasing department. There it is approved and a purchase order is written. The document is sent to the vendor, and a copy is sent to the receiving department. When the material is eventually received, a receiving report is produced that goes to the purchasing department and to the inventory clerk. The accounting department is also notified so that a check will be written and sent to the vendor. We could go into a lot more detail in describing the data processing tasks generated by the two physical events, stock reduction and order receipt, but it is obvious that one cannot study and understand business processes without at the same time being involved in the data processing function of business.

Figure 2-1 portrays the principal business functions performed in a typical manufacturing firm. It would be very difficult to obtain a clear understanding of how these functions are accomplished without considering the data processing system.

DATA PROCESSING FUNCTIONS

Just as there are overall business functions, such as production and sales, performed in a firm, so also are there basic functions in data processing. Data processing tasks are made up of a series of interrelated functions, the principal ones being data production, classification, sequencing, calculation, and transmission.

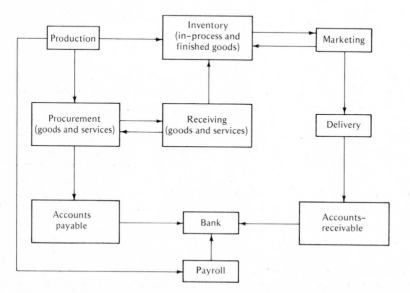

FIGURE 2-1   BUSINESS FUNCTIONS IN A MANUFACTURING FIRM.

DATA PRODUCTION

In the context of data processing, the term *data,* or *documentary data,* refers to recorded facts. Therefore, the contents of such activities as telephone conversations and committee discussions are not considered to be data from this standpoint.

Data is produced in several ways. A customer's purchase recorded manually on a sales slip constitutes the generation of data. A sales report which is derived from summarizing data on sales slips also exemplifies the generation of data.

Manually produced data is recorded on *source documents,* a term often inter-changeable with *business forms.* But in a more general context a source document may not be produced manually. For instance, the gas station attendant uses a credit card to inscribe part of the data on the source document.

Since we define data as recorded facts, it is obvious that *recording* is a necessary function in data processing. Some authors, in fact, choose to consider recording as a function distinct from data production or data origination. Recording media have certainly changed a great deal since Archimedes' drawings in the sand! Pencils, keyboards, and a variety of inscribers (credit card, stamp, check, magnetic ink, etc.) are among the many options available. Some special recording media and equipment are discussed later in this chapter.

The now familiar GIGO (garbage in, garbage out) motto signifies the importance of accuracy in data production and recording. In this respect two related data process-ing subfunctions are *data verification* and *data validation.* Verifying ascertains the accurate transcription from a source to the data recorded on a document: for example, ascertaining that the customer did indeed say 10 cases of oranges as written on the sales slip or ascertaining that the data entered on a punched card corresponds to the data written on the sales slip. Data validation refers to ascertaining the logical confor-mity of data to certain prescribed characteristics. For instance, if a code of 1 is used for male employees and a code of 2 for female, a validation test would ascertain that no 0s, 3s, or 4s, etc., were recorded for the sex code.

CLASSIFICATION

Data may be assigned to classes or categories according to the characteristics of the data (such as numeric or alphabetic) or according to the characteristics of the items that are referenced by given data. Typical classes are finished or in-process invento-ries, accounts-receivable, accounts-payable, and eastern and western sales territories.

Classification presupposes a logical scheme of assignment of objects to classes. As such, it is an information systems function. Typically, classification involves the use of codes or coded data so that the data is recorded to reflect the classification scheme. An example of such a code is the use of the numbers 01-16 to indicate the educational attainment of an employee on a personnel record.

SEQUENCING

The physical ordering or arrangement of data is the function of sequencing. Another term used for this function is *sorting.* Typically, data is sorted in ascending or descending order and in the numeric or alphabetic mode.

The sequencing of data is performed very extensively in business data processing. Data is meaningful only when arranged in the right order. Furthermore, the same data may yield different information when rearranged and processed in a different sequence. For example, sales data can be sequenced to yield information by product or resequenced to give sales territory information.

CALCULATION

This obvious function refers to performance of arithmetic computations—addition, subtraction, multiplication, and division. Other operations such as square roots or raising a number to a power are normally performed by a series of applications of these four basic operations.

TRANSMISSION

This function has become very important in the past 10 years with the formation of data processing networks that are geographically dispersed. In such long-distance transmission the function is automatically performed by hardware. In a more limited context, data is also moved or transmitted between parts of a computer system, such as from cards to internal storage and from magnetic tape to magnetic disk. From a computer programming standpoint, transmission in this context is extremely important to the efficient utilization of the available computer hardware.

REVIEW

1   In this section we have discussed five data processing functions: data production, classification, sequencing, calculation, and transmission. Of these, transferring data from cards to magnetic tape is an example of _____.

transmission

2   When the occurrence of a sale is recorded by the use of a credit card, the data processing function involved is _____.

data production

3   Of the five functions identified above, sorting the sales documents according to salespersons, so that appropriate commissions can be calculated, is an example of

_____.

sequencing

4   When sales invoices are coded according to the category of merchandise sold, the data processing function that has been accomplished by such encoding is called _____.

classification

5   Overall, we have suggested that the data processing system used in a firm is particularly important because senior executives [are / are not] in a position to observe actual operations on a continuous basis.

are not

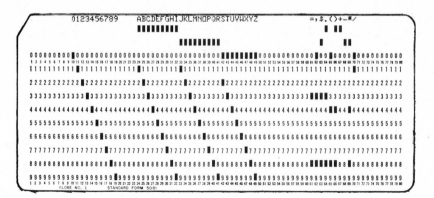

**FIGURE 2-2 IBM PUNCHED CARD ILLUSTRATING PUNCHED CODES FOR NUMBERS, LET-
TERS, AND SPECIAL CHARACTERS.**

DATA RECORDING

In the context of electronic data processing, perhaps the medium with which most
people are familiar is the punched card. Figure 2-2 illustrates the standard IBM card
with the punched codes in each column interpreted along the top of the card. The
card is a very frequently used data recording medium and contains 80 columns.
Since each column can be used to encode one character, the maximum number of
characters that can be recorded on a standard card is 80. In Figure 2-2 the 5 punched in
column 15 represents the numeric 5; the combination of 0 and 5 punched in column 45
represents the letter V; the combination of 0, 3, and 8 punched in column 62
represents a comma. The user need not be concerned about the particular codes that
represent different characters because these are automatically entered by the use of
the keypunch, which is the principal *data recording device* used in conjunction with
electronic data processing systems. A picture of a typical keypunch machine is
included in the appendix to this chapter, along with the instructions for using such a
machine. A keypunch is similar to a typewriter, the difference being that data is
recorded by being punched into cards rather than by being printed along the line of a
page.

A punched card is usually used to encode some one record or the facts associated
with some given transaction. For example, a card can be used to encode the name and
address of a customer. Figure 2-3 is an example of such a card with areas set aside to
contain data such as the customer number, name, etc. Another example is given in
Figure 2-4 showing a card that could be used to describe a particular sales transaction.
Because each card contains the facts associated with a particular record or transaction,
it is frequently referred to as a *unit record.* Punched card data processing methods
have been developed on the basis of the *unit record principle,* that is, the principle
that any one document should contain information relevant to a single record or
transaction only. An advantage of such a system is that a set of such cards can be sorted
and summarized in various ways, such as according to customer, according to items
sold, and according to salesperson.

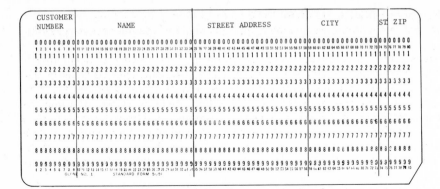

FIGURE 2-3   CUSTOMER CARD WITH FIELDS IDENTIFIED.

A field on a punched card is made up of one or more characters that are meaningful as a unit. Figure 2-3 contains six fields, beginning with "Customer Number" and ending with "ZIP." Figure 2-4 also contains six fields of data, but the fields do not encompass the full card in this case. Although the fields are preprinted on these two illustrations, the fields represented on a punched card are not necessarily identified on the card itself. For example, a punched card used as a check might not have such labels included on the card. Whether or not field labels are included, the data corresponding to a particular field must always be located in that field. Thus, a field may be larger than the number of characters to be included in it in any instance, but it can never be smaller. Alphabetic information is usually left-justified in a field; that is, punching begins in the first card column of the field and any blanks are in the right portion of the field. Numeric data is right-justified or punched according to a predesignated location for the decimal point, with so-called "leading" zeros punched in any positions in the left portion of the field that would otherwise be left blank. Because

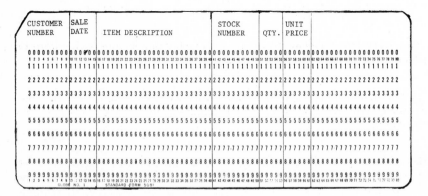

FIGURE 2-4   SALES TRANSACTION CARD WITH FIELDS IDENTIFIED.

blanks are not considered equivalent to zeros in COBOL programming, it is particularly important that numeric data which is right-justified include the necessary leading zeros.

Whereas punched cards as a data recording medium were first developed in conjunction with mechanized data processing (MDP), magnetic tape was developed in conjunction with electronic data processing (EDP). In most larger computer facilities, magnetic tape is now the principal data recording medium. However, often the data is first entered onto punched cards and then is transferred from the cards to reels of tape. The magnetic tape is very similar to the tape used with tape recorders. Data is encoded on the tape by means of magnetic charges on the surface coating of the plastic tape. Again, there is no reason for the user to be concerned about the details of the coding system.

In addition to punched cards, there are many other options for recording data. Keyboard-to-tape/disk devices record keystrokes from a keyboard onto magnetic tape or magnetic disk devices. Optical readers can be used to input data that is typewritten or carefully handwritten. Then there are magnetic ink inscribers and bar-coding devices as well as direct entry keyboards used with smaller computers to input data directly into the central storage.

REVIEW

1   The letters MDP stand for _____ _____ _____, and the letters
    EDP stand for _____ _____ _____.

*mechanized data processing; electronic
data processing*

2   The data recording medium which can be used with both MDP and EDP systems is
    the _____. Data is entered onto this medium by means of the _____

punched card; keypunch

3   The concept that each punched card should contain the facts associated with a
    single record or transaction only is called the _____ principle.

unit record

4   A series of card columns whose content is meaningful and should therefore be
    interpreted only as a unit is called a _____.

field

5   When entering data into a particular field of a punched card, alphabetic informa-
    tion is usually [left / right]-justified whereas numeric information is usually [left /
    right]-justified.

left; right

6   The data recording medium which can be processed much more rapidly than
    punched cards, and which has therefore become the principal data recording
    medium, is _____.

magnetic tape

INPUT/OUTPUT AND STORAGE DEVICES

In this section we consider the devices used to enter data into the computer, to obtain computer output, and to store data for eventual use by the computer. Figure 2-5 illustrates the relationship among input devices, output devices, and the central processing unit (CPU) of the computer. As indicated by the figure, when we say that data is being input into the computer, for example, what is really meant is that it is being read into the CPU of the computer. In the following section we further consider the characteristics of the CPU itself.

A variety of devices can be used to input data into the central processing unit of a computer system or output data from the CPU onto an external medium. The *input/output devices* discussed in this section give a brief understanding of the kinds of devices available. The card reader/card punch, magnetic tape drive, and cathode-ray tube (CRT) are examples of devices that can be used for input as well as output. On the other hand, a device used only for computer output is the printer.

Figure 2-6 portrays the several input-output devices that we discuss in this section. There are a number of additional devices that could be included in our discussion, but the ones included here are frequently used and are representative of the general features of such devices. As the name implies, the *card reader/card punch* can be used to enter data into the central processor from punched cards or to punch data taken from the CPU into punched cards. Within this device the card reader moves cards past a reading unit which converts the data on the cards into electronic form. On the other hand, the card punch automatically moves blank cards from the card hopper into a mechanism that punches data received from the CPU.

As contrasted to the card reader/card punch, the *magnetic tape drive* portrayed in Figure 2-6 is used for input from or output onto magnetic tape. The data recorded on magnetic tape is more compact than that recorded in the form of punched codes. For example, a reel of ½-inch tape, which holds 2,400 feet of tape, can contain the data punched on several hundred thousand punched cards.

Whereas the magnetic tape drive facilitates rapid input and output of data, the *cathode-ray tube* (CRT) facilitates human interaction in data analysis. Input is achieved through the keyboard illustrated on the display station in Figure 2-6, and output is presented visually on a cathode-ray screen similar in many respects to the picture tube of a television set. Any output that is desired in permanent form can be obtained by also directing it to the printer, described immediately below.

The *printer* is used only as an output device and provides a permanent visual record of selected data taken from the central processing unit of the computer system. A number of different printer models are available, with considerable variability in specific characteristics. The printers that are referred to as high-speed printers typically

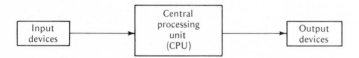

FIGURE 2-5   RELATIONSHIP OF INPUT DEVICES AND OUTPUT DEVICES TO THE CENTRAL PROCESSING UNIT (CPU).

(a)

(b)

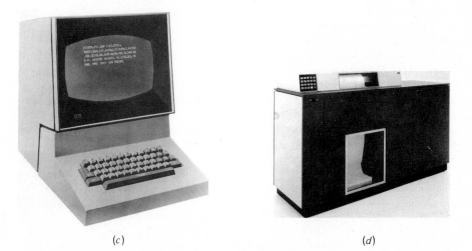

(c)   (d)

FIGURE 2-6   INPUT/OUTPUT DEVICES. (a) IBM 2540 CARD READER CARD PUNCH. (IBM CORPORA-
TION.) (b) UNIVAC MAGNETIC TAPE UNIT. (SPERRY RAND CORPORATION.) (c) IBM CATHODE-
RAY TUBE. (IBM CORPORATION.) (d) IBM 3211 PRINTER (IBM CORPORATION.)

produce over 2,000 lines of output per minute, with each line usually including either
120 or 132 alphanumeric characters. However, even this speed does not match the
processing time in the CPU, and therefore computer output is frequently obtained on
magnetic tape and such tape is then used to obtain printed output.

In addition to the need for input and output devices, use of the central processing
unit is enhanced by the availability of *external storage devices* which are directly

accessible to the CPU. These storage devices are called "external" because they are outside the CPU, which also contains a storage device. The CPU itself will be described in the following section. In a sense, external storage devices can be thought of as a special category of input/output devices, for they share the general input and output functions with the devices introduced above. However, their principal use is that of external storage which is relatively easily and quickly accessible for computer use, and we shall discuss these devices from the standpoint of their data storage features. The devices we discuss below as examples of such devices are magnetic drum storage, magnetic disk storage, data cell storage, and the cartridge system.

Figure 2-7 portrays the three examples of external storage devices which we discuss. A *magnetic drum* is a cylinder that rotates at a constant speed and has data recorded on its surface, which is coated with a magnetic material. Each track on the surface of the drum may have its own read/write head. This feature combined with the typical rotating speed of over 3,000 revolutions per minute makes for relatively rapid access to data. As for any recording medium utilizing magnetic codes, data recorded on the drum may be read repeatedly without loss, and the entry of new data in a particular storage location automatically erases the old data. Magnetic drums are frequently used to store computer programs and to store tables of values, such as actuarial tables, that are referred to repeatedly during computer operation.

Like drum storage, *magnetic disk* storage is an external storage device that also makes it possible to retrieve data in a random order with relatively high speed. For both these devices, the direct, or random, access capability can be contrasted with the sequential access capability associated with the use of magnetic tape as an external storage medium. Each disk storage unit consists of several thin disks, not unlike phonograph records, that are mounted on a vertical shaft. Both sides of each disk are coated with magnetic recording material, and each side is equipped with its own read/write assembly, thus making direct access feasible. Finally, the *data cell* and the *cartridge system* illustrated in Figure 2-7 are examples of direct access storage devices. These are capable of storing vast amounts of data—over 1 billion characters—and are used by very large organizations.

REVIEW

1   The devices used for the purpose of entering data into the central processing unit or for obtaining data from the CPU are referred to as _____ devices.

input/output

2   The input/output device used in conjunction with punched cards is the _____ _____.

card reader/card punch

3   Because of the advantages of speed and compact data representation, the input/output device with the greatest extent of use in data processing centers is the ____ _____.

magnetic tape drive

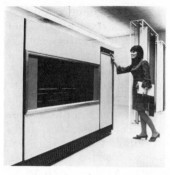

(a)

(b)

(c)

(d)

FIGURE 2-7 AUXILIARY STORAGE DEVICES. (a) UNIVAC FASTRAN III MAGNETIC DRUM. (SPERRY RAND CORPORATION.) (b) UNIVAC 8414 MAGNETIC DISK STORAGE. (SPERRY RAND CORPORATION.) (c) IBM 3321 DATA CELL UNIT. (IBM CORPORATION.) (d) IBM 3850 CARTRIDGE SYSTEM. (IBM CORPORATION.)

4 The device that uses a keyboard for input and provides visual output on a screen is the _____.

cathode-ray tube

5 Finally, the device used only for output which facilitates the preparation of reports is the _____.

printer

6 A storage device located outside the central processing unit (CPU) of the computer system is referred to as an _____ storage device. When data in such a device can be accessed in any desired order, the device is said to have _____ access capability.

external; direct (or random)

7 The external storage device which contains a rotating cylinder coated with magnetic material, and for which each track on the cylinder has its own read/write head, is the _____.

magnetic drum

8 The device which resembles a jukebox, because of the storage disks mounted on a vertical shaft, is the _____ storage unit.

magnetic disk

9 An example of a very high capacity external storage device is the _____.

data cell (or cartridge system)

THE CENTRAL PROCESSING UNIT (CPU)

In the preceding sections we have discussed data recording media and the devices that can be used for input into and output from the CPU. In general, all computer systems can be described as containing some kind of input devices, the central processing unit, and some kind of output devices.

Figure 2-8 illustrates the principal components of any computer system, with special attention given to the makeup of the central processing unit. As indicated, the three segments of the CPU are the internal storage, control unit, and arithmetic-logical unit. When a computer program or data is input into the CPU, it is in fact input into the *internal storage* of the CPU.

The control unit of the CPU serves to direct the sequence of computer system operation. From this standpoint, note that Figure 2-8 indicates that this control function extends to the input and output devices, and not just to the sequence of operations within the CPU. Finally, the *arithmetic-logical unit* is concerned with performing the arithmetic operations and logical comparisons designated in the computer program.

In terms of the overall sequence of events, a computer program is input into internal storage and then transmitted to the control unit, where it becomes the basis for overall sequencing and control of computer system operations. Data that is input into the internal storage of the CPU is available for processing by the arithmetic-logical

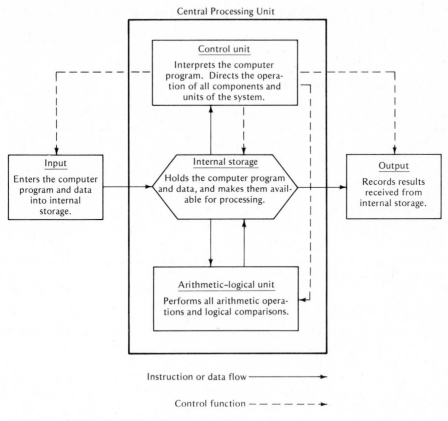

Central Processing Unit

Control unit

Interprets the computer program. Directs the operation of all components and units of the system.

Input

Enters the computer program and data into internal storage.

Internal storage

Holds the computer program and data, and makes them available for processing.

Output

Records results received from internal storage.

Arithmetic–logical unit

Performs all arithmetic operations and logical comparisons.

Instruction or data flow ⟶

Control function ⟶

FIGURE 2-8   COMPONENTS OF A COMPUTER SYSTEM.

unit, which conveys the results of the calculations and comparisons back to the internal storage. After the designated calculations and comparisons have been completed, output is obtained from the internal storage of the CPU.

REVIEW

1   The three components of any computer system are the input, central processing unit, and output. Both input and output are accomplished in conjunction with the _____ segment of the CPU.

internal storage

2   The segment of the CPU which is concerned with the overall sequencing of computer system operations is the _____ .

control unit

3 The segment of the CPU which is concerned with performing the required calculations and comparisons is the _____.

arithmetic-logical unit

COMPUTER GENERATIONS

Although the contents of this text are not technologically oriented, a brief consideration of the hardware advancements that have been made since the development of electronic computers is of interest in that these developments have had a direct bearing on the types of applications in which computers can be used.

The forerunners of modern computers were developed during the 1940s as special-purpose machines. The Mark I, which was developed by Howard Aiken at Harvard University, was a large electromechanical calculator designed to perform sequences of arithmetic calculations. The ENIAC, developed by Eckert and Mauchly at the University of Pennsylvania, was the first all-electronic sequential calculator. However, many would not consider ENIAC to be an electronic computer as such because it did not have the capability of storing a computer program in the central processing unit. The first electronic computers which included both the sequential processing capability and the stored program feature were the EDVAC developed in the United States and EDSAC developed in England.

Computers became commercially available during the early 1950s and have experienced very significant technological development since that time. The changes and improvements that have been made since the 1950s typically are described as having evolved through several distinguishable generations, or phases, of development.

First-generation computers were developed during the early 1950s and were characterized by the use of vacuum tubes as the principal electronic components. Because of the use of vacuum tubes, the machines were quite large, generated considerable heat, and had relatively high maintenance requirements because of tube failure. Computer speeds of first-generation machines typically were measured in milliseconds (thousands of a second). These machines had limited internal storage capacity, were punched card oriented, and had relatively slow input/output time. Therefore, these computers were most useful for scientific computing rather than administrative applications, as described in Chapter 1, in the section "Administrative Versus Scientific Applications of Computers."

Second-generation computers were developed in the late 1950s and were characterized by the use of solid-state electronic components in place of the vacuum tubes. The use of transistors and diodes in second-generation computers resulted in a reduction in the size of computer hardware, a considerable reduction in the heat being generated, and a marked improvement in the reliability of the system. The use of the smaller components also made it possible to increase the internal storage capacity of computers, increase computational speed, and improve input/output time. Computer speeds of second-generation machines typically were measured in microseconds (millionths of a second). Developments also included the capability of using magnetic tape as well as punched cards for input/output. The variety of possibilities led to an interest in developing separate computers for administrative applications as contrasted to scientific computing.

Third-generation computers were developed in the mid-1960s, and are characterized by the substitution of integrated circuits for the transistors of second-generation machines. Integrated circuits are microelectronic components each of which can perform the functions of hundreds of transistors. The operational result is a further marked improvement in internal storage capacity, computational speed, and input/ output time. Computer speeds of third-generation computers often are expressed in nanoseconds (billionths of a second). In general, there is also considerable versatility available with respect to the peripheral equipment (disk systems, drum files, etc.) that can be used with a third-generation computer and the software which is available for use. For this reason, a given third-generation machine can be used for either adminis- trative or scientific applications, and indeed a particular computer installation typically includes both kinds of applications.

Unlike the discrete developments that characterize the first three generations of computers, the *fourth-generation* computers appear to have developed in a more gradual, stepwise manner, and for this reason it is not yet entirely clear that a fourth- generation of change has yet been completed. Recent developments have included the use of large-scale integration (LSI) of circuitry, in which each small chip of silicon can perform the functions of thousands of transistors, thus further reducing the size of the electronic components used in computers. However, particular emphasis also has been placed on devices and developments that make it easier for administrators and others who are not computer professionals to use such systems. Along these lines, developments have been made in the use of timesharing terminals, the use of minicomputers and microcomputers, and the availability of more software for a variety of applications.

Computer system developments which are likely to continue include user-ori- ented machine instructions that minimize the necessity of having programming knowl- edge and the extensions of data base management systems which permit easy and immediate access to the data files of an organization. On the hardware size, the miniaturization of components is likely to continue for some time, leading to the development of more minicomputers and microcomputers and also making it possible to build in dual circuits (redundancy) so as to increase system reliability substantially.

REVIEW

1   As contrasted to the Mark I, the components of the ENIAC developed in the 1940s at the University of Pennsylvania were all electronic. However, many specialists in the computer field would not consider ENIAC to be an electronic computer because it did not have the capability of _____ in the central process- ing unit.

storing programs

2   In terms of electronic components used, first-generation computers are charac- terized by their use of _____.

vacuum tubes

3   The speeds of individual operations in first-generation computers typically were measured in terms of _____.

milliseconds (thousands of a second)

4   In terms of electronic components used, second-generation computers are char- acterized by their use of _____.

transistors

5   The speeds of individual operations in second-generation computers typically were measured in terms of _____.

microseconds (millionths of a second)

6   The use of integrated circuits in third-generation computers has resulted in individual operations in such computers often being measured in terms of

_____.

nanoseconds (billionths of a second)

7   The generation of computers in which there was some interest in differentiating scientific computers from those oriented toward administrative applications is the _____ -generation computers.

second

8   Extensive development of software and data base management systems is most characteristic of the _____-generation computer system.

fourth

EXERCISES

1   Discuss the statement "Managers monitor the course of organizational activity by seeing what the data processing system produces."

2   Name and explain the five basic functions of data processing discussed in the text.

3   In a manufacturing plant, workers punch a time clock which records their daily attendance at the plant. During the day as they start or finish work on a particular job, they fill in a labor ticket that identifies the job and shows the start and finish time for that job. At the end of the week, the time cards and labor tickets are processed for payroll and job accounting purposes.

   a   Design a validation test to be used with the time cards each week.
   b   Design a validation test for the labor tickets, i.e., a way to make sure that workers do not record unrealistic amounts of time spent on the different jobs.

4   In a data processing application an inventory report is produced that has the following form:

PART NUMBER	PREVIOUS BALANCE	AMOUNT PRODUCED	AMOUNT SOLD	NEW BALANCE
1234	100			
		80		
			60	
			40	
				80
21215	300			
			20	
			30	
				250

Design a validation test such that at the end of producing such a report we can be sure that the arithmetic has been performed correctly.

5   Develop a classification scheme that assigns a unique person-number code to a company with three departments and total employment of up to 5,000 people. Make sure that the code shows the department and the sex and provides for people hired and people terminated from the company.

6   Name and briefly describe the computer input/output devices discussed in the text.

7   A company records sales data on punched cards. For each item sold a card is punched containing item number (five digits), date, salesperson code (three digits), quantity, and price to the nearest cent. Design what you think would be suitable fields for the data. Explain any assumptions.

8   Consider how the developments in computer technology in the past 25 years relate to an increasing interest in management information systems.

APPENDIX: KEYPUNCH OPERATING INSTRUCTIONS

Figure 2-9 presents an overall view of a keypunch, and Figure 2-10 portrays the keyboard of this unit. Refer to these figures as you read the following instructions.

1 Make sure that the power switch is on. Turn on the PRINT toggle switch; it is located just above the keyboard. Make sure that the feed hopper has an adequate number of cards.
2 Press the FEED key to feed a card from the feed hopper.
3 Press the REG (register) key to position the card under the punching station.
4 *Punch alphabetic* information by pressing appropriate keys. Keys are labeled. In order to determine the column ready to be punched next, observe the indicator inside the glass cover located to the left of the feed hopper. *Punch numeric* information by holding down the NUM (numeric) key. Keys are labeled. *Space* by means of the long space bar.
5 To remove a card from the punching station, press the REL (release) key (in some keypunches the label is EJECT instead of REL). If you want to punch another card,

FIGURE 2-9   IBM 29 KEYPUNCH. (IBM CORPORATION.)

FIGURE 2-10   KEYBOARD CHART FOR THE IBM 29 KEYPUNCH. (IBM CORPORATION.)

go to reference point 2 above and repeat the cycle. If you have finished, press REL, then REG, then REL. The card will move to the output stacker in the upper left of the keypunch.

6   To duplicate a card that has just been punched, press the REL key to advance the card to the reading station. Press FEED, then REG. To duplicate a number of columns, press the DUP key. To punch in some columns, punch as usual.

7   To backspace, depress the backspace key located directly below the reading station of the punch.

8   For more efficient punching, turn on AUTO FEED toggle switch. Then depress FEED twice. After that, every time you depress REL a new card is fed and registered automatically, thus eliminating the need to depress FEED and REG every time. However, when making duplications or corrections, turn off the AUTO FEED switch.

Programming Concepts and COBOL Language

LEVELS OF COMPUTER LANGUAGES

A computer program is a set of instructions that directs a computer in the performance of a data processing task. A computer language is a set of characters, words, and syntactic rules that can be used to write a computer program. One of the most revolutionary developments associated with computer systems is that instructions are conveyed to the machine by means of a language. A little thought will reveal that, except for computers, people communicate with machines not by means of a language but by means of physical operations, such as turning a valve, striking a key, or depressing a pedal.

Every computer model has its own language, which is determined by its hardware structure. Such "native" computer languages are referred to as *machine languages*. These languages are, of course, machine dependent and are, at a first glance, highly obscure because they consist of long strings of numeric codes. Early computer programming was almost exclusively machine-language programming. Although machine language is natural to the hardware of a computer, it is quite unnatural to human programmers. A step in the direction of facilitating programming was taken with the development of *symbolic languages*. Symbolic languages use mnemonic codes to represent machine instructions. For instance, a machine instruction such as 21300400, meaning to add the value stored in location 400 to location 300, could be written as A SUM, TOTAL. Mnemonic codes are, of course, not understood by a computer, and therefore they have to be translated into machine-language form. An *assembler* is a machine-language program that translates symbolic language instructions into machine-language instructions. Symbolic languages are machine dependent in that a set of mnemonic codes is applicable only to a particular computer model. Therefore, the programmer has to be familiar with the particular instruction repertoire of the machine being programmed. This is a serious disadvantage when programming efforts are extensive and hardware is changing.

The next step in programming language development was the development of *higher-level languages* that are procedure oriented rather than machine oriented. Such languages focus on the data processing procedure to be accomplished, rather than on the coding requirements of particular machines. Further, higher-level languages are *not* machine dependent in that such programs are not restricted to use with particular computer models. Even though such instructions are not designed to correspond to the way a particular computer model operates, they must of course be executed on a particular machine. Again, the process of translation is used to obtain the required machine-language program. A computer program written in a higher-level language is referred to as a *source program*. A *compiler* is a machine-language program that translates (or compiles) the source program into a machine-language program, which is referred to as an *object* program. The object program is then input into the machine to perform the required task. Thus a compiler is a program whose function it is to convert source programs to object programs. The main difference between a compiler and an assembler is that *compilation* is a more complex process than *assembly*. Assembly typically involves a one-for-one translation from a mnemonic to a machine code, whereas compilation involves a many-for-one translation. One higher-level instruction may be the equivalent of several machine-level instructions.

Figure 3-1 illustrates the compilation and execution process. In the first phase the source program and the compiler serve as input into the central processing unit (CPU) of the computer. The output includes the object program, which is stored on a magnetic disk or tape device, and a listing of the source program on the printer, along with diagnostic error messages. If no serious errors are detected, the object program is automatically entered into the CPU of the computer. Based on the program instructions, input data are then read and analyzed, culminating with the required output.

One of the most frequently used higher-level languages is FORTRAN. It is a language best suited for computational tasks, although in recent versions it also has moderate data processing capabilities. COBOL was designed expressly for use in business data processing. It is a higher-level language, and as such it is machine independent, with minor exceptions. Historically, the language was first conceived at a Pentagon meeting in May 1959. At that meeting, representatives from government, business users, and computer manufacturers decided that it was feasible to proceed with the development of a higher-level language that would answer the needs of business data processing. An early version of the COBOL language appeared in December 1959. It was then followed by the COBOL-61, which has provided the basis

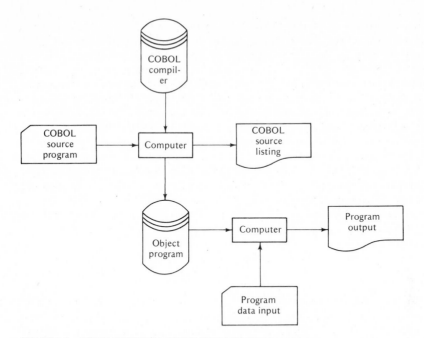

FIGURE 3-1 COBOL PROGRAM COMPILATION-EXECUTION PROCESS.

for the development of later versions. The next version was developed in 1965. However, it was not until August 1968 that a standard version of the language was approved by what is now called the American National Standards Institute (ANSI). This standard version, ANSI COBOL, was again revised in 1974 and has now been implemented by all major manufacturers and most well-managed computer installations. This text presents the great majority of commonly used elements of ANSI COBOL. A detailed and complete treatment of ANSI COBOL is appropriate for a computer manufacturer's reference manual rather than for an instructional text. Appendix B at the back of the book provides a description of the principal concepts underlying ANSI COBOL. However, this appendix will be meaningful to you only after you have become acquainted with the elements of COBOL programming.

One advantage of COBOL computer programs is that they can be substantially *self-documenting*. Self-documentation is a characteristic of a language that allows a reader of a program to understand its function and follow its processing steps. Documentation is very important because, like other aspects of business, data processing needs do not remain static. Making changes in programs, or *program maintenance*, is an ongoing activity in computer installations and may be performed by different people at different points in time. Thus, documentation is essential in order to avoid reprogramming. Although COBOL programs can be self-documenting, whether or not a particular COBOL program is self-documenting depends on the programmer. The language instructions are very English-like, but the programmer has substantial choice as to whether to make a program self-documenting or obscure.

Although COBOL has been available for a long time, its use substantially increased during the late 1960s and the 1970s. Widespread acceptance of the language coincided with the appearance of the standard version and with the development of efficient COBOL compilers. Many of today's compilers translate quickly and generate an efficient object program. In earlier years it was not unusual to find that compilation of a small program required about a half-hour and that the resulting object program ran slowly. Under such circumstances, computer installation managers tended to use lower-level symbolic languages that could be assembled (translated) more quickly and that resulted in more efficient object programs. Today, a COBOL program can be written in a shorter time than an assembly program for most data processing applications, and it can be run with about the same efficiency as a symbolic program written by a programmer of comparable competence. Thus, COBOL is now *the* language for administrative data processing, and one can reasonably predict that it will continue in this role for some time to come.

REVIEW

1   A computer program is essentially a set of instructions which directs the operation of a machine. When the set of instructions is written in a language that consists of a series of numeric codes which can be used with a particular computer model only, the language is referred to as a _____ language.

machine

2   The next step in the development of computer languages made possible the use of mnemonic codes, such as SUM, in place of numeric codes. As is the case for machine languages, such languages are also machine dependent. Because of the type of code system used, such languages are called _____ languages.

symbolic

3   The third step in the development of computer languages was the formulation of higher-level, or procedure-oriented, languages which [are also / are not] machine dependent. An example of such a language is _____.

are not; COBOL (or FORTRAN, BASIC, ALGOL, etc.)

4   Both symbolic languages and procedure-oriented languages have to be translated into machine-language form before they can be used to direct computer operations. The program which translates a symbolic language program into machine-language form is called a(n) _____, whereas the manufacturer-supplied program which translates a procedure-oriented language program is called a(n) _____ .

assembler; compiler

5   In the context of using a procedure-oriented language, the program written in such a language is often referred to as the _____ program, and the translated version of the program is referred to as the _____ program.

source; object

6 A principal reason for the substantial increase in the use of COBOL during the latter part of the 1960s and the 1970s was [the availability of efficient compilers / the development of new data processing needs].

the availability of efficient compilers

THE PROGRAMMING PROCESS

Programming is not a simple task but can best be thought of as a series of steps. These are task analysis, program flowcharting, program coding, program testing, and preparation for production.

It is imperative that the programmer clearly identify the data processing objective prior to writing program statements. *Task analysis* involves a thorough study of the computational methods used, the source of data input, and the desired form of output. Consultation with experts is very often part of task analysis. For example, accountants or tax specialists may be the source of defining the suitable or permissible method to be used in asset depreciation.

Depending on programmer preference and task complexity, task analysis may be followed by *program flowcharting*. A program flowchart is a graphic display of the computer processing required to accomplish the desired task. We will discuss flowcharting in a subsequent section of this chapter.

After a program flowchart has been drawn, the programmer proceeds with the actual *program coding,* or writing. These program instructions are then usually keypunched onto punched cards. In addition to the program itself, one needs *program control cards* which are peculiar to each computer installation. Typically, such cards identify the user (and possibly record the charges for the computer time used) and indicate the source language, the medium on which the object program is to be recorded, and other similar information. Figure 3-2 illustrates a typical COBOL program deck setup. The program control cards are the first cards to be input. They identify the user, indicate that the program is in COBOL, and specify some of the hardware to be used. Then follows the COBOL source program itself, which is a set of COBOL statements, followed by a card or cards indicating the end of the program. These cards serve to signal the compiler that the source program read-compile process should be terminated. The "Execute Program" instruction, which follows the source deck, directs the computer to enter the object program into internal storage and to proceed with program execution. As indicated in Figure 3-2, punched cards are the most common form of input, although occasionally the input may be on other media. The last card in the input deck contains a special code which signals the end of the data. This is a general deck setup. Each computer installation utilizes a specific form of program deck setup which may vary somewhat from this example.

The next step in the programming process is *program testing,* or *debugging.* Typically, a programmer's first few attempts to run a program will be unsuccessful. After each run, the computer (actually the compiler) issues a printer listing of the source program along with error diagnostic messages. Most of these messages refer to language errors, such as using the wrong verb, omitting a period, forgetting to close parentheses, and hundreds of similar possibilities. Debugging is concerned with

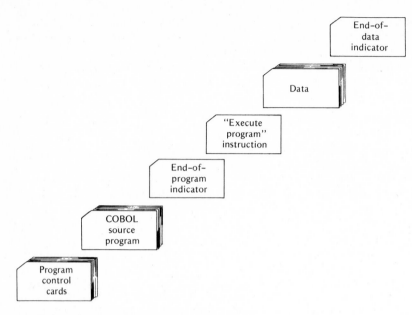

FIGURE 3-2   TYPICAL COBOL PROGRAM DECK SETUP.

making program corrections to eliminate language errors. In addition to language errors, a program may have logical errors. The program compiles and runs, but it does not produce correct results. Except for minor cases, the compiler cannot diagnose logical errors. For example, there is no way for the computer to detect an error in which the programmer wrote an instruction for multiplication instead of a required division. If the task analysis was thorough and the processing method clearly identified, it is much easier to locate logical errors if there are any.

Program testing can be a very extensive process. If the program performs a variety of functions, the programmer must choose the data input so that the program is executed under as many varied conditions as possible. From this standpoint, the program should be tested with data situations that are unlikely, as well as with those that are likely. In practice it is not unusual to find that after a "thoroughly" tested program has been running for some time a defect is discovered. Program testing is to some extent an art, and there is no general procedure by which one can be assured of detecting all errors, or bugs, in a large, complex program. Still, the skillful and conscientious programmer will reduce hidden bugs to a minimum.

Once the program has been tested, it is ready for the last step in the programming process, *preparation for production.* A principal part of this preparation is concerned with documenting the program. *Program documentation* involves attachment of explanations that describe the purpose of the program, the form of the input, the form of the output, the methods used in the processing steps, and the like. Good programming practice requires that a programmer complete a program and its documentation to the point where another programmer could step in and handle any desired modifications to the program with a minimum of reprogramming. In addition to program documentation, the programmer also prepares any instructions required by the computer operator during program execution.

In this section we have briefly described the five principal steps in the programming process: task analysis, program flowcharting, program coding, program testing, and preparation for production.

REVIEW

1 The first step in the computer programming process, which is concerned with a study of the required data processing, the type of input, and the required output, is called _____.

task analysis

2 After task analysis, a program flowchart may be prepared as a graphic display of the required sequence of computer data processing. The programmer then proceeds with the third step, which is _____.

program coding (or writing the program)

3 After the program has been written, it is executed with various data input in order to detect and correct any programming errors or omissions. This process is called

_____.

program testing (or debugging)

4 The last step in the programming process is called preparation for production. A principal part of this step is concerned with attaching explanations to the program so that it is understandable to another programmer. Such a set of explanations is called _____.

program documentation

THE OPERATING SYSTEM AND PROGRAM CONTROL CARDS

All modern computer systems are controlled by an *operating system* which consists of a set of programs designed to facilitate the automatic operation of the computer system and to reduce the programming task for system users. The heart of an operating system is the resident *supervisor* (*executive* and *monitor* are often used synonymously), which is a program that acts as the control module in the operating system. The computer operator loads the supervisor as the first task "each morning," and from then on the supervisor controls the operation, human intervention being required only to implement some exceptional procedure. The supervisor loads and executes other programs that are either part of the operating system or are submitted by users. When a program has finished being executed, control is resumed by the supervisor, which executes control functions until it transfers control to another program. When the machine is idle, the supervisor is in a "wait" state, waiting for the next program to be executed.

The motivation for the development of operating systems is related to the basic difference in speed between computer systems and human operators. In the early days of computing, a human operator took each program to be run, loaded it into the machine, and removed the associated output prior to loading the next program. As computers became faster and the number of users multiplied, it became obvious that the operating of computer systems had to be automated. In a modern computer system, this automation is achieved by the operating system. Human operators input the programs to be processed continuously (often simultaneously in different locations), while the operating system maintains control over the program-to-program execution sequence, checks availability of resources (tapes, disk space, printers) and, when needed, transfers control from one program to another in an attempt to maximize *throughput.*

The development of operating systems represents a major conceptual breakthrough and demands extensive programming efforts. In fact, programming is differentiated into systems programming (systems software is a synonym) and applications programming. *Systems programs* relate to operating systems and include supervisors, language processors, data management such as disk space allocation, and utilities. *Utilities* are programs that perform such standard tasks as copying data from cards to tape and dumping a tape on the printer. *Applications programs,* on the other hand, are oriented toward the use of the computer for some data processing task. A COBOL programmer is an applications programmer. All applications programs require the use of systems programs in their processing, and therefore it is essential to have a basic understanding of the operating system of the computer with which one is working.

Operating systems consist of hundreds of thousands, or even millions, of program instructions and require millions of dollars and many years of effort to develop. For these reasons, operating systems are considered an essential part of the equipment, are developed and maintained by each computer manufacturer, and are provided as part of the total cost of the equipment. Under such circumstances, you can see why each manufacturer has an operating system that differs from the others, and often has different operating systems for different computer models. Because of these differences, we cannot explain specifics in this text. We will, however, discuss the general concepts that relate COBOL programming to operating systems, and we will assume that the reader has access to information about the specific operating system used by his or her computer installation.

In order for a COBOL program to be run, the programmer needs to communicate certain things to the operating system. Typical areas of information include the following:

Identify the user as a legitimate user of the machine

Indicate the fact that a COBOL program is being used. (In a typical installation, programs are written in several languages and they need to be differentiated)

Request compilation

Indicate whether the compilation output (object program) is to be saved on disk, cards, tape, etc.

Request the use of tapes, disks, readers, printers, and other devices

Request execution of the compiled program

The communication process between the programmer and the operating system is effected by means of system commands known collectively as the Job Control Language (JCL). The JCL is of course not standardized. In general, the JCL is entered on cards or through an online keyboard terminal, such as a CRT. A typical procedure is to submit a COBOL program through the card reader. The JCL statements are punched onto cards referred to as *program control cards*. In general, there is a first card which identifies the user by account number or by name and may set parameters on maximum time, maximum number of pages, and the like. Then there are one or more JCL statements to invoke the compiler and to indicate the disposition of the object program. The source program follows, possibly with an end-of-program indicator. Then there are one or more JCL statements to ready the object program for execution. This is often referred to as a link-editing function and basically involves loading the program into memory along with a number of subprograms either requested by the programmer or automatically appended by the operating system. Finally, there is an execute type of instruction followed by the data (if on cards) and often by an end-of-data indicator.

Overall, then, program control cards serve to transmit certain categories of information to the operating system. On the basis of this information, execution of the program is scheduled and monitored by the supervisor, which is the systems program concerned with controlling the operation of the computer.

REVIEW

1   The entire set of programs designed by the computer manufacturer to facilitate the automatic operation of the computer is called the _____.

operating system

2   The particular program in the operating system which serves as a control module in the selection and scheduling of programs for execution is called the _____ _____.

supervisor (or executive or monitor)

3   The types of computer programs concerned with such functions as disk space allocation and copying data from cards to tape are called _____ programs.

systems (or utility)

4   The types of computer programs concerned with actual data processing tasks are called _____ programs.

applications

5   A programmer who uses COBOL as the programming language is a(n) [systems / applications] programmer.

applications

6   The communication process between the programmer and the operating system is carried out through the use of a set of commands called the _____ _____.

Job Control Language (JCL)

7 Typically, the JCL is input by means of punched cards, with one statement entered on each card. The several cards which constitute a set of such cards are called _____ cards.

program control

8 In terms of the sequence of cards required for executing a COBOL program, following the initial group of program control cards, the next set of cards typically includes the _____. Then certain additional program control cards are included, followed by the cards which contain the _____.

source program; data

PROGRAM FLOWCHARTING

A flowchart is a graphic outline of a computer program. As the title suggests, the flowchart identifies the steps needed in a data processing task and presents them with connecting lines and arrows to indicate the direction of flow, or sequence. Figure 3-3 illustrates some of the most frequently used flowcharting symbols.

To illustrate the use of some flowchart symbols, Figure 3-4 presents an example of a flowchart for a simple program designed to read 50 cards. Each card has a value representing a quantity. If the quantity is less than 100, the price is set at $10.00. If the quantity is 100 or greater, the price is set at $9.50. For each card record we print the quantity, the price, and the total. The program terminates when 50 cards have been read.

General input/output—indicates an operation of reading or writing.

Card input/output—indicates the I/O medium is punched cards.

Document input/output—used for printer output or for optical input from a source document.

Processing—indicates arithmetic operations, editing, moving of data, and the like.

FIGURE 3-3 COMMON FLOWCHARTING SYMBOLS.

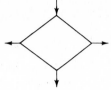

Decision—indicates a decision point. A test is performed and the program flow continues on each outgoing path conditional on the test.

Predefined process—indicates a number of processing steps whose detail is of no concern at this point. For example, "tax computation" may be one (predefined) step in a flowchart even though it is a complex procedure in itself.

Program comment or annotation—a comment or a description inside the box can be used to clarify some point of the flowchart.

On-page connector—indicates reference to another point in the flowchart on the same page.

Off-page connector—indicates reference to another point on a different page.

Terminal—indicates the beginning or end of a procedure.

Magnetic tape—indicates that input/output is from magnetic tape.

Magnetic disk—indicates that input/output is from magnetic disk.

Magnetic drum—indicates the use of magnetic drums for input/output.

FIGURE 3-3   COMMON FLOWCHARTING SYMBOLS (*continued*).

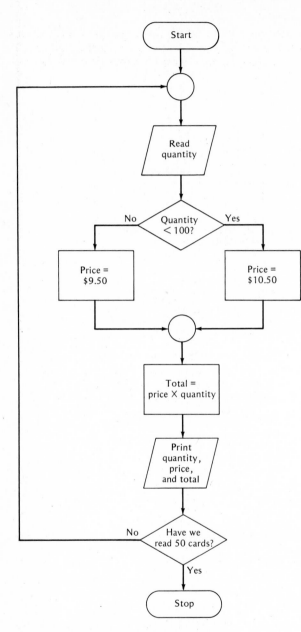

FIGURE 3-4 EXAMPLE OF A FLOWCHART.

50

All properly drawn flowcharts can be broken down into a few basic structures. Three such basic structures are included in Figure 3-4. One structure is the *sequence,* which depicts a series of consecutive tasks or operations. For example, the pair of tasks,

represents a sequence structure. Actually, with some minor exceptions, the entire flowchart in Figure 3-4 can be viewed as a sequence structure: a series of steps to be executed in the top-to-bottom order in which they are represented in the flowchart.

A second basic structure is the *if-then-else,* which is also called the condition structure, decision structure, or predicate structure. In Figure 3-4 we have

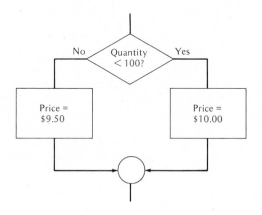

We test a condition and we perform one of two alternatives. In the example above, the condition "Quantity < 100?" is either true, and we execute the "Yes" branch, or it is not true, and we execute the "No" branch.

Sometimes one of the branches in a condition may be *null*. We test for a condition and if true we perform something; if false we do nothing. For example, suppose that the price is set at $10.00 and we give a discount to customers who brought 100 or more units:

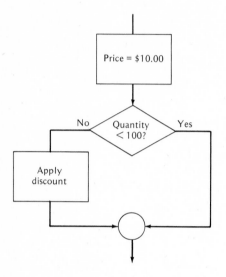

In this example the "Yes" branch is null, and it indicates that no action is taken as a result of the test.

It is also common to have a number of conditions in series. Suppose that we read a record from a file and we wish to print it if it is an hourly, skilled, nonunion employee. We would depict the screening as shown on the next page.

Notice that by use of the connector symbols (small circles), each condition and its outcomes can be identified easily. Such a series of dependent conditions is referred to as *nested* conditions. Thus the "Nonunion" condition is nested under the "Skilled" condition, which in turn is nested under the "Hourly" condition.

The third structure in Figure 3-4 is the *do-until,* shown on top of page 54.

We do a task (in this example a series of tasks) and perform a test; we then either repeat the task or we continue. If we substitute a general predefined process block for the detail of the original flowchart in Figure 3-4 we can represent the do-until in more abstract form, shown at the bottom of page 54.

The do-until is a *loop* structure. A loop is a structure that specifies repeated execution of program steps. Every properly structured loop should terminate, lest we have an *infinite* loop which can come about by logical error. In our example the loop terminates after we have read 50 cards.

A variation of the do-until loop is the do-while loop shown on page 55.

In a do-while loop we test first and if a condition holds we execute a task, repeating the process until the test reveals that the condition does not hold.

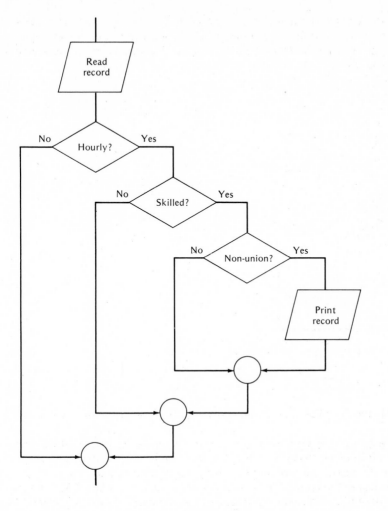

We conclude now our brief discussion of flowcharting concepts. A number of examples throughout the text further illustrate the flowcharting process. Also, the basic structures are discussed again in Chapter 9, "Structured Programming."

REVIEW

1 The sample flowchart in Figure 3-4 involves the use of several flowcharting symbols. With reference to Figure 3-4 only, one example of the use of the *decision* symbol is associated with the verbal description, "_____ _____."

Quantity < 100? (or: Have we read 50 cards?)

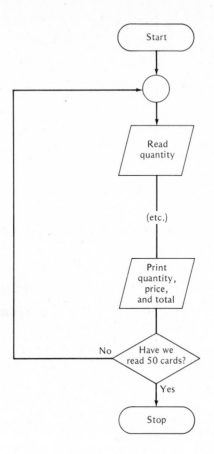

Do-until (abstracted)

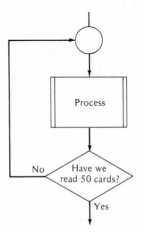

54

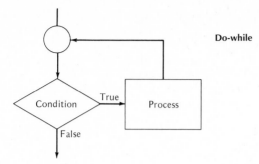

Do-while

2   An example of the use of the *terminal* symbol is associated with the verbal description "_____."

Start (or: Stop)

3   An example of the use of the *input/output* symbol is associated with the verbal description "_____."

Read quantity (or: Print quantity)

4   In terms of the logic of the program, note that the program will "stop" if all 50 cards have been read. On the other hand, if all 50 cards have not been read at the point in the flowchart where this test is made, the next verbal instruction executed will be "_____."

Read quantity

5   Of the three basic flowchart structures described in this section, the one that depicts a series of consecutive tasks or operations is the _____ structure.

sequence

6   A second basic flowchart structure is associated with testing a condition and performing one of two alternative tasks as a result of the test. This is called the _____ structure.

if-then-else

7   The third basic flowchart structure described in this section is used when a test is applied to determine whether a task (or series of tasks) should be repeated, or whether program execution should proceed to the next task. This is called the _____ structure.

do-until

ELEMENTS OF THE COBOL LANGUAGE

Any language can be described in terms of its *syntax* and its *semantics*. Syntax is concerned with the definition of what is legitimate in terms of the *form* of language structures. The semantics of a language defines the *meaning* implied by the different language structures. For example, in the English language, syntactical rules specify that "He study" is incorrect, but that "He studies" is correct. A language structure such as "The account balance is heavy" is syntactically correct, but it is semantically incorrect because proper understanding of the meaning of the words "account balance" and "heavy" indicates the statement to be meaningless. It is clear then that both syntax and semantics are required for proper use of a language.

Thus the task of learning a language such as COBOL is concerned with learning the rules for forming syntactically proper statements and understanding the computer operations generated by proper statements.

COBOL CHARACTER SET

The most basic and indivisible unit of the COBOL language is the *character*. The set of characters used to form COBOL source programs consists of the 51 characters listed in Figure 3-5.

COBOL WORDS

A sequence of continuous characters from the character set can form a *word*. There are two types of COBOL words, *reserved words* and *user-defined words*.

Reserved words are words that are defined both syntactically and semantically by the COBOL language. Appendix A presents a complete list of ANSI COBOL reserved words. The programmer cannot use any of these words except in the form specified by the language. Much of this text is devoted to explaining the use of such reserved words.

User-defined words are words supplied by the programmer (language user) in order to satisfy the format of a clause or statement in the language. A user-defined word may be 1 to 30 characters in length and may consist of letters, digits, and hyphens, except that a hyphen may not appear as the first or last character.

There is a total of 17 types of user-defined words, examples of which are condition-name, data-name, paragraph-name, record-name, and file-name. The reader will be exposed to different types of user-defined words as the text progresses. Special attention is given to data-names in the section that follows, because data-names are so frequently used.

CHARACTER	MEANING
0, 1, . . . , 9	Digit
A, B . . . , Z	Letter
	Space (blank)
( ) . "	Special symbols
+ − * /	
= $, ;	
< >	

FIGURE 3-5 THE SET OF CHARACTERS IN COBOL PROGRAMMING.

REVIEW

1   Study of the proper *form* of language structures concerns the _____ of the language, while study of the *meaning* of language structures concerns the _____ of the language.

syntax; semantics

2   The basic units of the COBOL language, such as the numbers 0 through 9 and the letters of the alphabet, are referred to as _____.

characters

3   COBOL words defined by the COBOL language and used only for particular purposes are called _____ words. On the other hand, words formulated by applications programmers are called _____ words.

reserved; user-defined

DATA-NAMES

Central storage or main storage in a computer can be thought of as a long string of character positions, with direct access available to any position. Both data and instructions are stored in internal storage, but from the programmer's viewpoint data storage is the most important concern. Data is stored in certain positions such that it can be referred to by a name or an address. In a procedure-oriented language such as COBOL, addresses are symbolic names and are called *data-names*. One way to view a computer program is to say that it consists of a set of instructions to manipulate central storage areas which are referenced by their corresponding data-names. The idea will become clear as we proceed, but first let us state the rules for forming data-names.

Data-names are coined at the discretion of the programmer, except that there are certain rules that must be followed:

1   A data-name can be up to 30 characters in length and can include alphabetic characters, numeric characters, and hyphens.
2   At least one character must be alphabetic.
3   The only special symbol permitted is the hyphen. A hyphen must always be embedded; that is, it cannot be the first or last character of the data-name.
4   Blanks cannot be included in the data-names.
5   Within the above rules the programmer may use any data-name, with the exception of the approximately 300 COBOL reserved words listed in Appendix A. (Manufacturers often add some of their own words to the ANSI list.)

Some examples of legitimate data-names are

HOURS

ENDING-INVENTORY

SALES-TAX-TOTAL

PREMIUM

A527157

31576X5

Of course, data-names do not have to be meaningful English words. A programmer can choose to use such data-names as X, Y, Z, X1, X2, and the like. However, even though such data-names are typically shorter than those that are inherently meaningful as names, they increase the likelihood of subsequent confusion. COBOL was specifically designed to allow self-documentation, which means that by reading the program one should be able to understand what the program does and what data it uses. The problem with using cryptic data-names is that their meanings may be forgotten by the programmer and are never understood by others unless a list of definitions is supplied.

Part of the programming job is to subdivide central storage into data units, such as characters, elementary or group items, and records. This is accomplished by the use of data-names in ways that can reflect the structure of the data involved. As a matter of fact, COBOL derives much of its suitability for administrative applications from the opportunity it provides to take explicit account of the structure of data.

As an example of the use of data-names, consider the following information that is to be stored internally:

RONALD JOHNSON
1057 MONTEREY DRIVE
TEMPE, ARIZONA 85282

Recall that internally the information will be stored as a continuous sequence of characters rather than as three lines. Assuming that it will be stored starting with storage position 101, we have the conceptual structure presented in Figure 3-6. The bottom row in the figure identifies the data as well as the data positions in internal storage, and the other rows refer to the labels by which reference can be made to the storage locations that contain particular kinds of information. In other words, in Figure 3-6 we have defined storage fields, and we have labeled them by the use of different data-names. For example, the label FIRST-NAME refers to storage positions 101–110. Correct computer programming relies on the use of unique data-names to identify unique positions in storage. Thus we can write instructions that direct the computer to take the data in columns 1–10 of a punched card and enter it in the storage location called FIRST-NAME. Obviously, the data-name FIRST-NAME must be unique to avoid ambiguity. Similarly, we could instruct the machine to print the contents of STREET on the high-speed printer, which would thereby make reference to the information held in storage positions 123–142.

Remember that a label or data-name, such as STREET, does not have any conceptual meaning for the computer as it would have for a person. We could just as well have used the data-name XYZ in our example. We simply indicate to the machine that something is to be done to or with the content of a storage location which has been labeled for reference purposes. If the label implies something about the meaning of the content to the programmer, it does not imply anything like that to the machine. Of course, it is a good habit to coin labels that convey meaning about the content to the programmer.

Referring again to Figure 3-6, notice that FIRST-NAME refers to storage positions 101–110, NAME refers to storage positions 101–122, and CUSTOMER-ADDRESS refers to storage positions 101–167, which include all the positions of this example. The way we have used the data-names allows us to reference data in accordance with their hierarchical structure. We can refer to the whole record, the group items in the record, or to the elementary items.

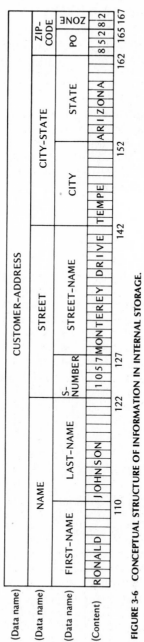

FIGURE 3-6 CONCEPTUAL STRUCTURE OF INFORMATION IN INTERNAL STORAGE.

REVIEW

1 In COBOL, a label for a field of data is appropriately called a(n) _____.

data-name

2 A data-name must be not more than _____ (number) characters in length and can include [alphabetic characters only / alphabetic and numeric characters].

30; alphabetic and numeric characters

3 Every data-name must include at least one [alphabetic / numeric] character, and the only special symbol permitted is the _____.

alphabetic; hyphen

4 Place a check mark before each of the following which is a legitimate data-name in COBOL.

a ____ INVENTORY
b ____ END OF YEAR BALANCE
c ____ 2735B5
d ____ 27-35B5
e ____ BALANCE-DUE-
f ____ 57
g ____ END-OF-YEAR-BALANCE-DUE-ON-ACCOUNT
h ____ CODE
i ____ BALANCE

a ✓
b *Spaces not allowed*
c ✓
d ✓
e *Hyphens must be embedded.*
f *At least one alphabetic character must be included.*
g *Must be less than 30 characters in length.*
h *A reserved COBOL word (a bit of a trick question—see Appendix A).*
i ✓

5 Each field of internal storage has a unique data-name, or label, associated with it. Each data-name [must / need not] be unique and [must / need not] imply something about the meaning of the content.

must; need not

6 Data-names can be so structured that data can be referenced according to hierarchical structure. When this is done, the labeled data fields will [all be separate and distinct / involve some overlap].

involve some overlap (e.g., "STREET" versus "NUMBER" in Figure 3-6)

THE HIERARCHICAL REPRESENTATION OF DATA

The example in Figure 3-6 in the preceding section demonstrates how data-names such as NAME can refer to groups of contiguous data-names. COBOL derives a great deal of its suitability for business applications from the fact that it allows the programmer to construct hierarchies of data structures.

A useful distinction is made between *elementary* and *group* items in COBOL. An elementary item has no subordinate parts. With reference to Figure 3-6, FIRST-NAME and ZONE exemplify the first and last of the eight elementary items from left to right. The data-name NAME, on the other hand, is an example of a group item. A group item may consist of one or more other group items, as is the case with CUSTOMER-ADDRESS in the illustration.

Reference to Figure 3-6 makes the concept of group item rather obvious. But in a programming language we cannot construct figures, and so we need a means of communicating the same information in symbolic form. The language provides such a symbolic form by means of the *level-number* form. Here is an example of how level numbers can represent the same hierarchical (grouping) structure as in Figure 3-6:

```
01   CUSTOMER-ADDRESS
        02   NAME
                03   FIRST-NAME
                03   LAST-NAME
        02   STREET
                03   S-NUMBER
                03   STREET-NAME
        02   CITY-STATE
                03   CITY
                03   STATE
        02   ZIP-CODE
                03   PO
                03   ZONE
```

The first level number 01 is associated with CUSTOMER-ADDRESS. An 01 level number indicates the highest level in a data hierarchy. Reference to the data-name at the 01 level is a reference to the entire data set, or *record*, as it is commonly called. There is only one data-name at the 01 level for each record, as it is the all-inclusive data-name. All data-names that follow this one and are part of this record have level numbers that are higher than 01 and, more specifically, in the allowable range 02–49.

The 02 NAME introduces NAME as a data-name subordinate to the 01 level. Reading from top to bottom corresponds to left to right in Figure 3-6. We observe a total of four data-names at the 02 level: NAME, STREET, CITY-STATE, and ZIP-CODE. Since they are all at the same level, 02, none of them is subordinate to the others in the group (but each is subordinate to the 01 level).

As in Figure 3-6, we are interested in specifying that NAME is a group item and that it consists of two other data-names, FIRST-NAME and LAST-NAME. This relationship is expressed by assigning the 02 level number to NAME and the 03 level number to FIRST-NAME and LAST-NAME. Notice that, as we read from top to bottom, STREET is not confused as being subordinate to NAME because both are assigned to the 02 level.

The indentations are preferred but not required. In addition, the level number need not increase by consecutive numbers. The following example illustrates these two points:

```
01   CUSTOMER-ADDRESS
03   NAME
05   FIRST-NAME
```

```
03   STREET
04   S-NUMBER
04   STREET-NAME
```

Notice the absence of indentation in the above example and observe that it is much harder to read and understand the expressed data hierarchy than in the preceding example. Also notice that level numbers do not increase by 1. The 03 NAME specifies that NAME is subordinate to CUSTOMER-ADDRESS, because 03 is greater than 01. Similarly, 05 FIRST-NAME is subordinate to NAME, because 05 is greater than 03. In the case of 04 S-NUMBER, it is understood that S-NUMBER is subordinate to the first data-name above it which has a lower level number. Thus, the 04 level is perfectly proper in the example, and it preserves the hierarchy of Figure 3-6. It should also be emphasized that, once NAME is assigned to the 03 level, STREET *must* also be assigned to the same level, since NAME and STREET have the same immediate superior, CUSTOMER-ADDRESS.

REVIEW

1   In COBOL programming, a data-name which has no subordinate items is called a(n) _____ item, while one that does have subordinate items is called a(n) _____ item.

elementary; group

2   The hierarchical level of a data item is indicated by the level number assigned to it. The item at the highest hierarchical level always has the [highest / lowest] level number assigned to it.

lowest

3   Whenever a data item in a record is a group item, the items subordinate to that item are assigned level numbers which are [higher / lower] than the level number of that item.

higher

CONSTANTS

It may have occured to you that a data-name in COBOL is analogous to the concept of a variable in algebra. It is a general symbol, or name, that can have many possible values. In addition to data-names, COBOL uses constants, and they are of three types: numeric literals, figurative constants, and nonnumeric literals. As an example of a *numeric literal,* suppose that the sales tax rate in a particular state is 0.04 of sales. Therefore, within the COBOL program we need a way in which we can multiply the amount of sales by 0.04. One way of accomplishing this *without* using a numeric literal is to define a storage field, assign a data-name, such as TAX-RATE, to it, and input the value 0.04 in the field. Conceptually, the internal storage location has the following structure:

TAX-RATE			(Data-name)
0	0	4	(Content)

The decimal point is not shown but is understood to be located in the appropriate position. With this approach, the reference to TAX-RATE will always make available the 0.04 value stored in this field. However, another option available in COBOL is simply to write the numeric literal 0.04 in the program itself and use this value directly. Essentially, we are saying that, if a value is a numeric constant, its data-name in internal storage is the same as its value. Conceptually, the internal storage location has the following structure:

004			(Data-name)
0	0	4	(Content)

Numeric literals without a decimal are understood to be integers (whole numbers). If a decimal is used, it must not be the last character. Thus, 35. is not correct, whereas 35.0 is acceptable. The reason for this rule is that in COBOL programming the period is always used to signal the end of a sentence, just as in English, and it would be ambiguous whether a point following a number is a decimal point or a period.

The second type of constant used in COBOL is the *figurative constant*. The most common figurative constants are ZERO, ZEROS, ZEROES, SPACE, and SPACES, although a few others are available. These refer to zeros or blanks, respectively. Their general use can be illustrated by the following brief examples. Suppose we want to set AMOUNT equal to zero. We can write MOVE ZERO TO AMOUNT to accomplish this objective. Similarly, if we wish to ascertain that blanks are contained in the field called TITLE, we can write MOVE SPACES TO TITLE. Figure 3-7 lists and defines the standard figurative constants used in COBOL programs.

In addition to numeric literals and figurative constants, the third class of constants is the *nonnumeric literal*. As contrasted to numeric literals and figurative constants, the nonnumeric literal is any alphanumeric value enclosed in quotation marks. For example, suppose we want to print the title INCOME STATEMENT. The words INCOME and STATEMENT are not intended to refer to data-names but, rather, we simply want these exact words printed. This can be done by enclosing them in quotation marks and using them as explained in the next chapter, in which the PROCEDURE DIVISION of COBOL will be described.

As an example of how a nonnumeric literal might be used in a decision context, suppose we want to know if a customer's last name is BROWN. We could write something like this:

ZERO ZEROS ZEROES	All three forms are equivalent, and they reference the value of zero. In an instruction such as MOVE ZEROS TO AMOUNT, the storage field AMOUNT would be filled by as many zeroes as there are positions in that field. Thus the context determines the number of occurrences of the character 0.
SPACE SPACES	Both forms are equivalent, and they reference one or more blanks, similar to the ZERO constant.
QUOTE QUOTES	Both forms are equivalent, and they reference the quotation mark.
HIGH–VALUE HIGH–VALUES	Both forms are equivalent, and they reference the highest value in the collating sequence for the particular computer system.
LOW–VALUE LOW–VALUES	Both forms are equivalent, and they reference the lowest value in the collating sequence for the particular computer system.
ALL literal	References one or more occurrences of the single character nonnumeric literal, as in MOVE ALL "A" TO HEADER, which results in the storage field HEADER being filled with A's.

FIGURE 3-7   FIGURATIVE CONSTANTS AND THEIR MEANINGS.

IF LAST-NAME IS EQUAL TO 'BROWN' (etc.)

Any letter, number, or special symbol can be enclosed in quotation marks with the exception of a quotation mark itself. If we want to use quotation marks as part of the literal, we can accomplish this by use of the QUOTE figurative constant as follows:

QUOTE 'TOTAL AMOUNT' QUOTE

In this example the word QUOTE indicates a quotation mark. The use of the figurative constant QUOTE before and after the nonnumeric literal will result in quotation marks being printed as part of the label. The quotation marks are printed as single or double marks, depending on the specific printer used.

Unlike a data-name, a nonnumeric literal can include blanks. Also, the nonnumeric literal can be composed entirely of numeric characters. This may seem like a contradiction, but it is not, since the term "nonnumeric" refers to how the characters are handled within the computer and not to their alphanumeric form as such.

REVIEW

1   In all, three classes of constants were discussed in this section. They are the
_____, _____; and _____.

numeric literal; figurative constant;
nonnumeric literal

2   In the following listing, place an NL before those expressions that can serve as numeric literals in a COBOL program, an FC for figurative constants, and a NON-L for nonnumeric literals; leave a blank for expressions not exemplifying any of the classes of constants.

a   ____ "DEPRECIATION SCHEDULE"
b   ____ "12%"
c   ____ 237
d   ____ INTEREST-DUE
e   ____ 125.
f   ____ ZEROS
g   ____ 25.32
h   ____ SPACES
i   ____ 100.0
j   ____ "SPACE"
k   ____ "325"

a   NON-L
b   NON-L
c   NL
d   *(No quotation marks.)*
e   *(Cannot end with a decimal point.)*
f   FC
g   NL
h   FC
i   NL
j   NON-L
k   NON-L

THE STRUCTURE OF COBOL PROGRAMS

COBOL programs are written according to a special structure which is organized into a hierarchy of parts. In terms of an overall outline, the structure of this hierarchy is described as follows. Much of this text is concerned with developing the detail associated with this structure.

A *character* is the lowest form in the program structure.

A *word* is made up of one or more characters.

A *clause* consists of characters and words and is used to specify an attribute of an entry.

A *statement* is a syntactically valid combination of words and characters written in the PROCEDURE DIVISION of a COBOL program and beginning with a verb.

A *sentence* is a sequence of one or more statements, the last of which is terminated by a period followed by a space.

A *paragraph* consists of one or more sentences.

A *section* consists of one or more paragraphs.

A *division* consists of one or more paragraphs or sections. Every COBOL program consists of four divisions in the following order: IDENTIFICATION DIVISION, ENVIRONMENT DIVISION, DATA DIVISION, and PROCEDURE DIVISION.

SAMPLE COBOL PROGRAM

Exhibit 3-1 illustrates a complete COBOL program. As is true for all COBOL programs, it consists of four divisions. The IDENTIFICATION DIVISION is written first, and it consists of one paragraph-name, in this case PROGRAM-ID, which identifies this program by the name LABELS.

The ENVIRONMENT DIVISION is written next. The basic function of this division is to specify the hardware required for this program.

The DATA DIVISION follows. It is used to identify the data-names that will be used in the program, as well as their data characteristics and hierarchical structure.

The last division is the PROCEDURE DIVISION, which constitutes the executable part of the program. In this division the programmer writes the specific instructions to be carried out by the computer. It is noticed that the instructions have the appearance of everyday language, which illustrates the self-documentation feature of the COBOL language.

The function of this sample program is to read cards containing three data fields and to print these fields on separate lines. Each card contains a name in columns 1–25, a street address in columns 26–50, and the city and state in columns 51–80. Output from two input data cards appears as follows:

ALLEN M. JOHNSON
1532 E. WASHINGTON ST.
CHICAGO, ILLINOIS 53186

PATRICIA K. WALTON
2252 PALM BOULEVARD
MIAMI, FLORIDA 31322

The program could be used with special adhesive labels so that a mailing could be made to a group of individuals whose names and addresses are recorded on punched cards.

THE COBOL CODING FORM

A special coding form used in writing COBOL source programs is illustrated in Exhibit 3-2, on which part of the program described in the preceding section is entered. This form has been prepared to coincide with the standard 80-column format of the punched card and therefore is particularly oriented toward applications in which the COBOL program is to be punched onto cards before input into the computer. This method of input is still typical in COBOL programming, although visual display keyboard terminals are on the uptrend.

EXHIBIT 3-1   SAMPLE COBOL PROGRAM

```
IDENTIFICATION DIVISION.
PROGRAM-ID. LABELS.

ENVIRONMENT DIVISION.
CONFIGURATION SECTION.
SOURCE-COMPUTER. ABC-480.
OBJECT-COMPUTER. ABC-480.
INPUT-OUTPUT SECTION.
FILE-CONTROL.
        SELECT CARDS-IN        ASSIGN TO CARD-READER-DEVICE.
        SELECT MAILING-LABELS ASSIGN TO PRINTER-DEVICE.

DATA DIVISION.

FILE SECTION.

FD   CARDS-IN
        LABEL RECORDS ARE OMITTED
        DATA RECORD IS CARD.
01   CARD.
     02 NAME        PICTURE IS X(25).
     02 STREET      PICTURE IS X(25).
     02 CITY        PICTURE IS X(30).

FD   MAILING-LABELS
        LABEL RECORDS ARE OMITTED
        DATA RECORD IS PRINT-RECORD.
01   PRINT-RECORD.
     02 PRINT-LINE PICTURE IS X(132).

WORKING-STORAGE SECTION.
01   END-OF-DATA-INDICATOR PICTURE IS XXX.


PROCEDURE DIVISION.
MAIN-LOGIC.
     OPEN INPUT  CARDS-IN
          OUTPUT MAILING-LABELS.

     MOVE 'NO' TO END-OF-DATA-INDICATOR.

     PERFORM READ-A-CARD.
     PERFORM READ-PRINT
          UNTIL END-OF-DATA-INDICATOR IS EQUAL TO 'YES'.

     CLOSE CARDS-IN
           MAILING-LABELS.
     STOP RUN.
*
READ-A-CARD.
     READ CARDS-IN RECORD
          AT END
             MOVE 'YES' TO END-OF-DATA-INDICATOR.

READ-PRINT.
     MOVE NAME TO PRINT-LINE
     WRITE PRINT-RECORD
          BEFORE ADVANCING 1 LINE.
     MOVE STREET TO PRINT-LINE.
     WRITE PRINT-RECORD
          BEFORE ADVANCING 1 LINE.
     MOVE CITY TO PRINT-LINE
     WRITE PRINT-RECORD
          BEFORE ADVANCING 4 LINES.

     PERFORM READ-A-CARD.
```

The first six positions of the COBOL Coding Form are reserved for the optional sequence number. The programmer may assign a sequence number to each program line so that they are numbered in order. A common practice is to use the first three columns as a page number corresponding to the number of coding form pages used. Then the next three columns indicate line numbers such as 010, 020, 030,. . . . Gaps

EXHIBIT 3-2 COBOL CODING FORM WITH SAMPLE COBOL PROGRAM

IBM

COBOL Coding Form

SYSTEM						PUNCHING INSTRUCTIONS			PAGE 1 OF 3
PROGRAM	LABELS				GRAPHIC		CARD		
PROGRAMMER		DATE FEB. '77			PUNCH		FORM #	*	IDENTIFICATION 73 80

SEQUENCE		CONT	A	B	COBOL STATEMENT
(PAGE)	(SERIAL)				
0 1				IDENTIFICATION DIVISION.
0 2				PROGRAM-ID. LABELS.
0 3				ENVIRONMENT DIVISION.
0 4				CONFIGURATION SECTION.
0 5				SOURCE-COMPUTER. ABC-480.
0 6				OBJECT-COMPUTER. ABC-480.
0 7				INPUT-OUTPUT SECTION.
0 8				FILE-CONTROL.
0 9				SELECT CARDS-IN ASSIGN TO CARD-READER-DEVICE.
1 0				SELECT MAILING-LABELS ASSIGN TO PRINTER-DEVICE.
1 1				DATA DIVISION.
1 2				FILE SECTION.
1 3			FD	CARDS-IN
1 4				LABEL RECORDS ARE OMITTED
1 5				DATA RECORD IS CARD.
1 6			01	CARD.
1 7				02 NAME PICTURE IS X(25).
1 8				02 STREET PICTURE IS X(25).
1 9				02 CITY PICTURE IS X(30).
2 0			FD	MAILING-LABELS
2 1				LABEL RECORDS ARE OMITTED
2 2				DATA RECORD IS PRINT-RECORD.
2 3			01	PRINT-RECORD.
2 4				02 PRINT-LINE PICTURE IS X(132).

*A standard card form, IBM Electro C61897, is available for punching source statements from this form.
Instructions for using this form are given in any IBM COBOL reference manual.
Address comments concerning this form to IBM Corporation, Programming Publications, 1271 Avenue of the Americas, New York, New York 10020.

Form No. X28-1464-4 U/M 025
Printed in U.S.A.

68

EXHIBIT 3-2 COBOL CODING FORM WITH SAMPLE COBOL PROGRAM (*continued*)

IBM COBOL Coding Form

SYSTEM			
PROGRAM	LABELS	PUNCHING INSTRUCTIONS	
PROGRAMMER	DATE FEB. '77	GRAPHIC / PUNCH	CARD FORM # / *

IDENTIFICATION 73 [ ] 80

```
01  WORKING-STORAGE SECTION.
02  01  END-OF-DATA-INDICATOR PICTURE IS XXX.
03  /.
04  PROCEDURE DIVISION.
05  MAIN-LOGIC.
06      OPEN INPUT CARDS-IN
07          OUTPUT MAILING-LABELS.
08      MOVE 'NO' TO END-OF-DATA-INDICATOR.
09      PERFORM READ-A-CARD
10      PERFORM READ-PRINT
11          UNTIL END-OF-DATA-INDICATOR IS EQUAL TO 'YES'.
12      CLOSE CARDS-IN
13          MAILING-LABELS.
14      STOP RUN.
15  *
16  READ-A-CARD.
17      READ CARDS-IN RECORD
18          AT END
19          MOVE 'YES' TO END-OF-DATA-INDICATOR.
20  READ-PRINT.
21      MOVE NAME TO PRINT-LINE
22      WRITE PRINT-RECORD
23          BEFORE ADVANCING 1 LINE.
24      MOVE STREET TO PRINT-LINE.
```

*A standard card form, IBM Electro C61897, is available for punching source statements from this form.
Instructions for using this form are given in any IBM COBOL reference manual.
Address comments concerning this form to IBM Corporation, Programming Publications, 1271 Avenue of the Americas, New York, New York 10020.

Form No. X28-1464-4 U/M 025
Printed in U.S.A.

69

are left in the sequence so that when program changes are made later new lines can be inserted without disrupting the previous sequence. For instance, a new line could be inserted between the second and third lines by assigning a line number of 025.

Column 7 is used mainly for continuation, and it is called the *indicator area*. When a word or literal cannot be completed on a line, it is continued on the next line starting with column 12 or to the right of it, and a hyphen (-) is entered in column 7 of that line to indicate the continuation. When a nonnumeric literal is being continued, not only do we enter a hyphen in column 7, but we also start the continued line with a quotation mark in column 12 or to the right of it and conclude with a quotation mark. For instance, we could have:

In this example the literal 'EXAMPLE CONTINUATION' does not fit on the line. Notice that in the continued line there is a hyphen in column 7, a quotation mark in column 12 (it could have been to the right of 12 as well), the remainder of the literal, and the closing quotation mark, for a total of three quotation marks. As a simplifying rule, the programmer should avoid continuations by not beginning a word or a literal that cannot be fully written on a given line.

Column 7 is also used to indicate that a line contains a comment entry by writing an asterisk (*). Whatever is written on such a line is listed with the source program but is not compiled. Comments can be used to enter explanations about a portion of the program. However, a well-written program should have a limited need for comments. As exemplified in Exhibit 3-2, the readability of a program is enhanced by leaving blank lines. This can be accomplished by leaving blank cards in the source program or by including cards with an asterisk in column 7. Finally, readability will be enhanced by causing a portion of the program to be listed on a new page, and this can be accomplished by entering a slash (/) in column 7.

REVIEW

1   The four divisions of a COBOL program are, in order, _____, _____, _____, and _____.

IDENTIFICATION; ENVIRONMENT;
DATA; PROCEDURE

2   The first six positions on the COBOL Coding Form are reserved for a sequence number, which typically includes a(n) _____ number and a(n) _____ number.

page; line

3   When a word or literal cannot be completed on a given line, a(n) _____ is entered in column 7 of [that line / the line on which the word is continued].

hyphen; the line on which the word is
continued

4 When a line contains only a comment entry, a(n) _____ is entered in column 7 of that line.

asterisk

5 When a line is to be printed on a new page in the printer listing of the program, a(n) _____ is entered in column 7 of that line.

slash

COBOL LANGUAGE FORMATS

We now describe the general method of presenting programming options. COBOL is characterized by great flexibility in the form of options available to the programmer. In order to communicate these options we use a *metalanguage,* a language about a language. The form of presentation used here is not unique to this book but is generally followed in all books concerned with COBOL program statements. The method is used in order to describe how each type of statement should be structured, and to identify the options available to the programmer for each type of statement. In other words, the style of presentation is necessary because we wish to talk about types of statements in general, rather than about specific and particular program instructions. For this purpose, then, the following set of conventions is followed:

1 Words presented in uppercase are always reserved COBOL words.
2 Uppercase words which are underlined are words that are required in the type of program statement being described. Uppercase words that are not underlined are optional and are used only to improve the readability of the program.
3 Lowercase words are used to indicate the points at which data-names or constants are to be supplied by the programmer. In addition to the words "data-name" and "literal," the term "identifier" is used to indicate a data-name, but it has a slightly broader meaning. It refers to either of the following cases: data-names that are unique in themselves, or data-names that are not unique in themselves but are made unique through *qualification.* Qualification is discussed in Chapter 5, "DATA DIVISION Features." For the time being you may safely assume the words "data-name" and "identifier" to be equivalent. Other lowercase words used to indicate items to be inserted by the programmer are:

file-name

record-name

integer

formula

condition

statement

any imperative statement

any sentence

4 Items enclosed in braces { } indicate that *one* of the enclosed items *must* be used.
5 Items enclosed in brackets [ ] indicate that the items are optional, and one of them *may* be used, at the option of the programmer.

6   An ellipsis (. . .) indicates that further information may be included in the program instruction, usually in the form of repeating the immediately preceding element any desired number of times.

As an example, consider the ADD statement. With the COBOL language format, a basic form of ADD is

$$\underline{\text{ADD}} \left\{ \begin{array}{l} \text{identifier-1} \\ \text{literal-1} \end{array} \right\} \left[\begin{array}{l} , \text{ identifier-2} \\ , \text{ literal-2} \end{array} \right] \dots \underline{\text{TO}} \text{ identifier-m}$$

If we apply the rules presented above, the word ADD is a reserved COBOL word because it is in uppercase, and it is required because it is underscored. The word TO is governed by the same rules. The braces following ADD indicate that one of the two alternatives enclosed *must* be used. Thus the required word ADD must be followed by either an identifier or a literal. Incidentally, it is also understood that, for this specific instruction, the identifier must be an elementary numeric (nonedited) field and the literal must be a numeric literal. The square brackets indicate that identifier-2 and literal-2 are both optional. In other words, the identifier or literal that immediately follows ADD may or may not be followed by a second identifer or literal. The commas are also optional; they may be included to improve readability, or they may be omitted. The ellipsis . . . indicates that the preceding element (in square brackets) may be repeated as many times as desired. Finally, the identifier-m indicates that there *must* be an identifier following the word TO. Note that it is not enclosed in braces, because it is the only option. Braces are used when we may choose among alternatives.

Utilizing the general format above, we see that the following examples are legitimate ADD statements.

ADD AMOUNT TO TOTAL
ADD 100 TO TOTAL
ADD REGULAR OVERTIME TO GROSS
ADD 10 BONUS 100.25 TO GROSS

REVIEW

1   In presenting COBOL statement instructions, words that are entirely in uppercase designate _____ words.

reserved COBOL

2   When a reserved COBOL word is underlined in the format presentation, this indicates that the word [may / must] be used as part of a program instruction.

must

3   Items to be inserted in the program instruction, such as data-names, identifiers, constants, and formulas, are indicated by [lowercase / uppercase] words.

lowercase

4   When two or more items are enclosed within brackets [ ], this indicates that one of them [may / must] be included in the program instruction. When two or more items are enclosed within braces { }, this indicates that one of them [may / must] be included.

may; must

5   To indicate that further information, such as additional data-names, can be included in an instruction, an ellipsis, which is three _____ is used.

periods

EXERCISES

1   In your own words, explain what is meant by a *computer language.*

2   Name and briefly discuss three levels of computer languages.

3   Explain the three related concepts *source program, object program,* and *compiler.* How do these three interrelate in a typical COBOL program run?

4   What does the following statement mean? "COBOL programs should be substantially self-documenting."

5   Programming is not a single step but is best thought of as a process. Discuss the steps involved in the programming process.

6   What is the *operating system* of a computer? How do *program control cards* relate to such a system?

7   Distinguish between language errors and logical errors in computer programming.

8   Give a brief history of the development of the COBOL language.

9   Draw a flowchart to correspond to the following verbal description: Start; set SUM and NUMBER-OF-VALUES to zero; input a record containing a value of INCOME, add this INCOME to the SUM, add 1 to NUMBER-OF-VALUES; if more records are available, input another record repeating the process, otherwise divide NUMBER-OF-VALUES into SUM giving an AVERAGE-INCOME; print the value of AVERAGE-INCOME and then stop.

10   Explain the concept associated with the hierarchical grouping of data in COBOL programming and describe how the hierarchical structure is represented in a COBOL program.

11   What is the difference between data-names and constants in COBOL?

12   Explain what is meant by a *figurative constant* and name some such constants.

13   Give the name and the role of each of the divisions that make up a COBOL program.

Writing
Complete Programs

INTRODUCTION

The purpose of this chapter is to provide a complete but rudimentary set of COBOL instructions so that the student can begin to write complete programs. In subsequent chapters we present additional statement types, as well as additional variations of statements presented in this chapter.

The chapter, by necessity, is lengthy. We recommend a quick initial reading of the entire chapter so as to grasp the entire set of ideas and to form a general framework within which to study the specific programming concepts included.

SAMPLE COBOL PROGRAM

A sample COBOL program is presented in Exhibit 4-1. This program will be used throughout this chapter to allow the reader to relate various types of language statements to a concrete case. The basic function of this program is the reading of card records containing employee salary data and printing a one-page report as presented in Exhibit 4-2. The program reads each employee record, determines the sex of the employee, and prints the name and salary. When all employee records have been input, the total and average salaries for men and women are printed and the program terminates.

EXHIBIT 4-1   SAMPLE COBOL PROGRAM

```
IDENTIFICATION DIVISION.
PROGRAM-ID. SALARY.


ENVIRONMENT DIVISION.
CONFIGURATION SECTION.
SOURCE-COMPUTER. ABC-480.
OBJECT-COMPUTER. ABC-480.
INPUT-OUTPUT SECTION.
FILE-CONTROL.
     SELECT CARD-FILE   ASSIGN TO  CARD-READER-DEVICE.
     SELECT PRINT-FILE  ASSIGN TO  PRINTER-DEVICE.


DATA DIVISION.

FILE SECTION.
FD   CARD-FILE
        LABEL RECORDS ARE OMITTED
        DATA RECORD IS CARD-IN.
01   CARD-IN.
     02 NAME-IN            PIC X(15).
     02 SEX-CODE           PIC 9.
     02 SALARY-IN          PIC 99999V99.


FD   PRINT-FILE
        LABEL RECORDS ARE OMITTED
        DATA RECORD IS PRINT-LINE.
01   PRINT-LINE.
     02 FILLER             PIC X(133).

WORKING-STORAGE SECTION.
01   NO-OF-MEN             PIC 99 VALUE ZERO.
01   NO-OF-WOMEN           PIC 99 VALUE ZERO.
01   MEN-TOTAL-SAL         PIC 9(7)V99 VALUE ZERO.
01   WOMEN-TOTAL-SAL       PIC 9(7)V99 VALUE ZERO.
01   END-OF-DATA-INDICATOR PIC XXX.

01   HEADER1.
     02 FILLER             PIC X VALUE SPACE.
     02 FILLER             PIC X(41) VALUE SPACES.
     02 FILLER             PIC X(13) VALUE 'ANNUAL SALARY'.

01   HEADER2.
     02 FILLER             PIC X VALUE SPACE.
     02 FILLER             PIC X(16) VALUE SPACES.
     02 FILLER             PIC X(42) VALUE
         'EMPLOYEE NAME            MEN            WOMEN'.

01   DATA-LINE.
     02 FILLER             PIC X      VALUE SPACES.
     02 FILLER             PIC X(15) VALUE SPACES.
     02 NAME-OUT           PIC X(15).
     02 FILLER             PIC X(5) VALUE SPACES.
     02 MEN-SAL-OUT        PIC ZZZ9999.99 BLANK WHEN ZERO.
     02 FILLER             PIC X(5)  VALUE SPACES.
     02 WOMEN-SAL-OUT      PIC ZZZ9999.99 BLANK WHEN ZERO.
```

In preparation for the program, we draw record layout forms to specify the input and output data formats, such as those presented in Exhibits 4-3 and 4-4. Such forms are useful during program development, and for future reference should the program need to be changed.

Exhibit 4-3 presents the input record layout. Data input will consist of card records, with one card per employee. Each card consists of four fields. The first one is the *name* in columns 1–15. It is followed by a one-digit *sex code* such that 1 = man, 2 = woman. The *salary* is a field of seven digits, the last two of which are decimal values. Columns 24–80 constitute the fourth field, which is unused by the program.

Exhibit 4-4 presents a print chart of the desired output. A two-line header is to be

EXHIBIT 4-1   SAMPLE COBOL PROGRAMS (*Continued*)

```
PROCEDURE DIVISION.
MAIN-LOGIC.
      OPEN INPUT CARD-FILE
           OUTPUT PRINT-FILE.

      WRITE PRINT-LINE FROM HEADER1
           AFTER ADVANCING PAGE.
      WRITE PRINT-LINE FROM HEADER2
           AFTER ADVANCING 2 LINES.

      MOVE SPACES TO PRINT-LINE
      WRITE PRINT-LINE
           BEFORE ADVANCING 2 LINES.

      MOVE 'NO' TO END-OF-DATA-INDICATOR.

      PERFORM READ-CARD.

      PERFORM PROCESS-AND-PRINT
           UNTIL END-OF-DATA-INDICATOR = 'YES'.

      PERFORM PRINT-SUMMARY.

      CLOSE CARD-FILE
            PRINT-FILE.
      STOP RUN.
PRINT-SUMMARY.
      MOVE ' T O T A L' TO NAME-OUT.
      MOVE MEN-TOTAL-SAL TO MEN-SAL-OUT.
      MOVE WOMEN-TOTAL-SAL TO WOMEN-SAL-OUT
      WRITE PRINT-LINE FROM DATA-LINE
            AFTER ADVANCING 3 LINES.
      MOVE ' A V E R A G E' TO NAME-OUT.
      DIVIDE NO-OF-MEN INTO MEN-TOTAL-SAL GIVING MEN-SAL-OUT.
      DIVIDE NO-OF-WOMEN INTO WOMEN-TOTAL-SAL GIVING WOMEN-SAL-OUT.
      WRITE PRINT-LINE FROM DATA-LINE
            AFTER ADVANCING 2 LINES.
READ-CARD.
      READ CARD-FILE RECORD
           AT END
              MOVE 'YES' TO END-OF-DATA-INDICATOR.
PROCESS-AND-PRINT.
      MOVE NAME-IN TO NAME-OUT.
      IF SEX-CODE = 1
         MOVE SALARY-IN TO MEN-SAL-OUT
         MOVE ZEROS TO WOMEN-SAL-OUT
         ADD 1 TO NO-OF-MEN
         ADD SALARY-IN TO MEN-TOTAL-SAL
      ELSE
         MOVE SALARY-IN TO WOMEN-SAL-OUT
         MOVE ZEROS TO MEN-SAL-OUT
         ADD 1 TO NO-OF-WOMEN
         ADD SALARY-IN TO WOMEN-TOTAL-SAL.
      WRITE PRINT-LINE FROM DATA-LINE
            BEFORE ADVANCING 1 LINE.

      PERFORM READ-CARD.
```

printed on print lines 1 and 3. Then the body of the report starts on line 5 and continues for as many lines as required (in this example we assume there are few enough records so that all the output will fit on one page). The X symbols represent individual print positions. Thus, for example, the men's *salary* field consists of a total of 10 print positions: 7 for the integer, 1 for the decimal point, and 2 positions to the right of the decimal point. At the bottom of the report, on an unspecified line (which depends on the number of employees), we will print the two lines with the total and the averages.

EXHIBIT 4-2   FORM OF OUTPUT FOR THE SAMPLE COBOL PROGRAM

	ANNUAL SALARY	
EMPLOYEE NAME	MEN	WOMEN
JONES, A.	18200.00	
ANDERSON, P.	12000.00	
ROBERTS, M.		15000.00
NICHOLSON, J.	19600.00	
PHILLIPS, P.		18500.00
WORK, A.		10000.00
TOTAL	49800.00	43500.00
AVERAGE	16600.00	14500.00

Figure 4-1 presents a flowchart of the program logic. The basic flow can be summarized as follows: Open the program files. Print the headers. Set the end-of-data-indicator switch to NO. Execute the Read-Card routine, which reads a data card, and if it is the end of the data sets the end-of-data-indicator switch to YES. Test to determine if the end of the data has been reached (end-of-data-indicator = YES). If it is not the end of the data, execute the Process-and-Print routine, otherwise print the totals, compute the averages, print the averages, and stop execution. The Process-and-Print routine checks to see if the card which was read pertains to a man (sex code = 1) or a woman (sex code ≠ 1). In either case we position the salary in the appropriate column, and we accumulate the number of employees and total salary for the respective category.

At this point the reader should reflect on the task and be sure to have the input, output, and program processing considerations clearly in mind. In the following sections we will study the task in terms of implementing it through COBOL programming.

EXHIBIT 4-3   LAYOUT OF INPUT FOR THE SAMPLE COBOL PROGRAM

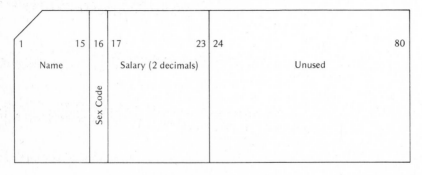

EXHIBIT 4-4 LAYOUT OF OUTPUT DATA FOR THE SAMPLE COBOL PROGRAM

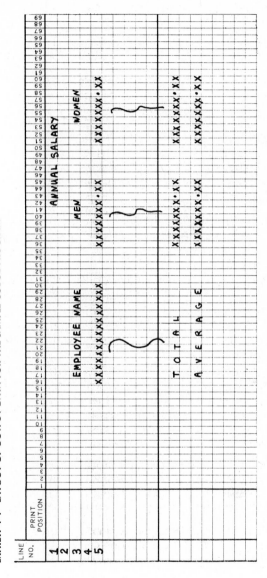

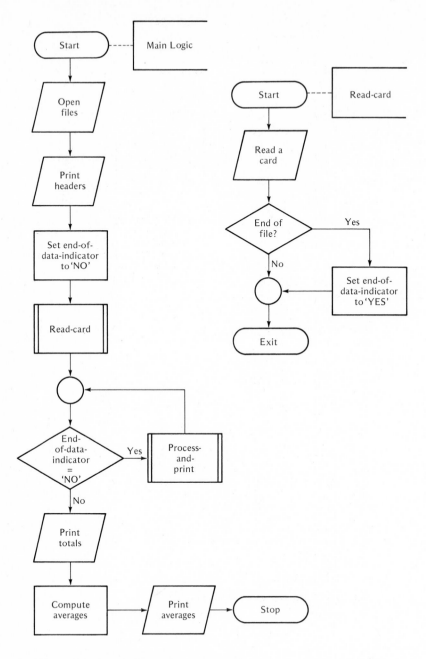

FIGURE 4-1   FLOWCHART FOR THE SAMPLE PROBLEM.

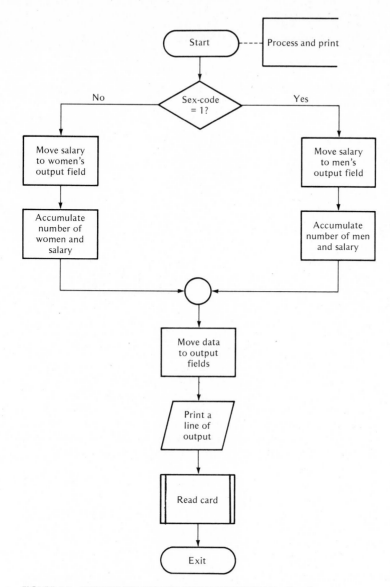

FIGURE 4-1   FLOWCHART FOR THE SAMPLE PROBLEM (*Continued*).

REVIEW

1   The purpose of the sample COBOL program described in this section is to perform an analysis using as input data the annual _____ of each employee.

salary

2 Of the two types of record layout forms which may be used in conjunction with writing a COBOL program, the one which describes the data to be processed is the _____ record layout.

input

3 Of the two types of record layout forms, the one which describes the desired printer output is called the _____ chart.

print

4 The overall program logic underlying a COBOL program can be developed and presented by the program _____.

flowchart

THE IDENTIFICATION DIVISION

The function of the IDENTIFICATION DIVISION is to supply information about the program to others who may read or use the program. On the COBOL Coding Form, we start in column 8 with the words IDENTIFICATION DIVISION. The first and only required paragraph is the PROGRAM-ID, which is followed by the program-name chosen by the programmer. As in the example, we may have:

IDENTIFICATION DIVISION
PROGRAM-ID. SALARY.

In this case, the word SALARY is the name the programmer has chosen to identify the program. This name must start with an alphabetic character and may consist of up to 30 alphabetic or numeric characters unless the specific compiler limits the number to fewer. The two lines above are sufficient content for the IDENTIFICATION DIVISION. All other paragraphs are optional, but if they are used, they must be written in the order shown. The following example includes optional paragraphs. The under-lined words are COBOL reserved words which are required; the other words are a matter of the programmer's choice.

IDENTIFICATION DIVISION.
PROGRAM-ID. SALARY.
AUTHOR. A. PHILIPPAKIS AND L. KAZMIER.
INSTALLATION. ARIZONA STATE UNIVERSITY.
DATE-WRITTEN. JANUARY 14, 1978.
DATE-COMPILED.
SECURITY. THIS PROGRAM RESTRICTED TO PERSONNEL WHO HAVE
      BEEN CLEARED BY THE CONTROLLER'S OFFICE.

All paragraph-names start in column 8 and, as indicated above, they are all optional with the exception of PROGRAM-ID. The compiler does not process what follows the COBOL words but only prints this content. Thus, after DATE-WRITTEN we could have written DURING THE SPRING OF 78. The compiler derives no more meaning from JANUARY than from the nonsense syllables AMZXAB. Therefore, the programmer should be concerned simply with choosing verbal descriptions that will be meaningful to the potential readers of the program.

Note that the DATE-COMPILED paragraph is left blank. The compiler will insert the actual date, and the source listing will include that date.

An entry in the IDENTIFICATION DIVISION may extend to more than one line, as illustrated above in the case of the SECURITY paragraph. In such a case the lines subsequent to the first one must all start in column 12 or to the right of column 12. The PROGRAM-ID paragraph, however, is restricted to one word which must not exceed 30 characters in length.

REVIEW

1 The order in which the four divisions of a COBOL program appear is _____, _____ , _____ , and _____ .

IDENTIFICATION; ENVIRONMENT;
DATA; PROCEDURE

2 Other than the division name itself, the only paragraph required in the IDENTIFI-CATION DIVISION is the one named _____ .

PROGRAM-ID

3 Although other entries in the IDENTIFICATION DIVISION may extend to more than one line, the PROGRAM-ID paragraph is normally restricted to one word which must not exceed _____ (number) characters in length.

30

4 Overall, the purpose of the IDENTIFICATION DIVISION of a COBOL program is to _____ .

describe the program to potential users
(etc.)

THE ENVIRONMENT DIVISION

A COBOL program written for one computer can normally be processed on another computer, with the exception of the ENVIRONMENT DIVISION portion of the program. The reason for this exception is that the specified equipment to be used in running the program is described in this division. Since the equipment at different computer centers differs in terms of manufacturer and model, the ENVIRONMENT DIVISION of a COBOL program has to be tailored to each computer installation. This may seem inconvenient, but consider also the advantages of this modular design of COBOL. Since equipment differences affect the ENVIRONMENT DIVISION only, this division of the program can be changed without rewriting any of the other three divisions.

The following illustration of an ENVIRONMENT DIVISION is reproduced from the sample program of Exhibit 4-1:

```
ENVIRONMENT DIVISION.
CONFIGURATION SECTION.
SOURCE-COMPUTER. ABC-480.
OBJECT-COMPUTER. ABC-480.
INPUT-OUTPUT SECTION.
FILE-CONTROL.
    SELECT CARD FILE ASSIGN TO CARD-READER-DEVICE.
    SELECT PRINT-FILE ASSIGN TO PRINTER-DEVICE.
```

There are two sections in this example division, the CONFIGURATION and the INPUT-OUTPUT. The SOURCE-COMPUTER and OBJECT-COMPUTER paragraphs serve documentation purposes. ABC-480 is fictitious in the example and would be replaced by a manufacturer's name and model number.

In this example there is one paragraph in the INPUT-OUTPUT SECTION, the FILE-CONTROL paragraph. The SELECT statement identifies the name of a file, in this case CARD-FILE. This file-name is the programmer's choice, and it is formed in compliance with COBOL name formation rules (although some compilers place further restrictions, such as that the first 12 characters must be unique). The ASSIGN statement declares that this file will be associated with the hardware device whose name follows, in this case, CARD-READER-DEVICE. Similarly, PRINT-FILE identifies another file-name, and the hardware device with which this file will be associated is PRINTER-DEVICE (thus, this file will include the output information). Device names are neither COBOL words nor programmer supplied, they are *implementor-names,* which means they are specific to the compiler used. Instead of the natural words shown in the example, the user of IBM compilers is likely to have entries of the following type:

```
SELECT CARD-FILE ASSIGN TO SYS005-UR-2540R-S.
SELECT PRINT-FILE ASSIGN TO SYS006-UT-1403-S.
```

In this case the terms SYS005-UR-2540R-S and SYS006-UT-1403-S stand for card reader and printer, respectively.

Apart from the specific computer name and card reader and printer designations, the entries shown in the example are sufficient to guide the student in writing ENVIRONMENT divisions for programs which involve input from the card reader and output on the printer. Later in the text additional considerations and options are discussed.

REVIEW

1   Of the four divisions of a COBOL program, the one written with an orientation to a particular computer center and its equipment is the _____ DIVISION.

ENVIRONMENT

2   The two sections of the ENVIRONMENT DIVISION are the CONFIGURATION SECTION and the INPUT-OUTPUT SECTION. Of these, the one which serves to

identify the equipment to be used and which is the only section specifically required is the _____ SECTION.

CONFIGURATION

3 The section of the ENVIRONMENT DIVISION concerned with the assignment of specified files to particular devises is the _____ SECTION.

INPUT-OUTPUT

4 Overall, the division of a COBOL program concerned with supplying general information about the program is the _____ DIVISION, whereas the division which specifies the equipment to be used is the _____ DIVISION.

IDENTIFICATION; ENVIRONMENT

THE DATA DIVISION

The DATA DIVISION identifies storage fields and their names. Commonly, it consists of two sections: the FILE and the WORKING-STORAGE sections. In its simplest form, the function of the FILE SECTION of the DATA DIVISION is to describe each file used in the program by specifying:

1 The name of the file
2 The name assigned to the record in the file
3 The hierarchical structure of the data fields in the record
4 The field size and type of data in each storage field of the record

The FILE SECTION of Exhibit 4-1 is reproduced below:

```
FILE SECTION.
FD CARD-FILE
     LABEL RECORDS ARE OMITTED
     DATA RECORD IS CARD-IN.
01   CARD-IN.
     02   NAME-IN              PIC X(15).
     02   SEX-CODE             PIC 9.
     02   SALARY-IN            PIC 99999V99.
FD   PRINT-FILE
     LABEL RECORDS ARE OMITTED
     DATA RECORD IS PRINT-LINE.
01   PRINT-LINE.
     02   FILLER               PIC X(133).
```

The designation FD is needed at the beginning of each file description; it stands for File Description. FD is always followed by a file-name, in this case, CARD-FILE for the first FD entry. The statement LABEL RECORDS ARE OMITTED indicates that this file has no labels. In a magnetic tape or disk file, label records are not omitted, but in a card file or a print file labels have no meaning. The use of labels is described in Chapter 10, "Magnetic Tape Files." For the time being, we will assume that labels are omitted. The next clause in the FD entry, DATA RECORD IS CARD-IN, identifies the name of the record in the file as CARD-IN. The word CARD-IN is the programmer's choice.

Following the FD entry a record description is written. The 01 level number introduces the record-name, CARD-IN. The following three entries describe the fields which are subordinate, or parts of the record. Each is introduced with the 02 level number, indicating that it is a subordinate field. PIC is an abbreviated form of PICTURE, an alternative form and a COBOL reserved word. The PIC clause is used to describe the size and data characteristics of the field, and the use of this clause is described later in this section in some detail. NAME-IN, SEX-CODE, and SALARY-IN are data-names coined by the programmer.

The second FD entry describes the PRINT-FILE associated with the printer. The record-name is PRINT-LINE, and it has one subordinate data field. FILLER is a COBOL reserved word. It is used optionally to name a field to which no specific mention will be made in the program. The use of FILLER eliminates the need to coin more data-names than needed. Since it is not used directly, FILLER can be used to name several fields without causing any problems of unique identification. An imperative rule of the language is that all references in a program must be made to unique field names. This rule is not violated by use of the nonunique name FILLER, because this field is not referenced in the program.

Storage fields associated with the file records receive data from or are used to send data to external input-output devices, such as card readers and printers. In addition to such storage fields, there is also a need for storage fields to store partial results, to save data for later computations, to store header data, and the like.

The following excerpt from Exhibit 4-1 illustrates a portion of the WORKING-STORAGE SECTION:

```
WORKING-STORAGE SECTION.
01   NO-OF-MEN            PIC 99 VALUE ZERO.
01   NO-OF-WOMEN          PIC 99 VALUE ZERO.
01   HEADER1.
     02   FILLER          PIC X    VALUE SPACE.
     02   FILLER          PIC X(41) VALUE SPACES.
     02   FILLER          PIC X(13) VALUE 'ANNUAL SALARY'.
```

The level number 01 is commonly used to introduce WORKING-STORAGE fields that are at the elementary level and therefore contain no subordinate fields. The 77 level may be used instead of 01 and traditionally 77 has been used for elementary WORKING-STORAGE fields. The most recent proposed standard COBOL has eliminated the use of level 77, since the 01 level performs the same function. However, the 77 has been in use for many years and will continue to exist in "old" programs. The VALUE clause is a means of initializing a field with the data specified; in the case of 01   NO-OF-MEN, the field is initialized to ZERO.

In addition to elementary fields, the WORKING-STORAGE section may contain group fields, such as HEADER1 in the illustration. The 01 level number introduces the record-name, HEADER1. There are three subordinate fields, all called FILLER in this case. The VALUE SPACES clause initializes the first two fields to blanks. It may seem odd that we use two fields to initialize the first 42 positions to blanks when one field could have been used. The reason is that in IBM computer systems the first position must always be blank because it is used for printer carriage control. Therefore it is a good practice always to initialize the first position to a blank no matter what fields follow this position. This matter is explained further in the next section of this chapter. The VALUE "ANNUAL SALARY" initializes the third FILLER fields to those characters. The name HEADER-1 can be used to refer to all of these FILLERS as one field. With reference to Exhibit 4-2, it is noticed that HEADER1 contains the data for the first header line in the output.

REVIEW

1   Of the four divisions of a COBOL program, the one concerned with the identification and description of storage fields is the _____ division.

DATA

2   After the DATA DIVISION and FILE SECTION have been identified in the program, the designation FD is used and is always followed by a file-name. FD is a reserved COBOL word and stands for _____.

File Description

3   A label as such is typically *not* attached to a file when the data is entered on [punched cards / magnetic tape].

punched cards

4   After the name of the file, the next item of information given in the FD entry is the name of the _____ contained in the file.

record

5   The level number assigned to the whole record is always _____ (number).

01

6   All fields in the record that are directly subordinate to the overall record commonly are assigned the level number _____ (number).

02 or higher

7   When a WORKING-STORAGE field is at the elementary level and therefore contains no subordinate fields, the level number assigned to the field is _____ (number).

01 or 77

8   An initial value can be established in a WORKING-STORAGE field by use of the _____ clause.

VALUE

9   The VALUE clause can be used in the WORKING-STORAGE SECTION to establish field values that are [numeric only / numeric or nonnumeric].

numeric or nonnumeric (for example, a nonnumeric literal such as 'ANNUAL SALARY' can be assigned)

THE PICTURE CLAUSE

Level numbers define the hierarchical structure of data items in a record, whereas data-names identify each field in the record by name. Beyond this, the PICTURE clause associated with each item is used to describe the field size and indicates such information as whether the field is numeric, alphabetic, or alphanumeric; whether it is computational or display; whether it contains editing characters; whether it contains a decimal point; and whether a numeric field can contain a negative value. All this is accomplished by use of the PICTURE clause.

The abbreviated form PIC is equally valid, and it is the form used in the example for no other reason than personal preference.

Referring to the sample program, we have an entry:

02 NAME-IN   PIC X(15).

The X is a PICTURE character which stands for an alphanumeric field. The (15) stands for the number of positions in the field, in this case 15. Thus X(15) indicates an alphanumeric field of 15 positions. Incidentally, data is referred to as alphanumeric, numeric, or alphabetic. In COBOL, an alphanumeric field can contain any legitimate COBOL character. A numeric field may contain only the digits 0–9 and an algebraic sign. An alphabetic field may contain the blank and any of the letters A–Z.

Another example of the PICTURE clause is:

02 SEX-CODE   PIC 9.

In this case the 9 indicates a numeric field of one position. The fact that there is only one 9 is the reason for the field size being 1. Contrast this to:

01 NO-OF-MEN   PIC 99 VALUE ZERO.

The statement above identifies a two-position numeric field. Thus, the number of 9s indicates the size of the field.

A decimal point is indicated with a V. The V PICTURE character shows the location of an *implied* decimal point. Consider the example:

02 SALARY-IN   PIC 99999V99.

The position of the V indicates that the first five character positions contain integer values and the last two positions in the field contain decimal values. It may be recalled that SALARY-IN refers to the data input from card columns 16–22 of the card input record. If on a given card these columns have 1254325 punched in them, the data will be read and stored as if it were 12,543.25 in ordinary language. Notice that the decimal point is not punched. Rather, the PICTURE provides the information to read in the last two digits as if they were entered to the right of a decimal point.

A PICTURE character may be repeated to indicate field size, or we may use parentheses enclosing a constant. Thus, we can have the following equivalent pairs of designations:

PIC 9999   is equivalent to 9(4)
PIC 99999V99   is equivalent to 9(5)V9(2)
PIC X(5)   is equivalent to XXXXX.

However, PIC X(42) cannot be written in the form of 42 X's because a rule of the language states that no more than 30 PICTURE characters can be used in a given clause—and it is a sensible rule, at least for the example.

So far we have discussed examples and rules concerned with forming alphanumeric and numeric fields, the latter with or without a decimal point. We will now consider *numeric edited* fields. In COBOL there is a definite distinction between numeric data used for computation and numeric data used for printing, which is referred to as edited data. Chapter 6 contains an expanded discussion of editing. At present we will consider two options exemplified in:

02 MEN-SAL-OUT   PIC ZZZ9999.99 BLANK WHEN ZERO.

The Z's are zero-suppress PICTURE characters. They imply that in this field of seven integers and two decimal positions any leading zeros in the first three positions should be replaced with blanks. Recall that numeric data do not include the blank. Thus, if we had a field which contained 0001234.56 and we wanted to print this data without the leading zeros, we would first move the data to an edited numeric field and then print the edited field. The other point to notice in this example is that a decimal point is included in the PICTURE character string. This is an editing decimal point, and it will be printed as such. In contrast, if we print a field which contains a V, no decimal point will be printed.

In a limited context, we have discussed the PICTURE clause for the following uses:

1 To define alphanumeric fields using the X PICTURE character
2 To define numeric fields using the 9 character
3 To define an implied decimal point using the V character
4 To suppress leading zeros by moving data in a numeric field to an edited numeric field using the Z character
5 To print a decimal point by moving data in an edited numeric field using the decimal (.) character

These rudimentary rules will suffice for the present. They will enable the student to write complete programs without being in full command of the PICTURE options which will be discussed further in Chapter 5, "DATA DIVISION Features."

REVIEW

1 The character in the PICTURE clause used to indicate that the field can contain alphabetic, numeric, or special symbols is the _____ character.

X

2 The character in the PICTURE clause which indicates that a field has numeric content only is the _____ character.

9

3 The character in the PICTURE clause which indicates the position of an assumed decimal point is the _____ character.

V

4 Either the V PICTURE character or the decimal (.) PICTURE character can be used to indicate the position of the decimal point. Of these, the one which requires use of a numeric edited field is the _____ character.

decimal (.)

5 The PICTURE character which serves the editing function of replacing leading zeros in a value with blanks is the _____ character.

Z

THE PROCEDURE DIVISION

The IDENTIFICATION, ENVIRONMENT, and DATA divisions in a COBOL program perform "housekeeping tasks" in that they provide background information so that the program can be executed after compilation. On the other hand, the instructions that directly result in execution of the program are given in the PROCEDURE DIVISION. Most of the instructions in the PROCEDURE DIVISION are instructions to operate on storage locations, or fields, that have been defined in the DATA DIVISION. Some verbal counterparts of PROCEDURE DIVISION instructions go like this: "Take the data punched onto a card and enter it into storage, according to the fields described by a record in the DATA DIVISION. Add the value of one data-name to that of another and place the result in a third data-name, all three data-names and their corresponding storage descriptions having been given in the DATA DIVISION. Output the contents of a storage location on the printer." The key words PROCEDURE DIVISION identify the beginning of this division and begin at the A Margin of the COBOL Coding Form, followed by a period. The division consists of paragraphs, each paragraph containing at least one sentence. Each paragraph starts with a paragraph-name beginning in column 8 (A Margin). Paragraph-names are coined by the programmer following the rules of data-name formation, with one additional option: Paragraph-names may be all-numeric. Sentences and statements are written in columns 12–72.

A PROCEDURE DIVISION may also consist of several sections, each one starting in column 8 with a section-name followed by the key word SECTION, as in TAX SECTION, where TAX is a programmer-chosen section-name. A section may contain several paragraphs. However, the need for sections occurs in large or sophisticated programs that are not likely to fall within the scope of a beginner's programming exercises.

In this chapter, we present some basic instructions used in the PROCEDURE DIVISION. Additional PROCEDURE DIVISION statements are described in Chapters 6 and 7.

The two most commonly used types of PROCEDURE DIVISION statements are imperative and conditional statements. An imperative statement consists of a verb that indicates action, plus appropriate operands involved in the action. In this chapter the following imperative verbs are discussed:

Input/output verbs: OPEN, READ, WRITE, CLOSE

Data transfer verb: MOVE

Arithmetic verbs: ADD, SUBTRACT, MULTIPLY, DIVIDE

Control verbs: PERFORM, GO TO, STOP

In addition to the four types of verbs, two basic conditional expressions are covered in this chapter: the IF and the AT END conditional expressions.

INPUT/OUTPUT VERBS

In this section we consider four input/output verbs: OPEN, READ, WRITE, and CLOSE.

Before an input or an output file can be used by the program it must be *opened*. It is not our purpose to go into any detail at this point, except to say that opening a file involves checking the availability of the device associated with the file. With reference to the first paragraph in Exhibit 4-1 the following statement can be seen:

OPEN INPUT   CARD-FILE
       OUTPUT PRINT-FILE.

The file named CARD-FILE is opened as input, and the file named PRINT-FILE is opened as output. Thus the OPEN verb declares the input or output function of the file. It will be recalled that the file names appear in two other divisions of the program. In the ENVIRONMENT DIVISION the two files were assigned to the card reader and printer, respectively, and in the DATA DIVISION the FD entries referenced each file. Thus, when references to files are made in the PROCEDURE DIVISION, it is understood that information about the files has already been given in the ENVIRONMENT and DATA divisions.

The basic format of the READ instruction is: READ file-name RECORD AT END imperative statement. In Exhibit 4-1, in the READ-CARD paragraph, the input instruction is

READ CARD-FILE RECORD
     AT END
          MOVE 'YES' TO END-OF-DATA-INDICATOR.

In the example program of Exhibit 4-1 we wish to read data punched onto cards. Each card is a record of the CARD-FILE whose record was named CARD-IN in the DATA DIVISION. It will be recalled that each card has the following fields:

CARD COLUMNS	CONTENT	DATA-NAME
1–15	Employee's name	NAME-IN
16	Sex code	SEX-CODE
17–23	Salary	SALARY-IN
24–80	Unused	FILLER

The representation of the data in internal storage and the assignment of data-names to storage positions can be represented by the following conceptual structure:

	CARD-IN			
Data-name	NAME-IN	SEX-CODE	SALARY-IN	FILLER
Columns	1 15	16	17 23	24 80

Thus when the command READ CARD-FILE RECORD is executed, the data contained in the next card in the card reader will thereafter be available by use of the data-name CARD-IN. Further, the data formerly contained in card columns 1–15 will be internally available by use of the data-name NAME-IN, the content of column 16 will be available under the name SEX-CODE, and the contents of columns 17–23 will be available under the name SALARY-IN.

Each execution of the READ statement causes the contents of a new card to go into CARD-IN and to erase the previous data contained in CARD-IN. This means that we normally process one record at a time and, when we read the next record, we have no use for the preceding one. If we do have further use for this record, then the data should be copied into another field to be saved for subsequent use.

As part of the READ instruction, we also need to indicate what the computer should do after all the input records have been read. The AT END clause serves this purpose. When a card is read, it is examined to see if it is an end-of-file card. The specific form of an end-of-file card differs according to the computer used, but in general it contains data codes which designate it as such. Only when such a card is read is the imperative statement following AT END executed. Thus AT END is a conditional clause; it indicates that the following statement should be executed if the card just read is an end-of-file card. In our sample program, the imperative statement following AT END enters a YES in the END-OF-DATA-INDICATOR field so that the program will be able to determine when all the data has been read in.

The output verb WRITE is similar to the input verb READ, except that reference is made to a record-name rather than a file-name. There are two basic forms illustrated in the sample program. The first one is

WRITE PRINT-LINE FROM HEADER1
    AFTER ADVANCING PAGE.

This in essence says to transfer the data in the field HEADER1 (FROM HEADER1) to PRINT-LINE, which is the record-name of the file associated with the printer, and to write the data in PRINT-LINE after skipping to the top of a new page (AFTER ADVANCING PAGE). PAGE is a COBOL reserved word which means the top of a new page on the printer.

Notice that in COBOL we do not write data directly. First we transfer it to the record of the output file, and then we write it. Now we can see why the DATA DIVISION definition of PRINT-LINE consisted of an X(133) field. It is simply a field to which we transfer whatever we want printed. For example, HEADER1 is a field which contains the first line of header data.

In the case of IBM COBOL compilers, if programmers wish to use all of the printer character positions, then they must provide for one more position than the print line. Thus if the printer we are using can print lines of 132 characters, we would write the following data record description:

01   PRINT-LINE   PIC X(133).

The first of these 133 positions is not printed. It is used for vertical spacing. The programmer should see to it that data fields to be printed have an extra first position containing a blank. For an IBM user the recommended data descriptions for HEADER 1 are as indicated in the DATA DIVISION in Exhibit 4-1:

01   HEADER1.
    02   FILLER   PIC X VALUE SPACE.

```
02  FILLER     PIC X(41) VALUE SPACES.
02  FILLER     PIC X(13) VALUE 'ANNUAL SALARY'.
```

Of the 42 blank spaces the first one will not be printed, but will be used by the system for carriage control instead. Thus, it is recommended that the programmer using IBM equipment write FILLER PIC X VALUE SPACE as the first field in all print records.

Compilers written by manufacturers other than IBM usually do not require the extra first print position. Thus, we would write:

```
01  PRINT-LINE.
    02  FILLER     PIC X(132).
         .
         .
         .
01  HEADER1.
    02  FILLER     PIC X(41) VALUE SPACES.
    02  FILLER     PIC X(13) VALUE 'ANNUAL SALARY'.
```

This approach is straightforward in that we specify only those print positions which are actually used for printed output.

A second example from Exhibit 4-1 illustrates another option of the ADVANCING clause:

```
WRITE PRINT-LINE FROM HEADER2
    AFTER ADVANCING 2 LINES.
```

In this case we print the contents of HEADER2 after the printer advances two lines, which leaves one blank line between the current and the preceding output. Thus to triple-space between lines we simply use AFTER ADVANCING 3 LINES, and in general the integer preceding the word LINES (or LINE) specifies the vertical spacing. In later chapters we will study additional options of the WRITE verb. As is always the case, the separate line spacing of the AFTER ADVANCING . . . clause is not required. However, we recommend it to enhance readability.

We conclude this discussion of input/output verbs with the CLOSE verb, which is used after a file is no longer needed and which must be used before the end of the program. At the end of the MAIN-LOGIC paragraph of Exhibit 4-1 we see:

```
CLOSE CARD-FILE
      PRINT-FILE.
```

The CLOSE verb is more meaningful in the context of magnetic tapes and disk files, but it is required for card and printer files as well. File-names are written on separate lines simply to enhance readability. CLOSE CARD-FILE PRINT-FILE would be equally acceptable in this case.

REVIEW

1 Input of data into the central storage of the computer is accomplished by executing a READ statement. Before a READ statement can be executed, a checking procedure must be carried out to determine file availability by executing a(n) _____ statement.

OPEN

2 As each record of a file is read into storage, the previous content of that storage location, which typically represents data from the preceding record which was read, is automatically [moved / erased].

erased

3 The part of the READ statement which indicates what should be done after all the records of the input file have been read is the _____ clause.

AT END

4 Output of data from a designated output file is accomplished by executing a(n) _____ instruction.

WRITE

5 Before a WRITE statement can be executed, availability of the output file must first be ascertained by executing an appropriate _____ statement.

OPEN

6 Data contained in a storage location can be transfered to an output file for subsequent output by use of the _____ option which is available with the write statement.

FROM

7 A further option available with the WRITE statement allows control of the vertical spacing in the printed output. The clause used to designate spacing instruction is the _____ clause.

ADVANCING

8 When a data processing operation is completed, the availability of both the input and output files that have been used should be terminated. This is accomplished by an appropriate _____ instruction.

CLOSE

DATA MOVEMENT

By data movement we mean the operation by which a value can be moved from one storage location to another. This result can be accomplished in the COBOL language by use of the verb MOVE. Consider, for example, the situation in which we initially have the following values in two storage locations with data-names A and B, respectively:

A		
0	3	5

B		
8	3	1

If we execute the instruction MOVE A TO B, the resulting values in the two storage locations will be as follows:

A		
0	3	5

B		
0	3	5

The verb MOVE causes the content of A to be copied into B, erasing the previous content of B. The general form of the MOVE instruction is

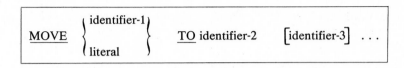

Some examples of the options available in writing MOVE instructions are

1 MOVE AMOUNT TO QUANTITY
2 MOVE 25.85 TO PRICE
3 MOVE ZEROES TO TOTAL
4 MOVE SPACES TO BLANKFIELD
5 MOVE "EXAMPLE" TO HEADING
6 MOVE "FOR THE YEAR 1970" TO TITLE, HEADER, SUBHEAD

Statements 2–5 are all concerned with literals. Statement 2 results in the value of a numeric constant being assigned to PRICE. Statements 3 and 4 are concerned with figurative constants. Finally, statements 5 and 6 are concerned with nonnumeric constants; in this case, anything enclosed within the quotation marks is transferred to the receiving field. In any use of the MOVE instruction, caution should be exercised so that the receiving field is not smaller than the sending field. If the receiving field is too small, truncation will result in the loss of part of the value or information being transferred. The rules for moving data are many and relate to the form of data moved. Two important points to remember are the following: Numeric data is aligned according to the decimal point. If the receiving field is larger than the sending, the extra positions are filled with zeros. If the receiving field is smaller, then truncation takes place as needed, to the right, left, or both right and left of the decimal point. In the following illustration the caret (˄) implies a decimal point.

SENDING FIELD   RESULT IN RECEIVING FIELD

| 0 | 1 | 3 | 5 | 2 |

| 0 | 0 | 1 | 3 | 5 | 2 | 0 |

| 2 | 5 | 2 | 3 | 5 |

| 2 | 5 | 2 | 3 | 5 |

| 2 | 5 | 2 | 3 | 5 |

| 5 | 2 | 3 | 5 |

| 2 | 5 | 2 | 3 | 5 |

| 5 | 2 | 3 |

For alphabetic or alphanumeric data, the data is left-justified in the receiving field (unless the programmer uses the JUSTIFIED RIGHT clause in the DATA DIVISION). If the receiving field is larger than the sending field, the additional positions are filled with blanks. If the receiving field is smaller, then truncation takes place from the right. The following examples illustrate some typical cases.

SENDING FIELD

B	O	N	A	N	Z	A

B	O	N	A	N	Z	A

B	O	N	A	N	Z	A

RECEIVING FIELD

B	O	N	A	N	Z	A	

B	O	N	A	N	Z	A

B	O	N	A	N

The MOVE verb may have as its operands elementary or group items. Thus it is possible to transfer the storage location of a character, a word, a group item, or an entire record.

A final point is that numeric data cannot be moved to an alphabetic field and alphabetic data cannot be moved to a field that has been designated a numeric field in the DATA DIVISION. On the other hand, alphabetic data can be moved to an alphanumeric field. Integer numeric data can be moved from an alphanumeric field to a numeric field. Numeric information can be moved to an alphanumeric field if the numeric value is an integer (whole number).

REVIEW

1   Assume that the storage location with data-names X, Y, and Z initially contains the values indicated on the first line of the table below. For each of the following MOVE instructions, indicate the value contained in each storage location after statement execution. Place a check after any statement that is not an executable MOVE instruction.

STATEMENT	X	Y	Z
Initial values	10	18	20
a MOVE X TO Y			
b MOVE X TO 15			
c MOVE 15 TO X			
d MOVE X TO Y Z			
e MOVE X TO Y, Z			
f MOVE ZEROES TO X, Y, Z			

a   10; 10; 20
b   √(incorrect form)
c   15; 18; 20
d   10; 10; 10
e   10; 10; 10
f   00; 00; 00

2   Assume that ORIGINAL has the data contents indicated below and that FINAL has the structure shown. Indicate the result of the instruction MOVE ORIGINAL TO FINAL in each case.

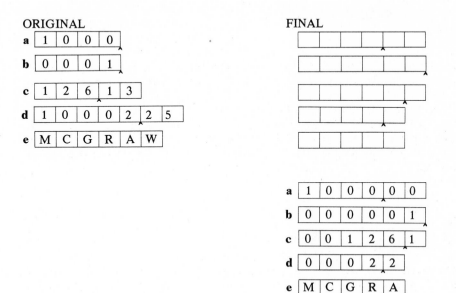

ORIGINAL

a [1 | 0 | 0 | 0]

b [0 | 0 | 0 | 1]

c [1 | 2 | 6 | 1 | 3]

d [1 | 0 | 0 | 0 | 2 | 2 | 5]

e [M | C | G | R | A | W]

FINAL

a [1 | 0 | 0 | 0 | 0 | 0]

b [0 | 0 | 0 | 0 | 0 | 1]

c [0 | 0 | 1 | 2 | 6 | 1]

d [0 | 0 | 0 | 2 | 2]

e [M | C | G | R | A]

3   For each of the following MOVE statements, indicate whether the statement is valid or invalid in COBOL by placing a check in the appropriate column.

SENDING FIELD	RECEIVING FIELD	VALID	INVALID
a Alphabetic	Numeric		
b Alphabetic	Alphanumeric		
c Numeric	Alphabetic		
d Numeric	Alphanumeric		
e Alphanumeric	Alphabetic		
f Alphanumeric	Numeric		

a   Invalid
b   Valid
c   Invalid
d   Valid for integers only
e   Valid for alphabetic contents only
f   Valid for integers only

ARITHMETIC VERBS

In this subsection we consider the use of four arithmetic verbs: ADD, SUBTRACT, MULTIPLY, DIVIDE.

The verb ADD is used to accomplish addition. As an example, suppose we have defined two storage fields in the DATA DIVISION, to which we have given the data-names SUBTOTAL and TOTAL. Assume that they contain the following values:

SUBTOTAL
0	1	0	0

TOTAL
0	0	2	3	2

If we write ADD SUBTOTAL TO TOTAL, the effect will be to increase the value of TOTAL by the value of SUBTOTAL, leaving the value of SUBTOTAL unchanged. Thus, execution of the instruction will result in:

SUBTOTAL
0	1	0	0

TOTAL
0	0	3	3	2

To illustrate another option in using the ADD instruction, suppose we want to add TOTAL and SUBTOTAL and to store the result in a field we call GRAND-TOTAL. To do this we can execute the instruction:

ADD TOTAL SUBTOTAL GIVING GRAND-TOTAL.

When this statement is executed, the original contents of TOTAL and SUBTOTAL are unaffected, and therefore the order of these two is immaterial.

In the Exhibit 4-1 sample program we find these examples:

ADD 1 TO NO-OF-MEN
ADD SALARY-IN TO MEN-TOTAL-SAL

The first example illustrates the use of a numeric constant as an operand of the ADD verb. Both examples illustrate the use of *accumulators*. If we check back in the WORKING-STORAGE SECTION of the DATA DIVISION, it will be observed that NO-OF-MEN and MEN-TOTAL-SAL were both initialized with a VALUE ZERO. This is necessary, since in the PROCEDURE DIVISION we say ADD . . . TO. . . . The initial contents of memory are, in general, not zero. Thus, if we have neglected to initialize the NO-OF-MEN field, for instance, we add 1 to nonzero and likely nonnumeric data with erroneous or unpredictable results. It should be emphasized that, when a field is defined as numeric (use of the 9 PICTURE character), it does not mean that it will necessarily contain numeric data. A good example is the common student error of not filling a numeric punched card field with leading zeros. Suppose that a field SALARY-IN PIC 99999V99 receives data from card columns 17–23 which have been punched as

| | 8 | 0 | 0 | 0 | 0 | 0 |

. The first position was left blank. The blank is a distinct character in the memory of a computer, and it is not the same as zero. Execution of ADD SALARY-IN TO MEN-TOTAL-SAL would result in erroneous arithmetic, since the addend would not be 8000.00 but "blank 8000.00" which is entirely incorrect.

In light of the above discussion, it should also be obvious now that arithmetic must be performed using fields defined as numeric fields in the DATA DIVISION. What may not be so obvious is that arithmetic *must not* be performed using numeric edited fields. Thus, fields whose PICTURE clauses contain Z's or editing decimal points (as well as other editing characters to be learned later) must not be operands in arithmetic statements. The 9 and the V, on the other hand, do define numeric items.

The verb SUBTRACT is used to accomplish arithmetic subtraction. It parallels the ADD verb in the two forms we will discuss in this section:

SUBTRACT AMOUNT FROM SUM
SUBTRACT AMOUNT FROM SUM GIVING BALANCE

The first example will cause the value of AMOUNT to be subtracted from the value of SUM, causing the content of SUM to change (unless AMOUNT is equal to zero). The second example causes the subtraction to take place, but the result is now stored in BALANCE, leaving AMOUNT *and* SUM unchanged.

At this point we take the opportunity to introduce the subject of negative numbers in COBOL. It is the responsibility of the programmer to define a field so that it can contain a negative value. Suppose we have:

02   AMOUNT   PIC 999
02   SUM   PIC 999

If AMOUNT contains the value 500 and SUM contains the value 100, the instruction SUBTRACT AMOUNT FROM SUM will cause SUM to contain 400, not −400. To avoid such problems we should have defined SUM in the DATA DIVISION as:

02   SUM PIC   S999.

The S PICTURE character designates a *signed* field and allows representation of negative values. As a general rule, all numeric fields should be signed. In the example of Exhibit 4-1 we did not do this because of the nature of the problem.

When punching negative data, the negative sign is *overpunched* in the rightmost column of the field. To overpunch the negative sign, when punching the rightmost digit, depress the MULTIPUNCH key on the upper left corner of the keyboard and hold it down while punching the digit *and* the negative sign. In this fashion both characters are entered in one column.

The verb MULTIPLY is used to accomplish multiplication. Consider these two forms:

MULTIPLY QUANTITY BY PRICE
MULTIPLY QUANTITY BY PRICE GIVING AMOUNT

The first instruction will cause the PRODUCT of QUANTITY and PRICE to be stored in PRICE. The second instruction will leave QUANTITY and PRICE unaffected, storing their product in AMOUNT.

The DIVIDE verb can be used as in:

DIVIDE PRICE INTO AMOUNT
DIVIDE NO-OF-MEN INTO MEN-TOTAL-SAL GIVING MEN-SAL-OUT

The first instruction will store the quotient of AMOUNT divided by PRICE in AMOUNT. The second example, taken from Exhibit 4-1, will store the quotient of MEN-TOTAL-SAL divided by NO-OF-MEN in MEN-SAL-OUT.

REVIEW

1 Assume that the storage locations with data-names X, Y, and Z initially, and before each statement, contain the values indicated on the first line of the table below. For each of the following COBOL statements indicate the value contained in each storage location after statement execution. Place a check after any statement that is not an executable ADD instruction.

STATEMENT	VALUE IN		
	X	Y	Z
Initial values	10	12	100
a ADD X TO Y			
b ADD X Y GIVING Z			
c ADD X Y			
d ADD Z TO Y			

a 10; 22; 100
b 10; 12; 22
c √(TO or GIVING is missing)
d 10; 112; 100

2 Assume that storage locations with data-names X, Y, and Z initially contain the values indicated on the first line of the table below. For each of the following COBOL statements indicate the value contained in each storage location after statement execution. Place a check after any statement that is not an executable SUBTRACT instruction.

STATEMENT	X	Y	Z
Initial values	90	30	20
a SUBTRACT Y FROM Z			
b SUBTRACT Z FROM Y			
c SUBTRACT Z FROM X GIVING Y			
d SUBTRACT X FROM Y GIVING Z			

a 90; 30; −10
b 90; 10; 20
c 90; 70; 20
d 90; 30; −60

3 Assume that the storage locations with data-names X, Y, and Z initially contain the values indicated on the first line of the table below. For each of the following COBOL statements, indicate the value contained in each storage location after statement execution. Place a check after any statement that is not an executable MULTIPLY or DIVIDE instruction.

STATEMENT	RESULTING VALUE IN		
	X	Y	Z
Initial values	90	30	10
a MULTIPLY Y BY Z			
b MULTIPLY Y BY Z GIVING X			
c MULTIPLY Z BY Y			
d DIVIDE X BY Z			
e DIVIDE Z INTO X			
f DIVIDE Z INTO X GIVING Y			

a 90; 30; 300
b 300; 30; 10
c 90; 300; 10
d √ (incorrect form)
e 9; 30; 10
f 90; 9; 10

4 If a field could conceivably contain a negative value, then in the DATA DIVISION the PICTURE clause for such a field should include the _____ PICTURE character as the leftmost character in the field.

S

CONDITIONAL EXPRESSIONS

We frequently wish to indicate that the execution of an instruction or a series of instructions is dependent on the presence or absence of some factor. For example, program instructions that result in an overdrawn statement being produced should be executed only if a checking account balance is negative. If the balance is not negative, these instructions should be bypassed. Similarly, if an employee is male, we may wish to execute certain instructions that accumulate totals for male employees. These statements are bypassed when the employee is classified as female, but in this case other program instructions might be executed to accumulate totals for female employees. Examples such as these are indicative of the need for conditional expressions. One specialized type of conditional expression is the AT END clause. The use of the AT

END clause makes it possible to designate which instructions are to be executed next, given that all records of the input file have been read; as contrasted to the situation in which they have not all been read. More general conditional expressions make use of the IF clause. In this section we present a basic set of applications for the IF statement. Additional options are described in Chapter 8, "Conditions and Conditional Statements."

For examples of the use of the conditional IF clause consider the following:

IF BALANCE IS GREATER THAN 82.50
IF NAME IS EQUAL TO "THOMPSON"
IF M-DATE IS NOT EQUAL TO "DECEMBER"
IF 35 IS LESS THAN COUNTER
IF "ABC 123" IS NOT EQUAL TO PARTCODE
IF AMOUNT IS EQUAL TO ZERO

The IF statement provides a test for a particular condition. If the specified condition is met, the instruction that directly follows the IF clause is executed. Otherwise, the next sentence in the program is executed. Suppose, for example, that a supplier gives a 0.03 volume discount for purchases of 1,000 units or more. Let QUANTITY and PRICE be the names of the storage locations that contain the data. We appropriately write in this case:

IF QUANTITY IS NOT LESS THAN 1000
    MULTIPLY 0.97 BY PRICE.
MULTIPLY PRICE BY QUANTITY GIVING TOTAL.

The effect of the above PROCEDURE DIVISION program segment is illustrated in the following flowchart:

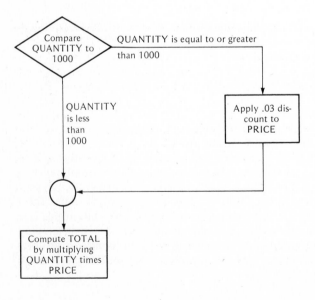

A second form of the conditional IF utilizes ELSE to specify the actions to be taken when the condition is not met. With respect to the preceding example suppose that the supplier gives a 0.01 discount to all customers but a 0.03 discount to purchasers of 1,000 or more units. We write:

IF QUANTITY IS LESS THAN 1000
    MULTIPLY 0.99 BY PRICE
ELSE
    MULTIPLY 0.97 BY PRICE.
MULTIPLY PRICE BY QUANTITY GIVING TOTAL.

The statement following the condition and preceding ELSE is executed if the condition is true. The statement following ELSE and preceding the next period is executed if the condition is false. With reference to the PROCESS-AND-PRINT paragraph of Exhibit 4-1, it should be noted that several statements (in the example, four) may precede or follow ELSE. In any case the period following ELSE is crucial, since it marks the end of the conditional sentence. Observe in the quantity discount example above that the MULTIPLY PRICE BY QUANTITY GIVING TOTAL statement is executed regardless of the truth or falsity of the condition. To understand the point even better we ask what would happen if the period after the words . . . 0.97 BY PRICE were removed in the example given above. The answer is that the TOTAL would be computed only if the condition QUANTITY IS LESS THAN 1000 is false.

The following operators may be used to form conditional expressions:

GREATER THAN	or	>
NOT GREATER THAN	or	NOT >
LESS THAN	or	<
NOT LESS THAN	or	NOT <
EQUAL TO	or	=
NOT EQUAL TO	or	NOT =

The words or symbols are equally valid, and the choice depends strictly on programmer preference.

A few words should be said about the way comparisons work. With respect to numeric items, the comparison is straightforward. Two data fields are compared with respect to their significant digits and algebraic sign, disregarding leading or trailing zeros. Thus 34.18 and 0034.180 are equal. With respect to alphabetic fields the comparison is also straightforward. If the fields compared are unequal, the smaller field is assumed to contain additional blanks to the right so as to match the size of the larger. Thus in the case of comparing $\boxed{M\,|\,A\,|\,N}$ to $\boxed{M\,|\,A\,|\,N\,|\,N}$ the characters are compared in pairs from left to right. The first pair is (M, M) and the last is (blank, N). In this case MAN is considered "smaller" than MANN. But $\boxed{M\,|\,A\,|\,N}$ and $\boxed{M\,|\,A\,|\,N\,|\,\,}$ are equal! Alphanumeric comparisons are based on an ordering of characters from highest to lowest called the *collating sequence* (see page 205). In all cases comparison proceeds in pairs of characters from left to right, but which character is smaller in such pairs as (*,$) and (=, 0) depends on the particular machine's collating sequence. If one were unaware of the existence of different collating sequences, one would be surprised to find that in some computers the blank is considered smaller than any digit, whereas in other computers the reverse is true.

REVIEW

1   Whereas the AT END clause is an example of a specialized conditional expression, more general conditional expressions make use of the _____ statement.

IF

2   If the condition specified in the IF clause is *not* met, then program execution continues with [the statement which directly follows the IF / the next sentence / the next paragraph].

the next sentence

3   In the comparison of numeric items −10.2 and 0.50 the larger item is _____.

0.50

4   When the alphabetic fields | A |
| B |R|O|W|N | and | B |R|I|T| | are compared, the larger one is the [A / B] field; this can be ascertained when the characters ___ and ___ are compared.

A; O; I

5   Alphanumeric comparisons are based on a special ordering of characters from lowest to highest, called the _____ sequence. This ordering [varies among computer manufacturers / is standard for all computer manufacturers].

collating; varies among computer
manufacturers

6   The option used in conjunction with the IF clause which makes it possible to execute one of two alternative statements (or sets of statements) without having to use two separate IF conditionals is the _____ option.

ELSE

7   Suppose that, if AMOUNT is greater than 10, PRICE should be discounted by 0.20. If AMOUNT is not greater than 10, PRICE should be discounted by 0.10. Write the COBOL program statement to achieve this result by using the ELSE option.

_____

_____

_____

_____

IF AMOUNT IS GREATER THAN 10
MULTIPLY 0.80 BY PRICE

ELSE

MULTIPLY 0.90 BY PRICE.
(*Note that* "MULTIPLY PRICE BY
0.80" *is not correct, because a literal
cannot follow* BY *when* GIVING *is not
used.*)

8.   For the question above, accomplish the same computational objective by using two separate IF statements.

_____

_____

_____

IF AMOUNT IS GREATER THAN 10
MULTIPLY 0.80 BY PRICE.
IF AMOUNT IS NOT GREATER THAN 10
MULTIPLY 0.90 BY PRICE.

CONTROL VERBS

Program instructions in the PROCEDURE DIVISION are executed in the order in which they are written, from top to bottom, except when control verbs interrupt this normal flow. In this section we discuss some basic forms of program control.

The PERFORM verb provides a powerful mechanism for program control. Referring to the MAIN-LOGIC paragraph of Exhibit 4-1 one can observe the instruction:

PERFORM READ-CARD.

READ-CARD is a paragraph-name. The effect of the instruction is to branch to the indicated paragraph, execute the instructions in that paragraph, and then return to the statement immediately following the PERFORM instruction (which in this case happens to be another PERFORM statement).

Two basic advantages are gained by using PERFORM in this program structure. The first one has to do with simplifying program logic. We can write one instruction to read a card and do whatever is associated with reading a card without bothering at this point with other details. Later we can work on the specifics of the performed paragraph. A second advantage can be seen by observing the last line of the program in Exhibit 4-1, which is PERFORM READ-CARD.

There were two instances in which we wanted a card to be read. Instead of writing the card-reading instructions twice in the desired places in the program, we made the card-reading instructions a separate paragraph executed under control of the PERFORM verb from two different places in the program. The following illustration depicts the control flow. The broken arrows indicate the return path from the performed paragraph.

(Program Instructions)

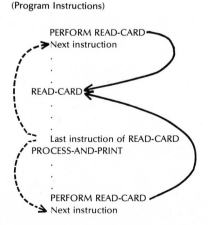

A second form of PERFORM provides the programmer with the ability to execute a paragraph or not execute it, depending on a condition. In the MAIN-LOGIC paragraph of Exhibit 4-1 we have:

PERFORM READ-CARD
PERFORM PROCESS-AND-PRINT
     UNTIL END-OF-DATA-INDICATOR = 'YES'.
etc.

In flowchart form the sentence can be represented as:

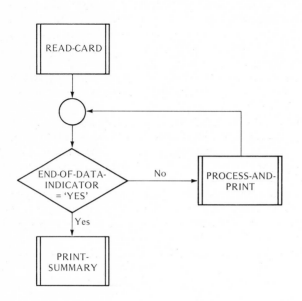

The END-OF-DATA-INDICATOR is tested for equality to YES. If it is not equal, the PROCESS-AND-PRINT paragraph is executed and we return to perform the test again. When the condition is met, PROCESS-AND-PRINT is not executed. Instead we continue with the next statement in the program, which is the PERFORM PRINT-SUM-MARY instruction in the Exhibit 4-1 sample program. It is important to note that the test is performed first and, if it is not met, then PERFORM PROCESS-AND-PRINT applies.

There are other forms of PERFORM statements, and these are described in Chapter 6. For now we will limit our attention to the two forms just described:

PERFORM paragraph-name.
PERFORM paragraph-name
    UNTIL condition.

Another control verb in COBOL is GO TO. Until recently it was one of the most used verbs in all programming languages. However, it has been found that its unrestricted use is likely to create difficulty in reading a program and to contribute to the development of error-prone programs. A controversy exists between those who feel that GO TO must never be used and those who feel that it should continue to be used under certain circumstances. In this book we refrain from the use of GO TO as much as possible. Still, programs written in the first quarter-century of programming history are full of GO TO statements, and the momentum of tradition is likely to result in some continued use of this control verb.

GO TO is an unconditional branch to a paragraph (or section) name. The object of a GO TO statement is a paragraph-name, and we can execute an individual sentence within a paragraph only by entering the paragraph from its beginning. Consider Exhibit 4-5. Note that there are two GO TO statements in the READING-DATA paragraph, and that they both make reference to paragraph-names. In one case reference is made to the paragraph-name in which the GO TO statement itself is included, because it is desired to repeat the instructions of that paragraph. Execution of a COBOL program always flows from the first to subsequent paragraphs, unless a transfer of control statement interrupts the flow. Therefore, in Exhibit 4-5 at the end of the STARTER paragraph we need not say GO TO READING-DATA, since program execution will automatically continue with the next paragraph.

Another control statement used in every COBOL program is STOP RUN, which terminates program execution. A program may contain more than one STOP RUN statement, depending on the logic of the program. As an example, we may wish to terminate execution on reading an error record, or we may wish to use STOP RUN after the program has completed its normal course. In Exhibit 4-5 the STOP RUN statement is the last one in the program. This does not have to be the case. STOP RUN signifies the logical end of the program. It should not be confused with the physical end of the program, which is indicated by a program control card that varies with the operating system used.

All files should be closed with the CLOSE verb prior to execution of the STOP RUN instruction.

EXHIBIT 4-5   AN EXAMPLE OF A PROCEDURE DIVISION USING GO TO

```
PROCEDURE DIVISION.
STARTER.
    OPEN INPUT ACCOUNTS-RECEIVABLE OUTPUT SUM-REPORT.
READING-DATA.
    READ ACCOUNTS-RECEIVABLE RECORD AT END GO TO WRAP-UP.
    IF AMOUNT IS GREATER THAN 500.00 MOVE RECEIVABLE TO REP-LINE.
    WRITE REP-LINE.
    ADD AMOUNT TO TOTAL.
    ADD 1 TO COUNTER.
    GO TO READING-DATA.
WRAP-UP.
    MOVE TOTAL TO EDTOTAL.
    DIVIDE COUNTER INTO TOTAL.
    MOVE TOTAL TO AVERAGE.
    MOVE SUMMARY TO REP-LINE WRITE REP-LINE.
    CLOSE ACCOUNTS-RECEIVABLE SUM-REPORT.
    STOP RUN.
```

REVIEW

1   The COBOL verbs which interrupt the normal sequential execution of program statements are called ——————— verbs.

control

2   The control verb which makes it possible to branch to a specified paragraph, execute it, and then return to the statement immediately following the statement containing the control verb is ———————.

PERFORM

3   The option available with the PERFORM verb which makes it possible to repeatedly execute a specified paragraph until a specified test condition is met is the ——————— option.

UNTIL

4   The COBOL verb that provides the programmer with the capability of achieving branching in a program without returning to the point of original branching is ———————.

GO TO

5   In order to continue program execution with the instructions in the next sequential paragraph of the PROCEDURE DIVISION, a GO TO statement [is / is not] required at the end of the preceding paragraph.

is not

6   The control statement used to terminate program execution is ———————.

STOP RUN

7   A STOP RUN statement [must appear only once / can appear in several places] in a program.

can appear in several places

8   STOP RUN [is / need not be] the last statement in a program.

need not be

EXERCISES

1   Write COBOL statements for the following computational tasks.

   a   Set TOTAL equal to the sum of SUBTOTAL-1 and SUBTOTAL-2.
   b   Add the value of BONUS to PAY.
   c   Calculate COMMISSION as the product of RATE and SALES.
   d   Make the value of SHARES equal to the number of shares that can be bought by DOLLARS at PRICE per share.

2   Write COBOL statements for the following data transfer tasks.

   a   Set the value of a data-name A equal to 150.
   b   Set the value of ACCUMULATOR equal to zero.
   c   Set HEADER equal to a string of the letter X.

d   Set TEST-VALUE equal to the highest character in the collating sequence of a given computer. (*Hint:* review the subject of *figurative constants*.)

e   Set the content of a storage field called MESSAGE to blank.

f   Set the content of MESSAGE to AMOUNT EXCEEDS LIMIT.

3   A storage field ABC was designed to contain a maximum of six alphanumeric characters. What will be the result of attempting to move the following data to it?

DATA	RESULT (CONTENT OF ABC)
STEVENSON	
ADAM	
BRINKS	
123456	
1234567	
123	

4   A storage field was designed to contain four numeric characters. What will be the result of attempting to MOVE the following numeric values to it?

NUMERIC VALUE	RESULT
1500	
150000	
13	

5   Write COBOL statements to exchange the contents of two fields, A and B.

6   Write COBOL statements to terminate a program if BALANCE is equal to zero.

7   Correct the following COBOL program segment:

PROCEDURE DIVISION.
FIRST-PARAGRAPH. READ CARD-FILE RECORD AT END etc.

8   Write a statement to make an output file called TRANSACTIONS-FILE available for subsequent use.

9   Write statements to determine if an output file called PAYABLES has all been read in and, if it has, to terminate the program at that point.

10 Write statements to print the (last) record of a file called FINAL-REPORT, making sure that the file is properly closed before the program terminates. The record of FINAL-REPORT is called MONTHLY-REPORT.

11 Write a statement to print a record called INVENTORY, using the contents of a storage area called EDITED-OUTPUT but without using the MOVE verb.

12 Write statements to print two records from a file whose record is called MONTHLY-REPORT, leaving two blank lines between the records. The first record will print the contents of HEADER-1 and the second will print the contents of HEADER-2.

13 Give a program instruction to execute next a paragraph called INTEREST-COMPUTATION.

14 If a paragraph consists of four sentences, can we write an instruction outside that paragraph to execute the third sentence next?

15 Write instructions to test if the MARITAL-STATUS-CODE is equal to 1 and, if it is, to execute a paragraph called SINGLES.

16 A storage field called SEX-CODE indicates whether a person is male or female (1 = male, 2 = female). Another field OCCUPATION contains the occupation of the person. Assuming the output record below, write COBOL statements to move the occupation to the appropriate place, making sure that if a person is male FEMALE-OCCUPATION is blank, and vice versa.

OTHER-DATA	MALE-OCCUPATION	FEMALE-OCCUPATION

17 A student is enrolled in HISTORY, ENGLISH, and ACCOUNTING, these three fields containing his corresponding numeric grades in those courses, using this scale: 4 = A, 3 = B, 2 = C, 1 = D, 0 = E. The history course is a two-credit course and the other two are three-credit courses. Write COBOL statements to calculate the grade point average and store it in GRADE-POINT. Use other storage fields of your choice.

18 The GROSS-PAY of an employee is calculated by multiplying REGULAR-HOURS by RATE and OVERTIME-HOURS by 1.50 of RATE. Write COBOL instructions to compute GROSS-PAY, using only one work-area field for intermediate results: WORK-AREA.

19 A card has been read containing the unit prices submitted by three vendors: PRICE1, PRICE2, PRICE3. It is desired to store in LOW-PRICE the smallest of the three prices. In case of ties, take any one of the equal items.

a Draw a flowchart and write COBOL statements to store the smallest price in LOW-PRICE.
b Describe what you would do if you had the task of finding the smallest of, say, 50 prices.

20 A deck of cards is being read from a file called CARDS. Each card contains, among other things, a field called AMOUNT. Draw a flowchart and write COBOL state-

ments to find the smallest value of AMOUNT read in and to store it in SMALLEST. Disregard ties. When all the cards have been read in, the program goes to the PROCESS-SMALLEST paragraph.

21 Is the following PROCEDURE DIVISION statement correct? ADD 3 TO FILLER.

22 Assume the following DATA DIVISION entries:

```
01   AMOUNT PICTURE 9(4).
01   DAYS-ELAPSED PICTURE X(9).
```

Are the following PROCEDURE DIVISION statements correct?

a MOVE "ZERO" TO AMOUNT.
b MOVE SPACES TO AMOUNT.
c ADD 50 TO DAYS-ELAPSED.
d MOVE ZERO TO DAYS-ELAPSED.
e MOVE "ZERO" TO DAYS-ELAPSED.

23 Referring to the schematic representation below, write a DATA DIVISION record description using the following information:

DEPT	2 letters
NAME	5 digits
RATE	4 digits, 2 decimal places, used for arithmetic
SKILL	1 letter
REGULAR	7 digits, 2 decimal places, used for arithmetic
OVERTIME	6 digits, 2 decimal places, used for arithmetic
SS-TAX	5 digits, 2 decimal places, used for arithmetic

PAY-RECORD					
EMPLOYEE		RATE	SKILL	YEAR-TO-DATE	
DEPT	NAME			GROSS	SS-TAX
				REGULAR OVERTIME	

24 Using the PERFORM verb write PROCEDURE DIVISION instructions to read 10 cards from a file called CARD-FILE, accumulating the sum of the values in a field called AMOUNT. (*Hint:* Set up a counter to count the cards read in and test for the value of the counter to determine termination.)

25 Carry out the same data processing task as in the preceding exercise, except do *not* use PERFORM. Instead, use the IF and GO TO instructions.

26 Punch and run the sample program given in this chapter in Exhibit 4-1. Use as input the sample data shown in Exhibit 4-2. Even though this exercise will not involve programming effort on your part, it will provide you with the opportunity to familiarize yourself with the ENVIRONMENT DIVISION entries pertinent to your computer, and the program-submission procedures of your installation.

27   Write a COBOL program that will take any deck of punched cards and list their contents on the printer. Another way of describing the program function is to say: Write an "80-80 card-to-printer lister."

28   It is desired to write a program to compute and print depreciation schedules, using the declining balance method. The input will consist of a deck of cards containing the following:

CARD COLUMNS	COBOL DATA-NAME
1–5	ASSET-NUMBER
6–14	ASSET-VALUE
15–16	RATE
17–18	YEARS

The ASSET-NUMBER is a five-digit identification code. ASSET-VALUE is the original value to be depreciated. RATE is the rate of depreciation, and finally YEARS is the number of years over which the asset will be depreciated.

   The following is an example of the desired output and also serves to illustrate the declining balance method.

ASSET 12345		ORIGINAL VALUE $1,000.00	RATE 0.20
YEAR	DEPRECIATION	ACCUMULATED DEPRECIATION	BOOK VALUE
1	$200.00	$200.00	$800.00
2	160.00	360.00	640.00
3	128.00	488.00	512.00
4	102.40	590.00	409.60
5	81.92	672.32	327.68

As indicated above, the rate—in this case 0.20—is successively multiplied by the declining book value to yield the annual depreciation.

   A list of file-, record-, and data-names to be used in the program is given on page 113, followed by pictorial descriptions on pages 114–115. Notice that the contents of non-FILLER data-names are left blank, since their content is variable.

Given the accompanying flowchart (pages 116–118) write the PROCEDURE DIVISION statements to carry out the steps indicated in the flowchart, using the data-names provided.

NAME	MEANING
ASSET-CARD	The record-name for the card input file
CARDS-IN	The file-name of the card input file
ASSET-NUMBER	The asset identification code
ASSET-VALUE	The original asset value
RATE	The rate of depreciation
YEARS	The number of years over which the asset will be depreciated
OUT-LINE	The record-name of the printer output file
PRINT-FILE	The output file-name
HEADER-1	A storage group field containing some nonnumeric literals such as "ASSET" along with space for the values to be printed as the first line of each output page
FILLER	A special kind of data-name that contains, in this program, either blanks or nonnumeric literals
NUMB	A storage field to which the ASSET-NUMBER read in is moved in preparation for output
ASSET	A storage field for the edited form of the ASSET-VALUE read in
RA	A storage field for the edited form of the RATE read in
HEADER-2	A storage field used to print the word ACCUMULATED in its proper place
HEADER-3	A group item to print the headers on top of the numerical values of the depreciation schedule
PRINT-LINE	A group item used to contain the edited form of the computation results
YEAR	A storage field containing the edited form of the YEARS (notice the plural) value read in
DEPRECIATION	The edited field for the depreciation value
ACCUM-DEP	The edited field for the accumulated depreciation value
BOOK-VALUE	The edited field for the book value at the end of each year
COUNTER	A storage field used to count the number of years for which depreciation values have been computed
ACCUMULATOR	A storage field for the unedited form of the accumulated depreciation value
WORK-AREA	A storage field containing the result of arithmetic operations prior to moving this result to the editing field DEPRECIATION

Record-name	ASSET-CARD				
Data-names	ASSET-NUMBER	ASSET-VALUE	RATE	YEARS	FILLER
Content					Blank
Positions	1–5	6–14	15–16	17–18	19–80

Record-name	OUT-LINE	
Data-names	FILLER	LINEOUT
Content		
Positions	1	2–133

Group-item-name	HEADER-1								
Data-names	FILLER	FILLER	NUMB	FILLER	FILLER	ASSET	FILLER	FILLER	RA
Content	ASSET	Blank		Blank	ORIG-INAL VALUE		Blank	RATE	
Positions	1–5	6–7	8–12	13–16	17–30	31–43	44–46	47–50	51–56

Group-item-name	HEADER-2	
Data-names	FILLER	FILLER
Content	Blank	ACCUMULATED
Positions	1–23	27–38

Group-item-name	HEADER-3						
Data-names	FILLER	FILLER	FILLER	FILLER	FILLER	FILLER	FILLER
Content	YEAR	Blank	DEPRECIA-TION	Blank	DEPRECIA-TION	Blank	BOOK-VALUE
Positions	1–4	5–8	9–20	21–26	27–38	39–42	46–55

Group-item-name	PRINT-LINE						
Data-names	YEAR	FILLER	DEPRECIA-TION	FILLER	ACCUM-DEP	FILLER	BOOK-VALUE
Content		Blank		Blank		Blank	
Positions	1–4	5–7	8–20	21–25	26–38	39–42	43–55

Temporary storage data-names	COUNTER	ACCUMULATOR	WORK-AREA
Contents			

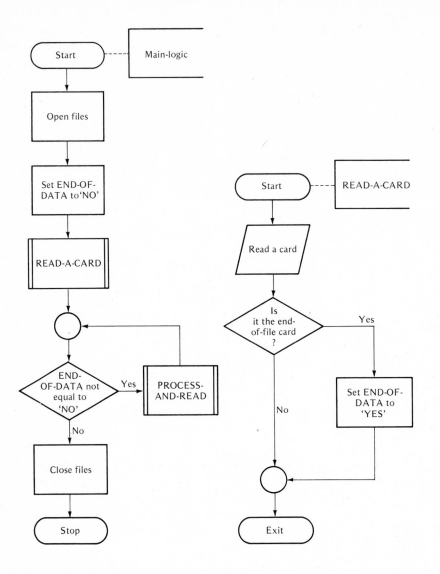

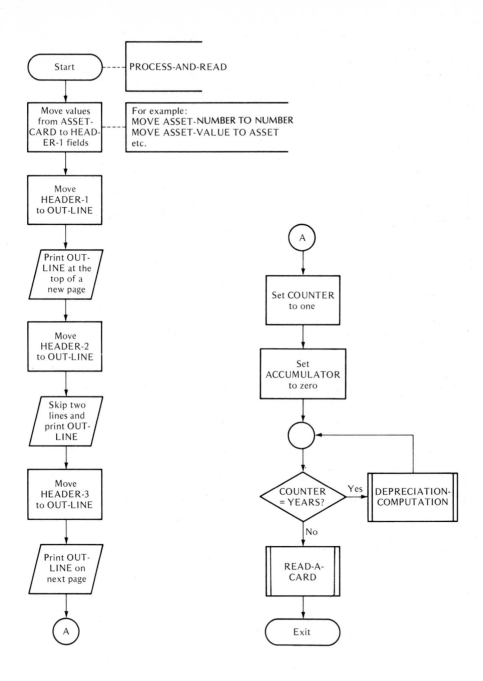

Start ----- PROCESS-AND-READ

Move values from ASSET-CARD to HEADER-1 fields

For example:
MOVE ASSET-NUMBER TO NUMBER
MOVE ASSET-VALUE TO ASSET
etc.

Move HEADER-1 to OUT-LINE

Print OUT-LINE at the top of a new page

Move HEADER-2 to OUT-LINE

Skip two lines and print OUT-LINE

Move HEADER-3 to OUT-LINE

Print OUT-LINE on next page

A

A

Set COUNTER to one

Set ACCUMULATOR to zero

COUNTER = YEARS?   Yes   DEPRECIATION-COMPUTATION

No

READ-A-CARD

Exit

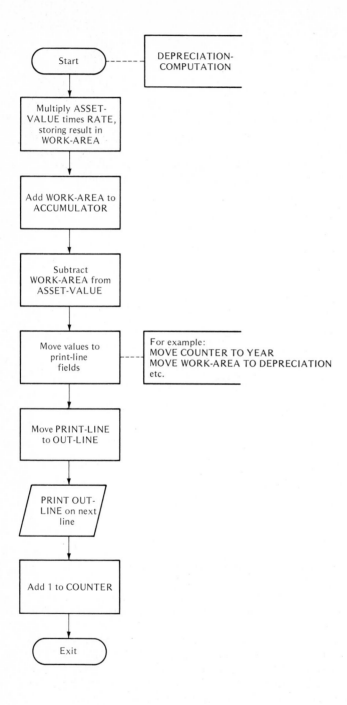

Start - - - - DEPRECIATION-COMPUTATION

Multiply ASSET-VALUE times RATE, storing result in WORK-AREA

Add WORK-AREA to ACCUMULATOR

Subtract WORK-AREA from ASSET-VALUE

Move values to print-line fields - - - For example:
MOVE COUNTER TO YEAR
MOVE WORK-AREA TO DEPRECIATION
etc.

Move PRINT-LINE to OUT-LINE

PRINT OUT-LINE on next line

Add 1 to COUNTER

Exit

DATA DIVISION
Features

INTRODUCTION

In the context of COBOL programming we are very much concerned about the physical and logical characteristics of data. The language acknowledges explicitly the multitude of data forms that can be used and provides the DATA DIVISION as the vehicle by which the programmer describes the desired specifications.

The DATA DIVISION can consist of one or more of these five sections: FILE SECTION, WORKING-STORAGE SECTION, LINKAGE SECTION, REPORT SECTION, and COMMUNICATION SECTION. We have already encountered the first two sections in Chapter 4, "Writing Complete Programs." The LINKAGE SECTION is discussed in Chapter 18, "Modular Programs and Subroutines." The REPORT SECTION is for use with a special feature, the *report writer*, which is discussed in Chapter 19, while the

COMMUNICATION SECTION can be used to access, process, and create messages for communicating with local and remote communication devices. Use of these language features is beyond the intended scope of this book.

The FILE SECTION is discussed extensively in Chapters 10 and 17, because the options presented are natural to the processing of magnetic tape and disk files. In this chapter we shall continue with the basic format used in Chapter 4:

FD   file-name LABEL RECORDS OMITTED
                DATA RECORD IS record-name

Following the FD entry we write the level number associated with each data-name, its PICTURE, etc.

THE PICTURE CLAUSE

We introduced the general form of the PICTURE clause in the examples presented in Chapter 4. We now describe PICTURE clause options in detail.

Level numbers define the hierarchical structure of data-items in a record, whereas data-names identify each field in the record by name. Beyond this, the PICTURE clause associated with each item is used to describe the field size and indicates such information as whether the field is numeric, alphabetic, or alphanumeric; whether it is computational or display; whether it contains editing characters; whether it contains a decimal point; and whether a numeric field can contain a negative value. All this is accomplished by use of the PICTURE clause. The general format for this clause is:

$$\left\{ \begin{array}{l} \text{PICTURE} \\ \text{PIC} \end{array} \right\} \text{ IS character-string}$$

We use the word PICTURE, or its abbreviated form PIC, and the optional word IS, and then we follow with a string of characters which are discussed below.

THE 9 PICTURE CHARACTER

The numeric 9 indicates that a storage position should only contain any of the numeric digits from 0 to 9. In this context, a blank is *not* considered equivalent to the numeric 0 and thus is not a numeric character. The field size of the item is indicated by the number of successively written 9s in the PICTURE clause. Thus PICTURE IS 999 means a field of three numeric positions. As indicated in Chapter 4, an alternative is to write a 9 followed by parentheses enclosing the number of positions in the field. For example, the statement 03 SUM PICTURE IS 9(5) indicates that SUM is a five-position numeric field. Some examples of using the 9 PICTURE character are as follows:

DESCRIPTION	NUMERIC VALUE	REPRESENTED IN STORAGE AS
02 SCHOOL-ENROLLMENT PICTURE IS 9(6)	12,327	012327
02 STOCK-ON-HAND PICTURE 9999	8,956	8956
04 POPULATION-OF-CITY PICTURE 9(10)	1,563,813	0001563813
03 UNION-MEMBERSHIP PICTURE IS 9999	285	0285

Again, note that a numeric field can contain only the digits 0–9. Blanks are *not* numeric characters. When punching data onto cards, you should be careful to zero-fill a field with leading zeros; otherwise you may be in for some surprising results. Thus in a field of six positions, the numeric value 532 should be punched as follows:

0	0	0	5	3	2

THE V PICTURE CHARACTER

The V character indicates the position of an assumed decimal point. "Assumed" means that the decimal point is not written as part of the field and therefore is not included as part of the field size. Instead, the information about decimal-point location is stored elsewhere in the computer, so that any arithmetic computations can be done correctly. For example, if two items are multiplied and each is assumed to have two positions to the right of the decimal, the product will be understood to have four positions to the right of the decimal point. If the V character is omitted, it is understood that the decimal point is at the extreme right of the numeric field. Therefore, it is not necessary to place a V as the last character in a PICTURE clause. Of course, no more than one V is permitted in a field. Note that, if we printed HOURS-WORKED without any editing, the value represented in storage, 385, would be printed *without a decimal*. Again, the V character establishes the *position* of the decimal for purposes of arithmetic manipulation but does not make the decimal point as such available for printout. Some examples of using the V character are given below. The caret (ʌ) indicates the position of the assumed decimal point.

DESCRIPTION	NUMERIC VALUE	REPRESENTED IN STORAGE AS
03 HOURS-WORKED PICTURE 99V9	38.50	38ʌ5
03 NET-PAY PICTURE 9(4)V99.	452.39	0452ʌ39
02 TON-CAPACITY PICTURE 999	550	550ʌ
02 BALANCE PICTURE 99999V99.	23561.00	2356100ʌ

THE P PICTURE CHARACTER

The P PICTURE character is used in conjunction with the V character to indicate the position of a decimal point in cases in which the decimal point is not within the number. This character is used, for example, when it is understood that a value held in storage represents thousands of units and we wish to indicate the decimal position for this value. The following examples indicate the use of this character; as before, the caret indicates the position of an assumed decimal point.

DESCRIPTION	NUMERIC VALUE	ARITHMETIC EQUIVALENT
02 AMOUNT PICTURE 99PPPV	12	12000ᴧ
02 AMOUNT PICTURE VP(3)9(4)	1023	ᴧ0001023

The P character is not used very much in COBOL applications to business problems. It is best suited to scientific computational needs which are not likely to be satisfied by COBOL anyway.

THE S PICTURE CHARACTER

The S character is used to designate a numeric field which is signed, i.e., which can be negative in value. In COBOL all fields are considered positive unless the S has been used. For instance, for a field containing the checking account balance of a bank customer, when the account is overdrawn, the only way the balance will become negative is to designate the balance field as a signed one by use of the S character. Otherwise, if the balance is $23.50 and a check is written for $50.00, the balance will become $26.50!

Only one S character may be used in a field, and it must be the leftmost character. The S is not counted in the size of the field, and therefore S99 is a field of two positions. In the examples below, the negative sign in machine representation is shown as a "—" on top of the rightmost digit in order to preserve the concept that it does not take up an extra position. For punched card data to be processed by use of a COBOL program, any negative number is so identified by punching the negative sign over the rightmost digit by multipunching. This means that, when you punch the rightmost digit, you depress the MULTI-PUNCH key and punch both the desired digit and the "—" sign in the same card column.

DESCRIPTION	NUMERIC VALUE	REPRESENTED IN STORAGE AS
02 BALANCE PICTURE S9999V99	156.29	015629
02 BALANCE PICTURE S9999V99	−1251.16	125116
02 BALANCE PICTURE S9(4)V99	−0.10	000010
02 BALANCE PICTURE 9(4)V99	−325.18	032518

THE X PICTURE CHARACTER

The X PICTURE character denotes that alphanumeric positions are contained in a field. NAME X(20), for example, signifies a field of 20 alphanumeric positions, which can include alphabetic characters, numeric characters, and special symbols. In the following examples, a "b" represents a blank space in the storage location. Notice that when the characters do not completely fill an X field they are left-justified, with blanks filling the remaining positions on the right.

DESCRIPTION	EXAMPLE	REPRESENTED IN STORAGE AS
02 PART-NAME PICTURE XXXXX	DIODE	DIODE
02 PART-NAME PICTURE X(5)	TUBE	TUBEb
02 NAME PICTURE X(20)	JOHN F. ANDREWS	JOHNbF.bANDREWSbbbbb
02 MESSAGE-CODE PICTURE X(8)	AB13C,$M	AB13C,$M

THE A PICTURE CHARACTER

The A PICTURE character is similar to the X character, except that it indicates that only alphabetic characters and blanks are contained in a field. Excluded therefore are numeric characters and special symbols. Since the first two statements in the examples above concerned storage locations containing only alphabetic information, the A PICTURE character could have been used instead of the X, as indicated below.

DESCRIPTION	EXAMPLE	REPRESENTED IN STORAGE AS
02 PART-NAME PICTURE AAAAA	DIODE	DIODE
02 PART-NAME PICTURE A(5)	TUBE	TUBEb

The reader is cautioned against using the A character in what seems a natural use: a field containing people's names. Names such as O'Neal do not consist of alphabetic characters alone. The X character is better suited for use in such fields.

REVIEW

1   We have thus far discussed six PICTURE characters that can be used in a PICTURE clause to describe the contents of a field. These are the 9, V, P, S, X, and A PICTURE characters. The character used to indicate that a field can contain either alphabetic, numeric, or special symbols is the _____ character, whereas the character that indicates alphabetic content only is the _____ character.

X; A

2 The character that indicates numeric content only is the _____ character. If the stored values can be negative as well as positive, the PICTURE clause should include the _____ character as the leftmost character.

9; S

3 In punching data, a negative value is indicated by multipunching a negative sign in the card column containing the [leftmost / rightmost] digit of the field.

rightmost

4 The character used to indicate the position of an assumed decimal point is the _____ character. This character is used only with PICTURE clauses which also contain the _____ PICTURE character.

V; 9

5 When we wish to identify the correct decimal position for a field whose numeric value is understood to be in thousands of units, we use the _____ PICTURE character.

P

6 When a value does not completely fill a numeric 9 field, the value is justified to the [right / left], and the extra positions are filled with [blanks / zeros].

right; zeros

7 When an item does not completely fill an A field or an X field, the item is justified to the [right / left], and the extra positions are filled with [blanks / zeros].

left; blanks

EDITING SYMBOLS

As contrasted to the field definition characters we have dicussed so far, the PICTURE characters that follow are editing symbols. The editing function involves a change in the form of data. For example, we may suppress leading zeros, we may use commas to make long numeric values more legible, we may insert a dollar sign in front of a value, etc. The purpose of editing is to make data more suitable for human reading. Thus editing in its most common use is associated with printing data on the printer. A great many of the applications of COBOL involve the production of reports that are to be read by people, and data editing enhances the visibility of data in such reports.

THE $ PICTURE INSERTION CHARACTER

By use of the $ PICTURE character the dollar sign is written in the position in which it is to appear in the output. Since the $ sign is counted in the size of the field, the field should be assigned at least one more position than the maximum number of significant digits expected. The $ may also be floated, by which we mean that it will not necessarily be entered in the leftmost position of a field but, rather, will be entered to the left of the first significant digit in the field and be preceded by blanks. For example, if we have the statement 02 SUM PICTURE $$$99, when a data value is to be entered in SUM, a test is performed. The leftmost digit is examined first. If it is zero, the next digit is examined. If this next digit is not zero, then the dollar sign is inserted directly to the left of it. For the PICTURE clause above, the $ sign can appear in any one of the first three positions, according to the value stored in the field. The following examples further illustrate the use of the $ PICTURE insertion character. The decimal point shown is an editing character discussed in the following section. The last example shows that, when the $ sign appears in all positions and the value is zero, the effect is to blank the field.

DESCRIPTION	NUMERIC VALUE	REPRESENTED IN STORAGE AS
02 SUM PICTURE $999.99	125.13	$125.13
02 SUM PICTURE $9(5).99	100.0	$00100.00
02 SUM PICTURE $$99.99	12.49	b$12.49
02 SUM PICTURE $$$9.99	150.10	$150.10
02 SUM PICTURE $$$$.99	0.15	bbb$.15
02 SUM PICTURE $$$$.$$	0.0	bbbbbbb

For the last example above, let us consider what the result in storage would be if the value to be written in SUM were 0.05. In this case, the presence of the . would stop the float, and the value would be represented in storage as bbb$.05. If the decimal point did not terminate the float, the result in storage would be bbbbb.$5, which is clearly not the desired representation. Therefore, the presence of the decimal point stops the float, *except* when the entire field is zero. Further examples involving use of the $ PICTURE character are included in the discussion immediately following.

THE . AND THE , PICTURE INSERTION CHARACTERS

Each of these insertion characters is used to indicate the position of the indicated character in the storage location. Because the . (decimal) PICTURE character indicates the position of the decimal point and serves to align the actual decimal values in the field, only one such character may appear in a field. Further, a field cannot contain both a V and a . PICTURE character. On the other hand, a field may include more than one , (comma) PICTURE character if the size of the field warrants it. The following examples illustrate the use of the . and the , PICTURE insertion characters in conjunction with the $ insertion characters. Notice some of these points. The $ float stops when either the first nonzero digit or the . or V is encountered. Again, the only exception is when the $ is written in all positions and the value is zero, in which case the entire field (including any . and ,) is blanked. If a comma happens to precede the first nonzero item, the comma is replaced by the dollar sign, which is the format generally desired for purposes of output.

DESCRIPTION	NUMERIC VALUE	REPRESENTED IN STORAGE AS
02 SUM PICTURE $9,999.99	2,350.22	$2,350.22
02 SUM PICTURE $9,999.99	150.31	$0,150.31
02 SUM PICTURE $$,999.99	150.31	bb$150.31
02 SUM PICTURE $$,$$$.99	25.40	bbb$25.40
02 SUM PICTURE $$,$$$.999	0.019	bbbbb$.019
02 SUM PICTURE $$,$$$.$$$	0.009	bbbbb$.009
02 SUM PICTURE $$,$$$.$$$	0.0	bbbbbbbbbb
02 SUM PICTURE $$,$$9.999	2,210.2	$2,210.200
02 SUM PICTURE $$,999.9	2,210.2	$2,210.2
02 SUM PICTURE $$,999.9	2,210.256	$2,210.2
02 SUM PICTURE $9,999.9999	23	$0,023.0000
02 SUM PICTURE $$,$$$.$$9	0.002	bbbbb$.002

THE Z PICTURE CHARACTER

The Z PICTURE character is used to replace leading zeros by blanks and thus performs a function identical to that of the floating $ character, except for insertion of the $ sign itself. As for the floating $, zero suppression terminates when the first nonzero digit or the . character is encountered, whichever occurs first. As with the $ PICTURE character, the only exception is when Z's have been designated for all positions in a field and the value to be inserted in that field is zero, in which case the entire field is blanked. The following examples illustrate the use of the Z PICTURE character.

DESCRIPTION			NUMERIC VALUE	REPRESENTED IN STORAGE AS
02	SUM PICTURE	Z99	25	b25
02	SUM PICTURE	ZZZ.99	25	b25.00
02	SUM PICTURE	ZZZ.99	0.10	bbb.10
02	SUM PICTURE	ZZZ.ZZZ	0.052	bbb.052
02	SUM PICTURE	ZZZ.ZZZ	0.0	bbbbbbb
02	SUM PICTURE	$ZZZ.9	13.2	$b13.2
02	SUM PICTURE	$ZZZZ.Z	13.2	$bb13.2
02	SUM PICTURE	$Z,ZZZ,ZZZ.ZZ	156,320.18	$bb156,320.18
02	SUM PICTURE	$Z,ZZZ,ZZZ.ZZ	3,156,320.18	$3,156,320.18
02	SUM PICTURE	$$,$$Z.999	0.001	bbbb$b.001

THE + and − PICTURE INSERTION CHARACTERS

Each of these editing characters can be inserted in the leftmost or rightmost position in a PICTURE. When the + character is used, any value that does not have an arithmetic sign associated with it is assigned a + sign. On the other hand, when the − PICTURE character is used, any value that does not have an arithmetic sign associated with it is represented in storage without a sign. In either case, a negative sign associated with a value is always represented in storage. The − PICTURE insertion character differs from the S character in that the use of the S character identifies a field as a signed one for computational purposes, but the sign does not occupy a position as such. Use of the − PICTURE character leads to a field in which the sign occupies a character position. The + character and the − character can also be floated, and in this respect are similar to the $ PICTURE character. However, the +, −, and $ are mutually exclusive as floating characters. If we want to have both $ float and + or − sign representation, we write the + or − to the right of the field, as illustrated in the last two examples that follow.

REVIEW

1 Several $ signs included in a PICTURE clause signify that [several dollar signs should appear in the output / the output should contain the dollar sign in one of several possible positions].

the output should contain the dollar sign in one of several possible positions

DESCRIPTION		NUMERIC VALUE	REPRESENTED IN STORAGE AS
02 BALANCE PICTURE	+999.9	35.2	+035.2
02 BALANCE PICTURE	999.9+	35.2	035.2+
02 BALANCE PICTURE	999.9+	−35.2	035.2−
02 BALANCE PICTURE	++9.9	−001.3	b−1.3
02 BALANCE PICTURE	+++9.99	.05	bb+0.05
02 BALANCE PICTURE	+++9.99	−.05	bb−0.05
02 BALANCE PICTURE	++++.++	.01	bbb+.01
02 BALANCE PICTURE	− − − −.− −	0.0	bbbbbbb
02 BALANCE PICTURE	−−99.99	−10.25	b−10.25
02 BALANCE PICTURE	−999.99	100.25	b100.25
02 BALANCE PICTURE	999.9−	−10.2	010.2−
02 BALANCE PICTURE	$$$$.99−	20.35	b$20.35b
02 BALANCE PICTURE	$$$$.99+	20.35	b$20.35+

2   Both the V PICTURE character and the . PICTURE character indicate _____ positions.

decimal point

3   The difference in the use of the V and the . PICTURE characters is that the V signifies an _____ decimal point, whereas the . signifies an _____ decimal point.

assumed; actual

4   In general, the $ float stops when the first nonzero digit is encountered or when the _____ PICTURE character is encountered. The only exception is when the value in the field is zero and the $ is written in all positions, in which case the field is filled with _____.

V or . (decimal); blanks

5   The PICTURE insertion character which is similar to the . PICTURE character but which can appear more than once in a field is the _____ PICTURE character.

, (comma)

6   The character in a PICTURE clause which is used to replace leading zeros in a value by blanks is the _____ PICTURE character.

Z

7   Representation of the algebraic sign of a numeric value is accomplished by use of the _____ or _____ PICTURE character.

+; −

8   If the − PICTURE insertion character is used, a value held in storage will have associated with it either a − sign or [+ / no] sign. If the + PICTURE character is used, a value held in storage will have associated with it either a + sign or [− / no] sign.

no; −

THE DB AND CR PICTURE CHARACTERS

In accounting applications there is often need to identify values that represent debits or credits. The COBOL language facilitates such differentiation by means of the

DB (debit) and CR (credit) editing characters. As indicated in the following exmples, the DB or CR symbol is written only to the right of a field in the PICTURE clause, and in both cases it is represented in storage for the purpose of subsequent output only when the value is negative.

DESCRIPTION	NUMERIC VALUE	REPRESENTED IN STORAGE AS
02 RECEIPT PICTURE $999.99DB	135.26	$135.26bb
02 RECEIPT PICTURE $999.99DB	−135.26	$135.26DB
02 RECEIPT PICTURE $,$$9.99CR	− 10.50	bb$10.50CR

Notice that the edited field does not provide for negative values as such. A value such as 10.50 would have been previously stored in a signed numeric field and then sent to the edited field. For example, if the original field is described by 03 PAY PICTURE S9(4)V99, then executing the instruction MOVE PAY TO RECEIPT will generate the stored content represented on the last line of the table above.

The following table summarizes the effects of the storage location associated with the use of the +, −, CR, and DB PICTURE editing symbols. Note that for positive values the + is included in the edited field only when the + PICTURE character appears in the PICTURE clause. Note also that for negative values the − sign is included in the edited field if either the + or − PICTURE character has been used, and that the CR or DB appears only if the numeric value is negative.

PICTURE CHARACTER USED	STORAGE REPRESENTATION WHEN VALUE IS POSITIVE	STORAGE REPRESENTATION WHEN VALUE IS NEGATIVE
+	+	−
−	Blank	−
DB	Blank	DB
CR	Blank	CR

THE B PICTURE CHARACTER

This is an insertion editing character resulting in blanks being entered in the designated positions. For example, suppose the first two characters in the storage location NAME always represent the initials of a person's first name and middle name, as follows: RBSMITH. If we wish to print the name with spaces included between the two initials and between the initials and the last name, we can set up the editing field 02 EDNAME PICTURE ABABA(10). Then if we execute the instruction MOVE NAME TO EDNAME and subsequently print the contents of EDNAME, the output will be R B SMITH.

THE 0 PICTURE CHARACTER

The zero insertion character causes zeros to be inserted in the positions in which it appears. For example, we can use this option if the value represented in the storage is understood to be in thousands and we want to edit it to show the full value. Thus if we had 1365 as the value of SUM and we set up EDSUM PICTURE 9(4)000, we could execute MOVE SUM TO EDSUM, giving the following result in EDSUM: 1365000.

THE * PICTURE CHARACTER

The * character is referred to as a check-protect character and is normally used to protect dollar amounts written on checks or other negotiable documents. As indicated by the following examples, it works very much like the floating $ or the Z PICTURE character. In this case, however, instead of the $ sign being floated or positions being filled with blanks, the * character is entered in each zero-suppressed position as designated in the PICTURE clause.

DESCRIPTION	NUMERIC VALUE	REPRESENTED IN STORAGE AS
02 CHECK-VALUE PICTURE $***.99	256.18	$256.18
02 CHECK-VALUE PICTURE $***.99	10.13	$*10.13
02 CHECK-VALUE PICTURE $***.99	0.15	$***.15

THE / PICTURE CHARACTER

Each / (stroke) in the PICTURE character string represents a character position into which the stroke character will be inserted. For example, suppose we have:

02   NUMERIC-DATE   PIC 9(6) VALUE 040778.
02   EDITED-DATE   PIC 99/99/99.

The instruction MOVE NUMERIC-DATE TO EDITED-DATE will cause EDITED-DATE to contain 04/07/78.

REVIEW

1   The editing characters that can be used in a PICTURE clause to identify debits and credits, respectively, are the _____ and the _____ characters.

DB; CR

2   In order for a DB or CR to be included in an editing field, the value entered in that field must be [positive / negative / positive for DB but negative for CR].

negative

3   The insertion editing character which results in blanks being entered in the designated positions is the _____ PICTURE character, whereas the insertion

editing character which results in zeros being entered in designated positions is the _____ PICTURE character.

B; 0

4   The insertion editing character which is referred to as the check-protect character is the _____ PICTURE character.

*

5   Use of the / (stroke) insertion character results in the stroke character being inserted in designated character positions [only when those positions are blank / to achieve visual separation of numeric values].

to achieve visual separation of numeric values

SUMMARY OF PICTURE CLAUSE OPTIONS

Table 5-1 lists all the PICTURE characters. As indicated, the characters that identify the type of content in a storage field are the 9, A, and X characters. Special purpose characters associated with numeric fields only are the V, P, and S characters. All the other characters listed in Table 5-1 are used for editing purposes.

Instead of listing the characters that can be used in PICTURE clauses, another way of summarizing the material presented in this section is to consider the categories of data that can be contained in a storage location and the PICTURE characters that can be used with each category. Accordingly, Table 5-2 identifies five categories of data: numeric, alphabetic, alphanumeric, numeric edited, and alphanumeric edited. Notice

TABLE 5-1   TYPES OF CHARACTERS AVAILABLE FOR USE IN PICTURE CLAUSES

TYPE OF CHARACTER	SYMBOL	USE
Field definition characters	9	Numeric field
	A	Alphabetic field
	X	Alphanumeric field
Numeric field special characters	V	Assumed decimal point
	P	Decimal scaling
	S	Operational (arithmetic) sign included
Editing characters	$	Dollar sign
	Z	Zero suppression
	*	Check protection
	.	Decimal point
	,	Comma
	+	Plus sign
	−	Minus sign
	DB	Debit
	CR	Credit
	B	Blank insertion
	0	Zero insertion
	/	Stroke insertion

TABLE 5-2   THE FIVE CATEGORIES OF DATA

Numeric items	The PICTURE may contain suitable combinations of the following characters: 9 V P and S.
Alphabetic items	The PICTURE clause contains only the A character.
Alphanumeric items	The PICTURE clause consists of A 9 and X characters. It cannot contain all A or all 9 characters, but it may contain a mixture of A and 9 characters.
Numeric edited items	The PICTURE clause can contain suitable combinations of the following characters: B P V Z 0 9 , . * + − CR DB $ and /.
Alphabetic edited items	The PICTURE clause can contain combinations of A and B characters.
Alphanumeric edited items	The PICTURE clause can contain combinations of the following characters: A X 9 B 0 and /.

that the PICTURE clause for alphanumeric items cannot contain all 9s or all A's; all 9s would be indicative of a numeric field, and all A's would indicate an alphabetic field. Note also that numeric edited items can include appropriate combinations of all 12 editing characters included in Table 5-1. On the other hand, alphabetic edited items can include the B (blank insertion) editing character only, whereas alphanumeric edited items can include the B and 0 (zero insertion) and / (stroke) editing characters only.

REVIEW

1   Three of the PICTURE characters we discussed are used for the purpose of defining the type of content in a storage field: the ___, ___, and ___ characters. On the other hand, the three special characters used in conjunction with computational numeric fields are the ___, ___, and ___ PICTURE characters. (Refer to Table 5-1 if you wish.)

9, A, X; V, P, S

2   The only editing PICTURE character used in conjunction with an alphabetic field is the ___ character, whereas the three editing characters which can be used in conjunction with an alphanumeric field are the ___, ___, and ___ PICTURE characters.

B; B, 0, /

THE BLANK WHEN ZERO CLAUSE

Use of this clause achieves the same result as Z PICTURE, but it is more general. Consider the statement 02 AMOUNT PIC ZZ9.99 BLANK WHEN ZERO. If AMOUNT contains a zero value, the field will be blanked (six blanks); otherwise the PICTURE string will provide the editing.

THE CURRENCY AND DECIMAL-POINT CLAUSES

COBOL has provisions for international usage. Changing the dollar sign and the convention of using a comma in lieu of a decimal point can be accommodated by means of two special clauses. These clauses are written in the SPECIAL-NAMES paragraph of the ENVIRONMENT DIVISION. It might seem inappropriate to introduce them at this point, but actually they are intrinsically related to the DATA DIVISION. The dollar sign of course is not the currency symbol for other nations. The programmer may specify the currency sign using the CURRENCY clause:

CURRENCY SIGN IS literal

For example, suppose that F is the currency sign. Then we would write CURRENCY SIGN IS 'F', and in PICTURE clauses we would use 'F' in place of $. THE CURRENCY SIGN *cannot* be chosen from the following: 0 through 9, A, B, C, D, L, P, R, S, V, X, Z, space, *, +,−, comma, ., (,), ", /, =.

In most countries outside the United States, the function of the decimal point and the comma are reversed. Thus, in Europe the numbers 1,35 and 2.534,99 are the equivalent of the American 1.35 and 2,534.99, respectively. To accomodate these different conventions we use the clause

DECIMAL-POINT IS COMMA

Once this clause has been used, the function of comma and period are exchanged in the character string of the PICTURE clause and in numeric literals. For example, it is correct to write

02   AMOUNT   PIC Z.ZZZ.ZZZ,ZZ

since the two decimal points have the same function as commas.

In a European COBOL program we might then have:

ENVIRONMENT DIVISION.
.
.
.
SPECIAL-NAMES. CURRENCY SIGN IS 'F'
      DECIMAL-POINT IS COMMA

REVIEW

1 In the event that an entire data field contains a zero value, the field can be output as all blanks by use of the _____ clause.

                                                    BLANK WHEN ZERO

2 The dollar sign can be changed to the appropriate symbol for another monetary system by use of the _____ clause.

                                                    CURRENCY

3 In monetary systems in which the decimal point and comma have functions opposite to those recognized in the United States, the interchange of these symbols can be achieved by use of the ———————————— clause.

DECIMAL-POINT

THE USAGE CLAUSE

Numeric data in a computer may be represented in one of two basic modes. They may be represented as character data or as numeric data. Both modes utilize binary characters (bits) of zero and one, but the meaning of a given bit depends on the coding method used.

In character mode each decimal digit in a number is represented by a group of binary bits. Commonly, either six or eight bits comprise each digit. Thus, in the six-bit Binary Coded Decimal (BCD) form, the decimal number 19 is represented as 000001001010. The first six bits represent the decimal digit 1, and the last six bits the digit 9. We should also mention two other commonly used coding schemes, the American Standard Code for Information Interchange (ASCII) and the Extended Binary Coded Decimal Interchange Code (EBCDIC), the latter used primarily by IBM.

Numeric data in numeric mode consists of binary bits that have positional values analogous to the decimal system. In the decimal system the first digit in the number 111 has meaning (100) entirely different from that of the third digit (1), even though they look alike. The string of binary bits 000001001010 viewed as a binary number signifies a quantity of 74, not 19, as it would in the BCD code described above. Actually, a variety of numeric coding schemes is in use. We mention their names for reference and direct the interested reader to other sources for explanation (most introductory EDP texts contain descriptions of such codes). The common coding forms are: fixed point binary, floating point of single or double precision, packed decimal, and zoned decimal.

The arithmetic registers of computers perform arithmetic with numeric data that is in numeric, not character, mode. If numeric data is represented in character mode, it must first be converted to numeric mode before arithmetic computations can be performed.

In COBOL, data in character mode is described as being in DISPLAY mode, while data in numeric mode is described as being in COMPUTATIONAL mode. DISPLAY is the default condition: All data items are assumed to be in DISPLAY mode unless they are declared to be COMPUTATIONAL. The declaration is done in the DATA DIVISION with the USAGE clause. Consider the following examples:

```
02  AMOUNT-1                    PIC 99.
02  AMOUNT-2                    PIC 99 USAGE DISPLAY.
02  AMOUNT-3                    PIC 99 USAGE COMPUTATIONAL.
02  AMOUNT-4                    PIC 99 USAGE COMP.
02  AMOUNT-5   USAGE COMP       PIC 99 VALUE ZERO.
```

The first example omits the USAGE clause, and the item will be in DISPLAY mode by default. The second example makes the declaration explicit. The third and fourth examples illustrate the COMPUTATIONAL declaration in full and abbreviated form, respectively. The last example illustrates the point that the order of USAGE, PIC, and VALUE is immaterial.

From a programming standpoint, omission of the USAGE clause seems to be the easiest course of action. From the standpoint of program running efficiency, however, significant savings can be achieved by using the COMPUTATIONAL form. Therefore we recommend that numeric fields in WORKING-STORAGE used for arithmetic be routinely defined as COMPUTATIONAL. Still, absence of the COMPUTATIONAL option does no harm in terms of the results. The compiler inserts the necessary instructions to convert a DISPLAY field into COMPUTATIONAL form prior to doing arithmetic, and then converts the result back into DISPLAY form before storing it in a DISPLAY field.

Data punched onto cards or entered via an online keyboard terminal is in DISPLAY mode, and thus no COMPUTATIONAL fields should be used in the record descriptions of such an input file in the FILE SECTION. Similarly, printing COMPUTATIONAL data makes no sense. However, COMPUTATIONAL data may be read from or written onto magnetic media, such as tapes and disks.

Most compilers specify different forms of COMPUTATIONAL. For instance, IBM and UNIVAC use COMPUTATIONAL-1 (or COMP-1) to define a single precision floating decimal field. ANSI COBOL recognizes only one form, COMPUTATIONAL(or COMP), and it is up to the implementor of the language to define the specific meaning of this standard term. Unless compelling reasons lead to the choice of nonstandard options, such as COMP-1, etc., the programmer will find it advantageous in the long run to stick with the standard.

THE SYNCHRONIZED CLAUSE

The USAGE COMPUTATIONAL option increases program running efficiency, but it does not do the whole job. The SYNCHRONIZED clause is needed to achieve additional execution efficiency. The need for the SYNCHRONIZED clause derives from the fact that COBOL is a general language, but computers of different manufacturers differ in structure. Consider this example.

```
01   FIELD-A.
     02   FIELD-B     PIC 9 USAGE COMP.
     02   FIELD-C     PIC 99 USAGE COMP.
```

In a straightforward fashion we defined two numeric computational fields of one- and two-decimal digits, respectively. In word-oriented computers, such as many UNIVAC, Honeywell, and CDC machines, both fields are stored in the same word, and arithmetic computations are not as efficient as when each field is stored in a separate word. In character-oriented computers, such as many IBM machines, arithmetic execution may not be as efficient as it could be, because the fields are not in proper storage boundaries. The SYNCHRONIZED clause can be used to improve efficiency in this simple example. Notice the SYNC abbreviation which is an alternative available.

```
01   FIELD-A.
     02   FIELD-B      PIC 9 USAGE COMP SYNCHRONIZED.
     02   FIELD-B      PIC 99 USAGE COMP SYNC.
```

However, the use of the option is not always this simple. For other variations, one should consult the manufacturer's manual for the computer being used.

We hasten to add that the SYNCHRONIZED option should be used sparingly. In order to achieve efficiency one must understand clearly the storage structure of a given computer, and the compiler's implementation of the SYNCHRONIZED option. Because this storage structure differs among computers, program compatability across different computers may be lost by use of the SYNCHRONIZED clause. The interested reader should study the manufacturer's manual for his or her own computer before using synchronization, and should consider use of the option only for programs that perform extensive numerical computation.

We digress for a moment to draw a brief comparison with the popular FORTRAN language. A user of that language may wonder why COBOL needs complications such as the SYNCHRONIZED clause, while FORTRAN does beautifully without any such considerations. FORTRAN achieves simplicity by limiting options and forcing uniformity. For instance, all numeric integer fields in FORTRAN occupy a full word (in a word-oriented machine), regardless of desired field size. In contrast, COBOL allows the programmer to define integer fields from 1 to 18 digits in size. The price of flexibility is complexity.

THE JUSTIFIED RIGHT CLAUSE

This option is used with elementary alphabetic or alphanumeric items only, and its effect is to override the convention of left-justifying nonnumeric data. Suppose we have the record description 02   TITLE   PIC X(10). If we write MOVE "JONES" to TITLE, the effect in TITLE will be | J | O | N | E | S | | | | | | , with the name left-justified. However, if in the DATA DIVISION we had written 02 TITLE PICTURE X(10) JUSTIFIED RIGHT, execution of the above MOVE instruction would result in | | | | | | J | O | N | E | S | in TITLE.

As indicated by the above example, the JUSTIFIED RIGHT clause is always used in conjunction with the PICTURE clause for elementary items. However, it cannot be used with level 66 or level 88 items. These two special-purpose levels are explained later in this chapter. In addition to arranging right-justification, the JUSTIFIED RIGHT clause also affects truncation. Without the JUSTIFIED RIGHT clause, truncation takes place from the right for alphabetic and alphanumeric data. When the JUSTIFIED RIGHT clause is used, truncation takes place from the left, as for numeric data.

REVIEW

1   Numeric data stored in a computer may be represented in one of two basic modes: as _____ data or as _____ data.

character; numeric

2 In order to perform arithmetic computations, numeric data must be in _____ mode.

numeric

3 In COBOL, the two modes in which data can be represented are DISPLAY and COMPUTATIONAL. The appropriate form of the data can be indicated by use of the _____ clause in the DATA DIVISION.

USAGE

4 When the USAGE clause is not used, the field is automatically defined as being [DISPLAY / COMPUTATIONAL] in form.

DISPLAY

5 The option which can be used in the DATA DIVISION to improve the efficiency of arithmetic execution by the assignment of appropriate storage boundaries is the _____ clause.

SYNCHRONIZED

6 Elementary alphabetic or alphanumeric items can be positioned in the rightmost portion of the field by use of the _____ clause in the DATA DIVISION.

JUSTIFIED RIGHT

QUALIFICATION

Up to this point in the book we have always indicated that every data-name must be unique in a given program. This requirement will now be modified by introducing the use of qualifiers, which retain the concept of unique data-names but expand the form to provide greater flexibility. A qualifier is a data-name of higher hierarchical level than the name it qualifies. The use of qualifiers results in having unique data-names for names that would otherwise not be unique, thus providing more flexibility in the assignment of data-names in the program. The following DATA DIVISION segment is an example of a case in which qualification would be necessary in the PROCEDURE DIVISION.

```
02  WEEKLY-TOTALS.
    03  HOURS           PICTURE 99V9.
    03  DEPARTMENT-NO   PICTURE 9(5).
02  MONTHLY-TOTALS.
    03  HOURS           PICTURE 999V9.
    03  (etc.)
```

Notice that HOURS seems to be used twice, but with respect to two different items, namely, the total hours for the week and the total hours for the month. If reference were made simply to HOURS, it would not be clear which storage field should be used. However, the use of qualifiers results in unique data-names and could be accomplished as follows in the PROCEDURE DIVISION instructions:

MOVE HOURS OF WEEKLY-TOTALS TO . . .
MOVE HOURS IN MONTHLY-TOTALS TO . . .

OF and IN in the above program statements are equivalent, and use of either word after a data-name serves to signal the use of a qualifier. Since a data-name that is not unique in the program must always be qualified, the use of nonunique names always results in longer statements in the PROCEDURE DIVISION. Despite this disadvantage, qualifiers are often used because they improve documentation. For instance, the statements in the above example make it quite clear that we are working with weekly and monthly hours, respectively.

A common use of qualifiers is with records that have some fields in common, such as master and transaction records. If an employee has an assigned identification number which is included in a master record as well as in a transaction record, the following type of instruction can be included in the PROCEDURE DIVISION:

IF EMPLOY-NUMBER IN MASTER-RECORD IS EQUAL TO
    EMPLOY-NUMBER IN TRANSACTION-RECORD . . .

Again, the documentation aspect of the program is enhanced in the above example in that it is quite clear what is being compared. A further use of the concept of nonunique data-names relates to the CORRESPONDING option, which is discussed in Chapter 6.

At times qualification requires several qualifiers. Consider the following example:

01 OLD-RECORD.	01 NEW-RECORD.
02 TODAYS-DATE . . .	02 TODAYS-DATE . . .
03 MONTH . . .	03 MONTH . . .
03 DAY . . .	03 DAY . . .
03 YEAR . . .	03 YEAR . . .
02 LAST-PERIODS-DATE	02 LAST-PERIODS-DATE . . .
03 MONTH . . .	03 MONTH . .
03 DAY . . .	03 DAY . . .
03 YEAR . . .	03 YEAR . . .
03 TOTAL . . .	03 TOTAL . . .

In the example above the OLD-RECORD and NEW-RECORD are assumed to be in the same program. Notice that there are four fields named MONTH. Thus a qualifier such as MONTH OF LAST-PERIODS-DATE does not provide a unique reference because there are two such fields, one in the OLD-RECORD and one in the NEW-RECORD. Therefore, two qualifiers are needed in order to reference a unique field such as

$$\text{MONTH} \begin{Bmatrix} \text{OF} \\ \text{IN} \end{Bmatrix} \text{LAST-PERIODS-DATE} \begin{Bmatrix} \text{OF} \\ \text{IN} \end{Bmatrix} \text{OLD-RECORD}$$

Since the TOTAL field in the above program example occurs only once in each record, only a single qualifier is required. Therefore, TOTAL IN OLD-RECORD is an adequate reference in this case. The use of two qualifiers such as TOTAL OF LAST-PERIODS-DATE IN OLD-RECORD is acceptable but unnecessary for the purpose of unique identification.

REVIEW

1   The use of qualifiers makes it possible to use the same data-name for variables that would otherwise have different data-names assigned to them. The main advantage of using qualifiers is that _____ is thereby improved.

documentation (or interpretation of the program, etc.)

2   When a qualifier is used, it always [precedes / follows] the referenced data-name, and its use is signaled by one of two words, _____ or _____.

follows; OF; IN

3   Qualifiers are frequently used when a master file record is updated, using data of individual transactions. Assume that the record-name for the master file is MAS-TER-RECORD and the record-name of the transactions file is TRANSACTION-RECORD. Both records contain a field called CUSTOMER-NUMBER. To determine that we are dealing with two records of the same customer we say: IF CUS-TOMER-NUMBER OF _____ IS EQUAL TO CUSTOMER-NUMBER OF _____.

MASTER-RECORD; TRANSACTION-RECORD (*either order*)

4   A sufficient number of qualifiers must be used to differentiate a particular data field from all other data fields in the program that are identified by the same data-name. Suppose that a qualifier is used with a data-name that is unique and thus requires no qualifier. From the standpoint of programming requirements, the qualifier is unnecessary [and the program will terminate / but will not affect program execution].

but will not affect program execution (again, such a qualifier might be used to improve documentation)

MULTIPLE DATA RECORDS

The following option is available in the file description to indicate the existence of more than one type of data record in the file.

FD file-name <u>LABEL</u> clause . . .

<u>DATA</u> $\begin{Bmatrix} \underline{RECORD}\ IS \\ \underline{RECORDS}\ ARE \end{Bmatrix}$ record-name-1 [record-name-2] . . .

Consider an example. Suppose that in a bank, customers may have three kinds of transactions: deposits, withdrawals, and change of address. A record containing information about a deposit or withdrawal has a different format than one pertaining to a change of address. We assume that all records identify the account by a five-digit number in the first five columns and the type of transaction by a transaction code in column 6. Then, if it is a deposit or withdrawal record, the amount is recorded in columns 7–12, while if it is a change of address the new address is recorded in columns 7–46. We can write the following data entries:

```
FD  TRANSACTION-FILE
    LABEL RECORDS OMITTED
    DATA RECORDS ARE FINANCIAL-REC
                    ADDRESS-REC.
01  FINANCIAL-REC.
    02  ACCOUNT        PIC 9(5).
    02  TRANS-CODE     PIC 9.
    02  AMOUNT         PIC 9(4)V99.
    02  FILLER         PIC X(38).
01  ADDRESS-REC.
    02  ACCOUNT        PIC 9(5).
    02  TRANS-CODE     PIC 9.
    02  NEW-ADDRESS    PIC X(44).
```

In this example, the FD entry has specified two types of data records, named FINANCIAL-REC and ADDRESS-REC. It is important to emphasize that physically, a record in this file will consist of 50 characters of data (the sum of all PIC clauses in either record description). Use of two record descriptions simply allows us to reference that data by different names and in different ways.

Both record names reference the entire 50 columns of data. Thus, MOVE FINANCIAL-REC or MOVE ADDRESS-REC do exactly the same thing, they move these 50 columns of data. Similarly, ACCOUNT of FINANCIAL-REC and ACCOUNT of ADDRESS-REC refer to the same first five columns of data, as do the TRANS-CODE names. However, AMOUNT refers to the data in columns 7–12 and, according to the PIC clause, it is assumed that the data is numeric. It should be recalled that a PICTURE clause simply specifies the storage allocation to data, and not the actual contents. The actual contents come about through input or move-type operations. Thus, if we were dealing with a change-of-address transaction and columns 7–12 contained the first six characters of the new address, a statement such as ADD 1 TO AMOUNT would produce unpredictable results, since we are performing arithmetic with nonnumeric data. More appropriately, we would first test to see what type of record we actually have before referencing the data in question. For this purpose assume that we use a code of 1 for a deposit, 2 for withdrawal, and 3 for change of address. We could write:

```
IF TRANS-CODE OF FINANCIAL-REC = 1
   PERFORM PROCESS-DEPOSIT.
```

The statement checks to see if column 6 contains the value 1. Notice that if we had used IF TRANS-CODE OF ADDRESS-REC = 1 it would be exactly the same thing, since both refer to column 6. To further clarify this point, we could have used this data description for ADDRESS-REC.

```
01  ADDRESS-REC.
    02  FILLER          PIC X(6).
    02  NEW-ADDRESS     PIC X(44).
```

Now ACCOUNT and TRANS-CODE need no qualification since they are unique names in FINANCIAL-REC. Use of TRANS-CODE still refers to column 6 of the data. Beginning students often equate the generic data-name FILLER with blank spaces. This should be a good point to discard any such misconception. In this example the FILLER in ADDRESS-REC refers to the first six columns which we know will contain data—the account number and the transaction code.

In general, a file may consist of more than one type of data record. As a rule, there should be a field which designates the type of record involved. In our example we used TRANS-CODE as a field which was in a fixed location no matter what the record type. Then we test the value of that field to ascertain the type of record. In general, this identifying field should be common to all record types, so that no matter what the data is in other fields, this field can be tested.

REVIEW

1   When there is more than one type of data record in a file, the file description in the DATA DIVISION should identify [only one / more than one] file-name.

only one

2   When there is more than one type of data record in a file, the file description in the DATA DIVISION should identify [only one / more than one] record-name.

more than one

3   A coded entry in a specified field serves to differentiate the different input records when there is more than one data record. Particularly when the records are of variable length, the differentiating field should be located in the [left / right] part of the record field.

left

4   In the case of multiple-type record files, at any given time the internal storage can contain [only one / more than one] type of record.

only one

THE REDEFINES CLAUSE

The REDEFINES clause can be used to allow the same storage location to be referenced by different data-names or to allow a regrouping or different description of the data in a particular storage location. The general format associated with the use of this option is:

```
level-number   data-name-1 REDEFINES data-name-2
```

The following example illustrates the use of this option:

```
01  SAMPLE.
    02  RECEIVABLE.
        03  CUSTOMER-NUMBER              PICTURE 9(8).
        03  CUSTOMER-NAME                PICTURE X(11).
        03  AMOUNT                       PICTURE 9(4)V99.
    02  PAYABLE REDEFINES RECEIVABLE.
        03  VENDOR-NUMBER                PICTURE 9(6).
        03  VENDOR-NAME                  PICTURE X(12).
        03  VENDOR-OWED-AMOUNT           PICTURE 9(5)V99.
```

In the above example, use of the REDEFINES option allows the data-names RECEIVABLE and PAYABLE to refer to the same 25 positions in internal storage. The format of these two data items in internal storage can be portrayed as follows:

In the above example, notice that the format of the data items was also changed by the use of the REDEFINES option, but that the overall size of the item was not changed.

It should be made clear that the redefinition applies to the storage area involved and not to the data that may be stored in that area at any point in time. The programmer is responsible for providing the necessary program logic so that correct reference is made to the actual data stored. In the example illustration above, if we write ADD VENDOR-OWED-AMOUNT TO . . . , the result will be to add the contents of the last seven storage positions, whatever these contents might be.

There are certain conditions under which the REDEFINES clause cannot be used. Two such conditions are

1 The REDEFINES clause cannot be used at the 01 level in the FILE SECTION. Recall that the use of multiple data records in the FD entry has the same effect as use of the REDEFINES option, in that it permits use of the same storage location for different records.

2 The REDEFINES clause cannot be used when the levels of data-name-1 and data-name-2 are different. Further, the level number must not be at the 66 or 88 level. These two special-purpose levels are explained in the following two sections.

REVIEW

1   The same storage location can be used in conjunction with two different data-
    names by use of the _____ clause.

    REDEFINES

2   When the REDEFINES option is used, the format of the data item [can / cannot]
    also be changed.

    can

3   Generally, the REDEFINES clause can be used when the two data items have the
    same level number. The exceptions are when the special purpose 66 or 88 level
    numbers are used and when the level number is at 01 in the _____
    SECTION, in which cases the REDEFINES clause cannot be used.

    FILE

THE RENAMES CLAUSE

The RENAMES clause provides the programmer with the capability of regrouping
elementary data items. In a sense it resembles the REDEFINES clause, except that it can
form a new grouping of data items which combines several items. Use of the RENAMES
clause is always signaled by the special 66 level number. The general format is

---

66 data-name-1 <u>RENAMES</u> data-name-2 [<u>THRU</u> data-name-3]

Consider the following example which includes use of the RENAMES clause.

```
01  TAX-RECORD.
    02  SOC-SEC-NUMBER          PICTURE X(9).
    02  NAME.
        03  FIRST-NAME          PICTURE X(10).
        03  INITIAL             PICTURE XX.
        03  LAST-NAME           PICTURE X(15).
    02  TOTALS-YEAR-TO-DATE.
        03  GROSS-PAY           PICTURE 9(8)V99.
        03  NET-PAY             PICTURE 9(8)V99.
        03  FED-TAX             PICTURE 9(6)V99.
        03  STATE-TAX           PICTURE 9(4)V99.
    66  LAST-GROSS RENAMES LAST-NAME THRU NET-PAY.
```

Schematically, the regrouping of data fields by use of the RENAMES clause in the
last statement can be portrayed as follows:

NAME				TOTALS-YEAR-TO-DATE			
SOC-SEC-NUMBER	FIRST-NAME	INITIAL	LAST-NAME	GROSS-PAY	NET-PAY	FED-TAX	STATE-TAX

LAST-GROSS

In the example, LAST-GROSS is a storage field that consists of the LAST-NAME, GROSS-PAY, and NET-PAY fields. In this way we can make reference to those three fields as one group, which would not be possible without use of the RENAMES clause.

There are other rules governing use of the RENAMES option, but they are beyond the scope of this text. The user should be aware that knowledge of additonal rules may be necessary for the successful use of the RENAMES option in more complex situations.

REVIEW

1   Elementary data items that are part of different storage fields can be regrouped and formed into a new field by use of the _____ clause.

RENAMES

2   The DATA DIVISION statement in which the RENAMES clause is used is always assigned the level number _____ (number).

66

CONDITION-NAMES

Recall that figurative constants are words that signify constant values. For example, the figurative constants ZERO and SPACES mean a value of zero and blanks, respectively. In effect, the use of condition-names enables the programmer to define additional figurative constants for use in the COBOL program. The use of this option is always indicated by the special level 88 entry whose format is

$$
88\ \text{data-name}\ \left\{ \begin{array}{l} \underline{\text{VALUE}}\ \text{IS} \\ \underline{\text{VALUES}}\ \text{ARE} \end{array} \right\}\ \text{literal-1}\ \ [\underline{\text{THRU}}\ \text{literal-2}]
$$

$$
[\text{literal-3}\ \ [\underline{\text{THRU}}\ \text{literal-4}]\ ]\ \ldots
$$

As an example of the use of condition-names, suppose that the personnel record used in a company contains, among other things, the number of years of education. The information is contained in a field called EDUCATION and is so coded that the number indicates the last school grade completed. Thus, a code number less than 12 indicates that the person did not complete high school, 12 indicates a high school graduate, 13–15 indicate some college education, 16 indicates a college graduate, and a number greater than 16 indicates some graduate or postgraduate work. If we wish to process for educational level, using these categories, we could write such PROCE-DURE DIVISION statements as: IF EDUCATION IS LESS THAN 12 . . IF EDUCATION IS EQUAL TO 12 . . . etc. However, an alternative is to define condition-names in the DATA DIVISION, which will then stand for the indicated values. Thus we can write:

```
01  PERSONNEL DATA.
    02  ID-NUMBER . . .
    02  NAME . . .
    02  ADDRESS . . .
    02  EDUCATION PICTURE IS 99.
        88  LESS-THAN-H-S-GRAD VALUES ARE 0 THRU 11.
        88  H-S-GRAD VALUE IS 12.
        88  SOME-COLLEGE VALUES ARE 13 THRU 15.
        88  COLLEGE-GRAD VALUE IS 16.
        88  POST-GRAD VALUES ARE 17 THRU 20.
```

With the above condition-names defined in the DATA DIVISION, they can then be used in PROCEDURE DIVISION statements. For example, the statement IF H-S-GRAD ADD 1 TO TOTAL1 is identical in result as the statement IF EDUCATION IS EQUAL TO 12 ADD 1 TO TOTAL1. Furthermore, the statement IF SOME-COLLEGE ADD 1 TO TOTAL2 is equivalent to a series of *nested* conditional statements (see Chapter 8) such as

```
IF EDUCATION IS LESS THAN 16
    IF EDUCATION IS GREATER THAN 12
        ADD 1 TO TOTAL2 . . . etc.
```

Thus, one advantage of using condition-names is that they allow the programmer to write complex tests in simple form in the PROCEDURE DIVISION. At the beginning of this section we indicated that the condition-name is like a figurative constant. As the result of reviewing the above example, it should now be clear that it is, except that the condition-name refers to a specific data-name only—EDUCATION in the above example.

REVIEW

1 The programmer can define figurative constants to be used in conjunction with a particular data-name by the use of _____.

condition-names

2 An entry in which a condition-name is defined is always assigned the level number _____ (number).

88

3 Suppose that for the data-name MARITAL-STATUS the possible values are 1 = married, 2 = divorced, 3 = widowed, 4 = single, and all other values are errors. Write suitable 88 level entries to define condition-names for

  a condition of being or having been married
  b condition of being single
  c condition of error code.

  03   MARITAL-STATUS PICTURE 9.
    88 _____
    88 _____
    88 _____

                                   a IS-OR-WAS-MARRIED VALUES ARE 1
                                       THRU 3.
                                   b SINGLE VALUE IS 4.
                                   c ERROR-CODE VALUES ARE ZERO 5
                                       THRU 9.

THE VALUE CLAUSE

In addition to defining storage fields with respect to form by using the PICTURE clause it is often desirable to assign initial values to WORKING-STORAGE fields. Such a value may remain unchanged throughout the program, such as a tax rate, or it may change in the course of program execution. Such initial values are generally not assigned to FILE SECTION items, since such fields either receive their data from the external medium or from some other storage location as the result of program execution.

As you may recall from previous examples, an initial value is assigned by the use of the VALUE clause. The general form of this clause is

$$\underline{\text{VALUE}} \text{ IS} \begin{Bmatrix} \text{numeric literal} \\ \text{figurative constant} \\ \text{nonnumeric literal} \end{Bmatrix}$$

The use of the VALUE clause is illustrated in the following examples. Notice that the order of the PICTURE and VALUE clauses is irrelevant, and that the use of the word IS is optional for each type of clause.

02 PAGE-TITLE VALUE IS "SAMPLE PROGRAM" PICTURE IS A(14).
02 TENTH-BAL PICTURE IS 99, VALUE 10.
02 TAX-RATE VALUE IS 0.03 PICTURE V99.
02 BLANKS-FIELD VALUE IS SPACES PICTURES X(20).
02 ACCUMULATOR PICTURE IS 9(8)V9(4) VALUE IS ZEROES.

At this point it should be noted that the VALUE clause associated with 88 level condition names is different from the VALUE clause used to assign initial values to storage positions.

REVIEW

1 Initial values can be assigned to WORKING-STORAGE fields by use of the _____ clause.

VALUE

2 The VALUE clause [always precedes / always follows / can either precede or follow] the PICTURE clause in a WORKING-STORAGE entry.

can either precede or follow

EXERCISES

1 True or false: The PICTURE clause can be used only with elementary items. Indicate the reason for your answer.

2 Indicate the size of each of the following fields:

PICTURE	SIZE
99V99	
9(3).9	
S999V9	
ZZ,ZZZ	
+(3).99	
$***,**9.99	
VPP99	
ZZZ000	

3 Suppose it has become necessary to change an existing COBOL program. The original version of the relevant DATA DIVISION entries is as follows:

02 FIELD-A
   03   FIELD-B
   03   FIELD-C
   03   FIELD-D
02 FIELD-E

In the revised version it is required that the fields be restructured so that (**a**) reference can be made to all the fields as one unit; (**b**) reference can be made to fields B and C as a unit; and (**c**) reference can be made to fields D and E as a unit. Show how this can be done.

4   Write DATA DIVISION entries for the WORKING-STORAGE record named SALES-DATA whose description is given below. Data are moved from the items whose PICTURE description is shown.

SOURCE ITEM PICTURE	RECEIVING ITEM-NAME	PRINT POSITIONS	EDITING REQUIRED
99999	SALE-NUMBER	1–5	Suppress all leading zeros.
		6–7	Blank
X(25)	NAME	8–32	None
		33–34	Blank
S9999V99	DOLLARS	35–?	Insert comma, decimal point. Dollar sign immediately to the left of leftmost nonzero digit. Show negative sign if negative.
		2 positions	Blank
S9(3)V9(4)	PROFIT		Show decimal point. Suppress leading zeros. Show negative sign to the left of leftmost nonzero digit.

5   Below are DATA DIVISION entries for fields that contain the data to be printed as the CHECK-REGISTER record. The output resulting from printing of the CHECK-REGISTER record should have approximately the following format (header titles are shown for clarity only).

VENDOR NAME	VENDOR NUMBER	CHECK NUMBER	DATE	DEBIT	DISCOUNT	CASH
ACME CORP.	1234	12345	01/03/72	$1,030.57	$20.13	$1,010.44

```
01  CHECK-NUMBER      PICTURE 9(5).
01  DEBIT             PICTURE 9(6)V99.
01  DISCOUNT          PICTURE 9(4)V99.
01  CASH              PICTURE 9(6)V99.
01  VENDOR-DATA.
    02  V-NAME        PICTURE X(15).
    02  V-NUMBER      PICTURE X(4).
01  DATE.
```

```
02  MONTH          PICTURE 99.
02  DAY            PICTURE 99.
02  YEAR           PICTURE 99.
```

Write DATA DIVISION entries to form the CHECK-REGISTER record so that the output is printed approximately in the desired format. (Make sure the date is in the form MM/DD/YY.)

6 It is required that two lines having the following general format be printed.

SUMMARY STATISTICS
AVERAGE BAL. $XXX,XXX.XX MAX $XXX,XXX.XX MIN $XXX,XXX.XX

Assume the following DATA DIVISION entries:

```
FD  PRINT-FILE LABEL RECORDS OMITTED DATA RECORD IS
      PRINT-LINE.
01  PRINT-LINE    PICTURE X(132).
WORKING-STORAGE SECTION.
01  MAX-BAL             PICTURE 9(6)V99.
01  MIN-BAL             PICTURE 9(6)V99.
01  AVER-BAL            PICTURE 9(6)V99.
```

Write WORKING-STORAGE SECTION entries to set up the required fields to print these two lines. Write the corresponding PROCEDURE DIVISION statements to accomplish the printing task.

7 A punched card file contains name and address data for college students and their parents or guardians. The file is so arranged that for each student there are two cards. The first card contains the name and address of the student, and the second card contains the name and address of parent or guardian. The card formats are as follows:

STUDENT CARD		PARENT CARD	
FIELD	CARD COLUMNS	FIELD	CARD COLUMNS
Student number	1–9	Student number	1–9
Student name	10–30	Parent name	10–30
Street	31–60	Street	31–60
City	61–79	City	61–79
Card code = 1	80	Card code = 2	80

a Write ENVIRONMENT and DATA DIVISION file and record entries to describe this card file.

b Write PROCEDURE DIVISION statements to read two consecutive cards, testing to ascertain that they are student and parent cards, respectively. When the first card is read, if it is a student card, it is stored in CARD-WORK-AREA. If the first card is not a student card or if the second card is not a parent card for the same student, the program branches to a paragraph ERROR-ROUTINE. If the cards are correct, the program branches to a paragraph called PROCESS.

8 In the diagram below there is a record called BIGFIELD. The numbers running from 1 to 13 indicate respective character positions. Thus, the record consists of 13 character positions. It is desired to be able to reference the following positions while also preserving the current structure of the record. Indicate how you would accomplish this objective.

a Reference 1, 2, 3, 4 by one name
b Reference 5, 6, 7 by one name
c Reference 8, 9, 10 by one name
d Reference 11, 12, 13 by one name
e Reference 1, 2, 3, 4, 5, 6, 7 by one name
f Reference 8, 9, 10, 11, 12, 13 by one name
g Reference 3, 4, 5, 6, 7, 8, 9, 10 by one name

BIGFIELD												
GROUP-A							GROUP-B					
AA		AB			AC		BA		BB		BC	
1	2	3	4	5	6	7	8	9	10	11	12	13

9 A wholesale distributor employs a number of salespeople in the five designated territories of a state. A coding method is used to denote a territory and a salesperson. The first digit indicates the territory and the second digit the individual salesperson.

TERRITORY	CODE
Southwest	11–16
Northwest	21–25
Central	31–38
Northeast	41–49
Southeast	51–54

a Write condition-name entries so that, given a value of SALES-CODE, we can determine the territory and be able to determine whether it is an error code. For example, codes 08 and 19 would be error codes.
b For certain purposes we are interested in testing whether a SALES-CODE value refers to the central or to the other territories. Set up condition-names that will enable us to test for central and noncentral territories.

PROCEDURE DIVISION Features I

INTRODUCTION

In Chapter 4 we presented a basic subset of language statements that enabled the student to write workable PROCEDURE DIVISION instructions. The purpose of this and the following chapter is to present additional options associated with the basic statements already presented and to add a number of new statement types. Completion of these two chapters will provide the student with a grasp of the fundamental PROCEDURE DIVISION statements. Additional statements and options are presented throughout most of the remaining chapters in reference to special purposes or functions, such as conditional statements, sequential file processing, merging, sorting, searching, direct access file processing, subprogramming, and report writing.

FILE-ORIENTED INPUT AND OUTPUT: OPEN, CLOSE, READ, WRITE

For review purposes, we present the basic formats of the four input and output verbs already discussed in Chapter 4.

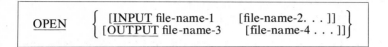

OPEN $\left\{ \begin{array}{ll} \text{[INPUT file-name-1} & \text{[file-name-2. . .]]} \\ \text{[OUTPUT file-name-3} & \text{[file-name-4 . . .]]} \end{array} \right\}$

CLOSE file-name-1   [file-name-2] . . .

READ   file-name RECORD [INTO identifier] AT END imperative
statement

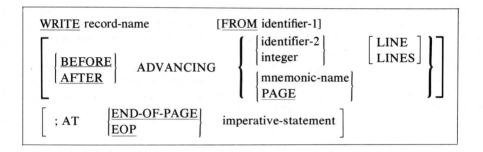

WRITE record-name   [FROM identifier-1]

$\left[\begin{array}{c} \text{BEFORE} \\ \text{AFTER} \end{array} \right]$ ADVANCING $\left\{ \begin{array}{l} \left\{ \begin{array}{l} \text{identifier-2} \\ \text{integer} \end{array} \right\} \left[\begin{array}{l} \text{LINE} \\ \text{LINES} \end{array} \right] \\ \left\{ \begin{array}{l} \text{mnemonic-name} \\ \text{PAGE} \end{array} \right\} \end{array} \right\}$

$\left[\text{; AT} \left\{ \begin{array}{l} \text{END-OF-PAGE} \\ \text{EOP} \end{array} \right\} \text{imperative-statement} \right]$

Special options and considerations with respect to the OPEN and CLOSE verbs are discussed in Chapter 10, "Magnetic Tape Files." For now, it will be recalled that an OPEN INPUT statement must be executed prior to inputing from a file, and that an OPEN OUTPUT must be executed prior to writing on a file. In relation to the READ statement, the INTO option causes an implicit move of the data record read into the specified identifier, thus making the data read in available in two places—the file record and the identifier associated with INTO.

The WRITE statement involves some new options. To review, the FROM option implies a move of data from identifier-1 to record-name. Use of the identifier-2 option in the ADVANCING clause can be illustrated by the following example.

Suppose that a sales invoice form has space for 10 items on each invoice, and we always wish to print the total billing on the last line of the invoice. We can use a storage field as a counter to keep track of the number of items on each invoice. Let us call this field KOUNT. If an invoice contains four items, the value stored in KOUNT will be 4; if an invoice contains six items, the value will be 6, and so on. In order to print the total billing on the last line of the invoice, the number of lines to be skipped will always be 10 spaces minus KOUNT. For this example, we are of course assuming that there will never be more than 10 items. Therefore, the following statements provide the basis for skipping the appropriate number of lines:

SUBTRACT KOUNT FROM 10 GIVING LINE-COUNT.
WRITE REP-LINE AFTER ADVANCING LINE-COUNT LINES.

When a mnemonic-name is used, it is specified in the SPECIAL-NAMES paragraph of the ENVIRONMENT DIVISION. Such mnemonic names are specified by the manufacturer. As an example, consider an IBM system where C01 is defined to mean channel 1 on the printer carriage control tape, where channel 1 defines the top of a printer page. We could have:

```
ENVIRONMENT DIVISION.
CONFIGURATION SECTION.
SOURCE-COMPUTER. IBM-370.
OBJECT-COMPUTER. IBM-370.
SPECIAL-NAMES
     C01 IS TOP-OF-PAGE.
INPUT-OUTPUT SECTION.
etc.
```

In the PROCEDURE DIVISION, the statement WRITE PRINT-RECORD AFTER ADVANCING TOP-OF-PAGE is understood to mean to skip to the top of a new page. Actually, the need to be able to skip to the top of a new page is universal enough for COBOL to include the reserved word PAGE as an option in WRITE, the use of which results in skipping to a new page.

AT END-OF-PAGE is a conditional statement. When specified, a check is made to determine if the END-OF-PAGE (abbreviated EOP) condition is met. If it is, then the imperative statement is executed. The END-OF-PAGE condition is defined by means of the LINAGE clause in the DATA DIVISION, which has the following format.

$$
\underline{\text{LINAGE}} \text{ IS} \left\{ \begin{array}{c} \text{data-name-1} \\ \text{integer-1} \end{array} \right\} \text{LINES} \left[, \text{WITH } \underline{\text{FOOTING}} \text{ AT} \left\{ \begin{array}{c} \text{data-name-2} \\ \text{integer-2} \end{array} \right\} \right]
$$

$$
\left[, \text{LINES AT } \underline{\text{TOP}} \left\{ \begin{array}{c} \text{data-name-3} \\ \text{integer-3} \end{array} \right\} \right] \left[, \text{LINES AT } \underline{\text{BOTTOM}} \left\{ \begin{array}{c} \text{data-name-4} \\ \text{integer-4} \end{array} \right\} \right]
$$

Let us consider an example. We want to produce a report with the following format.

LINE NUMBER	CONTENTS
1–5	Not used
6	The page header
7–56	The body of the report
57–59	The page totals
60–66	Not used

We could proceed as follows.

DATA DIVISION

.

.

.

FD PRINT-FILE LABEL RECORD OMITTED
          DATA RECORD IS PRINT-REC
          LINAGE IS 54 LINES
              WITH FOOTING AT 51
          LINES AT TOP 5
          LINES AT BOTTOM 7.

The page will consist of 66 lines which is the sum of the values referenced in each phrase, except for the FOOTING phrase. Five lines are unused at the top, and seven at the bottom.

In the PROCEDURE DIVISION the statement:

WRITE PRINT-REC FROM TOP-HEADER AFTER ADVANCING PAGE

will cause printing of the header on line 6 because now PAGE is associated with line 6, since LINES AT TOP 5 specifies that five lines be left blank at the top of the page. (TOP-HEADER in this example is assumed to contain the desired header.)

Now consider these statements:

WRITE PRINT-REC FROM BODY-OF-REPORT-LINE
    AFTER ADVANCING 1 LINE
    AT END-OF-PAGE PERFORM TOTALS.
TOTALS.
    WRITE PRINT-REC FROM TOTALS-LINE
        AFTER ADVANCING 3 LINES
    WRITE PRINT-REC FROM TOP-HEADER
        AFTER ADVANCING PAGE.

We keep printing data from BODY-OF-REPORT-LINE until we reach line 56, (51 + 5), which is defined as the footing: WITH FOOTING AT 51. At that point, the END-OF-PAGE condition holds and we PERFORM TOTALS, which prints data on line 59 (triple spacing) and then skips to the next page (line 6 of the next page) to print the page header TOP-HEADER.

A special counter is used whenever LINAGE is specified. It is called LINAGE-COUNTER, a COBOL reserved word. It is set to 1 when a print file is opened or when an ADVANCING PAGE is encountered. Afterward, the counter is automatically incremented the appropriate number of lines implied in each WRITE statement. When LINAGE-COUNTER is equal to the value of the FOOTING phrase, then an END-OF-PAGE condition occurs. The LINAGE-COUNTER may not be modified by the program, but it may be accessed. Thus, it is legitimate to write: IF LINAGE-COUNTER = 25 PERFORM MID-PAGE ROUTINE.

REVIEW

1   Prior to inputing data to be analyzed from a file, a(n) _____ statement must be executed.

                                                    OPEN INPUT

2 Prior to writing data on a file, a(n) _____ statement must be executed.

OPEN OUTPUT

3 The option whose use results in the same data being available in two different places after a READ statement is executed is the _____ option.

INTO

4 In conjunction with a WRITE statement, data are moved from an identifier-1 to a record-name by use of the _____ option.

FROM

5 The skipping of lines in conjunction with a WRITE statement is accomplished by use of the _____ clause.

ADVANCING

6 When an END-OF-PAGE (EOP) condition is specified in conjunction with a WRITE statement, then the description of the number of lines and their use has to be defined in a(n) _____ clause in the DATA DIVISION.

LINAGE

7 The special counter which is a reserved word and which is used implicitly whenever the LINAGE option is specified is the _____.

LINAGE-COUNTER

8 Assume these entries:

LINAGE IS 25 LINES
WITH FOOTING AT 21
LINES AT TOP 2
LINES AT BOTTOM 3

Fill in the missing members.

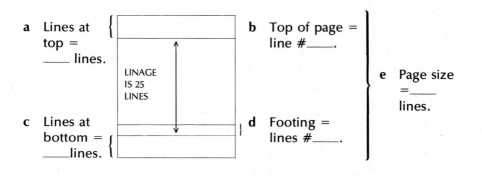

a Lines at top = ___ lines.

b Top of page = line #___.

c Lines at bottom = ___ lines.

d Footing = lines #___.

e Page size = ___ lines.

a 2
b 3
c 3
d 23 − 27
e 25 + 2 + 3 = 30

DATA-ORIENTED INPUT AND OUTPUT: ACCEPT, DISPLAY

Up to this point we have always discussed input and output in connection with files. Such is the normal use of input and output verbs, but it is also possible to execute input and output in conjunction with storage fields that are not part of any files. This is typically done to permit the input and/or output of short data items to or from devices such as the console typewriter and the printer. The verbs that allow such input and output are ACCEPT and DISPLAY. The general formats associated with use of the ACCEPT verb are

Format 1

```
ACCEPT identifier [FROM mnemonic-name]
```

Format 2

```
ACCEPT identifier FROM  { DATE }
                        { DAY  }
                        { TIME }
```

The first format can be used as in this example: ACCEPT STARTING-CHECK-NO FROM CONSOLE-TYPE. As a result of executing this instruction, the computer will input data into the STARTING-CHECK-NO storage field from the device previously defined as CONSOLE-TYPE in the SPECIAL-NAMES paragraph of the ENVIRONMENT DIVISION. If this device is a typewriter, further program execution is delayed until the operator types in the appropriate input. If the device is a card reader, the next card will be read, and data will be input into STARTING-CHECK-NO.

Data input via ACCEPT is treated as if it were alphanumeric with respect to positioning. Suppose that STARTING-CHECK-NO has been defined with a PICTURE 99999. If ACCEPT is executed with reference to the console typewriter and the operator types in 12345, the receiving field will contain 12345. On the other hand, if the operator types 12, the 12 will be stored *left-justified* in STARTING-CHECK-NO, and normally additional data will be requested. That is, the program will pause and wait for the remaining data. However, if the data were input from a card, the data (including blanks) present in the first five card columns will be stored in STARTING-CHECK-NO exactly as they were on the card.

The second format of ACCEPT can be used to move the contents of the COBOL predefined fields DATA, DAY, or TIME to a specified identifier. These latter three fields are not defined by the programmer but are made available by the compiler. Their *implicit definition is*

```
DATE    999999
DAY     99999
TIME    99999999.
```

The DATE field contains the year, month, and day. Assume that TODAY was defined:

```
02  TODAY.
    03  T-YEAR      PIC 99.
    03  T-MONTH     PIC 99.
    03  T-DAY       PIC 99.
```

The instruction ACCEPT TODAY FROM DATE issued on February 1, 1978, will cause the content of DATE, 780201, to be moved to TODAY.

The DAY field contains the year and the day of the year. Thus, July 1, 1979, will be stored as 79183.

TIME contains hours, minutes, seconds, and hundredths of a second based on elapsed time after midnight on a 24-hour-clock basis. Thus, 8:30 P.M. is stored as 20300000. The smallest value of TIME is 00000000, and the largest is 23595999.

The general format associated with use of the DISPLAY verb is

$$\underline{\text{DISPLAY}} \left\{ \begin{array}{l} \text{identifier-1} \\ \text{literal-1} \end{array} \right\} \left[\begin{array}{l} \text{, identifier-2} \\ \text{, literal-2} \end{array} \right] \ldots [\underline{\text{UPON}} \text{ mnemonic-name}]$$

Notice that DISPLAY can reference a series of identifiers or literals. Thus, we can write DISPLAY AMOUNT-A, "IS A VALUE OUT OF RANGE" UPON CONSOLE-TYPE. Execution of this statement will result in the contents of the storage field AMOUNT-A being typed on the console typewriter, followed by the literal message in the quotation marks.

In some computer installations ACCEPT and DISPLAY can be used only with devices predefined by the installation itself, and thus the device will not be named in the statement. For example, writing ACCEPT CODE-A may be valid and would refer to some specific device in the particular installation, such as the console typewriter or an alternate card reader. Similarly DISPLAY ERR-MESSAGE-1 may be valid in installations in which the DISPLAY verb is automatically associated with a particular device, such as the console typewriter, a card punch, or a printer.

Some installations also tend to use ACCEPT and DISPLAY as substitutes for READ and WRITE statements for card and printer files. For example, if the card reader is associated with ACCEPT and the printer is associated with DISPLAY, the programmer need not identify any files in the input and output statements. In an educational environment in which most input is from cards and most output is on the printer without any real "files" in use, the practice of using ACCEPT and DISPLAY may be expeditious. However, in a "real-world" environment the verbs ACCEPT and DISPLAY have limited usage as input and output verbs, because they lack the full power of READ and WRITE. A more common practice is to use DISPLAY for debugging purposes. For example, we can trace the contents of input records by the following approach:

```
READ INPUT-FILE RECORD AT END. . . .
DISPLAY REC-IN UPON PRINTER.
```

In this case REC-IN is assumed to be the name of the record read in, and we are displaying its contents on a device called PRINTER.

REVIEW

1 The verb used to input short data items not usually part of any file as such is the _____ verb, whereas the verb similarly used for short output, usually on the console typewriter, is _____ .

ACCEPT; DISPLAY

2 DATA input by use of the ACCEPT verb is always treated as being [alphabetic / numeric / alphanumeric].

alphanumeric

3 Because the DISPLAY verb can reference literals as well as identifiers, it can be used to convey certain _____ as well as data items.

messages (etc.)

4 Although the DISPLAY verb has limited use in computer programs for regular data processing applications, it is frequently used in conjunction with the _____ of computer programs.

debugging

DATA MOVEMENT: MOVE, MOVE CORRESPONDING

The use of the verb MOVE was described in Chapter 4, "Writing Complete Programs." The general format of this verb is

$$\underline{\text{MOVE}} \quad \left\{ \begin{array}{l} \text{identifier-1} \\ \text{literal} \end{array} \right\} \quad \underline{\text{TO}} \text{ identifier-2} \quad [\text{,identifier-3}] \ldots$$

While the use of the MOVE verb may seem straightforward, some points should be repeated from our original discussion in Chapter 4.

It will be recalled that the size and data description of the sending and receiving fields must be taken into account. For nonnumeric data alignment takes place at the left margin. For numeric data, alignment takes place with respect to the decimal point. Then, if the sending field is larger, excess digits are truncated on either side of the decimal point, while if the sending field is smaller, excess positions are zero-filled. Further, if the receiving field is a numeric edited field, data will be moved and edited according to the editing rules discussed in Chapter 5, "DATA DIVISION Features."

The level of a receiving field is also a factor. Data moved to a group item will always be treated as an alphanumeric move, regardless of the PICTURE clause of the elementary items. Consider these two group fields:

```
01  SENDING-FIELD.                    01  RECEIVING-FIELD.
    02  QUANTITY   PIC 99V9.              02  ED-QUANTITY   PIC Z9.9.
    02  PRICE      PIC 99V99.             02  ED-PRICE      PIC $$9.99.
```

MOVE SENDING-FIELD TO RECEIVING-FIELD will move the 7-character SENDING-FIELD to the 10-character RECEIVING-FIELD, left-justified, just like any alphanumeric move. The editing PICTURE characters in the elementary items of the RECEIVING-FIELD are inoperative. If we want the editing to take place, then we must move each elementary item individually, such as MOVE QUANTITY TO ED-QUANTITY, etc.

In a related context, moving zeros to a group item whose elementary items contain USAGE COMPUTATIONAL clauses may result in nonzero data. Consider this group-item:

```
01   GROUP-ITEM.
     02   AMOUNT-1     PIC 99V99 USAGE COMPUTATIONAL.
     02   AMOUNT-2     PIC 9999V99 USAGE COMPUTATIONAL.
```

A statement such as MOVE ZEROS TO GROUP-ITEM will move "character" zeros into GROUP-ITEM. A zero in character mode is different from a zero in binary numeric mode. Therefore, if we subsequently write ADD TOTAL TO AMOUNT-1, erroneous results will be obtained from the arithmetic operation, since AMOUNT-1 does not contain a zero value. To avoid such problems, we should move zeros to each individual numeric field which has been defined as USAGE COMPUTATIONAL. Thus MOVE ZERO TO AMOUNT-1, AMOUNT-2 would be the appropriate instruction for setting these two fields equal to zero. Of course, in the absence of the USAGE COMPUTATIONAL clauses, MOVE ZERO TO GROUP-ITEM would have resulted in proper zeros in the elementary fields.

We can summarize the legality of various types of MOVE statements as follows:

CATEGORY OF SENDING DATA ITEM	CATEGORY OF RECEIVING DATA ITEM		
	ALPHABETIC	ALPHANUMERIC ALPHANUMERIC EDITED	NUMERIC INTEGER NUMERIC NONINTEGER NUMERIC EDITED
ALPHABETIC	Yes	Yes	No
ALPHANUMERIC	Yes	Yes	Yes
ALPHANUMERIC EDITED	Yes	Yes	No
NUMERIC			
INTEGER	No	Yes	Yes
NONINTEGER	No	No	Yes
NUMERIC EDITED	No	Yes	No

In Chapter 5, "DATA DIVISION Features," we describe the concept of qualification. Briefly, this concept allows the programmer to use the same subordinate data-name in more than one place in the program, thus allowing nonunique data-names. The CORRESPONDING option, available for use with MOVE and with the arithmetic verbs, simplifies the program in cases in which the same operation is to be performed on one or several pairs of elementary, nonunique data-names. Let us take an example. Suppose we have the following two records:

```
01   PAY-RECORD.                    01   EDITED-RECORD.
     02   GROSS   PIC 9999V99.           02   GROSS       PIC ZZZ9.99.
```

02	NET	PIC 9999V99.	02	TAXES	PIC ZZ9.99.
02	TAXES	PIC 999V99.	02	NET	PIC ZZZ9.99.

If we want to move PAY-RECORD to EDITED-RECORD, we *cannot* do it in one statement. Writing MOVE PAY-RECORD to EDITED-RECORD would be incorrect, because the order of the variables NET and TAXES is not the same in the two records. Of course, the move could be accomplished by a separate MOVE statement for each of the three fields. However, the same result can be accomplished more easily by use of the CORRESPONDING option:

MOVE CORRESPONDING PAY-RECORD TO EDITED-RECORD.

The general format associated with the use of the CORRESPONDING option is

```
┌─────────────────────────────────────────────────────────────┐
│        ⎧ CORRESPONDING ⎫                                      │
│ MOVE   ⎨ ───────────── ⎬  identifier-1  TO  identifier-2      │
│        ⎩ CORR          ⎭                                      │
└─────────────────────────────────────────────────────────────┘
```

CORR is the abbreviated form of the option. Unlike the situation in the example above, the two data-names may contain only some items that correspond, as in the following example:

02 INSPECTION.	01 QUALITY-REPORT.
03 TOTAL-QUANTITY . . .	02 TOTAL-QUANTITY . . .
03 REJECTED . . .	02 QUALITY-RATIO . . .
03 ACCEPTED . . .	
03 QUALITY-RATIO . . .	

Executing the statement MOVE CORR INSPECTION TO QUALITY-REPORT will result in the two items or fields, TOTAL-QUANTITY and QUALITY-RATIO, being moved.

In order for the CORRESPONDING option to be used, there must be pairs of items having the same name in two group items, and at least one of the items in each pair must be elementary. Another rule to remember is that any items that are subordinate to identifier-1 and identifier-2 and have RENAMES, REDEFINES, or OCCURS clauses are ignored in the move. Therefore, we cannot use the MOVE CORRESPONDING option to move a table of values, for example. However, the identifier-1 and identifier-2 items may themselves have REDEFINES or OCCURS clauses or may be subordinate to data items with such clauses. (These clauses are discussed in later chapters.)

The CORRESPONDING option is also available with ADD and SUBTRACT, as can be observed in Appendix C, "Complete ANSI COBOL Language Formats." In general, the option should be avoided or used sparingly with respect to both MOVE and the arithmetic verbs. Use of the CORRESPONDING option may result in errors when programs are subsequently modified, and therefore most programming managers tend to limit or forbid use of this option.

REVIEW

1   When data is moved from a sending field to a receiving field, for nonnumeric data alignment takes place at the [left / right] margin.

left

2   When data is moved from a sending field to a receiving field, for numeric data alignment takes place in respect to the _____ .

decimal point

3   Data moved to a group item is always treated as [alphabetic / numeric / alphanumeric] data.

alphanumeric

4   If zeros are moved into a group item, such zeros will always be in the [character / binary numeric] mode.

character

5   The abbreviated form of the CORRESPONDING option is _____ . Use of this option in conjunction with the MOVE instruction results in transfer of only the _____ items contained in two records.

CORR; common (or corresponding)

6   When the MOVE CORRESPONDING option is used, an item will be moved if at least one of the items in each pair is at the _____ level and only if the receiving group item has an item with the same [storage capacity / name.]

elementary; name

7   The MOVE CORRESPONDING option can be used to move elementary items [including / but not including] tables of values at the elementary level.

but not including

PROCEDURE CONTROL: PERFORM

In the preceding two chapters we encountered the use of the PERFORM verb. In Chapter 14, "Table Handling," we will explore the full range of options associated with this very powerful verb. For now we limit our attention to presenting two basic formats used in previous examples.

The first and simplest format is

Format 1

PERFORM procedure-name

The word "procedure-name" refers either to a paragraph-name or a section-name in the PROCEDURE DIVISION. In the context of student programming exercises, sections are not common, and most often the object of PERFORM is a paragraph-name. The effect of PERFORM is to branch to the indicated paragraph, execute the instruction(s) in that paragraph, and then return to the statement immediately following the PERFORM instruction. In using Format 1 the paragraph to be performed should not contain a GO TO instruction, but may include another PERFORM statement.

As an example of the use of this format, suppose that we have the following two group items.

```
01  OUT-RECORD.
      02  ACCOUNT      PICTURE 9(6).
      02  FILLER       PICTURE X(5).
      02  NAME         PICTURE X(20).
      02  FILLER       PICTURE X(5).
      02  CHARGE       PICTURE ZZZZ.ZZ.
      02  FILLER       PICTURE X(5).
      02  PAYMENT      PICTURE ZZZZ,ZZ.

01  TRANSACTION.
      02  T-ACCOUNT    PICTURE 9(6).
      02  KODE         PICTURE 9.
      02  T-NAME       PICTURE X(20).
      02  AMOUNT       PICTURE 9(4)V99.
```

Further, suppose we are interested in producing a report that has the following general appearance:

ACCOUNT NUMBER	NAME	CHARGE	PAYMENT
11364	J. B. ANDERSON	135.16	
34125	R. C. BROWN		11.48
. . .	. . .	. . .	. . .

In other words, we want to list the account number and the name of each person involved in a transaction and also indicate the amount of charge or payment, according to the type of transaction. Let TRANSACTION contain a KODE such that a value of 1 indicates a CHARGE and a value of 2 indicates a PAYMENT, and assume that the codes are always correct. Now we can write:

```
IF KODE = 1
      PERFORM CHARGES
ELSE
      PERFORM PAYMENTS.
      .
      .
      .
CHARGES.
      MOVE AMOUNT TO CHARGE
      ADD AMOUNT TO TOTAL-CHARGES
      MOVE ZERO TO PAYMENT
      PERFORM PRINTING.
PAYMENTS.
      MOVE AMOUNT TO PAYMENT
      MOVE ZERO TO CHARGE
```

ADD AMOUNT TO TOTAL-PAYMENTS
    PERFORM PRINTING.
PRINTING.
    MOVE T-ACCOUNT TO ACCOUNT
    MOVE T-NAME TO NAME
    WRITE OUTPUT-RECORD FROM OUT-RECORD.

It should be noticed that the paragraphs CHARGES and PAYMENTS, which are objects of PERFORM, themselves invoke execution of the paragraph PRINTING by use of the PERFORM verb. Thus we have a case of *nested* PERFORM statements. Figure 6-1 presents a flowchart corresponding to the program statements.

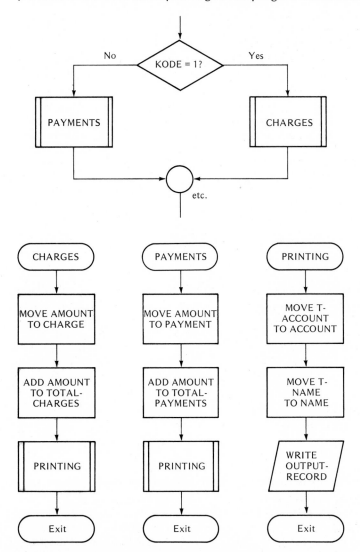

FIGURE 6-1   FLOWCHART FOR THE SAMPLE PROGRAM WHICH UTILIZES THE PERFORM VERB.

FORMAT 2 OF THE PERFORM VERB

This format permits execution of two or more consecutive paragraphs and then a return to the statement immediately following PERFORM:

Format 2

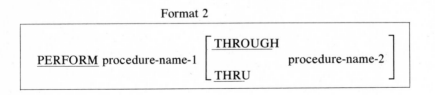

In the general format above, procedure-name-1 and procedure-name-2 refer to the first and last of a series of consecutive paragraphs. To illustrate the use of this option, let us look at an example which concerns the reading of a SALARY-REC which contains a SEX-CODE and a SALARY. Then we accumulate the total salaries separately for males and females, and we count the number of employees categorized as males and females, respectively. Finally, we print a line of output, LINEOUT, from an area called EDITED-DATA.

```
READ SALARY-REC AT END. . . .
PERFORM ACCUMULATION-BY-SEX THRU PRINTING.
    .
    .
    .
ACCUMULATION-BY-SEX.
    IF SEX-CODE = 1
        PERFORM MALES-TOTALS
    ELSE
        PERFORM FEMALES-TOTALS.
PRINTING.
    WRITE LINEOUT FROM EDITED-DATA . . .
    .
    .
    .
MALES-TOTALS.
    ADD SALARY TO MALE-SALARY.
    ADD 1 TO NUMBER-OF-MALES.
FEMALES-TOTALS.
    ADD SALARY TO FEMALE-SALARY.
    ADD 1 TO NUMBER-OF-FEMALES.
```

When the THRU option is exercised, it is possible to have one or more PERFORM statements included in the range of procedure-1 to procedure-2. These are nested PERFORM statements. It is also possible to have PERFORM statements whose range is totally outside the range of the first PERFORM. The following two examples illustrate the two permitted structures.

```
                          CORRECT STRUCTURE
A. ... PERFORM B THRU F.                              ┌─ B
B.                                                    │ ┌─ D
C. ... PERFORM D THRU E.                              │ │
D.                                                    │ └─ E
E.                                                    └─ F
F.
```

```
                          CORRECT STRUCTURE
A. ... PERFORM B THRU D.                        ┌─ B
B.                                              │         ... PERFORM M THRU Q.
C. ... PERFORM M THRU Q.                        │
D.                                              └─ D
G.
M.                                              ┌─ M
I.                                              │
Q.                                              └─ Q
```

The following example illustrates an incorrect structure.

```
                          INCORRECT STRUCTURE
A. ... PERFORM B THRU E.                           ┌─ B
B.                                                 │ ┌─ D
C. ... PERFORM D THRU F.                           │ │
D.                                                 │ │
E.                                                 └─┼─ E
F.                                                   └─ F
```

A variation of Format 2 of the PERFORM instruction incorporates the UNTIL clause and allows execution of one or more procedures as long as a specified condition is not met.

```
                               ┌┌ THROUGH ⎫                    ┐
PERFORM procedure-name-1       │┤         ⎬ procedure-name-2   │ UNTIL condition
                               └└ THRU    ⎭                    ┘
```

The beginning part of the example shown with Format 2 of PERFORM can be modified to utilize the UNTIL option.

READ SALARY-REC AT END MOVE ZERO TO END-OF-DATA.
PERFORM READING UNTIL END-OF-DATA = ZERO.
   etc.
READING.
   PERFORM ACCUMULATION-BY-SEX THRU PRINTING.
   READ SALARY-REC AT END MOVE ZERO TO END-OF-DATA.
ACCUMULATION-BY-SEX.
  .
  .
  .
  etc.

Paragraph READING is executed only if END-OF-DATA is *not* equal to zero. Thus the condition is tested prior to execution of the object of PERFORM. If the condition is true the first time, the object of PERFORM will never be executed. In flowchart form the PERFORM . . . UNTIL corresponds to a do-while structure:

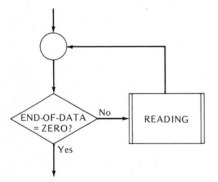

REVIEW

1 The COBOL verb used to execute a paragraph and return to the immediately following instruction is the _____ verb.

PERFORM

2 Whereas Format 1 of the PERFORM verb concerns the execution of a single paragraph (or section), Format 2 allows execution of [two / two or more] paragraphs.

two or more

3 Suppose four consecutive paragraphs are to be executed as a group. The Format 2 option of the PERFORM verb will include [two / four] procedure-names.

*two (only the first and last paragraphs in
the series are named)*

4   After execution of the paragraph(s) identified in the PERFORM instruction, execution of the program then continues with the statement immediately following [the identified paragraph(s) / the PERFORM instruction].

the PERFORM *instruction*

5   When the UNTIL option is used with the PERFORM verb, the condition is tested [before / after] the object of PERFORM is executed.

before

SAMPLE PROGRAM

We now present a complete program to provide another example of the programming process. We assume that a punched card file contains data on the number of vehicles passing a certain point on the highway. Each card contains an integer number in columns 1–4 corresponding to one day's traffic. We are interested in reading the card file and producing a report such as shown in Figure 6-2. For each week we list the daily data and a statistical summary for the week. It is assumed that as a maximum there may be 10 weeks of data. However, the last week of data may be a partial week— less than seven days.

Figure 6-3 presents a flowchart for the program. The program consists of seven modules, each corresponding to a paragraph in the PROCEDURE DIVISION. The MAIN-PROCEDURE summarizes the entire task logic. We use END-OF-DATA to check for the end of file condition and we use WEEK-COUNTER to count the weeks. Then, WEEKLY-ROUTINE is performed as long as the WEEK-COUNTER does not exceed 10, since we assume that there will be no more than 10 weeks of data.

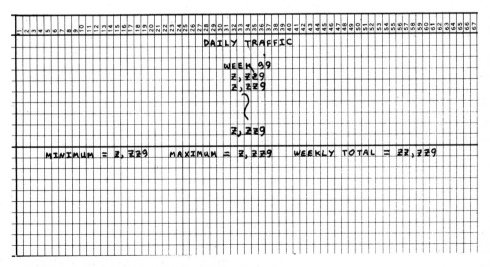

FIGURE 6-2   REPORT FORMAT FOR THE SAMPLE PROGRAM.

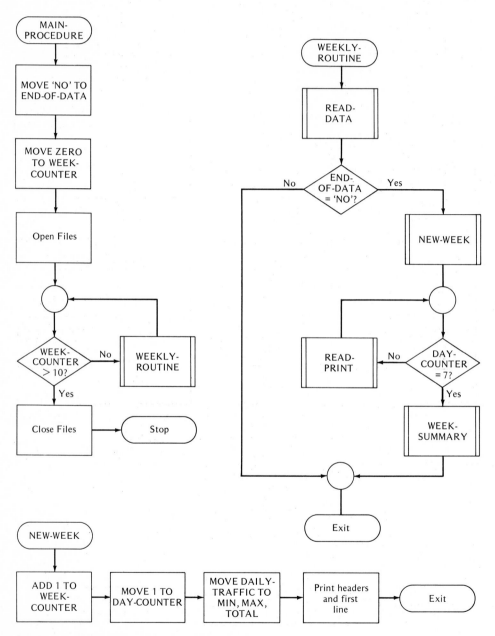

FIGURE 6-3   FLOWCHART FOR THE SAMPLE PROGRAM.

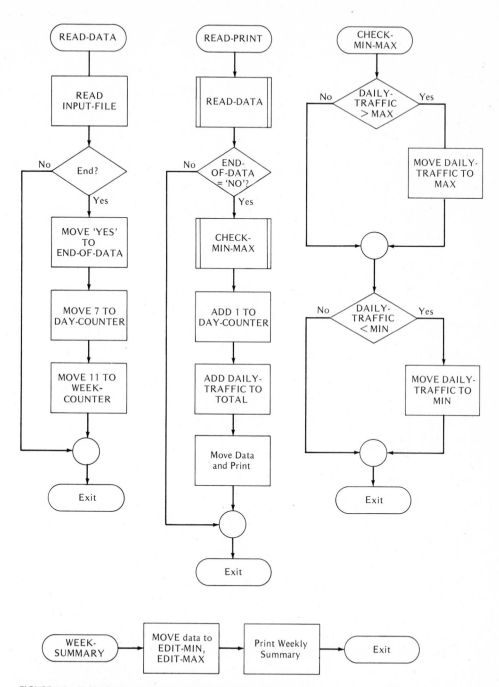

FIGURE 6-3 FLOWCHART FOR THE SAMPLE PROGRAM (*Continued*).

EXHIBIT 6-1 SAMPLE PROGRAM

```
IDENTIFICATION DIVISION.
PROGRAM-ID. TRAFFIC.
*
ENVIRONMENT DIVISION.
CONFIGURATION SECTION.
SOURCE-COMPUTER. ABC-480.
OBJECT-COMPUTER. ABC-480.
INPUT-OUTPUT SECTION.
FILE-CONTROL.
    SELECT INPUT-FILE   ASSIGN TO CARD-READER.
    SELECT OUTPUT-FILE  ASSIGN TO PRINTER.
DATA DIVISION.
FILE SECTION.
FD  INPUT-FILE   LABEL RECORDS OMITTED
                 DATA RECORD IS INPUT-REC.
01  INPUT-REC.
    02 DAILY-TRAFFIC   PIC 9(4).
    02 FILLER          PIC X(76).
FD  OUTPUT-FILE  LABEL RECORDS OMITTED
                 DATA RECORDS IS OUTPUT-REC.
01  OUTPUT-REC         PIC X(132).
WORKING-STORAGE SECTION.
01  END-OF-DATA        PIC XXX.
01  MIN               PIC 9(4).
01  MAX               PIC 9(4).
01  TOTAL             PIC 9(5).
01  DAY-COUNTER       PIC 9.
01  DAILY-LISTING.
    02 FILLER          PIC X(31) VALUE SPACES.
    02 EDIT-TRAFFIC    PIC Z,ZZ9.
01  PAGE-HEADER.
    02 FILLER          PIC X(27) VALUE SPACES.
    02 FILLER          PIC X(13) VALUE 'DAILY TRAFFIC'.
01  WEEK-HEADER.
    02 FILLER          PIC X(30) VALUE SPACES.
    02 FILLER          PIC X(5) VALUE 'WEEK '.
    02 WEEK-COUNTER    PIC 99.
01  STAT-SUMMARY.
    02 FILLER          PIC X(4) VALUE SPACES.
    02 FILLER          PIC X(10) VALUE 'MINIMUM = '.
    02 EDIT-MIN        PIC Z,ZZ9.
    02 FILLER          PIC X(3) VALUE SPACES.
    02 FILLER          PIC X(10) VALUE 'MAXIMUM = '.
    02 EDIT-MAX        PIC Z,ZZ9.
    02 FILLER          PIC X(3) VALUE SPACES.
    02 FILLER          PIC X(15) VALUE 'WEKKLY TOTAL = '.
    02 EDIT-TOTAL      PIC ZZ,ZZ9.
```

In the WEEKLY-ROUTINE the first task is to perform READ-DATA, which reads a card. If it is the end-of-file card we move YES to END-OF-DATA, 7 to DAY-COUNTER and 11 to WEEK-COUNTER. The last two items merit some explanation. First, observe that in the WEEKLY-ROUTINE there is a do-while loop which is executed as long as DAY-COUNTER does not equal 7—corresponding to the seven days of a week. However, if we read the end-of-file before we have processed seven cards, we can terminate the loop by setting DAY-COUNTER to 7. In a similar fashion, if we read the end-of-file before the tenth week, we can terminate the loop in the MAIN-PROCE-DURE by setting WEEK-COUNTER to 11.

Consider now the processing steps in WEEKLY-ROUTINE. We read a card. If it is not the end of the file we perform NEW-WEEK, which increments the WEEK-COUNTER by 1, sets DAY-COUNTER to 1 since we start a new week, saves the first day's input data (DAILY-TRAFFIC) in MIN, MAX, and TOTAL, prints the header for the week, and prints the first line. Thus NEW-WEEK handles the first card of each week. A little reflection will reveal that the first card of the week requires different processing than

EXHIBIT 6-1   SAMPLE PROGRAM (*Continued*)

```
PROCEDURE DIVISION.
MAIN-PROCEDURE.
    MOVE 'NO' TO END-OF-DATA
    MOVE ZERO TO WEEK-COUNTER
    OPEN INPUT INPUT-FILE
    OPEN OUTPUT OUTPUT-FILE
    PERFORM WEEKLY-ROUTINE
        UNTIL WEEK-COUNTER IS GREATER THAN 10.
*
    CLOSE INPUT-FILE
    CLOSE OUTPUT-FILE
    STOP RUN.
WEEKLY-ROUTINE.
    PERFORM READ-DATA
    IF END-OF-DATA = 'NO'
        PERFORM NEW-WEEK
        PERFORM READ-PRINT
            UNTIL DAY-COUNTER = 7
        PERFORM WEEK-SUMMARY.
READ-DATA.
    READ INPUT-FILE RECORD
        AT END MOVE 'YES' TO END-OF-DATA
            MOVE 7 TO DAY-COUNTER
            MOVE 11 TO WEEK-COUNTER.
NEW-WEEK.
    ADD 1 TO WEEK-COUNTER
    MOVE 1 TO DAY-COUNTER
    MOVE DAILY-TRAFFIC TO MIN
                           MAX
                           TOTAL
    WRITE OUTPUT-REC FROM PAGE-HEADER
        AFTER ADVANCING PAGE
    WRITE OUTPUT-REC FROM WEEK-HEADER
        AFTER ADVANCING 2 LINES
    MOVE SPACES TO OUTPUT-REC
    WRITE OUTPUT-REC AFTER ADVANCING 1 LINE.
    MOVE DAILY-TRAFFIC TO EDIT-TRAFFIC
    WRITE OUTPUT-REC FROM DAILY-LISTING
        AFTER ADVANCING 1 LINE.
READ-PRINT.
    PERFORM READ-DATA.
    IF END-OF-DATA = 'NO'
        PERFORM CHECK-MIN-MAX
        ADD 1 TO DAY-COUNTER
        ADD DAILY-TRAFFIC TO TOTAL
        MOVE DAILY-TRAFFIC TO EDIT-TRAFFIC
        WRITE OUTPUT-REC FROM DAILY-LISTING
            AFTER ADVANCING 1 LINE.
CHECK-MIN-MAX.
    IF DAILY-TRAFFIC IS GREATER THAN MAX
        MOVE DAILY-TRAFFIC TO MAX
    IF DAILY-TRAFFIC IS LESS THAN MIN
        MOVE DAILY-TRAFFIC TO MIN.
WEEK-SUMMARY.
    MOVE MIN TO EDIT-MIN
    MOVE MAX TO EDIT-MAX
    MOVE TOTAL TO EDIT-TOTAL
    WRITE OUTPUT-REC FROM STAT-SUMMARY
        AFTER ADVANCING 2 LINES.
```

the other cards, which can be handled identically to each other by means of a loop. This loop involves the READ-PRINT procedure in WEEKLY-ROUTINE. The READ-PRINT procedure handles processing of cards other than the first card of the week. Such processing involves determination of the minimum and maximum in the CHECK-MIN-MAX procedure, incrementing the DAY-COUNTER, accumulating the TOTAL for the week, and printing a line of output. The final step in WEEKLY-ROUTINE involves execution of the WEEK-SUMMARY, which moves data for editing and prints the summary line for the week.

At first blush the task seems simpler than it is. After all, we are only printing a very simple report! Yet, as is always the case, there are complicating details. In our program here, the complications arise from allowing for the possibility of the end-of-file condition to occur at any point in time.

Exhibit 6-1 presents a program written for this task. The flowchart of Figure 6-3 and the program in Exhibit 6-1 correspond very closely. The student will find it beneficial to study both the flowchart and the program in relationship to each other.

EXERCISES

1   Write a COBOL program that will read punched cards, edit the data, and print a report as indicated below.

Input

CARD COLUMNS	CONTENT
1–11	Social security number
12–23	Last name
24–32	First name
33–40	Blank
41–47	Annual earnings

Output
Not more than a page. Header at the top of the page, as follows:

SOCIAL SECURITY	LAST	FIRST	EARNINGS
XXX-XX-XXXX			$XX,XXX.XX
XXX-XX-XXXX			$XX,XXX.XX
	(etc.)		

Data
Punch four cards using social security numbers and names of your choice However, use these earnings:
$10,352.81
$ 5,863.98
$ 3,800.00
$ 691.12

2   Write a COBOL program to read a file of punched cards containing data about accounts-receivable and to print a summary of the overdue and forthcoming

receivables. An extended description follows, including flowcharts, variable names, and a partial DATA DIVISION. Thus the exercise is of moderate programming difficulty.

Input

Input consists of a deck of cards having the following design:

CARD COLUMNS	COBOL NAME
1–6	ACCOUNT-NO
7–8	FILLER (blank)
9–10	YEAR-DUE
11–13	DAY-DUE†
14–21	AMOUNT-DUE
22–80	FILLER (blank)

†The day on which the account receivable is due is expressed as a 3-digit number (Julian Calendar). Thus January 10 is 010, February 28 is 059, and December 25 is 359.

The first card in the deck is a special card containing today's date and year in columns 9–11 and 12–13, respectively. Alternatively, we may use ACCEPT . . . DAY to obtain today's date from the compiler, if this option is available. All other cards are cards pertaining to accounts-receivable.

The cards are sorted in ascending sequence on ACCOUNT-NO, and there should be only one card per account. The program checks for correct sequencing. Cards out of sequence are to be printed as shown on the sample output. Note that the data on such cards is excluded from the total.

DATA DIVISION

ALL DATA DIVISION entries are provided, except that you are asked to write WORKING-STORAGE entries to provide the header with the words STATUS, NUMBER OF ACCOUNTS, and DOLLAR VALUE.

```
DATA DIVISION.
FILE SECTION.
FD   REC-FILE LABEL RECORDS OMITTED DATA RECORD
     RECEIV-RECORD.
01   RECEIV-RECORD.
     02   ACCOUNT-NO          PICTURE 9(6).
     02   FILLER              PICTURE XX.
     02   DAY-DUE             PICTURE 999
     02   YEAR-DUE            PICTURE 99.
     02   AMOUNT-DUE          PICTURE 9(6)V99.
     02   FILLER              PICTURE X(59).
FD  REPORT-FILE LABEL RECORD OMITTED DATA RECORD
    REPORT-RECORD.
```

```
01   REPORT-RECORD          PICTURE X(132).
WORKING-STORAGE SECTION.
01   TODAY                  PICTURE 999.
01   THIS-YEAR              PICTURE 99.
01   PREVIOUS-ACCT-NO       PICTURE 9(6).
01   OVERDUE                PICTURE S9(6), USAGE
                            COMPUTATIONAL.
01   OVERDUE-AMOUNT         PICTURE S9(6)V99 USAGE
                            COMPUTATIONAL.
01   RECEIVABLE-AMOUNT      PICTURE S9(6)V99 USAGE
                            COMPUTATIONAL.
01   END-OF-DATA            PICTURE 9 VALUE ZERO.
01   ERROR-MESSAGE
     02   FILLER            PICTURE X(23) VALUE
          "ACCOUNT OUT OF SEQUENCE."
     02   FILLER            PICTURE XX VALUE SPACE.
     02   ERROR-NUMBER      PICTURE X(6).
01   RESULT.
     02   STATUS-TYPE       PICTURE X(13).
     02   FILLER            PICTURE X(9) VALUE SPACES.
     02   HOW-MANY          PICTURE ZZZ99.
     02   FILLER            PICTURE X(13), VALUE SPACES.
     02   DOLLAR-VALUE      PICTURE $$$,$$$.99.
```

A few data-names merit explanation

THIS-YEAR	Stores the current year as read in from the very first card of the input deck, or by use of the ACCEPT verb
TODAY	Stores today's data as read in from the very first card of the input deck or by use of the ACCEPT verb
PREVIOUS-ACCT-NO	Stores the previously read account number so that each card can be compared with the preceding one to see that they are in ascending sequence. Initially PREVIOUS-ACCT-NO is set equal to zero
OVERDUE	Stores the number of overdue accounts
OVERDUE-AMOUNT	Stores the total dollar value of overdue accounts
RECEIVABLE	Stores the number of accounts that are not overdue
RECEIVABLE-AMOUNT	Stores the total value of accounts that are not overdue

Sample input

```
        77101
012345  7709000010000
023567  7615000020020
001234  7614000030030
123456  7803000040040
```

Sample output

ACCOUNT OUT OF SEQUENCE 001234		
STATUS	NUMBER OF ACCOUNTS	DOLLAR VALUE
OVERDUE	02	$300.20
RECEIVABLE	01	$400.40
TOTALS	03	$700.60

Program flowchart
The flowchart for this program follows (pages 175–178).

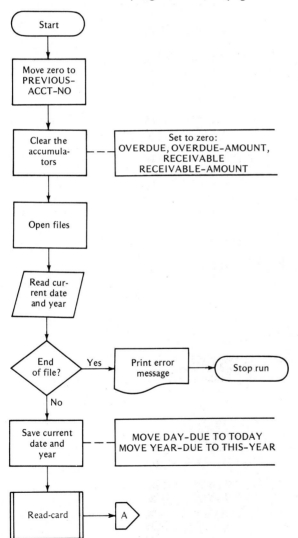

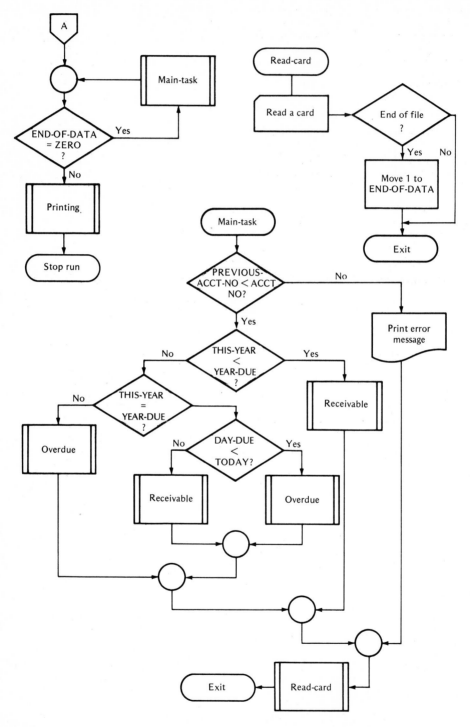

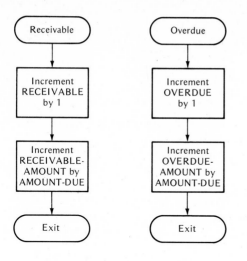

(The remainder of the flowchart for Exercise 2 is presented on page 178.)

(Continuation of flowchart for Exercise 2.)

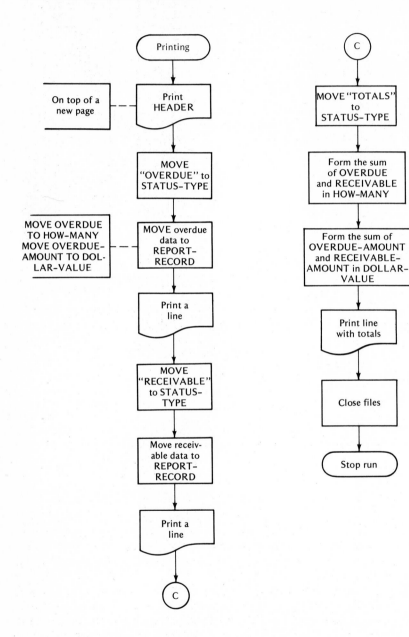

7

PROCEDURE DIVISION Features II

Arithmetic Verbs
The COMPUTE Verb
The STRING and UNSTRING Verbs
The INSPECT Verb
The COPY Verb
The GO TO . . . DEPENDING Verb
Exercises

ARITHMETIC VERBS

Two very useful options available with all arithmetic verbs are the ROUNDED and the ON SIZE ERROR clauses.

THE ROUNDED CLAUSE

A frequent need exists for rounding numeric values. For example, even though prices or rates of interest may be quoted to three or four decimal places, any billing must be rounded to two decimal places, since the smallest monetary unit is the cent. COBOL provides automatic rounding by use of the ROUNDED clause which can be used with all arithmetic verbs.

Execution of the statement ADD A TO B ROUNDED will result in a rounded number in B. If B was specified as containing two decimal places in the DATA DIVISION description, rounding is accomplished by adding 0.005 to the result of the addition and truncating the third place. Therefore, when the remainder which is to be dropped begins with a 5 or higher value, the number is rounded up; otherwise it is rounded down. If B was specified to contain one place to the right of the decimal, 0.05 is added to the result of the addition, and the second place is truncated.

EXHIBIT 7-1 STANDARD COBOL FORMATS FOR THE FOUR ARITHMETIC VERBS

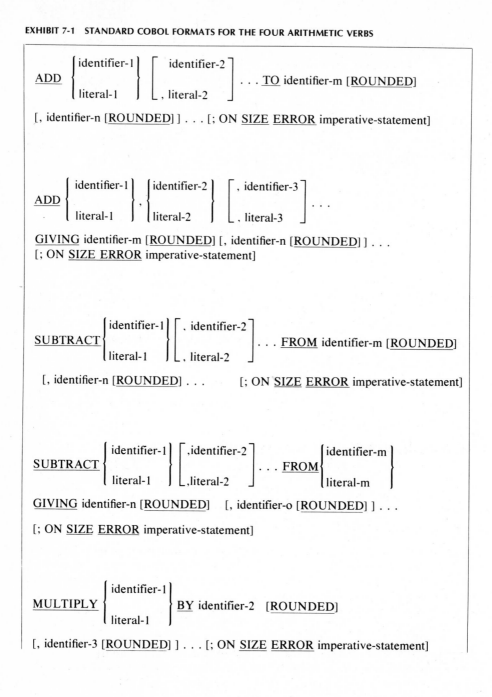

EXHIBIT 7-1   STANDARD COBOL FORMATS FOR THE FOUR ARITHMETIC VERBS (*Continued*)

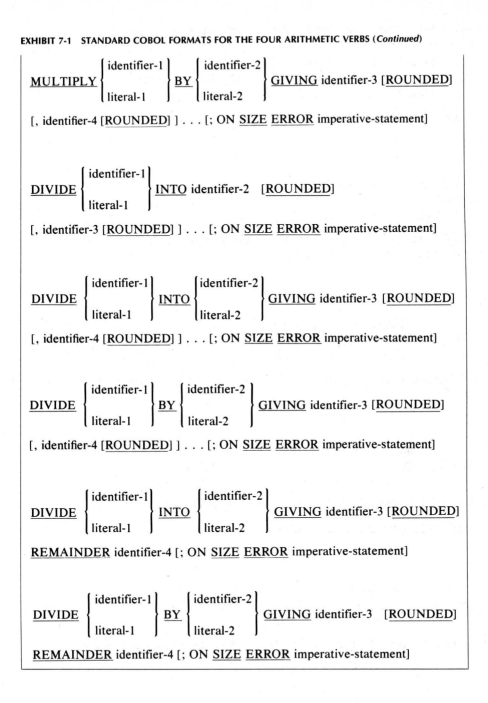

MULTIPLY $\left\{ \begin{array}{l} \text{identifier-1} \\ \text{literal-1} \end{array} \right\}$ BY $\left\{ \begin{array}{l} \text{identifier-2} \\ \text{literal-2} \end{array} \right\}$ GIVING identifier-3 [ROUNDED]

[, identifier-4 [ROUNDED]] . . . [; ON SIZE ERROR imperative-statement]

DIVIDE $\left\{ \begin{array}{l} \text{identifier-1} \\ \text{literal-1} \end{array} \right\}$ INTO identifier-2   [ROUNDED]

[, identifier-3 [ROUNDED]] . . . [; ON SIZE ERROR imperative-statement]

DIVIDE $\left\{ \begin{array}{l} \text{identifier-1} \\ \text{literal-1} \end{array} \right\}$ INTO $\left\{ \begin{array}{l} \text{identifier-2} \\ \text{literal-2} \end{array} \right\}$ GIVING identifier-3 [ROUNDED]

[, identifier-4 [ROUNDED]] . . . [; ON SIZE ERROR imperative-statement]

DIVIDE $\left\{ \begin{array}{l} \text{identifier-1} \\ \text{literal-1} \end{array} \right\}$ BY $\left\{ \begin{array}{l} \text{identifier-2} \\ \text{literal-2} \end{array} \right\}$ GIVING identifier-3 [ROUNDED]

[, identifier-4 [ROUNDED]] . . . [; ON SIZE ERROR imperative-statement]

DIVIDE $\left\{ \begin{array}{l} \text{identifier-1} \\ \text{literal-1} \end{array} \right\}$ INTO $\left\{ \begin{array}{l} \text{identifier-2} \\ \text{literal-2} \end{array} \right\}$ GIVING identifier-3 [ROUNDED]

REMAINDER identifier-4 [; ON SIZE ERROR imperative-statement]

DIVIDE $\left\{ \begin{array}{l} \text{identifier-1} \\ \text{literal-1} \end{array} \right\}$ BY $\left\{ \begin{array}{l} \text{identifier-2} \\ \text{literal-2} \end{array} \right\}$ GIVING identifier-3   [ROUNDED]

REMAINDER identifier-4 [; ON SIZE ERROR imperative-statement]

THE ON SIZE ERROR CLAUSE

The case may arise in which an arithmetic result is larger than anticipated, in terms of the number of digit positions available. For example, a construction worker earning $8.00 per hour should have a weekly gross pay well under $999.99. But suppose that by some mistake in the program, or more likely in the input, the computed weekly pay figure is over $1,000.00. Rather than allow truncation of this figure to occur, such "overflows" can be detected by use of the ON SIZE ERROR clause. For example, assume GROSS has PICTURE 999V99. We can write:

MULTIPLY RATE BY HOURS GIVING GROSS
    ON SIZE ERROR
    MOVE "GROSS PAY EXCEEDS $999.99" TO MESSAGE.

The ON SIZE ERROR clause is simply a conditional statement that says, if the size of a value does not fit in the field, do whatever is indicated in the statement that follows in that sentence. The statement that follows must be imperative; that is, it cannot be conditional. When ON SIZE ERROR is used and the condition is fulfilled, the arithmetic operand intended to receive the result is not altered from its previous value. In other words, it is as if the arithmetic operations had not happened.

In addition to "large" results, the ON SIZE ERROR condition is also fulfilled by a zero division. As you may recall from algebra, division by zero is an undefined operation yielding an "infinitely" large quotient.

Use of ON SIZE ERROR is advisable as a matter of programming routine. Otherwise, truncation of a value too large for a storage location will result in greater difficulty in detecting the associated error.

THE STANDARD FORMATS FOR ARITHMETIC VERBS

Exhibit 7-1 presents the standard COBOL formats for four arithmetic verbs: ADD, SUBTRACT, MULTIPLY, and DIVIDE. Since we are already familiar with the basic function of these verbs from Chapter 4, we study each verb by means of examples that illustrate the available options and their uses.

For the ADD verb, assume that the storage locations with data-names W, X, Y, and Z initially, and before each statement execution, contain the values indicated on the first line of the first table on page 183. For each of the following COBOL statements we indicate the value contained in each storage location after statement execution. All fields are assumed to contain three integer and two decimal places.

For the SUBTRACT verb, assume that the storage locations with data-names X, Y, and Z initially contain the values indicated on the first line of the second table on page 183. For each of the following COBOL statements, we indicate the value contained in each storage location after statement execution. All fields are assumed to be signed, consisting of three integer and two decimal places.

For the MULTIPLY verb, assume that the storage locations with data-names X, Y, and Z initially contain the values indicated on the first line of the first table on page 184. For each of the following COBOL statements, we indicate the value contained in each storage location after statement execution. All fields are assumed to be signed, consisting of three integer and two decimal places.

STATEMENT	VALUE IN			
	W	X	Y	Z
Initial values	15	10	12	100
ADD X TO Y	15	10	22	100
ADD W X TO Y	15	10	37	100
ADD 5, Y GIVING Z	15	10	12	17
ADD W, X, Y	Not executable—TO or GIVING is missing.			
ADD W, 3 X GIVING Z	15	10	12	28
ADD W 3 X TO Z	15	10	12	128
ADD X Z TO 3	Not executable—the numeric constant 3 cannot change in value.			
ADD W X GIVING Y	15	10	25	100
ADD X TO Y ROUNDED	15	10	22	100
ADD X 12.456 TO Y ROUNDED	15	10	34.46	100
ADD 1000 12.4 X TO Y	15	10	34.4	100 (Truncation occurs in the resulting value of Y.)
ADD 1000 12.4 X TO Y ROUNDED ON SIZE ERROR MOVE ZERO TO W	0	10	12	100 (Note that the value in Y is not altered.)
ADD X Y GIVING Z ROUNDED W ROUNDED	22	10	12	22

STATEMENT	X	Y	Z
Initial values	90	30	20
SUBTRACT Y FROM Z	90	30	−10
SUBTRACT Z FROM Y	90	10	20
SUBTRACT Y, Z FROM X	40	30	20
SUBTRACT 12, 18 FROM X	60	30	20
SUBTRACT Y, 25 FROM 100	Not executable—literal cannot follow FROM when the GIVING option is not used.		
SUBTRACT Z FROM X GIVING Y	90	70	20
SUBTRACT Y, 25 FROM 100 GIVING Z	90	30	45
SUBTRACT X 25.6 FROM Y ROUNDED	90	−85.6	20
SUBTRACT −1200.4 FROM Y ROUNDED ON SIZE ERROR MOVE +999.99 TO Z	90	30	999.99
SUBTRACT 10 FROM Z GIVING X, Y	10	10	20

Finally, for the DIVIDE verb, assume that the storage locations with data-names X, Y, and Z initially contain the values indicated on the first line of the second table on page 184. For each of the following COBOL statements, we indicate the value contained in each storage location after statement execution. All fields are assumed to be signed, consisting of three integer and two decimal places.

The above examples do not illustrate the REMAINDER option presented in Formats 4 and 5 of the DIVIDE verb. This option allows us to store the remainder from a division whose quotient is not exact.

STATEMENT	RESULTING VALUE IN		
	X	Y	Z
Initial values	90	30	10
MULTIPLY Y BY Z	90	30	300
MULTIPLY Y BY Z GIVING X	300	30	10
MULTIPLY Z BY Y	90	300	10
MULTIPLY Z BY 20	Not executable—literal cannot follow BY when the GIVING option is not used.		
MULTIPLY Z BY 20 GIVING X	200	30	10
MULTIPLY 2.5 BY X ROUNDED	225	30	10
MULTIPLY X BY Y ROUNDED	90	700	10
MULTIPLY 100.25 BY X ROUNDED ON SIZE ERROR MOVE ZERO TO Y	90	0	10
MULTIPLY X BY 10.2 GIVING Y, Z ROUNDED	90	918	918

STATEMENT	RESULTING VALUE IN		
	X	Y	Z
Initial values	90	30	10
DIVIDE X BY Z	Not executable—incorrect form.		
DIVIDE Z INTO X	9	30	10
DIVIDE Z INTO 100	Not executable—literal cannot follow INTO when GIVING option is not used.		
DIVIDE Z INTO 100 GIVING Y	90	10	10
DIVIDE 2 INTO Z GIVING X	5	30	10
DIVIDE X BY Z GIVING Y	90	9	10
DIVIDE 60 BY Y GIVING X	2	30	10
DIVIDE 12.2 INTO Y ROUNDED	90	2.46	10
DIVIDE 12.2 INTO X, Y ROUNDED	7.37	2.46	10
DIVIDE X INTO 10 GIVING Y, Z ROUNDED	90	.11	.11
DIVIDE X BY 10 GIVING Y, Z ROUNDED	90	9	9
DIVIDE 4.5 INTO X GIVING Y ROUNDED ON SIZE ERROR MOVE ZERO TO Z	90	20	10

Suppose that one share of a mutual fund sells for $30.00. The fund generates capital gains of $1.50 per share, and they are to be distributed in the form of additional shares, except that cash is paid in lieu of fractional shares. If NO-OF-SHARES represents the number of fund shares held by an investor, the additional shares and cash dividend can be computed as follows:

MULTIPLY 1.50 BY NO-OF-SHARES GIVING TOTAL-VALUE.
DIVIDE 30.00 INTO TOTAL-VALUE GIVING ADDITIONAL-SHARES
    REMAINDER CASH-DIVIDEND.

If NO-OF-SHARES = 50, then TOTAL-VALUE = 1.50 × 50 = 75.00. The number of additional shares is the *integer* quotient of 75.00/30.00 = 2. The remainder (CASH-DIVIDEND) is 75.00 − (2 × 30.00) = 15.00.

It should be noticed that, if ADDITIONAL-SHARES had been defined to two decimal places (e.g., 999V99), in the above example the quotient would have been 2.5 and the remainder zero. Thus, some care is needed in defining the precision of the quotient and the remainder fields in order to achieve the desired objective.

THE COMPUTE VERB

Use of the four arithmetic verbs we have studied thus far is particularly suitable for single arithmetic operations. But suppose it is required that an answer be obtained by use of such a formula as $a = 3b − c + b(d − 2)$. If we were to use the four arithmetic verbs to solve this equation, a large number of statements would be required. However, use of the COMPUTE verb along with symbolic arithmetic operators makes it possible to write compact arithmetic statements for mathematical expressions.

Table 7-1 lists the symbols used for the arithmetic operations addition, subtraction, multiplication, division, and exponentiation. Only the symbols for multiplication and exponentiation are different from the symbols commonly used in mathematics. In addition to the symbols, parentheses can be used to designate the order of operations. However, unlike their use in algebra, parentheses are never used to designate multiplication.

An arithmetic expression is formed by the use of arithmetic operators and data-names or literals. At least *one space must separate each operator symbol from the preceding and following data-names,* with parentheses used to designate or clarify the order of operations. Some examples of arithmetic expressions are

ALGEBRAIC EXPRESSION	COBOL ARITHMETIC EXPRESSION
$a + b$	A + B
$a − b + (a − 5)c$	A − B + (A − 5) * C
$a^2 − \dfrac{b + c}{2}$	A ** 2 -- (B + C) / 2

TABLE 7-1 THE FIVE ARITHMETIC OPERATIONS IN COBOL

+	Addition
—	Subtraction
*	Multiplication
/	Division
**	Exponentiation (raising to a power)

When parentheses are used, the operations within the parentheses are completed first, with order of priority given to the innermost sets, working from left to right in the arithmetic expression. In the absence of parentheses, the arithmetic operations are performed according to the following order of priority:

1 Exponentiation
2 Multiplication and division from left to right in the order written
3 Addition and subtraction from left to right in the order written

Consider the following COBOL examples:

COBOL ARITHMETIC EXPRESSION	ALGEBRAIC EXPRESSION
A + B / C	$a + \dfrac{b}{c}$
(A + B) / C	$\dfrac{a + b}{c}$
A + (B / C)	$a + \dfrac{b}{c}$

The first and third COBOL expressions above represent the same algebraic expression. This is so because division takes priority over addition. Nevertheless, it is good programming practice to include the parentheses in such cases, since documentation is thereby improved.

In addition to the five arithmetic operations, COBOL defines a *unary* operation. Standard COBOL defines both a "+" and a "−" unary operator. The meaning of the operator is simply to multiply a variable by + 1 or − 1, respectively. Thus, if we want to multiply variable B times the negative value of variable A, we could use the unary operator as follows:

$$B * (- A)$$

The − is the unary operator. Notice that it is written immediately after the left parenthesis, followed by a space and then the variable A. The requirement that the unary operator immediately follow a left parenthesis is an exception to the rule that a space must precede and follow an arithmetic operator. In the above example parentheses are used to avoid having two consecutive arithmetic operators.

Returning to the COMPUTE verb, we note that the general format associated with the use of this verb is

COMPUTE identifier-1 [ROUNDED] [, identifier-2 [ROUNDED]] . . .
= arithmetic-expression [; ON SIZE ERROR imperative-statement]

In its simplest form the COMPUTE verb has the same effect as the MOVE verb. For example, COMPUTE AMOUNT = TOTAL is the same as MOVE TOTAL TO AMOUNT. In a more typical use, however, COMPUTE stores the result of an arithmetic expression in a data field. An example is

COMPUTE GROSS = (REGULAR * WAGE) + 1.5 * (OVERTIME * WAGE).

Or, the COMPUTE verb can be used with the ROUNDED and ON SIZE ERROR options:

COMPUTE GROSS ROUNDED =
    (REGULAR * WAGE) + 1.5 * (OVERTIME * WAGE)
    ON SIZE ERROR
        PERFORM GROSS-TOO-BIG.

The arithmetic operators +, −, *, and / correspond to the verbs ADD, SUBTRACT, MULTIPLY, and DIVIDE, respectively. The arithmetic operator ** has no corresponding verb and can be used only with the COMPUTE verb. Since exponentiation is a general mathematical process, it can be used to extract roots as well as to raise numbers to various powers. Thus, A**2 means, a^2, but AA**0.5 means $\sqrt{A}$. This facility to extract roots increases the usefulness of the exponentiation operator. In general, however, COBOL has limited computational capabilities. COBOL programs are rarely written to accomplish tasks requiring complex computations. COBOL is used for data processing tasks rather than for computational tasks. Thus, logarithmic and trigonometric functions are not available in COBOL, although they are commonly available in other languages, such as FORTRAN and PL/1.

The identifier-1 in the COMPUTE format is the storage field that receives the results. It should be noted that it can be a numeric or numeric edited item. It really corresponds to the GIVING identifier clause in the other arithmetic verbs. All identifiers on the right-hand side, however, must be *elementary* numeric (nonedited) items.

REVIEW

1   As an alternative to the arithmetic verbs, arithmetic operators can be used in conjunction with the _____ verb.

                                                         COMPUTE

2   The arithmetic symbols used with the COMPUTE verb which indicate the operations addition, subtraction, division, and exponentiation are ____, ____, ____, ____, and _____, respectively.

                                                   +, −,, /, and ***

3   The COBOL arithmetic expression corresponding to the algebraic expression $a^2 - 2ac + c^2$ is _____.

                                (A ** 2) − (2 * A * C) + (C ** 2) *(See*
further comment in the next review item.)

4   Suppose that all the parentheses included in the above answer were omitted. The algebraic expression that corresponds to the resulting COBOL expression would be _____.

$a^2 - 2ac + c^2$ *(Discussion continued in the next review item).*

5   Therefore, because of the order in which the arithmetic operations are always performed, no parentheses are in fact required in the COBOL expression above. However, such parentheses are usually included to improve readability of the program. In the absence of parentheses, the order of priority for the arithmetic operations is such that _____ is always performed first, followed by _____ and _____, and culminating with _____ and _____.

exponentiation; multiplication; division; addition; subtraction

6   Typically, however, the use or nonuse of parentheses *does* make a difference in the way a COBOL arithmetic expression is evaluated. For each of the following COBOL expressions indicate the equivalent algebraic expression.

COBOL ARITHMETIC EXPRESSION	ALGEBRAIC EXPRESSION
((A + (B * C)) / D) ** 2	
(A + (B * C)) / D ** 2	
A + (B * C) / D ** 2	
A + B * C / D ** 2	

$$\left(\frac{a + bc}{d}\right)^2$$

$$\frac{a + bc}{d^2}$$

$$a + \frac{bc}{d^2}$$

$$a + \frac{bc}{d^2}$$

7   An example of the use of the unary operator in a simple COBOL expression involving multiplication is _____.

A * (− B) *(etc.)*

8   In the general format associated with the COMPUTE verb, the results of the arithmetic operation are stored in [identifier-1 / identifier-2].

identifier-1

THE STRING AND UNSTRING VERBS

These two verbs are designed to facilitate transfer of data from several sources into one destination and from one source to many destinations, respectively. In effect, use of these verbs allows one statement to be used in lieu of multiple uses of the MOVE verb and, possibly, in lieu of some DATA DIVISION entries.

We begin with two examples that illustrate uses of the STRING verb.

Suppose that EDIT-SOC-SEC contains a social security number, including hyphens after the third and fifth digits, as for instance '123-45-6789'. We wish to move the social security number to SOC-SEC while also removing the hyphens. The following data description entries are given.

```
01  SOC-SEC          PIC 9(9).
01  EDIT-SOC-SEC.
    02  PART-1        PIC 999.
    02  FILLER        PIC X      VALUE'-'.
    02  PART-2        PIC 99.
    02  FILLER        PIC X      VALUE '-'.
    02  PART-3        PIC 9999.
```

We now use the STRING statement:

```
STRING    PART-1      DELIMITED BY SIZE
          PART-2      DELIMITED BY SIZE
          PART-3      DELIMITED BY SIZE
   INTO   SOC-SEC.
```

The STRING here specifies moving the three fields PART-1, PART-2, PART-3 and positioning them adjacent to each other. The transfer of data can be thought of as taking place character by character. Thus, the data in PART-1 would be transferred into the first three positions of SOC-SEC, the data in PART-2 would be transferred into the next two positions of SOC-SEC, and so on. The DELIMITED BY SIZE clause specifies that the transfer of data from the associated field will stop (be delimited by) when as many characters have been transferred as the size of the source field. The next example illustrates the availability of other alternatives.

Assume that we want to print a report which lists a company name in columns 5–20, a city name starting with column 26, one blank space, and then the ZIP code. The source of data is VENDOR-RECORD.

```
01  VENDOR-RECORD.
    02  COMPANY-NAME    PIC X(15).
    02  STREET          PIC X(40).
    02  CITY-STATE      PIC X(20).
    02  ZIP             PIC 9(5).
```

The data in CITY-STATE is recorded so that the city name is followed by a comma, a space, and then the state code, e.g., LOS ANGELES, CA.

The output record is described as:

01   OUTPUT-REC   PIC X(132).

We use the STRING verb as follows:

MOVE SPACES TO OUTPUT-REC
MOVE 5 TO STARTING-PLACE.
STRING COMPANY-NAME DELIMITED BY SIZE, '   '
    CITY-STATE DELIMITED BY ','
    SPACE
    ZIP DELIMITED BY SIZE
INTO OUTPUT-REC
WITH POINTER STARTING-PLACE.

The first MOVE statement clears the output record of any previous contents. The second MOVE sets STARTING-PLACE to a value of 5 so that the beginning of data transfer into OUTPUT-REC will begin in column 5 (WITH POINTER STARTING-PLACE). Of course, STARTING-PLACE is an arbitrary name chosen by the programmer; but it must be an integer field for obvious reasons.

The STRING statement specifies that, in effect, five fields will be transferred: COMPANY-NAME, the nonnumeric literal '   ', CITY-STATE, the figurative constant SPACE, and ZIP. Thus, starting with column 5 of OUTPUT-REC, the entire (DELIMITED BY SIZE) COMPANY-NAME is transferred and it is followed by the five-blank nonnumeric constant. The next data to be transferred comes from CITY-STATE; the data is transferred character by character until a comma is encountered (DELIMITED BY ','). One blank follows (SPACE) and then the ZIP code. It should be pointed out that use of figurative constants such as SPACE or ZEROS, etc., always means one occurrence of the implied character. Thus we would obtain one blank even if we had used SPACES instead of SPACE.

The general format of STRING is as follows:

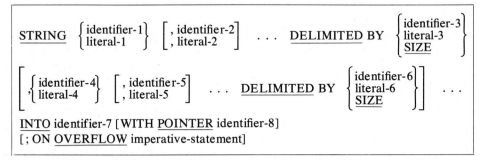

Our two examples have illustrated all but the OVERFLOW option. If the data specified to be transferred is longer than the size of the receiving item (identifier-7) during execution of a STRING statement, then the imperative statement of the OVERFLOW clause is executed. If the optional OVERFLOW is not used and the overflow condition arises, then the STRING operation is discontinued and the next program statement is executed. During execution identifier-8, if used, is incremented by one as each character is transferred. It is the value of this identifier which is checked to determine an overflow condition. If identifier-8 is not used, an implied counter is used to fulfill the same function.

The UNSTRING verb, as its name implies, acts in the reverse direction of the STRING verb. We present two examples to illustrate use of this verb.

Suppose that data is recorded in free form (without predefined fields) as follows:

TED S BROWN,4,15,3.52
TINA LORI CHRISTIANSON,1,12,2.50

As we can see, name fields are separated by one or more blank spaces, then commas separate the remaining three fields. We would like to move these data fields to a fixed format record.

```
01  STUDENT-RECORD.
    02  FIRST-NAME          PIC X(15).
    02  MIDDLE-NAME         PIC X(15).
    02  LAST-NAME           PIC X(20).
    02  CLASSIFICATION      PIC 9.
    02  CREDIT-LOAD         PIC 99.
    02  GPA                 PIC XXXX.
```

Assuming that the source data is in

```
01  FREE-FORM-RECORD     PIC X(57)
```

we can write:

```
UNSTRING   FREE-FORM-RECORD
           DELIMITED BY ALL SPACES OR ','
    INTO   FIRST-NAME
           MIDDLE-NAME
           LAST-NAME
           CLASSIFICATION
           CREDIT-LOAD
           GPA.
```

The DELIMITED clause specifies that fields in the source record are separated by one or more blank spaces (ALL SPACES), or single commas (OR ','). In essence, the source record is scanned character by character from left to right. When a blank or a comma appears it is assumed that a new field begins. The delimiters in this case are blanks or commas and they are not included in the data transfer, although the UNSTRING statement does include an option allowing the transfer of delimiters themselves.

Consider now a second example which expands on UNSTRING and illustrates combined use of STRING and UNSTRING.

Data records contain a number in columns 1–6, a name, and a header separated from each other by a dollar sign. As in the previous example, a delimiter such as a dollar sign can be used to allow recording of data without adherence to predefined field positions. When data length is highly variable, such free-form data can save a lot of space. Two sample records are as follows:

349687INTERNATIONAL TOOLS, INC. $ BALANCE SHEET $
135002ACME CORP. $ INCOME STATEMENT $

We are interested in printing the company name centered at column 40 on the top of a new page, followed by the name of the report on the third line, also centered at column 40. Solution of the problem involves separating the two fields, determining their size, and, on the basis of their size, centering the data in respect to column 40. We also assume that we wish to check that there are indeed two fields available in the relevant part of the source record. First we define some data fields:

01	FREE-FORM-RECORD	PIC X(46).
01	FIRST-LINE	PIC X(20).
01	SECOND-LINE	PIC X(20).
01	LENGTH-1	PIC 99.
01	LENGTH-2	PIC 99.
01	STARTING-POINT	PIC 99.
01	NO-OF-FIELDS	PIC 9.
01	OUTPUT-RECORD	PIC X(132),

Exhibit 7-2 presents a program segment written to accomplish the desired task. The NO-OF-FIELDS item is used to count the number of fields transferred. Notice its use in the TALLYING clause in the UNSTRING statement. The value 7 is moved to STARTING-POINT because the first six columns of FREE-FORM-RECORD contain a number which we wish to ignore. Notice the clause WITH POINTER STARTING-POINT. Using the $ as delimiter, we transfer data from the source record into two fields, FIRST-LINE and SECOND-LINE. In the process we obtain a count of the characters moved into each receiving field in LENGTH-1 and LENGTH-2, respectively. The COUNT option provides this length count. Finally, use of the OVERFLOW specifies execution of PERFORM ERROR-ROUTINE-1 if the data being transferred exceeds the size of the receiving field. This could happen in our example if the delimiting dollar sign was missing, or if one field was longer than 20 characters—the size specified for FIRST-LINE and SECOND-LINE.

After the UNSTRING statement we check to see that indeed we had two fields transferred; if not, we PERFORM ERROR-ROUTINE-2.

The PRINT-HEADERS paragraph computes the starting point of each line to the left of column 40. We divide the length of the field involved by 2 and we subtract this amount from 40. We then use the STRING verb to move the data, using LENGTH-1 as the pointer. Actually, it is the availability of the POINTER option in the STRING verb that makes it capable of achieving what the MOVE verb could not accomplish in this case. After the transfer of the data, we print the record and repeat the process for the next line of printed output. The general format of the UNSTRING verb is

```
UNSTRING identifier-1 [ DELIMITED BY [ALL] {identifier-2}
                                            {literal-1  } [ , OR

[ALL] {identifier-3} ]  . . . ] INTO identifier-4   [, DELIMITER IN identifier-5]
      {literal-2  }

[, COUNT IN identifier-6] [, identifier-7   [, DELIMITER IN identifier-8]

[, COUNT IN identifier-9]] . . . [WITH POINTER identifier-10]

[TALLYING IN identifier-11] [; ON OVERFLOW imperative-statement]
```

**EXHIBIT 7-2   EXAMPLE PROGRAM INVOLVING THE USE OF
UNSTRING AND STRING**

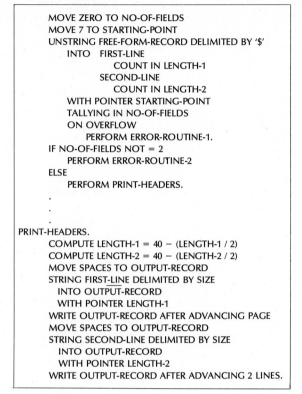

```
        MOVE ZERO TO NO-OF-FIELDS
        MOVE 7 TO STARTING-POINT
        UNSTRING FREE-FORM-RECORD DELIMITED BY '$'
            INTO   FIRST-LINE
                        COUNT IN LENGTH-1
                    SECOND-LINE
                        COUNT IN LENGTH-2
            WITH POINTER STARTING-POINT
            TALLYING IN NO-OF-FIELDS
            ON OVERFLOW
                    PERFORM ERROR-ROUTINE-1.
        IF NO-OF-FIELDS NOT = 2
            PERFORM ERROR-ROUTINE-2
        ELSE
                PERFORM PRINT-HEADERS.
        .
        .
        .
PRINT-HEADERS.
        COMPUTE LENGTH-1 = 40 − (LENGTH-1 / 2)
        COMPUTE LENGTH-2 = 40 − (LENGTH-2 / 2)
        MOVE SPACES TO OUTPUT-RECORD
        STRING FIRST-LINE DELIMITED BY SIZE
           INTO OUTPUT-RECORD
           WITH POINTER LENGTH-1
        WRITE OUTPUT-RECORD AFTER ADVANCING PAGE
        MOVE SPACES TO OUTPUT-RECORD
        STRING SECOND-LINE DELIMITED BY SIZE
           INTO OUTPUT-RECORD
           WITH POINTER LENGTH-2
        WRITE OUTPUT-RECORD AFTER ADVANCING 2 LINES.
```

We have illustrated all the options except the DELIMITER IN clause. When used, the clause specifies the identifier to be used to receive the delimiter(s). This option is used if we wish to move the delimiters themselves.

REVIEW

1   The verb which is used to transfer data from several sources to one destination is the _____ verb.

STRING

2   The verb which is used to transfer data from one source to many destinations is the _____ verb.

UNSTRING

3   When the DELIMITED BY SIZE clause is used in conjunction with the STRING verb, transfer of data from the sending field stops when the number of characters which have been transferred equals the size of the [sending / receiving] field.

sending

4   If an OVERFLOW clause is not used in conjunction with a STRING verb and an overflow condition occurs, then [the STRING operation / program execution] is terminated.

the STRING *operation*

5   Used in conjunction with the UNSTRING verb, the DELIMITED BY clause specifies the basis used to signal the beginning of a new record in the [sending / receiving] field.

sending

6   The clause which is used if delimiters themselves, such as commas or spaces, are to be transferred to receiving fields during the UNSTRING operation is called the _____ clause.

DELIMITER IN

THE INSPECT VERB

At times we need to access and manipulate individual characters in a field. One very common use is to edit input data, such as replacing leading blanks by zeros. COBOL now provides the INSPECT verb to accomplish such character manipulations. This verb replaces the EXAMINE verb which served a similar but more limited purpose in previous versions of the language.

The INSPECT verb is powerful but a bit complicated. Three formats are available, and these are presented in Appendix C, "Complete ANSI COBOL Language Formats." Discussion of the complete set of options would exceed the intended scope of this text. We present some examples to illustrate the basic options.

EXAMPLE 1   We want to replace all *leading* blanks by leading zeros in a field called TEST.
INSPECT TEST REPLACING LEADING ' ' BY '0'.

EXAMPLE 2   We want to replace *all* blanks by zeros in a field called TEST.
INSPECT TEST REPLACING ALL ' ' BY '0'.

EXAMPLE 3   We want to replace the first zero by a +.
INSPECT TEST REPLACING FIRST '0' BY '+'.

EXAMPLE 4   How many dollar signs are in TEST?
INSPECT TEST TALLYING COUNT-A FOR ALL '$'.

After the instruction is executed, the numeric field COUNT-A will contain a value equal to the number of $ in TEST. (COUNT-A would have been defined in the DATA DIVISION.)

EXAMPLE 5   How many zero characters are there to the left of the decimal and how many zeros are there to the right of the decimal point?
INSPECT TEST TALLYING COUNT-A FOR ALL '0' BEFORE INITIAL '.'
                       COUNT-B FOR ALL '0' AFTER '.'.

This instruction will result in COUNT-A containing the number of zeros before the decimal point and COUNT-B containing the number of zeros after the decimal point.

EXAMPLE 6   Count the number of dollar signs in TEST and replace all dollar signs after the first one by asterisks.
INSPECT TEST TALLYING COUNT-A FOR ALL '$'
    REPLACING ALL '$' BY '*' AFTER INITIAL '$'.

EXAMPLE 7   Assuming that TEST contains a name left-justified in TEST, how long is the name? (Unused positions are blank.)
INSPECT TEST TALLYING COUNT-A FOR CHARACTERS BEFORE
INITIAL ' '.

EXAMPLE 8   An untrained keypunch operator did not depress the numeric key; all numbers have been mispunched. For example, instead of a zero there is a /, instead of a 1 there is a U. Correct the data.

INSPECT TEST REPLACING ALL '/' BY '0'
                          'U' BY '1'
                          'I' BY '2'

                          .
                          .
                          .

                          '.' BY '9'.

THE COPY VERB

COBOL provides for a library facility. By "library" we mean a collection of COBOL source program elements recorded on tape or disk and accessible by reference to *text-names*. A well-planned and maintained library can reduce the time needed to write routines common to several programs, and it can serve to standardize such common routines.

For example, suppose we include the following statement in the DATA DIVISION:

01   INVENTORY-RECORD COPY MATERIAL-RECORD.

We obtain the following source program listing at compilation time. The C characters on the left margin indicate that these entries were copied.

```
     01   INVENTORY-RECORD COPY MATERIAL-RECORD.
C        02   PART-NUMBER                          PICTURE X(9).
C        02   PART-NAME                            PICTURE X(15).
C        02   STOCK-QUANTITY                       PICTURE 9(6).
```

We can use the copied items in the PROCEDURE DIVISION as if we had written their description in the DATA DIVISION of the current program. Notice that the record-name used in this program example, INVENTORY-RECORD, is not the same as the library-name for that record. Use of the same name is optional. It is of course good procedure to use the same name, so that comparison of different programs and communication between programmers are facilitated. The library simplifies program writing by standardizing records in different files, so that programs can be maintained and revised easily.

Building the library is commonly done outside the COBOL language by means of JCL (Job Control Language) statements. Use of a library is a very *local* practice, and we direct the readers to their own computer system for details.

THE GO TO . . . DEPENDING VERB

We have already used the GO TO control statement which unconditionally directs the program to a new paragraph. Another form of the GO TO statement allows conditional branching and has the following general format:

GO TO paragraph-name-1   paragraph-name-2   . . .   DEPENDING ON identifier.

This form of the GO TO statement allows conditional branching as follows: If the value of the identifier is 1, program execution branches to the first paragraph named. If it is 2, execution branches to the second paragraph named, and so on. Thus, the identifier must have a range of possible values from 1 to as many values as there are paragraph names listed. If the value of the identifier is outside the range in a particular instance, the GO TO statement is ignored. Of course, the identifier must be an integer and it must not be negative. As an example we might have students identified as freshmen through seniors by values of 1 through 4 stored in CLASS-CODE. We could write:

```
GO TO   PROCESS-FRESHMAN
        PROCESS-SOPHOMORE
        PROCESS-JUNIOR
        PROCESS-SENIOR
     DEPENDING ON CLASS-CODE.
PERFORM ERROR-PAR.
```

In this example CLASS-CODE is tested and program control branches to the respective paragraph. If CLASS-CODE contains a value outside of the range 1–4, then ERROR-PAR will be executed, since it is the next statement.

Use of this verb is discussed further in Chapter 9, "Structured Programming."

REVIEW

1 Individual characters in a field can be accessed and possibly changed by use of the _____ verb.

INSPECT

2 Use of the TALLYING option in conjunction with the INSPECT verb makes it possible to _____ designated characters.

count (etc.)

3 Use of the REPLACING option in conjunction with the INSPECT verb makes it possible to _____ designated characters.

change (etc.)

4 The verb which makes it possible to reference a precoded program segment from a library of such program segments is _____.

COPY

5 When the COPY verb is used to obtain a record description from a library, the record-name used in the program and in the library [must / need not] be the same.

need not

6 The form of the GO TO control statement which allows conditional branching requires use of the reserved COBOL word _____.

DEPENDING

7 In the conditional GO TO statement the value of the identifier determines the _____ to which branching occurs.

paragraph

8 When the DEPENDING option is used, the value of the identifier in the GO TO statement should not be negative or zero. If the value of the identifier is outside the range implied by the number of paragraphs listed, program execution [terminates / continues with the next statement].

continues with the next statement

EXERCISES

1 Write a COBOL program to compute depreciation schedules, using the declining balance method. Use the flowchart and program description given in Exercise 28 of Chapter 4.

2 Write a COBOL program to compute depreciation schedules, using the sum-of-the-digits method of depreciation. The sum-of-the-digits method works as follows: Suppose that you have an asset of original value $1,000.00 to be depreciated over 3 years, using the sum-of-the-digits method. Then the following table shows the nature of the calculations involved.

YEAR	DEPRECIATION RATE	DEPRECIATION
1	$\dfrac{3}{1+2+3} = \dfrac{3}{6}$	$1{,}000 \times \dfrac{3}{6} = 500.00$
2	$\dfrac{2}{1+2+3} = \dfrac{2}{6}$	$1{,}000 \times \dfrac{2}{6} = 333.33$
3	$\dfrac{1}{1+2+3} = \dfrac{1}{6}$	$1{,}000 \times \dfrac{1}{6} = 166.66$

Notice that the depreciation rate varies from year to year, but that the rate is applied to the same (original) asset dollar value. The rate consists of a denominator that is the sum of the digits from 1 up to the number of years over which the asset is to be depreciated. To test your understanding of the concept, compute the denominator value for 5 years. The answer is 15. The numerator of the depreciation rate varies from the number of years to 1 in steps of 1. Thus for a 5-year depreciation schedule the numerator values are: 5, 4, 3, 2, 1.

Input
Input is in the form of a deck of cards with the following data format:

CARD COLUMNS	CONTENT
1–5	Asset number
6–14	Original asset value in dollars and cents
15–16	Blank
17–18	Number of years over which the asset is to be depreciated
19–80	Blank

Output
The output should be on a new page for each asset and should have approximately the following format:

ASSET 12345	ORIGINAL VALUE		$1,000.00
YEAR	**DEPRECIATION**	**ACCUMULATED DEPRECIATION**	**BOOK VALUE**
1	$500.00	$ 500.00	$500.00
2	333.33	833.33	166.67
3	166.67	1,000.00	0.00

Note: In order always to show a final accumulated depreciation equal to the original value, and a final book value equal to zero, the depreciation of the last year is to be computed as follows:

Last year depreciation = original value − accumulated depreciation

Required

a Draw a flowchart of the program logic.
b Write and run a COBOL program to produce the desired output.

Use as test data that shown in the description above.

3 A deck of cards contains data about the inventory of a company. Each inventory item is identified by a unique item number. The deck of cards is sorted on item number. There are three types of cards in the deck. A *balance* card contains the amount in inventory as of the last time the data was processed. A *receipt* card contains the amount of a shipment received. An *issue* card contains the amount sold. For each shipment received and each sale made a separate card is punched. It is desired to read the cards, process the data, produce an inventory report on the printer, and produce a set of new balance cards on the card punch.

Input

CARD COLUMN	CONTENT
1–5	Item number
6–20	Part name (on balance cards only)
21	Card type code
	1 = balance
	2 = receipt
	3 = issue
22–25	Quantity

Note: The cards are sorted on item number. For each item, the balance card *precedes* the receipt and issue cards.

Sample input

```
01212TRANSFORMER    12350
01212               26000
01212               30150
01212               33050
01212               31600
01515GEAR TRAIN     11000
01515               30600
02010METAL PLATE    14000
```

Sample output
The printer output resulting from the sample input is

ITEM NUMBER	PART NAME	PREVIOUS BALANCE	NEW BALANCE
01212	TRANSFORMER	2350	3550
01515	GEAR TRAIN	1000	400
02010	METAL PLATE	4000	4000

The sample punched card output resulting from the same sample input is

01212TRANSFORMER	13550
01515GEAR TRAIN	10400
02010METAL PLATE	14000

These balance cards serve as input to the next program run, along with the receipt and issue cards punched between processing runs.

Required

a Draw a program flowchart.
b Write and run a COBOL program to accomplish the desired result. Assume all data is punched correctly.

4 The data processing objective of this program is to compute and print the monthly schedule of payments resulting from a credit purchase. Given the amount of the credit purchase and the number of monthly payments planned, the amount of the monthly payment is computed as follows:

$$\text{Payment due} = \frac{\text{amount of credit purchase}}{\text{number of payments}} + 0.015 \text{ of unpaid balance}$$

Of course, this formula presumes an interest charge of 0.015 per month on the unpaid balance in the account. For example, suppose that a customer has purchased an item valued at $1,200.00 and is going to pay for it over a 12-month period. The payment due at the end of the first month is

$$\text{Payment due} = \frac{\$1,200.00}{12} + 0.015 \ (\$1,200.00)$$
$$= \$100.00 + 0.015 \ (\$1,200.00) = \$100.00 + \$18.00 = \$118.00$$

Similarly, for the second month the payment is

$$\text{Payment due} = \frac{\$1,200.00}{12} + 0.015 \ (\$1,100.00)$$
$$= \$100.00 + 0.015 \ (\$1,100.00) = \$100.00 + \$16.50 = \$116.50$$

The monthly payment consists of a constant element, which is the original amount

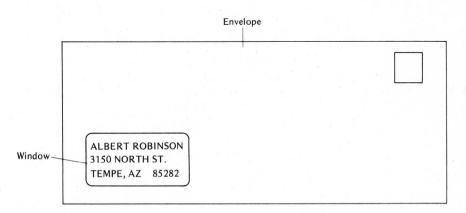

ABC COMPANY
5000 East Camelback Road
Phoenix, Arizona   85033

ALBERT ROBINSON
3150 NORTH ST.
TEMPE, AZ   85282

Fold here

SCHEDULE OF PAYMENTS

ORIGINAL AMOUNT $4,291.50

MONTH	INTEREST	TOTAL PAYMENT	UNPAID BALANCE
1	64.37	422.00	3,933.87
2	59.00	416.63	3,576.25
3	53.64	411.27	3,218.62
4	48.27	405.90	2,861.00
5	42.91	400.54	2,503.37
6	37.55	395.18	2,145.75
7	32.18	389.81	1,788.12
8	26.82	384.45	1,430.50
9	21.45	379.08	1,072.87
10	16.09	373.72	715.25
11	10.72	368.35	357.62
12	5.36	362.99	.00

Envelope

Window

ALBERT ROBINSON
3150 NORTH ST.
TEMPE, AZ   85282

of the credit purchase divided by the number of monthly payments, and a variable element, which is the monthly interest charge on the unpaid balance. With each monthly payment the unpaid balance is decreased by the amount of the constant element.

The desired output for this program is shown on page 201, in this case for a credit transaction of $4,291.50. In the figure it is assumed that the letterhead is preprinted, but that the name and address, all column headings, and the numeric values will be printed as the result of program execution. Since the column headings are always the same, in practice these headings would also be preprinted on the form in order to conserve computer time. However, in our example we will print the headings in order to illustrate how this can be accomplished through the use of COBOL. For each monthly payment the numeric information provided is the amount of monthly interest charge, the total payment due that month, and the unpaid balance remaining after that month. Note also that the spacing of the computer printout is designed for use with a window envelope, thereby eliminating the need for separate addressing of envelopes.

Program input

The input will consist of a deck of punched cards, with one card per customer. The layout of these data fields on the punched card is illustrated below.

CARD COLUMNS	CONTENTS
1–20	Customer's name
21–45	Number and street
46–70	City, state, and ZIP code
71–78	Amount of credit purchase
79–80	Number of monthly payments

Write a COBOL program to accomplish the task described above, given that $4,291.50 is to be repaid in 12 monthly installments and with a monthly interest rate of 1.5%.

Conditions and Conditional Statements

INTRODUCTION

Computer processors derive their logic capability from their ability to test for the truth or falsity of conditions. We can appreciate the fundamental nature of this ability by considering what computer programs would be like without conditional logic. In fact, it would be impossible to write most computer programs without the use of conditional instructions. The COBOL language recognizes the importance of this capability and provides a rich repertoire of conditions and conditional statements. We present the subject as a separate chapter, because of the number of conditions which can be tested, and to highlight the logical unity of various types of conditional statements.

We have already studied a number of conditional statements. First, we studied the IF conditional statement in Chapter 4, "Writing Complete Programs." In the same chapter we also discussed the AT END conditional clause, which is used in conjunction with input files. Finally, we studied the ON SIZE ERROR conditional clause, which is concerned with overflows resulting from arithmetic operations. In this section we expand on the subject of conditions and conditional statements by discussing six types of conditions: (1) relation conditions, (2) nested conditions, (3) class conditions, (4) sign conditions, (5) condition-name conditions, and (6) complex conditions. In general, a condition is an expression that is either true or false in a particular circumstance; that is, the condition either holds or it does not hold.

RELATION CONDITIONS

Such conditions are concerned with comparisons between two items. The type of comparison is indicated by the relational operator, which may be in the form of words or symbols. The relational operators available in COBOL are

LESS THAN   <

EQUAL TO   =

GREATER THAN >

The general format for relation conditions is

IF $\left\{\begin{array}{l}\text{identifier-1}\\\text{literal-1}\\\text{arithmetic-expression}\end{array}\right\}$ $\left\{\begin{array}{l}\text{IS [\underline{NOT}] \underline{LESS} THAN}\\\text{IS [\underline{NOT}] <}\\\text{IS [\underline{NOT}] \underline{EQUAL} TO}\\\text{IS [\underline{NOT}] =}\\\text{IS [\underline{NOT}] \underline{GREATER} THAN}\\\text{IS [\underline{NOT}] >}\end{array}\right\}$ $\left\{\begin{array}{l}\text{identifier-2}\\\text{literal-2}\\\text{arithmetic-expression-2}\end{array}\right\}$

Examples of the use of these additional features are

IF AMOUNT > 100 . . .

IF A + B = PRICE

IF A − B + 20 IS LESS THAN Q * A . . .

In the general format presented above, the first and second operands are often referred to as the subject and object of the condition, respectively. One additional point in this regard is that these two operands cannot both be literals. Thus the statement IF 3 IS GREATER THAN 2 is invalid. Of course, there is no reason why such a statement need ever be written, since the equality or inequality is predetermined by the statement itself and does not constitute a useful relational comparison.

The meaning of relational tests involving numeric values is obvious. If RATE-1 and RATE-2 are numeric fields, the conditional expression IF RATE-1 > RATE-2 PERFORM PAR-A leads to PAR-A whenever the numeric (algebraic) value of RATE-1 is greater than the numeric value of RATE-2 *regardless of the field size*.

With respect to nonnumeric comparisons, however, certain things are not so obvious. A comparison involving two alphabetic items proceeds from left to right in pairs of characters until the first unequal pair occurs. Thus, in comparing T H O R P to T H A L E S the first field is determined to be greater than the second when the O-A pair is compared. The size of the fields in this case is irrelevant. But suppose we are comparing the following two fields:

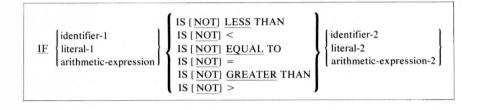

In this case the first field is considered smaller, since the first blank (from left to right) is considered smaller than the letter O.

As a third case of alphabetic comparison, consider this:

| S | M | I | T | H |

| S | M | I | T | H | | |

The two items are considered equal, even though their field size is unequal. In this case the blanks are ignored, which is consistent with the common-sense logic of the comparison.

Consider the following two alphanumeric fields:

| X | A | - | 1 | 1 | 4 |

| X | . | B | - | 3 |

Convention for determining the "larger" of the two does not exist. Still, these are legitimate fields in computer processing, and we must handle them. In this respect we rely on the *collating sequence* of a computer system, which varies with the computer used. The collating sequence is simply a defined sequence that states the relative rank of each possible character in a computer's storage. For example, in the widely used IBM System/370 computers the collating sequence for the following characters is as indicated by the order of listing:

blank

. (period or decimal point)

(

+ (plus sign)

)

- (hyphen or minus)

/

, (comma)

' (single quote)

" (double quote)

letters A–Z

numbers 0–9

Thus, when comparing 3-A/ and Z/9K, the 3-A/ is the greater.

The collating sequence used is defined by each manufacturer, and so no general collating sequence which applies to all computers can be defined.

REVIEW

1 Relation conditions are concerned with comparisons between two items. The words or symbols that serve to indicate the type of comparison to be made are called relational _____.

operators

2 As indicated above, relational operators can be in the form of either words or symbols. In the spaces below, enter the symbols that are equivalent to the listed relational operators:
LESS THAN _____
EQUAL TO _____
GREATER THAN _____

<; =; >

3 Of the following three relation conditions, the one that is invalid as a COBOL expression is the one identified by the letter [a / b / c].

a IF GROSS-PAY IS GREATER THAN 99 . . .
b IF 100 < ORDER-AMT . . .
c IF 500 > 400 . . .

c

4 An ordering which defines the relative rank of all the valid characters in a computer system is referred to as the _____ for the system.

collating sequence

NESTED CONDITIONS

Before discussing nested conditions, let us consider the general format for the IF statement.

IF condition	{ statement-1 NEXT SENTENCE }	{ ELSE statement-2 ELSE NEXT SENTENCE }

The possible unique structures are many and, since the IF statement is a very common and very useful program instruction, we will do well to spend some time studying it. Here are some of the forms we can have:

IF condition statement-1 . . .
IF condition statement-1 ELSE NEXT SENTENCE.
IF condition statement-1 ELSE statement-2.
IF condition NEXT SENTENCE ELSE statement-2.

Note that the first case shows that we can omit the ELSE portion. For example, we can write IF SUM-TAX < 50.00 MOVE ZERO TO DEDUCTIONS. The period following DEDUCTIONS signifies that the current sentence has ended. Thus the statement that follows will be the NEXT SENTENCE, and so it would be redundant to write ELSE NEXT SENTENCE, although it would not be wrong.

To enhance your understanding of conditional statements, study the following example.

```
IF AMOUNT IS GREATER THAN CREDIT LIMIT
     WRITE PRINT-LINE FROM CREDIT-OVERDRAW
ELSE
     MOVE AMOUNT TO BILLING-FIELD
     WRITE PRINT-LINE FROM BILL-AREA.
ADD AMOUNT TO TOTAL-VALUE.
```

With reference to the program statements and the flowchart on the next page, the program statements that correspond to the flowchart descriptions are as follows:

FLOWCHART DESCRIPTION	CORRESPONDING PROGRAM STATEMENT
Condition	IF AMOUNT IS GREATER THAN CREDIT-LIMIT
Statement-1	WRITE PRINT LINE FROM CREDIT-OVERDRAW
Statement-2	MOVE AMOUNT TO BILLING-FIELD WRITE PRINT-LINE FROM BILL-AREA
Next sentence	ADD AMOUNT TO TOTAL-VALUE

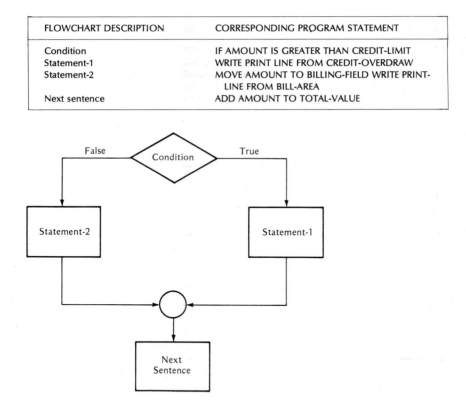

Notice that statement-1 and statement-2 need not be single statements. Statement-2 illustrates the case in which two statements are included.

The following program segment and flowchart illustrate another structure involving the NEXT SENTENCE:

```
IF A < B
      MOVE A TO SMALL
ELSE
      NEXT SENTENCE.
IF A = B
      NEXT SENTENCE
ELSE
      MOVE B TO SMALL.
MOVE SMALL TO EDIT-FIELD.
```

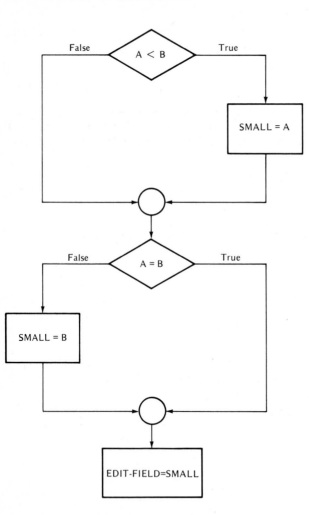

In the general format for the IF statement, statement-1 and statement-2 are not restricted to being imperative statements. Rather, they themselves may be conditional expressions, giving rise to the possibility of using nested IF statements. A relatively simple example of a nested IF statement, or a nested conditional, is the following:

IF AMOUNT IS LESS THAN 100
    IF AMOUNT IS GREATER THAN 50
        MOVE 0.3 TO RATE
    ELSE
        MOVE 0.4 TO RATE
ELSE
    MOVE 0.2 TO RATE

    The above COBOL statement corresponds to the following rule:

AMOUNT	RATE
Less than or equal to 50	0.4
Greater than 50 but less than 100	0.3
Equal to or greater than 100	0.2

    In order to interpret nested conditionals you will find it useful to look for the first ELSE; it always pertains to the immediately preceding IF. Then the second ELSE pertains to the IF just preceding the inner IF, and so on. Schematically, the relationships can be portrayed as follows:

IF ... IF ... IF ... ELSE ... ELSE ... ELSE ...

    In flowchart form the above example can be represented as follows:

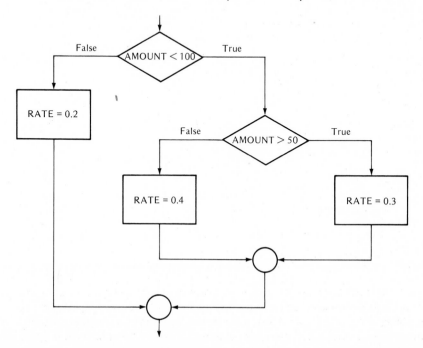

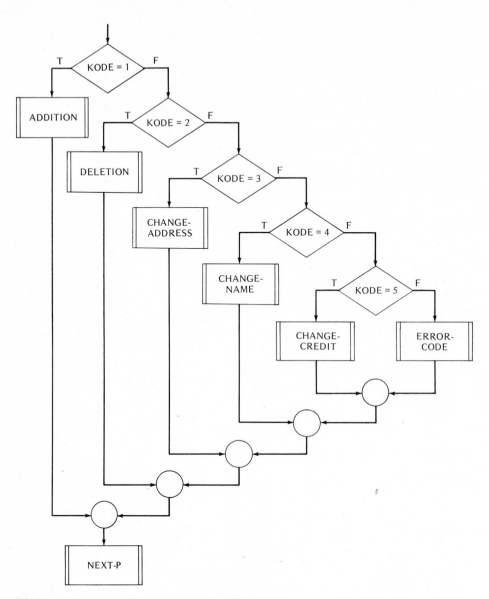

FIGURE 8-1   SAMPLE NESTED CONDITIONAL STRUCTURE.

Nested conditions can be very useful in writing program statements, but they can also be misused by nesting conditions so deeply that program logic is not easy to follow. Because nested conditions are important, we present some additional examples.

First, consider a code that can have legitimate values in the range 1–5. Figure 8-1 depicts a nested conditional structure that tests for the value of the code and executes a suitable procedure. In language form we could write:

```
IF KODE = 1
    PERFORM ADDITION
ELSE
    IF KODE = 2
        PERFORM DELETION
    ELSE
        IF KODE = 3
            PERFORM CHANGE-ADDRESS
        ELSE
            IF KODE = 4
                PERFORM CHANGE-NAME
            ELSE
                IF KODE = 5
                    PERFORM CHANGE-CREDIT
                ELSE
                    PERFORM ERROR-CODE.
PERFORM NEXT-P.
```

We have nested to five levels, which tests the limits of our ability to understand the program logic inherent in the nesting. In general, many programming managers advise against nesting more than three levels. In this particular example the structure is rather easy, however, because of the null alternatives involved. In this sense, we can say that even though we have nested to five levels, it is a "clean" program structure.

Alternately, we could use the GO TO . . . DEPENDING ON verb:

```
GO TO ADDITION
        DELETION
        CHANGE-ADDRESS
        CHANGE-NAME
        CHANGE-CREDIT
    DEPENDING ON T-CODE.
PERFORM ERROR-CODE.
GO TO GO-TO-COLLECTION.
ADDITION.
    .
    .
    .
GO TO GO-TO-COLLECTION.
DELETION.
    .
    .
    .
CHANGE-CREDIT.
    .
    .
    .
GO-TO-COLLECTION.
    PERFORM NEXT-P.
```

As a third alternative, we could use simple conditions:

IF T-CODE = 1 PERFORM ADDITION.
IF T-CODE = 2 PERFORM DELETION.
IF T-CODE = 3 PERFORM CHANGE-ADDRESS.
IF T-CODE = 4 PERFORM CHANGE-NAME.
IF T-CODE = 5 PERFORM CHANGE-CREDIT.
IF T-CODE < 1 PERFORM ERROR-CODE.
IF T-CODE > 5 PERFORM ERROR-CODE.
PERFORM NEXT-P.

In this case, the programming is simpler but there are two minor disadvantages.

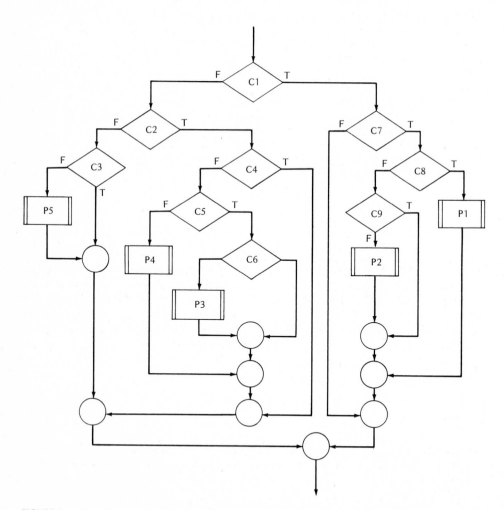

FIGURE 8-2   SAMPLE DEEPLY NESTED CONDITIONAL STRUCTURE.

First, it is not immediately obvious that only one of these seven conditions can be true, and therefore program clarity suffers. Second, all seven conditions will be tested before the PERFORM NEXT-P is executed, whereas in the nested and GO TO structures as soon as one condition holds, control moves to PERFORM NEXT-P immediately.

We next consider the example presented in Figure 8-2. It can be seen that the flowchart implies nested conditionals such as these:

```
IF  C1
    IF  C7
        IF  C8
            PERFORM P1
        ELSE
            IF NOT  C9
                PERFORM P2
            ELSE
                NEXT SENTENCE
ELSE
        IF  C2
            IF  C4
                NEXT SENTENCE
            ELSE
                IF  C5
                    IF  C6
                        NEXT SENTENCE
                    ELSE
                        PERFORM P3
                ELSE
                    PERFORM P4
        ELSE
            PERFORM P5.
```

It is obvious that the nesting has gone too far! What can we do to simplify the program structure? Figure 8-3 provides a suggested decomposition into several modules that are executed by use of PERFORM instructions. Notice that these modules are understandable, each by itself, and yet we do preserve their dependencies. Thus, rather than deep nesting, we suggest breaking down the program into several paragraphs containing simple or lightly nested conditional statements.

REVIEW

1 For the program instruction below, identify the program statement which corresponds to each IF statement element. Refer to the general format for the IF statement if you wish.

```
IF  QUANTITY < 100
    NEXT SENTENCE
```

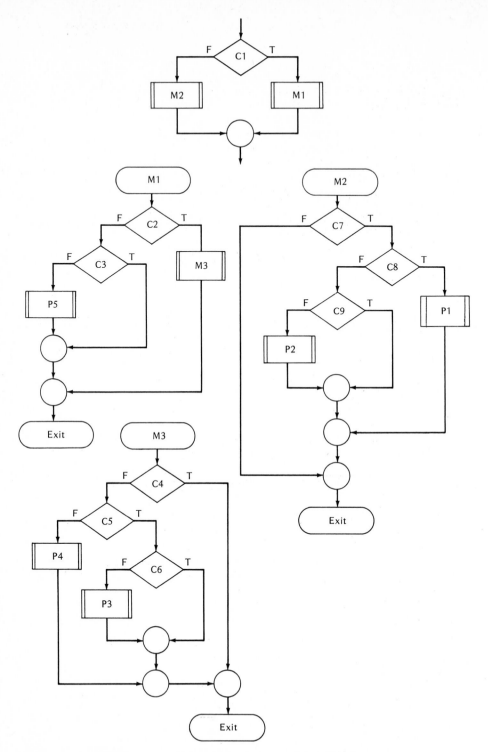

FIGURE 8-3   DECOMPOSITION OF A DEEPLY NESTED CONDITIONAL STRUCTURE.

ELSE
    MULTIPLY DISCOUNT BY PRICE.
MULTIPLY PRICE BY QUANTITY GIVING NET

IF STATEMENT ELEMENT	CORRESPONDING PROGRAM STATEMENT
a Condition	
b Statement-1	
c Statement-2	
d Next Sentence	

    a QUANTITY < 100
    b *Not used*
    c MULTIPLY DISCOUNT BY PRICE
    d MULTIPLY PRICE BY QUANTITY
        GIVING NET

2 Construct a flowchart for this program segment.

    IF   QUANTITY < 1000
        NEXT SENTENCE
    ELSE
        MULTIPLY DISCOUNT BY PRICE.
    MULTIPLY PRICE BY QUANTITY GIVING NET.

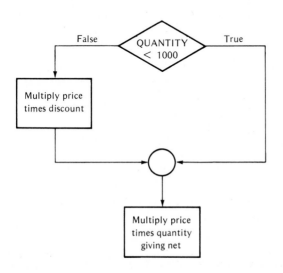

3   For the following COBOL statement complete the table below which summarizes the decision rule being used:

```
IF   GRSPAY < 1000.00
     IF   GRSPAY > 500.00
          MOVE 0.05 TO RETRMNT-DEDUC
     ELSE
          MOVE 0.03 TO RETRMNT-DEDUC
ELSE
     MOVE 0.07 TO RETRMNT-DEDUC.
```

AMOUNT OF GROSS PAY	RETIREMENT DEDUCTION RATE
Equal to or greater than 1,000	_____
Greater than 500 but less than 1,000	_____
Less than or equal to 500	_____

0.07; 0.05; 0.03

4   The type of conditional statement illustrated in the preceding question is usually referred to as a(n) _____ conditional.

nested

5   The logic associated with a deeply nested program structure can be clarified by decomposition of the program into several separate, but dependent, _____ _____ .

modules (or paragraphs)

CLASS CONDITIONS

The use of a class condition test makes it possible to determine whether the contents of a data field are numeric or alphabetic. Further, by the use of a combination of such conditionals we can also determine if the field contains alphanumeric data. The general format for the class condition test is

$$
\text{IF identifier IS } [\underline{\text{NOT}}] \begin{Bmatrix} \text{NUMERIC} \\ \text{ALPHABETIC} \end{Bmatrix}
$$

A data field is numeric if it contains only the digits 0–9, with or without an operational sign. Alphabetic items, on the other hand, consist of the letters A–Z and/or blanks. It is not valid to perform a NUMERIC class test on an alphabetic field or an ALPHABETIC class test on a numeric field. Thus, suppose we have the following DATA DIVISION specifications:

AMOUNT PICTURE 9(4)V99.
NAME   PICTURE A(15).

It would be improper to write:

IF AMOUNT IS ALPHABETIC . . . or IF NAME IS NUMERIC . . .

Instead, the AMOUNT field above can be tested to determine if the content is in fact NUMERIC or if it is NOT NUMERIC. Similarly, the NAME field can be tested only to determine if the content is ALPHABETIC or NOT ALPHABETIC. A common case of a numeric field not containing numeric data involves reading a field from a card which contains one or more blanks. Specifying the PICTURE with 9s does not guarantee that the field will contain numeric digits. Table 8-1 summarizes the valid uses of the class condition test for different kinds of fields. Note that any of the condition tests may be used with an alphanumeric field.

In general, the class condition test is useful as a check to determine if particular data classes contain the type of data as defined in the DATA DIVISION: numeric, alphabetic, or alphanumeric. The tests for NUMERIC and ALPHABETIC are straightforward, such as in:

IF AMOUNT IS NUMERIC . . .
IF NAME IS NOT ALPHABETIC . . .

In effect, the first statement above directly tests the appropriateness of the content in the numeric field called AMOUNT, whereas the second statement tests for inappropriateness of the content in the alphabetic field called NAME. Since an alphanumeric field can have both alphabetic and numeric content, the alphanumeric content can be ascertained indirectly by determining that the content is not entirely numeric and that it is not entirely alphabetic, as follows:

IF   FIELD-A IS NOT NUMERIC
    IF   FIELD-A IS NOT ALPHABETIC
        PERFORM ALPHA-NUM-PAR . . .

The class condition test cannot be used with numeric items whose USAGE has been declared COMPUTATIONAL. Thus the usage must be explicitly or implicitly DISPLAY, as discussed in Chapter 5, "DATA DIVISION Features."

TABLE 8-1   VALID USES OF THE CLASS CONDITION TEST FOR DIFFERENT KINDS OF FIELDS

FIELD CLASS	VALID TEST
Numeric	NUMERIC, NOT NUMERIC
Alphabetic	ALPHABETIC, NOT ALPHABETIC
Alphanumeric	NUMERIC, NOT NUMERIC, ALPHABETIC, NOT ALPHABETIC

SIGN CONDITIONS

The sign condition determines whether or not the algebraic value of an identifier or arithmetic expression is greater than less than, or equal to zero. The general format for the sign condition is

$$\underline{IF} \left\{ \begin{array}{l} \text{identifier} \\ \text{arithmetic-expression} \end{array} \right\} \text{IS} [\underline{NOT}] \left\{ \begin{array}{l} \underline{POSITIVE} \\ \underline{NEGATIVE} \\ \underline{ZERO} \end{array} \right\} \ldots$$

The subject of the condition must be a numeric field or arithmetic expression. If the value contained in the field is greater than zero it is POSITIVE, if the value is equal to zero it is ZERO, and if it is less than zero it is NEGATIVE.

As was true for the class condition test, the sign condition is frequently used as a check on the appropriateness of data. For example, if an inventory figure cannot be negative by definition, the presence of a negative value in such a field indicates some kind of error. In other circumstances, a zero or negative value in an inventory field might be indicative of an out-of-stock condition, and the test could be used to initiate a reordering procedure.

REVIEW

1   The purpose of a class condition test is to determine if the actual content of a storage field is _____, _____, or _____.

numeric; alphabetic; alphanumeric

2   Suppose that a field named VENDOR has been defined as an alphabetic field in the DATA DIVISION. If we wish to check for the possibility that numeric data have been entered into this field, we could do so by the statement: IF VENDOR IS _____.

NOT ALPHABETIC

3   Suppose that a field named ADDRESS has been defined as an alphanumeric field in the DATA DIVISION. If we wish to ascertain that the content of the field is in fact alphanumeric, we can do so by the statement _____ _____.

IF ADDRESS IS NOT NUMERIC IF
ADDRESS IS NOT ALPHABETIC

4   The sign condition can be used to test for three specific types of conditions in regard to the content held in a particular field: whether it is positive, _____, or _____. The subject of the sign condition must be a _____ field.

negative; zero; numeric

CONDITION-NAME CONDITIONS

In Chapter 5, "DATA DIVISION Features," we describe the use of condition-names, which are identified by level number 88. For completeness and later reference, we include such conditions here. For example, in the DATA DIVISION we have:

```
02   PAYROLL PICTURE 9.
        88   HOURLY VALUE 1.
        88   SALARY VALUE 2.
```

Then in the PROCEDURE DIVISION we can test the condition-name by a statement such as:

```
IF   HOURLY
        PERFORM HRLY-COMP
ELSE
        IF   SALARY
            PERFORM SALARY-COMP.
```

The above condition-name tests are equivalent to the following relational conditions tests in terms of the result:

```
IF   PAYROLL = 1
        PERFORM HRLY-COMP
ELSE
        IF   PAYROLL = 2
            PERFORM SALARY-COMP.
```

The use of the condition-name test, however, is generally preferred, because it represents better documentation by more clearly describing what is being tested in the PROCEDURE DIVISION statement itself.

COMPLEX CONDITIONS

It is possible to combine the simple (individual) conditionals we have described into complex conditionals by the use of the logical operators OR, AND, and NOT. OR means either or both, and AND means both. Thus, consider the following statement:

```
IF BALANCE IS NEGATIVE AND DAYS-OVERDUE > 10
        PERFORM PAR-A.
```

The instruction indicates that the program should execute PAR-A when both the balance is negative and the number of overdue days exceeds 10. On the other hand, consider the following statement:

```
IF INPUT-DATA IS NOT NUMERIC OR NAME-IS-MISSING
        MOVE 'CANT PROCESS, INCORRECT DATA' TO MESSAGE.
```

The program will move the indicated message to MESSAGE if either the input data is not numeric (perhaps because of a keying error) or the condition-name condition defined as NAME-IS-MISSING in the DATA DIVISION holds.

There is a rather complex set of rules associated with the writing and evaluation of complex conditionals. From the standpoint of the scope and orientation of this book, however, we shall limit our attention to the use of parentheses to clarify the meaning. For example, we can write:

IF (AGE IS GREATER THAN 28) OR ((EXPERIENCE = 4)
    AND (EDUCATION IS GREATER THAN HS)) . . .

The above condition holds either if age is greater than 28 or if both experience = 4 and education is greater than high school.

As another example consider the following:

IF ((KODE = 2) OR (KODE = 3)) AND (BALANCE-CODE = 1)
    MOVE SPACES TO ERROR-MESSAGE
    PERFORM OLD-ITEM-2.

In the above example the condition is true if BALANCE-CODE is equal to 1 and KODE is either equal to 2 *or* equal to 3.

Thus, by the use of complex conditionals we can write conditional tests that otherwise would require very long expressions consisting of several nested IF statements. Complex conditionals are particularly useful for selecting data from a file, since we can designate selective retrieval of records according to the presence or absence of complex conditions.

REVIEW

1 The conditional by which the type of record can be identified—for example, markup might vary according to the category of the item—is called the _____ test.

condition-name

2 Of course, the condition-name tested must be assigned in the DATA DIVISION as an 88 level statement, wherein it is also assigned a value. Although the condition could also be tested in the PROCEDURE DIVISION by testing the value, the condition-name test is usually preferred because it results in [greater programming accuracy / clearer documentation].

clearer documentation

3 As contrasted to simple conditionals, a combination of tests can be included in one statement by the use of _____ conditionals.

complex

4 The use of a complex conditional requires the use of one of the logical operators _____, _____, or _____.

OR; NOT; AND

5 When the logical operator OR is used in a complex conditional test, the presence of [either / both / either or both] of the conditional states constitutes a YES condition.

either or both

6 When the logical operator AND is used in a complex conditional test, the presence of [either / both / either or both] of the conditional states constitutes a YES condition.

both

EXERCISES

1 Write PROCEDURE DIVISION statements to implement the logic included in the following (unstructured) flowchart.

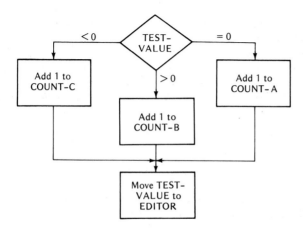

2 An input field has been defined as

03   IN-FIELD   PICTURE X(10).

Two other fields in WORKING-STORAGE have been defined as

01   AMOUNT   PICTURE 9 (10).
01   NAME   PICTURE A(10).

It is desired to test the content of IN-FIELD and, if it contains a number, to store it in AMOUNT; if it contains a name, to store it in NAME; and if a mixture of characters, to go to a paragraph called ERRORS.

a   Write PROCEDURE DIVISION statements to accomplish this task.
b   Suppose that, if the IN-FIELD contains a number, it is actually in dollars and cents. What would you do to make the number available in dollars and cents instead of as an integer? (*Hint:* Be careful!)

3 Using the 88 level number indicator in the DATA DIVISION and suitable condition-name clauses, the following obvious identifiers have been defined.

MALE

FEMALE

SINGLE-M

MARRIED-M

DIVORCED-M

WIDOWED-M

SINGLE-F

MARRIED-F

DIVORCED-F

WIDOWED-F

Assume we want to tabulate the number of individuals falling in the last eight classes, as, for example, the number of single males (SINGLE-M). We thus want to test the field containing the identifying code and ADD 1 TO the corresponding counter. Assume the following fields are to be used as counters: SM, MM, DM, WM, SF, MF, DF, WF (where SM stands for single males, etc.).

a Draw a flowchart corresponding to your program logic.

b Write *one* nested conditional expression to accomplish the required testing and tabulating.

4 Consider the following DATA DIVISION entries relating to a personnel record.

02 EDUCATION		PICTURE 99,
88 H-S GRAD	VALUE IS 12.	
88 COLLEGE-GRAD	VALUE IS 16.	
88 MASTERS-GRAD	VALUE IS 17.	
88 DOCTORATE-GRAD	VALUE IS 20.	
02 YEARS-OF-EXPERIENCE		PICTURE 99.
02 SEX		PICTURE 9.
88 MALE	VALUE 1.	
88 FEMALE	VALUE 2.	
02 GEOGRAPHIC-PREFERENCE		PICTURE 9.
88 EAST	VALUE 1.	
88 MIDWEST	VALUE 2.	
88 WEST	VALUE 3.	
88 SOUTH	VALUE 4.	
88 WILLING-TO-TRAVEL	VALUE 5.	

Suppose that we want to find individuals that fulfill one of these three requirements:

 i Five years of experience, male, high school graduate, willing to travel

 ii Male, one year of experience, master's degree, preferring the West or South

iii Three years of experience, female, doctorate, preferring the East

Write *one* compound conditional sentence to check whether a record in question fulfills the first, second, or third of these requirements. If one of these requirements is met, we WRITE PRINTLINE FROM NAME. If the requirement is not met, we go to PAR-A.

5   Consider the table of conditions below.

QUANTITY	PRICE	RATING	DISCOUNT
>100	>10	<2	0.05
>100	>10	≥2	0.10
>100	≤10	<2	0.15
>100	≤10	≥2	0.20
≤100	$\left\{\begin{array}{c}<\\=10\\>\end{array}\right\}$	$\left\{\begin{array}{c}<\\=2\\>\end{array}\right\}$	0.25

a   Write instructions *using nested if* to MOVE to DISCOUNT the value shown depending on the conditions.

b   Draw a structured flowchart corresponding to the data in the table.

6   Draw in flowchart form the following, where Ci stands for condition i and Fi stands for function (statement) i.

```
IF    C1
          AND (C2 OR C3)
        F1
        F2
ELSE
        IF   C3
                  OR (C6 AND C7)
              F3
        ELSE
              NEXT SENTENCE.
```

Structured Programming

INTRODUCTION

Data processing managers have become increasingly aware of the importance of the programming function in computer installations. In a typical case, programming and systems analysis efforts consume more than 50 percent of the annual budget. In addition, much of the programming effort is directed toward program *maintenance,* i.e., changes in or modifications to existing programs. In such an environment, traditional programming comes into conflict with cost management objectives. By traditional programming we mean programming generated as a form of personal art without adherence to established concepts and principles.

The traditional way has been to view programming as a personal creation by an individual. The characteristic of a good programmer has been the ability to write clever programs—"clever" often being synonymous with complex and obscure. The trouble is that obscure program codes are very difficult to understand by persons other than the author, and even the author may have difficulty when months or years intervene. The turnover in personnel and changing business requirements have forced attention on the need to write programs that are correct *and* easy to maintain. This need has been recognized and given prominence in the last few years, and considerable thought has been devoted to satisfying it.

The term "structured programming" has come to mean the collection of principles and practices that are directed toward developing correct programs which are easy to understand and to maintain. As with all new subjects, there is considerable disagreement and misunderstanding as to what structured programming is and is not.

PROGRAM STRUCTURE

A computer program is a set of instructions to a computer. But while the instructions are to be executed by the computer, the language in which we communicate these instructions is meant to be comprehensible to humans. High-level languages like COBOL are intended for human use in their direct form and are intended for machine use only indirectly, through compilation. Therefore, a basic principle of good programming is that *programs be understandable.*

A program that can be understood can be analyzed and tested for correctness. Incorrect programs have plagued computing from its early days. The most extreme manifestations of program errors make newspaper headlines, as when a wage earner receives a check for one million dollars, or a customer receives a bill for zero dollars. Another basic principle of good programming, then, is *to write correct programs.* In a more theoretical vein we talk of *proof of program correctness* as a reflection of efforts to prove in logical and unambiguous terms that a piece of program code is correct, i.e., that it does what it is intended to do and nothing else. Theoretical progress has been made only in very limited contexts, and at this time we cannot rely on formal theory to be our guide for producing correct programs. Instead, we rely on a number of rules and guides that are closer to common sense than they are to formal theory.

Program structure is a commonsense concept. It means that a program should not be "unstructured." The classic description of an unstructured program is the "spaghetti-bowl" program: a program whose logical flow is as tangled as this name implies. To understand a "spaghetti-bowl" type of program one has to untangle a terrible logical mess. Often, an unstructured program is so difficult to understand that instead of making a modification to it we find it easier to "scrap" the whole thing and start all over with a brand-new program. In contrast, a structured program is characterized by clarity and simplicity in its logical flow structure. It reads like ordinary language from beginning to end instead of branching from later paragraphs to earlier ones and back again like a tennis ball. So a simple, straight *flow of logic* is another principle of good programming.

Of course, programming tasks are by their nature complex. So we may raise the obvious question as to how we can avoid the inherent complexity of the task. Structured programs reduce and control complexity; they do not eliminate it. Further, structured programs achieve clarity and simplicity within the bounds of well-defined program segments or modules. Humans are characterized by a bounded rationality. We can only comprehend or attend to so much at a given time. So when confronted with a complex task we cope with it by breaking it down into smaller parts. In a similar way, structured programs consist of smaller interconnected parts. Each part or module is simple and comprehensible by itself, so that within each module we can achieve simplicity and clarity.

Special attention is required in specifying the interconnections between modules in a program. Preferably, a module exists as a separate entity that can be used in a variety of contexts without change, except in specifying the interconnection each time. In this way, a module may be worked on independently of the overall program of which it is a part, either initially or in subsequent modifications. A good example is a module that extracts the square root of a positive number. The specific computational procedure (algorithm) for extracting the square root can be developed independently of programs which may use the square root module. In this example the interconnection between the larger program and the square root module has the form: "Here is a number. Give me its square root."

We have thus discussed another principle of good programming: *A structured program should consist of interconnected modules, each module being simple and clear as to its purpose or task.*

A modular structure allows for abstraction and provides the mind with the ability to cope with complexity. We can understand an entire large program by abstracting from the details of each module to its basic purpose or function, and by focusing on the interrelationships between the modules. In practice, we develop modular structures by proceeding from the general to the specific, or by using what is widely known as the *top-down approach.* Suppose that we are to develop a payroll processing program. Utilizing the top-down approach we might proceed as follows:

The most abstract statement of the task is "Write payroll." We then proceed to break down this general statement to more specific statements, such as:

Edit input data

Process against master file

Output payroll checks and other reports.

Each of these broad functions can be subdivided into more specific ones, as for example:

Edit input data

Check for valid employee numbers

Check time card data against job tickets, etc.

Process against master file

Incorporate new hires

Compute gross pay, etc.

Compute state withholding tax

Compute F.I.C.A. tax

Without belaboring the point any further, it should be clear how specific tasks can be extracted from general ones. Each of the specific tasks eventually becomes a candidate for being developed into a program module.

It should be noted that in the process of developing the program structure we do not use a computer programming language. We write our thoughts in ordinary language with or without graphic aids such as arrows, boxes, brackets, etc. A widely used term is *pseudocode,* which stands for program description written in nonprogramming language. Some practitioners go so far as to adhere to certain rules of writing pseudocode. Our commonsense guide again tells us to use whatever form of language we find useful. To be sure, in a large installation, formal standards for writing pseudocode can play a beneficial role. But the absence of generally accepted standards precludes further discussion here. Pseudocode may be written in several levels of abstraction. In general we advise a one-page description of the total task, and then a description of each program module, with each module described on a separate page. These descriptions can serve as partial or even complete documentation of a program.

Thus far we have discussed the general characteristics, or principles, of structured programs. We now consider some specific forms of program structure by which these principles can be implemented.

REVIEW

1   The collection of principles and practices directed toward developing programs that are comparatively easy to understand and to change has come to be called _____ programming.

structured

2   Several commonsense principles underlying the development of structured programs were presented and discussed in this section. They are:

A program should be understandable.

A program should be correct.

A program should incorporate a simple, straight flow of logic.

A program should consist of interconnected modules, each module being simple and clear as to purpose or task.

3   A "spaghetti-bowl" program is one that is particularly lacking in terms of _____ _____ .

logical flow (etc.)

4   A program segment which is self-contained and structured for the purpose of accomplishing a specific task within an overall program is called a(n) _____.

module

5   The top-down approach to developing modular program structures involves working from the [specific / general] toward the [specific / general].

general; specific

6 A term which describes program segments written in ordinary language, rather than in a programming language, is ——————————————————.

pseudocode

FORMS OF PROGRAM STRUCTURE

A structured program can be completely developed using three basic forms of program structure: Sequence, If-then-else, and Do-while. One may encounter these as special terms which are written: SEQUENCE, IFTHENELSE, DOWHILE (pronounced as normal words). In flowchart form we represent them as follows:

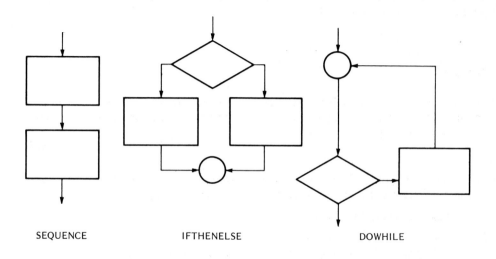

SEQUENCE   IFTHENELSE   DOWHILE

The SEQUENCE structure indicates the sequential flow of program logic. Each block may stand for a statement; it may stand for a whole module, or even a collection of modules. In COBOL we illustrate with statements in series, such as:

ADD SUBTOTAL GIVING GRAND-TOTAL
MOVE GRAND-TOTAL TO EDIT FIELD
WRITE PRINT-RECORD.

The IFTHENELSE structure indicates conditional program flow. The program takes one path or another, depending on whether a condition, often referred to as *predicate*, is true or false. In COBOL we implement the structure as follows:

IF AMOUNT IS GREATER THAN 100
    MULTIPLY 0.20 BY PRICE
ELSE
    MULTIPLY 0.10 BY PRICE.

We may have a case such that if a condition holds we do something, if not we continue in the program sequence.

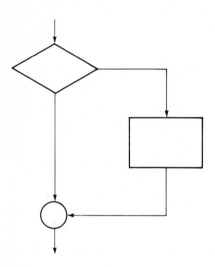

In COBOL we implement the structure by the omission of ELSE, as in the following:

IF AMOUNT IS GREATER THAN 100 MULTIPLY 0.20 BY PRICE.

The DOWHILE structure provides for a looping operation, that is, repetitive execution of a program segment. A loop is not infinite if it is correct. The predicate tests for a condition. If the condition holds, we exit from the loop; if not, we execute the instruction. Here is one COBOL example:

PERFORM PROCESS-AND-PRINT
    UNTIL END-OF-DATA-INDICATOR = ZERO.

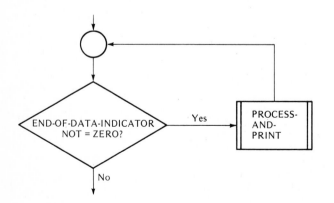

Next, consider this example:

```
MOVE 1 TO KOUNTER.
REPEAT.
    READ CARD-FILE RECORD . . .
    IF KOUNTER = 10
        GO TO OUT-OF-HERE
    ELSE
        ADD 1 TO KOUNTER
        GO TO REPEAT.
OUT-OF-HERE.
```

The reader may wish to flowchart the above example and then to modify it using the PERFORM verb instead. In this example GO TO is used twice. GO TO is generally considered an undesirable language form. Still, in the current example it can be argued that use of this control verb does no harm, and we present this example to dispel the notion that GO TO is necessarily harmful. Further, we want to point out that GO-TO-less programming is not synonymous with structured programming. A clear structure can be implemented with the use of a GO TO. On the other hand, indiscriminate use of GO TO is likely to lead to "spaghetti-bowl" programs, and for this reason it is preferable to refrain from using this verb when possible.

The above three basic structures will suffice to represent many programs. Still, it is often found convenient to introduce two more structures: DOUNTIL and CASE.

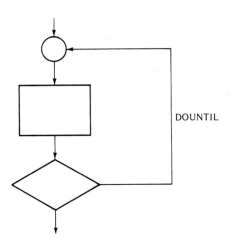

DOUNTIL

DOUNTIL resembles DOWHILE, except that the block precedes the test. Thus the block will be executed at least once. In COBOL we write:

```
PERFORM PROCESS-AND-PRINT.
PERFORM PROCESS-AND-PRINT
    UNTIL END-OF-DATA-INDICATOR = ZERO.
```

Notice that the above structure is a little awkward in COBOL, since we repeat one instruction. COBOL was not designed explicitly for structured programming, and therefore it requires some unnatural forms. Notice also that the UNTIL option is similar to DOWHILE, not DOUNTIL!

An alternate form using the GO TO is

```
REPEAT.
    PERFORM PROCESS-AND-PRINT.
    IF END-OF-DATA-INDICATOR = ZERO
        GO TO OUT-OF-HERE
    ELSE
        GO TO REPEAT.
OUT-OF-HERE.
```

The CASE structure is convenient when we have a large number of alternatives to be tested. Suppose that the marital status of an employee is coded as 1, 2, 3, 4, standing for single, married, divorced, and widowed, respectively (correctness of codes has been verified). We wish to count the number of employees belonging to each class. We have:

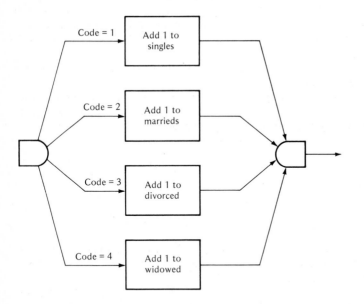

Assuming that KODE contains the marital status code we can use the GO TO . . . DEPENDING ON verb in COBOL as follows:

```
GO TO SINGLES, MARRIEDS, DIVORCED, WIDOWED
    DEPENDING ON KODE.
        :
        :
```

.
.
.

SINGLES.	ADD 1 TO SINGLES-COUNT
	GO TO NEXT-P.
MARRIEDS.	ADD 1 TO MARRIEDS-COUNT
	GO TO NEXT-P.
DIVORCED.	ADD 1 TO DIVORCED-COUNT
	GO TO NEXT-P.
WIDOWED.	ADD 1 TO WIDOWED-COUNT
	GO TO NEXT-P.

NEXT-P.
etc.

In this example the structure appears awkward. The reason is that each of the four processing paragraphs does something simple. If we imagine a more extended task performed for each case, however, then we can see the structure to be quite attractive. The convergence of all GO TO statements to NEXT-P is consistent with the general structured programming principle that each structured task should have one starting point and one ending point. Also, notice that GO TO is necessary in this structure. However, in order to preserve the proper structure, the paragraph referenced by GO TO must be physically located further down in the program than the point at which GO TO appears. Adherence to this rule meets the requirement that the program read in a forward direction.

The CASE structure may also be implemented in terms of nested IFTHENELSE structures, as exemplified on page 234.

Notice that each IFTHENELSE has a beginning and an end clearly marked by the use of collectors (circles). For instance, the collectors numbered 1, 2, and 3 mark the respective termination of each of the three IFTHENELSE structures. The subject of structured flowcharts is discussed more fully in the following section.

REVIEW

1 The three basic forms of program structure are SEQUENCE, IFTHENELSE, and DOWHILE. Of these, the one in which the program takes one path or another, depending on whether a condition is met, is _____.

IFTHENELSE

2 The program structure which results in repetitive execution of a program segment is _____.

DOWHILE

3 The program structure which simply involves a series of instructions which are executed in the order in which they are presented in the program is _____.

SEQUENCE

Nested IF implementation of CASE structure

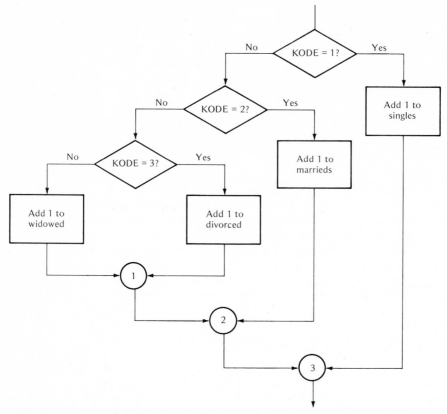

4   In addition to the three basic forms of program structure, two other forms are DOUNTIL and CASE. The structure which is similar to DOWHILE, except that the program segment which can be repeatedly executed will always be executed at least once, is ──────────.

DOUNTIL

5   The program structure in which the program takes one of several paths, typically depending on the value of a coded data item, is ──────────.

CASE

STRUCTURED FLOWCHARTS

Traditionally flowcharts have been used for two main purposes: to help the programmer develop the program logic, and to serve as documentation for a completed program. In recent years there has been some tendency to minimize the need

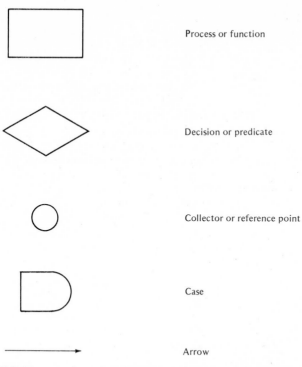

Process or function

Decision or predicate

Collector or reference point

Case

Arrow

FIGURE   9-1   IBM   STRUCTURED   PROGRAM   FLOWCHARTING SYMBOLS.

or even the usefulness of flowcharts. A case can be made that, if a programmer utilizes principles of good program structure, the program is self-documenting and therefore a flowchart is superfluous. Further, there are those who argue that in an environment where program modifications are frequent, redrawing flowcharts becomes cumbersome. We disagree with those who hold the extreme view that flowcharts are useless. Instead, we view flowcharting as a very useful tool for program development and documentation, but we acknowledge that the use of this programming aid should not be indiscriminate. In any case, for the beginning student use of programming flowcharts is invaluable, and we use flowcharts in this book for tasks that often are quite simple.

Structured flowcharts are intended to focus on the program logic rather than on the specific tasks to be performed by the program. As such, structured flowcharts tend to do away with special symbols for input/output, and the like. While there is no standard set of symbols, Figure 9-1 presents a set of flowcharting symbols adopted by IBM. A complete flowchart can be drawn using these symbols alone, although one may use standard flowcharting symbols as well. In any case, a structured flowchart has these main characteristics:

It is clear.

It is simple and easy to understand.

It has one clear beginning and one clear end.

It utilizes the five basic structures SEQUENCE, IFTHENELSE, DOWHILE, DOUNTIL, and CASE.

We now consider an example of a structured flowchart, although the flowcharts that have already appeared in this text also qualify as such examples. We assume the following task. A file consists of employee records. We are interested in preparing a report that shows average annual earnings for men and women and according to membership in a union. Employees are classified as hourly or salaried and as union or nonunion members on the basis of identifying data on each employee record. Figure 9-2 presents a structured flowchart designed to outline the processing logic. Since our purpose is to outline the processing logic, we omit such details as printing headers, moving and editing data, and opening and closing files.

Some points are worth considering with respect to the flowchart in Figure 9-2. First, notice the one-entry/one-exit feature. The flow is generally from beginning to end, allowing repetition of the main task of reading, testing, and accumulation by means of a DOUNTIL structure. If you have not noticed the DOUNTIL structure, consider this compressed version of Figure 9-2:

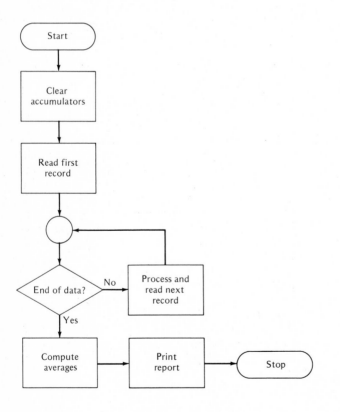

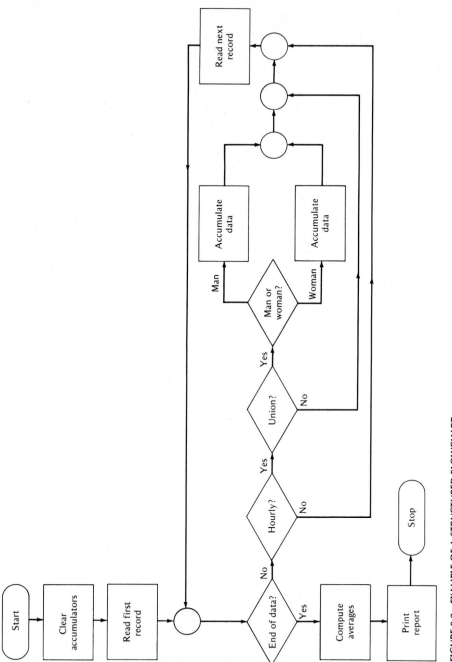

FIGURE 9-2 EXAMPLE OF A STRUCTURED FLOWCHART.

237

The Process and Read Next Record block stands for all the detail shown in Figure 9-2. The compressed version above makes clear the DOUNTIL structure and also illustrates a very important point. Because each segment has the one-entry/one-exit characteristic, in a structured flowchart we can represent a whole group of detailed tasks by one function or process symbol without affecting the validity of the overall structure. Thus, in the present example we could abstract a fairly complex structure into the simple Read and Process block. In a similar fashion we could abstract partially the nested IFTHENELSE structure as follows:

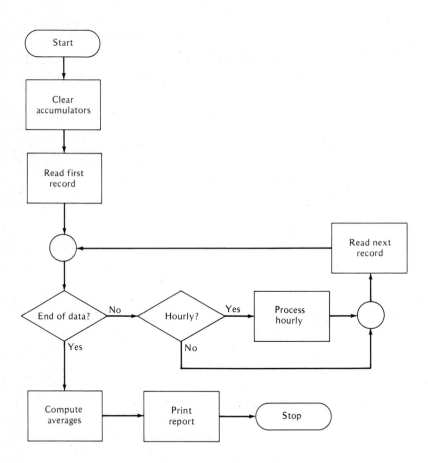

We now show that a record is tested for Hourly and it is either bypassed or processed depending on that particular attribute. This ability to abstract from the detail of a programming process can be reversed, of course. Thus, we can take the Process Hourly block and expand it into detail as an independent module:

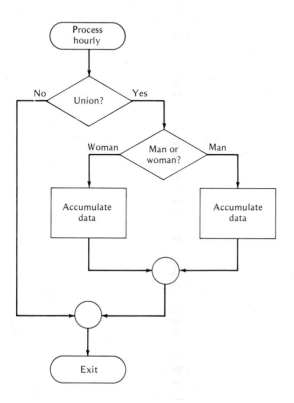

When we are at the early stages of program logic development we can draw flowcharts that concentrate on outlining the overall processing logic. Then we proceed to expand summary blocks into as much detail as needed without disturbing or altering the overall processing logic. In a reverse direction, if we are looking at a flowchart drawn by somebody else and we wish to "look at the forest rather than the trees," we can abstract from the detail within a logical framework or structure.

One useful way to depict the relationships among program modules is shown in Figure 9-3. Such a diagram presents control relationships among the modules of a program. Figure 9-3 illustrates that the Main Module invokes execution of Module A and Module B. Thus it is clear that these are dependent modules. Further, Module X is dependent upon Module A, while Module Y and Module Z are both dependent on Module B. Of course, this is a highly abstract representation. We do not show anything about the form of the dependency in such a diagram. For instance, whether A is

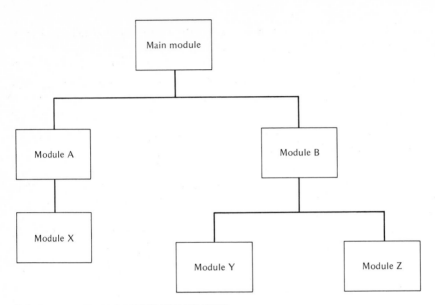

FIGURE 9-3   MODULE DEPENDENCIES DIAGRAM.

executed conditionally, or repetitively, or whatever. The main intent is to provide an accounting of the overall module relationships, and it is not uncommon to discover modules that are left unused in a program (unintentionally, of course).

REVIEW

1   Structured flowcharts are so constructed so as to focus on the [tasks / logic] inherent in the program.

logic

2   The four IBM structured programming symbols, other than the arrow, are portrayed below. The identifying letter of the one used to designate a collector or reference point is ———.

C

A   B   C   D

3 The identifying letter (above) of the structured flowchart symbol used to designate a process or function is _____.

B

4 The identifying letter (above) of the structured flowchart symbol used to designate use of the CASE program structure is _____.

D

5 The identifying letter (above) of the structured flowchart symbol used to designate a decision or predicate is _____.

A

6 A complete program flowchart for a complex programming process can be made more understandable by abstracting and thereby indentifying [detail / summary] modules in the program.

summary

STRUCTURED PROGRAMMING LOGIC

As we have already seen, structured programming relies heavily on the ability to break down a complex task into smaller simpler tasks whose details can be abstracted. Each of the component parts of a structured program is referred to as a module. A module in itself is a proper program structure: It has one entry and one exit, it reads naturally from top to bottom, and it may consist of any of the five basic program structures (SEQUENCE, IFTHENELSE, DOUNTIL, DOWHILE, CASE). The module is referenced by a name which should be as descriptive as possible. In COBOL that name is a paragraph- or section-name. A module should not exceed one page in length, so that it can be easily read. Finally, each module is executed by reference to it from another part of the program, usually through the PERFORM verb.

Figure 9-4 presents a general outline of structured programming logic. Note that there is a main logic module and a number of other, dependent, modules. The main logic part provides a summary of the program, and it is generally short enough that the essence of the entire program can be understood in the context of the main module. Notice that Module A, for instance, is executed under control of the Main Program Module. If the name of Module A is meaningful, say, Compute-State-Tax, we do not need to bother with the details of Module A. It may very well be the case that, as in the example, Module A is sufficiently large or complex that we need to break a Module X out of it—as might be the case for, say, out-of-state taxes. Thus, Module X is executed under the control of Module A which is in turn executed under the control of the main module. This nesting of modules is permissible and desirable. We only need to keep in mind that, as soon as the end of a module has been reached, we turn to the module which issued the execute instruction. Thus when Module X has been executed, we return to Instruction 2 of Module A and, as soon as Module A has been executed, we return to the EXECUTE MODULE B instruction of the Main Program Module.

The program structure described above is adequate for most data processing tasks. However, there are two conditions that restrict its use. Some tasks are common

```
Begin Main Program Module
    Instruction 1
    .
    .

    .
    Instruction M
    Execute Module A
    Execute Module B
    .
    .

    .
    Instruction n
End Main Program Module


Begin Module A
    Instruction 1
    Execute Module X
    .

    .

    .
    Instruction n
End Module A


Begin Module B
    Instruction 1
    .

    .

    .
    Instruction n
End Module B


Begin Module X
    Instruction 1
    .

    .

    .
    Instruction n
End Module X
```

FIGURE 9-4   A GENERAL OUTLINE OF STRUC-
TURED PROGRAMMING LOGIC.

to more than one program. Repeating the same instructions in each such program seems undesirable. The second case concerns large programming tasks. It is difficult for a team of programming staff members to work on the same program at the same time. It is easier to subdivide the composite task into *independent* program modules that can be written, compiled, and tested by individual programmers working independently of one another. This latter objective is achieved by using program subroutines, or subprograms. A program subroutine is a program just like any other program, except that it is not executable by itself; it can only be executed under control of another program. Program subroutines are the subject of Chapter 18, "Modular

Programs and Subroutines." It should be clear, however, that with or without the use of program subroutines the COBOL programmer can create modular, well-structured programs.

REVIEW

1　In the context of structured programming logic, the summary of the entire program is presented in the _____ module.

main program (or main logic)

2　In the context of structured programming logic, it [is / is not] possible for a dependent module to have another module dependent on it.

is (called nesting)

3　The objective of developing independent program modules which can be worked on by different programmers simultaneously can be achieved by the use of program _____.

subroutines (or subprograms)

EXERCISES

1　In your own words discuss the basic concepts involved in structured programming.

2　You are the manager of data processing. One of your experienced programmers comes to you with the following facts. An old program takes 10 minutes to run with specified data. A new version of this program using structured programming concepts requires 11 minutes for the identical data. The programmer points out that this 10 percent increase in running time is simply a waste, and he recommends that the staff stick with the old, efficient programming method. What would you do?

3　You are the manager of data processing and you decide to introduce structured programming. A one-day seminar is planned, and an outside consultant comes in and presents the subject. The next morning John Doe walks in your office and states that structured programming is Mickey-Mousey, a waste of time, and a perfect way to stifle the very creative elements that make a good programmer what he or she is. John Doe has been with the organization for 15 years and is considered a hot-shot by his peers. He has been writing the difficult programs, and he can always deal with modifications to older programs, which the younger programmers find difficult or impossible to do. How would you respond to John Doe?

4 An employee pays 0.0585 of her gross pay as F.I.C.A. taxes for the first $16,500 of her annual earnings. No F.I.C.A. is withheld for earnings over that amount. Assume the following self-defining COBOL data-names: YEAR-TO-DATE-GROSS, FICA, GROSS-PAY-THIS-WEEK. Draw a flowchart and write suitable COBOL statements to compute FICA. Call this set of statements the FICA-COMPUTATION paragraph and assume that after FICA is computed the program continues with a paragraph called MEDICAL-INSURANCE. (Make sure your logic handles the case where year-to-date earnings are, for example, $16,300 and this week's pay is, say, $380.00.) Draw a structured flowchart for the task of computing FICA in each weekly payroll.

5 Revise the following flowchart segment so that it is in proper structured form.

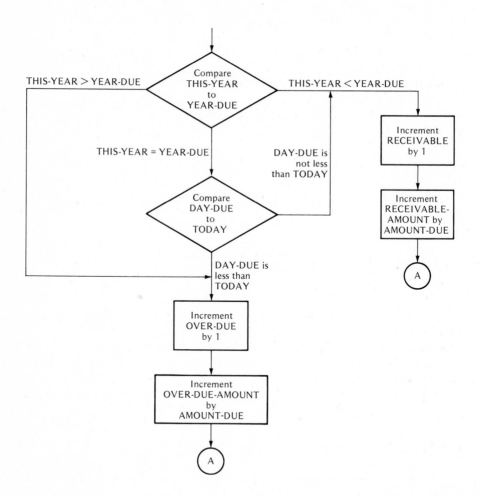

Magnetic Tape Files

INTRODUCTION

Business applications involve processing of voluminous data files that make it impractical to use punched cards. Cards can be read at speeds of only up to 1,500 cards per minute and can be punched at the rate of only about 500 cards per minute. Instead, magnetic tape has come to be a common file recording medium in data processing installations. It is not uncommon for a medium-sized data processing installation to have several thousand tape reels in its library.

PHYSICAL CHARACTERISTICS OF MAGNETIC TAPE

Typically, magnetic tape is a plastic tape which is ½ inch wide and comes in reels which are 2,400 feet in length, have a diameter of about 10½ inches, and weigh about 4 pounds each. One side of the plastic tape is coated with an iron oxide which is magnetically sensitive, and it is this surface that is used for the recording of data.

In terms of the information represented, magnetic tape consists of a long line of recorded symbols. Whereas printed data is entered on two-dimensional pages containing many lines per page, magnetic tape is equivalent to a narrow (one-line) but very long "page." The data is recorded in a string of successive positions, called *columns* or *frames*, with one data character per column. Each column is subdivided into a number of rows called *channels* or *tracks*. The magnetic state of each channel within each column is said to be binary, in that the presence of a particular magnetic state or *bit* is taken to represent a 1 and the absence of a bit represents a 0. The presence or absence of bits in the appropriate channels of a column represents a coded character in that column, very much like the presence or absence of holes in a single column of a punched card.

The number of columns per inch of magnetic tape is a measure of the density of the tape. Commonly, density is expressed in terms of bytes per inch (bpi), in which the term *byte* refers to the set of bits that can be entered in a single column of the tape. Typical tape densities are in the range of 800 to 1,600 bpi, although higher as well as lower densities are possible. This means that with an 800-bpi density we can record 800 columns of data on 1 inch of tape, which is equivalent to 10 fully punched 80-column cards. Theoretically, it is possible to record the contents of 288,000 cards on one 2,400-foot reel of 800-bpi tape (10 cards per inch × 12 inches per foot × 2,400 feet).

As indicated above, each channel or track within a column contains 1 bit, and the bit combinations in each column represent data characters according to the particular coding system used. Three coding systems frequently used are the seven-track code, nine-track code, and the binary code. In the case of the seven-track code, six tracks are used for data bits, and one track contains the *parity* bit portion used for increasing hardware operating accuracy. In the case of the nine-track code, eight tracks are used for data bits, and the ninth is the parity bit. Figure 10-1 shows some of the character code configurations for nine-track tape.

In the *binary coding system* data is recorded in terms of the binary system rather than in terms of alphabetic characters and decimal numeric values. For example, if a particular machine utilizes 36-bit binary words and seven-track tape is being used, six columns of the tape can be used to encode each binary word.

FIGURE 10-1   NINE-TRACK TAPE CODING.

REVIEW

1 Conceptually, magnetic tape consists of a long string of positions. Each position, or column, on a magnetic tape is subdivided into a number of rows which are called _____ .

channels (or tracks)

2 In each column of the tape, each channel has the capacity for one _____ of information.

bit

3 The density of information that can be entered on magnetic tape is typically expressed in terms of _____ (bpi).

bytes per inch

4 Three coding systems frequently used with magnetic tape are the seven-track code, the nine-track code, and the binary code. In the seven-track and nine-track codes one of the tracks is used for the _____ bit.

parity

5 As implied by the name, in the binary coding system all data are represented in the form of _____ .

binary digits

MAGNETIC TAPE UNITS

The magnetic tape unit is the specialized input/output device used for reading and writing magnetic tapes. As illustrated in Figure 10-2, it includes two reels. The file reel contains the tape to be read or to be written on, and the machine reel contains the tape that has already been processed. The tape is threaded through a read/write head capable of performing the functions of reading and writing, and thus the tape transport unit works very much like a home tape recorder.

As the tape advances past the read/write head, the rated speed of reading or writing is a function of two factors: the recording density of the tape and the linear speed of the tape drive. Thus, if the recording density is 800 bpi and the speed is 100 inches per second, the rated read/write speed will be 80,000 bytes per second. Typical ranges are from 40,000 to over 300,000 bytes per second, but much higher speeds are also possible.

REVIEW

1 The magnetic tape unit requires the use of two reels when it is used: the machine reel and the file reel. The reel which contains the tape to be written on or read is

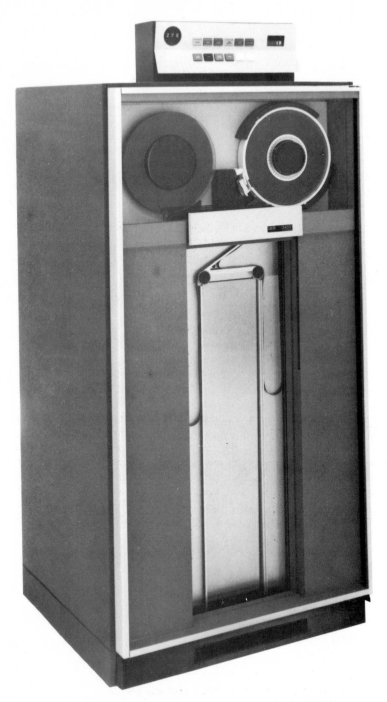

FIGURE 10-2   IBM 3420 MAGNETIC TAPE DRIVE. (IBM CORPORATION.)

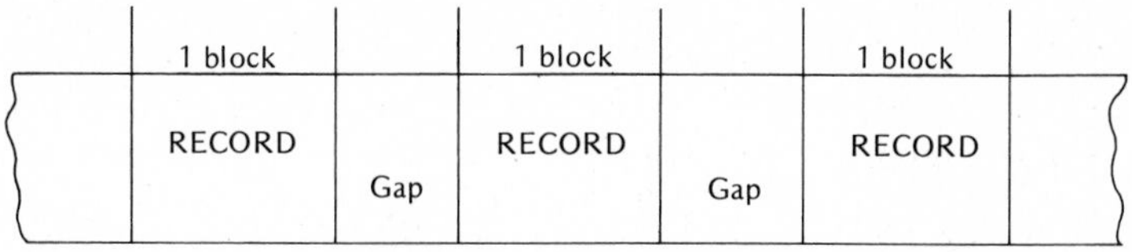

FIGURE 10-3   TAPE RECORDING FORMAT CONTAINING ONE RECORD PER BLOCK.

the _____ reel; and the reel that contains the tape that has already been processed is the _____ reel.

file; machine

2   The rated read/write speed of tape units typically varies between 40,000 and 300,000 bytes per second and is a function of the recording _____ of the tape and the linear _____ of the tape drive.

density; speed

TAPE RECORDS, BLOCKS, AND INTERBLOCK GAPS

Data is recorded on magnetic tape in the form of blocks. Each *block* consists of a grouping of data written (or read) in one continuous operation. Several formats are possible for the data to be included within a block. As a simplified example, suppose we are reading a file of cards which we want to record on tape. If we so choose, we can define each 80-column card as constituting one block. In this case we would have the recording format in Figure 10-3, which indicates that each block consists of one record.

Blocks are separated by a *gap,* which is a blank space about ½ inch in length. Gaps are required in order to differentiate different blocks of data, and the use of blocks may profoundly affect the *effective capacity* of processing. To illustrate, if we have a tape with a nominal capacity of 800 bpi and we record the contents of just one punched card per block, there will be a ½-inch blank for every ¹/₁₀ inch of data. Thus, for every foot of data on the tape there will be 5 feet of blank tape, which is hardly desirable. What can be done to improve matters? One thing we can do is simply to write several records per block, as illustrated in Figure 10-4.

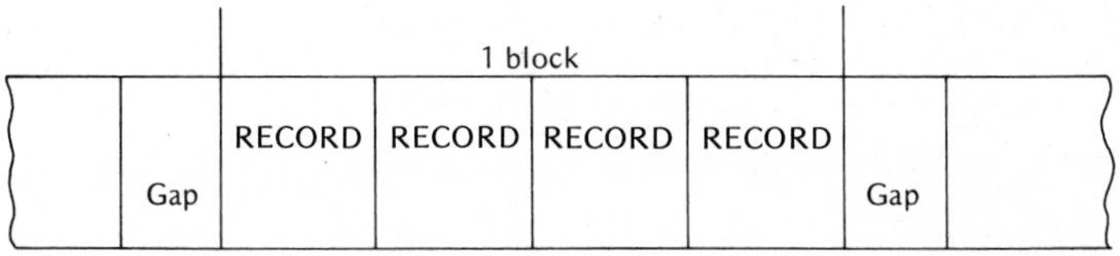

FIGURE 10-4   TAPE RECORDING FORMAT CONTAINING FOUR RECORDS PER BLOCK.

In this case four cards are read into storage, and we then write them as one block containing four records. Now for every $\frac{4}{10}$ inch of data there is $\frac{1}{2}$ inch of blank tape, which is a fourfold improvement but still is not very good. We may suggest: Why not read all the cards into storage and form one long block? The reason that this cannot usually be done is that internal storage is normally much smaller in capacity than the contents of a tape data file. For example, a file of 10,000 cards requires 800,000 bytes of internal storage capacity. Therefore, we have to strike a compromise between available storage capacity and the efficiency of tape input/output.

So far, we have discussed block size in terms of the number of records contained in each block. Actually, the size of each record is also of importance. In using magnetic tape the record size is not restricted to the 80 characters associated with puched cards, nor to any other particular limit. The records can be as long as is suitable for the applications involved. Furthermore, the records can be both fixed and variable in length. An example of a variable-length record is a record containing the transactions for the month for an individual checking account customer. The record for a customer who wrote 20 checks during the month is substantially shorter than the record of another customer who wrote 100 checks. And just as record size can be variable, so can the number of records per block. Overall, then, we can have fixed-length or variable-length records and fixed-length or variable-length blocks. Even though the block size is variable, its size obviously cannot be unlimited. The programmer has to define the maximum limit on block size in each tape operation.

One question perhaps remains to be answered. If variable-length records are written in a block, how can we distinguish between them? Typically, at the beginning of each record we have a control field that contains the length of the record. Thus, if we were forming a record which is to include the checks written by a bank customer, and if 15 characters are required to record the data of each check, we would increase the value of the record-length control field by 15 every time one more check was added to the record.

REVIEW

1   A grouping of data written on magnetic tape in one continuous operation, and which may include one or more records, is called a _____.

block

2   Because blocks of data have to be separated by the gap on the magnetic tape, it is more efficient to include [one / more than one] record in each block.

more than one

3   Before records from punched cards are entered onto magnetic tape they are first read into the internal storage of the computer. Therefore, an important factor which influences the block size used on the magnetic tape is the capacity of the [*internal storage* / *magnetic tape*].

internal storage

4 In addition to the number of records contained in each block, block size is also determined by the length of each record. Although both the record size and the block size can be fixed, variable size is possible [only for records / only for blocks / for both records and blocks].

for both records and blocks

5 When variable record lengths are used in a block, the records are differentiated from one another by the use of a control field which indicates the _____ of each record.

length (or size, etc.)

TAPE FILE ORGANIZATION FORMAT

In addition to data, other items of information are required in a tape file, as illustrated in Figure 10-5. These are now discussed in the sequential order indicated in the figure, from right to left.

BOT These letters stand for the beginning-of-tape marker, which is a reflective strip with an adhesive backing. The marker is attached several feet from the beginning of the tape and marks the beginning of usable tape. The portion of the tape that precedes the marker is used for threading the tape. The reflective marker identifies the starting point for tape use and is automatically sensed by the read/write head in both forward and rewind operations.

HEADER LABEL This is a block of data containing identifying information about the tape file. Normally, an external adhesive label is attached on the reel itself, so that a person can identify the contents of the reel by reading the adhesive label. However,

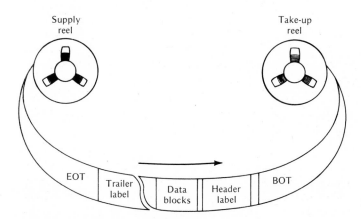

FIGURE 10-5 FORMAT OF INFORMATION ON A TAPE FILE.

because a computer center may have thousands of reels and the possibility exists that adhesive labels may be removed, a magnetic label is used and serves as a means of machine verification of the content of a reel of tape. The label typically contains such informations as:

File Identification	in terms of a file name or a file number
Retention Period	the date prior to which the tape cannot be overwritten
Creation Date	the date the file was established
Reel Sequence Number	the sequence number for a multivolume file that consists of several volumes (reels)

The header label not only serves as a means of verifying the correct identity of an input file but is also used as a means of preventing inadvertent overwriting on a reel used as output. Prior to writing the first block, the header label of an output file is read in, and the retention period is checked against the current date. If the retention period date is later than this date, a suitable error message will be generated for the operator.

TRAILER LABEL   This is a record written as the last record on the tape reel. Typically, it contains the same information as the header label, but in addition it contains a block count, which is a count of the number of data blocks written on the reel. This block count is used for control purposes. On a subsequent occasion when this file is input, the number of blocks read in by the program is accumulated and is compared with the block count recorded on the trailer label. If the two counts are not equal, there exists an indication of error.

The trailer label differs depending on whether a file is a single or a multivolume file. If it is a single-volume file, then the trailer is as described above. If it is a multivolume file, then the trailer label of each volume indicates the volume (reel) number as well.

EOT   The end-of-tape marker is again a reflective strip and serves to stop the tape drive in order to prevent the tape from dethreading. When the EOT marker is sensed, the tape drive will not advance forward even if a programming command so directs the computer. This safeguard is particularly important in the process of writing on a reel of tape, since it is inappropriate to continue writing right up to the physical end of the tape.

REVIEW

1   In this section we have described several items associated with a tape file: BOT marker, header label block, trailer label block, and EOT marker. The BOT marker is a reflective strip that signals the point at which [the tape physically begins / usable tape begins].

usable tape begins

2   The header label block is typically used [in addition to / in lieu of] an external adhesive label on the tape.

in addition to

3   For multireel files the trailer label signals the end of the reel and indicates that processing [should / should not] continue with another reel.

should

4   The EOT marker signals the physical end of the tape and prevents _____ .
_____ .

dethreading (or writing to the physical end of the tape, etc.)

TAPE FILE MAINTENANCE

The reading of magnetic tape involves a sequential access process. By "sequential access" we mean that access to a particular record can be obtained only by a sequential search that begins with the records that precede the one in question. If the records to be accessed are presented in a random order, access time with magnetic tape is relatively slow. To illustrate the point, if we had a dictionary of the English language written on a magnetic tape and we wished to look up a randomly ordered set of words, it would probably be more efficient to look up the words manually in a thumb-indexed dictionary. This is true despite the fact that a person can read a few words per second at the most, whereas the magnetic tape reads at a speed of many thousands of words per second. If, for example, we wanted to look up the words "rescind," "appeal," and "wonderful" in the order indicated, the limitation imposed by the sequential access feature is obvious. To begin with, the word "rescind" can be reached only by reading each word, starting with the words beginning with "a," bringing each word into memory, testing it to see if it matches "rescind," and then repeating the process for all other words until a match is found. A similar procedure would then be used for the other words whose definitions are to be found.

Files of data on magnetic tape are maintained or updated to reflect changes that take place. For example, suppose we have an inventory file on magnetic tape. During the week, we sell items from stock, receive additional shipments, and handle certain adjustments, such as returned items. In order to update the inventory file at the end of the week, it would be extremely inefficient to process each transaction in the random order in which it occurred, as illustrated by our dictionary example above. Instead, a typical procedure used is the one illustrated in Figure 10-6. Beginning with the top of the figure, we assume that the transactions were originally manually recorded and then were punched onto cards and transferred onto magnetic tape on a card-to-tape computer run. The transactions are sorted according to stock number after the card-to-tape conversion rather than before the conversion, because the transactions can be sorted faster and more reliably once the data is on tape. Then, the old master file is processed against the sorted transactions tape to produce the updated master tape. In addition, related stock status reports might be produced on the printer.

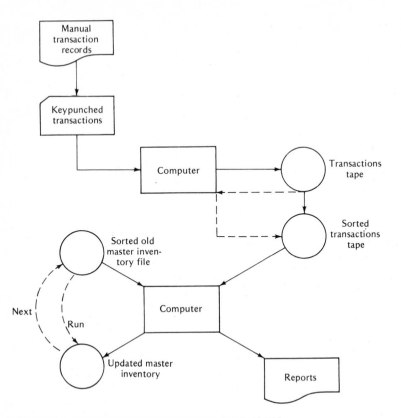

FIGURE 10-6   PROCEDURE USED FOR UPDATING A TAPE FILE.

As indicated by the dotted lines in Figure 10-6, what is now the updated master inventory file becomes the old master inventory file in the next update run, and the old master inventory file from the first run will be used for entry of the updated master inventory file on the next update run. This is known as a parent/child file relationship. However, the procedure we have described results in destruction of the prior week's file in each case, that is, the inventory file for the week preceding the one being updated. If we want to have more historical backup, we could use a third file in this procedure, giving rise to a grandparent/parent/child relationship. This is illustrated in Figure 10-7, in which it is assumed that the file is first created on January 1 and is revised on a weekly basis thereafter.

In order to update a master file, both the master file and the transactions file must be sorted on the same basis. Typically, they are sorted according to stock number, account number, employee number, or the like. To understand the updating procedure in greater detail, consider the flowchart in Figure 10-8. This flowchart is incomplete in that it ignores end-of-file conditions. A more thorough logic is presented in the section, "Example of File Update Logic," in the latter part of this chapter. In order to simplify our discussion, suppose that the master inventory file consists of just three inventory records arranged according to the following format:

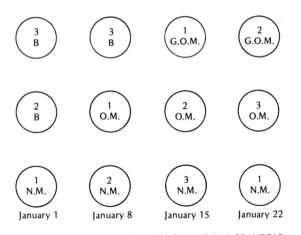

FIGURE 10-7   USE OF THREE REELS OF TAPE IN A GRANDPAR-ENT/PARENT/CHILD RELATIONSHIP. THE NUMBERS 1, 2, AND 3 IDENTIFY THE THREE TAPES. B = BLANK; N.M. = NEW (UPDATED) MASTER; O.M. = OLD MASTER; G.O.M. = GRAND OLD MASTER.

COLUMNS

	1–5 PART NUMBER	6–19 ITEM NAME	20–24 UNITS IN INVENTORY
Master Records			
First Record ⟶	03561	½ HP EL MOTOR	02000
Second Record ⟶	10513	TRANSFORMER	00800
Third Record ⟶	30561	GEAR TRAIN	07890

Suppose further that transactions are recorded on a tape file and that each transaction contains the stock number, a code (1 = receipt; 2 = issue), and an amount as follows:

COLUMNS

	1–5 PART NUMBER	6 CODE	7–11 AMOUNT
Transaction Records			
First Record ⟶	10513	2	00050
Second Record ⟶	10513	2	00100
Third Record ⟶	30561	2	03000
Fourth Record ⟶	30561	1	02200
Fifth Record ⟶	30561	2	00150

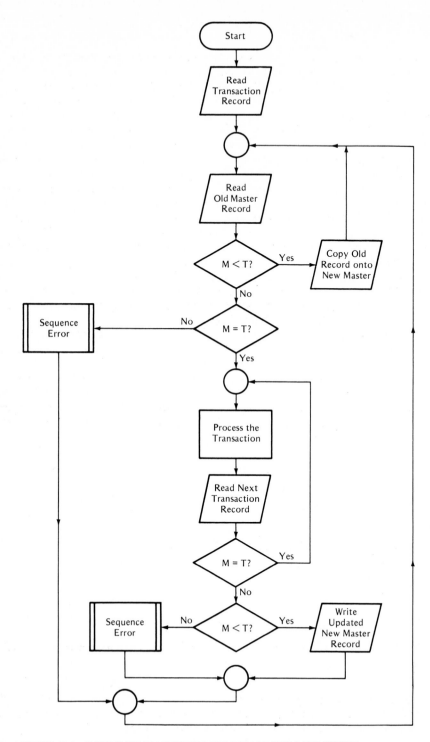

FIGURE 10-8   FLOWCHART ILLUSTRATING THE FILE UPDATING PROCEDURE.

Following the sequence of events on the flowchart of Figure 10-8, the first record of the master file (part number 03561) and the record of the first transaction (part number 10513) are read. The comparison indicates that the master stock number is less than the transaction stock number. This means that no transactions occurred for part number 03561, and therefore the entire record is written on the new master with no change. Following the sequence of the flowchart, the next master record is read (part number 10513). The first comparison indicates that the part number in the master record is not smaller than the part number in the transaction record. The second comparison indicates that they are equal. If they were not equal and therefore if the part number in the transaction record were smaller than the part number in the master record, this would have indicated an error condition involving an improper sequencing of one of the files. Once the equality has been established, the transaction is processed. In the case of the first transaction record this means that we check the code (2 = issue) and subtract the transaction amount (50) from the previous balance of 800.

Then we read the next transaction record. Its part number is equal to the part number in the previously read record, and so we are still dealing with the same part. We process this record and go on to read the next transaction record, which has a different part number. This means we have processed all the transactions for part number 10513. As indicated in Figure 10-8, next a comparison is made to determine if the new transaction part number is greater than the master part number with which we have been dealing. If it is less, the files have not been properly sorted. If no sequence error has occurred, the updated record will be written on the new master file.

The updating process continues in the way described above until all the transaction records have been read and processed, or until an error condition is detected. The reader should trace the logic associated with processing the remaining records and should check the results with the following figures, which show the new master records at the end of the updating process.

PART NUMBER	ITEM NAME	UNITS
03561	½ HP EL MOTOR	2000
10513	TRANSFORMER	650
30561	GEAR TRAIN	6940

REVIEW

1   The type of data access that is associated with the use of magnetic tape is called
_____ access.

sequential

2   The sequential access feature of magnetic tape makes it highly desirable that the master file and the transactions file to be used for the purpose of updating have items arranged in the [same / reverse] sequential order.

same

3   When only one backup file is kept in an updating procedure, the two files are called the new master and the old master. When a second historical backup file is kept, it is called the _____.

grand old master

4   In the comparisons made between the part number in the transaction record and the part number in the master record in our flowchart example, an error in sequencing was indicated if the transaction part number was [smaller / larger] than the master part number.

smaller (which would indicate that the
part number in the master file had already
been passed)

COBOL LANGUAGE INSTRUCTIONS FOR TAPE FILES

Business applications of COBOL most often involve data files recorded on magnetic tape. In fact, several COBOL instructions are meaningful only in reference to magnetic tape files. In the discussion below we describe those language instructions that are particularly pertinent to magnetic tape files. We will do so according to the program divisions. Of course, no special instructions are found in the IDENTIFICATION DIVISION.

ENVIRONMENT DIVISION INSTRUCTIONS
The following statements in the FILE-CONTROL paragraph of the INPUT-OUTPUT SECTION have special meaning with respect to tape files.

```
SELECT     [OPTIONAL]     file-name

     ASSIGN TO tape-unit-1     [, tape-unit-2]...


 ⎡                        ⎡ AREA  ⎤ ⎤
 ⎢ ; RESERVE integer-1    ⎢       ⎥ ⎥
 ⎣                        ⎣ AREAS ⎦ ⎦
```

The instruction for each file must start with the key word SELECT. OPTIONAL can only be used with input files, and its inclusion signifies that a file may or may not be present. In a tape file procedure we may have two input files: one containing current transactions, and the other, corrected previous error transactions. The second file may be declared OPTIONAL if we anticipate occasions of no previous error transactions. (Of course, the program logic is responsible for handling the presence or absence of an optional file.)

The "ASSIGN TO tape-unit" clause specifies that the tape unit is declared in different ways. In the case of IBM compilers we may use complex codes such as ASSIGN TO SYS005-UT-3410-S-MAST. Most other manufacturers use simpler codes, such as ASSIGN TO TAPE-UNIT MR02. Obviously, one has to consult local computer personnel for the prevailing terminology.

If the file consists of more than one reel, we may assign more than one tape unit to the file; hence the option "[, tape-unit-2] . . ." in the general instruction format above. Once the first reel is processed, processing will continue with the second reel and then any subsequent reels. If only one tape unit is used for a multireel file, the alternative procedure requires that the first reel be rewound and manually removed and that the new reel be threaded through before processing can continue. This matter is also discussed in connection with the CLOSE . . . FOR REMOVAL option later in this section.

The RESERVE clause given in the general instruction format above requires some explanation. The normal procedure with tape files is not to use this optional clause, in which case two areas, called *buffer areas,* are set aside in the internal storage of the computer for each file. This includes one necessary area plus one alternate area. The size of each area is equal to the block size in terms of the number of characters. The function of the alternate area is to make it possible to have overlap between input/ output and central processing. By "overlap" we mean that central processing can be applied to one set of data while another set is being read in or read out. This capability is particularly important in modern computer systems, for which central processing and input/output speeds are normally mismatched. If the RESERVE 1 AREA is used, no alternate buffer area is available and therefore no overlap is possible. Because the operating system routinely allocates a predetermined number of buffer areas, the RESERVE clause is seldom used.

The I-O-CONTROL paragraph of the INPUT-OUTPUT SECTION of the ENVIRON-MENT DIVISION can be used to express some aspects particular to tape files (page 260).

The RERUN clause can be used to instruct the computer to dump the program status as it is in internal storage onto a device—commonly a magnetic tape. Such a periodic recording of the program status permits restart of the program from the "middle," should an interruption become necessary. Such "checkpoints" are particularly useful in long program runs. For example, suppose a file update program has been running for 1 hour and there is a physical imperfection in the transactions tape, so that the last few transactions cannot be processed. Rather than correct the situation and rerun the entire program from its beginning, we could interrupt and restart it from the point where the last program status was recorded. The EVERY integer RECORDS clause specifies how often we record the program status. For example, we may have:

RERUN ON tape-unit-1 EVERY 1000 RECORDS OF TRANSACTION-FILE.

In the case of the above example, at most we would have to reprocess 1,000 TRANSACTION-FILE records should a program interruption occur. Additional options are available with the RERUN clause, which are self-explanatory for the most part, although their use is encountered in advanced applications and therefore we do not deliberate on them.

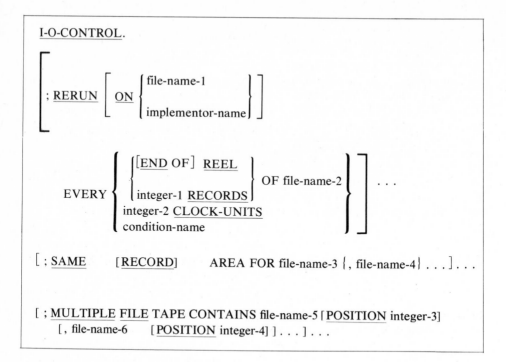

The SAME RECORD AREA clause allows two or more files to share the same internal storage area. This option would be used if the internal storage available were insufficient, and two files were not in use at the same time. As an example we have:

SAME RECORD AREA FOR MONTHLY-FILE, QUARTERLY-FILE.

The MULTIPLE FILE clause can be used when more than one file is recorded on the same tape reel. The POSITION integer specifies the relative position of the file—in effect, whether the file is in the first position, the second, the third, etc. For example,

MULTIPLE FILE TAPE CONTAINS WEEKLY-FILE POSITION 2, MONTHLY-FILE POSITION 4

could mean that WEEKLY-FILE is the second file in the reel and MONTHLY-FILE is the fourth file in the reel.

REVIEW

1   In the FILE-CONTROL SECTION of the ENVIRONMENT DIVISION the instruction for each file must start with the key word [SELECT / RESERVE], followed by the file-name.

SELECT

2   The ASSIGN TO tape-unit clause identifies the _____ to be used with each file.

tape unit

3   The number of tape units assigned to a file is usually [less than / equal to / greater than] the number of reels that make up that file.

equal to

4   If the RESERVE AREAS clause is not used in the FILE-CONTROL SECTION, then the number of storage areas, or buffers, that will be set aside for each file is _____ (number).

two

5   By the use of buffers the computer can be used more efficiently, because of the _____ made possible between input/output and central processing.

overlap

6   In the I-O-CONTROL paragraph of the INPUT-OUTPUT SECTION the RERUN clause is used to record program status [at periodic points during data processing / when an error condition is detected during the run].

at periodic points during data processing

7   The SAME RECORD AREA clause is generally used in order to conserve the number of [tape reels / storage areas] that need to be used.

storage areas

8   The MULTIPLE FILE clause is used in the INPUT-OUTPUT SECTION when more than one file is recorded on the same tape reel. The POSITION integer specified the relative position of the _____ on the _____.

file; reel

DATA DIVISION INSTRUCTIONS

The general format of instructions for the DATA DIVISION, some of which are particularly meaningful for tape files, is shown on the following page.

FD marks the beginning of a file description entry and is immediately followed by the name of the file. The name of the file has already been declared in the ENVIRON-MENT DIVISION, where it was assigned to a hardware device.

If tape records are grouped together, the BLOCK CONTAINS clause is used. If each record constitutes one block, the clause may be omitted or the equivalent BLOCK CONTAINS 1 RECORD can be used. When a block contains several records, then the clause must be used. Typically, this clause is used with the RECORDS option indicated above. In such a case it references the number of records per block. For example, if we have:

FD   TAPE-FILE BLOCK CONTAINS 10 RECORDS

each block will contain 10 records. However, if the records are of variable size, BLOCK CONTAINS 10 RECORDS will be interpreted to mean the maximum block size. Thus if the records varied between 10 and 100 characters (this would be so identified in the record description), BLOCK CONTAINS 10 RECORDS would mean that blocks can be

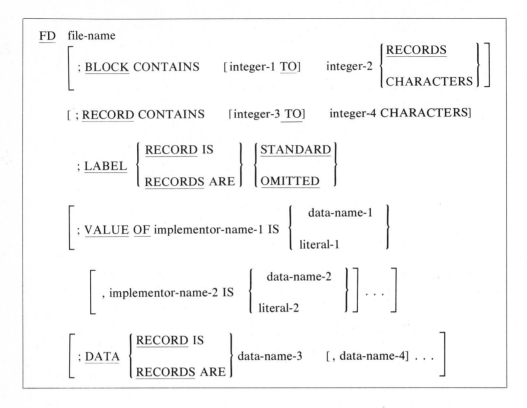

as short as 10 × 10 = 100 characters in length or as long as 10 × 100 = 1,000 characters in length. (Actually, the number of characters will be slightly different, depending on the *control fields* used by different compilers in recording variable-length blocks.)

If the option

FD   TAPE-FILE BLOCK CONTAINS 5 TO 12 RECORDS

were used, it would imply that the number of records per block may be a number between 5 and 12, again giving variable block size.

The option BLOCK CONTAINS integer CHARACTERS is used when the block contains "padding"—the last part of the block may consist of unusable characters. This could be the case when it is desired that block size be fixed but, because of variable record length, it is not possible to fill the entire block without splitting records across blocks.

RECORD CONTAINS [integer-1 TO] integer-2 CHARACTERS can be used for documentary purposes only. The record description will provide all such information to the compiler since, we recall, the record description specifies all the fields and their length. However, you may wonder how the record description is written for a variable-length record, such as corresponds to RECORD CONTAINS 20 TO 250 CHARACTERS. Up to now we have considered only fixed-length records. The subject will be covered in Chapter 14, "Table Handling," in reference to the OCCURS clause with the DEPENDING ON option.

The LABEL RECORDS clause is required for all files. The OMITTED option indicates that the file has no beginning or ending label. If the STANDARD option is used, it is understood to be the standard labels for the particular computer installation. The natural question may be: Granted that they are "standard" for an installation, how do we communicate in the context of the program what the label should be? We said earlier that the label record contains data that identifies the file, and obviously each file is uniquely identified. There are two basic ways of saying what the label contents should be. By the first approach (common in IBM computer systems), this information is communicated through program control cards submitted with the COBOL program. In other words, this information is not communicated, strictly speaking, in the COBOL program language. Another way of communicating the contents of label records is by use of the VALUE OF clause. For example, we could have for a particular case:

```
FD   PAYROLL-FILE BLOCK CONTAINS 10 RECORDS
       LABEL RECORDS ARE STANDARD
       VALUE OF IDENTIFICATION IS "A2359"
       RETENTION-PERIOD IS 090
       DATA RECORD IS PAY-REC.
```

In the above example the words IDENTIFICATION and RETENTION-PERIOD are meaningful in a particular installation, and they indicate that the STANDARD label contains a field called IDENTIFICATION whose content should be A2359. When the file is opened, the field is checked to ascertain that the A2359 data is there, in other words, that the correct tape has been mounted. The RETENTION-PERIOD field implies that this file cannot be written on until 90 days have elapsed. Of course, other similar fields are used in the VALUE clause option.

The example DATA RECORDS ARE REC-1, REC-2 implies that the file contains two types of records.

As a way of summarizing the discussion in this section, the following are examples of file descriptions in the DATA DIVISION that are concerned with magnetic tape files.

```
FD   TAPE-FILE-SAMPLE   BLOCK CONTAINS 10 RECORDS
                         RECORD CONTAINS 80 CHARACTERS
                         LABEL RECORDS ARE OMITTED
                         DATA RECORD IS SAMPLE-REC.

FD   FILE-A             BLOCK CONTAINS 600 CHARACTERS
                         LABEL RECORD IS STANDARD
                            VALUE OF IDENTIFICATION IS "A1-2B"
                         DATA RECORD IS REC.

FD   FILE-SIMPLE        LABEL RECORDS OMITTED
                         DATA RECORD IS SIMPLE-REC.
```

REVIEW

1   With reference to the sample file descriptions above, the names of the three files are _____, _____, and _____, respectively.

TAPE-FILE-SAMPLE; FILE-A; FILE-SIMPLE

2 The file description above in which each block contains one record is the [first / second / third] description. The file-description in which the record size can be variable is the [first / second / third] description.

third; second

3 The file description above which includes a label record is the [first / second / third] description. The file description which includes the optional VALUE OF clause is the [first / second / third] description.

second; second

PROCEDURE DIVISION INSTRUCTIONS

As with any file, prior to any reference to a tape file the file must be opened. The file is opened and declared to be input or output as follows:

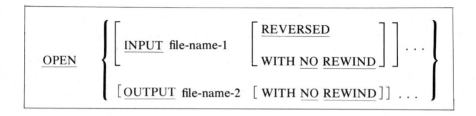

For input files the OPEN verb initiates a test of the label of the tape files if the label has not been omitted. For output files OPEN initiates the writing of a header (beginning of tape) label according to the specifications of the particular installation.

If an input file is designated with the OPTIONAL phrase in its SELECT clause, the first READ will cause the AT END condition to occur if the file is not present.

The REVERSED option can be used with tape files that can be read backward. When the REVERSED phrase is specified, the file is positioned at its end by execution of the OPEN statement.

If the INPUT . . . WITH NO REWIND option is used, the file must be at its beginning. If the option is omitted, then an OPEN command automatically rewinds the reel, if needed, and positions it at its beginning.

If the OUTPUT . . . WITH NO REWIND option is used, it normally means that a second or third (etc.) file will be recorded on the same reel. If OPEN OUTPUT file-name is used without the NO REWIND option, the file will be rewound to the beginning of the reel should it not be there when the OPEN instruction is executed.

Each tape file is closed as in the format at the top of page 265.

Prior to closing, a file must have been opened. "CLOSE file-name" results in end-of-file procedures. If label records have not been omitted, a trailer label is written and the tape is automatically rewound. If the option CLOSE file-name REEL is used, this results in closing that reel but not the file as such. Thus, the file itself will still be in an open status. The only circumstances under which the REEL option is used is in the case of multireel files, in which case the processing of a particular reel for a file may have been completed but other reels for the file might still remain to be processed. The NO

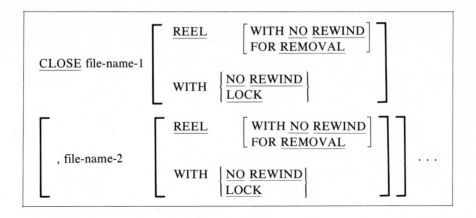

REWIND option prevents the rewinding that otherwise is automatically effected by the CLOSE verb. One circumstance in which the user would not want to rewind the tape is when a second file subsequently is to be read from or written on the same tape reel. When the LOCK option indicated above is used instead, the file is locked once the tape is rewound and can be reopened only by rerunning the entire program. The LOCK option thereby serves as protection against accidentally opening and misusing a file whose data has already been processed. The FOR REMOVAL option is used to allow the operator to intervene, remove the reel (at least, logically), and replace it with another reel. The specific procedure which should take place in conjunction with using the FOR REMOVAL option is not defined by COBOL. Rather, it is determined by the user.

The READ and WRITE verbs are the same for tape files as they are for other files. However, when tape records are organized into blocks, there are certain unique operations resulting from use of the standard input and output verbs. If blocked records are assumed, a READ file-name RECORD command will result in the first *whole* block being read from tape into the storage of the computer, rather than just the first record as such. However, only the first record is accessible to the programmer at this point. Conceptually, this can be represented as in Figure 10-9. The block buffer

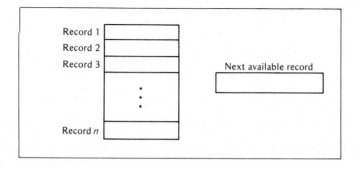

FIGURE 10-9   READING OF A BLOCK OF RECORDS WHEN A READ FILE-NAME RECORD COMMAND IS EXECUTED.

is filled with all the records in the block. Imagine then another field, call it "next available record," containing a copy of the first record. Now, when the READ command is executed a second time for the same file, no physical activity will take place at the tape unit. Rather, the second record will be transferred from the buffer to the "next available record." The process will continue in this way for each subsequent READ command until the last record of the block has been read. When the $(n + 1)$th record is to be read, the next block will be read into the buffer and the process repeated.

On the output side, when the first WRITE command is executed for a blocked tape file, no writing takes place on the tape. Rather, the first output record is written on the first cell of the buffer. As each subsequent WRITE command is executed, the records are accumulated in the buffer until the buffer is full, at which point a physical tape write will occur. The process continues in this fashion until all output records have been written on the tape.

REVIEW

1   As with any other type of input or output file, before any instruction can be executed for a tape file the file must be _____.

opened

2   When an input file is opened, a test is made of the _____ of the tape file as a matter of routine. When an output file is opened, a header _____ is written at the beginning of the tape according to the specifications of the computer installation.

label; label

3   The CLOSE file-name REEL option is used only in the case of _____ files.

multireel

4   The option in the closing routine which serves to protect the file from use (and misuse) is the [NO REWIND / LOCK] option, whereas the option that permits further use of the reel is the [NO REWIND / LOCK] option.

LOCK; NO REWIND

5   When there are several records in each block, execution of the READ command with a tape file results in one [record / block] being read.

block

6   In the case of executing either READ or WRITE statements, the block buffer is used for storing the contents of [one / several] records.

several

A SAMPLE CARD-TO-TAPE PROGRAM

In order to illustrate some of the concepts discussed in this chapter, we now present a sample program concerned with the use of tape files.

The programming objective is to transfer data from cards to tape, thus creating a tape file. The cards contain a part number in columns 1–5, an item-name in columns 6–19, and a quantity in columns 20–24. It is desired to record the data on the tape file, using a blocking factor of 5, that is, five records per block.

Exhibit 10-1 presents a COBOL program to accomplish the data processing task specified above. The program logic is straightforward. We will read cards and write

EXHIBIT 10-1   SAMPLE CARD-TO-TAPE PROGRAM

```
IDENTIFICATION DIVISION.
PROGRAM-ID. CARDTAPE.
ENVIRONMENT DIVISION.
CONFIGURATION SECTION.
SOURCE-COMPUTER.   Computer-name.
OBJECT-COMPUTER.   Computer-name.
INPUT-OUTPUT SECTION.
FILE-CONTROL.
     SELECT BALANCE-CARD   ASSIGN TO Card-reader.
     SELECT OLD-MASTER       ASSIGN TO Tape-unit-1.
DATA DIVISION.
FILE SECTION.
FD BALANCE-CARD, LABEL RECORD IS OMITTED
     DATA RECORD IS BAL-CARD.
01   BAL-CARD.
     02   BALANCE-DATA.
          03   ITEM-NUMBER                   PICTURE 99999.
          03   PART-NUMBER                   PICTURE X(14).
          03   ITEM-NAME                     PICTURE 99999.
     02   FILLER                             PICTURE X(56).
FD   OLD-MASTER, LABEL RECORDS OMITTED
     DATA RECORD IS OLD-BALANCE-RECORD
     BLOCK CONTAINS 5 RECORDS.
01   OLD-BALANCE-RECORD.
     02   NUMBER-IN-OLD-BALANCE             PICTURE 99999.
     02   NAME-IN-OLD-BALANCE              PICTURE X(14).
     02   QUANTITY-IN-OLD-BALANCE         PICTURE 99999.
WORKING-STORAGE SECTION.
01   END-OF-DATA                            PICTURE XXX.
PROCEDURE DIVISION.
MAIN-ROUTINE.
     MOVE 'NO' TO END-OF-DATA.
     OPEN INPUT BALANCE-CARD
          OUTPUT OLD-MASTER.
     READ BALANCE-CARD
          AT END MOVE 'YES' TO END-OF-DATA.
     PERFORM READ-WRITE
          UNTIL END-OF-DATA = 'YES'.
     CLOSE BALANCE-CARD OLD-MASTER.
     STOP RUN.
READ-WRITE.
     MOVE BALANCE-DATA TO OLD-BALANCE-RECORD
     WRITE OLD-BALANCE-RECORD.
     READ BALANCE-CARD
          AT END MOVE 'YES' TO END-OF-DATA.
```

them on tape until all the cards have been read. Note that, once the blocking factor is specified in the DATA DIVISION, the programmer need not consider that fact any more. The compiler automatically substitutes those instructions which accumulate five card records before writing the entire block of five records on the tape.

Notice that the DATA DIVISION entries are expressed in greater detail than is necessary in this application. If our sole interest were in simply copying data from cards onto tape, we could have written, for instance,

```
01   BAL-CARD.
     02   RELEVANT-DATA        PICTURE X(24).
     02   FILLER               PICTURE X(56).
01   OLD-BALANCE-RECORD        PICTURE X(24).
```

This arrangement would have simplified our DATA DIVISION. The sample program in Exhibit 10-1 provides an illustration for the more general case in which we may want to separate fields so that we can reference them in the course of program processing.

EXAMPLE OF FILE UPDATE LOGIC

The updating of sequential tape files is a common procedure in business data processing. The specific steps vary with each application. Still, we can discern a common logic characterizing all such update procedures, and we therefore present here an outline of this common logic. We believe that this suggested structure can serve as the basis for most sequential file updating procedures.

Exhibit 10-2 presents an outline of the program structure that can be used to update a tape file. A summary of the procedure is contained in the MAIN paragraph. Three program control switches are used: END-OF-T, END-OF-M, and END-OF-PROG. Initially, they are set to zero. When in the course of the program they are set to 1, they signify the end of transactions, the end of master file records, and the end of program, respectively.

Figure 10-10 presents flowcharts corresponding to the program outline. The student will find it instructive and effort-reducing to follow this outline in working assigned exercises concerned with file updating.

Exhibit 10-3 illustrates the application of the generalized updating outline to a specific simple task. Master records consist of a customer number, a customer name, and address. Transaction records consist of a customer number, a transaction code (1 = change name, 2 = change address), a name field, and an address field. The program is self-documenting and can be followed rather easily. The first part of the program illustrates the creation of a master file in the same program as the updating of that file. Such a practice may be desirable in a student environment where it is impractical to maintain permanent master files just for student programming purposes.

EXHIBIT 10-2   PROGRAM OUTLINE FOR A SEQUENTIAL FILE UPDATING PROCEDURE

```
MAIN.
    PERFORM INITIALIZATION.
    PERFORM READ-TRANS.
    PERFORM READ-MASTER.
    PERFORM PROCESSING
        UNTIL END-OF-PROG = 1.
    PERFORM WRAPUP.
    STOP RUN.

INITIALIZATION.
    OPEN FILES . . .
    MOVE ZERO TO   END-OF-T
                   END-OF-M
                   END-OF-PROG.
        .
        .
        .
    etc.

READ-TRANS.
    READ transaction-file RECORD
        AT END MOVE 1 TO END-OF-T.

READ-MASTER.
    READ mster-file RECORD
        AT END MOVE 1 TO END-OF-M.

WRAPUP.
        .
        .
        .
    CLOSE files
    etc.

PROCESSING.
    IF END-OF-T = 1
        PERFORM COPY-MASTER
            UNTIL END-OF-M = 1
        MOVE 1 TO END-OF-PROG
    ELSE
        IF END-OF-M = 1
            PERFORM LEFTOVER-TRANS
            MOVE 1 TO END-OF-PROG
        ELSE
            IF MASTER-NO < TRANSACTION-NO
                PERFORM COPY-MASTER
            ELSE
                IF MASTER-NO = TRANSACTION-NO
                    PERFORM-MATCHING
                ELSE
                    PERFORM SEQ-ERROR
                    or ADD-RECORD.
```

EXHIBIT 10-2 PROGRAM OUTLINE FOR A SEQUENTIAL FILE UPDATING PROCEDURE *(Continued)*

LEFT-OVER-TRANS.
    If new records can be added to the master file,
        PERFORM ADD-RECORD
           UNTIL END-OF-T = 1.
    If new records are not part of the procedure, then treat
    this as an error condition.

SEQ-ERROR.
    Possibly print an error message and/or bypass the current record,
    or set END-OF-PROG = 1 to terminate the run so that the files can
    be sorted in proper sequence.

MATCHING.
    PERFORM PROCESS-EQUAL
        UNTIL MASTER-NO NOT = TRANSACTION-NO
           OR END-OF-T = 1.
    IF MASTER-NO < TRANSACTION-NO
           OR END-OF-T = 1
        write new master record unless a deletion
        PERFORM READ-MASTER
    ELSE
        PERFORM SEQ-ERROR.

PROCESS-EQUAL.
    Do required processing.
    PERFORM READ-TRANS.

COPY-MASTER.
    Copy old master onto new master
    PERFORM READ-MASTER.

ADD-RECORD.
    Form a new record and write it on the updated file.
    PERFORM READ-TRANS.

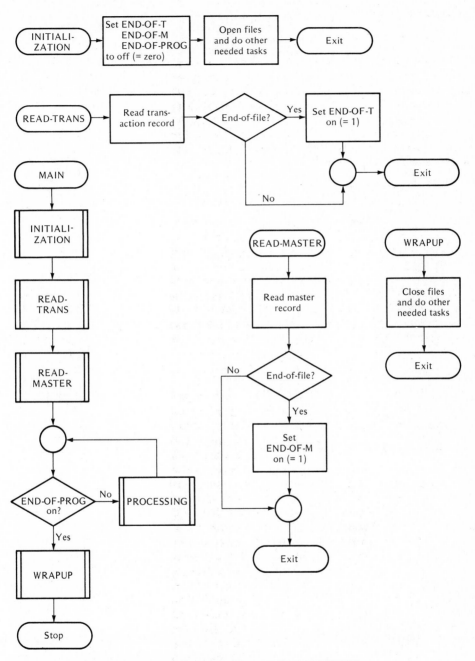

FIGURE 10-10   FLOWCHARTS FOR A SEQUENTIAL FILE UPDATING PROCEDURE.

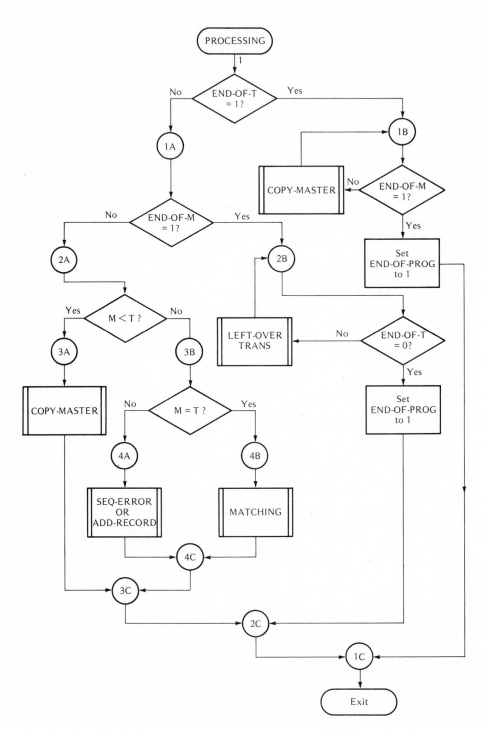

FIGURE 10-10 FLOWCHARTS FOR A SEQUENTIAL FILE UPDATING PROCEDURE *(Continued)*.

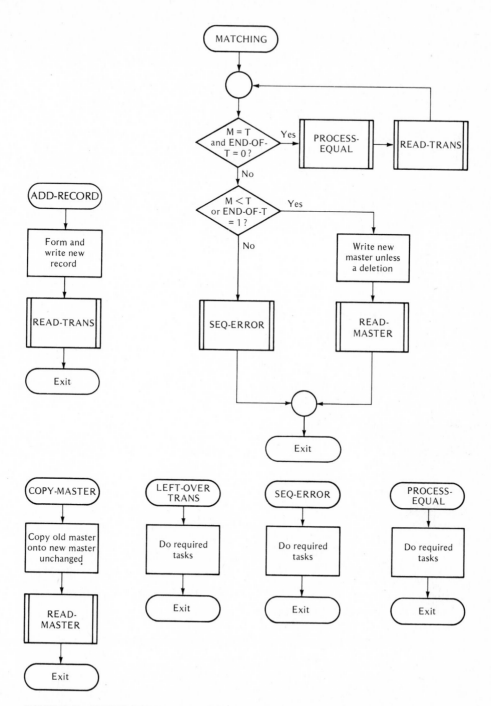

FIGURE 10-10   FLOWCHARTS FOR A SEQUENTIAL FILE UPDATING PROCEDURE *(Continued).*

EXHIBIT 10-3   SAMPLE SEQUENTIAL FILE UPDATING PROGRAM

```
IDENTIFICATION DIVISION.
PROGRAM-ID.  SIMPLEUPDATE.
ENVIRONMENT DIVISION.
CONFIGURATION SECTION.
SOURCE-COMPUTER.
OBJECT-COMPUTER.
INPUT-OUTPUT SECTION.
FILE-CONTROL.
    SELECT OLD-MASTER ASSIGN TO TAPEA.
    SELECT NEW-MASTER ASSIGN TO TAPEB.
    SELECT TRANS-FILE ASSIGN TO CARD-READER.
    SELECT PRINT-FILE ASSIGN TO PRINTER.
DATA DIVISION.
FILE SECTION.
FD  OLD-MASTER LABEL RECORDS OMITTED
                  BLOCK CONTAINS 5 RECORDS
                  DATA RECORD IS OLD-MASTER-REC.
01  OLD-MASTER-REC.
    02 CUST-NO-OM      PIC 99999.
    02 CUST-NAME-OM    PIC X(20).
    02 CUST-ADDRESS-OM PIC X(50).
*
FD  NEW-MASTER LABEL RECORDS OMITTED
                  BLOCK CONTAINS 5 RECORDS
                  DATA RECORD IS NEW-MASTER REC.
01  NEW-MASTER-REC.
    02 CUST-NO-NM      PIC 99999.
    02 CUST-NAME-NM    PIC X(20).
    02 CUST-ADDRESS-NM PIC X(50).
*
FD  TRANS-FILE LABEL RECORDS OMITTED
                  DATA RECORDS ARE MASTER-IMAGE
                  TRANSACTION-REC.
01  MASTER-IMAGE         PIC X(80).
*
01  TRANSACTION-REC.
    02 CUST-NO-T       PIC 99999.
    02 TRANS-CODE      PIC 9.
    02 CUST-NAME-T     PIC X(20).
    02 CUST-ADDRESS-T  PIC X(50).
    02 FILLER          PIC XXXX.
*
FD  PRINT-FILE LABEL RECORDS ARE OMITTED
                  DATA RECORD IS PRINT-REC.
01  PRINT-REC           PIC X(132).
*
WORKING-STORAGE SECTION.
01  END-OF-T           PIC 9.
01  END-OF-M           PIC 9.
01  END-OF-PROG        PIC 9.
01  ERROR-REC.
    02 FILLER              PIC X VALUE SPACE.
    02 TRANSACTION-IMAGE PIC X(71).
    02 FILLER              PIC X(5) VALUE SPACES.
    02 ERROR-MESSAGE    PIC X(55).

PROCEDURE DIVISION.
*
*
***THIS SECTION WILL READ CARDS AND TRANSFER THEM
*   ONTO THE OLD MASTER FILE, THUS CREATING AN OLD-MASTER.
*THIS IS A QUICK-AND-DIRTY WAY OF CREATING A FILE FOR
*   STUDENT USE
*
BUILD-MASTER SECTION.
*
MAIN-ROUTINE.
    MOVE ZERO TO END-OF-T.
    OPEN INPUT TRANS-FILE
         OUTPUT OLD-MASTER.
    READ TRANS-FILE AT END MOVE 1 TO END-OF-T.
    PERFORM READ-WRITE
        UNTIL END-OF-T = 1.
    CLOSE TRANS-FILE  OLD-MASTER
    GO TO UPDATE-MASTER.
*
READ-WRITE.
    WRITE OLD-MASTER-REC FROM MASTER-IMAGE.
    PERFORM READ-TRANS.
*
UPDATE-MASTER SECTION.
```

EXHIBIT 10-3   SAMPLE SEQUENTIAL FILE UPDATING PROGRAM *(Continued)*.

```
*
 MAIN-ROUTINE.
      PERFORM INITIALIZATION.
      PERFORM PROCESS-IT
          UNTIL END-OF-PROG = 1.
      CLOSE OLD-MASTER
            NEW-MASTER
            TRANS-FILE
            PRINT-FILE.
      STOP RUN.
*
 PROCESS-IT.
      IF END-OF-T = 1
          PERFORM COPY-MASTER
              UNTIL END-OF-M = 1
          MOVE 1 TO END-OF-PROG
      ELSE
          IF END-OF-M = 1
              PERFORM SEQUENCE-ERROR
              MOVE 1 TO END-OF-PROG
          ELSE
              PERFORM MATCHING.
*
 MATCHING.
      IF CUST-NO-T = CUST-NO-OM
          PERFORM PROCESS-EQUAL
      ELSE
          IF CUST-NO-T > CUST-NO-OM
              PERFORM COPY-MASTER
          ELSE
              PERFORM SEQUENCE-ERROR.

 PROCESS-EQUAL.
      IF TRANS-CODE = 1
          PERFORM CHANGE-NAME
      ELSE
          IF TRANS-CODE = 2
              PERFORM CHANGE-ADDRESS
          ELSE
              PERFORM CODE-ERROR.
      PERFORM READ-TRANS.

*
 INITIALIZATION.
      MOVE ZERO TO END-OF-T
                   END-OF-M
                   END-OF-PROG.
      OPEN INPUT  OLD-MASTER
                  TRANS-FILE

           OUTPUT NEW-MASTER
                  PRINT-FILE.
      PERFORM READ-TRANS.
      PERFORM READ-MASTER.
*
 READ-TRANS.
      READ TRANS-FILE RECORD AT END MOVE 1 TO END-OF-T.
 READ-MASTER.
      READ OLD-MASTER RECORD AT END MOVE 1 TO END-OF-M.
 CHANGE-NAME.
      MOVE CUST-NO-OM TO CUST-NO-NM
      MOVE CUST-NAME-T TO CUST-NAME-NM
      MOVE CUST-ADDRESS-OM TO CUST-ADDRESS-NM
      WRITE PRINT-REC FROM NEW-MASTER-REC AFTER 1 LINE
      WRITE NEW-MASTER-REC.
      PERFORM READ-MASTER.

*
 CHANGE-ADDRESS.
      MOVE CUST-NO-OM TO CUST-NO-NM
      MOVE CUST-NAME-OM TO CUST-NAME-NM
      MOVE CUST-ADDRESS-T TO CUST-ADDRESS-NM
      WRITE PRINT-REC FROM NEW-MASTER-REC AFTER 1 LINE
      WRITE NEW-MASTER-REC
      PERFORM READ-MASTER.
```

EXHIBIT 10-3 SAMPLE SEQUENTIAL FILE UPDATING PROGRAM *(Continued)*

```
*
 CODE-ERROR.
     MOVE TRANSACTION-REC TO TRANSACTION-IMAGE
     MOVE 'THIS TRANSACTION CONTAINS A CODE ERROR'
        TO ERROR-MESSAGE.
     WRITE PRINT-REC FROM ERROR-REC AFTER ADVANCING 1 LINE.
*
 SEQUENCE-ERROR.
     MOVE TRANSACTION-REC TO TRANSACTION-IMAGE
     MOVE 'THIS TRANSACTION IS OUT OF SEQUENCE'
        TO ERROR-MESSAGE
     WRITE PRINT-REC FROM ERROR-REC AFTER ADVANCING 1 LINE.
     MOVE OLD-MASTER-REC TO TRANSACTION-IMAGE
     MOVE 'CORRESPONDING MASTER RECORD' TO ERROR-MESSAGE
     WRITE PRINT-REC FROM ERROR-REC AFTER ADVANCING 1 LINE.
*
 COPY-MASTER.
     WRITE NEW-MASTER-REC FROM OLD-MASTER-REC
     WRITE PRINT-REC FROM OLD-MASTER-REC
     PERFORM READ-MASTER.
```

EXERCISES

1   A common business application involves the merging of two files to form one file. Perhaps you have been exposed to the card handling device called a *collator* which, among other functions, can take two card decks and merge them into one. If the two files are sorted, the merging procedure results in a new sorted file. In this case we want to merge two tape files so that the printed listing is in order.

Let us consider first the flowchart of the merging logic (page 277). We assume that we have two input tapes called TAPE-A and TAPE-B. The comparison of A to B refers to a comparison of the fields on the basis of which the two files are sorted.

Following are the first three program divisions to be used in this exercise. Assume that the merging is performed by comparisons of the A-NAME and B-NAME fields, but that the entire TA and TB records are printed.

```
IDENTIFICATION DIVISION.
PROGRAM-ID. MERGE.
ENVIRONMENT DIVISION.
CONFIGURATION SECTION.
SOURCE-COMPUTER. Computer-name.
OBJECT-COMPUTER. Computer-name
INPUT-OUTPUT SECTION.
FILE-CONTROL.
     SELECT LINE-IMAGE    ASSIGN TO    Printer-device.
     SELECT TAPE-A        ASSIGN TO    Tape-device-1.
     SELECT TAPE-B        ASSIGN TO    Tape-device-2.
DATA DIVISION.
FILE SECTION.
FD LINE-IMAGE LABEL RECORDS OMITTED DATA RECORD IS
     LINEOUT.
```

FLOWCHART FOR MERGING LOGIC

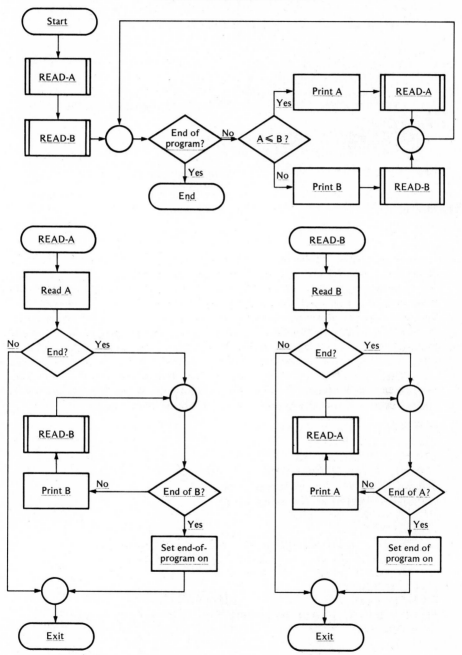

```
01  LINEOUT.
    02  OUT-1       PICTURE X(15).
    02  FILLER      PICTURE X(5).
    02  OUT-2       PICTURE X(65).
    02  FILLER      PICTURE X(47).
FD  TAPE-A LABEL RECORD OMITTED DATA RECORD IS TA.
01  TA.
    02  A-NAME      PICTURE X(15).
    02  A-REST      PICTURE X(65).
FD  TAPE-B LABEL RECORD OMITTED DATA RECORD IS TB.
01  TB.
    02  B-NAME      PICTURE X(15).
    02  B-REST      PICTURE X(65).
```

Write a PROCEDURE DIVISION to accomplish the merging task.

2   A company maintains inventory data on magnetic tape. The master file is sorted on part number and contains the following types of data for each item held in inventory.

FIELD	SIZE
Part number	5 numeric positions
Part name	15 alphanumeric positions
Quantity	5 numeric positions

For simplicity there are two types of transactions: receipts and issues. Each transaction is recorded on a punched card of the following format:

FIELD	SIZE
Part number	5 numeric positions
Transaction code	1 numeric position
1 = receipt	
2 = issue	
Quantity	5 numeric positions

Batches of transaction cards are accumulated and then processed to update the master file and to print a report which lists each part number, name, previous quantity balance, and new balance. When the transaction code is 1, the quantity is added; if the code is 2, the quantity is subtracted.

a Write a program to create the master file, on tape, from data on punched cards.

Sample input for the master tape

```
035611/2 HP EL MOTOR02000
10513TRANSFORMER      08000
30561GEAR  TRAIN-A    07890
30562GEAR  TRAIN-B    10250
30564GEAR  TRAIN-C    04650
30579GEAR  TRAIN-G    08529
40100STEEL  PLATE-1A  06099
40110STEEL  PLATE-2A  00852
40120STEEL  PLATE-3A  00996
40130STEEL  PLATE-4A  01250
40140STEEL  PLACE-5B  02899
40150STEEL  PLATE-3C  08192
51000BRASS  FTNGS-A   12695
51020BRASS  FTNGS-B   08569
51030BRASS  FTNGS-C   09992
60256BALL  BEARING-A201695
60257BALL  BEARING-A302561
60258BALL  BEARING-A410883
60259BALL  BEARING-A513429
60260BALL  BEARING-A608866
60261BALL  BEARING-A706219
```

b Draw a flowchart and write a program to update the master file, given a deck of transaction cards. The program should perform a sequence check to see that the cards are in the same sequence as the tape records. It is possible that some items may have no corresponding transactions, but no transactions are present for items not on the master tape.

Below is sample input for transactions (the master tape input is the same as shown in part a, above). The sample output is on page 281.

```
10513200200
10513110000
30562200500
30562200800
30562200900
30564108000
```

Sample input for transactions (continued)

40100112000
40100204000
40100203000
40140110000
51030200200
51030200965
60261200600
60261200500
60261200900
60261104000

3 The county assessor's office maintains a tape file of property owners, in the following (simplified) format:

Lot-number	9-digit code
Owner name	26 alphanumeric characters
Assessed valuation	8-digit field, including 2 decimal places

An update run involves reading card records and creating an updated tape file.

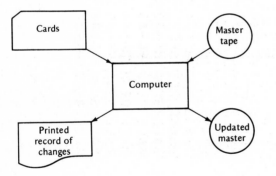

The input cards have the following format

Lot-number	9-digit code
Code	1-digit code

1 = change owner name
2 = change assessed valuation
3 = change both owner and valuation
4 = add to tax rolls
9 = remove from tax rolls

Owner name	26 characters
Assessed valuation	8 digits in dollars and cents

Sample Output

ITEM NUMBER	PART NAME	PREVIOUS BALANCE	NEW BALANCE
03561	1/2 HP EL MOTOR	2000	2000
10513	TRANSFORMER	8000	17800
30561	GEAR TRAIN-A	7890	7890
30562	GEAR TRAIN-B	10250	8050
30564	GEAR TRAIN-C	4650	12650
30579	GEAR TRAIN-G	8529	8529
40100	STEEL PLATE-1A	6099	11099
40110	STEEL PLATE-2A	0852	0852
40120	STEEL PLATE-3A	0996	0996
40130	STEEL PLATE-4A	1250	1250
40140	STEEL PLATE-5B	2899	12899
40150	STEEL PLATE-3C	8192	8192
51000	BRASS FTNGS-A	12695	12695
51020	BRASS FTNGS-B	8569	8569
51030	BRASS FTNGS-C	9992	8827
60256	BALL BEARING-A2	1695	1695
60257	BALL BEARING-A3	2561	2561
60258	BALL BEARING-A4	10883	10883
60259	BALL BEARING-A5	13429	13429
60260	BALL BEARING-A6	8866	8866
60261	BALL BEARING-A7	6219	8219

If a code of 1 is used, nothing is punched in the assessed valuation field. If a code of 2 is used, the owner field is blank, and a code of 9 implies that the card is blank from column 11 on.

The printer report should have the following approximate layout:

LOT NUMBER	OWNER	ASSESSED VALUE	NEW OWNER	NEW ASSESSMENT	OFF ROLLS
XXXXXXXXX	XXXXXXXX	$ XXXXXX.XX	XXXXXXXXX	$ XXXXXX.XX	
XXXXXXXXX	XXXXXXXX	XXXX.XX			***

Whenever an item is eliminated, it is signaled by three asterisks in the OFF ROLLS column.

Write a COBOL program to update such a file. The program should check for correct sequence in the card and tape records and for possibly erroneous codes in the card.

Sample master file

LOT NUMBER	OWNER NAME	ASSESSED VALUATION
000150000	JENKING, ANTHONY	10,872.00
000180000	ANDREWS, JULIA	256,237.00
000290000	THOMAS, THEODORE	162,116.00
000350000	MCDONALD, DONNA	769,276.00
000720000	MARTIN, JANE	99,998.00
001050000	RICHARDSON, PETER	820,600.00
001120000	SILVA, ROBIN	959,999.00

Sample card transaction records

LOT NUMBER	CODE	OWNER NAME	ASSESSED VALUATION
000180000	1	ANDREWS, THOMAS	
000290000	2		300,000.00
000720000	3	STEINMAN, WILLA	100,000.00
001050000	9		

Sample output (lack of space prevents showing the first name on the same line as the last name in the NEW OWNER column. However, on your output include this information on one line)

LOT NUMBER	OWNER	ASSESSED VALUE	NEW OWNER	NEW ASSESSMENT	OFF ROLLS
000150000	JENKING, ANTHONY	$ 10,872.00			
000180000	ANDREWS, JULIA	$256,237.00	ANDREWS, THOMAS		
000290000	THOMAS, THEODORE	$162,116.00		$300,000.00	
000350000	MCDONALD, DONNA	$769,276.00			
000720000	MARTIN, JANE	$ 99,998.00	STEINMAN, WILLA	$100,000.00	
001050000	RICHARDSON, PETER	$820,600.00			***
001120000	SILVA, ROBIN	$959,999.00			

4 A small publishing firm maintains a file of its magazine subscribers on magnetic tape. The magazine is published on a weekly schedule. Each week a computer program is run to print mailing labels for the current issue and to print notices to those subscribers whose subscription is about to expire.

The program runs in two phases. In the first phase the program reads a card containing the current date and then reads the master tape record by record. For each subscriber a test is performed to ascertain if the subscription has expired. If it has expired, the record is bypassed (this is not a realistic procedure but it is introduced to simplify the exercise). If the subscription has not expired, a mailing label is printed on the printer. If the subscription is going to expire within a certain period of time, note is made of the fact on a magnetic tape so that a subscription renewal reminder note may be mailed to the subscriber.

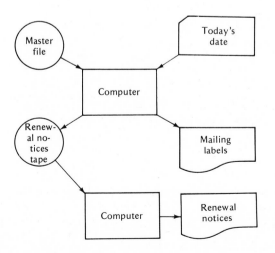

The following procedure is used in sending reminder notes. A first notice is sent if the subscription expires between the forty-fifth and thirty-eighth day from now. A second notice is sent if the subscription expires between the eighth and the fifteenth day from now. Looking at the diagram below, assume we are at point X. If the expiration date falls in the range D–E, we send a first notice. If it falls in

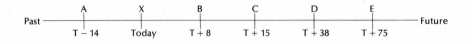

the range B–C, we send a second notice. If it falls to the *left* of A, the subscriber is bypassed. In other words, we continue to send the journal for 2 weeks past the expiration day (commonly done to ensure continuity for delayed subscription renewals).

Write a program to create the master file and to produce the type of output illustrated on page 286. The expiration day can be any day, and the program must be able to handle changes in years, for instance, the case where the current month is December and a subscription expires in January of the coming year.

Following is the input format to be used:

COLUMNS	MEANING
1–9	Customer code
10–30	Customer name
31–55	Street
56–70	State
71–75	ZIP code
76–80	Expiration date in Julian calendar form. The first two digits denote the year and the last three the day of expiration.

The expiration date is recorded in Julian calendar form, such that January 1 is 001, January 31 is 031, February 10 is 041, etc., as the last three digits.

Sample input

```
A19-HY139JAMES A. MCCORMICK  318 SOUTH LANE            MADISON, WI        5371077350
B28-NM318ABE KILIMANGARO     1936 N. MOUNTAINVIEW ST.  BOSTON, MA         0217578010
K23-MXN35PAUL S. BROOMFIELD  825 EAST BLACKTOP AVE.    LOS ANGELES     CA9006677300
N40-MA893ALEX V. MONTAGNE    193 SOUTH EDGWATER CIR.   CHICAGO, IL        6062077365
N41-31256DIANA A. FOREST     568 N. WASHINGTON ST.     LAS VEGAS, NV      8911178001
A13-B6358ROBERT L. ANDREWS   3182 WALNUT AVE.          ERIE, PA           1650377280
C21-K6399DONALD MUDD         562 NOLAN ST.             MIAMI, FL          3315277328
D21-K6400BRUCE BRIAN         1871 TYNDALL AVE.         PHOENIX, AZ        8502877327
D21-K6410JOHN JONES          132 PARK ST.              ATLANTA, GA        3032977297
D22-L1920DAVID BURR          6191 GRAND AVE.           KANSAS CITY, KS6610377290
D22-L1930JAMES LOFTON        3215 GEORGE ST.           BALTIMORE, MD      2120577298
D22-L5228JACOB STEIN         1817 LOYOLA DR.           ATHENS, OH         4570177325
```

Sample output (renewal notices assuming the current date to be 77290, on the Julian calendar)

PAUL S. BROOMFIELD
825 EAST BLACKTOP AVE.
LOS ANGELES, CA 90066

K23-MXN35

SECOND NOTICE

DEAR SUBSCRIBER.
    YOUR SUBSCRIPTION TO OUR MAGAZINE WILL EXPIRE IN 10 DAYS.
PLEASE RENEW YOUR SUBSCRIPTION BY COMPLETING AND RETURNING
THE ENCLOSED CARD. PROMPT ACTION IS URGED TO ASSURE YOU
OF UNINTERRUPTED SERVICE. IF YOU HAVE ALREADY SENT YOUR SUBSCRIPTION RENEWAL PLEASE
DISREGARD THIS NOTICE.

DONALD MUDD
562 NOLAN ST.
MIAMI, FL 33152

C21-K6399

FIRST NOTICE

DEAR SUBSCRIBER.
    YOUR SUBSCRIPTION TO OUR MAGAZINE WILL EXPIRE IN 38 DAYS.

286

PLEASE RENEW YOUR SUBSCRIPTION BY COMPLETING AND RETURNING
THE ENCLOSED CARD. PROMPT ACTION IS URGED TO ASSURE YOU
OF UNINTERRUPTED SERVICE. SENT YOUR SUBSCRIPTION RENEWAL PLEASE
IF YOU HAVE ALREADY SENT YOUR SUBSCRIPTION RENEWAL PLEASE
DISREGARD THIS NOTICE.

D22-L1930

JAMES LOFTON
3215 GEORGE ST.
BALTIMORE, MD 21205

SECOND NOTICE

DEAR SUBSCRIBER.
    YOUR SUBSCRIPTION TO OUR MAGAZINE WILL EXPIRE IN 08 DAYS.
PLEASE RENEW YOUR SUBSCRIPTION BY COMPLETING AND RETURNING
THE ENCLOSED CARD. PROMPT ACTION IS URGED TO ASSURE YOU
OF UNINTERRUPTED SERVICE. SENT YOUR SUBSCRIPTION RENEWAL PLEASE
IF YOU HAVE ALREADY SENT YOUR SUBSCRIPTION RENEWAL PLEASE
DISREGARD THIS NOTICE.

Sample output (mailing labels)

JAMES A. MCCORMICK   A19-HY139
318 SOUTH LANE
MADISON, WI   53710

ABE KILIMANGARO   B28-NM318
1936 N. MOUNTAINVIEW ST.
BOSTON, MA   02175

PAUL S. BROOMFIELD   K23-MXN35
825 EAST BLACKTOP AVE.
LOS ANGELES, CA   90066

ALEX V. MONTAGNE   N40-MA893
193 SOUTH EDGWATER CIR.
CHICAGO, IL   60620

DINA A. FOREST   N41-31256
568 N.WASHINGTON ST.
LAS VEGAS, NV   89111

ROBERT L. ANDREWS   A13-B6358
3182 WALNUT AVE.
ERIE, PA   16503

DONALD MUDD   C21-K6399
562 NOLAN ST.
MIAMI, FL   33152

BRUCE BRIAN   D21-K6400
1871 TYNDALL AVE.
PHOENIX, AZ   85022

JOHN JONES   D21-K6410
132 PARK ST.
ATLANTA, GA   30329

DAVID BURR   D22-L1920
6191 GRAND AVE.
KANSAS CITY, KS   66103

JAMES LOFTON   D22-L1930
3215 GEORGE ST.
BALTIMORE, MD   21205

JACOB STEIN   D22-L5228
1817 LOYOLA DR.
ATHENS, OH   45701

Batch Processing
of Sequential Files

INTRODUCTION

Information systems do not exist apart from organizational entities, but rather, they function in conjunction with ongoing *activity systems*. An activity system can be any complex task performed by such organizational entities as manufacturing plants, retail establishments, government agencies, military units, and nonprofit foundations. Information systems are designed to support activity systems by processing and storing information in such a way that a given information system reflects the state of the activity system. Specifically, the state of an activity system is indicated by the status of the files. In information systems, a *file* is a collection of data which has similar characteristics. Two kinds of files are generally identified in the context of batch processing of data: *Master files* and *Transactions*, or *Activity, files*.

Master files contain data which is relatively permanent in nature and which includes historical data up to some point in time at which the files were updated. Transactions files, on the other hand, contain temporary data to be used to alter and update Master files. Sometimes, however, legal or other institutional factors constrain us in the disposition of Transactions files. For example, a bank recording credit card charges may store such transactions data on magnetic tape or microfilm for use in subsequent audits or for questions that may arise about specific transactions.

Typically, the state of an activity system is very complex and is undergoing near-continuous change. The extent to which the information system indicates the state of the actual activity system is a function of the sophistication of the information system. In this context, a *real-time information system* is one which follows the evolving state of the activity system moment by moment. Very few real-time systems exist, because present costs of designing, implementing, and operating such systems generally outweigh the value of truly real-time information. Instead, *batch processing information systems* are used to indicate the state of the activity system at periodic, and usually scheduled, intervals. If we think of the state of the activity system as being affected by the occurrence of individual transactions, a real-time system can be described as being one in which transaction data is processed at the time of the occurrence of each transaction. In a batch processing system, however, transactions data is placed in "dead" storage for some period of time before being processed.

The maximum length of time and the average length of time that data is held in dead storage are measures of the real-timeness of an information system. If these values are equal to zero, the system is a perfectly real-time system. Let us consider an example. Suppose that transactions occur at a constant rate of, say, one every hour. This is of course a simplified assumption. Further, suppose that we schedule a batch processing operation every 10 hours and that this operation requires 2 hours of time. Incidentally, this required time includes other activities in addition to the computer processing as such. For example, the input has to be prepared before the computer processing can commence, and then the resulting reports have to be transmitted to the eventual users and await their attention. This is quite important. One can cite many examples of situations in which reports are issued on a daily basis to managers who,

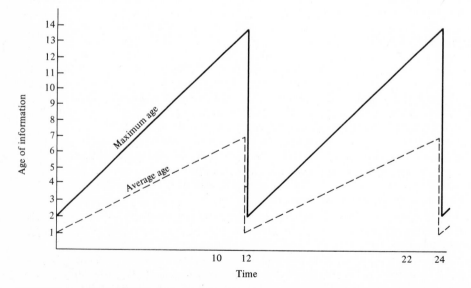

FIGURE 11-1   AGE OF INFORMATION AS A FUNCTION OF TIME WHEN TRANSACTIONS OCCUR AT A CONSTANT RATE BETWEEN BATCH PROCESSING RUNS.

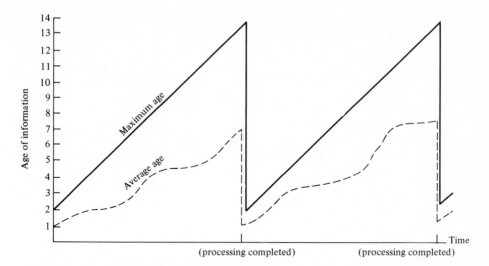

FIGURE 11-2   AGE OF INFORMATION AS A FUNCTION OF TIME WHEN TRANSACTIONS OCCUR AT A VARIABLE RATE BETWEEN BATCH PROCESSING RUNS.

because of competing duties, travel, and the like, do not study them thoroughly except on an occasional basis every few days. Thus, to assume that it takes 2 hours to process the accumulation of 10 hours of transactions by no means overstates the relative processing time.

Figure 11-1 represents the age of information as a function of time for the example we have been discussing. Notice that the lowest point on the maximum age scale is at 2 hours, and that this is the age of the information as soon as a batch is processed. The reason that the age does not drop to zero is that during the batch processing of transactions other transactions occur but must remain in dead storage until the next processing run. Following a batch processing run, the maximum age of the information increases until it reaches 14 hours just before the processing of the next batch is completed. Similarly, the average age at the time that a batch processing run is completed is 1 hour, and this value increases to 7 hours just before the processing of the next batch is completed. We have used hours in our illustration. We could have just as well used days or weeks or even months. The same principles would apply.

In a more generalized and more typical case, transactions would occur at random rather than fixed intervals, even though the pattern may be reflective of some fairly definite probability distribution. Assuming again a fixed interval between the batch processing runs, the age of information as a function of time can be represented as in Figure 11-2. In this case, the maximum age of an item of information increases linearly with time. But the average age increases unevenly because of the random intervals between individual transactions.

It is obvious that the more frequent the processing runs the lower will be the age of the information contained in a file. But we have certain conflicting objectives here. Each processing run involves a "get ready," or setup, cost. Time is required for programs to be loaded, special forms mounted, tape files retrieved and returned to the library, and many other such activities. Frequent processing of data batches would be very costly; so in general we try to balance frequency of updating against the cost of updating.

Figure 11-3 portrays the general relationship between the average age of information and the value of information. In general, the more timely the information the greater is its value. However, there may be a range of timeliness in which value is little affected. This is illustrated by the range in average age between points *a* and *b* in Figure 11-3. Then there may be a range in timeliness in which relatively small decreases in the average age of information result in relatively large decreases in the value of the information. This is illustrated by the form of the value curve between points *b* and *c* in Figure 11-3. Finally, after a certain point *(c)* further increases in the average age may have relatively little effect on information value. For example, a department manager in a retail store may not ascribe a great deal of difference to the value of sales information which is provided on a daily versus an hourly basis (*a* to *b* range). The value of sales information provided on a weekly basis would, however, be considerably less than that associated with the daily reports (*b* to *c* range). Finally, sales reports for periods beyond a weekly basis might differ little in value (beyond *c*) because of the general inadequacy of the data, assuming sales of a highly seasonal item. Of course, the time frame is dependent on the particular situation. In an airline reservation system the relevant time frame would be quite different from that of a department store, for example.

Figure 11-4 portrays the general relationship between the average age of information and the cost of producing the information. Daily batch processing is generally more costly than weekly processing. However, there may be diseconomies of scale

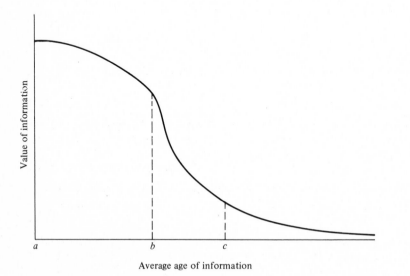

Average age of information

FIGURE 11-3   GENERAL RELATIONSHIP BETWEEN THE AVERAGE AGE OF INFORMA-
TION AND THE VALUE OF THE INFORMATION.

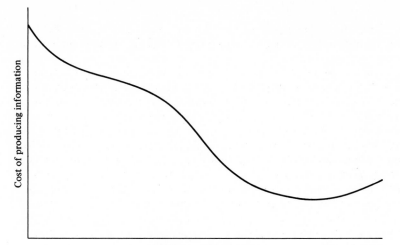

FIGURE 11-4   GENERAL RELATIONSHIP BETWEEN THE AVERAGE AGE OF INFORMATION AND THE COST OF PRODUCING THE INFORMATION.

when processing is too infrequent. For example, quarterly or annual processing could result in very large batches and difficulties in scheduling computer runs, thus resulting in higher average costs.

REVIEW

1   An effective information system is one which accurately reflects, or indicates, the state of the _____ system.

activity

2   The state of an activity system is indicated by the status of the files included in the information system. The two kinds of files identified in the context of batch processing are _____ files and _____ files.

Master; Transactions (or Activity)

3   An information system which follows the state of the activity system moment by moment would be referred to as a _____ information system.

real-time

4   In general, as the age of information increases, the value of the information [increases / decreases] and the cost of producing the information [increases / decreases].

decreases; decreases

MASTER FILE MAINTENANCE

File maintenance is a primary activity in the batch processing of sequential files. Although it is true that reports are the important result of data processing, it is necessary to maintain the Master files in order to produce the reports. Once the file is in the right state (updated and suitably ordered), report production is simply a matter of extracting the desired information. File maintenance and report production are frequently consolidated in the same run, but this need not be the case.

Since it is the transactions that affect the state of the Master file, which in turn reflects the state of the activity system, it is imperative that the transactions be screened for possible errors prior to being used to update the Master file. In this respect, it is useful to distinguish between data verification and data validation.

Verification is concerned with establishing that original data (usually manually produced) has been correctly transcribed into machine processable form. Verification is typically accomplished by duplicating the transcription effort, using suitable equipment. For example, the accuracy of input on punched cards can be ascertained by reentering the input by means of a verifier, which is similar to the keypunch in terms of physical appearance. Since verification which is achieved by duplicating the transcription effort is relatively costly, we should examine whether the value of such verification justifies the cost. For example, verification of hours worked is desirable in a payroll situation but may be questionable when data is to be used in summary form or for statistical analyses in which a small margin of error would not affect the usefulness of the report.

In addition to duplicating the data transcription, the accuracy of certain types of input can be verified by the use of self-checking numbers. A self-checking number is one which has a precalculated check digit appended to the basic number in order to detect keypunch or transmission errors. Normally, the check digit is used in conjunction with such identification codes as employee numbers, customer numbers, and part numbers. A self-checking number which includes the check digit will of course contain one more digit than the basic number. For example, a six-digit customer number would become a seven-digit number.

Although several techniques exist for calculating the check digit, the so-called "modulus 10 method" is most commonly used. The procedure is described and illustrated below. It should be noted, however, that several models of the IBM keypunch can be attached with a special device which will append the check digit to any number at the point of original determination of this digit. Therefore, the value of the check digit would not be determined manually.

The modulus 10 method of determining the value of the check digit can be described as follows:

1 The units (rightmost) position and every alternate position thereafter in the basic code number are multiplied by 2.
2 The individual digits in the product and the individual digits in the basic code number which were not multiplied by 2 are summed.
3 The sum is subtracted from the next-higher number ending in zero.
4 The difference is the check digit, which is to be appended to the basic code number in order to form the self-checking number.

Example:

Basic code number:	345798
Units and every alternate position:	4 7 8
Multiply by 2:	×2
Product:	956
Digits not multiplied by 2:	359
Sum of individual digits:	$9 + 5 + 6 + 3 + 5 + 9 = 37$
Next-higher number ending in zero:	40
Subtract sum of individual digits:	−37
Check digit:	3
Self-checking number:	3457983

When self-checking numbers are used, an error can be detected by the fact that the check digit is not appropriate for the basic number to which it is appended. It is possible that an incorrect basic number will have the same check digit as the original (correct) number. However, this can occur only if there is more than one keypunching or transcription error in the basic number, and it is therefore a rare occurrence.

As contrasted to verification, which is concerned with correct individual transcription, *validation* is concerned with the completeness and internal consistency of the set of data. The use of *control totals* is a very common approach to validation, and a *batch total* is one such control total. For example, a bank teller may produce a tape of the amounts deposited for batches of 50 deposits. These batch totals are identified with their corresponding batches and become part of the input for subsequent computer processing. The computer program duplicates the batch total accumulation process and compares these computer-generated totals with the totals determined manually. If they are not equal, an error has been made. In this example the most likely source of error is the transcription process from the manual deposit slip to the magnetically encoded document. Once an error has been detected, we need only search the particular batch in order to pinpoint the error entry or entries. As it can be seen, there is some advantage to keeping batch sizes small. If a batch contains 1,000 entries instead of the 50 described above, we might have to examine as many as 1,000 entries to locate the error.

A second type of control total is called a *hash total*. When a payroll file is formed, the hash total could be the sum of the social security numbers of all employees. In subsequent processing of this file the total could be formed again and compared with the previous total. If the two totals are not the same, this may indicate that one or more records were missed. The word "hash" indicates that the total has no meaning of its own and is used only for comparison purposes.

A third type of control total is often referred to as *crossfooting*. For example, the following relationship may apply to each item in an inventory file:

Opening balance + receipts − issues = on hand

Utilizing this known relationship, it must then be true that the totals for each of the four fields above for all items processed must also conform to the above formula.

As contrasted to the use of control totals, another form of validation relies on the use of *range checks*. This approach is based on the fact that classes of transactions must occur within certain numerical limits. For example, a transaction showing the

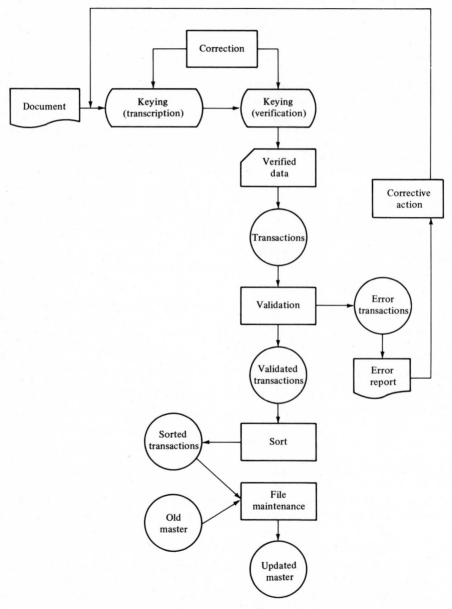

FIGURE 11-5   MASTER FILE UPDATE RUN WITH DATA VERIFICATION AND VALIDATION.

amount charged for a pair of shoes in a discount department store should not exceed $30. Similarly, the Internal Revenue Service can check to determine if deductions exceed a certain percent of income. In a particular form of the range check, we may check as to whether the amount sold is zero—thus performing a check to determine if the amount was left out. Such a determination is referred to as *completeness check*.

A third form of validation is referred to as a *consistency check*. Such checks are directed toward determining if the input data is consistent with known constraints of reality. For example, hourly rates of pay may always be expressed in dollars and cents rather than whole numbers, and the quantity of a particular item may always be in terms of pounds rather than some other unit of measurement.

The term *data editing* is often used in the context of data validation procedures, even though detection of errors as such may not be involved. Data editing is concerned mainly with accomplishing desired changes in the form of data. For example, blanks might be changed to leading zeros in a numeric field, and a date in the form of XX-XX-XX might be changed to the form XXXXXX, thereby eliminating the hyphens.

When an error is detected through the process of data validation, some corrective action must be taken. Ideally, the computer program should provide the corrective action which is necessary, and occasionally this is possible. But in most cases there is no way to correct the error based on the input data alone. Therefore, the fact that a certain type of error has been detected is reported either on magnetic tape for subsequent printer listing, directly on the printer, or directly on the console typewriter, for eventual manual correction. Figure 11-5 is a flowchart for a master file update run which includes data verification and validation. In this typical case, manual documents contain the original data which is punched and verified, then transferred to magnetic tape, validated, sorted, and finally processed to update the Master file. Depending on the extent of data validation, such procedures may be a subpart of the total update job or they may require a separate computer run. More often than not, validation procedures are a separate run, followed by a sort run, which is in turn followed by the main update run. Thus, computer programs concerned with updating Master files are not simple programs but rather are concerned with a series of complex tasks.

REVIEW

1 The procedures which are directed toward ascertaining that original data has been correctly transcribed are concerned with the general process called data _____.

verification

2 Data verification is typically accomplished by duplicating the transcription process, such as is involved when a verifier is used following keypunching. However, as an alternate to this approach certain types of numeric input, such as part numbers, can be verified as to accuracy by the use of _____ numbers.

self-checking

3 As contrasted to verification, data _____ is concerned with the completeness and internal consistency of a set of data, rather than the accuracy of individual transcriptions taken singly.

validation

4 Data validation is generally accomplished by making use of various types of _____ totals.

control

5 When the totals for groups of 100 sales transactions are included with the individual transaction values as the computer input, the type of control total being used for the purpose of validation is the _____ total.

batch

6 When the sum of all the customer numbers for accounts which have had a sales transaction is used for data validation purposes, the control total would be described as being a _____ total. On the other hand, the type of control total that is based on known numerical relationships among such totals as the total amount of payments and total account balances is referred to as _____.

hash; crossfooting

7 As contrasted to the use of control totals, the method of validation based on the fact that certain transactions can occur only within prescribed numerical limits involves the use of _____ checks. A third form of validation is based on the fact that transactions must conform to certain constraints of reality, such as being expressed in certain types of units, and this type of validation is therefore called a _____ check.

range; consistency

8 The procedure which is sometimes associated with validation procedures and which is concerned with changing the form of the input data, such as replacing "$" signs with zeros and eliminating commas included in numeric input, is called _____.

data editing

TRANSACTION RECORDS AND FILE MAINTENANCE

There are two basic types of transactions in Master file updating: transactions that change the values of fields in the Master records and transactions that result in whole records being added to or deleted from the file. For instance, in the updating of an inventory file the following types of transactions would result in changes in the values of the fields in the Master records:

Receipt transactions, indicating a shipment of items received from the vendor

Issue transactions, indicating items taken out of inventory for the purpose of sale to customers or for release to the production floor

Adjustment transactions, indicating corrections of errors, reconciliation of discrepancies between recorded data and physical inventory count, and the like

On-order transactions, indicating items ordered but not yet received

Committed-item transactions, indicating quantities encumbered or reserved for specified future issue

The program used in a file update process will examine the input transaction records, determine the transaction codes, and apply the appropriate adjustments to the records in the Master file. For example, for a receipt record corresponding amounts would be added to the "on hand" and "available" fields of the Master record for the item in question. Regardless of the specific processing required for such transactions, the final result is that the Master record is updated and written onto the new Master file.

The second type of transaction results in the addition or deletion of Master records. For example, in a payroll processing run we will typically have occasion to add new employees to the Master file or to delete some employee records from the file. To add a record to the Master file we simply encode the Transaction record to indicate the addition of a record and we include it in the appropriate sequence in the Transactions file. Normally, "add-type" transactions are longer than other types. In the payroll example, most of the usual transactions will involve only one punched card containing such input as employee number and hours worked. However, the formation of a Master record will probably require several cards for such information as full name and address, social security number, rate of pay, tax exemptions, and insurance and other deductions.

Once an add-type transaction is read, we may simply insert it in the updated file, or we may process any transactions which follow and which pertain to the new record. For example, it could be that we have a new employee and that he or she in fact worked during the pay period of concern. In addition to adding the record to the Master file we must also read the input regarding the amount of time worked and compute gross pay, taxes, and so on. Note that the inclusion of add-type transactions complicates the processing logic to some extent. In practice, it is not unusual to have one processing run in which the Master file is updated with respect to additions and deletions and to have a separate processing run which updates the file with respect to data modifications. This becomes desirable if the number of added or deleted records is large, as it might be for a magazine subscriber list or in a company that has substantial employee turnover.

Deletions from the file are also handled by submitting an encoded transaction record. At first it might seem a simple matter to delete a record from the file: simply do not write the old record in the updated Master file. Practical considerations dictate that a series of steps be followed in the case of deletions, however. For one thing, we will want to print full information regarding the deleted records so that the fact of deletion can be communicated to and reviewed by those who have managerial responsibility over the deleted items. Further, the deletion procedure itself has to take into consideration the continued need to work with the records in certain aspects. For example, in a payroll situation we may owe the employee some back pay and make appropriate adjustments for his or her deductions. We may still want to maintain the record (perhaps on a separate file) for such reasons as end-of-year tax reports and for reasons of recall in case the layoff proves to be temporary in nature.

In addition to transactions which change data on the records and those which alter the composition of the records in a file, there is a third type of transaction which logically could fall into the second category but which is usually considered to be a separate type of transaction. It often happens that we need to change the order of records in the Master file. One simple example would be the need to change the order of listing in an alphabetical file for women who are married and thus change their last names. If Miss Zacher marries and becomes Mrs. Brown, her record must be repositioned in the file. Another example would be that situation in which the employee identification number includes a department number and some employees are transferred between departments. With such examples in mind, let us consider two common ways for processing such changes.

One approach is to introduce two transactions in the same run. One involves the addition of a new record, and the other involves the deletion of an old one. In the example of the woman who changed her name from Zacher to Brown, we would provide an add-type transaction for Brown and a delete transaction for Zacher. If the volume of such changes is low, this is probably a satisfactory approach. However, if the volume of such transactions is high, this approach has the disadvantage that it requires whole new Master entries, which may involve considerable keypunching. For instance, in a university each student may have a record approximately 2,000 characters in length, containing his or her name, parents' names, local address, home address, transcript data, and so forth. The prospect of manually recreating a new

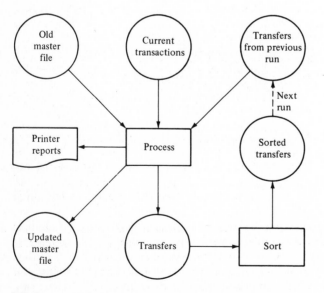

FIGURE 11-6   FILE UPDATING INVOLVING TRANSFER RECORDS.

Master record is undesirable, and the prospect of machine-punching the data from tape onto cards may require reading and searching an entire file consisting of several reels of tape.

An alternative approach by which the order of records in a Master file can be changed is to alter the record to be relocated, for example, by changing the last name and then writing this altered record on a special "transfer" tape and eliminating the record from the currently updated Master. This transfer tape is then sorted, and in the next run it is merged with the old Master file onto the updated Master. The process chart in Figure 11-6 presents the logic of the file processing in this case. By this approach we would read and merge the old Master file and the transfers-from-previous-run file as the current transactions are being processed. As the process is portrayed in Figure 11-6, five tape drives are required for each update run: one each for the input from the old Master file, current Transactions file, and transfers from previous run, and one each for output to the updated Master file and (new) transfers.

REVIEW

1   Of the two basic types of transactions in Master file updating, one is concerned with transactions which change the values of _____ contained in Master records, while the second is concerned with transactions which result in addition or deletion of whole _____ as such.

fields; Master records

2   Suppose an inventory file is updated and there have been no changes in the items held in inventory (although particular inventory levels have changed). Such an updating run would be entirely concerned with changing [values of fields in Master records / the record composition of the Master file].

values of fields in Master records

3   Given that employees have been added to and deleted from the payroll since the last payroll processing run, the type of transaction which is required is the type which is concerned with changing [values of fields in Master records / the record composition of the Master file].

the record composition of the Master file

4   A third type of transaction is concerned with changing the order of records held in a Master file. The most efficient way by which such a change can be accomplished is to alter the record to be relocated, write the record on a special _____ tape, and eliminate the record from the currently updated Master. On the next processing run the (then) old Master file is merged with the _____ tape from the previous run to form an updated _____.

transfer; transfer; Master file

ACTIVITY RATIOS AND FILE MAINTENANCE

The amount of activity over time is different for the various entries, or items, that constitute a Master file. For example, suppose we have a warehouse that stocks 20,000 parts. Some of them will experience daily activity, some may average one transaction a week, while others may have transactions just a few times a year. Let us say that we experience an average of 900 transactions a day and that these transactions are concerned with an average of 400 parts in the inventory system—that is, some parts have more than one transaction. Now suppose we update the Master file on a daily basis. Since 400 of the 20,000 parts were involved in the transactions, we say that the activity ratio is

$$\frac{400}{20,000} = \frac{1}{50} = 0.02$$

Thus, for every 50 records there will be one record for which some processing is done and 49 records will simply be copied from the old to the updated file. Obviously the part of the processing concerned with copying is unproductive. As an alternative to updating the file on a daily basis, we might consider processing the file once a week. On the average, there will now be more than 400 active parts per week. However, assuming that there are five working days per week, do not be misled into concluding that the number of active parts will be 400 per day $\times$ 5 days. Of the 400 average per day, there will be some parts that will be active every day or at least more than once a week. So we may have 1,200 active parts per week, resulting in the activity ratio

$$\frac{1,200}{20,000} = \frac{3}{50} = 0.06$$

The increase in the activity ratio from 0.02 to 0.06 in the above example represents an increase of 300 percent in the value of the ratio. In an extreme case, we may wish to process a batch of records only after a very high percentage—say 98 percent—have had some activity. But this requirement would generally conflict with the need for timely information, since it might well be months before 98 percent of the records experience activity. In a batch processing system we frequently have to balance information needs against data processing efficiency.

In some files the activity ratio is always high. For example, the payroll file for a manufacturing plant with 5,000 employees will include only a small percentage of "inactive" records on any given day (for those who were absent, on vacation, terminated, etc.). Yet payroll records are not processed daily just because the activity ratio is high. Rather, other factors determine the frequency of updating in this case.

When a file is large and activity variations are great, such a file is often subdivided into two Master files, one for "active" items and one for relatively "inactive" items. As a practical matter, it is not easy to specify the difference between these two groups of items. One possible way of making the distinction is to set some parameters on the activity. For example, active items might be defined as those which are involved in at least X transactions per designated period—say 10 transactions per month. All other items would then be considered inactive by definition. Another approach to distinguishing between active and inactive items is based on the nature of the items themselves. For example, we may know from experience that parts for automobiles that are eight years old or older are inactive, as are parts for the current model year. Parts for the other model years (one year to seven years old) would then be considered active.

When two Master files are used, some procedure is usually required for exit from one class of items and entry to the other class. The process chart in Figure 11-7 illustrates the basic procedure that is used. There are two types of processing runs, one for the active file and one for the inactive file. Typically, there will be several processing runs for the active file to each run of the inactive file. The input for the updating of the Active Master file includes the old Active Master, the transactions, and inactive records that have become active. The output consists of the updated Active Master, those transactions which do not pertain to active records, and those records which have become inactive.

In the maintenance of the inactive file, as portrayed in Figure 11-7, the input is the old Inactive Master, transactions of records not in the active file, and the (formerly) active records that are now inactive. For each of the latter two inputs several reels are typically merged because of there being several processing runs for the Active Master file for each processing run for the Inactive Master file. Two types of tape output are generated in addition to the updated Inactive Master file. One is concerned with error transactions—that is, transactions not applicable to either file. The other type includes the records that were inactive but now have had increased activity and therefore have been reclassified as being active. These reclassified records will be processed in the next maintenance run for the Active Master file.

REVIEW

1 If 300 of 1,000 items are involved in transactions during each week, on the average, the weekly activity ratio has the value: _____.

$$\frac{300}{1,000} = 0.30$$

2 For the example above, if the activity ratio is calculated for a typical 2-week period, the value of the ratio is likely to be [less than / equal to / greater than] the value 0.60.

less than

3 When activity variations among the records of a file are great, such a file is frequently subdivided into two Master files—one called the _____ Master file and the other called the _____ Master file.

Active; Inactive

DATA SEQUENCE AND FILE PROCESSING

The sequence by which data is ordered in a file is a very important matter in that the processing efficiency of a system is thereby directly affected. Sequential file

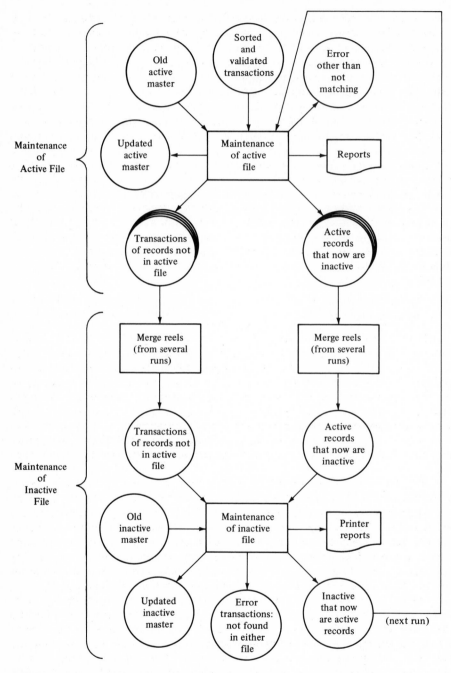

FIGURE 11-7   FILE MAINTENANCE WITH ACTIVE AND INACTIVE MASTER FILES.

processing requires that the files involved must be ordered in the same sequence. If one were to take a narrow view of file processing, one would consider the isolated jobs to be processed and proceed to order the file in the required order. For instance, to report sales by product, the file would be sorted according to product number and processed. Then, to report sales by month, the file would be ordered according to date and processed. This one-at-a-time consideration of processing runs overlooks the interactions that exist between different types of runs. The same file may be used for many processing runs, and it is the task of the systems designer to view as large a processing module as possible so that the processing runs can be scheduled efficiently.

Of particular importance is the process of sorting. Sorting is unproductive but necessary in sequential processing. In many installations sorting consumes 30 percent of the total processing time. While sorting is necessary, the amount of required sorting can be minimized by the appropriate ordering of the processing runs. For example, suppose we have a sales file sorted by *salesperson, product,* and *month of sale.* What this means is that the overall file is sorted according to salesperson-number, for each salesperson the sales are ordered according to product-number, and finally, for each product the sales are listed according to month of sale. Now, suppose the following two reports are required:

1   Sales by product by month
2   Sales by salesperson by month

Given the order of the sales file (salesperson, product, month) we should produce the second report first. The order of the sales file is already according to salesperson. In order to accumulate the monthly totals for each salesperson, 12 accumulators can be defined in internal storage for this purpose, thereby avoiding the necessity of sorting the original tape. After the monthly totals for a given salesperson have been output, the 12 accumulators are available for the next salesperson to be processed. After the second report is completed, the file can be sorted by product and month to produce the first report. On the other hand, if the reports were produced in the order indicated above, the file would have to be sorted prior to the production of *both* reports.

Another factor to be considered is the frequency of need for a particular report. Suppose that we have an inventory file sorted by project number and by part number. In other words, the part numbers are in sequenced order for each project number. If a report by part number is required every 3 months, the above ordering of the file makes sense. We need to sort the Master file by part number only once every 3 months because the file is maintained in the order of most frequent use. Of course, the transactions processed each week also have to be sorted according to project-number and part-number sequence, so as to be compatible with the inventory tape file.

If a report by part-number is required every week in addition to the report by project-number, it might be preferable to avoid the required sorting by maintaining two separate tape files for the same data but not in the same order. We would then have two processing runs. First, we could sort the transactions by project-number by part-number and update the project-part Master file. Then the transactions can be sorted by part-number by project-number to update the part-project Master file. This approach is predicated on the assumption that the transactions are fewer in number than the Master file records, and that it is therefore preferable to sort the transactions a second time rather than sort the Master file.

REVIEW

1 In this section we have considered some approaches by which the required sorting of a [set of transactions / tape file] can be minimized.

tape file

2 Sorting can be minimized by considering the interactions that exist between different types of runs and by considering the frequency of need for different reports. Where two different types of reports are required frequently, and relatively few transactions are involved, another possible way of minimizing the required amount of sorting is to maintain two separate [sets of transaction cards / tape files]—one for each type of required report.

tape files

DATA SEQUENCE AND CODES

The order, or sequence, of data organization and storage is a very important and complex matter. Data becomes meaningful as information when it is arranged in a suitable and logical manner for the use that is planned. Essential to such logical organization of data is a good classification system. Once a classification method has been designed, codes are assigned in accordance with the classification design. *Codes* can be defined as character strings that serve to identify the various class memberships of an item according to the classification system used. For example, a part code in a manufacturing company may identify the department that produces the part, the order number, and the physical characteristics of the product (such as size, weight, horsepower, and color), and so on.

In order to devise an efficient code it is imperative that the current or anticipated class structure of the objects or transactions of the activity system be studied. Thus, the development of a classification system and the corresponding codes may be an extended and difficult undertaking. In one case, a team of systems analysts worked for 2 years developing an efficient coding system for parts in a large diversified company with several plants and many different product lines. Part of the difficulty is associated with the dynamics of any ongoing situation. Products are added and deleted, new materials appear, and other companies may be merged with an existing one. Designing a class structure that can accommodate such a fluid environment is a challenging task.

A code is usually different from the commonly used name for an item, event, or transaction. After the development of mechanized data processing, numeric codes were often assigned because numeric codes can be processed much more efficiently than alphabetic codes with such equipment. However, today's electronic computers are practically as efficient with alphabetic as with numeric codes. The codes are assigned not so much to condense records as to assign objects and transactions to classes. For instance, a person's name provides no indication as to the department in which he or she works, and neither does his or her social security number. Therefore, an employee identification code number is typically assigned to each employee in an organization. Similarly, the commonly used names *electric motor* and *transformer* do not place these items in the *electrical equipment* class, although a different code system could achieve such identification.

In developing a coding system, some of the important questions to be raised are: What are the uses of the data? Does the prospective code satisfy as many classifications as the uses of the data require? To which subclasses does an item belong, in addition to the principal class membership? For example, an item in the major class *steel* could belong to the subclass *consumer* or *industrial*. Once the lowest subclass has been coded, a further code system may be developed to correspond to the different physical characteristics of the item or to the sequence of receipt, such as first-come first-coded.

A code should have the following desirable properties:

Precise.   The code should provide unique identification.

Concise.   The code should be as compact as possible. However, a code for human use may not be as concise as one used strictly for machine processing. For example, an automobile tire may have the designation 65013W4 (650 × 13 whitewall, 4-ply), which is not as concise as it could be but is easy for people to interpret.

Expandable.   The coding system should be so designed that future additions or deletions of classes can be accommodated.

REVIEW

1   The character strings that serve to identify the various class memberships of an item are called _____.

codes

2   The main disadvantage of comonly used names as codes is that [they do not provide all the required class identifications / they are too long for efficient computer processing].

they do not provide all the required class identifications

3   A code that is as compact as possible is described as being [precise / concise], while a code that provides unique identification is said to be [precise / concise].

concise; precise

CODING METHODS

There are many types of codes, but in this section we consider four basic types: sequence, group, mnemonic, and numeric-alphabetic.

Sequence codes consist of the assignment of a consecutive number to each item. For example, invoices could be numbered 06000, 06001, 06002, etc., like the numbering of checks in a checking account. This is the simplest type of coding method, but it is also least useful, since it identifies each item uniquely but does nothing to indicate the class membership of the item. Sequence codes are used in cases where the class is implicitly defined, as for an invoice file, or as a subcode to identify equal members of the same class.

Group codes consist of the assignment of specific character positions for class designation. For example, a code could consist of:

	GROUP 1	GROUP 2	GROUP 3
Code characters	XX	X	XXX

Thus, assuming a numeric code system, if group 1 is the material class, group 2 is a color class, and group 3 is a vendor code, we have the possibility of 100 material classes (0 through 99), 10 colors, and 1,000 vendors. Notice that by the use of this code system items can be referenced in respect to any or all of these three groups. For example, we can identify all items that belong to material class 20, all items handled by vendor 156, all items which belong to material class 39 *and* are supplied by vendor 865, and the like. However, as the code system is described above it is not capable of precise identification, since the code numbers for different items are not necessarily unique. In order to attain precision, another code group, or class, would have to be added. For example, suppose that material class 38 stands for cotton fiber and that there are 20 types of fiber supplied in 10 colors by 4 vendors. The group code described above can be expanded to provide for identification of the type of cotton fiber, thereby making possible precise identification:

	MATERIAL	TYPE	COLOR	VENDOR
Code characters	XX	XX	X	XXX

A code of 38133568 would designate an item with the following unique characteristics: material class 38, fiber type 13, color 3, and vendor 568.

Mnemonic codes consist of alphanumeric symbols that provide a mnemonic description of the item coded. That is, the codes are designed so that they are relatively easy to recognize and remember. Thus, we could have as an example:

ITEM	SIZE	COLOR	
S	15	WH	Shirt, size 15, white
S	16	GR	Shirt, size 16, green
B	36	BR	Belt, size 36, brown

Mnemonic codes are used in situations in which people need to use the codes, such as in retail stores and catalog order departments. Obviously, the mnemonic feature of a code is not relevant from the standpoint of computer processing.

Numeric-alphabetic codes consist of numeric codes such that the numeric sequence corresponds to the alphabetic sequence of the names of the items. They are frequently used by publishers of periodicals and in other situations in which there is need to maintain alphabetic order. Many possible coding systems are available, none of which is 100 percent precise without local modification. As an example of one simple system, we could have a letter code followed by a sequence code. The two-digit letter code in the code system below represents the first letter of the last name, while the four-digit sequence code allows for up to 9,999 names for each letter.

NAME	LETTER CODE	SEQUENCE CODE
Abrams, J	01	0001
Abrams, R	01	0002
Alberts, A	01	0003
.	.	.
.	.	.
.	.	.
Babcock, C	02	0001
.	.	.
.	.	.
Zambon, N	26	0001
Zenon, A	26	0002

In this sytem 26 × 9,999 unique codes are possible. However, if the list of names changes, a problem of insertions exists. Suppose we wish to add Adams to the list above. It is impossible to do so, because no sequence code is available for the proper positioning of Adams in the given list. In anticipation of such changes, unassigned numbers are frequently left between the assigned numbers. For example, the sequence code assigned to the first Abrams in the above list could be 0010, in anticipation of a later need to code a name such as Abbott, and Alberts could similarly be assigned the sequence code 0020. This method is likely to work well if we anticipate the relative frequency of use of the various first letters in names, perhaps by sampling telephone directories or business registers.

Note that the primary purpose of numeric-alphabetic codes is not to convert alphabetic information to numeric information but to condense the required code. Obviously, the numeric code can be made long enough—by providing two numbers per letter—so that every different name could be uniquely coded. But the resulting code would be twice as long as the original name!

Another useful code for large alphabetical files consisting of names is based on a numeric code formed by the following parts: the first letter of the last name, the second through the fifth letters of the last name as a unit, the month and year of birth, the sex, eye color, and height. This rather complex scheme is fully described in IBM reference manual F-20-8052-1, *A Unique Computable Name Code for Alphabetic Account Numbering*. The system was devised as the result of the observation by the Social Security Administration that while 1¼ million different last names exist in the United States, about 48 percent of the people have one of the 1,514 most common names.

REVIEW

1 The type of code which involves the assignment of a consecutive and unique number to each item is the _____ code.

sequence

2 The type of code which is usually alphanumeric and is constructed to be easy to interpret and understand for the human user is the _____ code.

mnemonic

3 The type of code which consists of different character positions of the code being assigned for different class and subclass designations is the _____ code.

group

4 Finally, the code system for which the numeric codes correspond to the alphabetic sequence of the uncoded items is the _____ code.

numeric-alphabetic

5 In general, the main objective associated with a group code is to achieve [as short a code number as possible / identification of as many classes as desired].

identification of as many classes as desired

EXERCISES

1 A local department store issues its own charge plates to its customers. Credit sales are processed on a batch basis and billing statements are mailed to customers. Customers return their payments along with a stub. Design a batch processing system to handle the credit sales of the department store. Describe the files that you would use and their maintenance. Also, design any manual procedures and forms that would be used.

2   Visit a data processing center and study one of their batch processing applications. Then write a report describing the application, including files, manual procedures, forms, validation or editing procedures, and relationship (if any) of this application to other applications at the center. Make an attempt to suggest modifications and improvements to the system.

3   A customer prepares a savings withdrawal slip for $340 for his account. The teller, mistakenly, subtracts $304 from the savings passbook and from the card. However, she does give him $340 cash as the withdrawal amount. Describe the controls you would build into the related batch processing system that would "catch" such errors and would provide for corrective action—manual or automated.

4   A grocery warehouse maintains an inventory of 15,000 different types of items. Some of these items are very active and others are relatively inactive. For example, certain soups and cereals have a high frequency of orders from the supermarkets supplied by this warehouse. Other items, like some canned gourmet foods, are ordered very sporadically.

   The current inventory processing system is a batch processing system, a run being made once a week.

   Suppose that we want to modify the system so that the Master file can be divided into two segments, one for the "active" records and one for the "inactive." Describe the steps that you would take in designing and then implementing such an Active-Inactive Master file inventory processing system.

5   It is desired to computerize some phases of the purchasing and receiving functions in a manufacturing company. Below is a verbal description of the procedure as this procedure is visualized by the manager of materials control. You are asked to draw flow diagrams showing input/output files and their processing such that the desired procedure could be computerized. The company has available a computer with card reader/card punch, one printer, and four magnetic tape units.

   A manually prepared requisition originates at the production and inventory control department. The requisition identifies the item by number and name and specifies the number, quantity, and date of shipment desired.

   Data are punched from the requisition for input into the computer. Obtained as output is a printed Requisition and Purchase History Review document which, in addition to the original requisition data, contains data on the last three purchases for the requisitioned item. Such a history includes date, purchase order number, vendor name, vendor code, quantity purchased, unit price, etc.

   The Requisition and Purchase History Review is given to the purchasing department where a buyer chooses the vendor, quantity, price, and so forth. The buyer's choice is punched onto a card containing requisition number, part number, vendor code, quantity, price, delivery, etc. The cards become input into a computer run for which the printed output is a purchase order in four copies (vendor, purchasing, requisitioning department, and accounting). The purchase order contains complete information, such as part number, part name, vendor name, code and address, quantity, and delivery date.

   As purchase orders are written, a second printer report is also produced for the receiving department. This report shows the purchase order number, vendor, quantity ordered, delivery date, and the like. When a shipment is received, the receiving department supplies data that is punched onto a card identifying the order, the quantity received, and the date of receipt.

As part of this system the following reports also are to be produced:

Twice a week:

a An Open Order Status report identifying the purchase order number, date, vendor name, vendor code, buyer code, quantity ordered, date shipment is due, quantity received (if partial shipment), and date of receipt. If shipment has been complete, the order is eliminated from this report. The report is prepared according to purchase number order.

b An Open Requisition report listing the requisitions for which no purchase orders have been issued yet. The report is in requisition number order.

c A Past Due Orders report listing only those open purchase orders for which shipment is overdue. The content for each line of the report is the same as the Open Order Status report.

Once each quarter:

a A Vendor Performance report identifying each purchase order issued during the quarter for each vendor. Data includes post office number, date, buyer code, quantity, price, total dollars, and any delivery variance from promised delivery date.

b A Buyer report listing the purchase orders issued for each buyer and including the same data as in the Vendor Performance report.

c A Purchase Activity report according to part number with the same purchase order date as the Vendor Performance report.

In your analysis of the case make sure to include a description of the files that you would maintain and show any processing that may be necessary to update such files. Also, supply verbal explanation or commentary to explain the flowcharts.

A Case Study in Sequential File Processing

Introduction
Master File Creation and Maintenance
Daily Processing
Monthly Statement Production
Exercises

INTRODUCTION

The objective of this chapter is to present a fairly extensive example of the implementation of sequential file processing logic and procedures.

In presenting this case, an effort has been made to balance the needs of students to deal with simplicity and the desire for exposure to some level of realistic complexity. Accordingly, we omit many details which would have to be included if this were an operational file processing system, so that students can grasp the essentials of the system without being overwhelmed with the details of such a system. Still, oversimplification has been avoided so as to dispel the notion that all tasks can be programmed with trivial effort.

The overall task relates to processing of customer transactions in a retail department store. In that context the following main processes take place:

Credit customers are identified by an account-number which is unique for each customer. Information on each customer is stored in a sequential file sorted on account-number. Each customer Master record contains such data as name, address, credit limit, balance, overdue balances, and other information.

Part of the task consists of creating this Master file and subsequently updating it with data that pertains to such things as additions of new customers, deletion of customers, name or address changes, credit limit changes("good credit" customers may be allowed to purchase larger amounts on credit, whereas "bad credit" customers may be limited to smaller amounts).

On a daily basis, customers are involved in such transactions as purchases, payments, returns, and adjustments (e.g., corrections). Their transactions take place at individual departments. At the "end of the day" a machine-readable transaction record is created by means of keypunching, or keying onto a key-to-tape or key-to-disk device. An alternative would involve a Point of Sale (POS) terminal such that transaction records are created at the time of occurrence and these records are stored on tape or disk to form a batch of transactions at the end of the day.

Each department submits a control total along with its batch of transactions. These batches are then processed through a program that checks for the accuracy, completeness, and validity of data. A Daily Transactions Register is produced for each department, reporting all transactions and any errors so that they can be corrected and submitted the next day.

The correct transactions are sorted on account number and then are processed against a Daily Master file. This Daily Master is a shortened version of the Master file and is used to prevent any abuses of the credit system. The department store bills customers once a month, but its financial officers want to be aware of any customers who attempt to run up a balance larger than their credit limit as such attempts may occur. To this purpose, a Daily Master file is maintained which contains account-number, current (as of this day) balance, and credit limit. This short Master file is updated daily. If today's transactions cause the balance to exceed the credit limit, a notice is printed to alert management of this fact.

At the end of the month the Daily Transaction files are merged onto one Cumulative Daily Transactions. This latter file along with the Daily Master and the Master file serve as input to a program that updates the Master and Daily Master files and produces the monthly billing statement sent to customers.

The above description outlines the overall system. We now proceed to study the tasks in greater detail.

MASTER FILE CREATION AND MAINTENANCE

Figure 12-1 shows a process chart for the procedure. We assume transaction records have been edited and are sorted on account-number (file sorting is discussed in Chapter 13). Notice that the Old Master is an optional file. That treatment allows us to create a New Master file without updating an old one by submitting a series of add-new-record transactions. As output we have a Master File Register report that lists the contents of the Master file and can be used for manual lookup. Error transactions, if any, are recorded on a file temporarily, so that the printer can be used for the Master File Register. Eventually, they are listed on the printer so that corrective action can be taken. Finally, an updated New Master file is created.

Figure 12-2 presents the layout of the Master file records. The first field contains the account-number which identifies each customer. Because of the critical nature of this item, account-numbers are assigned as a five-digit number with a simplified sixth check digit. The sixth digit is the truncated sum of the first five digits. For example, the check digit for account number 12345 would be 5 ($1 + 2 + 3 + 4 + 5 = 15$, but we truncate the 1 leaving 5). Therefore, the acount number is 123455. (This is not a very

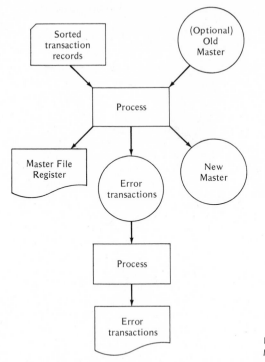

FIGURE 12-1 MASTER FILE CREATION AND
MAINTENANCE.

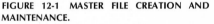

good check digit procedure, but we use it for simplicity. See page 295 for a description
of a more complicated but more reliable procedure.) Programs accessing account-
numbers will perform the check digit computation to verify that this is a (likely) valid
account number.

The next three fields contain information about the customer's name and address.
The credit limit field (OM-CREDIT-LIMIT) contains a value that has been determined by
the credit manager on the basis of the financial condition and experience with this
customer. The OM-BALANCE field normally shows the account balance as of the last
processing. The last field contains other data which we choose to ignore for simplicity.

The record layouts for transaction records are shown in Figure 12-3. Because one
card cannot contain all the necessary data to build a Master record, two record
descriptions are given—TRANSACTION-1 and TRANSACTION-2. Notice that for documentation all data names begin with a T, whereas Old Master data names begin with
OM. Column 7 of TRANSACTION-1 contains a transaction code as follows:

1 = add new customer record
2 = delete customer record
3 = change customer name
4 = change customer credit limit
5 = change name and credit limit
6 = change address
9 = no Old Master file is present (i.e., we intend to create one)

OLD-MAST-REC

OM-ACCOUNT-NO	OM-NAME	OM-ADDRESS		OM-CREDIT-LIMIT	OM-BALANCE	OM-OTHER-DATA
		OM-STREET	OM-CITY			
PIC 9(6)	PIC X(20)	PIC X(25)	PIC X(25)	PIC 9999V99	PIC S9(6)V99	PIC X(28)
1–6	7–26	27–51	52–76	77–82	83–90	91–108

FIGURE 12-2 MASTER FILE RECORD LAYOUT.

TRANSACTION-1

Record-name	TRANSACTION-1						
Data-name	T-ACCOUNT-NO	T-TRAN-CODE	T-CARD-CODE	T-NAME	T-CREDIT-LIMIT-A PIC X(6)	T-BALANCE-A PIC X(8)	FILLER
	PIC 9(6)	PIC 9	PIC 9	PIC X(30)	T-CREDIT-LIMIT PIC 9(4)V99	T-BALANCE PIC S9(6)V99	PIC X(38)
Columns	1-6	7	8	9-28	29-34	35-42	43-80

TRANSACTION-2

Columns	1-8	9-33	34-58	59-76	77-80
		T-ADDRESS			
Data-name	FILLER PIC X(8)	T-STREET PIC X(25)	T-CITY PIC X(25)	T-OTHER-DATA PIC X(18)	FILLER PIC X(4)
Record-name			TRANSACTION-2		

FIGURE 12-3   TRANSACTION RECORDS LAYOUT.

The T-CARD-CODE field in column 8 contains 2 if it is a TRANSACTION-2 type of record.

T-CREDIT-LIMIT is a redefinition of T-CREDIT-LIMIT-A so that the data can be referenced as if it were alphanumeric (for class condition testing) or numeric (for arithmetic data). In a similar way, T-BALANCE redefines T-BALANCE-A.

Exhibit 12-1 presents a program written to accomplish the Master file processing task. The student should spend some time reading it; when needed it will be helpful to flowchart the main modules. We proceed to make a few comments to highlight some aspects of the program.

Exhibit 12-2 illustrates two sets of data that can be used in conjunction with the program in Exhibit 12-1, one set to be used for the creation of the Master file and the second set to be used for updating that file. The first transaction card in this exhibit contains a 9 transaction code, which means that there is no Old Master file and therefore we proceed to the path that creates the Master file (see the CREATE-OR-UPDATE paragraph). If the transaction code of the first transaction record is a 9, the program executes the CREATE-MASTER paragraph which in turn invokes execution of the PROCESS-REMAINING-TRANS paragraph.

The PROCESS-REMAINING-TRANS routine reads pairs of cards and builds master records. When errors are encountered, an error message and the error transaction are written on the Error Transaction file. When all transactions have been read in, the program PERFORMS ERROR-LISTING, a routine that rewinds the Error Transaction file and lists the error transactions, if any.

When an update run is performed, the first transaction code is not equal to 9 and the program opens the Old Master file as input. Depending on the data, paragraphs such as MODIFY, DELETION, CHANGE-NAME, etc., are executed. Again, error transactions are accumulated on the Error Transaction file for subsequent listings.

Figure 12-4 presents a partial hierarchical procedure diagram for the program of Exhibit 12-1. Such a diagram displays which procedure, if any, is invoked by a given procedure. As it can be seen, there are several levels of dependency shown. Such a diagram identifies the dependency among paragraphs in terms of their execution. Specifically, the paragraph MAIN-PROCESSING in Figure 12-4 invokes execution of the four paragraphs STARTUP, CREATE-OR-UPDATE, UPDATE-ROUTINE, and ERROR-LISTING, which in turn invoke the execution of other paragraphs. Further, we can identify paragraphs that are not executed by the program (which can easily happen through oversight). Also, if we make a change to a paragraph, we can easily identify which additional procedures are going to have this change also incorporated into them, indirectly. The student will find it instructive to complete the diagram for the UPDATE-ROUTINE and ERROR-LISTING paragraphs.

DAILY PROCESSING

Each department generates daily transactions which are illustrated in Figure 12-5. In addition to the account-number, each transaction contains a one-digit code so that purchases, payments, returns, adjustments, and control-total are identified for processing. The control-total transaction is a special one. It is created by the department involved to be used as a control that all transactions have been transmitted and that all

EXHIBIT 12-1   A PROGRAM FOR MASTER FILE PROCESSING

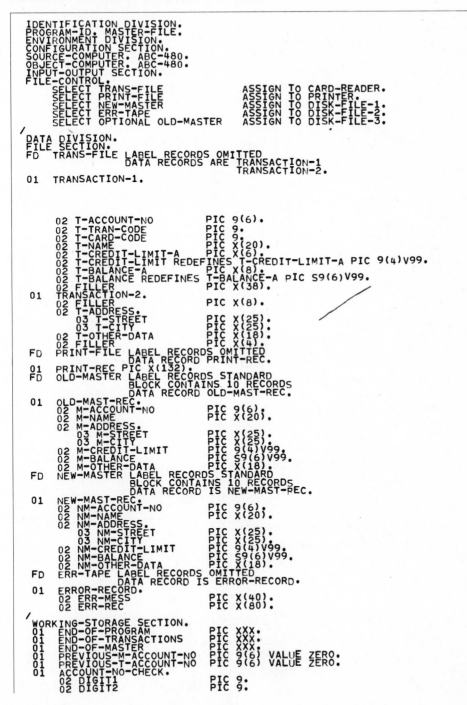

```
IDENTIFICATION DIVISION.
PROGRAM-ID. MASTER-FILE.
ENVIRONMENT DIVISION.
CONFIGURATION SECTION.
SOURCE-COMPUTER. ABC-480.
OBJECT-COMPUTER. ABC-480.
INPUT-OUTPUT SECTION.
FILE-CONTROL.
    SELECT TRANS-FILE           ASSIGN TO CARD-READER.
    SELECT PRINT-FILE           ASSIGN TO PRINTER.
    SELECT NEW-MASTER           ASSIGN TO DISK-FILE-1.
    SELECT ERR-TAPE             ASSIGN TO DISK-FILE-2.
    SELECT OPTIONAL OLD-MASTER  ASSIGN TO DISK-FILE-3.

DATA DIVISION.
FILE SECTION.
FD  TRANS-FILE LABEL RECORDS OMITTED
               DATA RECORDS ARE TRANSACTION-1
                                TRANSACTION-2.
01    TRANSACTION-1.


      02 T-ACCOUNT-NO          PIC 9(6).
      02 T-TRAN-CODE           PIC 9.
      02 T-CARD-CODE           PIC 9.
      02 T-NAME                PIC X(20).
      02 T-CREDIT-LIMIT-A      PIC X(6).
      02 T-CREDIT-LIMIT REDEFINES T-CREDIT-LIMIT-A PIC 9(4)V99.
      02 T-BALANCE-A           PIC X(8).
      02 T-BALANCE REDEFINES T-BALANCE-A PIC S9(6)V99.
      02 FILLER                PIC X(38).
01    TRANSACTION-2.
      02 FILLER                PIC X(8).
      02 T-ADDRESS.
         03 T-STREET           PIC X(25).
         03 T-CITY             PIC X(25).
      02 T-OTHER-DATA          PIC X(18).
      02 FILLER                PIC X(4).
FD  PRINT-FILE LABEL RECORDS OMITTED
               DATA RECORD PRINT-REC.
01    PRINT-REC PIC X(132).
FD  OLD-MASTER LABEL RECORDS STANDARD
               BLOCK CONTAINS 10 RECORDS
               DATA RECORD OLD-MAST-REC.
01    OLD-MAST-REC.
      02 M-ACCOUNT-NO          PIC 9(6).
      02 M-NAME                PIC X(20).
      02 M-ADDRESS.
         03 M-STREET           PIC X(25).
         03 M-CITY             PIC X(25).
      02 M-CREDIT-LIMIT        PIC 9(4)V99.
      02 M-BALANCE             PIC S9(6)V99.
      02 M-OTHER-DATA          PIC X(18).
FD  NEW-MASTER LABEL RECORDS STANDARD
               BLOCK CONTAINS 10 RECORDS
               DATA RECORD IS NEW-MAST-REC.
01    NEW-MAST-REC.
      02 NM-ACCOUNT-NO         PIC 9(6).
      02 NM-NAME               PIC X(20).
      02 NM-ADDRESS.
         03 NM-STREET          PIC X(25).
         03 NM-CITY            PIC X(25).
      02 NM-CREDIT-LIMIT       PIC 9(4)V99.
      02 NM-BALANCE            PIC S9(6)V99.
      02 NM-OTHER-DATA         PIC X(18).
FD  ERR-TAPE LABEL RECORDS OMITTED
             DATA RECORD IS ERROR-RECORD.
01    ERROR-RECORD.
      02 ERR-MESS              PIC X(40).
      02 ERR-REC               PIC X(80).

WORKING-STORAGE SECTION.
01    END-OF-PROGRAM           PIC XXX.
01    END-OF-TRANSACTIONS      PIC XXX.
01    END-OF-MASTER            PIC XXX.
01    PREVIOUS-M-ACCOUNT-NO    PIC 9(6) VALUE ZERO.
01    PREVIOUS-T-ACCOUNT-NO    PIC 9(6) VALUE ZERO.
01    ACCOUNT-NO-CHECK.
      02 DIGIT1                PIC 9.
      02 DIGIT2                PIC 9.
```

EXHIBIT 12-1   A PROGRAM FOR MASTER FILE PROCESSING *(Continued)*

```
        02 DIGIT3                PIC 9.
        02 DIGIT4                PIC 9.
        02 DIGIT5                PIC 9.
        02 CHECK-DIGIT           PIC 9.
    01  TRUNCATED-SUM            PIC 9.
    01  CHECK-ACCOUNT-NO         PIC XXX VALUE 'YES'.
        88 VALID-ACCOUNT-NO VALUE 'YES'.
    01  HEADER1.
        02 FILLER                PIC X(44) VALUE SPACES.
        02 FILLER                PIC X(28) VALUE
           'CUSTOMER MASTER FILE CHANGES'.
    01  HEADER2.
        02 FILLER                PIC X(54) VALUE SPACES.
        02 HEADER-DATE           PIC 99B99B99.
    01  HEADER3.
        02 FILLER                PIC X(28) VALUE
           ' ACC NO   TRANS               NAME'.
        02 FILLER                PIC X(12) VALUE SPACES.
        02 FILLER                PIC X(40) VALUE
           'STREET ADDRESS               CITY ADDRESS'.
        02 FILLER                PIC X(35) VALUE
           '          CR. LIMIT          BALANCE'.
    01  DATA-LINE.
        02 D-ACCOUNT-NO          PIC Z(7).
        02 FILLER                PIC XXXX VALUE SPACES.
        02 D-TRAN-CODE           PIC 9.
        02 FILLER                PIC XXXX VALUE SPACES.
        02 D-NAME                PIC X(22).
        02 D-STREET              PIC X(27).
        02 D-CITY                PIC X(28).
        02 D-CREDIT-LIMIT        PIC Z,ZZZ.99.
        02 FILLER                PIC XXX VALUE SPACES.
        02 D-BALANCE             PIC ZZ,ZZZ.99.
/
PROCEDURE DIVISION.

MAIN-PROCESSING.
    PERFORM STARTUP.

    PERFORM CREATE-OR-UPDATE

    PERFORM UPDATE-ROUTINE
        UNTIL END-OF-PROGRAM = 'YES'.

    PERFORM ERROR-LISTING.
    CLOSE TRANS-FILE
          PRINT-FILE
          NEW-MASTER
          OLD-MASTER
          ERR-TAPE.
    STOP RUN.


STARTUP.
    MOVE 'NO' TO END-OF-TRANSACTIONS
                 END-OF-MASTER
                 END-OF-PROGRAM
    OPEN INPUT   TRANS-FILE
         OUTPUT  PRINT-FILE
                 ERR-TAPE
                 NEW-MASTER.

    ACCEPT HEADER-DATE FROM DATE.

    WRITE PRINT-REC FROM HEADER1 AFTER ADVANCING PAGE.
    WRITE PRINT-REC FROM HEADER2 AFTER ADVANCING 1 LINE.
    WRITE PRINT-REC FROM HEADER3 AFTER ADVANCING 2 LINES.
CREATE-OR-UPDATE.
    READ TRANS-FILE RECORD
        AT END MOVE 'YES' TO END-OF-TRANSACTIONS.
    IF END-OF-TRANSACTIONS = 'YES'
        PERFORM NO-TRANSACTIONS
    ELSE
        IF T-TRAN-CODE = 9
           PERFORM CREATE-MASTER
        ELSE
           MOVE T-ACCOUNT-NO TO ACCOUNT-NO-CHECK
           PERFORM UPDATE-START.
```

EXHIBIT 12-1   A PROGRAM FOR MASTER FILE PROCESSING *(Continued)*

```
CREATE-MASTER.
    PERFORM READ-TRANS-START THRU READ-TRANS-END.
    IF END-OF-TRANSACTIONS = 'YES'
        PERFORM NO-TRANSACTIONS
    ELSE
            PERFORM PROCESS-REMAINING-TRANS.

UPDATE-START.
    IF NOT VALID-ACCOUNT-NO
    PERFORM READ-TRANS-START
        UNTIL VALID-ACCOUNT-NO.
    OPEN INPUT OLD-MASTER
    PERFORM READ-MASTER-START THRU READ-MASTER-END.

NO-TRANSACTIONS.
    MOVE ' NO TRANSACTIONS PRESENT,  RUN TERMINATED'
        TO PRINT-REC
    WRITE PRINT-REC AFTER ADVANCING 2 LINES
    MOVE 'YES' TO END-OF-PROGRAM.

READ-TRANS-START.
    READ TRANS-FILE RECORD
        AT END MOVE 'YES' TO END-OF-TRANSACTIONS
                MOVE 'YES' TO CHECK-ACCOUNT-NO.
    IF END-OF-TRANSACTIONS NOT = 'YES'
    MOVE T-ACCOUNT-NO TO ACCOUNT-NO-CHECK
    PERFORM CHECK-DIGIT-SUM
    IF NOT VALID-ACCOUNT-NO
        MOVE ' INVALID ACCOUNT NUMBER' TO ERR-MESS
        PERFORM LIST-WRONG-TRANS
    ELSE
        NEXT SENTENCE
    ELSE
        NEXT SENTENCE.

READ-TRANS-LOOP.
    PERFORM READ-TRANS-START
        UNTIL VALID-ACCOUNT-NO.

READ-TRANS-END.
    EXIT.

READ-MASTER-START.
    READ OLD-MASTER RECORD
        AT END MOVE 'YES' TO END-OF-MASTER
                MOVE 'YES' TO CHECK-ACCOUNT-NO.
    IF END-OF-MASTER NOT = 'YES'
    MOVE M-ACCOUNT-NO TO ACCOUNT-NO-CHECK
    PERFORM CHECK-DIGIT-SUM
    IF NOT VALID-ACCOUNT-NO
        MOVE ' INVALID ACCOUNT-NO IN MASTER FILE'
            TO PRINT-REC
        WRITE PRINT-REC AFTER 2
        WRITE PRINT-REC FROM OLD-MAST-REC AFTER 2
    ELSE
        NEXT SENTENCE
    ELSE
        NEXT SENTENCE.
READ-MASTER-LOOP.
    PERFORM READ-MASTER-START
        UNTIL VALID-ACCOUNT-NO.
READ-MASTER-END.
    EXIT.


CHECK-DIGIT-SUM.
    ADD DIGIT1 DIGIT2 DIGIT3 DIGIT4 DIGIT5
        GIVING TRUNCATED-SUM.
    IF TRUNCATED-SUM = CHECK-DIGIT
        MOVE 'YES' TO CHECK-ACCOUNT-NO
    ELSE
        MOVE 'NO' TO CHECK-ACCOUNT-NO.
```

EXHIBIT 12-1   A PROGRAM FOR MASTER FILE PROCESSING *(Continued)*

```
UPDATE-ROUTINE.
    IF END-OF-MASTER = 'YES'
        PERFORM PROCESS-REMAINING-TRANS
    ELSE
        IF END-OF-TRANSACTIONS = 'YES'
            PERFORM PROCESS-REMAINING-MASTER
        ELSE
            IF T-ACCOUNT-NO = M-ACCOUNT-NO
                PERFORM PROCESS-UPDATE
            ELSE
                IF T-ACCOUNT-NO > M-ACCOUNT-NO
                    PERFORM COPY-MASTER
                ELSE
                    PERFORM ADD-OR-ERROR.
PROCESS-REMAINING-TRANS.
    IF T-ACCOUNT-NO > PREVIOUS-T-ACCOUNT-NO
        AND T-ACCOUNT-NO > PREVIOUS-M-ACCOUNT-NO
        PERFORM ADD-RECORD
            UNTIL END-OF-TRANSACTIONS = 'YES'
    ELSE
        MOVE ' TRANSACTION RECORD OUT OF SEQUENCE RUN TERMINATED'
            TO ERR-MESS
        PERFORM LIST-WRONG-TRANS.
    MOVE 'YES' TO END-OF-PROGRAM.
ADD-RECORD.
    IF T-ACCOUNT-NO > PREVIOUS-T-ACCOUNT-NO
        AND T-TRAN-CODE = 1
        AND T-CARD-CODE = 1
        AND T-CREDIT-LIMIT-A IS NUMERIC
        AND T-BALANCE-A IS NUMERIC
        MOVE T-ACCOUNT-NO TO NM-ACCOUNT-NO, D-ACCOUNT-NO
        MOVE T-NAME TO NM-NAME, D-NAME
        MOVE T-CREDIT-LIMIT TO NM-CREDIT-LIMIT, D-CREDIT-LIMIT
        MOVE T-BALANCE TO NM-BALANCE, D-BALANCE
        MOVE T-ACCOUNT-NO TO PREVIOUS-T-ACCOUNT-NO
        PERFORM READ-SECOND-CARD
    ELSE
        MOVE ' ERRONEOUS TRANSACTION RECORD' TO ERR-MESS
        PERFORM LIST-WRONG-TRANS.
    PERFORM READ-TRANS-START THRU READ-TRANS-END.
READ-SECOND-CARD.
    PERFORM READ-TRANS-START THRU READ-TRANS-END.
    IF END-OF-TRANSACTIONS = 'NO'
        IF T-ACCOUNT-NO = PREVIOUS-T-ACCOUNT-NO
            AND T-CARD-CODE = 2
            MOVE T-STREET TO NM-STREET, D-STREET
            MOVE T-CITY TO NM-CITY, D-CITY
            MOVE T-OTHER-DATA TO NM-OTHER-DATA
            MOVE 1 TO D-TRAN-CODE
            WRITE NEW-MAST-REC
            WRITE PRINT-REC FROM DATA-LINE AFTER ADVANCING 1 LINE
            MOVE SPACES TO DATA-LINE
        ELSE
            MOVE ' SECOND CARD MISSING OR ERROR' TO ERR-MESS
            PERFORM LIST-WRONG-TRANS
    ELSE
        MOVE ' SECOND CARD MISSING FOR ADD TRANS AT END OF FILE'
            TO PRINT-REC
        WRITE PRINT-REC AFTER ADVANCING 2 LINES
        MOVE 'YES' TO END-OF-PROGRAM.
PROCESS-REMAINING-MASTER.
    PERFORM COPY-MASTER
        UNTIL END-OF-MASTER = 'YES'.
    MOVE 'YES' TO END-OF-PROGRAM.
COPY-MASTER.
    WRITE NEW-MAST-REC FROM OLD-MAST-REC.
    PERFORM READ-MASTER-START THRU READ-MASTER-END.
PROCESS-UPDATE.
    IF T-TRAN-CODE > 1
        AND T-TRAN-CODE < 9
        PERFORM MODIFY
    ELSE
```

EXHIBIT 12-1   A PROGRAM FOR MASTER FILE PROCESSING *(Continued)*

```
            MOVE ' WRONG TRANSACTION CODE' TO ERR-MESS
            PERFORM LIST-WRONG-TRANS
            PERFORM READ-TRANS-START THRU READ-TRANS-END.

   MODIFY.
        IF T-TRAN-CODE = 2
            PERFORM DELETION
        ELSE
            IF T-TRAN-CODE = 3
                PERFORM CHANGE-NAME
            ELSE
                IF T-TRAN-CODE = 4
                    PERFORM CHANGE-CREDIT
                ELSE
                    IF T-TRAN-CODE = 5
                        PERFORM CHANGE-NAME-CREDIT
                    ELSE
                        IF T-TRAN-CODE = 6
                            PERFORM CHANGE-ADDRESS
                        ELSE
                            MOVE ' WRONG TRANSACTION CODE' TO ERR-MESS
                            PERFORM LIST-WRONG-TRANS
                            PERFORM READ-TRANS-START THRU READ-TRANS-END.

   DELETION.
        MOVE T-ACCOUNT-NO TO PREVIOUS-T-ACCOUNT-NO
        PERFORM MOVE-OLD-MAST-TO-PRINT.
        PERFORM READ-TRANS-START THRU READ-TRANS-END.
        WRITE PRINT-REC FROM DATA-LINE AFTER ADVANCING 1 LINE.
        PERFORM READ-MASTER-START THRU READ-MASTER-END.
        MOVE M-ACCOUNT-NO TO PREVIOUS-M-ACCOUNT-NO.

   MOVE-OLD-MAST-TO-PRINT.
        MOVE T-ACCOUNT-NO TO D-ACCOUNT-NO.
        MOVE T-TRAN-CODE TO D-TRAN-CODE.
        MOVE M-NAME TO D-NAME
        MOVE M-STREET TO D-STREET
        MOVE M-CITY TO D-CITY
        MOVE M-CREDIT-LIMIT TO D-CREDIT-LIMIT
        MOVE M-BALANCE TO D-BALANCE.

   CHANGE-NAME.
        PERFORM MOVE-OLD-MAST-TO-PRINT.
        WRITE PRINT-REC FROM DATA-LINE AFTER ADVANCING 1 LINE.
        MOVE SPACES TO DATA-LINE
        MOVE T-NAME TO D-NAME
                        M-NAME
        WRITE PRINT-REC FROM DATA-LINE AFTER ADVANCING 1 LINE.
        PERFORM CHECK-FOR-ADDRESS-CHANGE.

   CHECK-FOR-ADDRESS-CHANGE.
        MOVE M-ACCOUNT-NO TO PREVIOUS-M-ACCOUNT-NO
        MOVE T-ACCOUNT-NO TO PREVIOUS-T-ACCOUNT-NO
        PERFORM READ-TRANS-START THRU READ-TRANS-END.
        IF T-ACCOUNT-NO = PREVIOUS-T-ACCOUNT-NO
            IF T-TRAN-CODE = 6
                MOVE SPACES TO DATA-LINE
                MOVE T-TRAN-CODE TO D-TRAN-CODE
                MOVE T-STREET TO D-STREET
                MOVE T-CITY   TO D-CITY
                WRITE PRINT-REC FROM DATA-LINE AFTER ADVANCING 1 LINE
                MOVE T-ADDRESS TO M-ADDRESS
                WRITE NEW-MAST-REC FROM OLD-MAST-REC
                PERFORM READ-TRANS-START THRU READ-TRANS-END
                PERFORM READ-MASTER-START THRU READ-MASTER-END
            ELSE
                MOVE ' INVALID TRANSACTION CODE' TO PRINT-REC
                WRITE PRINT-REC AFTER ADVANCING 2 LINES
                WRITE PRINT-REC FROM TRANSACTION-1
                    AFTER ADVANCING 1 LINE
        ELSE
            WRITE NEW-MAST-REC FROM OLD-MAST-REC.
            PERFORM READ-MASTER-START THRU READ-MASTER-END.

   CHANGE-CREDIT.
        PERFORM MOVE-OLD-MAST-TO-PRINT.
        WRITE PRINT-REC FROM DATA-LINE.
        MOVE SPACES TO DATA-LINE.
        MOVE T-CREDIT-LIMIT TO D-CREDIT-LIMIT
                               M-CREDIT-LIMIT
        WRITE PRINT-REC FROM DATA-LINE AFTER ADVANCING 1 LINE.
        PERFORM CHECK-FOR-ADDRESS-CHANGE.
```

EXHIBIT 12-1   A PROGRAM FOR MASTER FILE PROCESSING *(Continued)*

```
CHANGE-NAME-CREDIT.
    PERFORM MOVE-OLD-MAST-TO-PRINT.
    WRITE PRINT-REC FROM DATA-LINE AFTER ADVANCING 1 LINE.
    MOVE SPACES TO DATA-LINE
    MOVE T-NAME TO D-NAME
                    M-NAME
    MOVE T-CREDIT-LIMIT TO D-CREDIT-LIMIT
                           M-CREDIT-LIMIT
    WRITE PRINT-REC FROM DATA-LINE AFTER ADVANCING 1 LINE.
    PERFORM CHECK-FOR-ADDRESS-CHANGE.

CHANGE-ADDRESS.
    PERFORM MOVE-OLD-MAST-TO-PRINT.
    WRITE PRINT-REC FROM DATA-LINE AFTER ADVANCING 1 LINE.
    MOVE SPACES TO DATA-LINE
    MOVE T-STREET TO D-STREET
                     M-STREET
    MOVE T-CITY TO D-CITY
                   M-CITY
    WRITE PRINT-REC FROM DATA-LINE AFTER ADVANCING 1 LINE.
    WRITE NEW-MAST-REC FROM OLD-MAST-REC.
    PERFORM READ-TRANS-START THRU READ-TRANS-END.
    PERFORM READ-MASTER-START THRU READ-MASTER-END.

ADD-OR-ERROR.
    IF T-TRAN-CODE = 1
        PERFORM ADD-RECORD
    ELSE
        MOVE ' FILES OUT OF SEQUENCE JOB TERMINATED' TO ERR-MESS
        PERFORM LIST-WRONG-TRANS
        WRITE PRINT-REC FROM OLD-MAST-REC AFTER ADVANCING 2 LINES.

LIST-WRONG-TRANS.
    MOVE TRANSACTION-1 TO ERR-REC



    WRITE ERROR-RECORD.

ERROR-LISTING.
    CLOSE ERR-TAPE.
    OPEN INPUT ERR-TAPE.
    MOVE SPACES TO ERR-MESS.
    MOVE '*** E R R O R   L I S T I N G **' TO ERR-REC.
    WRITE PRINT-REC FROM ERROR-RECORD AFTER ADVANCING PAGE.
    MOVE 'NO' TO END-OF-PROGRAM
    READ ERR-TAPE RECORD
        AT END MOVE 'YES' TO END-OF-PROGRAM.
    IF END-OF-PROGRAM = 'YES'
        MOVE ' NO ERROR TRANSACTIONS' TO ERR-REC
        WRITE PRINT-REC FROM ERROR-RECORD AFTER 2
    ELSE NEXT SENTENCE.
    PERFORM ERR-LIST-1
        UNTIL END-OF-PROGRAM = 'YES'.

ERR-LIST-1.
    READ ERR-TAPE RECORD
        AT END MOVE 'YES' TO END-OF-PROGRAM.
    IF END-OF-PROGRAM NOT = 'YES'
        WRITE PRINT-REC FROM ERROR-RECORD
               AFTER ADVANCING 2 LINES
    ELSE
        NEXT SENTENCE.
```

dollar values (columns 28–33) have been entered correctly into the machine-processable transactions. One can visualize that a clerk in the department uses an adding machine or a "cash-register" tape to sum up all dollar values involved. This sum is the control total. When the transactions are read in, their dollar values are summed up and their sum is compared to the control-total. If the totals are different this fact is reported, so that management can investigate the cause of the discrepancy.

EXHIBIT 12-1   SAMPLE DATA WHICH CAN BE USED WITH THE PROGRAM IN

```
Sample file creation data:


       9
12345511JOHN L. ANDERSON        08000000015025
123455121020 NORTH 10TH STREET     ANYTOWN AZ 85280
13345611LINDA M. BREWSTER    10000000223000
133456121929 NORTHERN AVENUE       ANYTOWN AZ 85280
24567411LESLIE J. CROWN          08000000000000
245674121976 WASHINGTON BLVD.      ANYTOWN AZ 85280
31111711JAMES J. JONES          15000000060113
311117122020 VISTA DEL SOL         ANYTOWN AZ 85280
32222111PAT N. THOMPSON         08000000000000
3222211110 EAST PLAZA RD.          ANYTOWN AZ 85280
35123411JEAN L. PENDLETON      10000000055555
35123412888 WEST PLAZA RD.         ANYTOWN AZ 85280
41233811ELMER J. GUSTON        10000000000000
41233312350 SOUTHERN AVENUE        ANYTOWN AZ 85280




Sample file update data:


13345631LINDA K. STERN
133456621414 PRIMROSE LANE          ANYTOWN AZ 85280
15555111JIM N. PASTORE         08000000000000
1555511220 SOUTH RIDGE RD.         ANYTOWN AZ 85280
3512342
```

Exhibit 12-3 illustrates the format of the printed output of the daily transaction processing. The top report is a Daily Transactions Register with suitable column totals. Transaction dollar values are accumulated as records are read in. If the sum does not equal the department control total then the message ***OUT OF BALANCE is printed for the attention of management.

A second printed report details ERROR TRANSACTIONS for each department.

Figure 12-6 presents a process chart for daily processing. Correct transactions are sorted on account number and processed further. Incorrect transactions are corrected and fed back at a subsequent time.

The sorted correct transactions are processed against the Daily Master file. This file contains one record for each customer, consisting of account-number, credit limit, and balance. Its creation can be incorporated in the Master file creation and update process of Figure 12-1. As each new Master record is written, the relevant three fields can be sent to the Daily Master file. That procedure has not been included here in order to control complexity and to allow the opportunity to assign the modification as a programming assignment.

The transactions update the Daily Master. If the balance of a given customer exceeds the credit limit, then a credit control report is issued on the printer, identifying the customer. This report can be used by management to contact the customer or alert check-out clerks of the facts. In an actual application, a complete approach would require that we obtain the credit history for each customer who has exceeded the credit limit. However, our objective in this example is to understand sequential file processing logic—not the development of a complete credit control system.

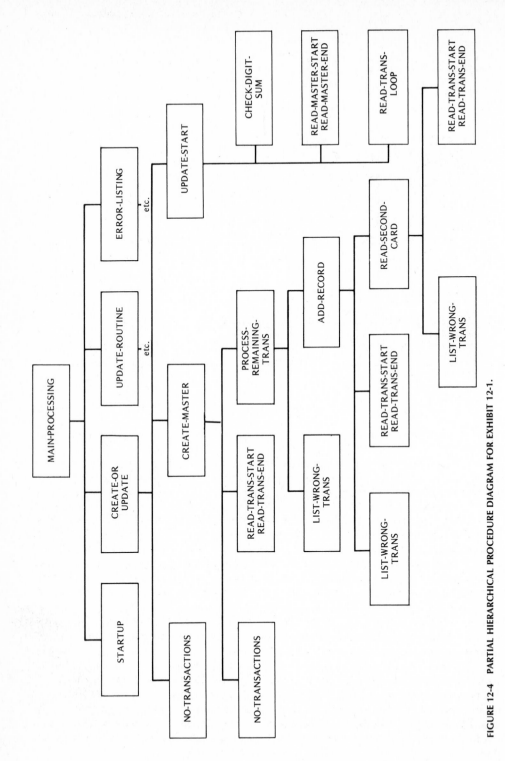

FIGURE 12-4 PARTIAL HIERARCHICAL PROCEDURE DIAGRAM FOR EXHIBIT 12-1.

DATA-NAME	COLUMNS	PURCHASE	PAYMENT	RETURN	ADJUSTMENT	CONTROL-TOTAL
ACCOUNT-NO	1–6	X	X	X	X	
TRANS-CODE		X	X	X	X	X
Purchase = 1		X				
Payment = 2			X			
Return = 3				X		
Adjustment = 4					X	
Control-total = 5						X
DATE	8–13	X	X	X	X	X
DEPT-NO	14–15	X	X	X	X	X
PRODUCT-NO	16–23	X		X		
QUANTITY	24–27	X		X		
DOLLAR-VALUE	28–33	X	X	X	X	X

FIGURE 12-5   DAILY TRANSACTIONS.

MONTHLY STATEMENT PRODUCTION

Figure 12-7 presents a process chart for the monthly statement production task. Every month customers receive a bill itemizing their account transactions. To begin with, the Daily Transaction files are merged to form one Cumulative Daily Transaction file. The merging could be taking place every day, every week, or at some other interval. If the only use of the Cumulative Daily Transactions file is at the end of the month, then it would, in general, be more efficient to wait for that time before merging the daily files.

In addition to the billing statement and the updating of the Daily Master and the Master files there would be a variety of reports produced for management use. Again, those considerations exceed our scope of interest.

Before concluding the description of this case, it should be emphasized that the updatings of the Master file as outlined in Figure 12-1 is a different task from the updating of the Master file in Figure 12-3. It is true that the two tasks could be combined into one by expanding the types of transactions and the processing functions to include all categories. We chose to separate the tasks for two reasons: first, in order to reduce the complexity of the task by breaking it into two different modules;

EXHIBIT 12-3   REPORT FORMAT FOR DAILY PROCESSING

DAILY TRANSACTIONS REGISTER (Report 1)
DD/MM/YR

DEPT NO XX

ACCOUNT	TRAN CODE	DATE	DEPT NO	PRODUCT NO	QUANTITY	PURCHASE	PAYMENT	RETURN	ADJUSTMENT
						XX	XX	XX	XX

TOTAL
DEPARTMENT CONTROL TOTAL XX
COMPUTED CONTROL TOTAL XX
***OUT OF BALANCE

ERROR TRANSACTIONS (Report 2)
DD/MM/YR

DEPT NO XX   BATCH DATE DD/MM/YR
List error transactions with a suitable error message

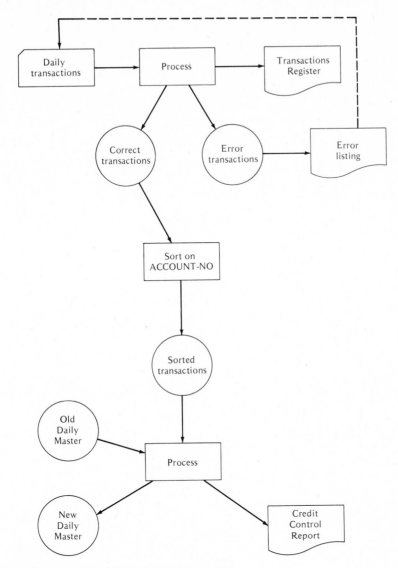

FIGURE 12-6   DAILY TRANSACTION PROCESSING.

and second, it is likely that the persons handling modifications to the Master file are different from the ones dealing with purchases, payments, etc. In that respect, it may make good sense to keep the Master file maintenance with respect to additions, deletions, address changes, etc., as a separate task from the financial updating of the Master file.

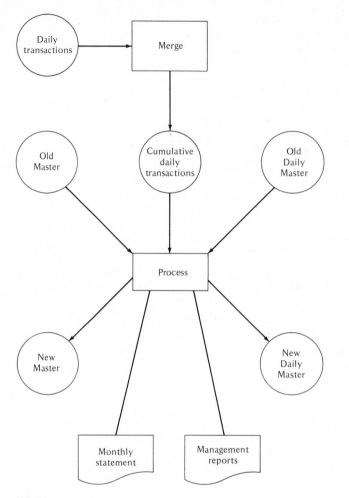

FIGURE 12-7   MONTHLY STATEMENT PRODUCTION.

EXERCISES

1   Use the following data as input and produce a Daily Transactions Register report and an Error Transactions report such as the ones illustrated in Exhibit 12-3.

```
        676042510                    005650
0135651760424101234567801000001000
0243211760424102345678900250011550
3111172760424102345678900050003100
```

```
      676042515              054000
5001283760424150010010000010000100
314525276042515092000000 05 001900
429780176042514003002000004002000
410235176042515004003000050010000
600220176042515005004000010020000
600220676042515005004000010020000
      676042520              656749
311117176042520010101000020002559
216481176042520020202000100010000
978565176042520030303001000030000
013565276032520040404001001468923
500128176042520050505050000145267
      676042540              006000
024320776042540010909090032001000
013565076042540020908080000000000
020215276042540030908080005005000
```

2 Modify the program of Exhibit 12-1 to incorporate the creation of a Daily Master file as discussed in the fifth paragraph of the Daily Processing section of this chapter.

13

Sorting and Merging Sequential Files

FILE SORTING

In our discussions of sequential tape file maintenance in the two preceding chapters, it was evident that sequential files must be sorted in sequence. The basis for the sequence is dictated by management needs. For example, in the processing of sales transactions, analysis may be required by product, by date, and by geographic area. In order to produce such a report, the data file has to be sorted so that the data is sequenced in the desired order.

File sorting is a complex task. Because it is so common, a number of file sorting procedures (algorithms) have been developed. Many algorithms are proprietary and therefore confidential. Still it is important to be familiar with the basic concepts, and therefore we undertake to present an elementary but basic description. Our purpose in this section is to provide an introduction to the concepts of file sorting by describing a rather basic file sorting procedure. This procedure involves two phases. In the first phase a group of records is read into central storage and an internal sort algorithm is applied to the records. The resulting set of sorted records is written by means of an output device, and another group of unsorted records is read into central storage. The process is repeated until all records have been processed. In the second phase a procedure involving repetitive merging of the sorted groups of records is used until the entire file is sorted. *Merging* is a process whereby two or more sequential files,

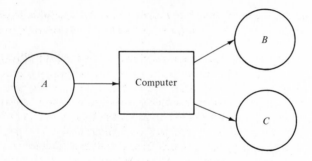

**FIGURE 13-1   CONFIGURATION OF INPUT AND OUTPUT ASSOCI-
ATED WITH THE FIRST STEP OF A FILE SORTING ROUTINE.**

each sorted in the same order, are combined to form one file in the same sort order as
the source files. The subject of file merging is discussed further in a later section of this
chapter.

In order to gain an overview of the two-phase file sorting procedure let us
consider an example.

Suppose that records with the following sort-key values are held on a reel of
magnetic tape and are to be sorted in ascending order: 50, 90, 10, 30, 120, 60, 20, 80. As
explained further in the next section of this chapter, a *sort key* is the designated field
which serves as the basis for sorting a file. In order to keep the illustration simple,
suppose that an internal sort algorithm will be employed to sort groups of just three
records at a time. Further, assume that four magnetic tape units are available. As the
first step in the sort routine, the original file tape is mounted on tape unit A and two
blank, or "scratch," tapes are mounted on units B and C for output. The general
configuration of input and output is represented in Figure 13-1.

The first three records (50, 90, 10) are read, sorted, and written on tape B. The next
group of three records (30, 120, 60) is then read, sorted, and written on tape C. The
reason that the second group of records is written on tape C rather than tape B is that
the smallest record in the group, record 30, is smaller than the highest record already
entered on tape B (record 90). If such were not the case, the second group of three
records would also be entered on tape B. The next group of records read is in fact the
last group in our example, and consists of the remaining two records. These two
records are sorted internally and then written on tape B. The reason that tape B is
chosen is that, even though the highest record on tape B (record 90) is larger than the
smallest record in the new group, that record is smaller than the highest record on
tape C (record 120). At the completion of this first phase of the sort routine, the
records are held on tapes B and C as follows:

CONTENTS OF B	CONTENTS OF C
10	30
50	60
90	120
20	
80	

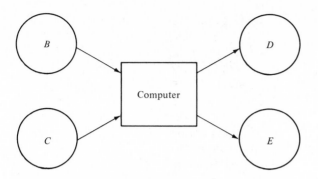

**FIGURE 13-2   CONFIGURATION OF INPUT AND OUTPUT ASSOCI-
ATED WITH THE SECOND STEP OF A FILE SORTING ROUTINE.**

Tapes B and C are now rewound and then opened as input tapes, while two other tapes, D and E, are mounted as output tapes. The general configuration of input and output for the second phase of the file sorting routine is illustrated in Figure 13-2. Incidentally, note that normally the original input tape (tape A) is set aside as backup in case something should go wrong during the sort, or in case the original record order of that tape is needed for subsequent processing.

With use of the configuration portrayed in Figure 13-2, tapes B and C are read for possible merging on tape D. Such a merging is accomplished up to the point of record 20. Because record 20 is lower than the preceding record 90, it is written on tape E. Similarly, record 80 is also smaller than record 90 and is also written on tape E. Finally, record 120, which is the last record read, is higher than both record 90 on tape D and record 80 on tape E. However, because it is closer to record 90 in terms of key value, it is written on tape D. Consequently, the result of the first merge is two sorted files, as follows:

CONTENTS OF D	CONTENTS OF E
10	20
30	80
50	
60	
90	
120	

All four file tapes are now rewound. Then, tapes D and E are used as input, and tapes B and C are used for output, with the objective of merging the two input files on tape B, if possible. The input/output configuration for this third step is portrayed in Figure 13-3.

Since tape files D and E are in sequence in the present example, this is the last merge required. All records will be written on tape B as one complete and sorted file.

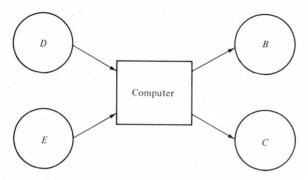

**FIGURE 13-3   CONFIGURATION OF INPUT AND OUTPUT ASSOCI-
ATED WITH THE THIRD STEP OF A FILE SORTING ROUTINE.**

Incidentally, the fact that the file has been completely sorted is determined by observing that all records are written on the same tape in the merge operation. The programming logic used is to set some data-name equal to some value, such as zero, at the start of the merge, and to change that value only if a record is written on the alternate tape. At the completion of the merge, the value of the data-name is tested. For the present example, the completion of the final merge results in the following contents for files B and C:

CONTENTS OF B	CONTENTS OF C
10	Blank
20	
30	
50	
60	
80	
90	
120	

Some observations regarding the sorting of files are in order. First, it is to our advantage to sort as large a group of records as possible in the internal sort phase of the sort routine. As the extreme case, if the group sorted internally is as large as the entire file, there will be no need for any subsequent merging. Of course, this is a trivial case. On the other hand, if each group sorted internally consists of one-half the file, only one tape merge will be required. In general, then, the larger the groups of records that are sorted in central storage, the smaller the number of merges required. The basic limitation is the central storage available. Central storage is generally measured in terms of thousands of characters of capacity, whereas typical data files include thousands of records.

Another point is that, the more tape units used, the faster the sort. If six tape units are used instead of four, fewer merges will be required. In general, however, we prefer an even number of tape units, so that the number of input and output units is equal.

Finally, since a great number of input/output operations occur during each merge operation, the records should be blocked in order to reduce the time devoted to such operations. But we should also observe that, in the internal sort phase of the overall sort procedure, the larger the output blocks used, the smaller the storage area available for the internal sort.

REVIEW

1   In order to sort a large data file, a combination of an internal file [sorting / merging] algorithm and an external file [sorting / merging] algorithm is typically used.

sorting; merging

2   In the internal sort phase of the file sorting procedure the group of records read into the computer at any one time usually constitutes [some / all] of the records in the given file.

some

3   The second phase of the file sorting procedure consists of repeated merging attempts involving two files until [both files are completely sorted / one sorted file and one blank file are produced].

one sorted file and one blank file are produced

COBOL SORT FEATURE

Since file sorting is frequently required in maintaining an information system, the COBOL language incorporates a sort feature which makes it possible to accomplish this operation with minimal programming. The programmer need not be concerned with the details of any sort algorithm in using this feature. Rather, one simply specifies the files to be sorted, the sort key (or keys) to be used, and any special procedures for the handling of files before or after the sort. We here illustrate the COBOL sort feature by means of two examples.

EXAMPLE 1

Assume that we have a tape file with the following record description in the DATA DIVISION:

```
01   INTAPE-RECORD.
     02   ACCOUNT-NUMBER      PICTURE 9(8).
     02   NAME                PICTURE X(20).
```

```
02  TRANS-DATE.
    03  DAY-OF-YEAR          PICTURE 999.
    03  YEAR                 PICTURE 99.
02  OTHER-DATA               PICTURE X(71).
```

Suppose we wish to sort the file in ascending sequence according to ACCOUNT-NUMBER and in descending sequence according to YEAR. That is, for each account all records are to be arranged from the most recent to the least recent YEAR. Also, assume that the sorted file is called SORTED-FILE and is to be available on tape unit 3. The sorting process can be portrayed as involving three files, INPUT-FILE, SORT-WORK-FILE, and SORTED-FILE, as follows:

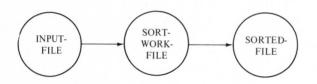

As discussed in the preceding section, in order to perform the sorting operation, there will be a need for more work tapes than the single SORT-WORK-FILE which the above diagram implies. Because the sorting procedure is preprogrammed, the programmer need not be concerned about the detail of the SORT-WORK-FILE. However, both the programmer and the computer operator should be aware that additional tape units should be assigned to the sorting task.

Exhibit 13-1 presents the COBOL program that can be used to sort the file described in the above example problem. In the ENVIRONMENT DIVISION, notice that three files are identified in the SELECT statements. Tape files are involved in the present problem, but the files could just as well have been stored on disk, for example.

In the DATA DIVISION the INPUT-FILE is described in the usual fashion. Notice, however, the SD (Sort Description) entry for the SORT-WORK-FILE. The level indicator SD indicates that this is the file to be used in conjunction with the sort routine. Notice also the absence of the LABEL RECORD clause. Some compilers permit the use of this clause, but ANSI COBOL excludes the option. The record description in the DATA DIVISION is straightforward and follows the usual format. The SORTED-FILE is an ordinary file. Notice that we chose to simplify the record description for this file by defining one overall PICTURE. Since the program is concerned only with sorting the file, there is no need to describe the parts of the records that constitute this file.

The relevant PROCEDURE DIVISION is simple and consists of just one paragraph. The SORT verb is very powerful in that the programmer need only specify the sort keys and the source and destination of the file records. The statement SORT SORT-WORK-FILE identifies the name of the file to be sorted—which should be the same file introduced by an SD entry in the DATA DIVISION. The ASCENDING KEY ACCOUNT-NUMBER-S clause specifies that the file is to be sorted in ascending ACCOUNT-NUMBER-S sequence. The DESCENDING KEY YEAR-S clause specifies that within each ACCOUNT-NUMBER-S we wish to sort in descending sequence with respect to the values contained in the YEAR-S field. Keep in mind that the key written first is the

EXHIBIT 13-1   SAMPLE SORT PROGRAM-1

```
IDENTIFICATION DIVISION.
PROGRAM-ID. SORT1.
REMARKS.   THIS PROGRAM ILLUSTRATES SORTING A SEQUENTIAL
     FILE CALLED INPUT-FILE AND MAKING THE SORTED FILE
     AVAILABLE IN SORTED-FILE.
ENVIRONMENT DIVISION.
CONFIGURATION SECTION.
SOURCE-COMPUTER. ABC-480.
OBJECT-COMPUTER. ABC-480.
INPUT-OUTPUT SECTION.
FILE-CONTROL.
     SELECT INPUT-FILE ASSIGN          TO CARD-READER.
     SELECT SORT-WORK-FILE     ASSIGN TO FILE-UNIT-1.
     SELECT SORTED-FILE ASSIGN         TO PRINTER.
DATA DIVISION.
FILE SECTION.
FD   INPUT-FILE LABEL RECORD OMITTED
     DATA RECORD IS INTAPE-RECORD.
01   INTAPE-RECORD.
     02   ACCOUNT-NUMBER             PICTURE 9(8).
     02   NAME                       PICTURE X(20).
     02   TRANSACTION-DATE.
          03   DAY-OF-YEAR           PICTURE 999.
          03   YEAR                  PICTURE 99.
     02 OTHER-DATA                   PICTURE X(71).
SD   SORT-WORK-FILE DATA RECORD IS WORK-RECORD.
01   WORK-RECORD.
     02   ACCOUNT-NUMBER-S           PICTURE 9(8).
     02   NAME-S                     PICTURE X(20).
     02   TRANSACTION-DATE-S.
          03   DAY-OF-YEAR           PICTURE 999.
          03   YEAR-S                PICTURE 99.
     02   OTHER-DATA                 PICTURE X(71).
FD   SORTED-FILE LABEL RECORD OMITTED
     DATA RECORD IS SORTED-RECORD.
01   SORTED-RECORD                   PICTURE X(104).
PROCEDURE DIVISION.
SORTING-PARAGRAPH.
     SORT SORT-WORK-FILE
     ON ASCENDING KEY ACCOUNT-NUMBER-S
     DESCENDING KEY YEAR-S
     USING INPUT-FILE
     GIVING SORTED-FILE.
     STOP RUN.
```

principal basis for the sort. Other keys are of decreasing sorting significance as we proceed from one to the next. For example, consider the following KEY clauses:

ASCENDING KEY STATE-NAME
ASCENDING KEY COUNTY-NAME
ASCENDING KEY CITY-NAME.

The order of listing of the above clauses indicates that STATE-NAME is the principal basis for the sort. Put another way, CITY-NAME will be sorted within COUNTY-NAME, and COUNTY-NAME will be sorted within STATE-NAME. Note that the sort keys are written according to the desired order of the sort, and not according to the order in which the keys appear in the record. For the example above it could very well be that the three fields used as sort keys are in the following physical order in the record: CITY-NAME, STATE-NAME, COUNTY-NAME.

The USING INPUT-FILE clause in Exhibit 13-1 specifies the file that is the source of the records, while the GIVING SORTED-FILE clause simply specifies the file on which the sort output is to be recorded. Finally, note that in the present example the programmer does *not* OPEN or CLOSE any of the three files involved. The use of the SORT verb automatically takes care of such procedures.

EXAMPLE 2

We now illustrate use of the COBOL sort feature with a more complex data processing task. Suppose we want to read a set of punched card records, add a field to each record to indicate its sequential order, sort the file, store the sorted file on magnetic tape, and finally, print the sorted tape as the output of the program. The process can be represented by the flowchart in Figure 13-4.

Exhibit 13-2 presents the COBOL program designed to accomplish the task described above. Notice that there are four files, called CARD-FILE, SORT-FILE, SORTED-FILE, and PRINT-FILE. DATA DIVISION entries follow the usual format, except for the use of SD to identify the SORT-FILE as the sort file, as was the case in the preceding example. In the present example the WORKING-STORAGE SECTION is used to form the SEQUENCE-NUMBER.

In the PROCEDURE DIVISION we first specify that we wish to sort the SORT-FILE on ASCENDING KEY NAME. Thus, the NAME field is the sort key. INPUT PROCEDURE IS READING-SEQUENCING indicates that records will become available to the SORT-FILE according to instructions contained in a section called READING-SEQUENCING. The first paragraph in the READING-SEQUENCING SECTION, called SET-UP, serves to open the CARD-FILE as input. Then we enter a loop involving the SEQ-RELEASE paragraph. Each card record is read, and in each case a four-digit sequence number is assigned to the field called DATA-TO-BE-INSERTED. Then we use the

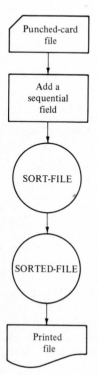

FIGURE 13-4 FLOWCHART FOR THE SAMPLE PROBLEM THAT INVOLVES USE OF THE SORT FEATURE.

EXHIBIT 13-2   SAMPLE SORT PROGRAM-2

```
IDENTIFICATION DIVISION.
PROGRAM-ID. SORT2
ENVIRONMENT DIVISION.
CONFIGURATION SECTION.
SOURCE-COMPUTER. ABC-480.
OBJECT-COMPUTER. ABC-480.
INPUT-OUTPUT SECTION.
FILE-CONTROL.
    SELECT  CARD-FILE ASSIGN     TO CARD-READER.
    SELECT SORT-FILE ASSIGN TO   FILE-UNIT-1.
    SELECT SORTED-FILE  ASSIGN TO FILE-UNIT-2.
    SELECT  PRINT-FILE ASSIGN    TO PRINTER.
DATA DIVISION.
FILE SECTION.
FD  CARD-FILE LABEL RECORD OMITTED
    DATA RECORD IS CARD-RECORD.
01  CARD-RECORD.
    02  FILLER                        PICTURE X(10).
    02  CARD-NAME                     PICTURE X(15).
    02  FILLER                        PICTURE X(51).
    02  DATA-TO-BE-INSERTED           PICTURE 9999.
SD  SORT-FILE DATA RECORD IS SORT-RECORD.
01  SORT-RECORD.
        02  DATA-FROM-CARD.
            03  FILLER                PICTURE X(10).
            03  NAME                  PICTURE X(15).
            03 FILLER                 PICTURE X(55).
FD  SORTED-FILE LABEL RECORD OMITTED
    DATA RECORD IS SORTED-RECORD.
01  SORTED-RECORD                     PICTURE X(80).
FD  PRINT-FILE LABEL RECORD OMITTED
    DATA RECORD IS PRINT-LINE.
01  PRINT-LINE.
    02  OUT-LINE                      PICTURE X(132).
WORKING-STORAGE SECTION.
01  END-OF-DATA          PIC XXX.
01  SEQUENCE-NUMBER      PIC 9(4).

PROCEDURE DIVISION.
MAIN-SORT-ROUTINE.
    MOVE ZERO TO SEQUENCE-NUMBER.

    SORT SORT-FILE ASCENDING KEY NAME
        INPUT    PROCEDURE IS READING-SEQUENCING
        OUTPUT   PROCEDURE IS RETURNING-PRINTING.

    STOP RUN.

READING-SEQUENCING SECTION.
SET-UP.
    OPEN INPUT CARD-FILE.
    MOVE 'NO' TO END-OF-DATA.
    PERFORM READ-DATA
    PERFORM SEQ-RELEASE
            UNTIL END-OF-DATA = 'YES'
    CLOSE CARD-FILE
    GO TO END-OF-SECTION.

READ-DATA.
    READ CARD-FILE RECORD
        AT END MOVE 'YES' TO END-OF-DATA.

SEQ-RELEASE.
    ADD 1 TO SEQUENCE-NUMBER.
    MOVE SEQUENCE-NUMBER TO DATA-TO-BE-INSERTED.
    RELEASE SORT-RECORD FROM CARD-RECORD.
    PERFORM READ-DATA.

END-OF-SECTION.
    EXIT.
```

EXHIBIT 13-2   SAMPLE SORT PROGRAM-2 *(Continued)*

```
RETURNING-PRINTING SECTION.
SET-UP.
    OPEN OUTPUT SORTED-FILE
                PRINT-FILE
    MOVE 'NO' TO END-OF-DATA
    PERFORM RETURN-DATA
    PERFORM WRITE-DATA
            UNTIL END-OF-DATA = 'YES'.
    CLOSE SORTED-FILE PRINT-FILE
    GO TO END-OF-SECTION.
RETURN-DATA.
    RETURN SORT-FILE RECORD INTO SORTED-RECORD
           AT END MOVE 'YES' TO END-OF-DATA.
WRITE-DATA.
    WRITE PRINT-LINE FROM SORTED-RECORD
    WRITE SORTED-RECORD.
    PERFORM RETURN-DATA.
END-OF-SECTION.
    EXIT.
```

RELEASE SORT-RECORD FROM CARD-RECORD statement. This simply says to move the contents of CARD-RECORD to SORT-RECORD and then to write the SORT-RECORD on its file. The RELEASE command can thus be thought of as a specialized form of the WRITE instruction.

The loop terminates when the last card is read, at which point the program branches to END-OF-SECTION, after CARD-FILE is closed. The END-OF-SECTION paragraph is the last paragraph of the READING-SEQUENCING SECTION, and is indicated by the EXIT verb. Recall that the execution of the READING-SEQUENCING SECTION was initiated by execution of the INPUT PROCEDURE statement in the SORTING-COMMAND paragraph. In fact, the INPUT PROCEDURE statement has the same effect as if we had written PERFORM READING-SEQUENCING SECTION. Program execution branches to that section and, when it is completed, the next statement in the SORTING-COMMAND paragraph is executed. The next statement in the present example is OUTPUT PROCEDURE IS RETURNING-PRINTING, which indicates the name of another section. Therefore, program execution then branches to the RETURNING-PRINTING SECTION.

The first paragraph of the RETURNING-PRINTING SECTION is the SET-UP, which opens the two output files. Then we PERFORM RETURN-DATA and enter a loop involving WRITE-DATA. The statement RETURN SORT-FILE RECORD INTO SORTED-RECORD is simply a special form of saying, "Read a record from the SORT-FILE and move it to the SORTED RECORD file." Notice the use of AT END which parallels the same clause used in connection with the READ verb. After each record is RETURNED, we employ an implicit move (FROM SORTED-RECORD) and we WRITE PRINT-LINE. Finally, we WRITE SORTED-RECORD on tape. The process is repeated until the END-OF-DATA = 'YES' condition holds. The SET-UP paragraph closes the files and END-OF-SECTION is executed next. Program control then returns to the statement which follows the statement, OUTPUT PROCEDURE IS RETURNING-PRINTING, because this is where the branching occurred. The statement in question is STOP RUN and signifies the logical end of the program.

Thus, in the above example we have demonstrated that, by using the INPUT PROCEDURE or the OUTPUT PROCEDURE option of the SORT verb, we can branch to another section of the program and perform any required data processing. By this approach the sorting function can be combined with any other program processing task. Frequently, for instance, it may be desirable to perform a sort in the "middle" of a processing job. The sort does not have to be considered a separate job. Rather, it can be embedded in the larger job.

REVIEW

1　The COBOL language feature by which a file can be sorted without having to write a sorting algorithm as such is called the _____ feature.

sort

2　In order to use the sort feature the programmer must specify the _____ to be sorted and the _____ to be used as the basis for the sort.

file; key (or keys)

3　If a file is to be sorted on the basis of more than one key, the key which is written [first / last] is the principal basis for the sort.

first

4ˋ　In the second example problem in this section two options of the SORT verb were used to branch to other parts of the program in order to perform required processing tasks. These were the _____ and _____ options of the SORT verb.

INPUT PROCEDURE; OUTPUT
PROCEDURE

SORT STATEMENT FORMATS

We now consider the COBOL format specifications that enable a programmer to use the sort feature. These format requirements are presented by division of the COBOL program.

IDENTIFICATION DIVISION

The usual format specifications are unaffected by the use of the SORT statement.

ENVIRONMENT DIVISION

In the FILE-CONTROL section we have the following:

FILE-CONTROL
    SELECT file-name ASSIGN TO device-name-1
    [device-name-2] . . . [OR device-name-3]
    [device-name-4] . . .

$$\left[\text{FOR } \underline{\text{MULTIPLE}} \left\{ \begin{array}{c} \underline{\text{REEL}} \\ \underline{\text{UNIT}} \end{array} \right\} \right] \dots .$$

The difference from the FILE-CONTROL formats previously discussed is the presence of the OR option. This option allows the output of the sort procedure to be available on one of the devices either preceding or following the OR. The programmer does not know which device it will be at the time of writing the program. The compiler automatically inserts instructions such that at execution time the program keeps track of the hardware device on which the sorted file was written, and when the program references the file the correct device is addressed.

In the I-O-CONTROL paragraph the format associated with use of the SORT option is

I-O-CONTROL
$$\left[\underline{\text{SAME}} \left\{ \begin{array}{c} \underline{\text{RECORD}} \\ \underline{\text{SORT}} \end{array} \right\} \text{AREA FOR file-name-1 [file-name-2] } \dots \right].$$

The SAME RECORD AREA option allows the sharing of the same storage location by several files, as indicated by the file-names which follow the clause. When this option is used, only one record is available at a given time, even though more than one file may have been opened. The reason for using this option is to save storage space. If the SAME SORT AREA clause is used, at least one of the files involved must be a sort file. Typically, this clause is used when more than one file is to be sorted. Some compilers treat this clause as a comment, since they provide their own space-saving routines.

DATA DIVISION
    In the DATA DIVISION the relevant format is

SD file-name

$$\left[\text{DATA} \left\{ \begin{array}{l} \underline{\text{RECORD}} \text{ IS} \\ \underline{\text{RECORDS}} \text{ ARE} \end{array} \right\} \text{data-name-1 [data-name-2]} \ldots \right]$$

[<u>RECORD</u> CONTAINS [integer-1 <u>TO</u>] integer-2 CHARACTERS].

The level indicator SD identifies the beginning of a sort file sort description. Notice that other than the SD the file description has the usual format. Notice also that there is no BLOCK CONTAINS option. Whether or not any blocking is possible or desirable is determined automatically by the preprogrammed sort routine.

PROCEDURE DIVISION
The SORT verb is the basic verb in the SORT option. The format is as follows:

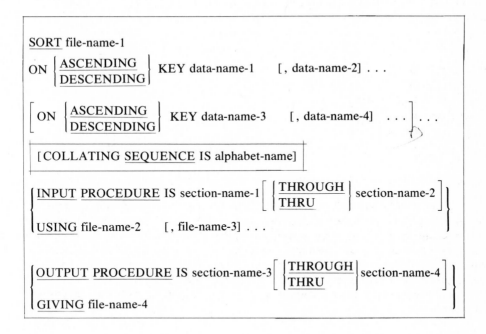

The verb SORT is always required. File-name-1 is the file designated in an SD entry in the DATA DIVISION. At least one KEY has to be specified. If more than one sort key is used and all are ascending (or all are descending), they can be written in the following form:

SORT file-name ON ASCENDING KEY ACCOUNT, NAME, YEAR.

In the above example we have specified an ascending sort by ACCOUNT, by NAME within ACCOUNT, and by YEAR within NAME. Or we could have used the word ASCENDING (or DESCENDING) in conjunction with each KEY as follows:

SORT file-name ON ASCENDING KEY ACCOUNT
        ON ASCENDING KEY NAME
        ON ASCENDING KEY YEAR.

The INPUT PROCEDURE and the OUTPUT PROCEDURE options refer to a section-name or a set of consecutive sections when the THRU option is exercised. The paragraphs in such sections specify the processing tasks to be performed prior to the sort (INPUT PROCEDURE) or after the sort (OUTPUT PROCEDURE). If the INPUT PROCEDURE is used, the verb RELEASE must be used somewhere in that procedure. If the OUTPUT PROCEDURE is used, the verb RETURN must be used somewhere in that procedure. The USING file-name-2 option is used when records are made available to the sort from file-name-2 without any processing. The GIVING file-name-4 option specifies that the sorted file is to be recorded on file-name-4.

The COLLATING SEQUENCE option allows the programmer to specify a particular collating sequence. In the SPECIAL-NAMES paragraph of the ENVIRONMENT DIVISION one can specify an alphabet name. For instance, we could have written:

SPECIAL-NAMES.
        THEIR-SET IS STANDARD-1
        OUR-SET IS NATIVE.

In this case the alphabet name THEIR-SET is associated with the ANSI standard character code set and therefore with that collating sequence. NATIVE is a COBOL word and specifies the computer's own set. Other options are also available but are uncommon in use.

The RELEASE verb discussed above has the following format:

RELEASE record-name [FROM identifier].

The RELEASE verb can be used only in a section referenced by the INPUT PROCEDURE of a SORT verb. The record-name in the above format refers to a record in the sort file. If the FROM option is used, the effect is to move the contents of identifier to the record-name and then to RELEASE. In effect, RELEASE is a specialized form of the WRITE verb.

The RETURN verb, which is used in conjunction with the OUTPUT PROCEDURE of a SORT verb, has the following format:

> RETURN file-name RECORD [INTO identifier]
> AT END imperative statement.

The RETURN verb has the effect of a READ verb. The file-name is the name of the sort file. When the INTO option is used, the effect is the same as execution of the longer instruction RETURN file-name MOVE record-name TO identifier. The AT END clause is required. The imperative statement identifies the processing to be performed after all the records have been returned from the sort file.

REVIEW

1   In the ENVIRONMENT DIVISION, the option which allows the output of the sort procedure to be available on one of several possible output devices is the _____ option.

                                                                                        OR

2   In the DATA DIVISION the file to be sorted is identified by the level indicator ___.
                                                              SD *(standing for Sort Description)*

3   If the INPUT PROCEDURE option is used in conjunction with the SORT verb, designated processing is performed [before / after] the sort, and the verb _____ must be used somewhere in the procedure.
                                                                          before; RELEASE

4   If the OUTPUT PROCEDURE option is used in conjunction with the SORT verb, designated processing is performed [before / after] the sort, and the verb _____ must be used somewhere in the procedure.
                                                                          after; RETURN

5   The RELEASE verb can be considered a specialized form of the _____ verb, while the RETURN verb can be considered a form of the _____ verb.
                                                                          WRITE; READ

FILE MERGING

Essentially, merging refers to the process by which two or more files, which are already sorted, are combined to form one file. Merging is often a required step in the process of sorting. Merging is also often used simply to combine two or more files without any further sorting activity. For example, the sales transactions in a department store might be processed on a daily basis, thus creating a daily sales tape sorted by item number. Then, at the end of each week it may be desirable to merge the several daily tapes to form a weekly sales tape for descriptive output and perhaps for batch processing use. The procedure of combining the several daily tapes to form one weekly tape exemplifies the merging process.

The simplest case of merging is the one in which there are two sorted files A and B, and they are merged to form one file. The process consists of reading a record from each input file, comparing the two records, and writing the "smaller" of the two onto the output file, based on a reference, or "sort key," field. Then another record is read from the file that supplied the last smaller record and the comparison is repeated. This process was discussed in Exercise 1 of Chapter 10 on "Magnetic Tape Files." In that exercise a flowchart of the merging process was presented, and this flowchart is here reproduced as Figure 13-5 for convenience of reference.

Suppose, however, that five daily transactions tapes are to be merged to form one tape. In such a case the process of merging requires a more complex logic. In each comparison five records are involved, one from each respective daily tape, and the smallest of the five is to be written on the output tape. The flowchart in Figure 13-6 indicates the essential logic of the comparisons which are required to find the smallest record. In this figure, A, B, C, D, and E are the five records from the five input files. File F is the output file. Notice that the process described in Figure 13-6 ignores end-of-file conditions. Incorporation of end-of-file condition processing would add considerable complexity to the logic of the procedure, as some reflection will reveal.

As compared with Figure 13-5, the description of the required procedure in Figure 13-6 indicates that required processing (that is, the number of comparisons) increases as the number of files to be merged is increased. We are often concerned with achieving an optimum balance between input/output and processing. In the case of merging two files it is easy to predict that input/output will be the time-consuming operation rather than processing. Of course, when merging two files the records will usually be blocked, so that we do not actually perform an input or output operation after every comparison, as implied by the flowchart in Figure 13-5. Still, the required processing is limited, and unless we have very fast input/output devices and a very slow central processor, the system will be I-O bound.

At the other extreme, one could consider the merging of 100 input files and could infer the likelihood of such a system being processing bound. Therefore, it must be that some optimum exists "between" the possible extremes. The actual optimum varies with the conditions associated with each merging task. Factors to be considered are the record size, sort-key size, blocking factor, central processor speed, and input/output speeds. When merging tape files, the choice of the optimum balance between input/output and processing is seldom self-evident. In most computer installations, however, the number of tape transport units is limited to perhaps four or six units. In such cases the rule of thumb would be to use all tape transport units available, realizing that even then the system is likely to be input/output bound. For example, suppose that we have 12 files to be merged. These files are identified by the letters A through L in Figure 13-7. If four tape transport units are available, three units would be used for input and one would be used for output. As illustrated in Figure 13-7, in such a case we could merge A, B, and C to form file 1, D, E, and F to form file 2, and G, H, and I to form file 3. Next we could merge files J and K (two-way merge) to form file 4. Then files 3, 4, and L can be merged to form file 5, and finally, files 1, 2, and 5 can be merged to form file 6.

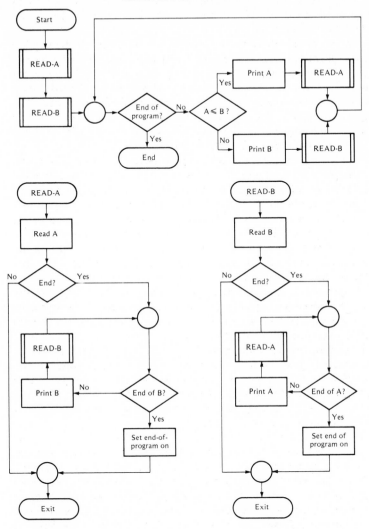

FLOWCHART FOR MERGING LOGIC

FIGURE 13-5 FLOWCHART FOR MERGING LOGIC.

An alternative way of merging the 12 files, which is not as efficient, would be to merge files J, K, and L to form one file, as illustrated in Figure 13-8. Notice, however, that this alternative merging procedure would take longer to accomplish. To see this, let us count the number of file passes that are required by each approach. By "file pass" we mean the process of inputting and merging the contents of a file with the contents of one or more other files. Thus, by the procedure portrayed in Figure 13-8

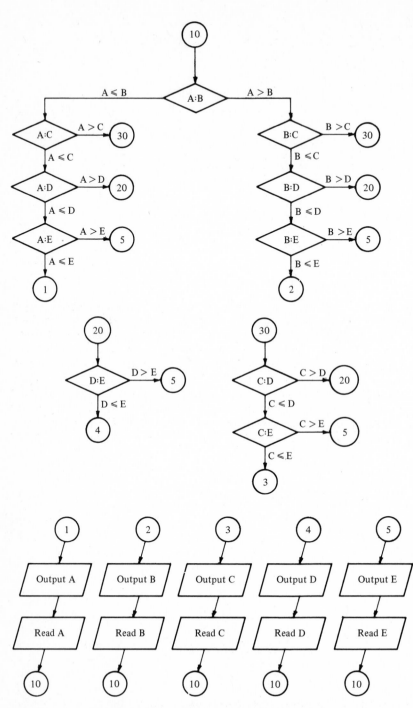

FIGURE 13-6   FLOWCHART FOR THE PROCESS OF MERGING FIVE FILES.

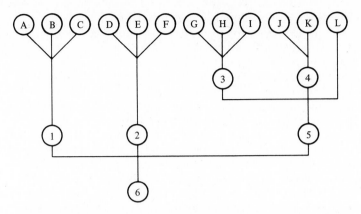

FIGURE 13-7   SCHEMATIC DIAGRAM FOR THE PROCESS OF MERGING 12 TAPE FILES BY THE USE OF FOUR TAPE TRANSPORT UNITS.

the formation of files 1, 2, 3, and 4 requires three file passes each. The formation of file 5 requires nine file passes because the contents of nine original input files are involved. Similarly, the formation of file 6 requires 12 file passes. Thus, in total 33 file passes are required to merge the files by the procedure portrayed in Figure 13-8. However, by the procedure portrayed in Figure 13-7 only 29 file passes are required (the student should satisfy himself that such is the case by analyzing Figure 13-7 in respect to the number of passes required). As it happens, given the 12 input files and four tape units the 29 file passes associated with the procedure in Figure 13-7 is the optimum result. A computational procedure, or algorithm, has been developed to determine the optimum merge configuration given the number of files to be merged

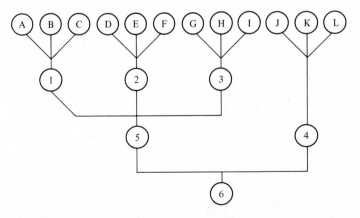

FIGURE 13-8   SCHEMATIC DIAGRAM FOR AN ALTERNATIVE WAY OF MERGING 12 TAPE FILES BY THE USE OF FOUR TAPE TRANSPORT UNITS.

and the tape units available, but this procedure is quite involved mathematically and beyond the scope of this book. However, the algorithm is included in most merge program packages, so that its application is automatic without the user having to determine the optimum merging routine for each situation.

Frequently, the files to be merged are not stored on magnetic tape. Rather, it may be that designated disk areas constitute "files." In such a case, the limitation of the number of available input/output units does not apply and the need to merge 50 files could conceivably be accomplished by one merge operation. However, our earlier-expressed concern about excessive processing time would have to be considered. If central processing time would far exceed input/output time, it is desirable to perform several merge operations with fewer files involved in each of the operations, thereby balancing input/output and processing time more closely and making it possible to overlap these two functions. Therefore, we may decide to merge seven files in each merge operation instead of merging all 50 in one operation. Again, a mathematical solution to such a problem is beyond the scope of this book, but optimum merge routines are included in most program packages.

As indicated in several places above, because the process of merging is frequently used and because the programming logic in a generalized context is not simple, most computer manufacturers supply "canned" merge packages for user application. Still, one should have a basic understanding of the merging logic even if he is not an author but a user of merge programs. Furthermore, merging is a fundamental operation in data processing and it is common that the application of merging logic is required in the processing of data held in central or auxiliary storage.

REVIEW

1   When two or more sequential files are combined to form one sequential file, the process is called _____.

merging

2   The simplest case of merging is the one in which _____ (number) files are merged.

two

3   In most computer installations, if all the tape transport units available are used to merge a relatively large number of tape files, the system is likely to be [input-output / processing] bound.

input-output

4   The optimum merge configuration to be used in merging several tape files generally is determined [by each user / by the merge program package].

by the merge program package

5   If a relatively large number of files which are stored on magnetic disk are merged in one operation, the system is likely to be [input-output / processing] bound.

processing

FILE MERGING WITH COBOL

Because it is frequently needed and of great importance, merging is implemented in COBOL as a very high-level language feature, in the form of the MERGE statement.

Let us consider an example. A business firm generates a sales history file at the

EXHIBIT 13-3   OUTLINE FOR A MERGE PROGRAM

```
FD   FIRST-QUARTER LABEL RECORDS STANDARD
                   DATA RECORD SALES-HISTORY.
01   SALES-HISTORY.
     02   DEPT-NO      PIC 999.
     02   PROD-NO      PIC 99999.
     .
     .
     .

FD   SECOND-QUARTER . . .
     .
     .
     .

FD   THIRD-QUARTER . . .
     .
     .
     .

FD   FOURTH-QUARTER . . .
     .
     .
     .

FD   YEARLY LABEL RECORDS STANDARD
           DATA RECORD   CUMULATIVE-SALES.
01   CUMULATIVE-SALES
     02   DEPT-NO     PIC 999.
     02   PROD-NO     PIC 99999.
.
.
.

SD   MERGE-FILE LABEL RECORDS OMITTED
               DATA RECORD   MERGE-RECORD.
01   MERGE-RECORD.
     02   DEPARTMENT     PIC 999.
     02   PRODUCT        PIC 99999.
.
.
.

PROCEDURE DIVISION.
.
.
.

     MERGE MERGE-FILE  ON ASCENDING KEY DEPARTMENT
                       ON ASCENDING KEY PRODUCT
          USING FIRST-QUARTER, SECOND-QUARTER,
                THIRD-QUARTER, FOURTH-QUARTER
          GIVING YEARLY.
```

end of the quarter. Each record in the file contains a department number and a product number, as well as many other fields. This quarterly file is sorted, with department number being the major sort key and product number being the minor sort key. At the end of the year we are interested in merging the four quarterly sales history files into one. Exhibit 13-3 presents an outline of the relevant parts of the program. Five files are introduced with an FD entry. Then the SD introduces the file to be used for the merge, which in this example is called MERGE-FILE. Notice that the data record description for this file corresponds to the record description of the four quarterly files. The merge statement in the PROCEDURE DIVISION references the SD file and specifies that the merge will proceed on the basis of DEPARTMENT being the major key and PRODUCT being the minor key. As is the case with the SORT verb, the keys decrease in significance in the order written. The ASCENDING option specifies that the next record of each of the four quarterly files will be examined, and the record sent to the output file next is the one which has the highest department number, or the highest product number if the department numbers are equal. If all four records have identical department and product values, then the records will be sent to the output file in the order in which the file names are written in the merge statement.

    The USING clause specifies the files to be merged, the input files. These files must be closed at the time of merging. Opening is carried out by the merge statement in an implicit fashion.

    The GIVING clause specifies the output file. This file will contain the combined set of the four quarterly files. This new file will be in the same sort order as the quarterly files. It should be emphasized that in order for the merge process to take place correctly the input files must be in the sort order indicated by the KEY specifications.

    The general format of MERGE is as follows:

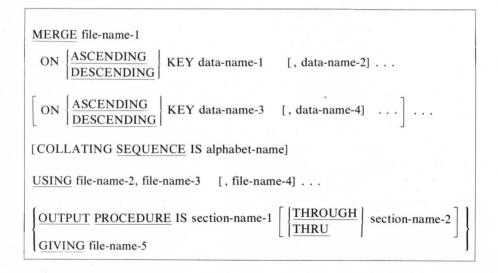

The OUTPUT PROCEDURE option parallels the one available with the SORT verb. A RETURN statement is used within the output procedure to make merged records available for processing, just as is the case with SORT. Unlike SORT, MERGE does not include any input procedure options. Thus the input files must be in proper form for merging before a MERGE instruction is executed.

REVIEW

1 The COBOL language feature by which monthly summaries of transactions can be combined to create an annual summary is the _____ statement.

MERGE

2 If 12 monthly summaries are to be combined to form an annual summary, then the number of FD entries required in the associated MERGE program is _____ (number).

13

3 In order for the merge process to take place correctly, it [is / is not] necessary that each input file be in the exact sort order indicated by the KEY specifications.

is

EXERCISES

1 A sort file has been defined as SORT-FILE and, in part, its data division entries include:

02   COURSE-CODE   PIC XXX.
02   COLLEGE   PIC 99.
02   COURSE-NAME   PIC X(6).

Considering the data presented below, write a SORT statement that could cause the sorted data shown. The original data comes from CARD-FILE and it is desired to have the sorted data in TAPE-FILE. Be sure to specify which are the major, intermediate, and minor sort keys.

ORIGINAL DATA	SORTED DATA
CIS20BILL	MGT10JILL
CIS30LINDA	QBA10BRENDA
QBA10BRENDA	CIS20MARY
CIS30XAVIER	CIS20JOHN
MGT10JILL	CIS20BILL
CIS20JOHN	CIS30XAVIER
CIS20MARY	CIS30LINDA

2   Using any data file available, write a program incorporating the COBOL sort feature to sort a file. For example, you could modify any of the exercises at the end of Chapter 10 to sort the master file or the transaction file in the required order.

3   Consider these as the contents of the four quarterly files discussed in the merging example. Show the content of the output file.

FIRST- QUARTER	SECOND- QUARTER	THIRD- QUARTER	FOURTH- QUARTER
345 12345	123 00112	345 56111	931 00001
345 25936	987 56111		999 99999
619 01110			

4   Using any two sorted data files, write a program incorporating the MERGE feature to combine them into one file.

Table
Handling

INTRODUCTION

A table, like a file, is a collection of logically related entries. Examples are tax rates for different municipalities in a metropolitan area, commission rates for different product classes, and income tax rates given different levels of income and numbers of dependents. Such data is normally short enough to be placed in central storage and thus constitute a table. Table handling is fundamental to data processing. COBOL recognizes this fact and includes specialized instructions for table definition and manipulation. We devote a separate chapter to the subject, because of its importance and complexity.

This chapter is concerned with the definition and processing of data in tables. In this context we also study advanced forms of the PERFORM verb which find their most powerful use in table handling applications.

SUBSCRIPTING AND THE OCCURS CLAUSE

A great deal of the documentation in COBOL derives from the use of appropriate data-names, that is, names that provide a direct clue to the type of data contained in the named storage location. There are situations, however, when practicality dictates that we dispense with the use of such names. For example, suppose we are processing data on the average income per household in each of the 50 states. If we chose to name the average income for each state uniquely, we could have such data-names as ALABAMA-INCOME, ALASKA-INCOME, and so on, for a total of 50 names. It is easy to imagine the problems that this practice would cause in the PROCEDURE DIVISION. For example, 50 MOVE statements would be required before the results could be printed.

The use of tables and subscripts is a programming feature that is particularly useful in such situations. A table is simply a set of values stored in consecutive storage locations and assigned one data-name. Reference to specific entries in the table is made by the use of the one name along with a subscript which identifies the location of the particular entry. Entries in a one-dimensional table are numbered sequentially 1, 2, 3, . . . on to the last. Thus, in our example of the average household income for the 50 states, imagine that we have a table of 50 entries. If the entries are arranged alphabetically and we wish to reference the average income for Arizona, the subscript will have a value of 3. Similarly, the subscripts for Washington and Wyoming will be 49 and 50, respectively. Use of the OCCURS clause in conjunction with the PICTURE clause enables the programmer to set up tables so that reference can be made to entire tables or individual values in tables by means of subscripts. A DATA DIVISION entry involving an OCCURS clause includes the data-name assigned to the table, the number of dimensions (up to three), the number of entries in each dimension, and the field characteristics of the entries. In this section we consider one-dimensional tables only, such as one for the average household income in the 50 states; a later section discusses two- and three-dimensional tables.

Assume that the data for average income is contained in a WORKING-STORAGE table, although it could be a FILE SECTION table just as well.

WORKING-STORAGE SECTION.
01 . . .
01 . . .
01   STATE-INCOME-TABLE.
       02   AVERAGE-INCOME OCCURS 50 TIMES   PICTURE 9(6)V99.

The OCCURS 50 TIMES clause sets up a table in storage that has the following conceptual structure:

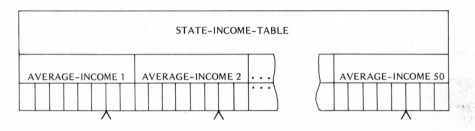

Execution of the PROCEDURE DIVISION statement MOVE STATE-INCOME-TABLE . . . will result in the entire table of 50 fields being moved. In order to move (or otherwise process) a single field or entry in the table the subscript is included in parentheses and separated from the name by a space as follows: MOVE AVERAGE-INCOME (12) TO. . . . This statement, of course, refers to the twelfth table entry.

The subscript may be a variable instead of a constant, but it must always be an integer (whole number). To understand the need for a subscript that is a variable, consider the following example. Suppose that some data cards have been read and have the following layout:

```
01  CARD.
    02  STATE-NUMBER     PICTURE 99.
    02  INCOME           PICTURE 9(6)V99.
```

Thus, the value in columns 1–2 is the number of the state when the states are listed alphabetically. The value in columns 3–10 is the average household income for that state. If the cards have not been arranged alphabetically, the following statement can be used to insert the income figure in the appropriate place in the table after the card has been read:

MOVE INCOME TO AVERAGE-INCOME (STATE-NUMBER)

With the insertion of this statement, if the state number were 49, the income value would be inserted in the forty-ninth entry of the average income table.

The OCCURS clause need not be used alone in a record, that is, other reference entries may be included as well. For example, the record might have been structured as follows:

```
01  STATE-INCOME-TABLE.
    02  AVERAGE-INCOME OCCURS 50 TIMES    PICTURE 9(6)V99.
    02  NATIONAL-AVERAGE                  PICTURE 9(6)V99.
```

However, notice that STATE-INCOME-TABLE now refers to more than the table of 50 entries. If we want to make specific reference to the table of 50 entries we will have to write something like this:

```
01  STATE-INCOME-TABLE.
    02  AV-TABLE.
        03  AVERAGE-INCOME OCCURS 50 TIMES    PICTURE 9(6)V99.
    02  NATIONAL-AVERAGE                      PICTURE 9(6)V99.
```

As a further illustration of a one-dimensional table, assume that we want to include the names of the states along with their corresponding average income figures:

```
01  STATE-INCOME-TABLE.
    02  NAME-INCOME OCCURS 50 TIMES.
        03  NAME      PICTURE X(12).
        03  INCOME    PICTURE 9(6)V99.
```

The OCCURS 50 TIMES clause sets up a table in storage that has the following structure:

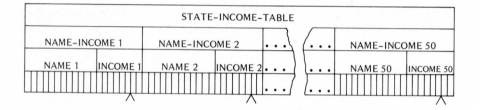

If we write NAME (1) we are referring to a storage field of 12 positions, whereas INCOME (1) refers to an eight-position field. If we write NAME-INCOME (1) we are referring to a storage field of 20 positions. Finally, STATE-INCOME-TABLE refers to the entire table of 100 fields.

REVIEW

1 The programmer can set up tables by using the _____ clause in the DATA DIVISION.

> OCCURS

2 The OCCURS clause indicates the number of _____ in the table.

> *entries (etc.)*

3 Suppose a STATE-POPULATION-TABLE is to include the population figures for all 50 states in alphabetical order. Complete the description below by writing the appropriate OCCURS clause. Assume that the PICTURE for POPULATION is 9(8).

01 STATE-POPULATION-TABLE.

_____

> 02 POPULATION OCCURS 50
> TIMES PICTURE 9(8).

4 Suppose that both the state names and the population figures are read in and we wish to set up a STATE-POPULATION-TABLE such that first the 50 state names are listed in the table, followed by the 50 population figures. Complete the description below, assuming that the PICTURE for NAME is X(12).

01 STATE-POPULATION-TABLE.

_____

_____

> 02 NAME OCCURS 50 TIMES
> PICTURE X(12).
> 02 POPULATION OCCURS 50
> TIMES PICTURE 9(8).

5 The table set up in the preceding question will have a total of 100 fields. After all data is read in, the content of NAME (1) will be the state name _____, and the content of POPULATION (50) will be the population figure for the state of _____ .

Alabama; Wyoming

AN EXAMPLE OF READING IN VALUES FOR A TABLE

Let us suppose that we have defined a tax table to contain 10 deduction rates.

```
01  TAX-TABLE.
    02  TAX-RATE OCCURS 10 TIMES    PICTURE V999.
```

We want to read in 10 values from punched cards. Assume that the punched card file is called RATE-FILE, and that the specific field containing the rate is called RATE. We will use a data-name N to specify the subscript value. Initially we want to read the first card and store the value of RATE in the first cell of the TAX-TABLE. Then we increase the value of N and repeat the process, storing each new value which is read into the Nth place of TAX-TABLE. Figure 14-1 presents the flowchart for this task. Notice that we account for the possibility of less than 10 cards in the input file, in which case we execute an error routine called NOT-ENOUGH-DATA. The following PROCEDURE DIVISION entries can accomplish the rate-reading objective:

```
        MOVE 'NO' TO DATA-END
        MOVE 1 TO N
        PERFORM TABLE-READ
            UNTIL N > 10 OR DATA-END = 'YES'.
        etc.
            .
            .
            .
TABLE-READ.
        READ RATE-FILE RECORD AT END MOVE 'YES' TO DATA-END.
        IF DATA-END = 'YES'
            PERFORM NOT-ENOUGH-DATA
        ELSE
            MOVE RATE TO TAX-RATE (N)
            ADD 1 TO N.
NOT-ENOUGH-DATA.
        etc.
```

AN EXAMPLE OF A TABLE OF CONSTANT VALUES

It is often desirable to build tables that contain specified constant values. One way to accomplish this objective is to define the table by using the OCCURS clause in the

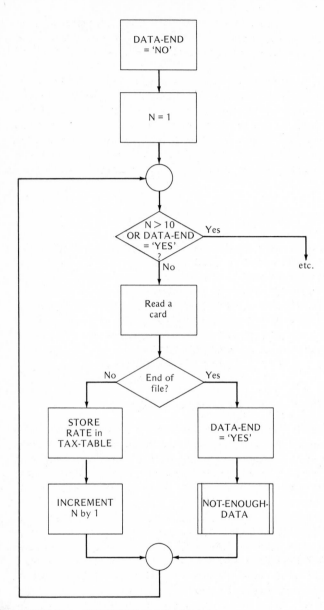

FIGURE 14-1   FLOWCHART FOR READING IN 10 TAX RATES.

DATA DIVISION and then, through suitable PROCEDURE DIVISION instructions, to read in the desired values. Yet, there is another way of initializing a table with constant values. The following example illustrates the joint use of the OCCURS and REDEFINES clauses to accomplish the task.

Suppose we want to have a table that contains the names of the 12 months of the year, so that we can reference these names by use of the table name and a subscript. For instance, we may want to reference the fifth month or the twelfth month, and so on. Using numeric values to reference the months is desirable, because arithmetic can be performed with numeric values. For instance, if we are on the sixth month and we want to reference the next month, we can simply add 1 to 6 and then make reference to the resulting month. The example below illustrates the common way of accomplishing this task.

```
01   MONTH-TABLE.
     02   JANUARY       PICTURE X(12) VALUE "JANUARY       ".
     02   FEBRUARY      PICTURE X(12) VALUE "FEBRUARY      ".
     02   MARCH         PICTURE X(12) VALUE "MARCH         ".
     02   APRIL         PICTURE X(12) VALUE "APRIL         ".
     02   MAY           PICTURE X(12) VALUE "MAY           ".
     02   JUNE          PICTURE X(12) VALUE "JUNE          ".
     02   JULY          PICTURE X(12) VALUE "JULY          ".
     02   AUGUST        PICTURE X(12) VALUE "AUGUST        ".
     02   SEPTEMBER     PICTURE X(12) VALUE "SEPTEMBER     ".
     02   OCTOBER       PICTURE X(12) VALUE "OCTOBER       ".
     02   NOVEMBER      PICTURE X(12) VALUE "NOVEMBER      ".
     02   DECEMBER      PICTURE X(12) VALUE "DECEMBER      ".
01   MONTHS REDEFINES MONTH-TABLE.
     02   MONTH         PICTURE X(12) OCCURS 12 TIMES.
```

Notice that the record MONTH-TABLE consists of 12 fields with each field conveniently named after each month. The VALUE clause is used to assign the constant (nonnumeric literal) values. Then the record called MONTHS is a table consisting of 12 entries. Each entry is referenced by the use of MONTH and a subscript. Thus, executing the instruction MOVE MONTH (3) TO PRINTAREA WRITE PRINTAREA results in the word MARCH being printed.

The procedure may seem unnecessarily roundabout. Let us justify the rationale. The VALUE clause cannot be used with the OCCURS clause. This makes sense, since the VALUE clause references *one* value and the OCCURS clause refers to several values. Thus, we use the REDEFINES clause with the OCCURS clause after we have described each individual field. Of course, all entries of MONTH-TABLE must be of equal field size for the procedure to accomplish the correct result.

A practical example is given using the table of months later in this chapter, in the section on the PERFORM verb.

TWO-DIMENSIONAL AND THREE-DIMENSIONAL TABLES

Two-dimensional tables require two subscripts to locate an individual entry, or field. As an example of a two-dimensional table, assume that a particular state has three state universities and it is desired to set up a table which will contain the enrollment figures for each university according to class standing: freshman, sophomore, junior, senior, and graduate. Conceptually, the following type of table is required.

ENROLLMENT

	UNIVERSITY		
YEAR	1	2	3
FR			
SO			
JR			
SR			
GR			

In order to set up the required storage locations the following DATA DIVISION entries can be written:

```
01  ENROLLMENT-TABLE.
      02  UNIVERSITY-NUMBER OCCURS 3 TIMES.
          03  YEAR OCCURS 5 TIMES     PICTURE 9(5).
```

Compilation of these DATA DIVISION statements results in the following conceptual storage layout.

ENROLLMENT-TABLE					
UNIVERSITY-NUMBER 1					UNIVERSITY-NUMBER 2
YEAR 1	YEAR 2	YEAR 3	YEAR 4	YEAR 5	. . .
					. . .

Thus, for each of the three universities there are five fields, corresponding to the five class-standing classifications. Notice that the level number of YEAR is lower (03) than that of UNIVERSITY-NUMBER (02). If the level number of YEAR were the same as that of UNIVERSITY-NUMBER, then the table would not be two-dimensional. To illustrate the use of the table, consider the following examples.

UNIVERSITY-NUMBER (3) refers to all five fields associated with the third university.

YEAR (2, 4) refers to the senior (4) enrollment in the second (2) university. YEAR must always be used with double subscripts. The first subscript refers to the superior hierarchical level (in this case, UNIVERSITY-NUMBER), and the second subscript refers to the entry in the YEAR table.

YEAR (5, 2) is incorrect, since only three values have been defined for UNIVERSITY-NUMBER. However, YEAR (2, 5) is correct and identifies the graduate student enrollment in the second university.

Notice that, even though we have defined a two-dimensional table (YEAR), we have also defined a one-dimensional table (UNIVERSITY-NUMBER) and one field (ENROLLMENT-TABLE). This again exemplifies the power of COBOL to reference data at different hierarchical levels with great flexibility.

Three-dimensional tables involve the use of three subscripts. We can illustrate the statements required to set up a three-dimensional table by adding a further breakdown by male and female to our two-dimensional example.

```
01  ENROLLMENT-TABLE.
      02   UNIVERSITY-NUMBER OCCURS 3 TIMES.
         03   YEAR OCCURS 5 TIMES.
            04   SEX OCCURS 2 TIMES      PICTURE 9(5).
```

Thus, SEX (2, 3, 1) refers to the enrollment of males (1) in the junior year (3) in the second university (2).

The following rules serve to summarize the requirements associated with the use of subscripted tables.

1 The OCCURS clause cannot apply to the 01 level. In other words, there cannot be a table of "records." However, this is a language rule and in no way prevents us from assigning a "record" to the 02 level and defining an 01-level name above it. This was the case in our first example:

```
01  STATE-INCOME-TABLE.
      02   AVERAGE-INCOME OCCURS 50 TIMES      PICTURE 9(6)V99.
```

2 The OCCURS clause cannot be used with 77 level items.
3 Subscripted tables may have one, two, or three dimensions.
4 The PICTURE clause applies to the elementary items only. Notice, for instance, the example of the three-dimensional table above.
5 Only one PICTURE description can be given for all like entries in a table, but there may be several entries that are not alike. The latter is exemplified by the example given earlier:

```
01  STATE-INCOME-TABLE.
      02   NAME-INCOME OCCURS 50 TIMES.
         03   NAME        PICTURE X(12).
         03   INCOME      PICTURE 9(6)V99.
```

The same PICTURE clause applies to all 50 NAME fields above. Thus, OCCURS is used for homogeneous sets of data.

6   The subscripts may be integer constants, or they may be integer variables. Their values must be positive; they must not be zero or negative.

7   The subscript or subscripts are enclosed in one set of parentheses and are separated from the table-name by a space. Multiple subscripts are separated from each other by *commas and spaces*. Examples are

A-TABLE (1)
A-TABLE (IDEN)
B-TABLE (3,   COUNT)
C-TABLE (GRADE,   CLASS,   YEAR)
C-TABLE (GRADE,   3,   YEAR)

REVIEW

1   In the two-dimensional ENROLLMENT-TABLE example, suppose we want UNIVERSITY-NUMBER to be at the lowest hierarchical level instead of YEAR. Write the appropriate statements below, using a PICTURE of 9(5) for the elementary field.

01   ENROLLMENT-TABLE.
02   _____
03   _____

YEAR OCCURS 5 TIMES.
UNIVERSITY-NUMBER
OCCURS 3 TIMES
PICTURE 9(5).

2   For the example in the preceding question, the location of juniors in the first university is referenced by the subscripted variable _____.

UNIVERSITY-NUMBER (3,   1)

3   The PICTURE clause is used only at the [highest / lowest] hierarchical level of a table.

lowest

4   The integer subscripts used in conjunction with subscripted variables [may / may not] be constant and [may / may not] be variables.

may; may

5   A subscript used in conjunction with subscripted variables [may / may not] be zero and [may / may not] have a negative value.

may not; may not

THE OCCURS . . . DEPENDING ON OPTION

Sometimes the number of entries in a table varies. The number of entries may be given by the value of a data-name. In such cases we may want to use the DEPENDING ON option of the OCCURS clause. Let us illustrate by an example.

In Chapter 10, "Magnetic Tape Files," we mentioned variable-sized tape records and deferred discussion until this point. We now illustrate the use of variable tape records with the OCCURS and DEPENDING ON clauses.

A bank utilizes magnetic tape to record the transactions of checking account customers. Some customers have a greater number of transactions than others; i.e., they write more checks or make more deposits. It seems natural that tape records should be variable. Let us assume the following record layout.

FIELD	NUMBER OF POSITIONS
Customer number	6
Number of transactions	3
Transaction code	1
Date	5
Amount	7
Transaction code	1
Date	5
Amount	7
(etc. for up to 100 transactions)	

This is a case where a record may contain from zero to 100 transactions. Notice that the minimum number of character positions is nine: six for the customer number and three for the number of transactions. The maximum size is 9 + (100 transactions × 13 characters per transaction) = 1,309. We can then have the following file description, assuming blocks of three records each.

```
FD   TAPE-FILE      BLOCK CONTAINS 3 RECORDS
                    RECORD CONTAINS 9 TO 1309 CHARACTERS
                    LABEL RECORD STANDARD
                    DATA RECORD IS CHECKING-ACCOUNT-RECORD.
01   CHECKING-ACCOUNT-RECORD.
     02   CUSTOMER-NUMBER              PICTURE 9(6).
     02   NUMBER-OF-TRANSACTIONS       PICTURE 999.
     02   TRANSACTION OCCURS 0 TO 100  TIMES DEPENDING ON
          NUMBER-OF-TRANSACTIONS.
          03   TRANSACTION-CODE        PICTURE 9.
          03   TRANSACTION-DATE        PICTURE 9(5).
          03   TRANSACTION-AMOUNT      PICTURE 9(5)V99.
```

Some comments are in order. First, the statement RECORD CONTAINS 9 TO 1309 CHARACTERS is optional, since the record description provides the same information. Notice also that it is possible in this case for TRANSACTION to occur *zero* times.

The general form of the DEPENDING ON option is

. . . OCCURS integer-1 TO integer-2 TIMES DEPENDING ON data-name.

REVIEW

1   The OCCURS . . . DEPENDING ON option can be used when the number of entries to be included in a table is [predetermined / variable].

variable

2   When the DEPENDING ON option is used, the word OCCURS in the program statement is always followed by a specified [value / range of values], and the ρhrase DEPENDING ON is always followed by a [data-name / specified value].

range of values; data-name

THE PERFORM VERB AND TABLE HANDLING

The PERFORM verb was introduced in Chapter 3 and then discussed further in Chapter 6. The following two basic formats have already been discussed:

Formats 1 and 2

PERFORM procedure-name

$$\underline{\text{PERFORM}}\text{ procedure-name-1 }\left[\begin{Bmatrix}\underline{\text{THROUGH}}\\\underline{\text{THRU}}\end{Bmatrix}\text{procedure-name-2}\right]$$

We now continue our study of the PERFORM verb, introducing additional formats and emphasizing the use of this verb for table handling applications.

FORMAT 3

As is true for all the remaining formats to be described, Format 3 of the PERFORM verb allows repetitive execution of program segments:

Format 3

$$\underline{\text{PERFORM}}\text{ procedure-name-1 }[\underline{\text{THRU}}\text{ procedure-name-2}]\begin{Bmatrix}\text{identifier}\\\text{integer}\end{Bmatrix}\text{TIMES}$$

As an example, suppose that we have monthly sales for the 12 months of the year and we wish to compute the average monthly sales. Assume that the data has been stored in SALES-TABLE:

```
01  SALES-TABLE.
    02  MONTHLY-SALES      PIC 9(6)V99 OCCURS 12 TIMES.
```

We can now write:

```
MOVE ZERO TO TOTAL-SALES
MOVE 1 TO N
PERFORM SUMMATION 12 TIMES
DIVIDE TOTAL-SALES BY 12 GIVING AVERAGE-SALES.
    .
    .
    .
etc.
SUMMATION.
    ADD MONTHLY-SALES (N) TO TOTAL-SALES
    ADD 1 TO N.
```

The identifier TIMES option is used in lieu of the integer TIMES option when the number of repetitive executions is variable. For example, suppose a bank computes the service charge on a checking account on the basis of the average balance. For simplicity, assume that the average is computed by adding up the balance after each transaction and then dividing by the number of transactions. Let us say that the individual balances are stored in a table called BAL-TABLE consisting of 100 cells, which is the maximum expected number of transactions. Let N stand for the number of transactions for each customer. Then we can write:

```
MOVE ZERO TO TOTAL. MOVE 1 TO K.
PERFORM SUMMING N TIMES.
DIVIDE N INTO TOTAL GIVING AVERAGE. . . .
    .
    .
    .
SUMMING. ADD BAL-TABLE (K) TO TOTAL. ADD 1 TO K.
```

In the above program segment the TOTAL register is initalized at ZERO, and K is initalized at 1. Since the SUMMING paragraph is then executed N times, the number of cells (K) of the BAL-TABLE that are added to the total is also N. Note this point, however. If the integer or the identifier used with PERFORM has a value of zero or is negative, the effect is that the object of PERFORM is *not* executed. For example, if we say PERFORM ABC M TIMES and M happens to have a value of 0 or is negative, ABC will not be executed at all; rather, the program will go on to the next statement. In effect, this fact allows for conditional execution of a procedure.

AN EXAMPLE OF THE PERFORM VERB

It is appropriate at this point to illustrate the use of PERFORM in the context of a complete program. The example illustrates the application of PERFORM, OCCURS, and REDEFINES, and the use of tables and subscripts. PERFORM is often used in conjunction with tables and subscripts, and therefore such a programming example is particularly appropriate. The function of the program is to output a sales forecast based on punched card input. The input values are as follows:

NEXT-MONTH   A numeric value that designates the first month to be included in the forecast

HOW-MANY-MONTHS   A two-digit number that designates the number of months to be included in the forcast

BASE   A dollar value used as the base for the forecast formula

COEFFICIENT   A numeric coefficient used in the forecast formula

The forecasting formula used is

$$F_i = B + cN$$

The forecast for month i (F_i) is equal to the base (B) plus a coefficient c times the number of months (N) from the starting point. If the first month is 2 (February), then the forecast for April will be

$$F_{April} = B + c(2)$$

Thus $N = 2$ in this case, since April is two months after February, which is the starting month.

If the following input is used, the resulting output is shown in Exhibit 14-1.

NEXT-MONTH   05
HOW-MANY-MONTHS   09
BASE   0010000000
COEFFICIENT   0000025000

A program listing is given in Exhibit 14-2. Notice that the setting up of the MONTH-TABLE in the WORKING-STORAGE SECTION is the same as presented in the earlier section, An Example of a Table of Constant Values.

In the PROCEDURE DIVISION the paragraph called CALCULATION-ROUTINE is performed HOW-MANY-MONTHS times. In this case the input field HOW-MANY-MONTHS contains the number of desired executions of the forecasting computation.

The MONTHS-FROM-NOW field corresponds to the N in the forecasting formula $F_i = B + cN$. Finally, the subscript WHICH-ONE is used to reference the name of the

EXHIBIT 14-1   ILLUSTRATIVE COMPUTER OUTPUT

	PROJECTED SALES
MAY	100250.00
JUNE	100500.00
JULY	100750.00
AUGUST	101000.00
SEPTEMBER	101250.00
OCTOBER	101500.00
NOVEMBER	101750.00
DECEMBER	102000.00
JANUARY	102250.00

month relating to each successive line of output. Since we have only 12 months, we may need to "wraparound" the MONTH-TABLE entries. For instance, if NEXT-MONTH = 5 and HOW-MANY-MONTHS = 9, the last month is not the thirteenth (4 + 9) but, instead, the first month of the next year. Thus, when the month subscript called WHICH-ONE exceeds 12, we subtract 12 from it to "bend" it down around the table.

FORMAT 4

The fourth format of PERFORM permits repetitive execution subject to a condition being fulfilled. We have already studied this format in Chapter 6, but we now consider its use in table handling.

EXHIBIT 14-2   SAMPLE FORECAST PROGRAM

```
IDENTIFICATION DIVISION.
PROGRAM-ID. FORECAST.
ENVIRONMENT DIVISION.
CONFIGURATION SECTION.
SOURCE-COMPUTER. ABC-480.
OBJECT-COMPUTER. ABC-480.
INPUT-OUTPUT SECTION.
FILE-CONTROL.
    SELECT INPUT-DATA ASSIGN TO CARD-READER.
    SELECT OUTPUT-FILE ASSIGN TO PRINTER.
*
DATA DIVISION.
FILE SECTION.
FD  INPUT-DATA LABEL RECORD OMITTED
                 DATA RECORD IS INCARD.
01   INCARD.
     02 NEXT-MONTH        PICTURE 99.
     02 HOW-MANY-MONTHS PICTURE 99.
     02 BASE             PICTURE S9(8)V99.
     02 COEFFICIENT      PICTURE S9(8)V99.
     02 FILLER           PICTURE X(56).
FD  OUTPUT-FILE LABEL RECORD OMITTED
                 DATA  RECORD OUT-LINE.
01   OUT-LINE PICTURE X(133).
*
WORKING-STORAGE SECTION.
01   WHICH-ONE          PIC 99.
01   MONTHS-FROM-NOW    PIC 99.
01   SALES             PIC S9(9)V99.
01   DATA-END          PIC XXX.
*
01   HEADER.
     02 FILLER           PICTURE X(15) VALUE SPACES.
     02 FILLER           PICTURE X(15) VALUE 'PROJECTED SALES'.
*
01   PRINT-RECORD.
     02 FILLER           PICTURE X VALUE SPACE.
     02 MONTH-NAME       PICTURE X(12).
     02 FILLER           PICTURE X(5) VALUE SPACES.
     02 EDIT-SALES       PICTURE ------99.99.
*
01   MONTH-TABLE.
     02 JANUARY          PICTURE X(12) VALUE 'JANUARY   '.
     02 FEBRUARY         PICTURE X(12) VALUE 'FEBRUARY  '.
     02 MARCH            PICTURE X(12) VALUE 'MARCH     '.
     02 APRIL            PICTURE X(12) VALUE 'APRIL     '.
     02 MAY              PICTURE X(12) VALUE 'MAY       '.
     02 JUNE             PICTURE X(12) VALUE 'JUNE      '.
     02 JULY             PICTURE X(12) VALUE 'JULY      '.
     02 AUGUST           PICTURE X(12) VALUE 'AUGUST    '.
     02 SEPTEMBER        PICTURE X(12) VALUE 'SEPTEMBER '.
     02 OCTOBER          PICTURE X(12) VALUE 'OCTOBER   '.
     02 NOVEMBER         PICTURE X(12) VALUE 'NOVEMBER  '.
     02 DECEMBER         PICTURE X(12) VALUE 'DECEMBER  '.
01   MONTHS REDEFINES MONTH-TABLE.
     02 MONTH            PICTURE X(12) OCCURS 12 TIMES.
```

EXHIBIT 14-2   SAMPLE FORECAST PROGRAM *(Continued)*

```
PROCEDURE DIVISION.
MAIN-ROUTINE.
    OPEN INPUT INPUT-DATA
    OPEN OUTPUT OUTPUT-FILE
    MOVE 'NO' TO DATA-END
    READ INPUT-DATA RECORD
        AT END MOVE 'YES' TO DATA-END.
*
    IF DATA-END = 'NO'
        WRITE OUT-LINE FROM HEADER AFTER PAGE
        MOVE SPACES TO OUT-LINE
        WRITE OUT-LINE AFTER ADVANCING 1 LINE
        MOVE ZERO TO MONTHS-FROM-NOW
        MOVE NEXT-MONTH TO WHICH-ONE
        PERFORM CALCULATION-ROUTINE
                HOW-MANY-MONTHS TIMES
    ELSE
        MOVE 'NO DATA AVAILABLE' TO OUT-LINE
        WRITE OUT-LINE AFTER 1 LINE.
*
*
    CLOSE INPUT-DATA, OUTPUT-FILE.
    STOP RUN.
*
CALCULATION-ROUTINE.
    ADD 1 TO MONTHS-FROM-NOW
    IF WHICH-ONE IS GREATER THAN 12
        SUBTRACT 12 FROM WHICH-ONE.
    COMPUTE SALES =
            MONTHS-FROM-NOW * COEFFICIENT.
    ADD BASE TO SALES.
    MOVE MONTH (WHICH-ONE) TO MONTH-NAME.
    MOVE SALES TO EDIT-SALES.
    WRITE OUT-LINE FROM PRINT-RECORD
            AFTER ADVANCING 1 LINE.
    ADD 1 TO WHICH-ONE.
```

Format 4

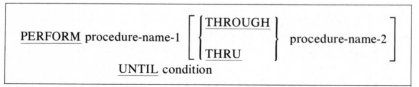

PERFORM procedure-name-1 $\left[\begin{Bmatrix} \text{THROUGH} \\ \text{THRU} \end{Bmatrix} \text{procedure-name-2}\right]$

UNDERLINE condition

For example, in the earlier section of this chapter, An Example of Reading in Values for a Table, we wrote:

PERFORM TABLE-READ
    UNTIL N > 10 OR DATA-END = 'YES'.

When the UNTIL option is used, a test is performed to determine if the condition is initially met. This test is performed prior to the first execution of the paragraphs that constitute the object of PERFORM. If the condition is met in the first place, the effect is to disregard the PERFORM verb.

The flowchart in Figure 14-2 indicates the control logic involved with the UNTIL option.

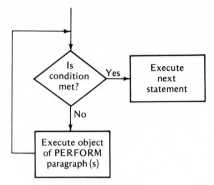

FIGURE 14-2   FLOWCHART ILLUSTRATING THE CONTROL LOGIC ASSOCIATED WITH USING THE UNTIL OPTION WITH THE PERFORM VERB.

REVIEW

1   The use of either Format 3 or Format 4 of the PERFORM verb allows _____ execution of program segments.

repetitive (etc.)

2   Suppose we are reading and accumulating certain figures for each of the 50 states in order to arrive at a national total. If the READ-TABLE paragraph, which is the object of PERFORM, immediately follows the PERFORM statement, we should write PERFORM READ-TABLE _____ TIMES.

49

3   In the question above, if we prefer to write "50 TIMES," possibly because this makes the program easier to read and interpret, we can do so by inserting a(n) _____ type of statement immediately after the statement which includes PERFORM.

GO TO

4   The object of PERFORM is not executed at all if the integer or data-name used with PERFORM has a _____ or _____ value.

zero; negative

5   When the THRU option associated with Formats 3 and 4 is used, more than one paragraph is included as the object of the PERFORM verb. In this case it is possible to have additional PERFORM verbs embedded in the object paragraphs, and these are called _____ PERFORM statements.

nested

6   Format 4 of the PERFORM verb allows repetitive execution of the object paragraph, or paragraphs subject to a condition being fulfilled. For example, such a statement might be MOVE 1 TO K. PERFORM BILLING _____ K > NUM-TRANSAC.

UNTIL

FORMAT 5

The fifth format option of the PERFORM verb is more elaborate than the others we have discussed to this point and is particularly suited for carrying out tasks which involve tables and subscripts.

Format 5

PERFORM procedure-name-1 [THRU procedure-name-2] VARYING

identifier-1 FROM $\left\{ \begin{array}{l} \text{identifier-2} \\ \text{literal-1} \end{array} \right\}$ BY $\left\{ \begin{array}{l} \text{identifier-3} \\ \text{literal-2} \end{array} \right\}$ UNTIL condition

It will be easier to understand the components of this option by first considering an example. Let us take the example discussed in relation to Format 3, which was

```
MOVE ZERO TO TOTAL-SALES
MOVE 1 TO N
PERFORM SUMMATION 12 TIMES.
DIVIDE TOTAL-SALES BY 12 GIVING AVERAGE-SALES.
    .
    .
    .
    etc.
SUMMATION.
    ADD MONTHLY-SALES (N) TO TOTAL-SALES
    ADD 1 TO N.
```

Now let us rewrite these instructions using the new format:

```
MOVE ZERO TO TOTAL-SALES
PERFORM SUMMATION VARYING N FROM 1 BY 1
    UNTIL N > 12.
DIVIDE TOTAL-SALES BY 12 GIVING AVERAGE-SALES.
    .
    .
    .
    etc.
SUMMATION.
    ADD MONTHLY-SALES (N) TO TOTAL-SALES.
```

The use of Format 5 allows us to execute an object paragraph or paragraphs while systematically varying an identifier. Of course, this identifier (in the above example, N) must have been defined in the DATA DIVISION.

Most often the identifier varied is used as a subscript, as in the example above. However, it could be used simply as a counter to control the number of executions of

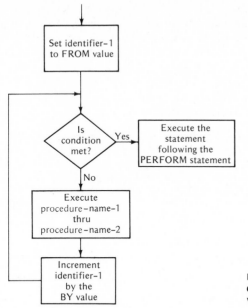

FIGURE 14-3 FLOWCHART ILLUSTRATING THE CONTROL LOGIC ASSOCIATED WITH USING THE VARYING OPTION WITH THE PERFORM VERB.

the object of the PERFORM verb. The flowchart in Figure 14-3 portrays the control logic involved in the execution of PERFORM with the VARYING option.

It is worthwhile to consider some further examples in order to illustrate the potential of Format 5. Let us say a home mortgage company issues a set of payment coupons at the beginning of each year. There are 12 coupons, numbered 1 to 12, each containing the name of the month in which the payment is due and the amount. What is required to prepare the coupons, then, is a repetitive execution (12 times) of a task with two variable factors: the coupon number (01 to 12) and the month-name. Of course, the amount of payment due will be the same for each of the months, and our present example is not concerned with the determination of this amount.

First, let us set up partial DATA DIVISION entries:

```
01  MONTHS-TABLE.
    02  MONTH PICTURE X(10) OCCURS 12 TIMES.
01  COUPON. (fillers skipped)
    02  COUPON-NUMBER PICTURE 99.
    02  MONTH-NAME PICTURE X(10).
    02  EDITED-AMOUNT PICTURE $$,$$9.99.
```

The MONTHS-TABLE will be filled with the names of the 12 months. Assume that the names are to be read from cards, the first card containing the name JANUARY and the twelfth card containing the name DECEMBER in a field called CARD-MONTH. The following PROCEDURE DIVISION program segment can be used to accomplish this task.

PERFORM MONTH-READER VARYING MONTH-NUMBER FROM 1
BY 1 UNTIL MONTH-NUMBER IS EQUAL TO 13.

.

.

.

MONTH-READER.
    READ MONTH-CARD RECORD AT END . . .
    MOVE CARD-MONTH TO MONTH (MONTH-NUMBER).

Recall that UNTIL MONTH-NUMBER IS EQUAL TO 13 is equivalent to writing UNTIL MONTH-NUMBER IS GREATER THAN 12.

Now, when the 12 month-names have been entered in the MONTHS-TABLE by execution of the above program segment, the set of statements required to print the 12 coupons, each with a coupon number, month-name, and edited amount, can be written as

LOOP-CONTROL.
    PERFORM COUPON-PRINTING VARYING KOUNT FROM 1 BY 1
    UNTIL KOUNT = 12.
COUPON-PRINTING.
    MOVE KOUNT TO COUPON-NUMBER.
    MOVE MONTH (KOUNT) TO MONTH-NAME.
    MOVE AMOUNT TO EDITED-AMOUNT.
    WRITE PRINT-LINE FROM COUPON.

Notice that the program segment says UNTIL KOUNT = 12. This will result in COUPON-PRINTING being executed 11 times under PERFORM control. After that, since COUPON-PRINTING is consecutive to the PERFORM statement, it will be executed once more through the natural sequence of the program. In addition, note that KOUNT, which is varied by PERFORM, is used in three ways:

1 To control the number of executions
2 As the coupon-number
3 As the subscript to retrieve the corresponding month-name from MONTHS-TABLE

It is now appropriate to review the overall procedure by which the VARYING option is carried out.

1 First, the identifier to be varied is set at its initial value, the value indicated by the clause

$$\underline{\text{FROM}} \left\{ \begin{array}{c} \text{identifier-2} \\ \text{literal} \end{array} \right\}$$

2 Then a test is made to determine if the condition specified by UNTIL is met. If it is met, PERFORM is skipped and control passes to the next statement. If the condition is not met, then the paragraph(s) specified is executed once.
3 Next, the value of the varied identifier is incremented by the amount shown in the clause

$$\underline{BY} \left\{ \begin{array}{l} \text{identifier-3} \\ \text{literal} \end{array} \right\}$$

4   The procedure in steps 2 and 3 is repeated.

The condition need not refer to the value of the identifier-1 which is varied, even though the examples above illustrate only such cases. The condition can refer to other identifiers, but it must in all cases refer to identifiers that have their values altered by the paragraphs under PERFORM control. Otherwise the loop will repeat indefinitely, as in the following example:

```
MOVE 10 TO AMOUNT
PERFORM ABC VARYING L FROM 1 BY 1
    UNTIL AMOUNT > 20.
ABC.
    WRITE REPORT LINE.
```

The problem with the above segment is that, whereas the value of L is being incremented, the value of AMOUNT is being tested. Since AMOUNT is never altered by the ABC paragraph, there will be no end to the loop!

Now consider one more example which further illustrates use of the VARYING option and utilizes the STRING verb discussed in Chapter 7, "PROCEDURE DIVISION Features II."

Suppose that a header is to be centered in respect to column 40 of a printed page. The size of the header is variable but it is always 20 or less characters long. The header is stored in the field called HEADER and we wish to move it and print it from the output record called OUTPUT-RECORD. Consider the following DATA and PROCEDURE DIVISION entries.

```
01  CHECK-FIELD    PIC X.
01  I              PIC 99.
01  HEADER.
    02  INDIV-CHAR PIC X OCCURS 20 TIMES.
        .
        .
        .
MOVE SPACE TO CHECK-FIELD
PERFORM DETERMINE-SIZE VARYING I FROM 20 BY -1
  UNTIL CHECK-FIELD NOT = SPACE
      OR I = ZERO.
ADD 1 TO I
COMPUTE I = 40 - (I / 2)
MOVE SPACES TO OUTPUT-RECORD
STRING HEADER DELIMITED BY SIZE
    INTO OUTPUT-RECORD
    WITH POINTER I.
WRITE OUTPUT-RECORD. . . .
```

.
.
.

DETERMINE-SIZE.
    IF INDIV-CHAR (I) NOT = SPACE
        MOVE 'X' TO CHECK-FIELD.

    The PERFORM DETERMINE-SIZE statement searches the HEADER field character by character from the right end of the field. When a nonblank character is encountered or the entire field has been searched we terminate the search. We then add 1 to I to restore it to the value that identifies the proper length. For example, if the data in HEADER consisted of ACME COMPANY the Y character would cause X to be moved to CHECK-FIELD. Then, by nature of the PERFORM VARYING, I would be incremented by −1 and would become 11 before the UNTIL test was executed. Thus the ADD 1 to I would restore I to the true length value of 12. Next, the procedure shows that we divide I by 2 and subtract this integer quotient from 40, which is the centering column. In this example, the data in HEADER is 12 characters long, thus I would I = 40 − 12/2 = 34. Then, use of the WITH POINTER I clause in the STRING verb would move the HEADER data into OUTPUT-RECORD beginning with column 34.

FORMAT 6

    The sixth format of the PERFORM represents some rather complex options that may require some practice in order to master them.

Format 6

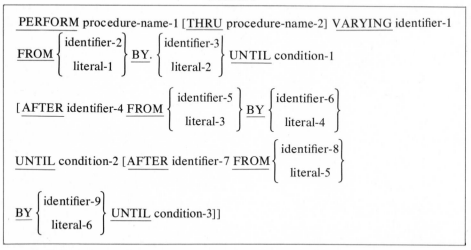

    To illustrate the general idea suppose that we have enrollment figures for six state colleges each with four years of class levels subdivided into male and female students. We are interested in forming the sum of enrollment for all colleges and all students.

01   ENROLLMENT-TABLE.
    02   COLLEGE OCCURS 6 TIMES.

```
03   CLASS-LEVEL OCCURS 4 TIMES.
     04   STUDENT OCCURS 2 TIMES PIC 9999.
```

.
.
.

```
MOVE ZERO TO TOTAL-ENROLLMENT
PERFORM SUMMATION
     VARYING I FROM 1 BY 1
          UNTIL I > 6
     AFTER J FROM 1 BY 1
          UNTIL J > 4
     AFTER K FROM 1 BY 1
          UNTIL K > 2.
```

.
.
.

```
SUMMATION.
     ADD STUDENT (I,   J,   K) TO TOTAL-ENROLLMENT.
```

The table below shows the variation of the three subscripts I, J, and K. The identifier associated with the second AFTER varies the fastest, the identifier associated with the first AFTER varies next fastest, and the identifier following the VARYING varies the slowest. Thus, SUMMATION will be executed 48 times (6 × 4 × 2), in total.

I	J	K
1	1	1
1	1	2
1	2	1
1	2	2
.	.	.
.	.	.
.	.	.
1	4	1
1	4	2
2	1	1
2	1	2
2	2	1
.	.	.
.	.	.
.	.	.
6	4	2

SAMPLE PROGRAM

Punched cards contain a quarter value in column 1, a region value in column 2, and a sales amount in columns 3–5. We want to read such a card file and produce a report that shows sales by quarter and region, as follows:

QUARTER	REGION			
	EAST	SOUTH	MIDWEST	WEST
1				
2		10		
3				
4				

Exhibit 14-3 presents a program written to accomplish the task. The data is accumulated in a two-dimensional table

```
01  SALES-TABLE.
    02  QUARTER-DATA OCCURS 4 TIMES.
        03  SALES OCCURS 4 TIMES PIC 9(5).
```

EXHIBIT 14-3   PROGRAM FOR A QUARTERLY REPORT

```
    IDENTIFICATION DIVISION.
    PROGRAM-ID. TABLES.
*
    ENVIRONMENT DIVISION.
    CONFIGURATION SECTION.
    SOURCE-COMPUTER. ABC-480.
    OBJECT-COMPUTER. ABC-480.
    INPUT-OUTPUT SECTION.
    FILE-CONTROL.
        SELECT INPUT-FILE  ASSIGN TO CARD-READER.
        SELECT OUTPUT-FILE ASSIGN TO PRINTER.
*
    DATA DIVISION.
    FILE SECTION.
    FD  INPUT-FILE LABEL RECORD OMITTED
                   DATA RECORD IS INPUT-RECORD.
    01  INPUT-RECORD.
        02 QUARTER         PIC 9.
        02 REGION          PIC 9.
        02 AMOUNT          PIC 999.
        02 FILLER          PIC X(75).
    FD  OUTPUT-FILE LABEL RECORD OMITTED
                    DATA RECORD IS OUTPUT-RECORD.
    01  OUTPUT-RECORD  PIC X(132).
*
    WORKING-STORAGE SECTION.
    01  END-OF-DATA    PIC XXX.
*
    01  SALES-TABLE.
        02 MONTH-DATA OCCURS 4 TIMES.
           03 SALES OCCURS 4 TIMES PIC 9(5).
*
    01  HEADER-1.
        02 FILLER PIC X(27) VALUE SPACES.
        02 FILLER PIC X(6)  VALUE 'REGION'.
    01  HEADER-2.
        02 FILLER PIC X(17) VALUE ' QUARTER     EAST'.
        02 FILLER PIC X(6)  VALUE SPACES.
        02 FILLER PIC X(9)  VALUE 'SOUTH   '.
        02 FILLER PIC X(15) VALUE 'MIDWEST   WEST'.
```

EXHIBIT 14-3   PROGRAM FOR A QUARTERLY REPORT *(Continued)*

```
*
 01    OUTPUT-LINE.
       02 FILLER              PIC X(5).
       02 QUARTER-OUT         PIC 9.
       02 FILLER              PIC X(4).
       02 DATA-OUT OCCURS 4 TIMES.
          03 FILLER           PIC XX.
          03 REGION-OUT       PIC ZZ,ZZZ.
          03 FILLER           PIC XX.

 PROCEDURE DIVISION.
 MAIN-ROUTINE.
       OPEN INPUT  INPUT-FILE
            OUTPUT OUTPUT-FILE.
       MOVE 'NO' TO END-OF-DATA.
       MOVE ZERO TO SALES-TABLE.
*
       PERFORM READ-DATA.
       PERFORM READ-ACCUMULATE
          UNTIL END-OF-DATA = 'YES'.
*
       PERFORM HEADERS
*
       PERFORM PRINT-TABLE VARYING QUARTER FROM 1 BY 1
                    UNTIL QUARTER IS GREATER THAN 4.
*
       CLOSE INPUT-FILE, OUTPUT-FILE.
       STOP RUN.
*
 READ-DATA.
       READ INPUT-FILE AT END MOVE 'YES' TO END-OF-DATA.
*
 READ-ACCUMULATE.
       ADD AMOUNT TO SALES (QUARTER, REGION)
       PERFORM READ-DATA.
*
 HEADERS.
       WRITE OUTPUT-RECORD FROM HEADER-1 AFTER ADVANCING PAGE
       WRITE OUTPUT-RECORD FROM HEADER-2
          AFTER ADVANCING 3 LINES.
*
 PRINT-TABLE.
       MOVE SPACES TO OUTPUT-LINE.
       PERFORM MOVE-DATA VARYING REGION FROM 1 BY 1
                    UNTIL REGION IS GREATER THAN 4.
       MOVE QUARTER TO QUARTER-OUT.
       WRITE OUTPUT-RECORD FROM OUTPUT-LINE
          AFTER ADVANCING 2 LINES.
*
 MOVE-DATA.
       MOVE SALES (QUARTER, REGION) TO REGION-OUT (REGION).
```

The PROCEDURE DIVISION is quite straightforward, but it requires some study by the student. Notice that in the READ-ACCUMULATE paragraph the QUARTER and REGION values which are read in from a card are used as subscripts. Thus a card which contains 12010 would mean to add 010 (AMOUNT) to the SALES (1, 2) cell of the SALES-TABLE. This addition is carried out for as long as there are cards available. Since we are adding to existing values, we make sure that all cells of the table have zeros as the initial values simply by saying MOVE ZERO TO SALES-TABLE. This move to the group level ensures zeros at the elementary level as well.

It should also be noted that we have a nested PERFORM structure in this program. We PERFORM PRINT-TABLE VARYING QUARTER, whereas in PRINT-TABLE we PERFORM MOVE-DATA VARYING REGION. Thus MOVE-DATA is executed four times for each execution of PRINT-TABLE and it allows us to move the four region values for each quarter to their editing field. A review of OUTPUT-LINE in the DATA DIVISION will reveal that we have defined a table (DATA-OUT); it is to this table that we move data in the MOVE-DATA paragraph.

REVIEW

1 By the use of Format 5 of the PERFORM verb, control of PERFORM is associated with systematically incrementing the value of a(n) _____.

identifier

2 The key programming word that indicates that an identifier is to be systematically varied is the word _____.

VARYING

3 The test made to determine if the condition specified for terminating PERFORM control has been met is indicated by the reserved COBOL word _____.

UNTIL

4 If the identifier being incremented in a Format 5 PERFORM instruction is not the same as the identifier being tested, the result is that [the PERFORM is skipped / looping continues indefinitely].

looping continues indefinitely

5 The Format 6 option of the PERFORM verb extends the efficiency of COBOL by allowing the programmer systematically to vary up to _____ (number) identifiers in a nested fashion.

three

THE EXIT VERB

The series of procedures specified by the PERFORM verb must culminate at a single end point. Where this would not otherwise be the case, the EXIT verb is used to provide an artificial end point. Let us illustrate the function of the EXIT command by a specific example. Suppose we have a TABLE that consists of 20 cells and we want to determine how many cells have a value of zero and how many contain a positive value (we are not interested in negatives). This can be accomplished by executing the following program segment:

```
    MOVE ZERO TO COUNTER
    PERFORM TESTING THRU LOOP-END
        VARYING I FROM 1 BY 1 UNTIL I = 20.
TESTING.
    IF TABLE (I) < ZERO GO TO LOOP-END.
    IF TABLE (I) = ZERO
        ADD 1 TO ZERO-COUNT
        GO TO LOOP-END
    ELSE
        ADD 1 TO POSITIVE-COUNT.
LOOP-END.
    EXIT.
```

As is the case in the above example, the EXIT verb must occupy a paragraph by itself. The LOOP-END is a kind of dummy paragraph that allows control to remain with the PERFORM verb. Note that in the absence of the LOOP-END paragraph we cannot very easily bypass the intervening statements in the TESTING paragraph. It is also important to note that the use of EXIT is not reserved for situations involving PERFORM verb control. If somehow the dummy paragraph is entered without being under the control of PERFORM, there is no effect, and program execution continues with the next paragraph.

REVIEW

1   In cases in which the procedures specified by the PERFORM verb do not culminate at a single point, such a point can be provided by use of the _____ verb.

EXIT

2   The EXIT verb is always located in a paragraph of its own. If execution of this paragraph is attempted in the absence of PERFORM control, program execution will then [stop / continue with the next paragraph].

continue with the next paragraph

EXERCISES

1   Write DATA DIVISION entries to set up a table which is to contain annual dollar sales for the years 1966–1978. No value will exceed $100,000,000.00.

2   Write DATA DIVISION entries to set up a table to contain dollar and unit sales for the years 1966–1978. It is desired to be able to reference the dollar sales or the unit sales individually for each year, as well as to reference as a group the dollar sales and unit sales pertaining to a given year. The general format of the table is as follows:

Year	Dollar sales	Unit sales
1966		
1967		
⋮	⋮	⋮
1978		

3   Use DATA DIVISION entries to form a table containing the names of the days of the week so that the names are referenced by a subscript, i.e., Monday by a subscript 1, and Sunday by a subscript 7.

4   A marketing survey conducted by a company involved administering a questionnaire of 25 questions. The responses to each question have been coded by a one-digit code, ranging from 0 to 9. It is desired to accumulate a table of the responses to each of the 25 questions as shown in the following diagram. Write DATA DIVISION entries to form such a table. It should be possible to make reference to each individual cell in the table, as well as each row (question).

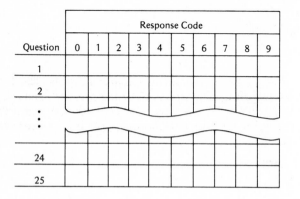

5   Assume that TAX-TABLE contains 30 values (V999). Write the PROCEDURE and DATA DIVISION statements required to print the contents of the table in the following formats.

a   Print the 30 values in one column of 30 lines.
b   Print the 30 values seven per line for as many lines as are needed.

6   Suppose that the following table contains 20 values.

```
01  SALES-DATA-TABLE.
    02  SALES-TERRITORY OCCURS 5 TIMES.
        03  QUARTER-SALES OCCURS 4 TIMES      PICTURE 9(6)V99.
```

It is desired to read in the data and produce the report on page 386. Input columns representing sales territories. Write the necessary program instructions.

7   For the following table, write the necessary program instructions to find the smallest value and place it in SMALLEST. Disregard the possibility of ties.

```
02  TABLE OCCURS 50 TIMES      PICTURE X(12).
```

8   In the following two-dimensional table it is desired to form the sum of each row and the sum of each column, as well as the grand total. The results of the

summations are to be saved, so that they can be printed later in the program. Write relevant DATA and PROCEDURE DIVISION entries.

01 SALES-DATA-TABLE.
   02 SALES-TERRITORY OCCURS 5 TIMES.
      03 QUARTER-SALES OCCURS 4 TIMES   PICTURE 9(6)V99.

9 Card records contain sales data as follows:

COLUMNS	
1–5	Amount (whole dollar)
6	Region code: 1 = West, 2 = Midwest
	3 = South, 4 = East
7–8	Month code (numeric)

It is desired to read in the data and produce the report on page 386. Input records which contain error region codes, error month codes, or nonnumeric amounts should be excluded from the tabulation and are to be printed with a suitable error message. Data is shown below. Write a program to produce such a table.

00133412	00156208	20200410
00096410	00171307	00900309
00085201	00145405	00100106
00099101	00201403	00500206
00110202	00300302	/ 560507
00100303	00152201	70082 01
00050405	00118408	00233102
00040004	00190406	00422109
00030704	00150309	00150212
00018103	00160110	00050211
00025302	00213211	00060412
00020401	00115112	00030411
00010106	00118109	0015412
00123102	00219208	00018311
00185303	00300402	00072312
00197308	00200203	00035211
00142409	00145302	00150303
00356407	00142304	00160202
00428407	00140205	00110101
00234202	00150207	00200204
00152103	00160108	00220308
00123101	00152109	00183407
01100205	00202100	00157301
01200307	00200312	00085409
00142211	00145311	00096110

ACME CORPORATION
SALES ANALYSIS REPORT

MONTH	WEST	MIDWEST	SOUTH	EAST	MONTHLY TOTAL	PERCENT OF YEAR TOTAL
JANUARY						
FEBRUARY						
MARCH						
APRIL						
MAY						
JUNE						
JULY						
AUGUST						
SEPTEMBER						
OCTOBER						
NOVEMBER						
DECEMBER						
TOTAL						
PERCENT OF TOTAL						

Table Sorting and Searching

INTERNAL SORTING

Internal sorting is concerned with the sorting procedures (algorithms) used with tables of data held in central storage. A considerable number of such methods exist, and we consider only the principal ones in the following sections. The names used below do not necessarily represent standard nomenclature, because there are no commonly used names for many of these algorithms.

LINEAR SEARCH SORT ALGORITHM

Suppose we have a table of 100 records in the internal storage of a computer. First, we define another table with the same storage capacity. Then we examine each record of the original table in succession, looking for the smallest record. This smallest record is copied as the first entry in the alternate table and it is deleted from the first table. The process is repeated, each time finding the smallest remaining record and recording it in successive places in the alternate table until all the records in the original table have been stored in the alternate table. The linear search sort algorithm is a simple one conceptually, but it is very inefficient. For one thing, it requires twice the amount of storage as the table to be sorted. For another thing, it requires as many searches through the original table as there are entries in the table. Thus, if the table to be sorted contains 100 records, we will search 100 times 100 records each time = 10,000 records.

INTERCHANGE SORT ALGORITHMS

Three versions of the interchange sort approach can be distinguished, and these are individually described below. Fundamental to all these algorithms is the interchange of two elements. Suppose that we have RECORD-1 and RECORD-2 and we want to interchange them. The procedure by which this can be accomplished requires the use of a third storage location; call it TEMPORARY-STORAGE. A description of the process by which the interchange is accomplished is presented in Figure 15-1. As the first step, RECORD-1 is moved to TEMPORARY-STORAGE to save it. Then RECORD-2 is moved to RECORD-1. Finally, the content of TEMPORARY-STORAGE is moved to RECORD-2. We now describe the three variations of the interchange sort algorithm.

By the *linear search-interchange algorithm* a search is made through the table comparing the first record with every other record in the table. Each record that is smaller than the first record is interchanged with it. Of course, this might involve more than one interchange, since the first record might be interchanged with the fifth and then that record might be interchanged with the ninth record, for example. One such pass through the table results in the smallest record being the first entry in the table. The process is then repeated beginning with the second entry in the table, resulting in the second smallest value being placed as the second entry in the table. On the third pass the process begins with the third entry, and so on to the record before the last. Thus for a table with N records, N − 1 repetitions of the procedure are required. Given a table with 10 records, for example, once the appropriate value to be placed in the ninth entry has been determined, the tenth entry automatically contains the highest record.

The *adjacent comparison-interchange algorithm* involves comparison of adjacent records and interchange where appropriate, as implied by the name of this technique.

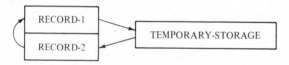

FIGURE 15-1   SCHEMATIC DIAGRAM FOR THE INTERCHANGE
OF TWO ELEMENTS IN STORAGE BY THE USE OF A THIRD
STORAGE LOCATION.

Specifically, in the first pass the first entry is compared with the second, the second with the third, and so on until the (N−1)th record is compared with the Nth record in the table. The two records being compared each time are interchanged whenever the second record is smaller than the first record, assuming that the file is being sorted into ascending order. If no interchange was necessary during an entire pass, this means that the table is already in order. Otherwise, at least one more pass is required.

By the adjacent comparison approach, at the end of the first pass the largest record is driven to the bottom of the table. Thus in the second pass through the table N-1 table entries are considered, in the third pass N-2 are considered, and so forth. Thus the table is sorted from the last entry up, and every pass through the table involves a smaller table for comparisons and interchanges. Eventually only two elements remain to be considered—the first and the second.

Typically, however, the table will come to be sorted correctly before all possible passes through the table are made by the adjacent comparison approach. As indicated above, the fact that no interchange is necessary during a pass through the table serves to indicate that the table is already correctly sorted. In order to avoid unnecessary passes through the table, it is useful to incorporate a procedure by which such a situation can be detected. One way of doing this is to initialize a data-name with a value such as zero, and to change the value to 1 with the occurrence of any interchange. At the end of each pass the value of the data-name is tested. If the value is zero, the table is sorted. If the value is 1, at least one more pass is required.

The procedure associated with the adjacent comparison-interchange algorithm will now be illustrated by means of a COBOL program, which is presented in Exhibit 15-1.

The input consists of 80-column punched cards. Each card record consists of two fields, NAME-IN and FILLER. The NAME-IN will be used as the sort key while FILLER is assumed to contain other data. Data is read in by execution of the READ-DATA-IN SECTION, which stores the records in a table called ENTIRE-TABLE. Notice that N is a counter that represents the number of records read (maximum of 50).

The sorting operation takes place in the SORT-DATA SECTION. The PERFORM OUTER-LOOP is executed as long as TEST is not equal to "SORTED" and as long as I is not equal to N-1. This instruction, in essence, says to keep going through the table as long as it is not sorted after each pass through, but in any case not to go through more than N-1 times. In the OUTER-LOOP paragraph, TEST is set to the value 'SORTED' so that if no interchange takes place that value will stay as such and will terminate execution of the OUTER-LOOP paragraph. Each time through, M is decreased by 1, since the table is effectively shortened as the largest value floats to the bottom. The PERFORM PAIRED-COMPARISONS instruction allows us to compare M-1 pairs and interchange their values as needed.

The PRINT-DATA SECTION simply lists the data on the printer for visual review.

Finally, the third version of the interchange sort algorithm is the *bubble sort-interchange algorithm*. Use of this method results in the first part of the table being sorted first, and in this sense it can be viewed as a top-down algorithm as contrasted to the bottom-up sort process associated with adjacent comparison. By the bubble sort-interchange method the first step is that the second record is compared with the first, and if necessary, they are interchanged. Then the third record is compared with the second. If these two records are interchanged, the (new) second record is compared with the first, interchanging if necessary. Next, the fourth and third record are compared for possible interchange. Again, if an interchange occurs, we go "upward" and compare the third with the second record and then possibly the second with the first record. Thus, at each stage a record rises like a bubble to find its proper place, and hence the name "bubble sort" which is applied to this algorithm.

As an example of using the bubble sort-interchange algorithm consider the following set of six records with sort-keys as indicated:

5

8

10

11

9

15

Comparison of the second and first records results in no interchange. Similarly, comparison of the third and second and of the fourth and third records results in no interchange. However, when the fifth and fourth records are compared (9 and 11) an interchange results. Following this, comparison of the fourth and third records (9 and

EXHIBIT 15-1   COBOL INTERNAL SORT PROGRAM UTILIZING THE ADJACENT COMPARISON-INTERCHANGE ALGORITHM

```
IDENTIFICATION DIVISION.
PROGRAM-ID. INSORT.
*
ENVIRONMENT DIVISION.
CONFIGURATION SECTION.
SOURCE-COMPUTER. ABC-480.
OBJECT-COMPUTER. ABC-480.
INPUT-OUTPUT SECTION.
FILE-CONTROL.
    SELECT INPUT-FILE  ASSIGN TO CARD-READER.
    SELECT OUTPUT-FILE ASSIGN TO PRINTER.
*
DATA DIVISION.
FILE SECTION.
FD  INPUT-FILE  LABEL RECORD OMITTED
                DATA RECORD CARD-RECORD.
01  CARD-RECORD.
    02 NAME-IN          PIC X(15).
    02 FILLER           PIC X(65).
FD  OUTPUT-FILE LABEL RECORD OMITTED
                DATA RECORD PRINT-RECORD.
01  PRINT-RECORD        PIC X(132).
*
WORKING-STORAGE SECTION.
01  ENTIRE-TABLE.
    02 TABLE-REC OCCURS 50 TIMES.
       03 NAME          PIC X(15).
       03 FILLER        PIC X(65).
01  DATA-END            PIC XXX.
01  TEST                PIC X(8).
01  N                   PIC 99.
01  I                   PIC 99.
01  J                   PIC 99.
01  K                   PIC 99.
01  M                   PIC 99.
01  TEMP-STORE          PIC X(80).
/
PROCEDURE DIVISION.
MAIN-ROUTINE.
    OPEN INPUT   INPUT-FILE
         OUTPUT OUTPUT-FILE
    PERFORM READ-DATA-IN
    PERFORM SORT-DATA.
    PERFORM PRINT-DATA.
*
    CLOSE INPUT-FILE, OUTPUT-FILE
    STOP RUN.
```

EXHIBIT 15-1   COBOL INTERNAL SORT PROGRAM UTILIZING THE ADJACENT COMPARI-SON-INTERCHANGE ALGORITHM *(Continued)*

```
*
 READ-DATA-IN SECTION.
 SET-UP-TO-READ.
       MOVE 'NO' TO DATA-END.
       MOVE ZERO TO N.
       PERFORM READ-DATA
       PERFORM STORE-READ
               UNTIL DATA-END = 'YES'
                  OR N = 50.
       GO TO EXIT-READ.
 READ-DATA.
       READ INPUT-FILE AT END MOVE 'YES' TO DATA-END.
 STORE-READ.
       ADD 1 TO N
       MOVE CARD-RECORD TO TABLE-REC (N)
       PERFORM READ-DATA.
 EXIT-READ.
       EXIT.
*
 SORT-DATA SECTION.
 SET-UP-TO-SORT.
       MOVE 'UNSORTED' TO TEST
       MOVE N TO M
       PERFORM OUTER-LOOP VARYING I FROM 1 BY 1
                          UNTIL TEST = 'SORTED'
                             OR I = N - 1.
       GO TO SORT-ENDED.
*
 OUTER-LOOP.
       MOVE 'SORTED' TO TEST
       COMPUTE  M = M - 1
       PERFORM PAIRED-COMPARISONS VARYING J FROM 1 BY 1
                          UNTIL J > M.
 PAIRED-COMPARISONS.
       COMPUTE K = 1 + J
       IF NAME (J) IS GREATER THAN NAME (K)
          MOVE TABLE-REC (J) TO TEMP-STORE
          MOVE TABLE-REC (K) TO TABLE-REC (J)
          MOVE TEMP-STORE TO TABLE-REC (K)
          MOVE 'UNSORTED' TO TEST
       ELSE
          NEXT SENTENCE.
 SORT-ENDED.
       EXIT.
*
 PRINT-DATA SECTION.
 PRINT-ROUTINE.
       PERFORM PRINTOUT VARYING I FROM 1 BY 1
                        UNTIL I IS GREATER THAN N.
       GO TO PRINT-END.
 PRINTOUT.
       MOVE TABLE-REC (I) TO PRINT-RECORD
       WRITE PRINT-RECORD AFTER ADVANCING 1 LINE.
 PRINT-END.
       EXIT.
```

10) results in another interchange, but then the comparison of the third and second records (9 and 8) results in no further interchange. Finally, the sixth and fifth records are compared (15 and 11). Since this is the last pair of records and no interchange is required, the sort routine is completed.

REVIEW

1   As contrasted to merging, which is concerned with combining two or more files, the process which is concerned with arranging a single file in a designated sequential order is called _____.

sorting

2 Thus far, we have described two categories of methods that can be used for internal sorting. By "internal sorting" we mean the sorting of a table held in the _____ of the computer.

internal (or central) storage

3 By the linear search sort algorithm an alternate table is set up in internal storage with the same dimensions as the original data table. The records from the original table are then moved one at a time to the new table, with the first record to be moved being the record with the [smallest / largest] sort-key.

smallest

4 If 200 records are to be sorted by the linear search sort algorithm, a total of _____ (number) record searches will have to be performed.

40,000

5 Three versions of the interchange sort algorithm have been described in this section. The feature which is common to all these versions is that in each approach _____ (number) records are compared each time for possible interchange.

two

6 In the linear search-interchange algorithm the first record in the table is compared with every other record, with the result that after the first pass the smallest record is located in the first position in the table. For a table with 200 records, _____ (number) passes through the table are required to complete the sorting process.

199

7 By the adjacent comparison-interchange algorithm all adjacent records are compared and interchanged, when necessary, during each pass through the table. The fact that the table is correctly sorted is indicated when _____ (number) interchanges are required during a particular pass through the table.

0 (or no)

8 The third version of the interchange sort algorithm is the bubble sort-interchange algorithm. By this approach, each record is properly placed before subsequent records are considered, resulting in the [first / last] part of the table being sorted first and thereby requiring _____ (number) passes for a table of N records.

first; one

MERGING SORT ALGORITHM

Thus far, we have described two categories of methods that can be used for the purpose of internal sorting: the linear search sort algorithm and the interchange sort algorithms, with the latter approach including three different versions. We now describe a third major method, the merging sort algorithm. The basic idea underlying this approach is that repetitive merging of files will lead to a sorted file. In general, suppose we have a table of N records. We can think of this table as consisting of N files of one record each. Pairs of these "files" can be merged, giving rise to N/2 sorted files. Pairs of these N/2 files can then be merged, giving N/4 sorted files. We continue until we have N/N files, or one sorted file.

As a more specific example of the application of the merging sort algorithm, consider the example presented in Figure 15-2. In this example, N = 11. Merging pairs of "files" consisting of one record each results in N/2 = 11/2 = 5.5 = 6 sorted files (notice that when N is odd we "round up" the number of files, with the last file containing fewer records than the other files). The second merge in Figure 15-2 results in 6/2 = 3 sorted files. Notice that each of these three files is sorted as a result of the merge procedure. For example, merging of the two files containing records (15, 20) and (10, 50) resulted in the merged and sorted file (10, 15, 20, 50). In a similar fashion, a third and finally fourth merge procedure is carried out, resulting in one completely sorted file.

In using the merging sort algorithm we are in fact not restricted to the merging of pairs. We can just as well merge triplets or quadruplets of files, or whatever. In the extreme case we can conceive of merging all N files of one record each during one merge procedure. Such an approach is the equivalent of the linear search sort algorithm discussed earlier in this section.

CHAINED RECORDS SORT ALGORITHM

The methods of sorting that have been considered thus far all require the movement of records—such as in the interchange algorithms, for example. Since the time required to transfer a record from one storage location to another increases with the size of the record, it would be desirable to sort records that are relatively long without having to move them. This can be accomplished by the use of the chained records sort algorithm, but at the cost of additional storage requirements. By the use of this method two additional fields are defined for each record of a given table of records. The first field, call it the predecessor field, contains a value that defines the

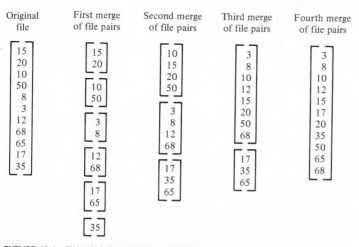

FIGURE 15-2   EXAMPLE OF THE APPLICATION OF THE MERGING SORT ALGORITHM.

location of the record that logically precedes the record in question. The other field, call it the successor field, contains a value that defines the location of the record that logically follows the given record. If such predecessor and successor fields are defined for each record, we say that we have a fully chained set of records. Such a set has both a forward and backward chain, since given any particular record we can determine all the records that precede it and all the records that follow it. In order to designate the first and last records of the file, the first can be assigned a predecessor value of zero while the last record can be assigned a successor value of zero.

In order to illustrate the procedure associated with the chained records sort algorithm, let us consider the table defined by the following DATA DIVISION statements.

01 STORAGE-BANK.

    02 STORE OCCURS 50 TIMES.

        03 DATA-STORE.

            04 KEY-FIELD   PICTURE 9(5).

            04 DATA-FIELD   PICTURE X(75).

        03 PREDECESSOR   PICTURE 99.

        03 SUCCESSOR   PICTURE 99.

Conceptually, the table defined by the above statements has the following structure:

STORE			
DATA-STORE		PREDECESSOR	SUCCESSOR
KEY-FIELD	DATA-FIELD		

Thus, STORE(1) refers to the first line of the table, which is the first physical record. Similarly, DATA-STORE(1) refers to the first two fields of the first record while PREDECESSOR(1) and SUCCESSOR(1) refer to the predecessor and successor values of the first record in the table. Assume that the data to be stored consists of five records whose KEY-FIELDS are 3200, 3900, 2000, 4000, and 3500. For simplicity we ignore the DATA-FIELD values, although it should be noted that this field would usually be the largest of the several fields. In addition, it is useful to define the following data-names, whose values will be stored outside the table as such:

NEXT-PLACE = the next entry in the table

FIRST-PLACE = the physical position of the record which is logically the first entry in the table

LAST-PLACE = the physical position of the record which is logically the last entry in the table

For the five records whose keys are 3200, 3900, 2000, 4000, and 3500, respectively, we now consider the effects of entering each of these records to the table described above in a sequential fashion.

FIRST RECORD ENTERED

KEY-FIELD	DATA-FIELD	PREDECESSOR	SUCCESSOR
3200		00	00

NEXT-PLACE = 2. FIRST-PLACE = 1, LAST-PLACE = 1.

Since there is only one record in the table at this point, the PREDECESSOR and SUCCESSOR fields are both set equal to zero. Similarly, this one record is both the FIRST-PLACE and LAST-PLACE entry in the table. The value of NEXT-PLACE indicates that the second record will be considered next.

SECOND RECORD ENTERED

KEY-FIELD	DATA-FIELD	PREDECESSOR	SUCCESSOR
3200		00	02
3900		01	00

NEXT-PLACE = 3. FIRST-PLACE = 1. LAST-PLACE = 2.

The KEY-FIELD of the second record is higher than the KEY-FIELD of the first record; therefore, the second record logically succeeds the first and SUCCESSOR(1) = 02. However, the first record is not logically preceded by any other record, and hence

PREDECESSOR(1) = 00. Similarly, PREDECESSOR(2) = 01 and SUCCESSOR(2) = 00. The FIRST-PLACE in the table is at record 1 while the LAST-PLACE is at record 2.

THIRD RECORD ENTERED

KEY-FIELD	DATA-FIELD	PREDECESSOR	SUCCESSOR
3200		03	02
3900		01	00
2000		00	01

NEXT-PLACE = 4, FIRST-PLACE = 3, LAST-PLACE = 2.

The KEY-FIELD of the third record (2000) is compared with the KEY-FIELD of LAST-PLACE (3900), and it is found to be smaller. The third record is then compared with the predecessor of LAST-PLACE record (3200), and it is again found to be smaller. However, because no other predecessor record exists, the search is completed and the predecessor and successor values are changed as indicated above.

The effects of processing the fourth and fifth records are illustrated in the following two tables. Note the logic of the changes in the predecessor and successor values in each table.

FOURTH RECORD ENTERED

KEY-FIELD	DATA-FIELD	PREDECESSOR	SUCCESSOR
3200		03	02
3900		01	04
2000		00	01
4000		02	00

NEXT-PLACE = 5, FIRST-PLACE = 3, LAST-PLACE = 4.

FIFTH RECORD ENTERED

KEY-FIELD	DATA-FIELD	PREDECESSOR	SUCCESSOR
3200		03	05
3900		05	04
2000		00	01
4000		02	00
3500		01	02

NEXT-PLACE = 6, FIRST-PLACE = 3, LAST-PLACE = 4.

Given the completed table above, suppose we wish to output the records in this table in ascending sequence. The contents of FIRST-PLACE indicates the location of the first record, that is, the record with the smallest key value. In the above example it is the third record, with the associated KEY-FIELD value of 2000. If the location of this record had not been stored in FIRST-PLACE, it could have been determined by checking the value of each PREDECESSOR field until the one with a value of zero was found. Of course, once the first record is identified, the location of each record which follows is determined by reference to the SUCCESSOR field. Execution of the following PROCEDURE DIVISION statements will result in printed output of the sorted array, with a total of NEXT-PLACE minus 1 records being included in the output.

```
MOVE FIRST-PLACE TO M.
PERFORM PRINTING VARYING N FROM 1 BY 1
UNTIL N = NEXT-PLACE.
    .
    .
    .
PRINTING.
    MOVE DATA STORE(M) TO PRINT-RECORD.
    WRITE PRINT-RECORD.
    MOVE SUCCESSOR(M) TO M.
```

The sort algorithms described in this section are not the only ones available, but they are the ones frequently used and give an indication of the different approaches that can be followed to sort records held in internal storage. In order to achieve a fast sort in respect to particular data circumstances more complex algorithms have been developed. Some of these are proprietary in nature and are not available for general free distribution.

REVIEW

1 The basic idea underlying the merging sort algorithm is that repetitive merging of files will lead to a sorted file. Since we generally begin by merging pairs of "files" which contain only one record each, given N records at the end of the first merge, there are [N / 2N / $\frac{N}{2}$] files.

$$\frac{N}{2}$$

2 Suppose a file containing seven records is to be sorted by use of the merging sort algorithm. By the usual approach of merging pairs of files _____ (number) merges will be required to produce one completely sorted file.

three

3 The chained records sort algorithm differs from all the other sort methods described in this section in that it [does / does not] require that records be moved in order to achieve output which is sorted.

does not

4 The chained records sort algorithm eliminates the time required to move records in internal storage at the price of increased storage requirement. In order to use this algorithm two fields were added to each record in internal storage in the example used in this section. These fields were called _____ and _____ in our example.

PREDECESSOR; SUCCESSOR

5 Although the first logical record can be determined by finding the record for which SUCCESSOR = _____ (value), the necessity of such a search was eliminated in the example in this section by defining the storage location, which we called _____.

0; FIRST-PLACE

TABLE SEARCHING

The use of a dictionary to look up the meanings of words is perhaps the most common example of the need to search a table or file for particular entries. Other examples are a sales tax table used by a cashier, an income tax table used by a taxpayer, a rate table used by an electric utility to compute a customer's bill, a listing of rooms available in a hotel, and a list of football tickets available for a football game. File searching is an all-pervasive data processing function. Fundamental to all information systems is the function of accessing a record from a file and using it in some way.

File organization is basic to our ability to search for a record in a file. For example, a file might be organized as a sequential file, in which case finding a particular record requires the accessing of all preceding records. On the other hand, the file might be organized on an indexed sequential basis, in which case the index file is used to determine the neighborhood of the record being sought. Finally, if the file is a direct access file, a mathematical calculation yields the address of the record being sought. The three principal methods of file organization are discussed in Chapter 16, on "Direct Access Files."

In many situations a "file" is short enough to be entirely contained in internal storage. In such a case it is referred to as a "table." Where we *search* a file, it is often said that we *look up* a table. The terminology associated with tables differs somewhat from that associated with files, but the concepts are basically the same. However, the techniques by which the concepts are implemented are often different. For example, chaining of records by the use of linkage fields and the setting up of overflow areas is common practice in respect to files but uncommon for stored tables.

A table, like a file, is a collection of logically related entries. Examples would be tax rates for different municipalities in a metropolitan area, commission rates for different product classes, and tax rates given different numbers of dependents. Such data is normally short enough to be placed in central storage and thus constitutes a "table." As in the case of a file, a table can be organized for sequential, indexed sequential, or direct access. In the following sections we discuss certain methods for accessing the records contained in a table. Such methods are frequently called table look-up methods. During this discussion we will refer to the concepts of keys, records, and tables. Therefore, it is appropriate to describe these concepts at this point.

A record which is sought is always identified by a *key,* such as a part number, first and last name, and the like. A *table* is made up of a group of *records,* and each record has a field for the key, or identifier. Usually, there will be other data in each record besides the key, but sometimes the key field comprises the entire content. An example would be a table of names. In any event, the key is the relevant item of information from the standpoint of the search. To find a record in a table means to find a key which matches the key of the record being sought.

REVIEW

1   A file can be organized as a _____ file, an _____ file, or a _____ file.

> *sequential; indexed sequential;*
> *direct access*

2   When a "file" is entirely included in the central storage of a computer, it is appropriately called a _____.

> *table*

3   Chaining and linking are frequently used techniques in respect to the storage of records in [files / tables].

> *files*

4   A table is made up of a group of records. The record which is sought in a table is always identified by the value or information contained in the _____ field of the record.

> *key*

LINEAR SEARCH

In a linear search we employ the access method common to sequential files: beginning with the first record we access all records in sequential order until the desired record is found. This method can be applied to a table organized on any basis. However, two different versions of the method can be used with sorted and unsorted tables, respectively. If a table is sorted, that is, sequentially ordered, there is no need to continue the search when the point at which the record would have been stored has been passed. The flowchart in Figure 15-3 presents the logic of linear search for a sequentially organized table. Assume that T is the name of the table and therefore T(I) is a subscripted reference to the Ith entry of the table. The subscript I is initialized to a value of 1. We compare X, the key of the record we are seeking, to T(I), the key of the Ith record in the table. If X is less than T(I), this indicates that the point at which the record being sought would have been stored has been passed, and therefore the record is not contained in the table. For instance, if we are seeking employee-number 123 and the current (Ith) record being investigated has a value of 152, there is no point to continuing the search. All records subsequent to 152 will have key numbers larger than 152. On the other hand, as long as X is greater than T(I) we continue to increment the value of I, but with the provision that I should not exceed N, which is the number of records in the table. We repeat the process until either the record is found or it can be established that the record is not in the table.

The linear search method is generally the simplest procedure to use. It is particularly well suited for unsorted tables, since the method does not require that the table be in any particular order. In practice, many tables are unsorted. If the membership of a table is dynamic, that is, changing often, it may be very costly in terms of overall efficiency to sort the table every time an entry is added to or deleted from the table. Furthermore, it may be that other uses of the data require an order that is based on a different key from the one under consideration. The task of sorting the table in one order and then resorting back to the original order may not be worth the effort. For example, suppose we are processing daily credit purchases which have been sorted by customer number. For credit screening purposes we may want to identify the customers who made purchases of $10,000 or more. If we have a block of 20 customers as a table in central storage, it is much simpler to employ a linear search rather than to sort the records by amount of purchase and then back to customer number. Of course, for an unsorted table the search should continue until all entries have been checked, since the record which is sought can be in any location in the table.

The logic of the linear search strategy presented in Figure 15-3 may be unnecessarily simpleminded if the sorted table to be searched is fairly large. For example, suppose we have a sorted table of 500 entries. If the record which we are seeking is located toward the end of the table, it would seem that there should be some way by which the search can be "speeded up" to get to the table area in which the record is located. A typical variation of the linear search method by which this can be accomplished is to make the increment of the subscript greater than 1 if the record being sought has a key greater than the record which has just been investigated in the table. For example, an increment of 10 could be used until a "greater than" condition is found. Then we could backtrack to search the remaining nine records in the group. Figure 15-4 illustrates the basic logic of the procedure. Initially, the increment variable K is set equal to 10. As long as X > T(I), the procedure is repeated. Finally, when X < T(I) we set

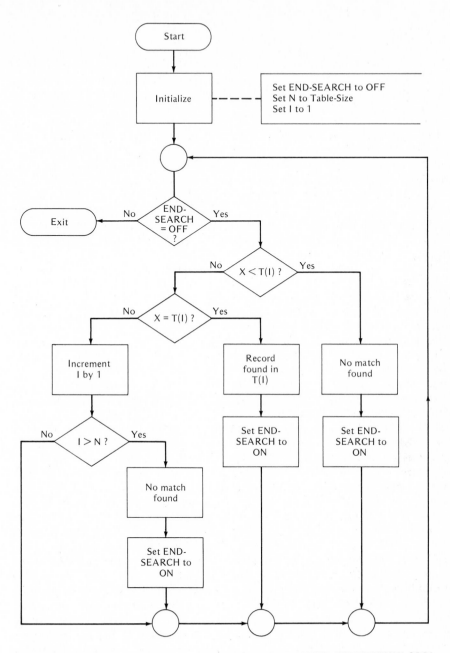

FIGURE 15-3   FLOWCHART FOR THE LINEAR SEARCH OF A SORTED (SEQUENTIALLY ORGA-NIZED) TABLE.

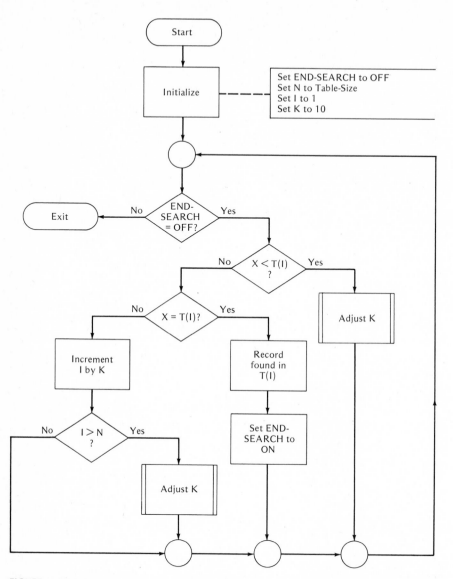

FIGURE 15-4 FLOWCHART FOR THE LINEAR SEARCH OF A SORTED TABLE USING AN INCREMENT OF 10.

K = 1 and subtract 9 from the value of I. Subtracting 9 from I brings us back to the first record of the immediately preceding group of nine records, and subsequent repetitions of the search are then based on incrementing the value of I by 1.

As we increment the value of I by K, such as 10, it is possible that the resulting

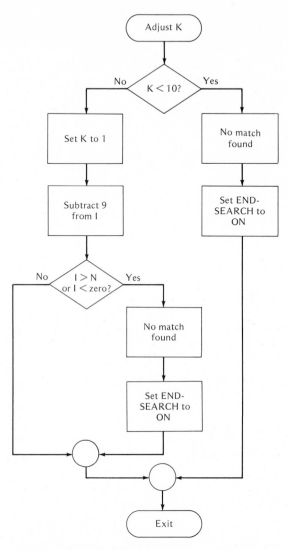

FIGURE 15-4 FLOWCHART FOR THE LINEAR SEARCH OF A SORTED TABLE USING AN INCREMENT OF 10 *(Continued).*

value of I will exceed the table size. For example, for a table with 105 entries and with K = 10, adding 10 to 101 would result in the attempt to search the nonexistent 111th entry. In Figure 15-4, notice that when the value of I exceeds the table size, the subroutine Adjust K is followed, by which we go back where we left off before the preceding increment of 10 (at the 102nd entry in this case). If the record being sought has a key larger than any entry in the table, processing is again directed to the subroutine when I once again exceeds table size. But in this second case K < 10 and so program execution is terminated with no match having been found.

The increment size of 10 is here used only as a convenient example, and is not necessarily an efficient increment. As a matter of fact, when we consider the binary search increment in the next section we shall see that a "dynamic" increment value related to powers of 2 is a more efficient increment size.

Another variation of the linear search method takes account of the fact that for a given table the likelihood of the need to access a particular entry is not the same for all entries in the table. If the table is formed so that the most frequently used entries are placed first, the average access time per search will be reduced. In general, therefore, it is desirable to load a table in the inverse order of usage, with the most frequently used records being placed at the beginning of the table.

REVIEW

1   The table-searching method by which each record is checked in sequential order until the desired record is found is called the _____ method.

linear search

2   When a table is sorted, the linear search for a record can be terminated, even though the record has not been found, if the end of the table has been reached or if _____

_____.

the point at which the record would have been stored has been passed (etc.)

3   If an unsorted table is searched by the linear search method, the search is terminated only when _____.

the end of the table has been reached

4   The process of searching a relatively large table can be speeded up by making the _____ value associated with the linear search greater than 1.

increment

5   Based on the example flowchart presented in this section, suppose that an increment value of K = 8 is used in conjunction with a linear search of a table. If it is found that the key value X is less than the record value in a particular comparison, K is set equal to _____ (value) and _____ (value) is subtracted from the value of I.

1; 7

6   In general, the time required for searching a table is minimized when the table is arranged according to [increasing / decreasing] order of usage of the records.

decreasing (since the most active records would be listed first)

BINARY SEARCH

Binary search is also referred to as dichotomous search. It has the feature that each comparison eliminates from further consideration half the entries that could contain the record being sought. The method requires that the table be sorted. We begin by investigating the record at the midpoint of the table. If that record is not the one being sought, it can be determined whether that record is smaller or larger than the one being sought, thereby eliminating half the records from further consideration. For example, if the midpoint record is larger than the one being sought, the record being sought must be in the first half of the table, if it is included in the table at all. Conversely, if the midpoint record is smaller than the record being sought, the first half of the table can be eliminated from further consideration. After half the table is eliminated from consideration, we proceed to the midpoint of the remaining half and again compare the record with the record being sought. The procedure is repeated until the record being sought is found or until it can be concluded that the record is not included in the table. The flowchart in Figure 15-5 presents the logic associated with the binary search method.

Referring to Figure 15-5, we begin by setting two data-names, LO and HI, equal to zero and to the table size plus 1, respectively. The midpoint of the table, MID, is determined by adding LO to HI, dividing by 2, and rounding any fraction upward. Thus, if LO = 0 and HI = 9 for a table with eight entries, MID = $(0 + 9)/2 = 4.5$, which is rounded to 5. MID is then used as the subscript of T, and the value of the record sought, X, is compared with the MIDth record in the table. If X is less than T(MID), the record being sought could only be located below the MID position, and therefore we set HI = MID. Similar reasoning leads to setting LO = MID when X is greater than T(MID). Then the difference between HI and LO is checked. If it is less than 2, and since any fractional value would have been rounded upward, this indicates that the last record checked was the last possible location at which the record being sought might have been located, and that the record being sought is not in the table. For example, for a table with eight entries the first MID = 5, as above. Suppose X > T(MID). Then LO = MID = 5 and HI − LO = 9 − 5 = 4, which is *not* less than 2. The value of MID in the next loop is $(5 + 9)/2 = 7$. Again, suppose X > T(MID). Then LO = 7 and HI − LO = 9 − 7 = 2. The next MID = $(7 + 9)/2 = 8$. If X is unequal to T(MID), the HI − LO comparison will yield one of these two results: If X < T(MID), then HI − LO = 8 − 8 = 0. If X > T(MID), then HI − LO = 9 − 8 = 1. In either case the expression HI − LO will be less than 2 and the search will be terminated with no match found.

Figure 15-6 illustrates the procedure by which the name "Myrtle" would be found in an alphabetically ordered list by means of the binary search method. Notice that a match occurred on the third item considered. If we had been looking for "Mark," one more time through the loop would have been required, for a total of four look-ups. With a table size of 11, four look-ups is in fact the maximum number that can be required, as explained below.

The binary search method is a relatively fast search procedure. It is interesting to note that through practical experience most people use a loose form of binary search. In using a dictionary, if we have "overshot" the point of the entry we may flip back a few pages and again determine the direction of the desired entry. Similarly, a secretary looking in an alphabetical file takes something like midpoint jumps to locate a desired

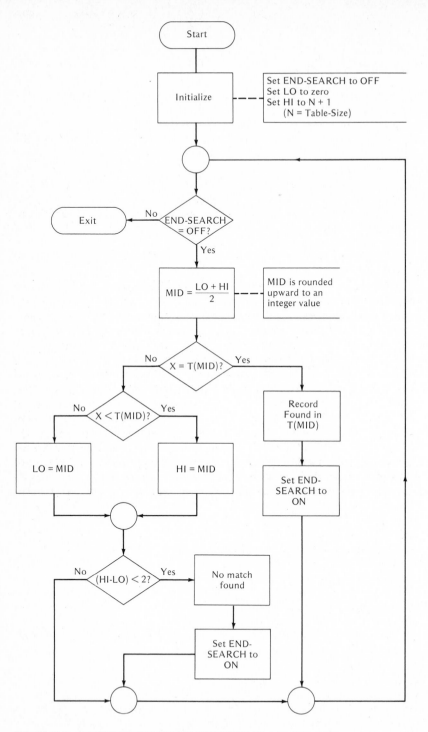

FIGURE 15-5 FLOWCHART FOR THE BINARY SEARCH OF A SORTED TABLE.

Table entries

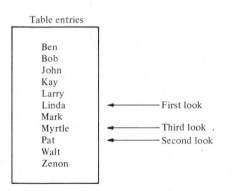

Ben
Bob
John
Kay
Larry
Linda
Mark
Myrtle
Pat
Walt
Zenon

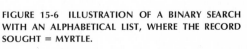

First look

Third look .

Second look

FIGURE 15-6   ILLUSTRATION OF A BINARY SEARCH WITH AN ALPHABETICAL LIST, WHERE THE RECORD SOUGHT = MYRTLE.

name quickly. The relative efficiency of the binary search becomes more pronounced as the table size is increased. This is so because the maximum number of comparisons required by this method increases only linearly while table size increases exponentially. Table 15-1 presents the mathematical relationship which is involved. Thus, for example, whereas a table with 15 entries requires a maximum of four comparisons, a table with 255 entries requires a maximum of just eight comparisons.

For the reason described above, the binary search method also becomes increasingly more efficient than the linear search method as table size is increased. The general comparison is presented in Table 15-2, for which the increment associated with the linear search is 1. The table sizes listed in the first column of Table 15-2 increase exponentially. Note that the maximum number of comparisons for the linear search method also increases exponentially, whereas the maximum number of comparisons for the binary search method increases approximately on a linear basis. The "average" figures reported in Table 15-2 are based on the assumption that the records being sought are randomly and uniformly distributed in the tables. That is, they have

TABLE 15-1   MAXIMUM NUMBER OF COMPARISONS REQUIRED BY THE BINARY SEARCH METHOD FOR TABLES OF VARIOUS SIZES

TABLE SIZE		MAXIMUM NUMBER OF COMPARISONS
RANGE	AS A POWER OF 2	
1	2^0	1
2	2^1	2
3–4	2^2	3
5–7	less than 2^3	3
8–15	less than 2^4	4
16–31	less than 2^5	5
32–63	less than 2^6	6
64–127	less than 2^7	7
128–255	less than 2^8	8
256–511	less than 2^9	9

TABLE 15-2   LINEAR AND BINARY SEARCH COMPARED

	NUMBER OF COMPARISONS			
	LINEAR		BINARY	
TABLE SIZE	MAXIMUM	AVERAGE	MAXIMUM	AVERAGE
5	5	3	3	2
10	10	5	4	3
50	50	25	6	5
100	100	50	7	6
1,000	1,000	500	10	9
10,000	10,000	5,000	14	13
100,000	100,000	50,000	17	16

not been ordered according to frequency of use. As can be seen in the table, the binary search method outperforms the linear search method by a wide margin especially when the table size is relatively large. However, the binary search method requires longer execution time because it involves the use of division, and this arithmetic operation is relatively slow as compared with addition or subtraction. Still, if we assume that a binary search requires five times the amount of time per comparison as does linear search, then the breakeven point in choosing between the two methods is at a table size of about 25. Thus, except for small tables which include fewer than 25 entries binary search will be faster than linear search. Remember, though, that the binary method specifically requires that the table be sorted whereas linear search can be used with either a sorted or unsorted table. The time required to sort a table may then have to be balanced against the search time saved by the binary method. If the membership of a table is stable and the table is used frequently, binary search is likely to be the best choice. Otherwise, linear search may be preferred.

REVIEW

1   The table search procedure by which each comparison eliminates from consideration half the entries that could contain the record being sought is called

_____.

binary search

2   Suppose that a sorted table contains 30 entries. By the logic of the binary search method the initial value of LO is set equal to _____ and the initial value of HI is set equal to _____.

0; 31

3   For the example above, the value of MID in the first loop through the program would be _____ (value).

16

4 Continuing with the above example, suppose that in the first comparison X < T(MID). Then for the purpose of the next comparison LO = _____, HI = _____, and MID = _____.

0; 16; 8

5 Suppose that a table is increased exponentially in size. The maximum number of required comparisons by the linear search method would increase [linearly / exponentially] while the maximum number of comparisons by the binary search method would increase [linearly / exponentially].

exponentially; linearly

6 Given that a table is sorted, the binary search method is generally faster than the linear search method when the number of entries in the table is equal to at least _____ (number).

25

PROBABILISTIC SEARCH

It is often possible to estimate the approximate table position of a record based on the record key of the required record. For example, suppose that a manufacturing plant has been in operation for 2 years. At the time of initial employment each employee was assigned a unique employee-number, beginning with 1001 and continuing in consecutive and ascending order. The employee-numbers for individuals who have terminated employment with the company have not been reassigned. The table has no gaps, however. At the present time there are 600 employees with the highest employee-number being 1700. Because the range 1001 to 1700 includes 700 numbers, this indicates that 100 employees have terminated employment with the company during the 2-year period. If we need to look up the name and address of employee-number 1265, it is possible to estimate the position of this record. For instance, we might reason: The range of employee-numbers is 1001 to 1700. Employee-number 1265 would be in the 265th position in the table if the total of 100 vacancies in the table was not a factor. Assuming these 100 vacancies are uniformly distributed over the entire range of 700 numbers, there are about 15 gaps for each 100 numbers. Thus, a good estimate of the table position for employee-number 1265 would be $265 + (\frac{15}{100} \times 265) =$ $265 + 40 = 305$. We would then begin our search in the 305th position. If the record there is higher than the one sought, a linear search would continue in a backward direction. If the record in that position is smaller, the linear search would proceed in a forward direction.

The critical question in using probabilistic search is how the formula, or algorithm, is determined for identifying the first position to be searched. There is no general formula that can be used. Rather, each situation has to be analyzed individually in attempting to determine a formula by which table position can be estimated given the value of the key. In statistical analysis, a formula by which one variable is estimated given the value of a second variable is called a regression equation. The general form of the regression equation when the relationship between the two variables is "linear" is $Y = a + bX$. In this equation, Y is the estimated value of the table position, a and b are constants which can be computed based on the data, and X is the given key value of the record being sought. A regression equation can be graphically represented by a regression line. Figure 15-7 portrays a regression line for a situation in which there is a linear relationship between key number and table position. Referring to Figure 15-7, note that the fact that the relationship is linear results in the regression line being a straight line. The line represents the series of values one obtains in solving for Y given the general equation $Y = a + bX$. This form of the regression equation results in a straight regression line because the increase in the value of Y is proportional to the increase in the value of X. Also, note that given the value of X, which is the key value of the record being sought, the position of the record is not determined with certainty. That is, there is "scatter" of the actual position values in respect to the regression line. This scatter, or discrepancy, is indicative of the probabilistic ingredient included in the search procedure.

Often, the relationship between the record key and table position will follow a curvilinear form rather than being linear. In such a case a number of different forms of the regression equation may be appropriate, depending on whether the curved regression line is exponential or other nonlinear form. Figure 15-8 portrays a nonlinear regression model in which the curve is exponential in form. The general form of the regression equation for such a curve is $Y = ab^x$. Standard mathematical techniques exist by which it can be determined if the data can be represented adequately by any one form of the possible regression equations for curves. Sometimes no standard form can be used to represent the relationship.

In general, probabilistic search is a useful technique when table size is large, table membership is stable, and its usage will be great enough to warrant the special effort. In Chapter 16, "Direct Access Files," we discuss randomizing routines that can be used to transform a record key to an address. Such randomizing methods fall into the

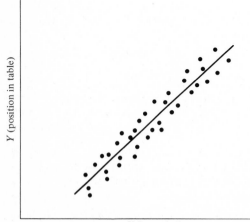

FIGURE 15-7   REGRESSION LINE WHEN THE KEY VALUES AND THE TABLE POSITIONS OF THE RECORDS HAVE A LINEAR RELATIONSHIP.

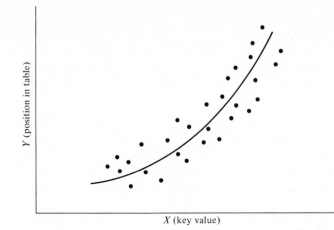

FIGURE 15-8 REGRESSION CURVE WHEN THE KEY VALUES AND THE TABLE POSITIONS OF THE RECORDS HAVE AN EXPONENTIAL RELATIONSHIP.

present probabilistic search category. One difficulty with randomizing routines is that synonyms occur, and therefore no unique relationship exists between a key and its location. Still, the randomizing routine takes us to the neighborhood of the record location. Once there, a method such as linear search can be used to find the record being sought.

REVIEW

1   When a formula, or algorithm, is used to determine the approximate table position of a record based on its key value, the search method is called _____ search.

probabilistic

2   In statistical analysis, the general equation by which the value of a variable is estimated based on the value of another variable is called a _____ equation.

regression

3   The regression equation for a straight line is of the general form $Y = a + bX$. If this equation is used to estimate the table position for a record, the value of the record key is represented by the symbol _____ in the equation.

X

4   If the record being sought is not at the location determined by the formula or equation used in conjunction with probabilistic search, the search typically continues from that point by the use of the _____ method.

linear search

DIRECT SEARCH

If we think of linear search as the method that requires the most extended search, then *direct search* refers to the other extreme, in which no search is required. Direct search implies that the key of the record indicates its position in the table without any ambiguity or uncertainty. Thus, in such a case we need only "look up" the entry rather than "search" for it.

A coding method can often provide a direct relationship between a record and its position in a table. Consider some examples. A coding method in which a "1" is assigned as the key for first grade enrollment, "2" for second grade enrollment, and so on to "12" for twelfth-grade enrollment could provide direct reference between grade level and entry position. For example, enrollment in the seventh grade could be determined by reference to the seventh entry in the table. Furthermore, if the table contained enrollment figures for a school district which includes 10 schools, the schools could also be sequentially numbered from 1 to 10 and a two-dimensional subscript reference could be used to determine the table entry containing the enrollment in a particular grade of a particular school. For example, the subscript (8, 4) would indicate the enrollment in the eighth grade of the fourth school. As another example, we could maintain an insurance table for premium rates by age beginning with age 1 to age 99. In this case the premium rate for a person who is 24 years of age would be the twenty-fourth entry in the table.

Another form of direct search is made possible by an arithmetic transformation of the key value of the record. For example, the check numbers for a month may begin at 1324 but be consecutively numbered from that point. Thus, in order to look up check number 1520 in a table we could transform the check number to the table position by subtracting 1323, thereby identifying the position as being 197. The transformation can also involve more than a simple arithmetic operation. For instance, we may have a transformation algorithm such that "April 10" is converted to "100," for the 100th day of the year for most years, and to "101" for leap years. As another example, suppose a withholding-tax table has the following form:

WEEKLY INCOME	NUMBER OF EXEMPTIONS						
	1	2	3	4	. . .	9	10
$ 60							
62							
64							
.							
.							
.							
496							
498							
500							

Given a weekly income X and an exemption value Y, we could determine the position of the table entry for the appropriate withholding amount by the following transformation: First divide X by 2 and obtain an integer quotient. Then subtract 29 from the integer quotient to obtain the subscript for the income class. Finally, the value of Y can be used directly as the subscript for the exemption class. To illustrate, suppose that the weekly earnings $X = \$123.45$ and exemption code $Y = 4$. We then compute: $X/2 = 123.45/2 = 61.725 = 61$ truncated to an integer. Then $61 - 29 = 32$, which identifies the thirty-second row in the table as being the appropriate row. The tax rate is determined by reference to row 32, column 4.

A third approach which serves as a basis for using the direct search method is based on a two-phased search. This approach is useful for tables that have some gaps in the key numbers and for which the records are relatively long, and it is based on setting up an *index table* that includes a position for every possible number in the key sequence. The content of each entry in this index table is the position number of the corresponding record, with a "0" (or any other designated code) being used with key numbers for which there is no record. To illustrate, suppose that we have the following table of just five records, for simplicity:

RECORD TABLE	
KEY	OTHER DATA (300 CHARACTERS)
101	
102	
107	
108	
110	

Notice that no records exist for keys 103, 104, 105, 106, and 109 in the table above, and thus there are gaps in the key sequence. As the first phase in the transformation, we can subtract 100 from the key to determine the table position in the index table. The index table would then have the following form:

INDEX TABLE
1
2
0
0
0
0
3
4
0
5

Thus, for record 107 the value 100 is subtracted to determine the position in the index table as being the seventh entry. Reference to this seventh entry then indicates that the record being sought is the third entry in the record table. Since there is no record with the key 104, the index table indicates a record position of "0" for this record.

The reason for using the index table is to save storage space, as contrasted to the possible approach of leaving blank spaces in the record table for the nonexistent records. Normally the index entries are only a few digits in length, so that allowing an entry for each gap does not waste much space. The records themselves should be relatively long in order to justify the additional table, however. Note that in the example above the data in each record occupies 300 characters. Thus, without very much wasted space the use of an index table can make possible the use of the direct search method.

While direct search is desirable, it is often impractical. Either with or without the use of an index table, direct search requires a one-for-one correspondence between each possible key and each record position. The number of gaps in a particular code system may be such that it is impossible to provide a storage position for every possible key.

REVIEW

1   The table-searching method by which the key of the record can be used to determine the exact position of the record in the table is called _____.

direct search

2   The form of direct search by which the code directly indicates the position of the record in the table can be used [with one-dimensional tables only / with any table].

with any table

3   Another form of direct search is made possible by an arithmetic transformation of the record key. By this approach, if the record keys are numbered sequentially from 335 to 420, each key could be transformed to the appropriate table position by subtracting _____ from each key value.

334

4   A third approach that makes it possible to use direct search is particularly appropriate when there are gaps in the record keys and the records are relatively long. By this approach an _____ table is constructed for use with the table to be searched.

index

TABLE SEARCHING WITH COBOL

The use of a dictionary to look up the meaning of words is perhaps the most common example of the need to search a table or file for particular entries. In the context of data processing, searching tables to find particular entries stored in them is a fundamental process. Because of the frequency with which table searching is used in computer programs, the COBOL language includes a specialized set of instructions to facilitate the programming task. Suppose, for example, that a company maintains a list of office employees in alphabetical order. There are 400 employees, and each is assigned a four-digit employee identification number. Because of coding requirements, such as having the departmental identification included in the code, there is no correspondence between the numeric order of the identification numbers and the alphabetic order of employee names. The DATA DIVISION statements which describe the table can be written as follows:

```
01   DATA-TABLE.
     02   NAME-NUMBER OCCURS 400 TIMES.
          03   NAME          PICTURE X(16).
          03   EMPL-NO       PICTURE 9999.
```

In this section we consider two data processing tasks. First, given the name of an employee, determine his or her employee-number. Second, given the employee-number, determine his or her name. Also, the procedures to be used with both sorted and unsorted tables are described below.

SEARCHING A SORTED TABLE

Assume that the table is sorted on the NAME field. Since the table will be searched by reference to the NAME field, the record description entry can be written in such a way as to indicate the fact that the table is sorted on NAME in ascending order. Further, the record description can be so written that reference to table entries can be made by use of a variant of the subscript concept, called an *index*. Thus, in place of the table description in the general DATA DIVISION statements cited above, the following statements can be written:

```
01   DATA-TABLE.
     02   NAME-NUMBER OCCURS 400 TIMES
          ASCENDING KEY IS NAME
          INDEXED BY WHICH-ONE.
          03   NAME          PICTURE X(16).
          03   EMPL-NO       PICTURE 9999.
```

Notice the ASCENDING KEY IS statement, which indicates that the item defined by the OCCURS clause is sorted in ascending sequence. The INDEXED BY WHICH-ONE clause defines WHICH-ONE as an index for NAME-NUMBER. Unlike a subscript, an index is *not* defined or described by a DATA DIVISION entry and PICTURE clause. It is a numeric field, normally binary, whose length is defined by the compiler used. If we write NAME (WHICH-ONE), we thus reference an entry in the table just as with the use of a regular subscript. However, unlike a subscript, the value of WHICH-ONE is defined by one of three verbs: the SET, SEARCH, or PERFORM verb. Rather than elaborating further on the use of WHICH-ONE as an index, the following example is used to provide additional understanding of this option.

Suppose that EMPL-NAME is a field that contains a name for which we want to determine the associated employee-number. In order to accomplish this task we can execute the following PROCEDURE DIVISION statements:

```
SEARCH ALL NAME-NUMBER
    AT END PERFORM CANT-FIND
    WHEN NAME (WHICH-ONE) = EMPL-NAME
        MOVE EMPL-NO (WHICH-ONE) TO EDIT-NUMBER.
```

The instruction SEARCH ALL NAME-NUMBER indicates that all the entries in the NAME-NUMBER table should be searched. Recall that in the DATA DIVISION the OCCURS clause defined ASCENDING KEY IS NAME. Therefore, the search is conducted with respect to the NAME field. If no match is found, the AT END clause is executed. As the table is searched, the procedure is to vary WHICH-ONE and to compare the resulting NAME (WHICH-ONE) to EMPL-NAME. If the two match, the MOVE statement which follows the WHEN is executed next and the search terminates. If no match is found, WHICH-ONE is changed to a new value and the procedure is repeated until the entire table has been searched. But how is the value of WHICH-ONE varied? The instructions are included in the compiler. Since the table in the present example is sorted, it is likely that the compiler will provide instructions for a binary search. If a linear search were used, the values of WHICH-ONE in this example would be 1, 2, 3, . . . , 399, 400. Again, note that the search procedure is automatically supplied by the compiler, so that the programmer need not write any of the detailed instructions for this search. When a match is found, program execution is transferred to the instruction MOVE EMPL-NO (WHICH-ONE) TO EDIT-NUMBER following the WHEN. Notice that WHICH-ONE has the reference value of the record for which the match occurred. Thus, it is used as a subscript, or index, to reference the corresponding EMPL-NO.

AN ALTERNATIVE APPROACH FOR SORTED TABLES

We now demonstrate some options with respect to the above search procedure by using an alternate approach to the task. First, we rewrite the DATA DIVISION entries as follows:

```
01   DATA-TABLE.
    02   NAME OCCURS 400 TIMES
         ASCENDING KEY IS NAME
         INDEXED BY NAME-INDEX
         PICTURE IS X(16).
    02   EMPL-NO OCCURS 400 TIMES
         INDEXED BY NO-INDEX
         PICTURE 9999.
```

In effect two tables are defined, one called NAME and the other called EMPL-NO. The NAME table is sorted on ascending sequence and is indexed by NAME-INDEX, while the EMPL-NO table is indexed by NO- INDEX. Of course, the two PICTURE descriptions refer to the NAME and EMPL-NO fields, respectively, and *not* to the index names.

In relation to the above DATA DIVISION statements the following PROCEDURE DIVISION statements can then be written:

```
SET NAME-INDEX TO 1.
SEARCH NAME VARYING NO-INDEX
   AT END PERFORM NO-MATCH
   WHEN EMPL-NAME = NAME(NAME-INDEX)
      MOVE EMPL-NO(NO-INDEX) TO EDIT-FIELD.
```

The SEARCH statement contains the VARYING option, which in effect indicates that NO-INDEX is to be varied in the same way as the index of the table being searched, in this case, NAME-INDEX. Thus, for example, when NAME-INDEX = 10, then NO-INDEX is also equal to 10. As a result, the EMPL-NO (NO-INDEX) referred to in the MOVE statement corresponds to the NAME for which a match was found. If a match occurred in the thirty-fourth position of the NAME table, for example, NAME-INDEX and NO-INDEX would both have a value of 34. Thus, the employee-number which is output corresponds to the name of the employee for which a match was found.

SEARCHING AN UNSORTED TABLE

We now consider the search procedure that can be used with an unsorted table. Further, though it makes no difference in the general procedure used, we shall now assume we have an employee-number and we wish to find the corresponding name, rather than vice versa. The relevant DATA DIVISION entries can be written as follows:

```
01  DATA-TABLE.
    02  NAME-NUMBER OCCURS 400 TIMES INDEXED BY N.
        03  NAME      PICTURE X(16).
        03  EMPL-NO   PICTURE 9999.
```

The NAME-NUMBER table is indexed by N, which is an index-name of our choice. Assume that the employee-number in question is stored in EMPLOYEE-NUMBER. In the PROCEDURE DIVISION we can write:

```
SET N TO 1.
SEARCH NAME-NUMBER
   AT END PERFORM NO-MATCH
   WHEN EMPLOYEE-NUMBER = EMPL-NO(N)
      MOVE NAME(N) TO EDIT-NAME.
```

The value of N is initialized at 1 by the statement SET N TO 1. Since the table has not been sorted (and particularly, since it has not been sorted with respect to EMPL-NO), a linear search will be performed beginning with the first entry of the table. If we have a reason to begin the search at another point, either constant or variable, such statements as SET N TO 52 or SET N TO FIRST-VALUE can be written. Notice that the SEARCH verb does not include use of the ALL option. The ALL option can be used only with tables that have the KEY option in OCCURS, that is, only with sorted tables. The search procedure followed is to vary N from its first value of 1 by increments of 1 up to the last value (in this case 400), each time testing to determine if EMPLOYEE-NUMBER equals EMPL-NO (N). If a match is found, NAME(N) is moved to EDIT-NAME so that it can be output. If no match is found in the entire table, AT END is executed.

REVIEW

1   The variant of the subscript concept, which can be used to reference table entries, is called a(n) _____.

index

2   The value of an index used to reference table entries is defined by one of three verbs: SET, SEARCH, or PERFORM. If a SEARCH instruction is executed and no match is found in the data table, the _____ clause is always executed.

AT END

3   By the alternative approach for determining the employee-number given the name of the employee, two tables were defined, one for NAME and the other for EMPL-NO. The index number associated with EMPL-NO was set equal to the index of the NAME table being searched by use of the _____ option.

VARYING

4   When an unsorted table is searched, the method always used is _____ search.

linear

COBOL LANGUAGE OPTIONS IN TABLE SEARCHING

Now that we have explored the basic ideas associated with table searching by means of examples, we can turn our attention to a formal consideration of the language options. We do not consider all the possible options that could be used, but rather, we describe the basic ones.

THE OCCURS CLAUSE

First, let us consider the format associated with the OCCURS clause:

```
OCCURS integer TIMES
    ⎡⎰ASCENDING ⎱              ⎤
    ⎣⎱DESCENDING⎰ KEY IS data-name-1 [ data-name-2] . . . ⎦

    [ INDEXED BY index-name-1 [ index-name-2] . . .]
```

Some examples may help illustrate the available forms of the OCCURS option.

```
02   SAMPLE OCCURS 100 TIMES
     ASCENDING KEY IS YEAR MONTH.

     03   OTHER-DATA       PICTURE X(20).
     03   MONTH            PICTURE 99.
     03   YEAR             PICTURE 99.
     03   REST-OF-IT       PICTURE X(40).
```

In the above example there are two keys, YEAR and MONTH. Keys are listed in decreasing order of significance. Thus, the months are sorted in ascending sequence within the years, which are also in ascending sequence. As the example illustrates, the order in which the keys appear in the KEY clause is *not* related to their physical order in the record.

```
02   SAMPLE PICTURE 9(8) OCCURS 100 TIMES
     INDEXED BY N.
```

In the above case we specify an index called N, presumably for the purpose of later using this index in a SEARCH statement.

THE USAGE CLAUSE

Consider now the USAGE clause. We can specify that the USAGE of a data item is INDEX, so that the item can be used in conjunction with SET, SEARCH, or PERFORM statements. You may recall that USAGE IS DISPLAY and USAGE IS COMPUTATIONAL are the other available options:

$$
\underline{\text{USAGE}} \text{ IS } \left\{ \begin{array}{l} \underline{\text{DISPLAY}} \\ \underline{\text{COMPUTATIONAL}} \\ \underline{\text{INDEX}} \end{array} \right\}
$$

As an example of using the USAGE clause consider the following program segment:

```
01   SAMPLE.
     02   FIRST-PART     PICTURE X(10).
     02   K USAGE IS INDEX.
```

The item called K in the above example is an INDEX item, and therefore no PICTURE clause is given. All index items are handled according to the rules associated with particular computer systems. Normally, index items are in binary form.

THE SEARCH VERB

Consider now the SEARCH verb, which is the cornerstone of a search instruction. Two principal formats are available, as follows:

Format 1

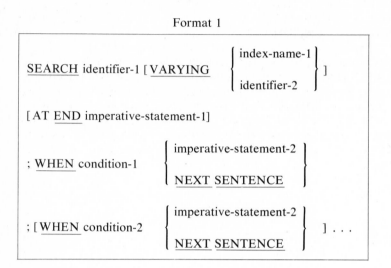

Format 2

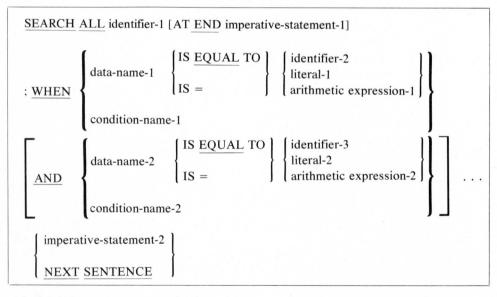

In Format 1, identifier-1 is an item whose description in the DATA DIVISION contains an OCCURS and an INDEXED BY clause. When the VARYING option is used, index-name-2 or identifier-2 is varied in the same way as the index specified in the relevant INDEXED BY clause. Identifier-2 must have been specified as USAGE IS INDEX, or it must be an elementary integer item. The AT END clause is optional. If it is omitted, program control will pass to the next sentence when the table has been searched and no match has been found. If AT END is included and imperative-statement-1 does not terminate with GO TO, a branch to the next sentence will be made (in effect bypassing the WHEN clauses). WHEN introduces another form of conditional expression.

Format 2 is used with sorted tables, that is, tables for which the OCCURS clause contains a KEY in addition to the INDEXED BY option. The search may be a binary search, or any other method included in a particular compiler. However, as far as the programmer is concerned, only the instructions included in Format 2 are required.

Notice in Format 2 that only one WHEN option is available, but multiple AND conditions are allowed. Thus all the conditions must be true in order for the search to be satisfied. In contrast, whenever multiple WHEN statements are used in Format 1, any one of these conditions being true constitutes a sufficient reason for search termination.

THE SET VERB

Basically, the SET verb is a variation of MOVE and provides a way of handling index items. Two formats are available, as follows:

Format 1

$$\underline{\text{SET}} \left\{ \begin{array}{l} \text{index-name-1 [index-name-2]} \ldots \\ \\ \text{identifier-1 [identifier-2]} \ldots \end{array} \right\} \underline{\text{TO}} \left\{ \begin{array}{l} \text{index-name-3} \\ \text{identifier-3} \\ \text{integer-1} \end{array} \right\}$$

Format 2

$$\underline{\text{SET}} \text{ index-name-1 [index-name-2]} \ldots \left\{ \begin{array}{l} \underline{\text{UP BY}} \\ \underline{\text{DOWN}} \ \underline{\text{BY}} \end{array} \right\} \left\{ \begin{array}{l} \text{identifier-1} \\ \text{integer-1} \end{array} \right\}$$

In Format 1, if we use index-name-1, we can set it equal to index-name-3, identifier-3, or literal-1. If identifier-3 is used, it must be defined as an elementary integer item, while if integer-1 is used, it must be a positive integer. If we set identifier-1 and it has not been defined by a USAGE IS INDEX clause, it can only be set to index-name-3.

If we write SET A TO B, we are basically moving the value of B to A. In this way we can transfer data to an index item or an identifier for use in a SEARCH or for use after a SEARCH. For instance, we may have two tables, one INDEXED BY A and the other INDEXED BY B. After performing a search and finding a match on the first table, we may want to reference the corresponding entry in the second table. We then SET B TO A so that B can be used as a subscript or index in the second table.

In Format 2 we can increase or decrease the value of index-name-1 either by a positive integer (literal-1) or by the value of identifier-1, which must be a field that has not been defined as USAGE IS INDEX. The effect of UP BY is to increase the value of index-name-1, while the effect of DOWN BY is to increase index-name-1 by the indicated decrement.

REVIEW

1   The COBOL language option used to indicate the total number of table entries and to identify the key or keys associated with the records is the _____ clause.

OCCURS

2   The COBOL option used to identify a particular data item as being an index is the _____ clause.

USAGE

3   The COBOL verb which identifies the table to be searched and also includes options to indicate what should be done when a match is found as well as when it is not found is _____.

SEARCH

4   The·COBOL verb which is a variation of the MOVE verb and which provides the basis for designating the value to be assigned to an INDEX is the _____.

SET

EXAMPLES OF INDEXING AND SEARCHING

Perhaps it will provide a useful review to consider some examples to help tie together the language formats. Suppose we have 100 students who took an examination consisting of eight parts, each individually scored. The names of the students as well as the scores are internally stored in the table described by the DATA DIVISION entries below.

```
01   EXAM-TABLE.
     02   STUDENTS OCCURS 100 TIMES
          INDEXED BY S.
          03   NAMES     PICTURE X(16).
          03   SCORES    PICTURE 999V9
               OCCURS 8 TIMES
               INDEXED BY Q.
```

First, let us consider the case in which we want to identify the students who had a perfect score (100.0) in any of the eight sections of the examination. When such a condition is found, the student's name is to be printed. The following PROCEDURE DIVISION statements can be written to accomplish this task:

```
SET S TO 1.
PERFORM SEARCHING 99 TIMES.
SEARCHING.
    SET Q TO 1.
    SEARCH SCORES
        WHEN SCORES(S, Q) EQUAL TO 100.0
        MOVE NAMES(S) TO PRINT-FIELD
        WRITE PRINT-LINE.
    SET S UP BY 1.
NEXT-P.
```

In the above program segment the index-name S is initialized to the value of 1, and then a PERFORM loop is entered. The paragraph called SEARCHING searches the table of SCORES, which is two-dimensional. Notice that when S = 1, Q is varied under the control of the SEARCH verb from 1 to 8. When a value of 100.0 is encountered, the NAMES field is moved and printed. The SEARCH verb is like a PERFORM verb in that it executes a repetitive procedure, comparing the score on each of the eight parts of the examination to 100.0. After all eight parts of the examination for the first student have been searched or a perfect score has been found, program execution branches to the statement SET S UP BY 1, and execution of the SEARCHING paragraph is repeated under the control of the PERFORM verb. After the ninety-ninth execution of the SEARCHING paragraph the paragraph is executed once more, since it immediately follows the PERFORM statement.

As another brief example of table searching, assume we have the following table defined in the DATA DIVISION:

```
01  TABLE.
    02  SALES-TOTALS     PICTURE 9(6)V99
        OCCURS 12 TIMES
        INDEXED BY N.
```

Suppose we want to find the largest value in the above table and store it in LARGE. This can be accomplished by the following PROCEDURE DIVISION statements:

```
            MOVE SALES-TOTALS(1) TO LARGE.
            SET N TO 2.
ABC.        SEARCH SALES-TOTALS AT END GO TO BCD
                WHEN LARGE IS LESS THAN SALES-TOTALS(N)
                MOVE SALES-TOTALS(N) TO LARGE.
            GO TO ABC.
BCD.        (etc.)
```

When program execution enters paragraph BCD in the above program segment, LARGE will contain the largest value in SALES-TOTALS (or in the case of ties, the first of the largest values).

EXERCISES

1 Write suitable COBOL statements to sort a table of N (N ≤ 100) numeric values using the linear search sort algorithm.

2 Write suitable COBOL statements to sort a table of N (N ≤ 100) numeric values using the bubble sort-interchange algorithm.

3 Suppose that we have a table that contains the following data:

10	12	04	08	03

If we were using the adjacent comparison-interchange algorithm and if a pair comparison takes 1 microsecond and a pair interchange takes 5 microseconds, what would be the total comparison time and what would be the total interchange time? Be sure to justify your results.

4 Use the chained records sort algorithm in this exercise, which requires the inputting of data, sorting, and outputting the sorted data. The input will be in punched cards in the following format. Allow for a maximum of 50 cards of input.

CARD COLUMNS	FIELD
1–4	sort key, numeric
5–8	alphanumeric data

The output should consist of three pages.

a As each record is read in, it is output on the printer.

b After the entire table is read in and predecessor and successor values have been assigned, output the table in its stored sequence in the following format:

RECORD	IDENTIFIER	DATA	PREDECESSOR	SUCCESSOR
1	XX	XXXXetc.	XX	XX
2	XX	XXXX	XX	XX
3	XX	XXXX	XX	XX
.	.	.	.	.
.	.	.	.	.
.	.	.	.	.

c   The table is printed in its sorted (ascending) sequence in the following format:

RECORD	IDENTIFIER	DATA	PREDECESSOR	SUCCESSOR
XXX	XXX	XXXX	XX	XX

5   Write a COBOL program segment to perform a search in a sorted table called TABLE, searching for an entry that matches THIS-RECORD. If a match is found, the program goes to the paragraph MATCHED; otherwise it goes to the paragraph NO-MATCH. Use I to hold the position of the matching table entry, if there is a match.

Assume the following data descriptions:

```
01   THIS-RECORD      PICTURE X(12).
01   I                PICTURE 999.
01   TABLE.
     02   CELL         PICTURE X(12) OCCURS 100 TIMES
                       INDEXED BY N.
```

6   How does COBOL differentiate between searching sorted and unsorted tables?

7   What is the difference between an index and a subscript in COBOL?

8   Review the meaning of the following search-related COBOL features, explaining the use of each feature:

a   OCCURS accompanied by the ASCENDING, (DESCENDING) KEY options.
b   INDEXED BY
c   USAGE IS INDEX
d   SEARCH and its several optional forms
e   SET TO, and SET UP BY or SET DOWN BY

9   Incorporate the indexing capability of COBOL in a program you have written previously, and use the SEARCH verb in conjunction with any required search.

Direct
Access Files

DIRECT ACCESS STORAGE

Direct access is a property of storage devices and refers to the capability of reaching any storage location in the same time interval as for any other designated location. The only truly direct access storage device available in computer systems today is internal storage. Access to any location in internal storage requires a fixed time length, namely, the access time associated with the computer system.

However, certain devices outside of central storage offer access times that at least approximate the direct access feature. Such capability is provided mainly by the use of magnetic disks and magnetic drums, although cartridge systems and data cells are also available. These devices are not really direct access devices as defined above, but they are capable of accessing any available storage location in a short enough time so that the practical result approximates that associated with direct access.

As contrasted to sequential access storage, such as by magnetic tape or punched cards, direct access storage (DAS) devices have the following distinguishing characteristics:

1   They have the capability of reaching a record in storage by following a direct path to that storage location. This is analogous to using a thumb-indexed dictionary. On the other hand, tape files can reach a record only by sequentially accessing every record preceding the one which is sought. Furthermore the "forward" capability of being able to read records from the back toward the front is generally absent for sequential access storage (but there are some tape drives that can read backward).
2   In order to change a particular record in a DAS file, it is not necessary to create a brand-new file as is the case with tape files. Instead, the particular record can be accessed, updated, and replaced in its original location without disturbing the other records.

In the following paragraphs we consider some applications in which the direct access feature is particularly desirable.

ONLINE SYSTEMS

Such systems involve the receipt of data directly from the point of origin, usually through a variety of input/output terminal devices with telecommunication capabilities. For example, a credit card system needs to be accessible to retailers to check on the credit status of customers. Similar access may be desirable in an airlines reservation system or a parts inventory system. In such systems the transactions typically occur in random order. If flight information were stored on magnetic tape, for example, it would be very difficult to respond to a series of randomly ordered flight status and reservations requests.

MULTIPLE-FILE UPDATING

A particular segment of information frequently cuts across organizational lines and files in its effects. The payment submitted by a customer affects the accounts-receivable file, the cash-on-hand, and the credit file. Instead of sorting the payment transactions for each file, all files can be updated with one run if they are held in DAS devices. Similarly, if the customer has submitted a payment and also has changed addresses, both the accounts-receivable and name-address files need to be changed.

FILES WITH LOW ACTIVITY

When DAS files are used, only the records that show activity need to be updated. Thus, if only 100 of 6,000 master records show any activity, the other 5,900 records need not be handled. Particularly when the activity ratio is low, this results in considerable savings in required processing time. However, one point that should not be overlooked is that there is no father/son file relationship when a DAS file is updated. So how can subsequent detection of errors be achieved and an audit trail be provided? One possibility is to write the old master file (before updating) on another disk for backup purposes. But this amounts to a kind of sequential processing and would largely offset the advantages of the direct access feature. Instead, more elaborate label checking procedures have been established with direct access storage devices in order to minimize the possibility of errors, and methods independent of the system itself are established by which regeneration of the earlier states of the file can be accomplished, such as creation of *journal* files.

MULTIPLE LOOKUPS

Suppose that a municipal sales tax has to be added to invoice amounts, with the tax rate varying according to municipality. In a batch system we could sort all transactions by city, then process them against the tax table and enter the rate applicable to each transaction. Then we would sort by customer again and process the transactions. With direct access files two runs would not be required. Instead, the table of tax rates can be stored on disk and can be accessed for each transaction without the need for sorting the transactions according to municipality.

USE AS TEMPORARY STORAGE

The use of a DAS device can simplify the storage of information which is not necessary to be maintained as part of a permanent record file. For example, as part of the procedure associated with printing bank account statements the accounts that are overdrawn can be entered on disk for subsequent printing of overdraw notices. As another example, suppose that sales invoices are processed daily but that sales commissions are processed every 2 weeks. As each invoice is processed in a batch system the commission associated with the sale could be entered directly in the salesperson's disk record. Throughout this section we have not suggested that disk storage is always to be preferred. Rather, the principal storage possibilities of disk, tape, and cards need to be evaluated and compared in respect to the particular objectives of a data processing system.

REVIEW

1   The type of storage device for which any record can be reached in about the same interval of time is called a _____ storage device.

direct access

2   The direct access storage (DAS) device with which we shall be principally concerned in this chapter is the magnetic _____.

disk

3   As contrasted to magnetic tape storage, DAS devices have the capability of following a [direct / sequential] path to a storage location, and the updating of DAS files results in the existence of [an old and new master / a new master only].

direct; a new master only

4   An information system which involves receipt of data directly from the point of origin, such as in an airline reservation system, is called an _____ system.

online

5   A number of situations were described in which direct access files are particularly appropriate. One general factor associated with the use of a direct access file is that transactions [need to be / need not be] sorted for the purpose of updating such a file.

need not be

CHARACTERISTICS OF MAGNETIC DISK STORAGE

A magnetic disk is a magnetically sensitive circular surface resembling a phonograph record. Data is recorded on this disk surface in designated circular bands called *tracks*. Figure 16-1 portrays a magnetic disk storage device and includes a diagram of tracks on the surface of a disk. Typically there are several hundred usable tracks on the surface of a magnetic disk. Each track can contain a few thousand characters around its circular length. Each track is separate from the others, and all tracks have the same capacity, even though the circles become smaller as we move away from the periphery. Tracks are referenced in numeric order from 0 up to the last. Thus, if we have 200 tracks, the first is designated track 000 and the last as track 199.

A *disk pack* refers to a group of disks stacked on a vertical spindle parallel to each other, but physically separated from one another. Such packs are normally removable as a unit, so that we can change disk packs for the same reasons that we change reels of magnetic tape. A disk pack of six disks has 10 usable surfaces, because the top and bottom surfaces of the two outer disks are not used since they are more exposed to handling and to the possibility of being "scratched."

A *cylinder* refers to a set of tracks having the same track number and belonging to the same disk pack. In other words, track 1 of each disk surface in a disk pack constitutes cylinder 1. Thus, if each disk surface has 200 tracks, there are 200 cylinders in such a disk pack. Therefore, unique reference to particular tracks can be made in terms of cylinder and track number. If a disk pack of 10 surfaces is assumed, cylinder 5, track 3 identifies the fifth track of the third surface. Tracks are, in fact, referenced in this way.

Typically, for each disk surface there is a read/write head—a device that can read data from or write data on the surface. These heads are fixed to a vertical column and can move as a unit toward the center or away from the center of the disk pack. Figure 16-2 illustrates the read/write head mechanism. Suppose that all 10 read/write heads are positioned over the tracks that constitute cylinder 1, and imagine the disk pack to be rotating rapidly about its axis. It can be seen that every position of every track 1 will pass under its respective read/write head. Since the read/write heads can move from track to track in a horizontal motion, and since the disks rotate, we can see that we can have direct access to any track in the disk pack. In the preceding paragraph we pointed out that reference to individual tracks is made in terms of cylinder and track number. A more common way of expressing this is to say that tracks are referenced by cylinder-head number. Thus we can instruct the system to read the data in the track identified by cylinder 10, head 5.

A widely used disk device is the IBM 3330. A disk pack in this system consists of 11 disks (20 recording surfaces). Each disk surface consists of 400 tracks, with a capacity of

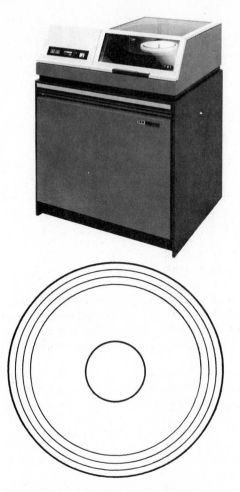

FIGURE 16-1 MAGNETIC DISK STORAGE DEVICE AND SCHEMATIC REPRESENTATION OF TRACKS ON A DISK SURFACE. (IBM CORPORATION.)

about 13,000 bytes per track. Data is transferred from the disk system to central storage, and vice versa, at the rate of 806,000 bytes per second. The time required for the read/write head to reach a given track depends on the distance between the current and the desired position of the head. Once the right track has been accessed, on the average it takes 8.4 milliseconds to access a specific record on a given track. The IBM 3330 and many other disk systems like it exemplify the great capacity and access speed available in modern direct access devices.

Although the cylinder/track organization is widely used, there are alternatives. Some disk systems consist of a *head-per-track* arrangement. Instead of a movable read/write head there is one head for each track. This arrangement eliminates mechanical

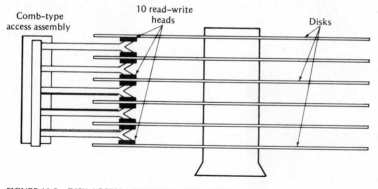

FIGURE 16-2 DISK ACCESS MECHANISM. (IBM CORPORATION.)

movement, and therefore the average access time is increased substantially. However, the cost of such disks limits their feasibility for large storage files. In some disk systems, instead of referring to cylinders and tracks, one refers to *sectors*, or *segments*, and tracks. A sector is a fixed portion of a track and is addressable. For example, if we had 10 surfaces with 200 tracks per surface and 10 sectors per track, we would assign sector addresses from 00000 to 19999 (10 surfaces × 200 tracks × 10 sectors = 20,000 sectors).

This brief description of the hardware associated with magnetic disk storage should be only a starting point for the interested reader. With this coverage of the hardware essentials as a foundation, in the next section we consider basic ways of recording data on magnetic disk.

REVIEW

1 A group of magnetic disks stacked on a vertical shaft in a parallel fashion is called a(n) _____.

disk pack

2 The magnetically sensitive circular bands on the surface of a magnetic disk are called _____.

tracks

3 A set of tracks having the same track number and belonging to the same disk pack is called a _____.

cylinder

4 Typically, a disk pack containing six disks has _____ (number) read/write heads. Reference to individual tracks is made in terms of [head-cylinder / cylinder-head] number.

10; cylinder-head

5   Typically, each cylinder-head (track) location contains [only one / several] records.

several

6   When a disk device involves reference to sectors, this indicates that the device [is / is not] organized on a cylinder/track basis.

is not

RECORDING DATA ON DISK

Data can be recorded on disk tracks with or without the use of *keys*. A key is a label that is used to identify a particular record. For instance, it may be a part number, social security number, name, or the like. A key is required whenever the location of the record cannot be specified exactly. Thus, if we want the third record on a specific track, no key is required. But if we want the record of customer number 2734 without reference to a specific storage location, a key is required.

Special fields are utilized to identify records. Since these are not standard, we will consider a typical layout. As indicated in Figure 16-3, the beginning of a track is indicated by the beginning-of-track mark (BT). As for magnetic tape, fields are separated by a gap (G). The home address field (HA) consists of four fields in the illustration in Figure 16-3: an indicator for track condition (TC) signals as to whether the track is operative or defective; then the cylinder number (CY) and head number (HD) serve to identify the track in terms of cylinder-head location; finally, the error-checking code (EC) is a field that contains a value for error-checking purposes, to verify that the data is written or read correctly. The track descriptor record (TDR) serves to indicate an alternative track if the given track is defective, in addition to other functions not of concern to the user. Many disk systems contain "spare" tracks that are used as alternates whenever a track becomes defective; this avoids the necessity of terminating a job "in the middle" or recreating an entire file because of difficulty with one or two tracks.

A record is designated by a beginning-of-record mark (BR) so that the system has a basis for sensing the beginning of a record as such. After the gap there is a control area (CA), illustrated in Figure 16-3, which contains several fields: a track condition description (TC) indicates whether the track is operative, as was the case in the home address field. A cylinder number (CY) and head number (HD) identify the track, while the record number (RN) identifies the sequential order of the record on the track. A key-length field (KL) indicates the length of the key; if no key is being used, this field has a value of zero. The data-length field (DL) indicates the number of positions in the record itself. Finally, the error-checking code (EC) is again used for error-checking purposes.

The control area (CA) is so positioned that when the appropriate record is found by reference to the information stored in this area the record itself can be read during the same rotation of the disk, since the data area (DA) which includes the record itself follows the control area. For instance, if we wished to read the fourth record in cylinder 10, track 8, the CA field of the first three records on the track would be read, but the records as such would be bypassed. When the CA field of the fourth record is

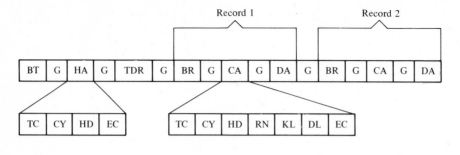

BT   Beginning-of-track mark
 G   Gap
HA   Home address
     TC   Track condition
     CY   Cylinder number
     HD   Head number
     EC   Error-checking code
TDR Track description record
BR   Beginning-of-record mark
CA   Control area
     TC   Track condition
     CY   Cylinder number
     HD   Head number
     RN   Record number
     KL   Keylength (if no key = 0)
     DL   Data-length; the number of characters in DA
     EC   Error-checking code
DA   Data area, the record itself

FIGURE 16-3   TYPICAL LAYOUT OF THE FIELDS ON A TRACK IN DISK STORAGE WHEN DATA IS RECORDED WITHOUT THE USE OF KEYS.

read, the record will be recognized as being the appropriate one (RN = 4) and the record will be read according to the record length defined in the DL field of the control area. Note that the schematic diagram in Figure 16-3 does not portray the relative lengths of the several fields. The data area often consists of hundreds of characters, and thus is much longer than the identification and control fields which precede it on the track. Also, the designation of just a DA field following CA is based on the assumption that a key was not used.

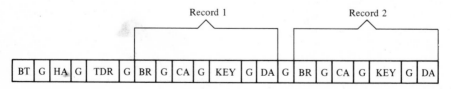

FIGURE 16-4   GENERAL LAYOUT OF THE FIELDS ON A TRACK WHEN DATA IS RECORDED WITH ASSOCIATED KEYS.

The layout of each record on the track when a key is used is illustrated in Figure 16-4. Of course, in this case the KL field in the associated control area will indicate the length of the key, rather than containing a value of zero. In many disk systems the length of the key is limited to 255 bytes. In contrast to the layout when no key is used, after the CA and following the gap there is the key (KEY) field. As indicated earlier in this section, this key is used as a label to identify a specific record. Of course, identifying information may be contained in the data area (DA) itself. But the use of the KEY field makes it possible to check the identification of a record in the disk control unit before it is transferred to the central processor, thus conserving central processor time.

REVIEW

1 A label which is used to identify a particular record on a disk is called a _____

key

2 A number of special fields are used to identify the track location and the records on the track. The key-length (KL) field is in the control area which [precedes / follows] the data for each record and which [is omitted / has a value of zero] when no key is used.

precedes; has a value of zero

3 In general, the major part of each record on a disk track is devoted to the [control area (CA) / data area (DA)].

data area (DA)

4 When a key is not used, the identification of a record [cannot be checked / can usually still be checked in the central processor].

can usually still be checked
in the central processor

DATA RECORD FORMATS

In terms of the organization of data records as such on a track, we can classify the method as being one of four types. Although the detail of each format may vary somewhat from that given below, the format specifications which are described are the ones that are most generally used.

FIXED, UNBLOCKED

Each record in the file is of the same record length, and each record is individually placed on the track.

FIXED, BLOCKED

Each record is of the same length, but two or more records are grouped to form a block. In this case the KEY field is the key for the last record in the block. However, each record in the block has an assigned key to differentiate it from the other records in the block during actual reading of the records as such.

VARIABLE, UNBLOCKED

The length of the records in the file is variable. One field indicates the length of the block, including the field in question, while another field indicates the length of the data record, also including that field. Note that the existence of these two fields essentially represents a duplication of the same information. However, the information is different for the case of variable blocked records, to be discussed next. For the present case, if a record has 4 bytes (characters) in each of these two fields and a logical record of 17 bytes, the format will be as follows:

| 0 | 0 | 2 | 5 | 0 | 0 | 2 | 1 | T | H | E | | D | A | T | A | | I | S | | H | E | R | E |

VARIABLE, BLOCKED

Records are of variable length, and each data area contains two or more records. Again, each data area (DA) contains a field indicating the number of bytes per block, including the field in question, and each record is preceded by another field indicating the number of bytes in the record, including the field in question. For example, suppose that a block consists of 36 bytes. The first record consists of 13 bytes and has a key whose value is KEY1. The second record consists of 19 bytes and has a key whose value is KEY2. The format of this particular block will be as follows:

| 0 | 0 | 3 | 6 | 0 | 0 | 1 | 3 | K | E | Y | 1 | S | H | O | R | T | 0 | 0 | 1 | 9 | K | E | Y | 2 | L | O | N | G | | R | E | C | O | R | D |

length of record

Again, note that the "36" in the above segment is the length of the entire block, while the "13" and "19" represent the length of each record, including respective KEY fields in this case.

The total number of bytes available for actual data is dependent on the number of records defined per track, because of the gaps and control areas associated with each record. Table 16-1 indicates the maximum bytes per record and the maximum bytes available per track for the IBM 2311 disk system, given various numbers of records per track and assuming the use of a KEY field in the data area. Note that the values in Table 16-1 indicate data capacity as such. For example, with five records per track and with the use of a key with each record, each record can include up to 632 bytes of information.

TABLE 16-1 AVAILABLE BYTES PER RECORD AND PER TRACK IN THE IBM 2311 DISK SYSTEM, GIVEN THE USE OF A KEY

RECORDS PER TRACK	BYTES PER RECORD	BYTES PER TRACK
1	3,605	3,605
2	1,720	3,440
3	1,111	3,333
4	811	3,244
5	632	3,160
6	512	3,072

REVIEW

1 Of the standard formats of data organization, the format which involves records of the same length but with two or more records per block is referred to as _____.

fixed blocked

2 The type of standard format of data organization which involves only one record per block, but with a length that may vary from block to block, is referred to as _____.

variable, unblocked

3 In the case of the variable record-length format, two types of fields precede the record itself in the data area. The first indicates the total number of bytes in the _____, while the second indicates the total number of bytes in the _____.

block; record

4 In addition to the physical storage capacity associated with a particular data system, the total number of bytes available for actual data in each track is dependent on the number of _____ defined for that track.

records

FILE ORGANIZATION METHODS

The availability of DAS devices provides processing options that are not available with sequential file media such as magnetic tapes. It is important that files be so organized that efficient processing can be accomplished by matching file data characteristics, processing method, and file organization. For example, given a situation in which the transactions are always available in sequential order, it would be very inefficient to have the disk file organized on a random basis.

Basically, three methods of file organization are available in disk systems: sequential, indexed sequential, and relative file organization. *Sequential* file organization indicates that the records in the file are positioned in a sequential order, such as according to part number. *Indexed sequential* file organization is one in which the records are filed sequentially, but a table (index) is available which identifies the location of groups of records, thereby reducing access time. *Relative* file organization is such that the logical order and physical order of the records do not necessarily correspond with one another. For such a file, a technique, or rule, is required to determine the location of the record in the disk system.

The remainder of this chapter will be devoted to a detailed discussion regarding the use of the three file organization methods. In making a choice among these methods, the following general factors should be considered.

STATIC VERSUS DYNAMIC FILE MEMBERSHIP

A file that has a relatively low number of additions and deletions of records during each period is described as being *static,* and a file with a high number of additions and deletions is described as being *dynamic.*

PERCENT OF ACTIVITY

Optimum file organization is particularly important for highly active files and less important for relatively inactive files. A small percentage of improvement in the processing of a highly active file with 10,000 transactions daily may result in a large savings in terms of processing time saved. Conversely, a large percentage of improvement in efficiency for relatively inactive files may result in small improvements in terms of processing time saved.

DISTRIBUTION OF ACTIVITY

Records that have high activity may be so grouped so as to increase processing efficiency. For example, active records can be stored in adjoining cylinders so as to minimize access time, rather than being randomly located throughout all available cylinders.

REVIEW

1   Whereas sequential file organization indicates a sequential ordering of the records in a file, the type of file organization in which the records are ordered sequentially but can be accessed rather directly as part of a group, much as with a thumb-indexed dictionary, is the _____ file organization.

indexed sequential

2   The type of file organization for which the logical order and physical order of records do not usually correspond with one another is the _____ file organization.

relative

3   A file that has a relatively high number of record additions and deletions from period to period is said to be _____, while a file with a relatively low number of additions and deletions is said to be _____.

dynamic; static

4 Improvements in processing efficiency as indicated by overall time saved are usually best attained by giving principal attention to the files [for which greatest improvement is possible / which are most active].

which are most active

SEQUENTIAL FILE ORGANIZATION

Even though a file is stored on a direct access device, it may have a sequential organization. For instance, a payroll file may be stored in ascending employee number sequence with the first employee number being located in the first track of the first cylinder. A key is unnecessary in such a file unless we also expect to use the file in conjunction with nonsequential processing. A disk file that is sequentially organized is much like sequential files stored on magnetic tape. As such, in order to alter the membership of the file by adding or deleting records, the entire file has to be rewritten. However, unlike tape files the file need not be rewritten in order to update the contents of individual records in the file.

The time required for the actual processing of a sequential file is relatively low. For example, suppose that we have a payroll file of 6,000 records and that every employee record is to be processed. Let us assume that there are 4 records per track, each 811 bytes in length and stored sequentially. Thus, the file occupies 1,500 tracks. Since there are 10 tracks per cylinder, the file occupies 150 of the 200 cylinders available in the disk pack used with the IBM 2311 system. For simplicity, assume also that the read/write head is at cylinder 00 at the beginning of file processing. Then the time required to process the 40 records on the first cylinder 00 is:

Average rotational delay	12.5 ms
Read record (811 bytes)	5.2
Processing plus rotational delay	19.8
Write updated record	5.2
Verify updated record	25.0
Total	67.7 ms × 40 records = 2,708
Movement to next cylinder	25
Total for each group of 40 records	2,733

Total for 150 groups of 40 records =
2,733 × 150 = 409,950 ms = 409.9 sec = 6.8 min

The value of 12.5 milliseconds for average rotational delay is based on the assumption that one-half revolution of the disk will be required, on the average, in order to locate the desired record on the track. On the other hand, the value of 19.8 milliseconds for processing and rotational delay before writing is the minimum value based on the assumption that processing will be completed in time to write the result after just one rotation of the disk (note that the sum of read record, processing, and rotational delay is 25 milliseconds). Although some processing tasks would require more than 19.8 milliseconds, thus resulting in a larger overall time estimate being required, the typical processing tasks associated with file updating could easily be completed within the time available in one rotation of the disk.

Sequential files need not be processed sequentially. They can also be processed randomly by employing a search method. Suppose we have a customer file of 10,000 records and 200 transactions occurred during a particular time period. Instead of sorting the customer transactions, we could take them in a random order and employ a search technique. The most obvious but least efficient search method would be to start searching with the first record in the file until the appropriate record is found. On the average, we would have to access half the file for each transaction. Thus, for the 200 transactions we would have $200 \times \frac{1}{2}(10,000) = 1,000,000$ accesses! A more efficient method, such as binary search, would typically be used. Such alternative methods are described in Chapter 15, "Table Sorting and Searching."

Overall, sequential files are particularly appropriate for files of high activity, such as payroll files, and in situations in which the transactions are presorted according to the order of the file.

REVIEW

1 When a sequential disk file is used in conjunction with sorted transactions, a key to identify the record is [necessary / unnecessary].

unnecessary

2 Sequential organization of a disk file is particularly appropriate for files of [low / high] activity.

high

INDEXED SEQUENTIAL FILE ORGANIZATION

This form of file organization represents something of a balance between sequential file organization and relative file organization. It allows sequential storage but facilitates random accessing or processing. The method utilizes an index table which indicates the approximate storage location for a given record. An indexed sequential file consists of two principal components: the main file and the index.

The *main file* is the storage area which includes the records in sequential order. It consists of two segments, namely, the *prime* area and the *overflow* area. The prime area is loaded with the records in sequential order when the file is first created, whereas the overflow area is designed to accommodate additions to the file. Through linkage techniques explained below, a logical sequence is retained in the file even though the writing of records in overflow breaks the correspondence between logical and physical order which is typical of sequential files.

The *index*, or index file, is frequently subdivided into two hierarchical levels, although for very large files it may be desirable to have more than two levels. As an illustration, we shall use an index file consisting of two levels: the cylinder index and the track index. Each record in the cylinder index consists of two fields. These fields are indicated by the second and third columns of Table 16-2. The first column, the cylinder number, is provided in the table to facilitate exposition and is not part of the cylinder index as such. The first field contains the value of the key associated with the highest (and therefore last) record in the corresponding cylinder. In the table, the highest record in the first cylinder of the file has the key 1250.

**TABLE 16-2   A CYLINDER INDEX FOR AN INDEXED
SEQUENTIAL FILE**

CYLINDER NUMBER	HIGHEST KEY IN CYLINDER	ADDRESS OF TRACK INDEX FOR CYLINDER
000	1250	0000
001	6900	0010
002	11300	0020

Each cylinder is provided with a track index for that cylinder. This track index commonly is written in the first track of the cylinder and may occupy all or part of that track. The second field in each cylinder index record contains the address of the track index for the corresponding cylinder. Thus, in our example in Table 16-2 the track index for the first cylinder is located in track address 0000 (cylinder 000, track 0).

In seeking a record in the file, the key of that record is compared with the keys in the cylinder index. For instance, if we are seeking record number 3200, the fact that the highest record in the first cylinder has a key of 1250 indicates that record 3200 is not in the first cylinder. The next comparison indicates that record 3200 is located in the second cylinder (if it is even included in the file), because the highest key in that cylinder is 6900, which is higher than 3200. The corresponding track address of 0010 indicates that as a next step the system will seek cylinder 001, track 0, to examine the track index for further directional information.

Now consider the track index portrayed in Table 16-3. The information in the column headed "Track Address of Track Index" is not really recorded as such but is included in the table to facilitate exposition. The track address is part of the information recorded in each track, as explained in the earlier section, Recording Data on

TABLE 16-3   A TRACK INDEX FOR AN INDEXED SEQUENTIAL FILE

TRACK ADDRESS OF TRACK INDEX	PRIME INDEX		OVERFLOW INDEX	
	KEY OF HIGHEST RECORD	ADDRESS OF TRACK	KEY OF HIGHEST RECORD	ADDRESS OF TRACK
0000	32	0001	***	***
0000	68	0002	79	01081
0000	125	0003	198	01083
0000	369	0004	***	***
.	.	.	.	.
.	.	.	.	.
.	.	.	.	.
0000	1250	0009	***	***
0010	1310	0011	1750	01121
0010	1990	0012	***	***
.	.	.	.	.
.	.	.	.	.
.	.	.	.	.
0010	6418	0019	6900	01123

Disk. Each record in the track index consists of two areas, the *prime index* and the *overflow index*. Each of these two areas consists of two fields. One field is reserved for the key and the other for the address. The key field indicates the key of the highest (last) record in the corresponding track. Thus, in Table 16-3 the highest record in track 0001 of the prime track area is the record whose key has a value of 32. Still considering the prime index, it can be seen that track 2 in cylinder 000 contains a record whose key is 68 as the highest record in the track. Further down, notice that track 0011 (cylinder 001, track 1) contains a record whose key is 1310 as the highest record in the track. As indicated in the first column of Table 16-3, the track index for a cylinder is recorded in the first track of each cylinder, tracks 0000 and 0010 in this case.

In order to illustrate the concept of the overflow index and the meaning of the associated track index it will be helpful to consider Table 16-4 in conjunction with Table 16-3. Table 16-4 indicates all record keys of the records stored in tracks 1, 2, 3, and 4 of the first (000) cylinder of the file. For simplicity we consider only four tracks, even though normally a greater number would be used. Notice that each track contains six records. We will make reference to these records by means of the respective keys which are listed in Table 16-4. The first track has 21 as the lowest-valued record and 32 as the last record. Referring to the track index in Table 16-3, the prime index associated with the first track indicates that the key of the highest record is 32, which matches the highest-valued record for that track in Table 16-4. The entries for the overflow index of the first track are asterisked in Table 16-3, indicating that no such entries have been made. That is, there were no overflow entries for track 1 of cylinder 000.

As indicated by the prime index for the second track in Table 16-3, the highest record in this track is 68. The corresponding entries in the overflow index for this track indicate 79 as the key of the highest record and 01081 as the address. Referring again to Table 16-4, notice the track whose home address is 0108 (second line from the bottom in the table). This track is a track in a cylinder which has been reserved for overflow records. The track address of 01081 cited above refers to cylinder 010, track 8, record 1. Because this is the address at which overflow begins for prime track 2, this means that this overflow address includes records that logically belong between the second and third prime tracks, that is, records whose key is higher than 68 and lower than 100. The key of the highest record in overflow for prime track 2 is 79, as indicated by the

TABLE 16-4   RECORDS STORED IN TRACKS 1–4 OF CYLINDER 000 FOR THE SAMPLE ILLUSTRATION

TRACK HOME ADDRESS	RECORDS IN TRACK					
0001	21	25	26	29	30	32
0002	40	50	54	55	61	68
0003	100	101	119	120	121	125
0004	210	250	260	271	305	369
.	.	.	.	.	.	.
.	.	.	.	.	.	.
.	.	.	.	.	.	.
0108	74	79	172	176	182	185
0109	192	198				

overflow index for the second track in Table 16-4. Notice that the first record is 74 and the second record is 79. Thus, there are in fact two records that represent overflow from track 2, and the second one has a key of 79. What caused the overflow in this case? Basically, after the file was created, two records were added to the track. Since the number of records exceeded the track capacity by two records, these records became overflow.

To further illustrate the concept of overflow, in Table 16-3 the prime index for the third track of cylinder 000 indicates that the highest record in that track has a key of 125. This corresponds with the highest key for track 3 listed in Table 16-4. The overflow index for this track in Table 16-3 indicates that there are one or more overflow records for this track, with the last one having a key of 198. Further, the overflow begins in cylinder 010, track 8, with 3 (address 01083). In Table 16-4 we can observe that the last two records of this overflow are stored in a different track, track 0109. Thus record 198, which is the one identified in the overflow index, is in fact located in a track different from the track address referenced by the overflow index because the referenced overflow track was itself overfilled. How such additional overflow is accomplished will be explained in the next section of this chapter.

Referring again to the track index in Table 16-3, notice that the key of the highest record in track 9 is 1250 and that this is also the highest key in the cylinder, since the corresponding overflow index is asterisked. Then refer back to the cylinder index in Table 16-2 and notice that 1250 is the key for cylinder 000, the first cylinder in the file. The highest key in the second cylinder (cylinder 001) is indicated as being 6900 in Table 16-2. Referring to the track index in Table 16-3, notice that this record is in the overflow area for cylinder 001, track 9, which is located in cylinder 011, track 2. Thus, the cylinder index identifies the highest key in the conceptual cylinder, whether or not the key is located in the same physical cylinder. In the case of overflow, there will generally be a difference between the conceptual cylinder and physical cylinder of the record with the highest key.

Thus, we have illustrated the nature of the cylinder index and track index as these relate to the identification of records stored in particular tracks, either prime or overflow. The basic reason for the development of a two-level index is to reduce access time. The cylinder index is often small enough so that it can be entered in internal storage. A quick reference to it provides the address of the track index. Then, the track index also consists of only a few entries, and the address of the record which is sought can be determined rather quickly. If the index were one-level, the required search process would take considerably longer. As an analogy, consider the familiar example in which a general library directory placed at the main entrance directs you to the third floor for the business and social science collection. Such a directory is equivalent to a cylinder index, and once you consult the directory your further concern is only in reference to the detailed directory on the third floor. In the absence of the main library directory, a systematic approach would require that directories on all floors beginning with the first floor be consulted until the required item is found.

REVIEW

1   The type of disk file organization which allows sequential storage but facilitates random accessing or processing is called _____ file organization.

indexed sequential

2   The *main file* in an indexed sequential file includes two types of file storage areas, referred to as the _____ area and the _____ area.

prime; overflow

3   The index file used in conjunction with an indexed sequential file is frequently subdivided into two or more hierarchical levels. In the example in this section, two levels were used, namely, a _____ index and a _____ index.

cylinder; track

4   Suppose that we have determined that a particular record is located in cylinder 5 of an indexed sequential file. The track location for this record could then be determined by reference to the track index for this cylinder, which would generally be located in the cylinder-track address_____.

0050 (since the track address is commonly written in the first track of the designated cylinder)

5   The track index for each cylinder indicates the keys of the [lowest / highest] records in the prime area and in the overflow area for each _____.

highest; track

6   A cylinder index identifies the key of the highest record stored in the [physical / conceptual] cylinder of interest.

conceptual

ADDING RECORDS TO AN INDEXED SEQUENTIAL FILE

We now consider the process of adding records to an indexed sequential file. Study of this section will further clarify the processes of indexing and overflow and will introduce you to the concepts of linkage and file chaining.

For convenience of reference, Tables 16-2, 16-3, and 16-4 are herewith repeated. Now, suppose that we need to add record 31 to the indexed sequential file portrayed in Table 16-4. Logically, this record should be located in the first prime track because it is smaller than the highest record in that track. When such a situation occurs, the new record is inserted in the appropriate location, and the last record in that track is then "bumped" into overflow. In this particular case, record 31 replaces record 32 and record 32 is written in overflow. The content of track 0001 is now as follows:

TRACK HOME ADDRESS	RECORDS IN TRACK					
0001	21	25	26	29	30	31

The next available space for overflow is in cylinder 010, track 9, record 3 (see the last line of Table 16-4), and this is the location in which record 32 is written. Since the

**TABLE 16-2   A CYLINDER INDEX FOR AN INDEXED
SEQUENTIAL FILE**

CYLINDER NUMBER	HIGHEST KEY IN CYLINDER	ADDRESS OF TRACK INDEX FOR CYLINDER
000	1250	0000
001	6900	0010
002	11300	0020

TABLE 16-3   A TRACK INDEX FOR AN INDEXED SEQUENTIAL FILE

TRACK ADDRESS OF TRACK INDEX	PRIME INDEX		OVERFLOW INDEX	
	KEY OF HIGHEST RECORD	ADDRESS OF TRACK	KEY OF HIGHEST RECORD	ADDRESS OF TRACK
0000	32	0001	***	***
0000	68	0002	79	01081
0000	125	0003	198	01083
0000	369	0004	***	***
.	.	.	.	.
.	.	.	.	.
.	.	.	.	.
0000	1250	0009	***	***
0010	1310	0011	1750	01121
0010	1990	0012	***	***
.	.	.	.	.
.	.	.	.	.
0010	6418	0019	6900	01123

**TABLE 16-4   RECORDS STORED IN TRACKS 1–4 OF
CYLINDER 000 FOR THE SAMPLE ILLUSTRATION**

TRACK HOME ADDRESS	RECORDS IN TRACK					
0001	21	25	26	29	30	32
0002	40	50	54	55	61	68
0003	100	101	119	120	121	125
0004	210	250	260	271	305	369
.	.	.	.	.	.	.
.	.	.	.	.	.	.
.	.	.	.	.	.	.
0108	74	79	172	176	182	185
0109	192	198				

overflow index for track 1 was previously empty (see line 1 of Table 16-3), we now enter the key of the record that has been placed in overflow (32) and the associated address (01093), as indicated below. Notice that the prime index was also changed to reflect the fact that the highest key in track 1 is now 31, instead of 32.

TRACK ADDRESS OF TRACK INDEX	PRIME INDEX		OVERFLOW INDEX	
	KEY OF HIGHEST RECORD	ADDRESS OF TRACK	KEY OF HIGHEST RECORD	ADDRESS OF TRACK
0000	31	0001	32	01093

Next, let us consider the addition of record 75 to this record file. As indicated in Table 16-3, this key is higher than the highest record in the second prime track but lower than the highest record in the overflow for this track. Therefore, record 75 will be written in the overflow for the second track. The next available overflow space is cylinder 010, track 9, record position 4, since record 32 was written in position 3 of this cylinder and track.

Referring to Table 16-4, note that record 75 will be physically separated from records 74 and 79, between which it logically belongs in the context of a sequential file. In order to achieve logical contiguity in the face of physical separation, the concept of chaining with linkage fields is employed.

As records are written in overflow a linkage field is included with each record. Linkage fields are not required with records in a prime track, because such records are always stored sequentially according to record keys. However, for overflow records linkage fields serve to identify the location of the next sequential record, which may or may not be contiguous to the record in question. Table 16-5 presents the overflow tracks previously included in Table 16-4 but in addition identifies the linkage field associated with each record in overflow. In track 0108 the first record has a key of 74 and a linkage value of 01082, which means that the next record in the sequence is located in track 0108, record 2 (the next physical record, in this case). The link field of record 79 is asterisked, which indicates the end of the particular sequence. Recall that records 74 and 79 were the only two records which represented the overflow from prime track 0002. The third record has a key of 172 and it is the first record of the chain representing the overflow from prime track 0003, as indicated in Table 16-3, which

TABLE 16-5 OVERFLOW RECORDS ILLUSTRATING THE USE OF LINKAGE FIELDS

TRACK HOME ADDRESS	RECORD 1		RECORD 2		RECORD 3		. . .	RECORD 6	
	KEY	LINK	KEY	LINK	KEY	LINK	. . .	KEY	LINK
0108	74	01082	79	***	172	01084	. . .	185	01091
0109	192	01092	198	***	32	***			

identifies the address of the first overflow record for prime track 0003 as 01083, or the third record in track 0108. The records are consecutively ordered in the remaining positions in this track, and the last record in the track, record 185, has a link to the first record of the next track (linkage value 01091). Record 198 has an asterisked link field because it is the last record of this chain. Finally, record 32 does not have a link value because it is the only overflow record from prime track 0001.

Now, let us again consider the addition of record 75 in the overflow of this indexed sequential file. As described in the discussion above, the next available overflow space is in track 0109, record 4. In order to establish appropriate linkage, a link value of 01082 is included with record 75, as indicated in Table 16-6. In addition, in order to have appropriate linkage to record 75, the linkage of record 74 is changed from 01082 to 01094. The overflow index in the prime track is not changed, however, because the last overflow record is still 79 and the address of the first overflow record is still 01081.

The final example involves the addition of record 200 to this indexed sequential file. Referring to Table 16-3, it can be seen that the key of the last record in the overflow of track 0003 is 198, while the key of the last record in prime track 0004 is 369. Therefore, record 200 would be entered in prime track 0004. By reference to Table 16-4 we can see that record 200 will be placed in the first record position in the track, with the subsequent records then being moved back by one record position and record 369 being moved to overflow. The next available space in overflow is record 5 in track 0109. Thus the track index will now have the following conceptual form:

TRACK ADDRESS OF TRACK INDEX	PRIME INDEX		OVERFLOW INDEX	
	KEY OF HIGHEST RECORD	ADDRESS OF TRACK	KEY OF HIGHEST RECORD	ADDRESS OF TRACK
0000	31	0001	32	01093
0000	68	0002	79	01081
0000	125	0003	198	01083
0000	305	0004	369	01095

Similarly, the overflow track 0109 will now have the following content:

HOME ADDRESS	RECORD 1		RECORD 2		RECORD 3		RECORD 4		RECORD 5	
	KEY	LINK	KEY	LINK	KEY	LINK	KEY	LINK	KEY	LINK
0109	192	01092	198	***	32	***	75	01082	369	***

Since the record with the key 369 is the only record in overflow for prime track 0004, the link field for this record does not contain the key of any other record.

The examples and explanations above have demonstrated the important charac-

TABLE 16-6   ADDITION OF A RECORD IN OVERFLOW

HOME ADDRESS	RECORD 1		RECORD 2		RECORD 3		RECORD 4	
	KEY	LINK	KEY	LINK	KEY	LINK	KEY	LINK
0108	74	01094	79	***	172	01084		
0109	192	01092	198	***	32	***	75	01082

teristics of indexed sequential files. The use of such files is extensive in business data processing systems because they have some of the advantages of sequential files while also providing random access capability. In the next section of this chapter we demonstrate how such a file can be used in conjunction with either sequential or direct access file processing.

REVIEW

1   When a record which is to be added to an indexed sequential file should logically be located within a prime track, [the record is placed in that track and the last record is "bumped" into overflow / the record in question is entered directly into overflow].

> *the record is placed in that track and the*
> *last record is "bumped" into overflow*

2   When a record which is to be added to an indexed sequential file should logically be located within a particular track in overflow, [it is located in the appropriate position and other records are "bumped" / it is located in the next available position in overflow].

> *it is located in the next available position*
> *in overflow*

3   In order to achieve logical continuity of the records in overflow for records which may be physically separated, a _____ field is included with each record to identify the location of the next sequential record, if it is located in overflow.

> *linkage (or link)*

4   The concept of file chaining is particularly concerned with identifying the appropriate sequencing of records in the [prime / overflow] area of the data file.

> *overflow*

SEQUENTIAL AND RANDOM ACCESS WITH AN INDEXED SEQUENTIAL FILE

Suppose that an indexed sequential file has already been established and we wish to process it in a sequential order. Figure 16-5 presents a flowchart which indicates the

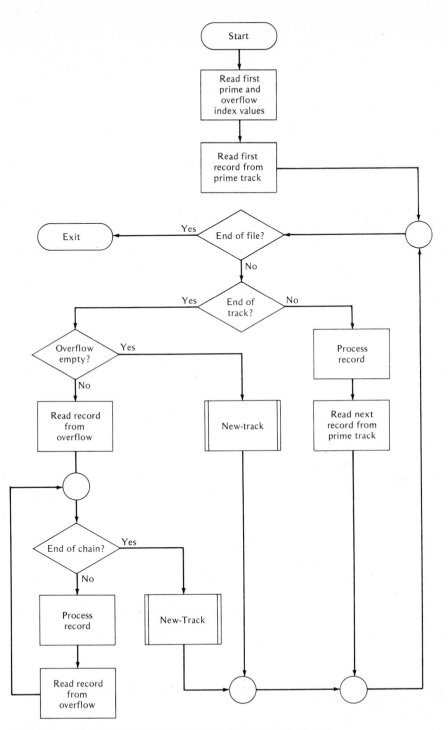

FIGURE 16-5 SEQUENTIAL ACCESS WITH AN INDEXED SEQUENTIAL FILE.

449

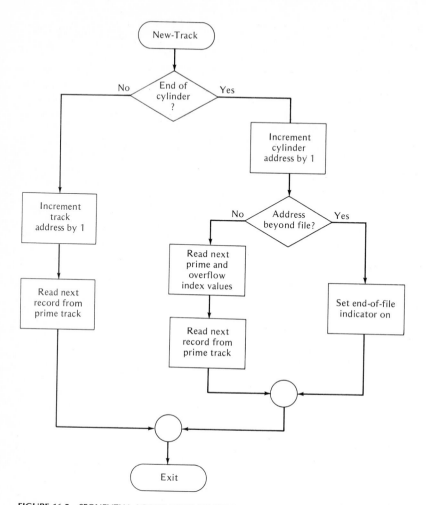

FIGURE 16-5   SEQUENTIAL ACCESS WITH AN INDEXED SEQUENTIAL FILE *(Continued).*

accessing logic associated with sequential processing. Briefly, we begin with the cylinder index, which directs us to the first track index. From the track index we process all the records, both prime and overflow, for the cylinder. These processing steps are repeated for all the cylinders contained in the file. When the last record in the last cylinder and track is processed, the overall processing of the file is completed.

The main appeal of an indexed sequential file, however, is the capability of processing such a file randomly. Figure 16-6 presents a flowchart which indicates the accessing logic associated with random access. Given the key associated with a record, the cylinder index is searched. The search may be sequential or binary, as explained in Chapter 15, "Table Sorting and Searching." We then access the corresponding track index, which indicates whether the record is located in the prime or overflow area. The appropriate area is searched for a key equal condition. If the format for all the records includes the use of keys, the disk control system can usually search each track for a key equal condition without transferring each record into internal storage. Thus, in one rotation of the disk all the records of a track can be searched, and if found, the record which is sought can be transferred to internal storage for appropriate processing.

In the chapter which follows we illustrate the implementation of file processing using disk files in COBOL. As will be obvious in that chapter, the programmer using COBOL has limited responsibility in regard to the accessing logic. Most of the steps have been incorporated into the language processor and are carried out automatically without the use of instructions from the programmer. Still, it is useful, if not necessary, to understand the basic logic and programming steps associated with processing an indexed sequential file.

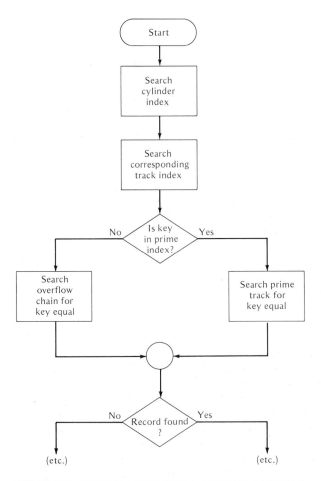

FIGURE 16-6   RANDOM ACCESS WITH AN INDEXED SEQUENTIAL FILE.

We have not mentioned the deletion of records from an indexed sequential file. Normally, when a record is to be deleted, a special code is used to denote the fact. By this approach, the record is not physically deleted immediately. Rather, it remains in the file until the file is recreated, at which point the records containing a deletion code are omitted. Consider that an indexed sequential file is in essence a sequential file. As such, immediate physical deletion would result in one of two conditions. One condition would be a "hole" in the sequence of records, while the other would involve a shuffling upward of all subsequent records to close the resulting gap. The use of a deletion code is preferable to either of these conditions.

From time to time an indexed sequential file has to be recreated. In addition to removing deleted records, it is also desirable to recreate such files in order to reduce processing delays resulting from having a large number of records in overflow. Thus, a file may be re-created on a periodic basis or whenever the overflow records exceed a designated number.

REVIEW

1   When an indexed sequential file is processed in a sequential order, [all / selected] records are processed for all the cylinders contained in the file.

all

2   When an indexed sequential file is processed in a random order, a search routine is used which requires identification of the _____ associated with each record to be accessed.

key

3   If a record is to be deleted from an indexed sequential file, normally it is [immediately removed / "tagged" with a deletion code for removal when the file is recreated].

"tagged" with a deletion code for removal
when the file is recreated

RELATIVE FILE ORGANIZATION AND THE DIVISION REMAINDER METHOD

Relative, or direct, file organization is based on establishing a relationship between a record key and the physical position of the record in the file. In this manner a direct path can be taken to a record, resulting in the capability of random access and random processing of records contained in a file.

Perhaps the most obvious form of relative or direct organization is to use a record key that has a one-to-one correspondence with the physical positions of records. For example, if we assign employee-numbers from 0001 to 9999, we can store the 0001 employee-number record in the first position of track 000, the next record in the second position of that track, and so on in a consecutive order. Thus, accessing the record of employee-number 0369 would be accomplished by using the number as the disk address. A slight modification of this system is represented by transforming the employee-number to an address by adding or subtracting a constant. For example, if employee-numbers range from 02000 to 10000, we could subtract 1999 from each number to determine the disk address.

Although the system of using the record key to indicate the disk address would be generally desirable, it is seldom in fact feasible. In the case of a personnel file, for example, the employee code numbers may range from 02000 to 10000, but with a large number of currently inactive codes and with the total number of employees being well below the total range of numbers. This means that we would waste a lot of disk space if a space were reserved for each possible record key. It might be argued that the solution to this problem is to fill in the gaps in the numbering system. This solution may not be feasible for a number of reasons. First, if a person terminates employment with the company, we would not want to reassign his code to another individual for at least a given time period in order to avoid confusion in records. Further, some code numbers within the sequence might never be assigned on the basis of the coding system being used. For example, the first two digits might designate department-number while the next three digits might be used to designate employee-number within each department. Using such a system, if department 3 has 150 employees, the last employee-number for that department would be 03150 while the first employee-number in the next consecutive department would be 04001, resulting in a large block of unassigned numbers within the sequence.

Because of the difficulties cited above, a so-called randomizing technique of some kind is generally used to assign disk addresses to records, and then to locate these records once they have been placed in storage. Basically, a randomizing technique is a computational procedure by which key numbers are converted into file addresses. At the start of this discussion it should be pointed out that one problem associated with the use of any randomizing technique is that of *synonyms*—two or more different keys which convert to the same address. Therefore, one desirable feature of a good randomizing method is that the number of synonyms is minimized.

One way of minimizing the number of synonyms is to allow a lot of space for storage of the file, thus reducing the probability that two keys will convert to the same address. In this respect, the concept of the *packing factor* indicates the ratio of the actual number of records to the total number of storage spaces assigned. For example, if a file contains 10,000 records and it is packed at 80 percent, then 12,500 spaces have been assigned to the file. Obviously, the higher the packing factor, the greater the number of synonyms that will occur.

The most frequently used randomizing method is the division remainder method. As for any such technique, the division remainder method is used for a twofold purpose: to determine the position of each record in conjunction with a direct access file and to achieve about an equal distribution of the records in the range of disk addresses assigned to the file. We shall describe this method by means of a numerical example. Suppose a file consists of 10,000 records, and that we assign the 12,000 disk storage spaces which are numbered 00000 to 11999 to this file. Further, assume that the record keys range in value from 001000 to 9999999. The following steps illustrate the application of the division remainder method to determine the storage location for the record whose key is 0235670:

1   Reduce the key range to the storage address range by dividing the key by the prime number which is closest to the highest address assigned to the file. A prime number is a number that is evenly divisible only by itself and by 1. An abbreviated table of prime numbers is presented in Table 16-7. In the present case, the closest prime number to address 11999 is 11987. Therefore, we divide the key by this number to the point of obtaining the whole-number quotient and determining the value of the remainder:

$$\frac{0235670}{11987} = 19 \text{ with the remainder } 7917$$

2   The remainder associated with the division in step 1 is used to determine the track address by dividing the remainder by the number of records per track as follows:

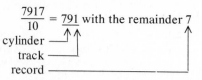

Thus, record number 0235670 would be located in cylinder 79, track 1, record 7. As another example, the storage location for the record whose key is 9999999 would be determined as follows:

$$\frac{9999999}{11987} = 835 \text{ with remainder } 2854$$

TABLE 16-7   TABLE OF SOME PRIME NUMBERS

NUMBER	NEAREST PRIME NUMBER
500	499
1,000	997
5,000	4,999
6,000	5,987
7,000	6,997
8,000	7,993
9,000	8,899
10,000	9,973
12,000	11,987
14,000	13,999
16,000	15,991
18,000	17,989
20,000	19,997
22,000	21,991
32,000	31,991
42,000	41,999
52,000	53,993

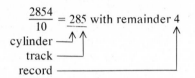

$$\frac{2854}{10} = \underline{285} \text{ with remainder } 4$$

cylinder
track
record

Note that this record, which has the highest-numbered key, is not the last record in the file. The application of the division remainder technique results in a randomized location of the records in respect to the key numbers.

REVIEW

1   The type of file organization associated with the need to access records in a nonsequential order is the _____ file organization.

relative (or direct)

2   Use of the record key to indicate directly the disk address in a relative file (is / is not) generally feasible in a random file system.

is not

3   A randomizing technique is generally used in conjunction with direct access files in order to determine the storage location of each record. The particular technique which is most frequently used is called the _____ method.

division remainder

4   One problem associated with any randomizing method is that associated with two or more keys converting to the same storage address. Such repetitions are called _____.

synonyms

OTHER RANDOMIZING METHODS

DIGIT ANALYSIS METHOD

By this method a frequency count is performed in regard to the number of times each of the 10 digits occurs in each of the positions included in the record key. For example, Table 16-8 presents a frequency count for the number of times each digit occurred in a five-position numeric key for 2,800 records. In this tabulation we can observe that digits 0–9 occur with approximately uniform distribution in key positions 2, 3, and 5. Therefore, if a three-digit address were required, the digits in these three positions in the record keys could be used. Given that there are 2,800 records, however, a four-digit address would be required. Suppose we desire the first digit to be a 0, 1, 2, or 3 only. Such assignment can be made with about equal frequency for each digit by using a rule such as the following: assign a "0" when digits in positions 2 and 3 both contain odd numbers, a "1" if position 2 is odd and position 3 is even, a "2"

TABLE 16-8 FREQUENCY OF OCCURRENCE OF THE DIGITS 1–9 FOR 2,800 FIVE-POSITION KEYS

	KEY POSITION				
DIGIT	1	2	3	4	5
0	2026				
1	618	250	218	1012	260
2	128	395	391	185	382
3	23	263	389	299	271
4	5	298	330	52	302
5		335	299	101	387
6		303	339	18	299
7		289	308	134	301
8		267	267	999	245
9		400	259		353

if position 2 is even and position 3 is odd, or a "3" if positions 2 and 3 both contain even numbers. Thus, the address for key 16258 would be 3628: the "3" from the fact that positions 2 and 3 both contain even numbers and the "628" from key positions 2, 3, and 5. Other rules for prefixing additional digits can be formulated for different circumstances. In any event, the digit analysis method relies on the digits in some of the key positions being approximately equally distributed. If such is not the case, the method cannot be used with good results.

MID-SQUARE METHOD

The record key is multiplied by itself, and the product is truncated from left to right so as to form a number equal to the desired address length. Thus key 16258 would be squared to give 264322564. To form a four-digit address, this number is truncated from the left, resulting in the address 2564.

FOLDING

The key is separated into two parts which are then added together to form the address. For example, suppose key 1234567 is to be transformed into a four-digit address. We can add the first four positions to the last three positions to form the address, or in this case, 1234 + 567 = 1801. As another possibility, we can begin with the middle four digits and add the other digits as follows:

In general, the concept of folding does not refer to one standard method, but rather to a general class of possibilities.

ALPHABETIC KEYS

It is possible, and sometimes common, that the key is alphabetic, as in the case of a student file which utilizes an alphabetic key. In order to determine a numeric address, a procedure is defined by which letters are transformed to numbers. These numbers might then be used as addresses or, more likely, be used in conjunction with one of the randomizing techniques discussed above. Thus, if the transformation rule is that A = 00, B = 01, . . . , Z = 25, ADAM would become 00030012. Of course, other transformation rules are possible, such as A = 11, B = 12, . . . , Z = 36.

The randomizing methods that have been discussed are not the only ones that can be used, but they do represent the principal techniques. As indicated previously, the division remainder technique is used most frequently and generally works at least as well as other methods. But special circumstances may make some other method desirable for a given file.

REVIEW

1   The randomizing method for which the digits in at least some of the key positions must be dispersed about equally in terms of value is the _____ method.

digit analysis

2   The randomizing method in which the key is multiplied by itself as part of the procedure for determining the address for the record is the _____ method.

mid-square

3   The randomizing method in which one part of a key number is added to another part of the number to form the address is the _____ method.

folding

4   Because an alphabetic key would frequently vary in length, such a key is generally transformed [directly into a numeric address / into a numeric code for subsequent determination of an address].

into a numeric code for subsequent determination of an address

5   The randomization technique most frequently used in conjunction with random, or direct, file organization is the _____ method.

division remainder

HANDLING OF SYNONYMS

When two or more key values are converted to the same address, the usual solution to such a storage problem is to utilize the concept of overflow. The most straightforward approach is to file the record in the next available space. Suppose that the storage location for a record has been computed to be cylinder 79, track 1, record 7, but that another record has already been stored in that location. The record which is now to be stored is thus a synonym. In order to assign a storage position to the synonym we can next check record position 8, then position 9, then, if necessary, even proceed to different tracks and different cylinders until an available space is found. How can we determine which record is stored in the original position, and also, how can we subsequently determine the location of the synonym? The *key* of the record provides the basis for both procedures. If the record in question is not found in the first computed location, as determined by some randomizing method, the search continues into the adjoining higher-numbered positions and then proceeds back to the beginning of the file if necessary until the record is found.

If the packing factor is high, with relatively few open spaces included in the file, a great number of synonyms are likely to be formed and chain reactions will result. That is, an overflow record will occupy a space which would normally have been occupied by another record, and that record will similarly take the place of another record, and so on. The result is slow average access due to required search for particular records. If the packing factor is low, there is more unused storage space but more rapid access. In general, a packing factor of about 80 percent is satisfactory.

In addition to using a lower packing factor, there are three specific procedures by which the search problems associated with synonyms can be minimized.

1 Compute only a cylinder and track location by the randomizing method being used, rather than cylinder, track, and record position. Then assign records within each track sequentially according to time of original entry. By this approach the procedure associated with overflow will be used less frequently, since the computed storage location contains several positions. The term *bucket* denotes the allocation of several records to one address. Thus, a bucket size of 1 would imply an address which specifies a cylinder-track-record position. A bucket size of 10 would mean that 10 records can be stored in each address, which would be indicative of a cylinder-track.

2 Include a linkage field in the record stored in a location for which a synonym exists. Thus, if a record is to be stored in location 7917 but a record has already been placed there, the synonym is stored in the next available position and the location of that position is entered in the linkage field of the first record. If a third record also has the same address, the second record would contain the linkage to the third record, and so on. By this approach we take a direct path to the next record rather than following a sequential search, thereby reducing average access time.

3 Subdivide the allotted storage spaces into two areas, the main and the overflow. For example, suppose 10,000 records are to be stored in 15,000 possible locations. The first 12,000 locations can be designated as the main storage area, with the other 3,000 designated as the overflow area. All address computations would be made in respect to the main storage area. If the computed address is already in use, we add the computed address to the base address of the overflow area. For example, suppose the main area includes addresses 00000–11999, overflow includes 12000–14999, and the address computed is 7917. In this case, the base address of the overflow area is 12000 and therefore 7917 + 12000 = 19917. But this number exceeds the highest allotted address (14999). The procedure to follow in such cases is to subtract the highest allotted address from the computed overflow address (19917 − 14999 = 4918) and again add the result to the base address (4918 + 12000 = 16918). However, the recomputed address is still outside the limits of the file; so

the procedure is repeated until an acceptable address is obtained. In this case, one further repetition is required: $16918 - 14999 = 1919$; $1919 + 12000 = 13919$. If it should occur that this is also a duplicate address, one of three methods can be used to determine the address: next available space, next available space with use of a linking field, or prior designation of a second overflow area with repetition of the above procedure for determining the overflow address.

It is often useful to perform a statistical analysis of the records in a file in order to subdivide the file according to extent of activity. Suppose that for a file of 10,000 records 3,000 of the records account for 80 percent of the file activity. In such a case these 3,000 records should be stored first, thereby minimizing the number of times that such records are synonyms, and when a synonym does occur, assuring that the substitute address will not in general be far removed from the original address. After the active records are loaded, the less active group should be loaded. Of course, we might subdivide the file into several groups rather than only two, in which case the groups would be stored in order of decreasing activity.

Addition of records to a random file over an extended period of time requires no special consideration beyond the methods already discussed, since it does not matter whether the records are being stored during just one computer run or over a series of weeks or months. However, one consideration is important in respect to additions being made over a period of time. The change in the size of the file may result in a packing factor that is too large. In general, it is good practice to recreate random files at some regular interval of time, with the length of the interval depending on the add-delete activity, the nature of the business, the use of the files, and the like.

REVIEW

1 When a synonym occurs while attempting storage of a record in a random file, the usual solution to the storage problem is to store the record in _____ _____.

the next available space

2 In general, there are more synonyms and more chain reactions as the packing factor gets [smaller / larger]. A packing factor of about ____ percent has been found satisfactory for most random files.

larger; 80

3 A bucket size of 10 would be indicative of an address which is a [cylinder-track / cylinder-track-record]. The use of a bucket size larger than 1 results in [fewer / more] synonyms occurring, in general.

cylinder-track; fewer

4 The use of a linkage field in conjunction with synonyms makes it possible to [reduce the number of synonyms / reduce the average access time for locating synonyms].

reduce the average access time for
locating synonyms

5   If the allotted storage space for a file is divided into main and overflow areas, the initial address computations are made in respect to [the main area only / the entire allotted storage area].

the main area only

6   If a file is subdivided into subgroups according to extent of activity, the group of records which should be loaded first is the group with [least / most] activity.

most

EXERCISES

1   Discuss characteristics of data processing applications that make direct access features particularly desirable. Give examples of each application type.

2   Review the factors that affect the time to access a record from a file that is organized as a direct file.

3   If you were choosing among disks produced by a number of manufacturers, what performance factors would you want to consider?

4   Consider two typical business data processing applications: inventory and payroll. Using general guidelines, which application would be better suited to direct file organization and which would be better suited to random processing?

5   Describe the three file organization methods discussed in the text, and give an example application in which you would use each type of organization.

6   In direct file organization the record keys precede the data. Why are the keys so positioned?

7   It is suggested that we use the randomizing routine to compute cylinder, track, and record number within track. It is countersuggested that computing record number is unnecessary and that cylinder and track number are enough locational information. Why is it that the second suggestion may or may not be true?

8   Suppose that a file is organized as indexed sequential but it is stored on a drum. If you were to design an index, would you make it different from the disk-type index discussed in the text?

9   A savings and loan institution has a few thousand customers who maintain deposit accounts. The master file is updated on a batch basis every night. The question has been raised as to whether the transactions should be sorted and the master file updated as a sequential file or whether the master file should be direct so that the transactions can be processed in a random order. Give your reasoning on what you would consider in making a choice.

10 As records are added to an indexed sequential file the average access time increases because we have to follow the chain in the overflow records. What data would you collect in order to establish a rule as to how many record additions would be required before a recreation of the file is desirable?

Direct
Access Files and COBOL

INTRODUCTION

In the preceding chapter we discussed the storage, organization, and processing of data files on direct access devices, such as disks. This chapter introduces the reader to the implementation of direct access file processing using the COBOL language. Because some COBOL features are specifically designed for direct access files, several new language features are introduced.

COBOL LANGUAGE INSTRUCTIONS
FOR SEQUENTIAL FILES

Relatively few new language statements are required for the processing of a disk file that is sequential in terms of file organization. The presentation in this section is organized according to the four divisions of a COBOL program.

IDENTIFICATION DIVISION

The contents of this division are not affected by the use of a sequential magnetic disk file.

ENVIRONMENT DIVISION

The SELECT sentence of the FILE-CONTROL paragraph may contain information about the fact that this file is organized sequentially. This option depends on the way the manufacturer designates the device name. For example, in an IBM compiler the statement, SELECT file-name ASSIGN TO device-name, may require a special code in the device name designation that signifies the organization of the file.

At this point it will be appropriate to clarify the possible question of device designation. We may ask: Can we have more than one file per disk pack and, if so, how do we allocate certain cylinders or sectors to one file or to another? The answer to the first question is that it is, in fact, possible to have several files stored in the same pack. The assignment of specific areas to each file is normally accomplished by the use of JCL (Job Control Language) instructions. In other words, this file storage allocation is done *outside* the COBOL language statements as such.

Since IBM computers are so common, it may be worthwhile to mention that a WRITE-VERIFY option is available for disk files being updated when using IBM equipment. If this option is specified when an updated record is rewritten on the disk, it is immediately verified. The option is specified in the I-O-CONTROL paragraph as follows:

ENVIRONMENT DIVISION.
FILE-CONTROL.
I-O-CONTROL
APPLY WRITE-VERIFY ON file-name.

This WRITE-VERIFY clause applies to IBM compilers regardless of whether the file is sequential, direct, or indexed.

DATA DIVISION

No new COBOL statements are associated with the use of sequential disk files for this division. However, LABEL RECORDS ARE STANDARD is often a requirement. The BLOCK CONTAINS clause is also allowed, as it is with magnetic tape files.

PROCEDURE DIVISION

Different statements apply, depending on whether a disk file is used as input, as output, or as both input and output, i.e., updated.

For input files we simply use the OPEN INPUT, READ, and CLOSE routine as before (as with magnetic tape files, in Chapter 10). The AT END clause associated with READ has the same meaning as before but is slightly modified if we take account of the different hardware involved; that is, we reach the end of a disk file rather than the end of a tape. Typically, the last record in the file contains special codes to designate it the last record.

For *output* files we use OPEN OUTPUT as usual, and we use CLOSE as if the file were sequential on tape. While the programming instructions remain the same, the physical process is a little different. For instance, the concept of *rewinding* a magnetic tape is not meaningful for a disk file. Still, it should be kept in mind that label records are used with disk files, and that OPEN and CLOSE cause routine label processing in a fashion analogous to processing with magnetic tape.

For update files it is possible to have the updated records simply replace the old records in the same physical locations. Thus, such a file cannot be considered either INPUT or OUTPUT. Instead, it is declared to be I-O, which stands for input-output. Such a designation makes it possible to read from and write on the same file. There are two new options shown in the general format:

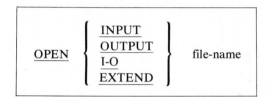

In order to update a sequential file on disk we use "OPEN I-O file-name." Then, after issuing a READ verb that accesses the record to be updated, we use the REWRITE verb to replace the updated record in the same file instead of WRITE on a different file. It will be recalled that with magnetic tape files we must read a record from one file and MOVE and write the updated record on a new file. The format of the REWRITE statement is as follows:

> <u>REWRITE</u> record-name [<u>FROM</u> identifier]

It should be noted that REWRITE can only be used to update an existing file. If we are creating a file, we use the WRITE verb.

Again with reference to the OPEN verb, the EXTEND option causes the file to be positioned immediately following the last logical record of that file. Subsequent WRITE statements referencing the file will add records to the file as though the file had been opened with the OUTPUT option. Notice that EXTEND allows records to be added at the end of a file, and not "in between." A common student error is to ignore the fact that sequential disk file organization implies the very same constraints in processing logic that we encounter with magnetic tape. Even though the file is on disk, to access the one-thousandth record requires that we first access sequentially the preceding 999 records. EXTEND is the only option that allows a shortcut, and it is only useful for additions at the end of the file.

Based on the above description, it can be seen that sequential file processing using disks entails relatively few new ideas in the COBOL language. Exhibit 17-1 presents the relevant skeleton of instructions for a program that reads transaction cards containing an identifying account number and a quantity, which is used to update a corresponding quantity field in the disk file record. Apart from the language

EXHIBIT 17-1   OUTLINE OF A COBOL PROGRAM FOR UPDATING A SEQUENTIAL DISK FILE

```
ENVIRONMENT DIVISION.
FILE-CONTROL.
      SELECT CARD-FILE ASSIGN TO card-reader.
      SELECT DISK-FILE ASSIGN TO disk-device.
DATA DIVISION.
FILE SECTION.
FD   CARD-FILE LABEL RECORD OMITTED
      DATA RECORD IS DATA-CARD.
01   DATA-CARD.
      02   ACCOUNT-NO                        PICTURE 9(5).
      02   QUANTITY                          PICTURE 9(6)V99.
      02   FILLER                            PICTURE X(67).
FD   DISK-FILE LABEL RECORDS ARE STANDARD
      DATA RECORD IS DISK-REC.
01   DISK-REC.
      02   ACCOUNT-NO                        PICTURE 9(5).
      02   QUANTITY                          PICTURE 9(8)V99.
      02   OTHER-DATA                        PICTURE X(105).
PROCEDURE DIVISION.
SETTING-UP.
      OPEN I-O DISK-FILE.
      OPEN INPUT CARD-FILE.
MAIN-LOGIC.
      PERFORM INPUTTING-DISK.
      PERFORM INPUTTING-CARD.
      PERFORM UPDATING
            UNTIL end condition.
      CLOSE CARD-FILE, DISK-FILE.
      STOP RUN.
INPUTTING-DISK.
      READ DISK-FILE RECORD AT END . . .
INPUTTING-CARD.
      READ CARD-FILE RECORD AT END . . .
UPDATING.
      IF ACCOUNT-NO OF DATA-CARD = ACCOUNT-NO OF DISK-REC
            PERFORM PROCESSING
            REWRITE DISK-REC
      ELSE . . .
            .
            .
            .
PROCESSING,
etc.
```

changes, the logic remains the same as for updating a magnetic tape file. The only difference is that we need not WRITE master records for which there are no corresponding transactions. Since we are not creating a new, updated disk file, there is no need to rewrite that which is already there. Therefore the program logic must provide for the REWRITE statement to be executed only for those disk records for which we have card (transaction) records. Of course, all the disk records are read, since this is a sequential file and the records are accessed sequentially.

REVIEW

1   When using magnetic disk storage, the assignment of more than one file to a particular disk pack is [possible / a programming error].

possible

2   The instruction used to open a sequential disk file for the purpose of updating the file is OPEN [INPUT file-name / I-O file-name / OUTPUT file-name].

I-O file-name

3   After a record in a sequential file has been accessed for the purpose of updating, the updated record is replaced in the original file location by use of the _____ verb.

REWRITE

4   Use of the EXTEND option with the OPEN verb causes the file to be positioned [at the first / after the last] record of the file.

after the last

5   The program example in the last part of this section is concerned with file [creation / retrieval / updating] for a sequential disk file.

updating

CREATION OF AN INDEXED FILE

An indexed file may be created with minimal effort on the part of the programmer. The source records must first be sorted in ascending sequence on a data field which will serve as a sort key for the file. It should be kept in mind that an indexed file is a sequential file, and therefore the records are positioned in ascending order. We consider an example to illustrate the process.

Source records which contain data about vendors are available on punched cards. Columns 1–8 contain an identifier which is unique for each vendor, columns 9–68 contain other relevant data, and columns 69–80 are unused. We desire to copy these records on disk, forming an indexed file sorted on the basis of the data in columns 1–8. Each disk record will consist of 68 characters.

First we sort the source records on columns 1–8. In the following sample data the records are already sorted, except for the fifth record (37654310), which is purposely placed out of order to illustrate the effects of such a condition.

```
12345678ACME-10
22345678ACME-20
35120001ACME-30
37654310ACME-40
35290001ACME-50
45678912ACME-60
49678912ACME-70
54371203ACME-80
58120000ACME-90
60000000ACME-92
70000000ACME-93
80000000ACME-94
99999999ACME-99
```

Exhibit 17-2 presents a COBOL program written to create an indexed file.

Notice the SELECT statement. ACCESS IS SEQUENTIAL specifies that the access mode for this file is sequential. ORGANIZATION IS INDEXED specifies that this is an indexed file. RECORD KEY IS VENDOR-NUMBER specifies that there is a field called VENDOR-NUMBER which is a field in the file record and which serves as the sort key for the file. In other words, the file will be in ascending order of VENDOR-NUMBER values.

In the DATA DIVISION in Exhibit 17-2 observe that VENDOR-NUMBER is a field in the record description of the indexed file (DISKFILE). The current ANSI COBOL standard specifies that RECORD KEY be a field in the file record and that it must be alphanumeric. At the time of this writing different compilers handle the process differently. For example, IBM compilers require that the first field in the record be a deletion code set to LOW-VALUES by the programmer to indicate that a record exists (that it has not been deleted—which could happen in subsequent processing of the file). Therefore, if you are using such a compiler, VENDOR-NUMBER cannot be the first field in the record. As another example of variable practice, some UNIVAC compilers use the term ACTUAL KEY instead of RECORD KEY and allow that key to be a field in WORKING-STORAGE. We anticipate that such variations from the standard will have been removed from current practice by the time this book is published. Still, many programs have been written under the old guidelines, and one can expect to continue seeing these variations in existing programs.

In the PROCEDURE DIVISION of Exhibit 17-2 the relevant part is

```
FILE-CREATE.
    MOVE VENDOR-INDENT TO VENDOR-NUMBER
    MOVE VENDOR-DATA OF CARD TO VENDOR-DATA OF
        DISK-RECORD
    WRITE DISK-RECORD
        INVALID KEY PERFORM ERROR-CASE.
    PERFORM READ-CARD.
```

We move VENDOR-INDENT, a field in the input card, to VENDOR-NUMBER, which was declared to be the RECORD KEY in the SELECT statement. The move of VENDOR-DATA simply transfers the other fields of the source record to the output record. The WRITE statement now includes the INVALID KEY condition. This condition

EXHIBIT 17-2   A COBOL PROGRAM TO CREATE AN INDEXED FILE

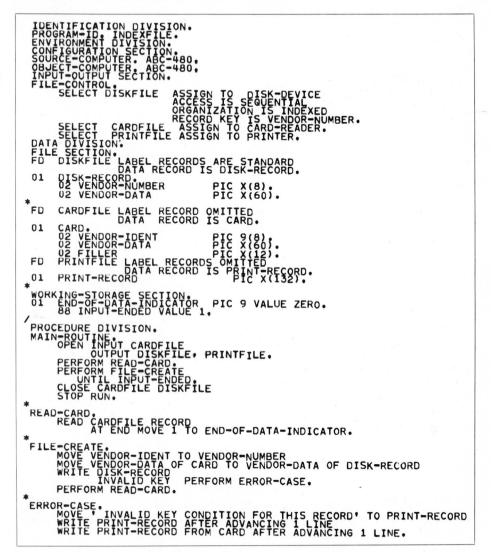

```
IDENTIFICATION DIVISION.
PROGRAM-ID. INDEXFILE.
ENVIRONMENT DIVISION.
CONFIGURATION SECTION.
SOURCE-COMPUTER. ABC-480.
OBJECT-COMPUTER. ABC-480.
INPUT-OUTPUT SECTION.
FILE-CONTROL.
     SELECT DISKFILE    ASSIGN TO   DISK-DEVICE
                        ACCESS IS SEQUENTIAL
                        ORGANIZATION IS INDEXED
                        RECORD KEY IS VENDOR-NUMBER.
     SELECT  CARDFILE   ASSIGN TO CARD-READER.
     SELECT  PRINTFILE ASSIGN TO PRINTER.
DATA DIVISION.
FILE SECTION.
FD   DISKFILE LABEL RECORDS ARE STANDARD
              DATA RECORD IS DISK-RECORD.
01   DISK-RECORD.
     02 VENDOR-NUMBER        PIC X(8).
     02 VENDOR-DATA          PIC X(60).
*
 FD  CARDFILE LABEL RECORD OMITTED
              DATA  RECORD IS CARD.
01   CARD.
     02 VENDOR-IDENT         PIC 9(8).
     02 VENDOR-DATA          PIC X(60).
     02 FILLER               PIC X(12).
FD   PRINTFILE LABEL RECORDS OMITTED
              DATA RECORD IS PRINT-RECORD.
01   PRINT-RECORD           PIC X(132).
*
WORKING-STORAGE SECTION.
01   END-OF-DATA-INDICATOR  PIC 9 VALUE ZERO.
     88 INPUT-ENDED VALUE 1.
/
PROCEDURE DIVISION.
MAIN-ROUTINE.
     OPEN INPUT CARDFILE
          OUTPUT DISKFILE, PRINTFILE.
     PERFORM READ-CARD.
     PERFORM FILE-CREATE
        UNTIL INPUT-ENDED.
     CLOSE CARDFILE DISKFILE
     STOP RUN.
*
 READ-CARD.
     READ CARDFILE RECORD
          AT END MOVE 1 TO END-OF-DATA-INDICATOR.
*
 FILE-CREATE.
     MOVE VENDOR-IDENT TO VENDOR-NUMBER
     MOVE VENDOR-DATA OF CARD TO VENDOR-DATA OF DISK-RECORD
     WRITE DISK-RECORD
          INVALID KEY  PERFORM ERROR-CASE.
     PERFORM READ-CARD.
*
 ERROR-CASE.
     MOVE ' INVALID KEY CONDITION FOR THIS RECORD' TO PRINT-RECORD
     WRITE PRINT-RECORD AFTER ADVANCING 1 LINE
     WRITE PRINT-RECORD FROM CARD AFTER ADVANCING 1 LINE.
```

is true whenever the record key of the record about to be written is not greater than the key of the preceding record in the file. If the INVALID KEY condition is true, we execute the imperative statement that follows—in this case PERFORM ERROR-CASE. Reviewing ERROR-CASE in Exhibit 17-2 we observe that we print an error message and list the error record. Using the sample input data presented earlier we would receive one error message and the fifth record would be printed, since it is the one record out of sequence.

Creation of an indexed file is a complex task; yet the language is very high level with respect to this task. The programmer need write very few instructions to invoke the procedures necessary for the task. In review, these instructions involve a few clauses in the SELECT statement, provision for a record key in the record description of the file, and moving data to the output record in the PROCEDURE DIVISION. In the following section we study these specialized instructions in a more thorough and comprehensive framework.

REVIEW

1 An indexed file essentially is a [sequential / direct] file.

sequential

2 In the ENVIRONMENT DIVISION, after the file is described as being SEQUENTIAL and INDEXED, the basis on which the file is sorted is identified by the COBOL reserved words _____.

RECORD KEY

3 The current ANSI COBOL standard specifies that RECORD KEY be alphanumeric and that it [must / need not] be a field in the file record.

must

4 The fact that one or more records to be written in an indexed file are not in the appropriate sequence is detected and identified by using the _____ option in conjunction with the WRITE statement.

INVALID KEY

COBOL LANGUAGE INSTRUCTIONS
FOR INDEXED FILES

Indexed files are in very wide use. Even though the early standard version of COBOL had no provision for them, the use of such files increased substantially in the early 1970s. As a consequence, each manufacturer developed his own program instructions and procedures. The current version of ANSI COBOL does contain language formats for indexed files, and we present these here. It should be noted that many programs were written in the prestandard era, and it will be natural to find continued adherence to manufacturer-dependent versions for some years to come. Fortunately, the current variations among manufacturers and the standard are not great, and the reader of this text should need only minimal changes to adopt the standard to a local version, if it is necessary to do so.

There are two divisions that involve special instructions—the ENVIRONMENT and the PROCEDURE divisions.

ENVIRONMENT DIVISION

In the ENVIRONMENT DIVISION we encounter some new options based on the following format:

```
SELECT file-name ASSIGN to implementor-name
   ; ORGANIZATION IS INDEXED

   ┌                           ┌ SEQUENTIAL ┐ ┐
   │ ; ACCESS MODE IS          │ RANDOM     │ │
   └                           └ DYNAMIC    ┘ ┘

   ; RECORD KEY IS data-name-1
   [ALTERNATE RECORD KEY IS data-name-2 [WITH DUPLICATES]]
```

The ORGANIZATION statement specifies that this will be an indexed file and will ultimately invoke the program routines which will create or use the index. COBOL is a very high-level language in this option. Creation and use of the index is a complex procedure, yet the programmer need only write one statement.

The ACCESS MODE clause specifies the way records in the file will be accessed. ACCESS MODE IS SEQUENTIAL specifies that records will be accessed in ascending order of the record key. Omission of the ACCESS clause defaults to the SEQUENTIAL option. Thus, up to now our omission of this clause from programming considerations in this book has implied the sequential access mode. The RANDOM option specifies that the order in which records are accessed will be controlled by the programmer. This control is accomplished by moving the value of the key of the desired record into the RECORD KEY field and then issuing an input-output command (READ, WRITE, REWRITE, DELETE).

The DYNAMIC option allows the programmer to change at will from sequential access to random access using appropriate forms of input-output statements. This option is not implemented in some compilers. In its absence, the file for a given program must be declared to be either in SEQUENTIAL or in RANDOM access mode, but not in both modes in the same program.

We repeat here a point made in the previous section on creating an indexed file. When the file is first being created, it *must* be in sequential access mode. In subsequent uses it may be in any of the three options, SEQUENTIAL, RANDOM, or DYNAMIC.

RECORD KEY references a data-name which must be a field within the record description of the file. In case of multiple records a field from any record description may be given. RECORD KEY specifies the field on the basis of which the file is sorted. The ALTERNATE RECORD option specifies a record key that is an alternate record key for the file. When alternate keys are used, we can access records either on the basis of the *prime* key specified in the RECORD KEY clause or on the basis of another ALTERNATE RECORD KEY. The file of course is always sorted on the basis of the prime record key. The DUPLICATES phrase specifies that the value of the associated alternate record key may be duplicated within any of the records in the file. In the absence of this phrase the presence of duplicate key values is an error condition. Notice that duplicate key values are permitted for alternate keys. Each record must have a unique prime key. An example of alternate key values that are duplicates may be the ZIP code in a record where the ZIP code was specified as an alternate record key. Such a key allows the accessing of a record with a specified ZIP code—with recognition that the record so accessed will not be unique with respect to this (alternate) key value.

REVIEW

1   In the SELECT statement in the ENVIRONMENT DIVISION, the fact that a file is to be set up as an indexed file is specified in the _____ statement.

ORGANIZATION

2   A file organized as an indexed file [can / cannot] be accessed in a sequential manner.

can

3   Omission of the ACCESS clause in the SELECT statement for an indexed file results in the file having to be accessed by the [sequential / random] mode.

sequential

4   The ACCESS MODE option which allows the programmer to change at will from sequential access to random access is called the _____ mode.

DYNAMIC

5   When the ALTERNATE RECORD KEY is used to access a record in a file, the file has to be sorted on the basis of the [prime / alternate] key.

prime

6   The ALTERNATE KEY associated with a record [must / need not] be a unique key value in the file.

need not

PROCEDURE DIVISION

An indexed file can be opened as INPUT, OUTPUT, or I-O (input-output). Table 17-1 summarizes the permissible input-output statements for each of these options, depending on the access mode specified.

Reading records from an indexed file is accomplished using one of two formats:

Format 1

```
READ file-name [NEXT] RECORD [INTO identifier]
      [; AT END imperative-statement]
```

Format 2

```
READ file-name RECORD   [INTO identifier]
   [; KEY IS data-name]
   [; INVALID KEY imperative-statement]
```

The first format must be used if the SEQUENTIAL access mode has been specified either explicitly or implicitly (by default). The NEXT phrase must be specified when a file is declared to be in the DYNAMIC access mode and records are to be retrieved sequentially. Execution of READ . . . NEXT RECORD retrieves from the file the next record whose record key is higher than the one accessed previously. From a logical standpoint, READ . . . NEXT operates identically to READ in a sequential magnetic tape file. We use the qualification "from a logical standpoint," because in an indexed file the physical and logical order may not be in direct correspondence. This happens when an indexed file has new records added to it. Instead of "squeezing" them in between existing records, they are put in a physically separate location (overflow) and connected by address pointers to the records that logically precede and follow them.

The AT END clause has the same meaning as in a sequential file.

Format 2 is used for files in RANDOM access mode; it is also used when records are to be retrieved randomly from a file in DYNAMIC access mode. The KEY clause references the data-name specified as a key either in the RECORD KEY or the ALTERNATE RECORD KEY clauses. If the KEY clause is omitted in the Format 2 READ statement, the prime key (RECORD KEY) of the file is assumed by default. The INVALID KEY condition holds when no record can be located whose record key matches the

TABLE 17-1   PERMISSIBLE INPUT-OUTPUT STATEMENTS

FILE ACCESS MODE	STATEMENT	OPEN MODE		
		INPUT	OUTPUT	I-O
Sequential	READ	X		X
	WRITE		X	
	REWRITE			X
	START	X		X
	DELETE			X
Random	READ	X		X
	WRITE		X	X
	REWRITE			X
	START			
	DELETE			X
Dynamic	READ	X		X
	WRITE		X	X
	REWRITE			X
	START	X		X
	DELETE			X

value of the data-name specified or implied by the KEY IS clause. For instance, we may have:

MOVE 123456789 TO SOC-SEC-NO.
READ STUDENT-MASTER RECORD
    KEY IS SOC-SEC-NO
    INVALID KEY PERFORM ERROR-READ.

In the above example, ERROR-READ will be executed if no record in the file has a SOC-SEC-NO key equal to 123456789.

Records are recorded in the file by use of the WRITE statement:

<u>WRITE</u> record-name [<u>FROM</u> identifier] [; <u>INVALID</u> KEY imperative-statement]

When a file is being created, WRITE is used as illustrated in the previous section. After a file has been created, WRITE is used to add new records to the file. As always, the proper value is moved to the prime record key, and the execution of WRITE causes the new record to be inserted in the correct logical position within the file. The INVALID KEY condition is true under the following circumstances: (1) The file has been opened as OUTPUT, and the value of the prime record key is not greater than the value of the prime record key of the previous record; (2) the file has been opened as I-O, and the value of the prime record key is equal to the value of the prime record key of a record already existing in the file; (3) an attempt is being made to write more records than can be accommodated by the available disk storage.

The INVALID KEY clause appears as an option in the general format. From the viewpoint of this text it is required. It is *not* required whenever the programmer provides for the same effect as the INVALID KEY clause by use of the USE verb. However, a discussion of the USE verb is beyond the scope of this book, since it is employed in more advanced applications than the ones reasonable for student environments. Therefore WRITE should include the INVALID KEY clause.

In updating tasks REWRITE is used to replace a record existing in the file.

<u>REWRITE</u> record-name [<u>FROM</u> identifier] [; <u>INVALID</u> KEY imperative-statement]

At the time of execution of REWRITE the file must be open in the I-O mode. The record being replaced is the one whose key matches the value of the prime record key. The INVALID KEY holds when the value of the record key in the record to be replaced does not match the value of the record key of the last record read, or the value of the record key does not equal the record key of any record existing in the file.

The DELETE statement logically removes a record from an indexed file.

DELETE file-name RECORD [; INVALID KEY imperative-statement]

A DELETE command can only be executed if the file has been opened in I-O mode. If the file was declared to be in a SEQUENTIAL access mode, the INVALID KEY must *not* be specified; a DELETE statement must have been preceded by a successful READ statement, which precludes the possibility of any INVALID KEY condition—the AT END associated with READ serves in lieu of INVALID KEY in such a case.

If the file has been declared to be in RANDOM or DYNAMIC access mode, INVALID KEY is true when the file does not contain a record whose prime record key value matches the value of the record key. Thus the programmer is responsible for moving the key value of the record to be deleted to RECORD KEY.

The START verb allows sequential retrieval of records from a point other than the beginning of the file. Thus it is possible to retrieve records sequentially starting with some record in the "middle" of the file.

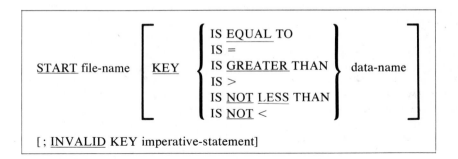

The file must be in SEQUENTIAL or DYNAMIC access mode and must be open in the INPUT or I-O mode at the time START is executed. The KEY phrase may be omitted, in which case EQUAL is implied. In essence, the START statement means to position the file to that record whose record key satisfies the explicit or implicit KEY condition. For example, if CUSTOMER-NAME is a record key and we want to retrieve the records of customers whose names begin with M or higher, we can write:

MOVE 'M' TO CUSTOMER-NAME
START CUSTOMER-FILE
    KEY IS NOT LESS THAN CUSTOMER-NAME
    INVALID KEY PERFORM ERROR-START.

MOVE in the above program segment is an alphanumeric move resulting in CUSTOMER-NAME containing the letter M and blanks to the right of M. The KEY IS

NOT LESS condition specifies that we want to position the file to the first record whose key is not less than the letter M; in other words, it will be the first name that begins with the letter M. A READ statement then retrieves that record, and subsequent READ statement execution retrieves the following records sequentially.

The data-name in the KEY phrase can be either a record key (specified as RECORD KEY, or ALTERNATE RECORD KEY), or it may be a data item subordinate to a record key, provided that the data item is the first (leftmost) field in the record key. In other words we can specify the "first part" of a record key.

The INVALID condition is true if the KEY condition cannot be met. For example, consider the following program segment:

```
MOVE 'MICHNER' TO CUSTOMER-NAME.
START CUSTOMER-FILE
      KEY IS EQUAL TO CUSTOMER-NAME
      INVALID KEY PERFORM ERROR-START.
```

ERROR-START will be executed if there is no customer in the file whose record key is equal to 'MICHNER'.

REVIEW

1   In the PROCEDURE DIVISION, reading records from an indexed file is accomplished by using the _____ verb.

> READ

2   Whenever records in an indexed file are to be retrieved randomly, the _____ clause indicates the data-name to be used to identify each record.

> KEY

3   If the KEY clause is omitted in conjunction with random retrieval of records, the basis for identifying each record is the [RECORD KEY / ALTERNATE RECORD KEY].

> RECORD KEY

4   In the PROCEDURE DIVISION, records are added to an indexed file by using the _____ verb.

> WRITE

5   Execution of a WRITE statement to add a record to an indexed file results in the record being added [at the end of the file / in the correct logical position within the file].

> *in the correct logical position within the file*

6   The verb that is used to replace a record held in an indexed file is _____.

> REWRITE

7   In order for a REWRITE instruction to be executed, the file must be open in _____ mode.

> I-O

8 The verb used to remove a record from an indexed file is ⎯⎯⎯⎯⎯⎯.

DELETE

9 A DELETE command can only be executed if the file has been opened in ⎯⎯⎯ mode.

I-O

10 The verb which makes possible the sequential retrieval of records from a point other than the beginning of the file is ⎯⎯⎯⎯⎯⎯.

START

11 In conjunction with executing a START statement, the data-name used as the key [must / need not] have been previously specified as RECORD KEY or ALTERNATE RECORD KEY.

need not

AN EXAMPLE OF PROCESSING AN INDEXED FILE

We present an example which illustrates use of most of the language statements and options presented in the preceding section. The example involves processing the vendor file created by the example program in Exhibit 17-2. We now give the following record description to the file:

```
FD   DISKFILE LABEL RECORDS ARE STANDARD
              DATA RECORD IS DISK-RECORD.
01   DISK-RECORD.
     02 VENDOR-NUMBER      PIC X(8).
     02 VENDOR-NAME        PIC X(15).
     02 VENDOR-ADDRESS     PIC X(45).
```

Transaction records are submitted through a CARDFILE and have the following record description:

```
01   CARD.
     02 TRANS-CODE                                  PIC 9.
         88  CHANGE-ADDRESS                         VALUE 1.
         88  ADD-VENDOR                             VALUE 2.
         88  DELETE-VENDOR                          VALUE 3.
         88  ERROR-CODE VALUES ARE ZERO, 4 THRU 9.
     02 VENDOR-IDENT                                PIC 9(8).
     02 VENDOR-NAME                                 PIC X(15).
     02 VENDOR-ADDRESS                              PIC X(45).
     02 FILLER                                      PIC X(11).
```

It is apparent from the self-documenting nature of the above record description that we are interested in changing the address of a vendor, and adding or deleting vendors.

Exhibit 17-3 presents the complete program. Notice in the ENVIRONMENT DIVI-

EXHIBIT 17-3 SAMPLE PROGRAM TO ILLUSTRATE PROCESSING OF AN INDEXED FILE

```
    IDENTIFICATION DIVISION.
    PROGRAM-ID. UPDATEISAM.
    ENVIRONMENT DIVISION.
    CONFIGURATION SECTION.
    SOURCE-COMPUTER. ABC-480.
    OBJECT-COMPUTER. ABC-480.
    INPUT-OUTPUT SECTION.
    FILE-CONTROL.
        SELECT DISKFILE ASSIGN TO MASS-STORAGE-ISAMFILE
                            ORGANIZATION IS INDEXED
                            ACCESS MODE IS DYNAMIC
                            RECORD KEY IS VENDOR-NUMBER.
*
        SELECT CARDFILE ASSIGN TO CARD-READER.
        SELECT PRINTFILE ASSIGN TO PRINTER.
    DATA DIVISION.
    FILE SECTION.
    FD  DISKFILE LABEL RECORDS ARE STANDARD
                    DATA RECORD IS DISK-RECORD.
    01  DISK-RECORD.
        02 VENDOR-NUMBER        PIC X(8).
        02 VENDOR-NAME          PIC X(15).
        02 VENDOR-ADDRESS       PIC X(45).
    FD  CARDFILE LABEL RECORDS ARE OMITTED
                    DATA RECORD IS CARD.
    01  CARD.
        02 TRANS-CODE           PIC 9.
            88 CHANGE-ADDRESS    VALUE 1.
            88 ADD-VENDOR        VALUE 2.
            88 DELETE-VENDOR     VALUE 3.
            88 ERROR-CODE        VALUES ARE ZERO, 4 THRU 9.
        02 VENDOR-IDENT         PIC 9(8).
        02 VENDOR-NAME          PIC X(15).
        02 VENDOR-ADDRESS       PIC X(45).
        02 FILLER               PIC X(11).
    FD  PRINTFILE LABEL RECORD OMITTED
                    DATA RECORD PRINTLINE.
    01  PRINTLINE               PIC X(132).
*
    WORKING-STORAGE SECTION.
    01  END-OF-DATA-INDICATOR   PIC 9 VALUE ZERO.
        88 INPUT-ENDED VALUE 1.

    PROCEDURE DIVISION.
    MAIN-ROUTINE.
*
*   THIS PORTION ILLUSTRATES RANDOM UPDATING OF INDEXED FILE
*
        OPEN INPUT  CARDFILE
             OUTPUT PRINTFILE
             I-O    DISKFILE.
        MOVE ' LISTING FROM UPDATE PORTION' TO PRINTLINE
        WRITE PRINTLINE AFTER ADVANCING PAGE.
        PERFORM READ-CARD.
        PERFORM UPDATE
            UNTIL INPUT-ENDED.
        CLOSE DISKFILE.
*
*   THIS PORTION ILLUSTRATES SEQUENTIAL RETRIEVAL.
*
        MOVE ZERO TO END-OF-DATA-INDICATOR.
        MOVE ' LISTING FROM SEQUENTIAL RETRIEVAL' TO PRINTLINE
        WRITE PRINTLINE AFTER ADVANCING 5 LINES.
        OPEN INPUT DISKFILE
        PERFORM READ-DISK.
        PERFORM LISTING
            UNTIL INPUT-ENDED.
        CLOSE DISKFILE.
*
*   THIS PORTION ILLUSTRATES USE OF THE START VERB.
*
        MOVE ZERO TO END-OF-DATA-INDICATOR
        MOVE 35290001 TO VENDOR-NUMBER
        OPEN INPUT DISKFILE
        START DISKFILE KEY IS GREATER THAN VENDOR-NUMBER
              INVALID KEY MOVE 1 TO END-OF-DATA-INDICATOR.
        MOVE   LISTING FROM USE OF START VERB' TO PRINTLINE
        WRITE PRINTLINE AFTER ADVANCING 5 LINES
        PERFORM READ-DISK
        PERFORM LISTING
            UNTIL INPUT-ENDED
        CLOSE DISKFILE.
*
        STOP RUN.
```

EXHIBIT 17-3 SAMPLE PROGRAM TO ILLUSTRATE PROCESSING OF AN INDEXED FILE *(Continued)*.

```
 READ-CARD.
     READ CARDFILE RECORD
            AT END MOVE 1 TO END-OF-DATA-INDICATOR.
*
 UPDATE.
     MOVE VENDOR-IDENT OF CARD TO VENDOR-NUMBER.
     IF CHANGE-ADDRESS
        PERFORM ADDRESS-1 THRU ADDRESS-3
     ELSE
        IF ADD-VENDOR
           PERFORM ADDITION-1 THRU ADDITION-3
        ELSE
           IF DELETE-VENDOR
              PERFORM DELETION-1 THRU DELETION-3
           ELSE
              PERFORM ERROR-CARD.
     PERFORM READ-CARD.
*
 ADDRESS-1.
     READ DISKFILE RECORD
            INVALID KEY GO TO ADDRESS-2-0.
     MOVE VENDOR-ADDRESS OF CARD TO VENDOR-ADDRESS OF DISK-RECORD.
     REWRITE DISK-RECORD
              INVALID KEY GO TO ADDRESS-2-1.
     GO TO ADDRESS-3.
 ADDRESS-2-0.
     MOVE ' CANNOT FIND DISK RECORD FOR THIS CARD ' TO PRINTLINE
     WRITE PRINTLINE AFTER ADVANCING 1 LINE.
     WRITE PRINTLINE FROM CARD AFTER ADVANCING 1 LINE.
     GO TO ADDRESS-3.
 ADDRESS-2-1.
     MOVE ' CANNOT REWRITE THIS RECORD' TO PRINTLINE
     WRITE PRINTLINE AFTER ADVANCING 1 LINE.
     WRITE PRINTLINE FROM DISK-RECORD AFTER ADVANCING 1 LINE.
     GO TO ADDRESS-3.
 ADDRESS-3.
     EXIT.
*
 ADDITION-1.
     MOVE VENDOR-NAME    OF CARD TO VENDOR-NAME   OF DISK-RECORD
     MOVE VENDOR-ADDRESS OF CARD TO VENDOR-ADDRESS OF DISK-RECORD
     WRITE DISK-RECORD
            INVALID KEY GO TO ADDITION-2.
     GO TO ADDITION-3.
 ADDITION-2.
     MOVE ' CANNOT CREATE A RECORD FROM THIS CARD' TO PRINTLINE
     WRITE PRINTLINE AFTER ADVANCING 1 LINE
     WRITE PRINTLINE FROM CARD AFTER ADVANCING 1 LINE.
     GO TO ADDITION-3.
 ADDITION-3.
     EXIT.
*
 DELETION-1.
     DELETE DISK-RECORD
            INVALID KEY GO TO DELETION-2.
     GO TO DELETION-3.
 DELETION-2.
     MOVE ' CANNOT DELETE RECORD SPECIFIED BY THIS CARD'
          TO PRINTLINE
     WRITE PRINTLINE AFTER ADVANCING 1 LINE
     WRITE PRINTLINE FROM CARD AFTER ADVANCING 1 LINE
     GO TO DELETION-3.
 DELETION-3.
     EXIT.
*
 ERROR-CARD.
     MOVE ' WRONG TRANSACTION CODE IN CARD' TO PRINTLINE
     WRITE PRINTLINE AFTER ADVANCING 1 LINE
     WRITE PRINTLINE FROM CARD AFTER ADVANCING 1 LINE.
*
 READ-DISK.
     READ DISKFILE NEXT RECORD
            AT END MOVE 1 TO END-OF-DATA-INDICATOR.
*
 LISTING.
     WRITE PRINTLINE FROM DISK-RECORD AFTER ADVANCING 1 LINE.
     PERFORM READ-DISK.
```

SION that DISKFILE is in DYNAMIC access mode and that VENDOR-NUMBER is the record key. The PROCEDURE DIVISION is self-documenting and consists of three control portions which illustrate random updating, sequential retrieval, and use of the START verb, respectively. The first portion illustrates random access and updating. The following sample input records were used.

```
211111111ACME-01     ADDED RECORD
135120001            NEW ADDRESS
497654310            ERROR CODE TEST = 4
349678912            DELETE
160000000            NEW ADDRESS
349678912            DELETE PREVIOUSLY DELETED
169743210            CHANGE NONEXISTING
```

We have written comments instead of data to simplify debugging. For instance, the first record has a code of 2 (column 1), which means to add a new vendor whose number is 11111111. Instead of address we have written the comment ADDED RECORD.

Studying Exhibit 17-3, we can see that the UPDATE paragraph analyzes the transaction code, and then we execute the ADDRESS, ADDITION, DELETION, or ERROR-CARD paragraph. Each of these paragraphs illustrates, respectively: the replacing of a record (REWRITE), the addition of a record (WRITE), the deletion of a record (DELETE), and the handling of INVALID KEY conditions.

In the second portion of the MAIN-ROUTINE procedure we illustrate sequential retrieval. When OPEN INPUT DISKFILE is executed, the open instruction causes the file to be positioned at the beginning, so that when the first READ DISKFILE NEXT RECORD is executed, the first record is retrieved.

The third portion of the MAIN-ROUTINE illustrates use of the START verb:

```
MOVE 35290001 TO VENDOR-NUMBER.
START DISKFILE KEY IS GREATER THAN VENDOR-NUMBER
    INVALID KEY MOVE 1 TO END-OF-DATA-INDICATOR.
```

In this illustration we want to retrieve sequentially all records whose key is greater than 35290001. The record whose key equals 35290001 will not be retrieved, since the GREATER THAN option is used.

Exhibit 17-4 shows the output resulting from executing the program in Exhibit 17-3. The reader will find it useful to run the programs in Exhibits 17-2 and 17-3 and obtain the results shown in Exhibit 17-4. Since compilers differ, some changes to "localize" the programs may be necessary, and the task may prove worth the effort. Of course, the small volume of data involved allows easy desk-checking of the program.

RELATIVE FILE ORGANIZATION

A relative file consists of records identified by a key that contains information about the location of a record in the file. In an indexed file the identifier key has to be looked up in the index in order to determine the (approximate) location of a record in

EXHIBIT 17-4   SAMPLE OUTPUT FROM THE PROGRAM IN EXHIBIT 17-3

```
LISTING FROM UPDATE PORTION
WRONG TRANSACTION CODE IN CARD
497654310              ERROR CODE TEST = 4
 CANNOT DELETE RECORD SPECIFIED BY THIS CARD
349678912              DELETE PREVIOUSLY DELETED
 CANNOT FIND DISK RECORD FOR THIS CARD
169743210              CHANGE NON-EXISTING



LISTING FROM SEQUENTIAL RETRIEVAL
11111111ACME-01        ADDED RECORD
12345678ACME-10
22345678ACME-20
35120001ACME-30        NEW ADDRESS
37654310ACME-40
45678912ACME-60
54371203ACME-80
58120000ACME-90
60000000ACME-92        NEW ADDRESS
70000000ACME-93
80000000ACME-94
99999999ACME-99



LISTING FROM USE OF START VERB
37654310ACME-40
45678912ACME-60
54371203ACME-80
58120000ACME-90
60000000ACME-92        NEW ADDRESS
70000000ACME-93
80000000ACME-94
99999999ACME-99
```

the file. In contrast, record keys in a relative file contain information about the locations of records. At first it seems that doing away with the index is an appealing feature. In principle, relative files are the best organization method for direct access files. In practice, there are complicating factors that make relative file organization difficult to implement for the general case. Thus indexed files are widely used, while relative files are in rare use.

From the standpoint of programming requirements, relative files have a great deal of similarity to indexed files. Most of the COBOL language instructions discussed earlier in connection with indexed files are directly applicable to relative files as well. Still, there are differences, especially at the conceptual level.

As always, each record contains a unique identifier or key. This key may be in a form that references a location directly, or it may have to be manipulated by the programmer to transform the value of the identifier key to a file record location. Suppose that 5000 inventory parts are identified by a four-digit number ranging from 0001 to 5000. We can create a relative file such that part number 0001 occupies the first record space, part number 0002 occupies the second space, and so on. On the other hand, suppose that each part is identified by an eight-digit code based on a classification scheme that takes account of different product classes and product characteristics. An eight-digit code can range from 00000001 to 99999999. A relative file of over 99 million spaces is impractical if we only have 5000 parts. Still we can create a relative file by taking the part code and transforming it to one of 5000 possible record file spaces.

There are several such *key-to-address transformation* methods, but one is in wide use, the *division remainder* method. In general, these methods are concerned with converting a code (numeric, alphabetic, or alphanumeric) to a location address through a *randomizing* routine. Given a code value, the generated address has, in theory, equal chance of being any one of the possible file record addresses. One of the difficulties inherent in the process is that more than one code value might transform to the same address, creating a condition known as a *synonym*. The incidence of synonyms is reduced by allowing for vacant spaces in the file. Thus we might allocate 6000 record spaces for a 5000-record file, thereby substantially reducing the incidence of synonyms. The ratio of record spaces used to total spaces is called the packing factor, and an 0.80 packing factor is adequate in most cases. Of course, no matter what the packing factor, the probability of synonyms occurring is greater than zero. Two common methods are in use for handling synonyms. During the creation of the file, when a synonym occurs, we scan the following record locations until we find the first vacant location and store the record there (thereby setting the stage for possible "chain reactions"). When retrieving a record, we retrieve the record in the original location; if it is not the one we want, we keep searching in succeeding locations. Recall that each record is uniquely identified by a code, so that we can identify a record apart from its location. Sometimes a file is structured so that each record contains a field that points to the location of the next synonym, thereby reducing the number of searches necessary. A second method of handling synonyms is to allocate a separate *overflow* space to contain records which are synonyms. When a record cannot go to its address because it is already occupied, it is placed in the overflow. The overflow may be searched serially, or there may be a pointer field in the record of original location identifying the location of the synonym. All of these matters were considered in greater detail in Chapter 16.

Matters such as key-to-address transformations and handling of synonyms are not acknowledged by the language. COBOL assumes that the programmer handles these. The language provides only the basic mechanism by which relative files can be created and processed.

The relevant ENVIRONMENT DIVISION format for relative files is as follows:

```
SELECT file-name ASSIGN TO implementor-name
  ; ORGANIZATION IS RELATIVE

[                    { SEQUENTIAL    [, RELATIVE KEY IS data-name] }   ]
[ ; ACCESS MODE IS   { RANDOM                                      }   ]
[                    { DYNAMIC         , RELATIVE KEY IS data-name  }   ]
```

ORGANIZATION IS RELATIVE has the obvious meaning. The ACCESS MODE clause has the same meaning as discussed for indexed files. Notice, however, RELATIVE KEY as contrasted to RECORD KEY. The data-name specified as RELATIVE KEY *must* be a WORKING-STORAGE unsigned integer item. Its function is to contain the location address for the record about to be accessed, or the location of the record that was just accessed.

The reader should be clear on the role of RELATIVE KEY, which is different from the RECORD KEY of indexed files. RECORD KEY is part of the file record. RELATIVE KEY is an item apart from the record. Given a record, the value of its identifier field is taken by the programmer and transformed through a key-to-address routine to give a location address stored in the RELATIVE KEY field, as portrayed below.

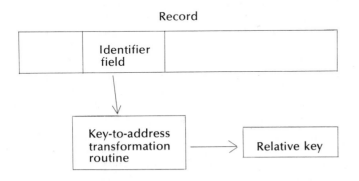

In the next section we explain one method of generating relative key values.

A relative file may be created either sequentially or randomly. If it is to be created sequentially, we omit the RELATIVE KEY clause—an option shown in the ENVIRON-MENT DIVISION format above. In the format, observe that the RELATIVE KEY clause is required if the access mode is RANDOM or DYNAMIC. To create the file sequentially we can write:

SELECT file-name ASSIGN TO device
    ORGANIZATION IS RELATIVE
    ACCESS MODE IS SEQUENTIAL.

Then, in the PROCEDURE DIVISION we open the file as OUTPUT and we WRITE record-name. The first execution of WRITE records in the first record location, the second execution records in the second location, and so on. If we want to retrieve the record in the one-hundredth location on a subsequent occasion, we will have to put the value 100 in RELATIVE KEY and then read.

The WRITE verb has the same format as presented for indexed files. The INVALID KEY clause applies when we try to write more records than can be accommodated in the allocated space, or when we try to write on a space already written on (synonym). Of course, file space is allocated using JCL statements.

A relative file may also be created randomly, in which case we use ACCESS MODE IS RANDOM RELATIVE KEY IS. . . . In a later section we present an example illustrating the process.

Records are read from a relative file using one of two formats:

Format 1

```
 READ file-name [ NEXT] RECORD [ INTO identifier]
        [ ; AT END imperative-statement]
```

Format 2

```
READ file-name RECORD [ INTO identifier]
     [ , INVALID KEY imperative statement]
```

Format 1 must be used if records are retrieved in sequential mode. NEXT must be used if DYNAMIC access mode is specified and records are retrieved sequentially.

Format 2 is used when the access mode is RANDOM, or when the access mode is DYNAMIC and records are retrieved in random order. The INVALID KEY condition occurs when RELATIVE KEY contains an address pointing to a record that was previously deleted (see DELETE verb below), or to an address beyond the boundaries of the file.

A record may be updated using REWRITE, which has the same format as for indexed files. This verb functions in the same way as discussed for indexed files, with the exception that RELATIVE KEY contains the address of the record to be replaced.

Records may be deleted from the file using DELETE, just as is done with sequential files.

Sequential retrieval of records may be accomplished using the SEQUENTIAL or DYNAMIC access mode, the issuance of an OPEN INPUT instruction, and repetitive execution of READ or READ NEXT. Whenever sequential retrieval is desired from a point other than the beginning of a file, then the START command can be used. The same format applies as for indexed files, except that the starting record location is placed in the RELATIVE KEY field.

REVIEW

1 A key-to-address transformation method is concerned with converting a key code to a _____.

location address

2 When two different code values are converted to the same location address by the use of a randomizing routine, it is said that a _____ has been produced.

synonym

3 The ratio of number of record spaces used to the total number of record spaces available for a record file is called the _____ factor.

packing

4 When a synonym has occurred, two common solutions to assigning a storage location are to search the following record locations for the first vacant location and to allocate a separate _____ space to contain all records which are synonyms.

overflow

5 The location address determined by a key-to-address routine is stored in the _____ field.

RELATIVE KEY

6 For an indexed file the RECORD KEY [is / is not] part of the original file record. For a relative file the RELATIVE KEY [is / is not] part of the original file record.

is; is not

7 In the SELECT statement of the ENVIRONMENT DIVISION, the RELATIVE KEY clause is not needed and is omitted if the file is to be created [sequentially / randomly].

sequentially

8 One particular adverse consequence associated with creating a relative file sequentially is the absence of any vacant _____ locations between the stored file records.

storage

9 Records stored sequentially in a relative file [can / cannot] be accessed randomly.

can

10 Records stored randomly in a relative field [can / cannot] be accessed sequentially.

can

AN EXAMPLE OF CREATING A RELATIVE FILE

A punched card file is to be transferred to disk, organized as a relative file. For simplicity, we assume that there will be no more than 50 records. Each card contains an ITEM-NUMBER in columns 1–5 and an ITEM-NAME in columns 6–25. Disk records will have identical format.

We shall use ITEM-NUMBER as the identifier for each record and we shall compute disk addresses using this identifier and the prime number 47. We assume that our operating system takes care of cylinder, track, and record references, and indeed this is typically the case. Therefore, by using the division remainder technique we convert each ITEM-NUMBER value to a (relative) disk address in the range 1–50.

Exhibit 17-5 presents a program written to create such a relative file. In the MAIN-ROUTINE we PERFORM ZERO-DISK as many times as the value of MAX-NO-OF-

LOCATIONS which we have set to 50 in the DATA DIVISION. The function of ZERO-DISK is to set to zero the ITEM-NUMBER value of each *possible* disk record. We do this in order to have a means of identifying which disk spaces are vacant. Along these lines, note the condition name VACANT-SPACE under ITEM-NUMBER of the DISK-RECORD.

The next main task in the MAIN-ROUTINE is repeated execution of READ-PROCESS-CARD, whose function can be outlined as follows. We read each card record and compute its corresponding address (LOCATION-ADDRESS) in the RANDOMIZE-READ paragraph. We then access the contents of the record specified by LOCATION-ADDRESS. If that space is vacant, we write a record there; if not vacant, we proceed to search for a vacant space in consecutive locations. In order to prevent infinite looping if all 50 locations of the file become occupied, we have used a LOOP-FLAG and a STARTING-ADDRESS. Let us explain by use of an example: Suppose that a record

EXHIBIT 17-5   A COBOL PROGRAM TO CREATE A RELATIVE FILE

```
        IDENTIFICATION DIVISION.
       *PROGRAM-ID. RELATIVE-FILE.
       *
        ENVIRONMENT DIVISION.
        CONFIGURATION SECTION.
        SOURCE-COMPUTER.
        OBJECT-COMPUTER.
        INPUT-OUTPUT SECTION.
        FILE-CONTROL.
            SELECT DISK-FILE        ASSIGN TO DISK-DEVICE
                                    ORGANIZATION IS RELATIVE
                                    ACCESS MODE IS RANDOM
                                    RELATIVE KEY IS LOCATION-ADDRESS
       *
            SELECT CARD-FILE        ASSIGN TO CARD-READER.
            SELECT PRINT-FILE       ASSIGN TO PRINTER.
       *
       *
        DATA DIVISION.
        FILE SECTION.
        FD  DISK-FILE        LABEL RECORDS OMITTED
                             DATA RECORD IS DISK-RECORD
                             RECORD CONTAINS 25 CHARACTERS.
        01  DISK-RECORD.
            02  ITEM-NUMBER     PIC 9(5).
                88 VACANT-SPACE VALUE ZEROS.
            02  ITEM-NAME       PIC X(20).
       *
        FD  CARD-FILE        LABEL RECORDS OMITTED
                             DATA RECORD IS CARD-RECORD.
        01  CARD-RECORD.
            02  ITEM-NUMBER     PIC 9(5).
            02  ITEM-NAME       PIC X(20).
            02  FILLER          PIC X(55).
       *
        FD  PRINT-FILE       LABEL RECORDS OMITTED
                             DATA RECORD IS PRINT-RECORD.
        01  PRINT-RECORD     PIC X(132).
       *
       *
        WORKING-STORAGE SECTION.
        01  END-OF-DATA          PIC XXX.
        01  LOOP-FLAG            PIC 9.
        01  LOCATION-ADDRESS     PIC 999.
        01  STARTING-ADDRESS     PIC 999.
        01  PRIME-NUMBER         PIC 99 VALUE 47.
        01  WORKFIELD            PIC S99999 USAGE COMP.
        01  QUOTIENT             PIC S999   USAGE COMP.
        01  PRODUCT              PIC S99999 USAGE COMP.
        01  I                    PIC 999.
        01  ERROR-RECORD.
            02  FILLER           PIC X VALUE SPACE.
            02  ERROR-LOCATION   PIC ZZ999.
            02  FILLER           PIC XX VALUE SPACE.
            02  ERR-MESSAGE      PIC X(50).
        01  MAX-NO-OF-LOCATIONS  PIC 999 VALUE 50.
```

converts to location 40. We set LOOP-FLAG to zero and STARTING-ADDRESS to 40. If location 40 is already occupied, we increment LOCATION-ADDRESS to 41 and check to determine if that space is vacant. If all locations between 40 and 50 are occupied, we should check location 1 as the next consecutive space after 50 (hence the instruction IF LOCATION-ADDRESS > MAX-NO-OF-LOCATIONS SUBTRACT MAX-NO-OF LOCA-TIONS FROM LOCATION-ADDRESS in the HANDLE-SYNONYMS paragraph). In the event that the entire file is full, our LOCATION-ADDRESS would eventually become equal to the STARTING-ADDRESS, indicating that we have come full circle. At that point we set LOOP-FLAG to 1 and we generate an error message and a program termination (see MOVE 'YES' TO END-OF-DATA in LOAD-RECORD paragraph).

The procedure illustrated here can be used to update a relative file as well as to create it. Exercise 4 at the end of the chapter provides an opportunity to create and update a relative file.

EXHIBIT 17-5   A COBOL PROGRAM TO CREATE A RELATIVE FILE *(Continued)*

```
PROCEDURE DIVISION.
MAIN-ROUTINE.
    MOVE 'NO' TO END-OF-DATA
    OPEN INPUT  CARD-FILE
    OPEN OUTPUT DISK-FILE
                PRINT-FILE.
*
    PERFORM ZERO-DISK
            VARYING I FROM 1 BY 1 UNTIL I >  MAX-NO-OF-LOCATIONS.
*
    CLOSE DISK-FILE.
*
    OPEN I-O DISK-FILE
*
    PERFORM READ-PROCESS-CARD
            UNTIL END-OF-DATA = 'YES'.
*
    CLOSE CARD-FILE
          PRINT-FILE
          DISK-FILE.
    STOP RUN.
*
*
ZERO-DISK.
    MOVE I TO LOCATION-ADDRESS
    MOVE ZERO TO ITEM-NUMBER OF DISK-RECORD
    WRITE DISK-RECORD
          INVALID KEY PERFORM CANT-ACCESS.
*
READ-PROCESS-CARD.
    READ CARD-FILE RECORD
         AT END MOVE 'YES' TO END-OF-DATA.
    IF END-OF-DATA = 'NO'
       PERFORM LOAD-RECORD.
*
LOAD-RECORD.
    PERFORM RANDOMIZE-READ
    IF VACANT-SPACE
       NEXT SENTENCE
    ELSE
       MOVE LOCATION-ADDRESS TO STARTING-ADDRESS
       MOVE ZERO TO LOOP-FLAG
       PERFORM HANDLE-SYNONYMS
               UNTIL VACANT-SPACE
                  OR LOOP-FLAG = 1.
*
    IF LOOP-FLAG = 1
       MOVE 'YES' TO END-OF-DATA
    ELSE
       MOVE CARD-RECORD TO DISK-RECORD
       WRITE DISK-RECORD
             INVALID KEY PERFORM CANT-ACCESS.
```

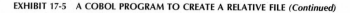

EXHIBIT 17-5   A COBOL PROGRAM TO CREATE A RELATIVE FILE *(Continued)*

```
*
 RANDOMIZE-READ.
     MOVE ITEM-NUMBER OF CARD-RECORD TO WORKFIELD
     DIVIDE PRIME-NUMBER INTO WORKFIELD GIVING QUOTIENT
     MULTIPLY QUOTIENT BY PRIME-NUMBER GIVING PRODUCT
     SUBTRACT PRODUCT FROM WORKFIELD GIVING LOCATION-ADDRESS.
*
* WE COULD ALSO WRITE
*     DIVIDE PRIME-NUMBER INTO WORKFIELD
*          REMAINDER LOCATION-ADDRESS
*
     MOVE ZERO TO LOOP-FLAG
     MOVE LOCATION-ADDRESS TO STARTING-ADDRESS
     READ DISK-FILE RECORD
          INVALID KEY PERFORM CANT-ACCESS.
*
 HANDLE-SYNONYMS.
     ADD 1 TO LOCATION-ADDRESS
     IF LOCATION-ADDRESS > MAX-NO-OF-LOCATIONS
        SUBTRACT MAX-NO-OF-LOCATIONS FROM LOCATION-ADDRESS.
*
     IF LOCATION-ADDRESS = STARTING-ADDRESS
        MOVE ITEM-NUMBER OF DISK-RECORD TO ERROR-LOCATION
        MOVE 'CANNOT LOCATE THIS RECORD' TO ERR-MESSAGE
        WRITE PRINT-RECORD FROM ERROR-RECORD AFTER 2 LINES
        MOVE 1 TO LOOP-FLAG
     ELSE
        READ DISK-FILE RECORD
             INVALID KEY PERFORM CANT-ACCESS.
*
 CANT-ACCESS.
     MOVE LOCATION-ADDRESS TO ERROR-LOCATION
     MOVE 'THIS RECORD LOCATION CAUSED INVALID KEY'
          TO ERR-MESSAGE
     WRITE PRINT-RECORD FROM ERROR-RECORD AFTER 2 LINES.
```

EXERCISES

1   In updating a sequential file, all records in the master file are read, but only those records for which there are transactions are updated. Therefore if in reading a master record it is determined that the record has no corresponding transactions, we will want to bypass that record. On the other hand, if transactions have been processed, we will want to rewrite the updated record in its place on the disk.

    Draw a flowchart of the programming logic that will accomplish this selective rewriting of master records.

2   Refer to Exercise 2 of Chapter 10 for the program description.

  a   Create the master file on disk, using input from punched cards. Use sequential file organization.

  b   Update the master file on a sequential basis.

3   Refer to Exercise 2 of Chapter 10 for the program description.

  a   Create the master file as an indexed file, using part-number as the RECORD KEY.

  b   Update the master file on a random basis, using part-number as the RECORD KEY.

4   A manufacturer of three product classes has a sales force consisting of 100 salespeople, each person assigned a unique salesperson-number of five digits.

Salespeople are paid on commission, receiving monthly commission benefits as well as an annual bonus based on monthly performance. It is desired to maintain commission data for each salesperson by product class and by month on a disk file.

a Create a relative file that will contain a record of the commission data for each salesperson in the following form. Salesperson-number will serve for the RELATIVE KEY.

FIELD	FIELD SIZE
Salesperson-number	5 digits
Salesperson-name	
Last name	15 characters
First name	10 characters
Middle initial	1 character
Commission totals by product class (3 classes) and by month (12 months).	Each total can be as large as 999,999.99. Note: There will be 36 totals.

The file is created by reading one card per salesperson containing salesperson-number and salesperson-name fields. After the randomizing technique has been employed to determine the disk location, all commission totals (36 fields) are set to zero. Then the record is written on the disk.

b Update this file, using sales transaction data punched on cards. Use salesperson-number as the RELATIVE KEY.

The transaction cards have the following layout:

CARD COLUMNS	FIELD
1–5	Salesperson-number
6	Commission code (based on product class)
	1 = 0.02 of sales
	2 = 0.03 of sales
	3 = 0.05 of sales
7–8	Month code (from 01 to 12)
9–14	Sales value in dollars and cents

Assume that the transaction cards are sorted by salesperson number. Therefore we need access the relevant master record only once for each set of cards corresponding to one salesperson. Of course we may have transactions for only *some* of the salespeople.

As each salesperson is processed, we want to print on the printer a report as follows:

CURRENT COMMISSION DATA			
		TOTALS	
PERSON NUMBER	NAME	THIS MONTH	YEAR-TO-DATE
12345	LAST FIRST M.	$ 870.35	$18,562.40
24966	LAST FIRST M.	1020.20	12,112.96
.	.	.	.
.	.	.	.
.	.	.	.
.	.	.	.
.	.	.	.

In other words, we want to accumulate the commissions, regardless of product class, for the current month and to accumulate the year-to-date totals for all months through the present one.

Modular Programs and Subroutines

Introduction
An Example of Main and Subroutine Structure
Exercises

INTRODUCTION

Chapter 9, "Structured Programming," described the basic concepts of modular program structure. Throughout this book we have utilized the PERFORM verb as the basic control mechanism for implementing modular program structure. Still, it is often desirable to program a task in terms of one *main* program and one or more *subroutines* or *subprograms*. In such a structure the main program is the executable program. Subprograms can be written and compiled independently, but they can only be executed in conjunction with a main program. There are two basic reasons why subprograms are desirable.

Whenever a task is either too large for one person or the time available requires the formation of a project team, then subroutines are a natural way of partitioning one task among several persons. Because subprograms can be compiled independently, each team member can work individually to develop and test a portion of the total task. Communication among the team members is limited to brief coordinative activities assigned to a *chief programmer* who is responsible for the overall project design and for effective and efficient interfacing *between* subtasks partitioned out as subroutines.

A second major reason for using subroutines is the frequent need to incorporate the same task into more than one program. In such a case a subroutine that is written and tested once can be recorded in a program library and can be used by several programs, thus avoiding the "reinvention-of-the-wheel" syndrome that often plagues ill-managed data processing staffs.

When using subroutines, there is one *main program* and one or more subroutines. The main program initiates and controls execution involving the execution of subroutines and, eventually, termination of the job. A given subroutine may be called into execution by the main program, or it may be called by another subroutine. However, in a given program there must be at least one call issued by the main program, and that must be the first call. After that point, subroutines may call each other—although they cannot call themselves (recursion is not allowed). You may have noticed the use of the word "call." It is standard terminology in reference to subroutine execution, and it is so implemented in COBOL in the verb CALL.

We will explain the implementation of program subroutines using an example.

AN EXAMPLE OF MAIN AND SUBROUTINE STRUCTURE

The task is concerned with checking for errors in punched card data pertaining to an inventory. The data items have the following format:

CARD COLUMNS	FIELD NAME
1–5	ITEM-NUMBER
6–20	ITEM-NAME
21	ITEM-CODE
22–26	QUANTITY

The basic checking procedure is concerned with the value of ITEM-CODE, because this signifies the type of record. A "1" means that the QUANTITY field contains the previous balance for the item specified by ITEM-NUMBER, a "2" indicates the receipt of goods, and a "3" indicates the issue of goods from inventory. Any other code is an error. We assume that the cards are sorted so that all cards of the same item number are grouped together and the card with a "1" in column 21 leads the group. We recognize four types of error conditions:

DUPLICATE BALANCE CARD   This condition arises whenever more than one card in a group of the same item number has a code of 1.

MISPLACED BALANCE CARD   A card with a code of 1 exists, but it is not the first in the group.

BALANCE CARD MISSING   The first card in a group is not a code 1 card.

INCORRECT CODE   A code other than 1, 2, or 3 exists.

On detection of a card meeting one of these conditions the card is printed with the corresponding explanatory error message so that it can be corrected.

In addition to the error messages we also desire a summary of totals as shown in Exhibit 18-1, which illustrates a set of sample input records and the resulting sample output.

We decide to use a subroutine to check for data validity. Our immediate reason for using a subroutine is to illustrate the process. In general, it is desirable to use a

EXHIBIT 18-1   SAMPLE INPUT AND OUTPUT FOR THE INVENTORY EXAMPLE

```
12345TEST-ITEM-1    100100
12345TEST-ITEM-1    200100
12345TEST-ITEM-1    300200
23456TEST-ITEM-2    300010
34567TEST-ITEM-3    100020
34567TEST-ITEM-3    200100
34567TEST-ITEM-3    300050
45678TEST-ITEM-4    200100
45678TEST-ITEM-4    100100
45678TEST-ITEM-4    300100
45678TEST-ITEM-4    100200
56789TEST-ITEM-5    100100
56789TEST-ITEM-5    40050
56789TEST-ITEM-5    300020
67890TEST-ITEM-6    100300
67890TEST-ITEM-6    300100
78901TEST-ITEM-7    100400
78901TEST-ITEM-7    100300
89012TEST-ITEM-8    100200


23456TEST-ITEM-2    300010    DUPLICATE BALANCE CARD
45678TEST-ITEM-4    200100    DUPLICATE BALANCE CARD
45678TEST-ITEM-4    100100    MISPLACED BALANCE CARD
45678TEST-ITEM-4    300100    BALANCE CARD MISSING
45678TEST-ITEM-4    100200    MISPLACED BALANCE CARD
56789TEST-ITEM-5    40050     INCORRECT CODE
78901TEST-ITEM-7    100300    DUPLICATE BALANCE CARD


VALID RECORDS =                    012

INVALID RECORDS =                  007

BALANCE TOTAL =                    1120

RECEIPTS TOTAL =                   200

ISSUES TOTAL    =                  370
```

subroutine if changes in the type of data checking are possible, so that such changes can be made in the subroutine independently of the main program. We proceed to define the function of the main program and the subprograms as follows:

MAIN PROGRAM   Reads each data card. Gives each card to the subroutine to check if it contains valid data. If execution of the subroutine indicates that the data is not valid, the card is printed along with an error message. If execution of the subroutine indicates that the data is valid, then we accumulate the proper totals. We then proceed to read another card. When all the cards have been read, we print a summary of the accumulated totals and terminate the program.

SUBROUTINE   The subprogram receives a data card from the main program. It checks for errors. If an error is found, an appropriate error message is supplied to the main program. If no error is found, a blank error message is supplied to the main program. Then the subroutine terminates. The four error messages are:

DUPLICATE BALANCE CARD
MISPLACED BALANCE CARD
BALANCE CARD MISSING
INCORRECT CODE

From the preceding discussion we can see that, in order for the process to be completed, the main program must make the data which has been read available to the subroutine, and the subroutine must make an appropriate error message available to the main program. The need to pass data to and from a called program is almost always present when using subroutines. We refer to such data items as the *arguments* in a call statement.

In our example we need the value of ITEM-CODE as one argument. We also need to provide the subroutine with the value of ITEM-NUMBER. However, the values of ITEM-NAME and QUANTITY are not needed by the subroutine, and therefore are not specified as arguments. As we have already stated, another argument is an error message. But we also need to specify some additional arguments. Suppose that we have item number 12345 with a code of 1. If the previous card was also item number 12345 with a code of 1, we have the case of a duplicate balance card, but with the data otherwise being correct. Therefore, the item number of the previous item must be known, and we specify an argument to contain that value. In addition, we need to know whether a correctly placed balance card has been encountered or not, in order to differentiate between a misplaced balance card and a duplicate balance card. We set up a field as an argument to serve in this capacity. When a new item number is encountered, we place a 1 in this argument if the code is 1; otherwise we use a 2. For example, when we encounter a code of 1 on the third card of a given item, it is a case of a misplaced balance card if the indicator argument has a value of 2.

The two arguments just discussed, the value of the previous item number and the indicator for a correctly placed balance card, are needed only by the subroutine. The question can be raised as to why they are designated arguments rather than just data-names in the subroutine. The reason for designating them as arguments is in order to adhere to a very important rule of good modular programming practice: A *subroutine should be like a black box; its output should be strictly dependent on the input, and not on any "remembered" state of the subroutine that resulted from a previous call.* This rule is imperative when a subroutine is called by several other subroutines in the same program, and it is a good rule to follow even for a simple case, as in our example. Therefore, if the content of a data field used by a subroutine changes from call to call, it is a good procedure to include such a data field in the argument list.

In a subroutine the arguments are specified in a special section of the DATA DIVISION, the LINKAGE SECTION. For our example the section can be written as follows:

```
LINKAGE SECTION.
77   ERROR-MESSAGE            PIC X(25).
01   OTHER-DATA.
     02   PREVIOUS-ITEM       PIC 99999.
     02   CURRENT-ITEM        PIC 99999.
     02   KODE                PIC 9.
     02   BALANCE-CODE        PIC 9.
```

In this case there are two arguments, one an elementary level 77 field, and the other a group 01 field. We have made these choices to illustrate the available options. Equally acceptable is the incorporation of ERROR-MESSAGE as an 02 field in OTHER-DATA, or designating the four 02 level items as 77 level items.

Exhibit 18-2 presents a complete listing of the subroutine, including the LINKAGE

SECTION, we have just discussed. It will be noticed that a WORKING-STORAGE SECTION is also used, and in this case it consists of the four error-messages. The absence of a FILE SECTION is explained by the fact that in this example the subroutine is not involved in input or output operations. The PROCEDURE DIVISION requires some explanation. First, note that the division heading is followed by the word USING, which is followed by the list of arguments written in the LINKAGE SECTION. We have written the two arguments on separate lines for better visibility. This is especially useful if the argument list is long. Another characteristic of a subroutine is that there should be no STOP RUN statement. Instead we use the EXIT PROGRAM statement to

EXHIBIT 18-2   LISTING OF THE SUBROUTINE FOR THE INVENTORY DATA CHECKING EXAMPLE

```
IDENTIFICATION DIVISION.
PROGRAM-ID. EDIT-PROGRAM.
ENVIRONMENT DIVISION.
CONFIGURATION SECTION.
SOURCE-COMPUTER. ABC-480.
OBJECT-COMPUTER. ABC-480.
DATA DIVISION.

WORKING-STORAGE SECTION.
77   MESSAGE-1   PIC X(22) VALUE 'DUPLICATE BALANCE CARD'.
77   MESSAGE-2   PIC X(22) VALUE 'MISPLACED BALANCE CARD'.
77   MESSAGE-3   PIC X(20) VALUE 'BALANCE CARD MISSING'.
77   MESSAGE-4   PIC X(14) VALUE 'INCORRECT CODE'.

LINKAGE SECTION.
77   ERROR-MESSAGE          PIC X(25).
01   OTHER-DATA.
     02 PREVIOUS-ITEM        PIC 99999.
     02 CURRENT-ITEM         PIC 99999.
     02 KODE                 PIC 9.
     02 BALANCE-CODE         PIC 9.

PROCEDURE DIVISION  USING   ERROR-MESSAGE
                            OTHER-DATA.
MAIN-CHECK.
    IF PREVIOUS-ITEM = CURRENT-ITEM
       PERFORM OLD-ITEM-1 THRU OLD-ITEM-2
    ELSE
       PERFORM NEW-ITEM-1.

GO-BACK.
    EXIT PROGRAM.

OLD-ITEM-1.
    IF ((KODE = 2) OR (KODE = 3)) AND (BALANCE-CODE = 1)
       MOVE SPACES TO ERROR-MESSAGE
       GO TO OLD-ITEM-2.
    IF (KODE = 1) AND (BALANCE-CODE = 1)
       MOVE MESSAGE-1 TO ERROR-MESSAGE
       GO TO OLD-ITEM-2.
    IF (KODE = 1) AND (BALANCE-CODE = 2)
       MOVE MESSAGE-2 TO ERROR-MESSAGE
       GO TO OLD-ITEM-2.
    IF ((KODE = 2) OR (KODE = 3)) AND (BALANCE-CODE = 2)
       MOVE MESSAGE-3 TO ERROR-MESSAGE
       GO TO OLD-ITEM-2.
    IF (KODE = ZERO) OR (KODE > 3)
       MOVE MESSAGE-4 TO ERROR-MESSAGE
       GO TO OLD-ITEM-2.
OLD-ITEM-2.
    EXIT.
NEW-ITEM-1.
    MOVE CURRENT-ITEM TO PREVIOUS-ITEM.
    IF KODE = 1
       MOVE SPACES TO ERROR-MESSAGE
       MOVE 1 TO BALANCE-CODE
    ELSE
       MOVE MESSAGE-1 TO ERROR-MESSAGE
       MOVE 2 TO BALANCE-CODE.
```

indicate termination of the subroutine. The use of this statement can be seen in the GO-BACK paragraph. Recall that termination of a subroutine does not mean termination of the program. It simply denotes that we return to the program that called the subroutine, and continue with the next instruction of that calling program.

To review, then, there are three special aspects of a subroutine. The presence of a LINKAGE SECTION, the USING clause in the PROCEDURE DIVISION heading, and use of the EXIT PROGRAM in place of STOP RUN. A subroutine may use no arguments and therefore neither LINKAGE nor USING will be required, but such a situation is infrequent.

Exhibit 18-3 presents a complete listing of the main program. First we direct our

EXHIBIT 18-3   LISTING OF THE MAIN PROGRAM FOR THE INVENTORY CHECKING EXAMPLE

```
IDENTIFICATION DIVISION.
PROGRAM-ID. MAIN-PROGRAM.
ENVIRONMENT DIVISION.
CONFIGURATION SECTION.
SOURCE-COMPUTER. ABC-480.
OBJECT-COMPUTER. ABC-480.
INPUT-OUTPUT SECTION.
FILE-CONTROL.
    SELECT CARD-FILE  ASSIGN TO CARD-READER-DEVICE.
    SELECT PRINT-FILE ASSIGN TO PRINTER-DEVICE.
DATA DIVISION.

FILE SECTION.
FD  CARD-FILE
        LABEL RECORDS ARE OMITTED
        DATA RECORD IS CARD-RECORD.
01  CARD-RECORD.
    02 ITEM-NUMBER       PIC 99999.
    02 ITEM-NAME         PIC X(15).
    02 ITEM-CODE         PIC 9.
    02 QUANTITY          PIC 99999.
    02 FILLER            PIC X(54).
FD  PRINT-FILE
        LABEL RECORD OMITTED
        DATA RECORD IS PRINT-LINE.
01  PRINT-LINE.
    02 FILLER            PIC X.
    02 PART-1            PIC X(26).
    02 FILLER            PIC XXXX.
    02 PART-2            PIC X(25).
    02 FILLER            PIC X(79).

WORKING-STORAGE SECTION.
77  VALID-RECORDS        PIC 999999 USAGE COMPUTATIONAL VALUE ZEROS.
77  INVALID-RECORDS      PIC 999999 USAGE COMPUTATIONAL VALUE ZEROS.
77  ERROR-MESSAGE        PIC X(25).
77  END-OF-DATA          PIC 9.
77  EDIT-FIELD           PIC ZZZZZ999.
77  BALANCE-TOTAL        PIC  9(8) USAGE COMPUTATIONAL VALUE ZEROS.
77  RECEIPTS-TOTAL       PIC  9(8) USAGE COMPUTATIONAL VALUE ZEROS.
77  ISSUES-TOTAL         PIC  9(8) USAGE COMPUTATIONAL VALUE ZEROS.
01  CALL-ARGUMENTS.
    02 OLD-ITEM          PIC 99999.
    02 NEW-ITEM          PIC 99999.
    02 KODE              PIC 9.
    02 BALANCE-CODE      PIC 9.

PROCEDURE DIVISION.
SET-UP.
    OPEN INPUT CARD-FILE
         OUTPUT PRINT-FILE.
    MOVE ZEROS TO OLD-ITEM.
    MOVE ZERO TO END-OF-DATA.
    PERFORM READ-CARD.
MAIN-LOGIC.
    PERFORM CHECK-ROUTINE
        UNTIL END-OF-DATA = 1
    PERFORM PRINT-SUMMARY.
    CLOSE CARD-FILE  PRINT-FILE.
JOB-END.
    STOP RUN.
```

EXHIBIT 18-3   LISTING OF THE MAIN PROGRAM FOR THE INVENTORY CHECKING EXAMPLE
(Continued)

```
READ-CARD.
    READ CARD-FILE
        AT END
            MOVE 1 TO END-OF-DATA.
    MOVE ITEM-NUMBER TO NEW-ITEM.
    MOVE ITEM-CODE TO KODE.
CHECK-ROUTINE.
    CALL 'EDIT-PROGRAM' USING ERROR-MESSAGE
                             CALL-ARGUMENTS.
    IF ERROR-MESSAGE = SPACES
        ADD 1 TO VALID-RECORDS
        PERFORM ACCUMULATE-ROUTINE
    ELSE
        MOVE SPACES TO PRINT-LINE
        MOVE CARD-RECORD TO PART-1
        MOVE ERROR-MESSAGE TO PART-2
        WRITE PRINT-LINE BEFORE ADVANCING 1 LINE
        ADD 1 TO INVALID-RECORDS.
    PERFORM READ-CARD.
ACCUMULATE-ROUTINE.
    IF KODE = 1
        ADD QUANTITY TO BALANCE-TOTAL.
    IF KODE = 2
        ADD QUANTITY TO RECEIPTS-TOTAL.
    IF KODE = 3
        ADD QUANTITY TO ISSUES-TOTAL.

PRINT-SUMMARY.
    MOVE SPACES TO PRINT-LINE
    MOVE VALID-RECORDS TO EDIT-FIELD
    MOVE EDIT-FIELD TO PART-2
    MOVE 'VALID RECORDS = ' TO PART-1
    WRITE PRINT-LINE AFTER ADVANCING PAGE.
    MOVE SPACES TO PRINT-LINE
    MOVE INVALID-RECORDS TO EDIT-FIELD
    MOVE EDIT-FIELD TO PART-2
    MOVE 'INVALID RECORDS = ' TO PART-1
    WRITE PRINT-LINE AFTER ADVANCING 2 LINES
    MOVE SPACES TO PRINT-LINE
    MOVE BALANCE-TOTAL TO EDIT-FIELD
    MOVE EDIT-FIELD TO PART-2
    MOVE 'BALANCE TOTAL = ' TO PART-1
    WRITE PRINT-LINE AFTER ADVANCING 2 LINES
    MOVE SPACES TO PRINT-LINE
    MOVE RECEIPTS-TOTAL TO EDIT-FIELD
    MOVE EDIT-FIELD TO PART-2
    MOVE 'RECEIPTS TOTAL = ' TO PART-1
    WRITE PRINT-LINE AFTER ADVANCING 2 LINES
    MOVE SPACES TO PRINT-LINE
    MOVE ISSUES-TOTAL TO EDIT-FIELD
    MOVE EDIT-FIELD TO PART-2
    MOVE 'ISSUES TOTAL   =' TO PART-1
    WRITE PRINT-LINE AFTER ADVANCING 2 LINES.
```

attention to the CHECK-ROUTINE paragraph in the PROCEDURE DIVISION. Notice the sentence:

CALL 'EDIT-PROGRAM' USING ERROR-MESSAGE
                         CALL-ARGUMENTS.

CALL is very similar to PERFORM, except that the object of CALL is a *separately compiled* subroutine instead of a paragraph in the program. A CALL statement in essence is an instruction to execute the specified subroutine-name, which is the program-name given in the PROGRAM-ID paragraph of the subroutine. The USING clause introduces the argument list. In this case the first argument is ERROR-MESSAGE, which is a level 77 WORKING-STORAGE field. The PICTURE associated with this field is X(25), which is identical to the one in the subroutine. The second argument is called CALL-ARGUMENTS, and it is a level 01 WORKING-STORAGE field. Reviewing the subroutine arguments and contrasting them to the main program we have:

MAIN PROGRAM	SUBROUTINE
. . . WORKING STORAGE SECTION . . .	LINKAGE SECTION.
77 ERROR-MESSAGE PIC X(25). . . .	77 ERROR-MESSAGE PIC X(25).

01   CALL-ARGUMENTS.
    02 OLD-ITEM   PIC 99999.
    02 NEW-ITEM   PIC 99999.
    02 KODE   PIC 9.
    02 BALANCE-CODE PIC 9.
.
.
.
.
	01 OTHER-DATA.
	    02 PREVIOUS-ITEM PIC 999999.
	    02 CURRENT-ITEM PIC 99999.
	    02 KODE PIC 9.
	    02 BALANCE-CODE PIC 9.

CALL 'EDIT-PROGRAM' USING
    ERROR-MESSAGE CALL-ARGUMENTS.
	PROCEDURE DIVISION USING ERROR-MESSAGE
	                          OTHER-DATA.

We note that the second argument in CALL and the second argument in the PROCEDURE DIVISION USING clause of the subroutine are named differently, as are some of the subordinate fields. This is permissible and a reasonable thing to do. The arguments in a subroutine are often referred to as "dummy" arguments. At compilation time they are not translated to specific storage locations. Instead, subroutines are "link-edited" to the main programs via JCL statements, and at that point the storage addresses allocated to the arguments in the main program are substituted for the "dummy" addresses in the subroutine. Thus, the specific data-names used may be similar or they may be different. What must be identical, however, are the number of arguments and the PICTURE description of the arguments in the calling and called program. In our example, ERROR-MESSAGE is so named in both programs. However, what is called NEW-ITEM in the main program is called CURRENT-ITEM in the subprogram; but they both refer to storage locations 6–10 of the group field named CALL-ARGUMENTS in the main program.

Arguments must be defined at the 77 or 01 level and may be defined in the FILE, the WORKING-STORAGE, or LINKAGE SECTION. A subprogram which calls another subprogram may have an argument in its CALL statement which is defined in its own LINKAGE SECTION. A main program never contains a LINKAGE SECTION.

Thus far we have discussed how to set up subprograms and how the CALL verb operates. In order to actually run a program subroutine JCL statements are required, but these vary with the installation and therefore we cannot present such information in this text. In general we can use one of two approaches. First, we can compile and debug a subprogram and store it on disk or tape. Then when we compile the main program, we submit information that the subroutine called by the program is already stored in a specified place on disk or tape. Alternately, the subroutine and the main program can be submitted together in the same computer run, with JCL instructions that the subroutine is available in the same run.

The program in Exhibits 18-2 and 18-3 are substantially self-documenting. However, it may be worthwhile to comment on some of the programming features and logic incorporated in the subprogram in Exhibit 18-2. The OLD-ITEM-1 paragraph incorporates the use of complex conditions using the AND and OR operators along with parentheses. Parentheses are used to clarify the condition specified. For instance, the condition "(KODE = 2) or (KODE = 3) AND (BALANCE-CODE = 1)" can be described in the following table:

CONDITION VALUE	KODE	BALANCE-CODE
True	2	1
True	3	1
False	All other combinations	

The use of compound conditions facilitates logical testing, which otherwise is difficult to do with simple conditions. Incidentally, the task of checking the data in this program is conceptually rather difficult, because it is hard to determine clearly all the possibilities. A good tool for such applications is a *decision table,* which facilitates complete enumeration of all the possibilities. Table 18-1 presents a decision table which was constructed to facilitate writing the subroutine. Without its use, the programming task is rather difficult.

TABLE 18-1   DECISION TABLE FOR THE INVENTORY EXAMPLE

	POSSIBILITY							
CONDITION	1	2	3	4	5	6	7	8
PREVIOUS-ITEM = CURRENT-ITEM	X	X	X					
PREVIOUS-ITEM = CURRENT-ITEM				X	X	X	X	X
KODE = 1	X			X	X			
KODE = 2 OR 3		X				X		X
KODE = 1 OR 2 OR 3			X				X	
BALANCE-CODE = 1				X		X		
BALANCE-CODE = 2					X			X
ACTION	1	2	3	4	5	6	7	8
BLANK ERROR MESSAGE	X					X		
DUPLICATE BALANCE CARD				X				
MISPLACED BALANCE CARD					X			
BALANCE CARD MISSING		X	X					X
INCORRECT CODE							X	

A few words on the use of GO TO in the subroutine are warranted. First notice that each GO TO refers to a paragraph further down in the program, so that we are causing no backtracking. Then notice that we can replace each GO TO by a period. Since the conditions are mutually exclusive, if one of the first three conditions is true, then the subsequent ones must be false, and correct logic will be preserved. But we would be testing conditions unnecessarily. We have positioned the first condition in that particular position because that is the condition that we expect to prevail most of the time. Omission of GO TO would cause all four conditions to be tested, when in fact the first one is the only one needed in most instances.

REVIEW

1 When using subroutines, there is one _____ and one or more _____.

main program; subroutines

2 The data items passed to and from a called program (subroutine) are referred to as the _____ in the CALL statement.

arguments

3 The COBOL verb which is similar to PERFORM, except that the object is a separately compiled subroutine instead of a paragraph in the program, is _____.

CALL

4 The item-name assigned to an argument in the main program and assigned to that argument in the subroutine [must / need not] be the same.

need not

5 The PICTURE description of an argument in the main program and the description in the subroutine [must / need not] be the same.

must

6 The type of analytical table which is useful for portraying all the possible combinations of results which can be encountered in a checking procedure is a(n) _____.

decision table

EXERCISES

1 Discuss two main reasons for using subprograms.

2 Employees pay 5.85 percent of their first $16,500 annual earnings as F.I.C.A. tax. We are interested in writing a subroutine which will compute the F.I.C.A. tax for each employee. Outline a skeleton program structure for a main program and a subroutine. The main program calls the subroutine to compute the F.I.C.A. tax. Be sure to show all relevant aspects of the structure, including argument definition and PROCEDURE DIVISION statements.

3   Draw a structured flowchart corresponding to the subroutine in Exhibit 18-2. (Represent the corresponding conditions by abbreviated labels, such as C-1 = the first condition, etc.)

4   Write Exercise 28 of Chapter 4 dealing with a depreciation schedule as a main program and subroutine. The main program should read in the data and print the headers. Then it calls a subroutine which computes and prints the depreciation schedule. The main program reads new data and repeats the cycle until all input data has been read and processed.

Under the above requirement a printer file has to be available for both the main program and the subroutine. Some help will be needed from someone who knows your installation in order to avoid erroneous use of OPEN, CLOSE, and WRITE sequences. If you find this to be a problem, try the assignment doing all the printing, including the header, in the subroutine.

The Report Writer Feature

INTRODUCTION

The Report Writer module provides the facility for producing reports by specifying the physical appearance of a report rather than requiring specification of the detailed procedures necessary to produce the report. For most reports, the Report Writer facility will prove an advantage by reducing program logic requirements and reducing errors. The Report Writer is part of the COBOL language and it can be incorporated in any program, except in cases of small system compilers which do not include this feature.

Our description of the Report Writer begins with a basic example in an attempt to impart an overall view of the use of this language feature. Then additional capabilities are discussed in the context of a more advanced example and some modifications of that example. Finally, the formal language skeleton is presented along with explanations. Full treatment of the Report Writer is beyond the scope of this text, and would require considerable additional space. Still, this discussion will provide sufficient information to enable the programmer to produce most of the kinds of reports generated in practice.

A BASIC EXAMPLE

The Report Writer focuses the attention of the programmer on the format of the desired report. It is for this reason that it is almost imperative that one begin with a layout of the report. Most professionals utilize special printer chart forms, such as shown in Figure 19-1, to lay out the report format. Students may utilize 80-column COBOL coding forms or simply use plain paper with suitable annotations.

Figure 19-1 presents the desired report format for the basic example. In this case, there are five parts to the report. The first one is a *report heading,* a title for the report. Such a heading will appear only once in a report, and in this example, we desire it to be on a separate page. Then, there is the *page heading.* This is a heading that we want to have printed at the beginning of each page of the report. The report *detail* consists of the actual data of the report. In this case, we require four fields for each line of report detail. The first field includes 18 alphanumerics in columns 4–21, the second field includes two numerics in columns 27–28, the third field includes four alphanumerics in columns 39–42, and the fourth field is a numeric edited field in columns 52–61. A *page footing* is desired consisting of the literal PAGE and a Z9 field to print the page number. Finally, corresponding to the report heading we desire a *report footing,* which will be printed at the very end of the report. In the Report Writer terminology, the report heading, the page heading, the detail, the page footing and the report footing are called *report groups.* Additional report groups will be described later.

Now that we have described the horizontal format for each report group we turn our attention to the vertical format of the report. Most reports consist of pages. For this example, we assume that a page consists of 25 lines. Within the per-page limit of 25 lines, we define the desired vertical layout as shown in Figure 19-1.

Notice that the report heading will start on line 12 of the first page and will end on line 18. No other data will be presented on that page.

The page heading will appear on line 5, and since in this case it consists of only one line it will also end on line 5. The first detail line will start on line 7 (thus double spacing between it and the page heading) while the last detail line will be printed on line 19. Then, the page footing will appear on line 23 while the report footing will appear on line 25 of the last page only.

Figure 19-2 presents the header page, page 2, and the last page of the report. The design of the report format constitutes the major conceptual effort in report writing. The next step consists of translating the two dimensional layout to COBOL instructions.

Let us assume that our task is defined as follows. We desire to read data from a card file and to produce a report with the format presented in Figure 19-1. The card file records have the following record description:

CARD COLUMN	DATA-NAME	PICTURE
1–18	DEPARTMENT-IN	X(18)
19–20	MONTH-IN	99
21–24	PRODUCT-CODE-IN	X(4)
25–32	INVOICE-TOTALS-IN	9(6)V99
34–80	FILLER	X(48)

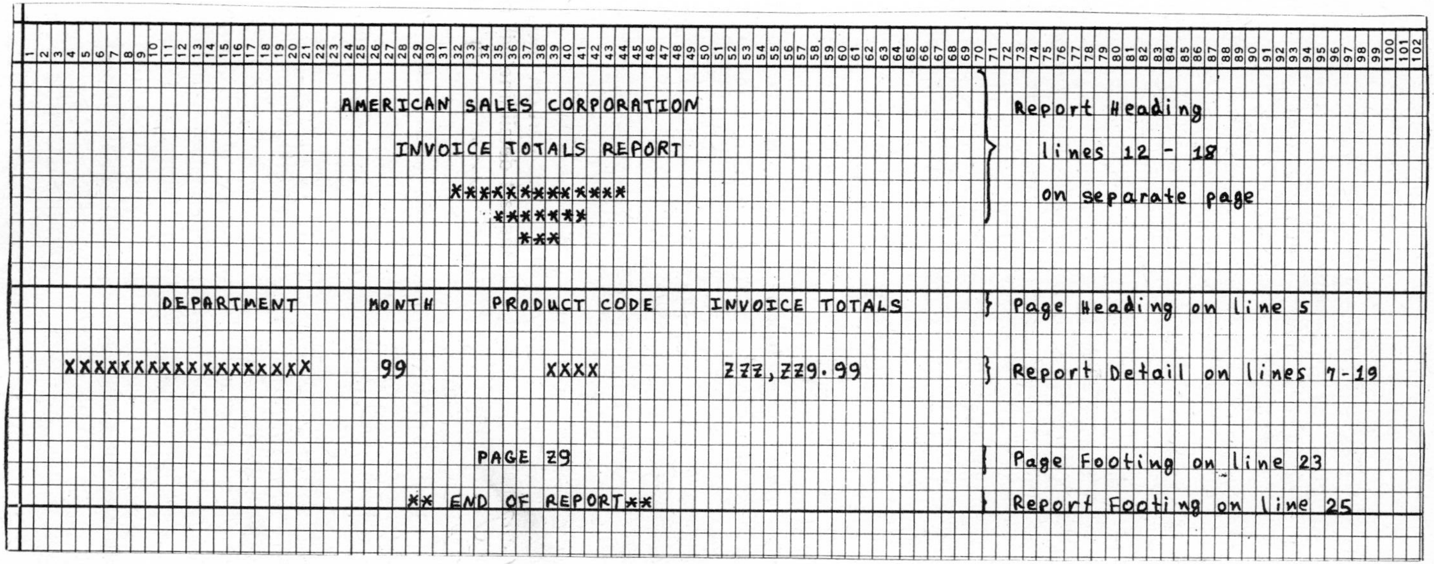

FIGURE 19-1 DESIRED REPORT FORMAT.

Report Heading AMERICAN SALES CORPORATION   *first Page only*
                  INVOICE TOTALS REPORT
                  ****
                  ****
                  ***

Prog heading DEPARTMENT   MONTH   PRODUCT CODE   INVOICE-TOTALS *each page*

            APPLIANCES   01   A-10   100.25
            APPLIANCES   01   A-11   25.25
            APPLIANCES   01   A-15   250.00
            APPLIANCES   01   B-13   83.00
            APPLIANCES   01   B-20   9,008.30
detail   APPLIANCES   01   B-21   150.50
            APPLIANCES   01   B-22   326.60
            APPLIANCES   01   C-10   8.90
            APPLIANCES   02   A-10   90.20
            APPLIANCES   02   A-15   85.37
            APPLIANCES   02   A-25   654.92
            APPLIANCES   02   B-18   870.00
            APPLIANCES   02   B-20   50.00

                                PAGE   2

                DEPARTMENT   MONTH   PRODUCT CODE   INVOICE-TOTALS

            CHILDRENS CLOTHING 03   1-16   118.42
            CHILDRENS CLOTHING 03   1-17   100.00
            CHILDRENS CLOTHING 03   1-18   20.00
            CHILDRENS CLOTHING 03   1-19   70.00
            CHILDRENS CLOTHING 03   1-20   79.85
detail   CHILDRENS CLOTHING 03   1-21   85.42
            CHILDRENS CLOTHING 03   1-22   160.66
            CHILDRENS CLOTHING 03   1-23   158.18
            CHILDRENS CLOTHING 03   1-24   750.00

Page footing   PAGE   6   *Page footing*
Report footing   **END OF REPORT**   *last Page only*

FIGURE 19-2   HEADER PAGE, PAGE 2, AND LAST PAGE OF THE REQUIRED REPORT.

Our task will involve reading a card and printing a line showing the data read in a report which includes page headings, specified horizontal and vertical spacing, and page and report footings. Exhibit 19-1 presents the first part of a program written to accomplish this task. It will be noted that it is just like any COBOL program so far, with one file assigned to CARD-READER and another file assigned to the PRINTER. The FD entry and the record description for CARD-IN are typical of COBOL programs in general.

It is desired to produce the report on the device called PRINTER (as indicated by the SELECT statement in the ENVIRONMENT DIVISION). Since this will be a report produced by the Report Writer, the FD for REPORTFILE is as follows:

FD   REPORTFILE
        LABEL RECORDS ARE OMITTED
        REPORT IS INVOICE-REPORT.

EXHIBIT 19-1   FIRST PART OF THE COBOL PROGRAM FOR THE BASIC EXAMPLE

```
IDENTIFICATION DIVISION.
PROGRAM-ID. REPGEN1.

ENVIRONMENT DIVISION.
CONFIGURATION SECTION.
SOURCE-COMPUTER. ABC-480.
OBJECT-COMPUTER. ABC-480.
INPUT-OUTPUT SECTION.
FILE-CONTROL.
    SELECT CARDFILE    ASSIGN TO CARD-READER.
    SELECT REPORTFILE ASSIGN TO PRINTER.

DATA DIVISION.
FILE SECTION.
FD  CARDFILE
       LABEL RECORDS ARE OMITTED
       DATA RECORD IS CARD-IN.
01   CARD-IN.
     02 DEPARTMENT-IN        PIC X(18).
     02 MONTH-IN             PIC 99.
     02 PRODUCT-CODE-IN      PIC X(4).
     02 INVOICE-TOTALS-IN    PIC 9(6)V99.
     02 FILLER              PIC X(48).
```

The terms REPORTFILE and INVOICE-REPORT are arbitrary choices of the program author. That the LABEL RECORDS ARE OMITTED is no surprise since this is a printer file, but they could have been STANDARD if, for example, the report were to be produced on tape (for eventual transmission to printer or display terminal). What is new is the REPORT IS clause. Instead of saying DATA RECORD IS, as is the case for other files, we now use the reserved word REPORT IS.

Exhibit 19-2 presents the complete COBOL program. Notice that following the FILE SECTION of the DATA DIVISION and the WORKING-STORAGE SECTION we write the REPORT SECTION.

The Report Descriptor (RD) entry parallels the File Descriptor (FD) entry of an ordinary file. The report-name in RD INVOICE-REPORT must be the same as in the FD entry of the report file, where the REPORT IS clause gives the report-name. The PAGE clause is optional, but it is commonly used unless we simply desire a report that is continuous and not broken into pages (in other words, a report consisting of one long page). In the example we have:

```
RD   INVOICE-REPORT
        PAGE LIMIT IS 25 LINES
        HEADING 5
        FIRST DETAIL 7
        LAST DETAIL 19.
```

The indentations and the separate lines are used here for visual clarity; the RD must appear in columns 8–9 and the other clauses must be in column 12 or to the right of 12. PAGE LIMIT IS 25 LINES defines the page size in terms of vertical lines. This page size has nothing to do with the physical size of the paper which is defined by the crease. It should be kept in mind that the space between pages is controlled by the printer carriage control tape, which is designated by the operator, or which reflects the convention of each computer installation.

The HEADING 5 entry in Exhibit 19-2 means that page or report headings will start on line 5. In our example the report heading is on a separate page, and therefore the

EXHIBIT 19-2   THE COMPLETE COBOL PROGRAM FOR THE BASIC EXAMPLE

```
IDENTIFICATION DIVISION.
PROGRAM-ID. REPGEN1.

ENVIRONMENT DIVISION.
CONFIGURATION SECTION.
SOURCE-COMPUTER. ABC-480.
OBJECT-COMPUTER. ABC-480.
INPUT-OUTPUT SECTION.
FILE-CONTROL.
    SELECT CARDFILE    ASSIGN TO CARD-READER.
    SELECT REPORTFILE ASSIGN TO PRINTER.

DATA DIVISION.
FILE SECTION.
FD  CARDFILE
        LABEL RECORDS ARE OMITTED
        DATA RECORD IS CARD-IN.
01  CARD-IN.
    02 DEPARTMENT-IN         PIC X(18).
    02 MONTH-IN              PIC 99.
    02 PRODUCT-CODE-IN       PIC X(4).
    02 INVOICE-TOTALS-IN     PIC 9(6)V99.
    02 FILLER                PIC X(48).

FD  REPORTFILE
        LABEL RECORDS ARE OMITTED
        REPORT IS INVOICE-REPORT.

WORKING-STORAGE SECTION.
01  END-OF-DATA          PIC XXX.

REPORT SECTION.
RD  INVOICE-REPORT
        PAGE LIMIT IS 25 LINES
            HEADING 5
            FIRST DETAIL 7
            LAST  DETAIL 19.

01  TYPE IS REPORT HEADING
        NEXT GROUP NEXT PAGE.
    02 LINE NUMBER IS 12
        COLUMN NUMBER IS 24
        PICTURE IS A(26)
        VALUE IS 'AMERICAN SALES CORPORATION'.
    02 LINE NUMBER IS PLUS 2
        COLUMN NUMBER IS 28
        PICTURE IS X(21)
        VALUE IS 'INVOICE TOTALS REPORT'.
    02 LINE NUMBER IS PLUS 2
        COLUMN NUMBER  IS 32
        PICTURE IS X(13)
        VALUE IS ALL '*'.
    02 LINE NUMBER IS PLUS 1
        COLUMN NUMBER IS 35
        PICTURE IS X(7)
        VALUE ALL '*'.
    02 LINE NUMBER IS PLUS 1
        COLUMN NUMBER IS 37
        PICTURE IS XXX
        VALUE '***'.
01  TYPE PAGE HEADING
```

line number 5 is relevant for the page heading only. The entries for FIRST DETAIL and LAST DETAIL define the inclusive range of lines on which detail report lines can be written.

It will be noted that in this example no mention is made in the PAGE entry about the page and report footing. The omission is intentional, so that the example can provide an illustration of defining vertical positioning apart from the PAGE option. A later example will include another option (FOOTING) in the PAGE description.

After the RD entry, it will be noted that there are five report groups described, with each at the 01 level:

EXHIBIT 19-2 THE COMPLETE COBOL PROGRAM FOR THE BASIC EXAMPLE
(Continued)

```
        LINE NUMBER IS 5.
        02 COLUMN NUMBER IS 11
            PICTURE IS X(20)
            VALUE IS 'DEPARTMENT        MONTH'.
        02 COLUMN NUMBER IS 35
            PICTURE IS X(30)
            VALUE IS 'PRODUCT CODE      INVOICE-TOTALS'.

01  INVOICE-DATA
        TYPE IS DETAIL
        LINE NUMBER IS PLUS 1.
        02 COLUMN NUMBER IS 4
            PICTURE IS X(18)
            SOURCE IS DEPARTMENT-IN.
        02 COLUMN NUMBER IS 27
            PICTURE IS 99
            SOURCE IS MONTH-IN.
        02 COLUMN NUMBER IS 39
            SOURCE IS PRODUCT-CODE-IN
            PICTURE IS X(4).
        02 COLUMN NUMBER IS 52
            PICTURE IS ZZZ,ZZ9.99
            SOURCE IS INVOICE-TOTALS-IN.

01  TYPE PAGE FOOTING.
        02 LINE 23.
            03 COLUMN 34
                PIC AAAA
                VALUE 'PAGE'.
            03 COLUMN 40
                PIC Z9
                SOURCE IS PAGE-COUNTER.
01  TYPE REPORT FOOTING
        LINE 25.
        02 COLUMN 30
        VALUE '**END OF REPORT**'
        PIC X(17).


PROCEDURE DIVISION.
SET-UP.
        OPEN INPUT  CARDFILE
             OUTPUT REPORTFILE.
        MOVE 'NO' TO END-OF-DATA
        READ CARDFILE RECORD
            AT END MOVE 'YES' TO END-OF-DATA.      manipulation.
        INITIATE INVOICE-REPORT.
        PERFORM READ-PRINT
            UNTIL END-OF-DATA = 'YES'.
        TERMINATE INVOICE-REPORT
        CLOSE CARDFILE REPORTFILE
        STOP RUN.
READ-PRINT.
        GENERATE INVOICE-DATA.              → manipulation
        READ CARDFILE RECORD
            AT END MOVE 'YES' TO END-OF-DATA.
```

01   TYPE IS REPORT HEADING. . . .

   .
   .
   .

.01   TYPE PAGE HEADING. . . .

   .
   .
   .

01   INVOICE-DATA TYPE IS DETAIL. . . .

   .
   .
   .

01   TYPE PAGE FOOTING. . . .

    .

    .

    .

01   TYPE REPORT FOOTING. . . .

    Each 01 level in Exhibit 19-2 introduces a report group in a fashion analogous to the record descriptions in an ordinary file. A report group may consist of one or several lines of output, and within each line there may be one or several fields. Following is a description of each report group and an explanation of the options used.

    The first report group is

```
01   TYPE IS REPORT HEADING
        NEXT GROUP NEXT PAGE.
     02   LINE NUMBER IS 12
          COLUMN NUMBER IS 24
          PICTURE IS A(26)
          VALUE IS 'AMERICAN SALES CORPORATION'.
     02   LINE NUMBER IS PLUS 2
          COLUMN NUMBER IS 28
          PICTURE IS X(21)
          VALUE IS 'INVOICE TOTALS REPORT'.
     02   LINE NUMBER IS PLUS 2
          COLUMN NUMBER IS 32
          PICTURE IS X(13)
          VALUE ALL '*'.
     02   LINE NUMBER IS PLUS 1
          COLUMN NUMBER IS 35
          PICTURE IS X(7)
          VALUE ALL '*'.
     02   LINE NUMBER IS PLUS 1
          COLUMN NUMBER IS 37
          PICTURE IS XXX
          VALUE '***'.
```

    The 01-level number introduces a new report group. The reserved words TYPE IS REPORT HEADING declare the type of report group about to be described. The NEXT GROUP specifies the positioning of the next group, and NEXT PAGE specifies that it should be on the next page. It will be recalled that the report heading was to be on a page by itself.

    At the 02 level there are five entries. In this case each represents one line. The level numbers used are in the range 01–49 as usual. The first 02-level entry reads:

```
02   LINE NUMBER IS 12
     COLUMN NUMBER IS 24
     PICTURE IS A(26)
     VALUE IS 'AMERICAN SALES CORPORATION'.
```

    The LINE NUMBER IS 12 specifies that we want this item to be printed on line 12. Then, in column 24 (COLUMN NUMBER IS 24) we want to print a field whose PICTURE IS A(26) and whose content is supplied by the VALUE clause.

The second 02-level entry illustrates what is called *relative* line spacing with the option LINE NUMBER IS PLUS 2, meaning to double space from the previous line. In our example the previous line was number 12, which was specified by *absolute* line spacing. Therefore, the PLUS 2 in this case has the same effect as having said LINE NUMBER IS 14.

The remaining three 02-level entries of this report group are similar to the first two and have the purpose of printing three lines of asterisks for visual effect.

The second report group in Exhibit 19-2—remember a report group is introduced by an 01 level—is TYPE PAGE HEADING, which implies that this information will be printed once for each page as a heading on the page. The LINE NUMBER IS 5 specifies that the page heading will be printed on line 5. Notice that for this report group, the LINE clause is not given at the 02 level, unlike the previous report group, the REPORT HEADING. The reason for the difference is that the PAGE HEADING will consist of one line only and so the LINE clause can be included in the 01 level.

Two 02-level entries now introduce two fields, one starting in column 11, the other starting in column 35. They both contain literals specified by VALUE clauses. The presence of two fields is simply for illustration. One longer field would have the same effect as two shorter ones, since the intent is simply to print a heading.

The third report group described is given a data-name (INVOICE-DATA) and is TYPE DETAIL. The data-name is optional for the other report groups but is required for this one because later on, in the PROCEDURE DIVISION, we will want to make direct reference to this report group. The first field of this group is

```
02   COLUMN NUMBER IS 4
     PICTURE IS X(18)
     SOURCE IS DEPARTMENT-IN.
```

The SOURCE clause specifies the source of the contents of this field. It is analogous in effect to a MOVE DEPARTMENT-IN TO the X(18) field starting in column 4. Whenever this report group is to be printed, the data contained in the field DEPARTMENT-IN will be moved to the current field. (It will be recalled that DEPART-MENT-IN was a field in the card input file, in this example.)

The remaining three fields of the INVOICE-DATA report group specify the location and source for the remainder of the line.

The next 01-level entry in Exhibit 19-2 introduces a TYPE PAGE FOOTING, which will be printed once for each page. The page footing will consist of one line of output as specified by 02 LINE 23. Notice that, for illustration of the available options, the LINE clause has been given its own 02 level, and that the IS has been omitted, being optional in all cases. There are two fields in that line, each introduced at the 03 level (it could have been 04 or higher just as well). The first field starts at column 34 and has the VALUE clause, the second field is in columns 40–41 and has the SOURCE IS PAGE-COUNTER clause. The PAGE-COUNTER is a COBOL reserved word. It is a counter that contains an integer value indicating the page number of the current page. The counter is updated automatically each time a new page is to be printed, and so no special instructions along this line are required. However, the programmer may access (but not alter) the content of PAGE-COUNTER both in the REPORT SECTION and in the PROCEDURE DIVISION. The effect of this page footing report group will be to print the page number at the bottom of each page, as can be observed in Figure 19-2.

The final report group described in Exhibit 19-2 is TYPE REPORT FOOTING, which will be printed at the end of the report at the bottom of the last page, on line 25.

Completion of the REPORT SECTION constitutes the end of the major task in the use of the report writer. The PROCEDURE DIVISION for this example is rather simple:

```
PROCEDURE DIVISION.
SET-UP.
    OPEN INPUT CARDFILE
        OUTPUT REPORTFILE.
    MOVE 'NO' TO END-OF-DATA
    READ CARDFILE RECORD
        AT END MOVE 'YES' TO END-OF-DATA.
    INITIATE INVOICE-REPORT.
    PERFORM READ-PRINT
        UNTIL END-OF-DATA = 'YES'.
    TERMINATE INVOICE-REPORT
    CLOSE CARDFILE REPORTFILE
    STOP RUN.
READ-PRINT.
    GENERATE INVOICE-DATA.
    READ CARDFILE RECORD
        AT END MOVE 'YES' TO END-OF-DATA.
```

First the files are opened. Then the INITIATE INVOICE-REPORT is an instruction analogous to OPEN for files. For instance, the INITIATE will cause the PAGE-COUNTER to be set to zero. Other actions resulting from the INITIATE will be described later. For now, it will suffice to say that before a report can be written the INITIATE command must be issued once—and only once.

In the READ-PRINT paragraph the procedure consists of reading a record from the CARDFILE and then we GENERATE INVOICE-DATA. It will be recalled that INVOICE-DATA was the data-name that we gave to the TYPE IS DETAIL report group. As a result of executing the GENERATE instruction, the Report Writer will control the printing of all other report groups (REPORT HEADING, PAGE HEADING, PAGE FOOTING) used in this example. Thus, use the Report Writer is concerned mainly with report format specifications, not with procedure specifications.

When all the records from CARDFILE have been processed, we TERMINATE INVOICE-REPORT in the JOB-END paragraph. As a result of the TERMINATE the report footing will be printed. The TERMINATE is analogous to CLOSE.

REVIEW

1 The Report Writer module of COBOL makes it possible for the programmer to arrange production of a report by specifying the [programming procedures / format] associated with the report.

format

2 In the terminology of the Report Writer, such parts of the report as the report heading, page heading, and page footing are called report _____.

groups

3 Typically, the first step associated with using the Report Writer is to lay out the desired format of the report on a _____ chart.

printer

4 When the Report Writer module is used, the format of the report is described in the _____ DIVISION of the COBOL program.

DATA

5 In the DATA DIVISION of the COBOL program, the section in which the report format is described, and which typically follows the FILE SECTION and the WORKING STORAGE SECTION, is the _____.

REPORT SECTION

6 In the REPORT SECTION of the DATA DIVISION, each of the report groups associated with the report is assigned to the _____ -level number.

01

7 Within each report group in the REPORT SECTION, each item of output typically is described at the _____ -level number when several items (usually lines) are included.

02

8 When the Report Writer module is used, then in the PROCEDURE DIVISION the _____ command must be executed after the OPEN command for the files and before the report can be printed.

INITIATE

9 In the PROCEDURE DIVISION, the printed output for all of the report groups is achieved by execution of the _____ command.

GENERATE

10 When the Report Writer module is used, the PROCEDURE DIVISION command which is analogous to the CLOSE, and which also results in the report footing being printed, is the _____ command.

TERMINATE

CONTROL BREAKS IN REPORT WRITING

The basic purpose of the example which follows is to introduce the concept of *control breaks*. In addition, other features of the Report Writer will be illustrated.

Most reports pertain to data that is associated with categories which bear a hierarchical relation to each other. Very often the categories correspond to organizational departments or groupings. For instance, suppose that we are producing a report listing alphabetically the enrollment for a college. We have students enrolled in a section, sections belonging to a course, courses belonging to a department, and departments belonging to a college. Suppose that we are interested in having the enrollment report in a way that makes these relationships meaningful. To achieve this objective, we designate that each section begin on a new page with a header, that there be a header for each course, and that there be a header for each department.

Further, we designate that enrollment be reported for each section, for each course, for each department, and for the entire college.

In the context of the recurring control breaks in the above example, we would say that we have three control breaks: section, course, and department. We speak of department as the *major* control, course as the *intermediate,* and section as the *minor* control. Of course we may have more than three control levels, each subordinate to its superior and all subordinate to one—the major control.

As the report is being produced we want to *break* the routine whenever a new section, a new course, or a new department begins. The *control* is based on the content of the fields that designate the section, course, and department. We would expect that the Report Writer would check the section, for instance, and if it changes we would want to print the total enrollment for the section just listed. But it may be that the section did not change (say section 1 of a one-section course) but the course number changed from CIS-302 to CIS-402. The report writer then must also be checking the course designation to capture the change. A similar checking procedure is required for department designation.

The highest level of control break is called the *final* control, which is of course nonrecurring. In essence, it is a means of controlling the Report Writer action when all the detail data has been processed. In the registration example, a final control break would occur when the last department in the college has been processed and we are ready to report the enrollment for the entire college.

Related to the control breaks, the Report Writer enables the user to present report groups that are called *control headings* and *control footings* in the report. A control heading is a report group (one or more lines of output) that is presented when a control break occurs. For example, a control heading specified for the department field could be used to print the department name and start a new page. As the name implies, a control footing is a report group that is presented at the end of a group and before the next category begins. In our example, at the end of each course we might desire a control footing to write the accumulated total enrollment of all the sections in that course. Typically, control footings are used for accumulating and reporting totals, while control headings are used for printing headers.

It should be noted that the control fields and the sort order of the input file are related. In our example we would expect that the data have been sorted by student within section, by section within course, by course within department, and by department within the college. This sorting would be appropriate to establish control breaks that treat department as a more inclusive control than course, course as more inclusive than section, etc.

The desire to designate hierarchically related control fields and to take actions dependent on the contents of these fields is very common in report production, and is implemented in the Report Writer module of COBOL.

REVIEW

1   When control breaks are used in conjunction with the Report Writer, the category which is at the highest hierarchical level compared with the other categories is termed the _____ control.

major

2 In addition to major control break, other levels of such breaks are _____
and _____ controls.

intermediate; minor

3 When all data has been processed, the last break is associated with the output of
grand totals for all of the categories and is called the _____ control break.

final

4 A heading (or footing) which is printed just before (or just after) a data group
which is associated with a control break is called a _____ heading (or
footing).

control

AN EXAMPLE WITH CONTROL BREAKS

We begin with a description of the desired report, in terms of the format of the
layout and in terms of the content. In discussing the basic example earlier, we
illustrated the process of developing the report specifications. At this point we assume
that the task specification stage has been completed, and we proceed to illustrate the
desired report by presenting three sample pages in Figures 19-3a, 19-3b, and 19-3c.
Notice that this report essentially is a revised version of the first example in this
chapter.

Figure 19-3a presents the first page of the report. The report header is now on the
same page as the first page header and the first page detail. The page header has been
modified by dropping the column DEPARTMENT and adding two new columns,
MONTH TOTAL and DEPT. TOTAL.

A new report group appears which consists of the fixed header DEPARTMENT:
and the department name (in the case of the first page it is APPLIANCES). This type of
header is absent from the second page (Figure 19-3b) because we desire that department name be printed only at the start of a new department listing.

The page footing remains the same as in the previous example.

Figure 19-3b presents the second page of the report and serves to illustrate the
accumulation of month and department totals. The page is short because the end of
the first department (APPLIANCES) occurs on this page and we desire to start each
department at the top of a new page. The line of asterisks is used for visual effect.

Figure 19-3c presents the last page of the report. One item deserves special
attention. It is the line GRAND TOTAL FOR INVOICE REPORT. The purpose is to show
the grand total of all invoice totals processed in this report. It is, therefore, produced
as a *final* control footing.

Now that we have a clear visualization of the desired report, let us consider the
programming aspects. Exhibit 19-3 presents the entire program from which the sample
report pages were produced. Up to the REPORT SECTION the program is identical to
the one used in the basic example.

The Report Descriptor (RD) entry specifies the fields that will be used for control
break purposes.

```
RD  INVOICE-REPORT
        CONTROLS ARE FINAL
            DEPARTMENT-IN
            MONTH-IN
```

(handwritten annotation: Group Predicate) DEPARTMENT: APPLIANCES *(handwritten annotation: report heading)*

AMERICAN SALES CORPORATION
INVOICE TOTALS REPORT

MONTH	PRODUCT CODE	INVOICE-TOTALS	MONTH TOTAL	DEPT. TOTAL
01	A-10	100.25		
	A-11	25.25		
	A-15	250.00		
	B-13	283.00		
	B-20	9,008.30		
	B-21	150.50		
	B-22	326.60		
	C-10	8.90		
			9,952.80	

(handwritten annotation: Control heading) *(handwritten annotation: Control footing)*

PAGE 1   *(handwritten annotation: page footing)*

(a)

MONTH	PRODUCT CODE	INVOICE-TOTALS	MONTH TOTAL	DEPT. TOTAL
02	A-10	90.20		
	A-15	85.37		
	A-25	654.92		
	B-18	870.00		
	B-20	50.00		
			1,750.49	
03	A-15	15.00		
	B-20	182.18		
			197.18	
				11,900.47

(handwritten annotation: Group Indicate)

****

PAGE 2

(b)

FIGURE 19-3 (a) FIRST PAGE OF THE REPORT. (b) SECOND PAGE OF THE REPORT.

MONTH	PRODUCT CODE	INVOICE-TOTALS	MONTH TOTAL	DEPT. TOTAL
03	1-19	70.00		
	1-20	79.85		
	1-21	85.42		
	1-22	160.66		
	1-23	158.18		
	1-24	750.00		
			2,041.16	5,157.10

****
****

GRAND TOTAL FOR INVOICE REPORT   19,289.69   *Grand footing Amt*

Report footing

PAGE   7

END OF REPORT

(c)

FIGURE 19-3 (*Continued*)   (c) LAST PAGE OF THE REPORT.

EXHIBIT 19-3 COBOL PROGRAM FOR THE EXAMPLE WITH CONTROL BREAKS

```
IDENTIFICATION DIVISION.
PROGRAM-ID. REPGEN2.

ENVIRONMENT DIVISION.
CONFIGURATION SECTION.
SOURCE-COMPUTER. ABC-480.
OBJECT-COMPUTER. ABC-480.
INPUT-OUTPUT SECTION.
FILE-CONTROL.
      SELECT CARDFILE   ASSIGN TO CARD-READER.
      SELECT REPORTFILE ASSIGN TO PRINTER.


DATA DIVISION.
FILE SECTION.
FD  CARDFILE
      LABEL RECORDS ARE OMITTED
      DATA RECORD IS CARD-IN.
01   CARD-IN.
      02 DEPARTMENT-IN        PIC X(18).
      02 MONTH-IN             PIC 99.
      02 PRODUCT-CODE-IN      PIC X(4).
      02 INVOICE-TOTALS-IN    PIC 9(6)V99.
      02 FILLER              PIC X(48).

FD  REPORTFILE
      LABEL RECORDS ARE OMITTED
      REPORT IS INVOICE-REPORT.
WORKING-STORAGE SECTION.
01   END-OF-DATA          PIC XXX.

REPORT SECTION.
RD  INVOICE-REPORT
      CONTROLS ARE FINAL
                   DEPARTMENT-IN
                   MONTH-IN
      PAGE LIMIT IS 25 LINES
            HEADING 2
            FIRST DETAIL 5
            LAST DETAIL 18
            FOOTING 20.

01 TYPE IS REPORT HEADING.
      02 LINE IS 2
         COLUMN NUMBER IS 35
         PICTURE IS A(26)
         VALUE IS 'AMERICAN SALES CORPORATION'.
      02 LINE NUMBER IS PLUS 2
         COLUMN NUMBER IS 38
         PICTURE IS X(21)
         VALUE IS 'INVOICE TOTALS REPORT'.

01  PAGE-TOP TYPE IS PAGE HEADING
         LINE NUMBER IS PLUS 2.
      02 COLUMN NUMBER IS 25
         PICTURE IS XXXXX
         VALUE IS 'MONTH'.
      02 COLUMN NUMBER IS 35
         PICTURE IS X(30)
         VALUE IS 'PRODUCT CODE      INVOICE-TOTALS'.
      03 COLUMN NUMBER IS 72
         VALUE IS 'MONTH TOTAL   DEPT. TOTAL'
         PICTURE IS X(25).

01 TYPE IS CONTROL HEADING DEPARTMENT-IN
         LINE NUMBER IS PLUS 2
         NEXT GROUP IS PLUS 2.
      02 COLUMN 6
         PICTURE X(11)
         VALUE 'DEPARTMENT:'.
      02 COLUMN 18
         PICTURE X(18)
         SOURCE DEPARTMENT-IN.


01  INVOICE-DATA
         TYPE IS DETAIL
         LINE NUMBER IS PLUS 1.
```

EXHIBIT 19-3   COBOL PROGRAM FOR THE EXAMPLE WITH CONTROL BREAKS
(Continued)

```
        02 COLUMN NUMBER IS 4
           PIC IS X(18)
           SOURCE IS DEPARTMENT-IN
           GROUP INDICATE.
        02 COLUMN NUMBER IS 27
           PICTURE IS 99
           SOURCE IS MONTH-IN
           GROUP INDICATE.
           02 COLUMN NUMBER IS 39
           SOURCE IS PRODUCT-CODE-IN
           PIC X(4).
        02 COLUMN NUMBER IS 52
           PIC IS ZZZ,ZZ9.99
           SOURCE IS INVOICE-TOTALS-IN.

    01  TYPE IS CONTROL FOOTING MONTH-IN
           LINE NUMBER IS PLUS 1.
        02 MONTH-TOTAL
           COLUMN NUMBER IS 69
           PICTURE IS Z,ZZZ,ZZ9.99
           SUM INVOICE-TOTALS-IN.

    01  DEPT-TOTAL   TYPE IS CONTROL FOOTING DEPARTMENT-IN
           NEXT GROUP NEXT PAGE.
        02 LINE NUMBER PLUS 1                  — 02 Dept-total
           COLUMN NUMBER IS 82
           PICTURE IS ZZ,ZZZZ,ZZ9.99
           SUM MONTH-TOTAL.
        02 LINE NUMBER IS PLUS 2
           PICTURE IS X(95)
           VALUE ALL '*'
           COLUMN NUMBER IS 2.

    01  TYPE IS CONTROL FOOTING FINAL.
        02 LINE NUMBER IS PLUS 2
           COLUMN NUMBER 2
           PICTURE X(95)
           VALUE ALL '*'.
        02 LINE NUMBER PLUS 2.
           03 COLUMN NUMBER 36
              PIC X(30)
              VALUE 'GRAND TOTAL FOR INVOICE REPORT'.
           03 COLUMN NUMBER 66
              PIC ZZZ,ZZZ,ZZ9.99
              SUM INVOICE-TOTALS-IN.
    01  TYPE PAGE FOOTING.
        02 LINE 23.
           03 COLUMN 46
              PIC AAAA
              VALUE 'PAGE'.
           03 COLUMN 54
              PIC Z9
              SOURCE IS PAGE-COUNTER.
    01  TYPE REPORT FOOTING
           LINE NUMBER IS PLUS 2.
        02 COLUMN NUMBER IS 41
           PICTURE X(17)
           VALUE '**END OF REPORT**'.


    PROCEDURE DIVISION.
    SET-UP.
        OPEN INPUT  CARDFILE
             OUTPUT REPORTFILE.
        MOVE 'NO' TO END-OF-DATA
        INITIATE INVOICE-REPORT
        READ CARDFILE RECORD
             AT END MOVE 'YES' TO END-OF-DATA.
        PERFORM READ-PRINT
             UNTIL END-OF-DATA = 'YES'.
        TERMINATE INVOICE-REPORT
        CLOSE CARDFILE REPORTFILE
        STOP RUN.
    READ-PRINT.
        GENERATE INVOICE-DATA.
        READ CARDFILE RECORD
             AT END MOVE 'YES' TO END-OF-DATA.
```

There are three control breaks specified. One is declared with the reserved word FINAL. This is always the most inclusive control in the hierarchy. The next control field is DEPARTMENT-IN which is a field in the input record. The minor control is MONTH-IN which is also a field in the input record. The order of writeup establishes the hierarchy. The FINAL must be the first control (if used); then the remaining order is established. Thus if instead of having written MONTH-IN as the last item we had written it as the second, we would have established DEPARTMENT-IN as the minor control.

In the present example we want control footings for month and department. Referring back to Figures 19-3a, 19-3b, and 19-3c, it should be noted that the data presented to the Report Writer was sorted by month within department. If the data had been sorted by department within month, then given the hierarchy of FINAL, DEPARTMENT-IN, MONTH-IN, the report would be different. The difference would be that department totals would be produced for all departments for each month. Thus, it is important to relate the input file sort order with the control breaks desired and, when required, sort the input file in a different order or change the format of the report.

The PAGE clause in the RD entry in Exhibit 19-3 is similar in form to the basic example. The FOOTING 20 clause specifies that line 20 will be the last line number on which a CONTROL FOOTING report group may be presented. PAGE FOOTING and REPORT FOOTING report groups must follow the line number 20.

The REPORT HEADING group is specified to begin on LINE 2. The absence of NEXT GROUP NEXT PAGE (as contrasted to Exhibit 19-2) implies that this heading will be on the first page of the report, along with the page heading.

The next report group is

```
01   PAGE-TOP TYPE IS PAGE HEADING
        LINE NUMBER IS PLUS 2.
        etc.
```

For illustration, a data-name (PAGE-TOP) has been assigned to this TYPE PAGE HEADING report group, and this heading begins two lines below the previous line printed. Referring back to the REPORT HEADING description, it will be observed that the report heading begins on line 2 and consists of two lines with double spacing (PLUS 2). Thus, the report heading will be printed on lines 2–4, and the page heading will begin on line 6 of the first page. On subsequent pages, however, the report heading will not be printed. Then the page heading will start on line 4, which is determined as follows: The PAGE clause established line 2 as the first line on which a heading (HEADING 2) can be printed. Since the PAGE HEADING has relative spacing (LINE NUMBER IS PLUS 2), it follows that the page heading will start on line 4 of the second and subsequent pages.

The next report group in Exhibit 19-3 is

```
01   TYPE IS CONTROL HEADING DEPARTMENT-IN
        LINE NUMBER IS PLUS 2
        NEXT GROUP IS PLUS 2.
     02   COLUMN 6
        PICTURE X(11)
        VALUE 'DEPARTMENT:'.
```

```
02  COLUMN 18
    PICTURE X(18)
    SOURCE DEPARTMENT-IN.
```

This is a CONTROL HEADING group and it will be printed every time that the field DEPARTMENT-IN changes value. Refering to Figures 19-3a, 19-3b, and 19-3c, the header DEPARTMENT: XXXXXXXXXXXXXXXXXX (where the X's stand for the department name) is printed only when a new department is introduced in the input stream. (The fact that the field DEPARTMENT-IN is used both as a control heading break and as a source field is just a coincidence in this example.)

The clauses LINE NUMBER IS PLUS 2, NEXT GROUP IS PLUS 2 specify that this report group will be printed two lines after the previous report group (the page header) and that the next group (which is a detail report group in this example) will be presented two lines below, thus double spacing before and after. The two 02 fields are similar to the type we have already discussed in the basic example.

The next report group specified in Exhibit 19-3 is 01 INVOICE-DATA TYPE IS DETAIL LINE NUMBER IS PLUS 1. As in the previous example, this will be the report group referenced in the GENERATE statement in the PROCEDURE DIVISION. The only difference between this and the corresponding group in the basic example is the use of the GROUP INDICATE clause. Specifically, we have:

```
02  COLUMN NUMBER IS 4
    PIC IS X(18)
    SOURCE IS DEPARTMENT-IN
    GROUP INDICATE.
```

The effect of the GROUP INDICATE is to print the data only at the beginning of a report, at the beginning of each page, and after each control break. This clause has also been specified for the data in column 27 whose source is MONTH-IN. A glance at the sample report output in Figures 19-3a, 19-3b, and 19-3c will show the effect of the GROUP INDICATE. A good contrast is provided by the absence of this clause in the description of the detail group of the basic example.

The next report group in Exhibit 19-3 is

```
01  TYPE IS CONTROL FOOTING MONTH-IN
        LINE NUMBER IS PLUS 1.
    02  MONTH-TOTAL
        COLUMN NUMBER IS 69
        PICTURE IS Z,ZZZ,ZZ9.99
        SUM INVOICE-TOTALS-IN.
```

The TYPE clause specifies this to be a CONTROL FOOTING associated with the data-name MONTH-IN, which is a data-name in the input file record. The meaning of this control footing is that whenever the value of the data-name MONTH-IN changes, a control break will occur which will, in turn, result in printing the edited sum of the values of the data-name INVOICE-TOTALS-IN in column 69 of the next line. As each detail group is presented, the sum of the INVOICE-TOTALS-IN fields is formed in the MONTH-TOTAL field.

The ability to specify summation fields whose data is printed as a result of control breaks is a fundamental capability of the Report Writer. A sum counter is initially set to zero by the Report Writer. Then, as each detail line is presented, the specified data is added to this sum counter. When a control break occurs the value of the sum counter is printed and then it is reset to zero. In the present example a name has been given to the accumulator: MONTH-TOTAL. As each input card is read and a detail report line is printed MONTH-TOTAL is incremented by the value of INVOICE-TOTALS-IN. Then, when MONTH-IN changes value, the edited value of MONTH-TOTAL will be printed starting in column 69. Referring back to Figure 19-3a, it will be observed that when the month changed from 01 to 02 a month total of 9,952.80 was printed.

The next report group introduced in Exhibit 19-3 is

01   DEPT-TOTAL TYPE IS CONTROL FOOTING DEPARTMENT-IN
        NEXT GROUP NEXT PAGE.

The effect of this control footing is to sum the values of the MONTH-TOTAL sum counter (SUM MONTH-TOTAL) and to print the edited sum starting in column 82 of the next line. Reference to Figures 19-3a, 19-3b, and 19-3c reveals that this sum counter is printed only when the department changes; thus all the month totals for a given department are printed before the department total. Referring back to the CONTROLS ARE FINAL DEPARTMENT-IN MONTH-IN serves to remind us that in this hierarchy of control breaks the MONTH-IN is subordinate to DEPARTMENT-IN. Thus the expected order of control footings is that several MONTH-TOTALS will be printed for each DEPT-TOTAL.

Incidentally, the order in which the control footing report groups are written is immaterial. The logic of report presentation is not related to the order in which the report groups are specified in the program.

Two additional features of the DEPT-TOTAL report group deserve attention. The NEXT GROUP NEXT PAGE clause specifies that after this group we want to start a new page. The second feature is that this group consists of two lines. The first one prints the value of the sum counter while the second line consists of asterisks.

The next group is

01   TYPE IS CONTROL FOOTING FINAL.

No name is given to this report group (names are optional). This kind of control footing will be printed after all control breaks have occurred, since it is the highest in the control hierarchy. Thus, after the last detail group has been presented and after all the control footings have been presented then the final control footing is presented in the report. In a sense it resembles a report footing, except that SUM clauses can only appear in control footing groups and, therefore, a CONTROL FOOTING FINAL is necessary.

The SUM INVOICE-TOTALS-IN specifies that this sum counter (and we have given it no name) will accumulate the sums of the INVOICE-TOTALS-IN values. Actually, it would be advisable to have said SUM DEPT-TOTAL to reduce the required number of additions, in a fashion similar to the SUM MONTH-TOTAL specified for the DEPT-TOTAL group. This inadvisable variation is shown here to illustrate the options available. If the report consisted of thousands of lines the extra additions might be considered a substantial inefficiency.

One point needs clarification. Referring to Figure 19-3c, the question may be raised: Why is not the final control footing printed on a new page, since the previous control footing (DEPT-TOTAL) contained the NEXT GROUP NEXT PAGE clause? The reason is that the NEXT GROUP clause is ignored when it is specified on a control footing report group that is at a level other than the highest level at which a control break is detected. In this case, a final control footing is at a higher level, and therefore the NEXT GROUP clause associated with the DEPT-TOTAL control footing group is ignored.

The PAGE FOOTING and REPORT FOOTING groups in Exhibit 19-3 are similar to the ones in the basic example in Exhibit 19-2.

The PROCEDURE DIVISION is identical to the one in the basic example, illustrating that the differences in the resulting report are attributable to the differences in the report description, rather than in the procedures specified.

REVIEW

1 In the RD entry in the REPORT SECTION of the DATA DIVISION, if the FINAL control break is used then it must be the [first one / last one] listed.

first one

2 When the major report groups are described at the 01 level in the DATA DIVISION, then the CONTROL HEADING and CONTROL FOOTING groups are described at the [01 / 02] level.

01

3 The effect of the GROUP INDICATE clause in the description of a report group is to print the associated information only at the beginning of the report, at the beginning of each _____, and after each _____.

page; control break

4 The data name which is associated with either a CONTROL HEADING or a CONTROL FOOTING must be a data name in the _____ file record.

input

5 A CONTROL HEADING report group typically involves the specification of descriptive _____ headings.

column (or report, etc.)

6 A CONTROL FOOTING report group typically involves the specification of various _____ which are to be reported.

sums (or totals, etc.)

7 Even though a report footing has been specified, it is also necessary to specify a FINAL control footing if the output of a _____ clause is desired at the end of the report.

SUM

AN EXAMPLE USING DECLARATIVES

Figure 19-4 illustrates the output of what appears to be the report discussed in the more advanced example, with one exception: The line PAGE TOTAL = 10,783.29 is new. Suppose then that we are interested in showing a page total for the invoice-totals

AMERICAN SALES CORPORATION

INVOICE TOTALS REPORT

DEPARTMENT	MONTH	PRODUCT CODE	INVOICE-TOTALS	MONTH TOTAL	DEPT. TOTAL
APPLIANCES	01	A-10	100.25		
		A-11	25.25		
		A-15	250.00		
		B-13	83.00		
		B-20	9,008.30		
		B-21	150.50		
		B-22	326.60		
		C-10	8.90		
APPLIANCES	02	A-10	90.20	9,952.80	
		A-15	85.37		
		A-25	654.92		

PAGE TOTAL =   10,783.29

PAGE   1

FIGURE 19-4 OUTPUT RESULTING FROM THE MODIFIED PROGRAM USING DECLARATIVES.

EXHIBIT 19-4   REVISED PROGRAM FOR THE MORE ADVANCED EXAMPLE, USING DECLARATIVES

```
        .
        .  (as before)
        .
 FD REPORTFILE
        LABEL RECORDS ARE OMITTED
        REPORT IS INVOICE-REPORT.
 WORKING-STORAGE SECTION.
 01   END-OF-DATA          PIC XXX.
 01   PAGE-ACCUMULATOR   PIC 9(7)V99.

 REPORT SECTION.
        .
        .  (as before)
        .
 01   TYPE PAGE FOOTING.
      02 LINE 21.
         03 COLUMN 34
            PIC A(12)
            VALUE 'PAGE TOTAL ='.
         03 COLUMN 49
            PIC ZZ,ZZZ,ZZ9.99
            SOURCE PAGE-ACCUMULATOR.
      02 LINE 23.
         03 COLUMN 46
            PIC AAAA
            VALUE 'PAGE'.
         03 COLUMN 52
            PIC Z9
            SOURCE IS PAGE-COUNTER.

 01   TYPE REPORT FOOTING
      LINE NUMBER IS PLUS 2.
      02 COLUMN NUMBER IS 41
         PICTURE X(17)
         VALUE '**END OF REPORT**'.


 PROCEDURE DIVISION.

 DECLARATIVES.
 PAGE-END SECTION.
      USE BEFORE REPORTING PAGE-TOP.

 PAR-A.
      MOVE ZEROS TO PAGE-ACCUMULATOR.
 PAR-B.
      EXIT.
 END DECLARATIVES.

 PROCEDURAL SECTION.
 SET-UP.
      OPEN INPUT  CARDFILE
           OUTPUT REPORTFILE.
      MOVE 'NO' TO END-OF-DATA
      INITIATE INVOICE-REPORT
      READ CARDFILE RECORD
           AT END MOVE 'YES' TO END-OF-DATA.
      PERFORM READ-PRINT
           UNTIL END-OF-DATA = 'YES'.
      TERMINATE INVOICE-REPORT
      CLOSE CARDFILE REPORTFILE
      STOP RUN.
 READ-PRINT.
      GENERATE INVOICE-DATA.
      ADD INVOICE-TOTALS-IN TO PAGE-ACCUMULATOR
      READ CARDFILE RECORD
           AT END MOVE 'YES' TO END-OF-DATA.
```

printed on that page. This example will serve as a vehicle to illustrate how the programmer can specify procedures other than those made possible by the standard report groups.

What we desire is the summation of the invoice totals and printing them at the bottom of the page but above the page footing. In a sense, we desire a control break associated with the end of a page. But the rules of the CONTROLS clause specify that we must not use control breaks associated with data names defined in the REPORT SECTION. Further, a SUM counter cannot be used except with CONTROL FOOTING report groups.

In order to proceed directly to the illustration, consider the modification to the more advanced example in Exhibit 19-4. A WORKING-STORAGE field has been added, PAGE-ACCUMULATOR. Then, in the PROCEDURE DIVISION, the reserved word DECLARATIVES introduces a special purpose section, in this example the PAGE-END SECTION. The USE verb specifies the condition under which the procedures in the DECLARATIVES portion will be executed, and in this case it is BEFORE REPORTING PAGE-TOP. It will be recalled that PAGE-TOP was the name given to the page heading report group. Thus, the procedures specified in this section will be executed before printing the page header. Now looking at PAR-A, the simple task of MOVE ZEROS TO PAGE-ACCUMULATOR is the only procedure specified in this section (PAR-B simply contains an EXIT command). In essence, then, we have said: Before printing the heading on each page, zero out the working-storage field called PAGE-ACCUMULA-TOR. The END DECLARATIVES marks the end of the declarative part of the PROCE-DURE DIVISION.

In the SET-UP paragraph the MOVE ZERO TO PAGE ACCUMULATOR simply serves to set the initial value before the report begins (a VALUE clause in the WORKING-STORAGE would have had the same effect). In the READ-PRINT paragraph observe the two statements:

GENERATE INVOICE-DATA.
ADD INVOICE-TOTALS-IN TO PAGE-ACCUMULATOR.

After each report detail group is generated the value of PAGE-ACCUMULATOR is incremented by the amount of INVOICE-TOTALS-IN. When a page footing is printed, the value of PAGE-ACCUMULATOR serves as the SOURCE. Then, the declarative portion takes effect, before the next page heading is printed, and the PAGE-ACCUMU-LATOR is set to zero to begin again the new page accumulation.

REVIEW

1   The reserved word DECLARATIVES is used to introduce special purpose sections in the _____ DIVISION of a COBOL program.

PROCEDURE

2   The verb which specifies the condition under which the procedures under DECLARATIVES are to be executed is the _____ verb.

USE

3 When presentation of the DECLARATIVES in the PROCEDURE DIVISION has been completed, this is indicated by the command _____.

END DECLARATIVES

LANGUAGE SPECIFICATIONS FOR THE COBOL REPORT WRITER

A complete language specification description is beyond the scope of the present discussion. However, a full list of the language options is included in Appendix C of this book. In the following description only a few of the options are highlighted.

1 $\begin{Bmatrix} \underline{CONTROL}\ IS \\ \underline{CONTROLS}\ ARE \end{Bmatrix}$ $\begin{Bmatrix} \text{data-name-1 [,data-name-2]} \ldots \\ \underline{FINAL}\ \text{[,data-name-1 [,data-name-2]} \ldots] \end{Bmatrix}$

Data-name-1 and data-name-2 must not be defined in the Report Section. FINAL, if specified, is the highest control, data-name-1 is the major control, data-name-2 is an intermediate control, etc. The last data-name specified is the minor control.

2 $\underline{GROUP}$ INDICATE

The GROUP INDICATE clause specifies that the associated printable item is presented only on the first occurrence of the associated report group, after a control break or page advance.

3 $\underline{LINE}$ NUMBER IS $\begin{Bmatrix} \text{integer-1 [ON } \underline{NEXT}\ \underline{PAGE}] \\ \underline{PLUS}\ \text{integer-2} \end{Bmatrix}$

This clause specifies vertical positioning information for the associated report group.

Integer-1 and integer-2 must not be specified in such a way as to cause any line of a report group to be presented outside of the vertical subdivisions of the page designated for the report group type, as defined by the PAGE clause (see discussion of the PAGE clause).

Within a given report group, an entry that contains a LINE NUMBER clause must not contain a subordinate entry that also contains a LINE NUMBER clause.

Within a given report description entry a NEXT PAGE phrase can appear only once and, if present, must be in the first LINE NUMBER clause in that report group.

A LINE NUMBER clause with the NEXT PAGE phrase can appear only in the description of the CONTROL HEADING, DETAIL, CONTROL FOOTING and REPORT FOOTING groups.

The first LINE NUMBER clause specified within a PAGE FOOTING report group must be an absolute LINE NUMBER clause.

4 $\underline{NEXT}$ GROUP IS $\begin{Bmatrix} \text{integer-1} \\ \underline{PLUS}\ \text{integer-2} \\ \underline{NEXT}\ \underline{PAGE} \end{Bmatrix}$

The NEXT GROUP clause specifies information for vertical positioning following presentation of the last line of a report group. However, it is ignored when it is specified on a CONTROL FOOTING report group which is at a level other than the highest level at which a control break is detected.

The NEXT PAGE phrase of the NEXT GROUP clause must not be specified in a PAGE FOOTING report group.

The NEXT GROUP clause must not be specified in a REPORT FOOTING or PAGE HEADING report group.

5 $\underline{\text{PAGE}}$ $\begin{bmatrix} \text{LIMIT IS} \\ \text{LIMITS ARE} \end{bmatrix}$ integer-1 $\begin{bmatrix} \text{LINE} \\ \text{LINES} \end{bmatrix}$

[,$\underline{\text{HEADING}}$ integer-2] [,$\underline{\text{FIRST}}$ $\underline{\text{DETAIL}}$ integer-3]

[,$\underline{\text{LAST}}$ $\underline{\text{DETAIL}}$ integer-4] [,$\underline{\text{FOOTING}}$ integer-5]

The PAGE clause defines the length of a page and the vertical subdivisions within which report groups are presented. The order of writing HEADING, FIRST DETAIL, LAST DETAIL and FOOTING is immaterial.

Use of the PAGE clause defines certain page regions which are described in Format 5, above. In this format, the integer-1, integer-2, etc., refer to the operands of the PAGE clause. As an illustration of using the table, notice that CONTROL FOOTING report groups are allocated the region between integer-3 and integer-5. Thus, if the PAGE clause had contained FIRST DETAIL 6, FOOTING 20, the CONTROL FOOTING report group description should not contain, for example, an absolute LINE NUMBER clause referring to line 22.

6 $\underline{\text{SOURCE}}$ IS identifier-1

The SOURCE clause identifies the sending data item that is moved to an associated printable item defined within a report group description entry.

Identifier-1 may be defined in any section of the DATA DIVISION. If identifier-1 is a REPORT SECTION item, it can only be PAGE-COUNTER, LINE-COUNTER, or a sum counter.

7 {$\underline{\text{SUM}}$ identifier-1 [,identifier-2]. . .

[$\underline{\text{UPON}}$ data name-1 [,data-name-2] . . .]} . . .

$\begin{bmatrix} \underline{\text{RESET ON}} \begin{Bmatrix} \text{data-name-3} \\ \underline{\text{FINAL}} \end{Bmatrix} \end{bmatrix}$

The SUM clause establishes a sum counter and names the data items to be summed.

When more than one identifier is used the sum counter is incremented by the sum of the identifiers. Thus:

03   EX-TOTAL PIC Z(6).99 SUM DAT1, DAT2

indicates that EX-TOTAL will be incremented by both the value of DAT1 and DAT2 each time a summation is indicated. If DAT1 and DAT2 are items described in the same report group and on the same line, we refer to this sum as a *crossfooting,* as in the example below:

DAT1	DAT2	EX-TOTAL
20	30	50

In contrast to crossfooting, we refer to *rolling forward* as the summation of sum counters at a lower hierarchical level. Thus:

02   DEPT-TOTAL PIC ZZ,ZZZ,ZZ9.99 COLUMN 69
     SUM MONTH-TOTAL

where MONTH-TOTAL was a sum counter specified earlier, represents an example of a *rolling forward* total.

A SUM clause can appear only in the description of a CONTROL FOOTING report group.

The UPON phrase provides the capability to accomplish selective subtotaling for the detail report groups named in the phrase.

The RESET option inhibits automatic resetting to zero upon the occurrence of a control break. Thus the sum counter can be zeroed only when a control break occurs for data-name-3, or on the occurrence of FINAL. The latter case represents an accumulation for the entire report.

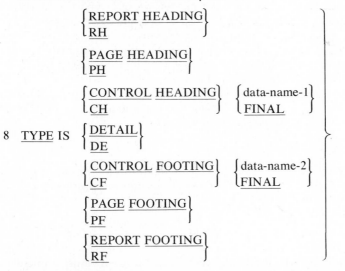

The TYPE clause specifies the particular type of report group that is described by this entry. Each option can be abbreviated in a two-letter word.

In a complete report format the following general outline occurs:

REPORT HEADING   *(one time only)*
PAGE HEADING

.
.

.

CONTROL HEADING   *Repeated*
                   as many
DETAIL   *times*   *Repeated for*
                   as   *as many pages*
CONTROL FOOTING   *needed*   *as needed*

.
.

.

PAGE FOOTING
REPORT FOOTING   *(one time only)*

9   INITIATE report-name

The INITIATE statement causes the system to begin processing a report. As part of the initialization procedure, all sum counters are set to zero, and so is PAGE-COUNTER and LINE-COUNTER.

10   GENERATE $\left\{ \begin{array}{l} \text{data-name} \\ \text{report-name} \end{array} \right\}$

The GENERATE statement directs the production of a report in accordance with the report description in the REPORT SECTION of the DATA DIVISION. Data-name is a TYPE DETAIL report group. If report-name is used, no detail report groups are printed, and instead we produce what is called a summary report.

The GENERATE statement causes report generation, including handling of control breaks, the start of page procedures, etc.

A report may contain more than one type of detail report group. In such a case there will be more than one GENERATE statement in the PROCEDURE DIVISION, each referencing the proper detail group.

11   TERMINATE report-name

The TERMINATE statement causes the completion of the report processing. All CONTROL FOOTING and REPORT FOOTING groups are produced.

12   USE BEFORE REPORTING identifier

The USE statement specifies PROCEDURE DIVISION statements that are executed just before a report group named in the REPORT SECTION of the DATA DIVISION is produced. The USE statement, when present, must immediately follow a section header in the declaratives section, and must be followed by a period followed by a space.

The identifier is a report group.

EXERCISES

1 A card file contains data pertaining to student grades. Each card record consists of:

COLUMNS	CONTENT
1–15	Student name
16–27	Course name
28	Credits
29	Grade (A, B, C, D, or F)

It is desired to print a report as outlined on the print chart below.

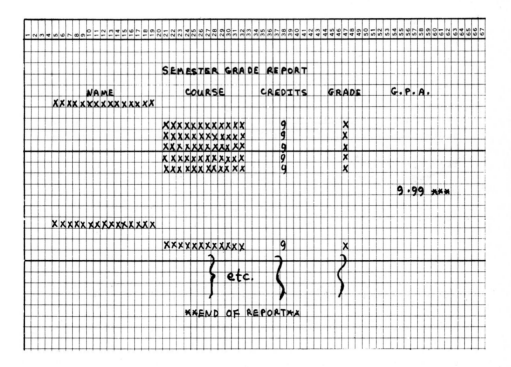

The report heading "SEMESTER GRADE REPORT" will be printed on the first page only.

For page size limits use:

PAGE LIMIT IS 40 LINES
HEADING 3
FIRST DETAIL 5
LAST DETAIL 37.

Each student is enrolled in five courses.

A report footing is printed at the end of the report, as shown.

The grade point average (GPA) is computed by considering

A = 4, B = 3, C = 2, D = 1, F = 0 points.

Hint: You may find it useful to use two DECLARATIVES procedures; one to compute the GPA before printing the line containing the GPA, and one to clear the total credits accumulator which you will need to sum up the credits for each student.

2 Incorporate the Report Writer feature into a program which you have already written.

Data Base Concepts

INTRODUCTION

Organizations are complex systems. They consist of distinct individual subsystems which are interrelated. The main force that interrelates subsystems is the information flow across organizational units. As managers acquire experience and develop sophistication in the use of computer systems, they become very aware of the need to integrate information flows and to understand the relationships existent in organizational data. Figure 20-1 illustrates the complex interrelationships of data flows in a manufacturing organization. Attempts to deal efficiently with such complex systems of data have lead to the development of the data base approach.

The term *data base* can be defined in several ways. But the most meaningful way from the standpoint of the design of an information system is that it is a collection of interrelated data. Implicit in this definition is the capability to define interrelationships among data, to minimize redundancy (duplication of data), to store data in such ways that it can be retrieved to satisfy a variety of user needs, and to modify the stored data as needed.

In many respects the data base approach is characterized by the word *efficiency*. In principle, one can do anything with non-data base systems as with data base systems. In practice, the cost of doing certain things without the benefit of the data base approach is so prohibitive that the possibility is dismissed. There are two main contributors to such prohibitive costs. First, data redundancy leads to extreme storage

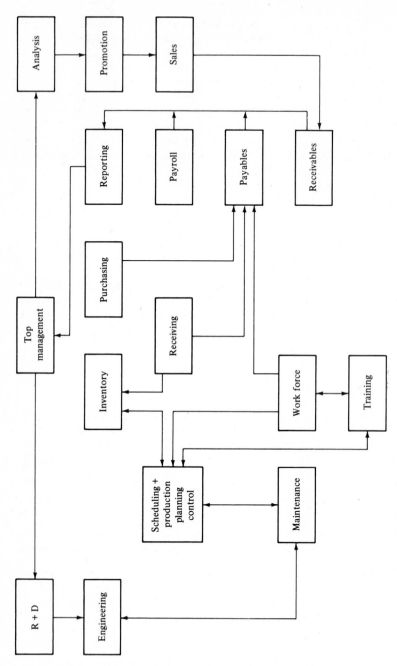

FIGURE 20-1   POSSIBLE PATHS OF INFORMATION FLOW IN A MANUFACTURING FIRM.

requirements. Second, searching time becomes uncontrolled as we need to access entire files to locate the data of interest. Consider an example. Bank customers maintain checking and/or savings accounts. There are two basic questions that we might want to ask: What accounts does a given customer have? What customers have a savings account (or, alternatively, a checking account)? A file designed to answer the first question would consist of records in customer number order, each record identifying the customer and his or her checking and/or savings account. If we want to ascertain which customers maintain a savings account we would have to read every single customer record to select those with a savings account. Alternately, we could think of a file whose records consist of the checking accounts first followed by the savings accounts, in order of account numbers. This file can be used for efficiently ascertaining which customers maintain a savings account, but it requires a complete file reading to determine the accounts held by a given customer. If we maintain two files, both types of questions can be answered efficiently, but we incur the inefficiency of storing the same data twice, and having two files to update whenever we need to make a change in the data. If we maintain only one file then we avoid redundancy but we incur inefficiency in accessing data for the type of question for which the file was not intended.

This brief example illustrates the issues and needs that have brought about the development of the data base approach. In the following section we review the characteristics of the non-data base approach. By far the majority of existing information systems are not data base oriented, and therefore it is useful to consider the differences between the two approaches.

REVIEW

1   An information system which makes it possible to define interrelationships in the data, minimize redundancy, retrieve data in a variety of ways, and modify the stored data can appropriately be called a _____ information system.

data base

2   In general, any report that be obtained using a data base system [can / cannot] also be obtained using a non-data base system.

can

3   The two main contributors to high cost when a variety of reports are obtained from a non-data base system are _____ in data and computer time used for

_____.

redundancy; searching files

4   Most information systems now in existence can be characterized as being [data base / non-data base] systems.

non-data base

DATA BASE DESIGN—TRADITIONAL APPROACH

All business information systems involve a data base. From one system to the next the difference is in the degree of specific structure and implementation. Many information systems are manual. This is particularly likely in a small firm, but it is not uncommon to find manual system segments in large organizations as well. We shall consider a "typical" manual system in order to describe the usual characteristics of manual systems. Data generation is always associated with a paper form or source document of some kind. With rare exceptions, the source document is produced in several copies. The generating department retains one copy while the other copies are distributed to other organizational areas. The copy in the originating department is filed and is eventually processed with other such transactions, usually on a periodic basis. Thus, the important characteristics of a manual system are the physical movement of paper forms, the existence of departmental files, and the departmental processing of the data on the forms.

As a brief illustration of a manual information system, take the case of a sales order received by a manufacturing company. The sales order is written up in several copies. The customer receives the original, with one copy being retained by the sales department. A copy of the sales order is sent to the accounts receivable department. The credit department receives a copy of the sales order for the purpose of evaluating and authorizing credit. This copy is then forwarded to the materials management department, and in the inventory control section a determination is made as to whether or not the order can be filled from existing stock. Given that there is enough stock, a form is prepared and sent to the shipping department for use as a shipping document. After the material is delivered, the signed shipping document acknowledging receipt is sent to the accounts receivable department, and this document is matched up with the appropriate sales order copy as the basis for preparing the customer billing.

As illustrated by the above example, the need to integrate the diverse activities in an organization leads to the physical movement of the paper forms from one department to another. Each department maintains its own files and performs some of its own data processing. Departmental files contain data pertaining to the specific functions performed by that department. Still, as the fact of multiple copies of the same form attests, many of the departmental files are duplicates of each other. Of course, even in a manual system certain central files exist, and normally these are accounting files which contain financial data. Since such diverse areas as sales, inventory, and payroll can all be expressed in terms of dollars, financial files can be centralized and need not be maintained separately by each department.

When electronic data processing was developed, it was first viewed as a promising avenue for improving efficiency. The first logical approach to increasing efficiency is to decrease input while maintaining the output, as discussed in Chapter 1, "Management Information Systems." Therefore, the focus of early attention was the decrease in processing costs. The orientation was as follows: Here is data processing task X; let us use electronic data processing to do it better, cheaper, and faster. Of course, computer equipment did not come in small modules but, rather, was more efficiently acquired as one large unit. Therefore, a *central* data processing facility became a technological necessity. Still, the central location of data processing did not prevent the continued adherence to the functional approach to file organization and data analysis. The idea that each organizational function needs its own files was pervasive.

Furthermore, although paper forms in multiple copies were no longer required, it was considered necessary to maintain multiple copies of data records in different magnetic tape files. Often the main reason given was the sort order. The operations manager wanted the sales data organized by product, the sales manager by customer, and the like. The data processing task did not change in its concept, even though the electronic computer had been applied to the task. The transactions batches were processed against several files for the purpose of the file updating and preparing reports. What changed were the specifics of data processing implementation. Instead of departmental clerical personnel doing the detailed work, it was done by the computer in the central facility. Actually, the concept of segmented file structure mushroomed. The capability of computers to process data so as to produce different types of reports was applied to satisfy managers' increasing interests in a variety of reports. But the technical details associated with computer programming and file processing made it necessary to proliferate the number of files. Once a master file was formed it was not desirable to erase it and to regenerate it each time it was needed. A little reflection on the specifics of batch processing of sequential files will lead one to the conclusion that it is not practical to keep master file data in one central file, because the entire file would have to be processed whenever we wished to output anything from that file.

The use of the past tense throughout the above description is not meant to imply past practice in a chronological sense. The functional approach to information systems is still, by far, the prevalent mode of operation and design. It is a stage of development that almost all data processing organizations go through, and the approach eases the transition from manual to electronic processing. Furthermore, the approach has the appeal that it parallels organizational functions and therefore seems like a natural basis for file organization.

The disadvantages of the functional approach to file organization stem primarily from the dynamics of business. Sooner or later managers come to the realization that a computerized information system is a means not only of doing a given job better but also of doing a different job. As managers gain experience in the use of the information system, demands increase that the system be more responsive to their interests in new types of data analysis. If not by deliberate study, managers find the functional system inadequate by accident. The shock comes when a manager places a seemingly routine request: To restructure a report so that it contains, say, a comparative column for some data. The response comes that the requested analysis would involve a major project because it would affect 15 programs and the re-creation of 10 files. The realization comes that a good system is not one that is designed to do a given job well but, rather, one that can cope with changes in required analyses. Functional systems are so crystallized that an attempt to restructure them makes them come apart.

Overall, there are, in fact, two management forces that lead to eventual dissatisfaction with functional system design. One is that as managers gain experience as users of an information system they move in the direction of wanting to change the scope and flexibility of data analysis. The second force is associated with the fact that information systems gradually find users in the upper echelons of management. As top managers become involved, they place informational demands on the system that are contrary to the concept of functionalization. Top managers tend to take a total view of the organization and are therefore likely to request analyses that transcend departmental boundaries as well as organizational levels. It then becomes apparent that the organization chart with its horizontal functional divisions and its vertical managerial echelons is not a suitable prototype for the architecture of data base design.

Throughout the past decade the general trend has been the increasing integration of data files. Carried to its extreme, such integration would culminate in *one* central data base integrating all data from all functions. This trend, however, has been modified recently as a result of the development of *minicomputers* and *distributed data systems.*

The availability of low-cost, high-performance minicomputers has brought about an emerging reversal in the singular trend of data centralization. Distributed data systems utilize small computers interconnected with each other and with the central (large) computer of the organization. Functional data pertinent to a limited organizational domain is maintained locally, thereby giving use again to the old concept of functional data files, while data pertaining to other functions becomes part of the central data base. For example, a local insurance office could maintain a local data base of its own clients using a minicomputer. Through data communications, such decentralized data bases are available to the central corporate data base for consolidation. In this respect, emerging distributed data systems tend to achieve both the advantages of local, functional data for local use, as well as central, integrated data for uses based on interrelationships in organizational functions.

REVIEW

1   In a manual information system the source document is almost always prepared [as a single copy / in several copies].

in several copies

2   In order to initiate required action in each of the several departments involved, in a manual system it is typical that _____ move from department to department.

paper forms (etc.)

3   The immediate reaction to the implementation of centralized electronic data processing was [continued adherence to / abandonment of] the functional approach to file organization.

continued adherence to

4   Because the functional approach to file organization was maintained even after introduction of computers, the number of files maintained in such systems tended to [decrease / remain stable / increase].

increase

5   Two management forces that lead to dissatisfaction with the functional approach to file organization are the desire by managers for more data analysis flexibility as they gain familiarity with computerized information systems and the increasing role of _____ managers as users of such systems.

top

6   One particular hardware development which has made possible the maintenance of decentralized, functional files while also having these files available as part of a centralized data base is the development of _____.

minicomputers

DATA STRUCTURES

An important characteristic of the data base approach is the ability to represent interrelationships among data items. There are two levels of data structure that can be considered: logical structure and physical structure. The *logical data structure* is concerned with the defined data relationships apart from their physical recording. *Physical data structure* is concerned with the actual storage representation of data and its relationships. In this section we consider four basic types of logical data structure: flat files, tree hierarchies, networks, and the relational model.

FLAT FILES

The file structures that we have so far considered in this book are called *flat files*. We have viewed files as collections of records, each record consisting of a number of fields such as shown in Figure 20-2. In the more generalized context of data-base terminology, a record may also be called a *segment* or a *tuple*. Each row in Figure 20-2 constitutes a record. Each record is identified by a unique key, called the *entity identifier* or the *primary key*. In Figure 20-2 the EMPLOYEE-NUMBER is an example of an entity identifier. The term *attribute* is often used in lieu of the term field. Thus, a column in Figure 20-2, such as WAGE RATE, constitutes an entity attribute. Flat files are often ordered on the basis of the entity identifier values, thereby establishing a logical relationship between records. However, no relationships are implied between the other attributes in the record.

TREE HIERARCHIES

A hierarchical data structure represents a relationship between a *parent* and a *child* data item. The relationship can be depicted in graphic form as a *tree*, as illustrated in Figure 20-3. At the head of the tree there is an element called the *root;* all other elements are hierarchically lower and are referred to as *nodes* in the tree. A node which has other dependent nodes is a parent element, while the dependent nodes are called the children. Children of the same parent are called (logical) *twins*. A node with no children is called a *leaf*.

The specific characteristic of a hierarchical structure is that each child has only one parent. (We will contrast this characteristic to network structures in the next section.)

Trees may be *balanced* (each parent has an equal number of children) or *unbalanced*. Balanced trees may be *binary* (each parent has two children).

EMPLOYEE-NUMBER	DEPARTMENT	SKILL CODE	WAGE RATE	YEAR-TO-DATE GROSS
1234	10	A	3	10000
5678	20	B	1	7500
9101	10	L	2	8425

FIGURE 20-2   AN EXAMPLE OF A FLAT FILE.

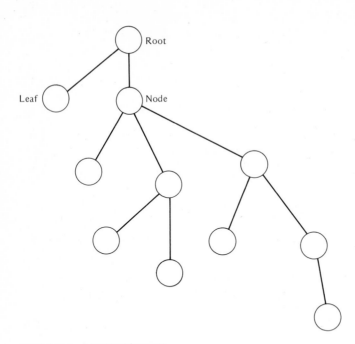

FIGURE 20-3   A TREE STRUCTURE.

An alternative to the parent-child terminology is *owner-member*. A hierarchy can be represented by a so-called *CODASYL set* as illustrated in Figure 20-4. The set terminology comes from the data base specifications of CODASYL.

Consider Figure 20-5, illustrating the hierarchical structure for a personnel file. The DEPT RECORD serves as the root of the tree hierarchy. EMPLOYEE RECORD and DEPT JOB RECORD are children of the root. Finally, EMPLOYEE RECORD is the parent to three logical children records: MAILING ADDRESS, JOB HISTORY, and DEPENDENTS.

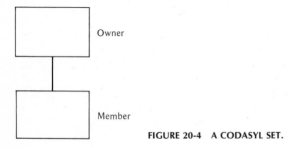

FIGURE 20-4   A CODASYL SET.

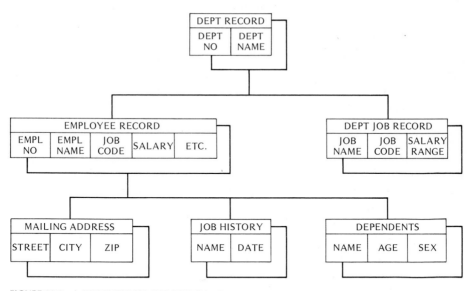

FIGURE 20-5   A HIERARCHICAL FILE STRUCTURE.

NETWORKS

A *network* is a data structure such that a child in a hierarchy may have more than one parent. Consider a case where a company operates on the basis of projects. Employees are assigned to projects and machines are used by projects. The logical relationships are represented in Figure 20-6. A specific illustration is given in Figure 20-7, which is based on three employees, two projects, and three machines. The connecting lines indicate the relationships. For instance, Employee 1 has three parents, Project 1 and Machines 1 and 2. Similarly, Project 1 can be viewed to have as parents Machines 1 and 3 and Employees 1, 2, and 3.

Figure 20-8 illustrates the decomposition of the example network into six set hierarchies, while Figure 20-9 illustrates that the network could also be represented by six flat files (at the cost of great redundancy).

THE RELATIONAL MODEL

The relational model is based on the fact that any data structure can be reduced to a set of flat files provided that some redundancy is allowed. A *relation* is a two-dimensional table. The table consists of rows called *tuples* and a fixed number of columns such that the data in a column represents a homogeneous set—the data represents values for the same attribute. The data base user is equipped with language operators which enable the formation of new tables (relations) by means of extracting a subset of columns, a subset of rows, or by combining columns and rows from two or more tables.

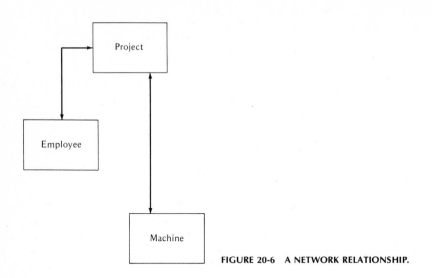

FIGURE 20-6 A NETWORK RELATIONSHIP.

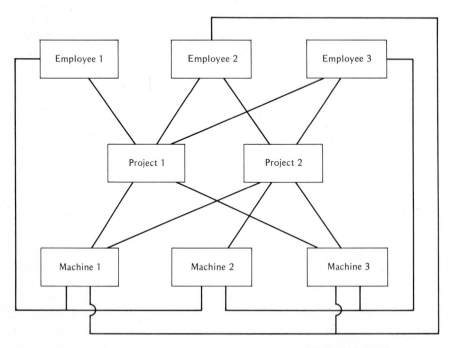

FIGURE 20-7 AN EXAMPLE OF A NETWORK STRUCTURE WITH THREE RECORD TYPES.

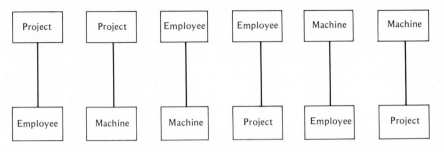

FIGURE 20-8 SUBSTITUTION OF SIX SET HIERARCHIES FOR A NETWORK.

Consider Figure 20-10, which represents two relations, Project and Employee. The Project Table consists of two rows and two columns while the Employee Table consists of five rows and two columns. Relationships can be formed by reference to these tables. Suppose that we present the request: Identify the employees who worked on Project 2. This request could be satisfied by forming a new table that would consist of the second and fifth rows of the Employee Table, as follows:

```
El    P2
E3    P2
```

As another example, consider the request: Find the customer names for the projects on which Employee 3 (E3) worked. This request would be satisfied by joining the fourth and fifth rows of the Employee Table and the two rows of the Project Table to form a new table:

EMPLOYEE NO	PROJECT NO		PROJECT NO	CUSTOMER NAME		CUSTOMER NAME
E3	P1	+	P1	Jones	=	Jones
E3	P2		P2	Smith		Smith

The appeal of the relational model is based on two factors. First, the concept of tabular structure seems easy to understand by users in general. In contrast, hierarchies

P1	E1	P1	M1	E1	M1	E1	P1	M1	E1	M1	P1
P1	E2	P1	M3	E1	M2	E2	P1	M1	E2	M1	P2
P1	E3	P2	M1	E2	M1	E2	P2	M2	E1	M2	P2
P2	E2	P2	M2	E2	M3	E3	P1	M2	E3	M3	P1
P2	E3	P2	M3	E3	M2	E3	P2	M3	E2	M3	P2
				E3	M3			M3	E3		

FIGURE 20-9   REPRESENTATION OF THE NETWORK AS SIX FLAT FILES.

PROJECT TABLE

PROJECT NO	CUSTOMER NAME
P1	Jones
P2	Smith

EMPLOYEE TABLE

EMPLOYEE NO	PROJECT NO
E1	P1
E1	P2
E2	P1
E3	P1
E3	P2

FIGURE 20-10   AN EXAMPLE OF A RELATIONAL MODEL DATA REPRESENTATION.

and networks can become quite complex and difficult to comprehend. The second advantage of the relational model is that it is based on a formal rational model whose logical manipulation can be described by means of a mathematical system of *relational algebra* or *relational calculus*.

REVIEW

1   The data structure concepts which are concerned with defined data relationships, but not the physical recording of the data, are associated with _____ data structure.

logical

2   In the flat file structure, if each column represents a data field, or attribute, then each row represents a _____ .

record

3   In the generalized terminology associated with data base concepts, a record is called a _____ or a _____ .

segment; tuple

4   In the flat file structure, each record is uniquely identified by one of the attributes which is used as the _____ .

entity identifier (or primary key)

5   In hierarchical tree structures, the element at the head of the tree is called the _____, while all other elements, which are hierarchically lower, are called _____ .

root; nodes

6   In hierarchical tree structures, a node which has other dependent nodes is called a _____ element, while the dependent nodes are called _____ .

parent; children

7   In hierarchical tree structures, a parent [can / cannot] have more than one child, and a child [can / cannot] have more than one parent.

can; cannot

8 In the network structure, a parent [can / cannot] have more than one child, and a child [can / cannot] have more than one parent.

can; can

9 If a file which has a network structure is represented by several flat files instead, the result is that there will be considerable _____ in data.

redundancy

10 When the relational model is used as the basis for logical data structure, the *relation* of interest can always be graphically portrayed as a two-dimensional _____.

table

11 The rows (or tuples) and columns which define a particular relation in the relational model are always extracted from [one / two / two or more] other data tables.

two or more

12 In comparison with hierarchical tree structures and network structures logical data structures which follow the relational model are generally [easier / more difficult] to understand.

easier

POINTER STRUCTURES

The preceding section presented the basic concepts associated with logical data structures. Our ability to understand and communicate logical structure concepts is dependent on our use of graphic representations. But computers can store characters of data, not graphic figures, and thus we must use some other method of representation when it comes to considerations of *physical data structures*. *Pointers* provide us with an effective physical means of implementing logical data relationships in computer storage. A pointer is a data-item whose value is the storage address of some other data-item. Commonly, a pointer is a record field which contains the storage address of some other record. (The reader may recall encountering the concept of pointers in Chapter 16, "Direct Access Files," in connection with the linkage of overflow records in indexed sequential files.)

In this section we present some of the common pointer structures. It should be recognized, however, that there are many other pointer structures that are also used.

LIST CHAINS

A list is a data structure such that there is one starting (head) record, and each record (including the head) contains a pointer to the next record in sequence. The last record in the sequence has a special pointer value to indicate the end of the list chain. Figure 20-11 represents a simple list structure for five "Project Records." The spatial separation of the records is intended to represent the possible physical separations that may exist between records. The arrows in Figure 20-11 provide a pictorial view of the pointer structure. In computer storage the value stored in the pointer field gives the storage address of the record to which the arrow points in the figure.

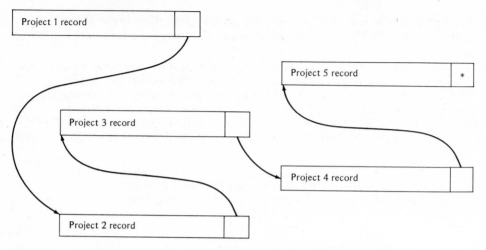

FIGURE 20-11   A SIMPLE LIST STRUCTURE.

The basic advantage of a simple list chain is that we may preserve logical order even though we may have "random" physical order. One disadvantage is that it is a forward-only system. If we have accessed a particular record through a chain of pointers and we wish to access its logical predecessor, there is no way to go backward. Figure 20-12 shows how we can have both forward and backward access capability by

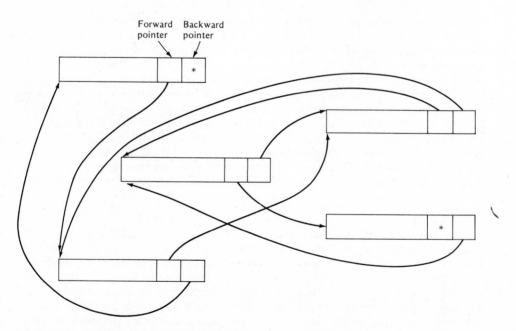

FIGURE 20-12   A LIST CHAIN WITH FORWARD AND BACKWARD POINTERS.

utilizing two pointers in each record. One pointer gives the storage address of the succeeding record while the other pointer gives the storage address of the preceding record.

Figure 20-13 illustrates the applications of two-way pointers in the case of hierarchical structure involving two projects and the relationships of employees and machines assigned to projects. We form two list chains, one for each project. The Project records serve as heads of their respective chains. Each Employee record contains two pointers. One pointer points to the next employee record for Project 1 while the other pointer points to the next employee record for Project 2. The

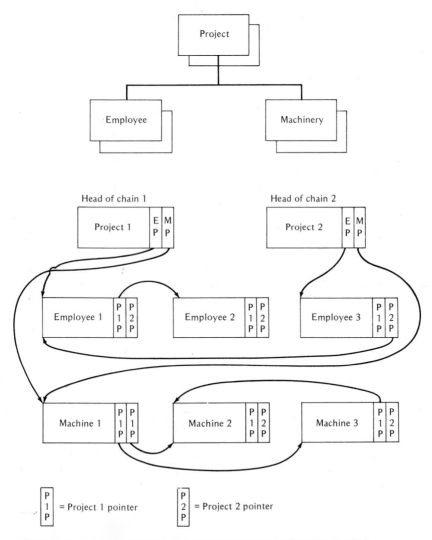

FIGURE 20-13   AN ILLUSTRATION OF A LIST CHAIN WITH TWO-WAY POINTERS.

employee pointer (EP) in the Project 1 record points to Employee 1. The Project 1 Pointer (P1P) in the Employee 1 record points to the Employee 2 record, which is the end of the chain. With respect to the Project 2 chain it should be noted that the first record in the employee chain is Employee 3, which is followed by Employee 1. This last example illustrates the ability of pointer structures to represent logical orders which are impossible as physical orders without redundancy. Specifically, the Employee 1 record is first in the Project 1 chain while it is last in the Project 2 chain.

The machine records also contain two pointers in a fashion analogous to that of the employee records.

RINGS

A ring is a list chain such that the last record in the chain points to the head record. Figure 20-14 shows a simple ring structure. A ring provides an access path that is circular, and care must be taken to distinguish the head record. Suppose that in a ring of 500 records we are looking for a record which does not exist. We could have an infinite loop if we did not mark the header record as such.

Sometimes it is desirable to be able to return to the head of a chain from the record which we have just accessed without completing the entire path of the ring. Figure 20-15 illustrates the use of two pointers for quick return to the head record. One pointer points to the next record while the other points to the head record.

Reviewing Figure 20-15, it can be seen that the pointer structure allows return to the head of the chain, but is inefficient for returning to the predecessor record. Thus in such a ring of 500 records if we had accessed the 300th logical record and we wanted to access the 299th logical record, we would have to access all records from the first record (head) to the 299th record. We could consider the use of a third pointer to identify the predessor record if we anticipate frequent need to backtrack. Obviously, pointer systems can proliferate as we strive for flexibility and efficiency. For instance, it is possible to have pointers that allow for "big jumps" instead of one record at a time. In general, as the number of pointers increases file updating becomes more complex, since additions or deletions to the file require changes in many pointers.

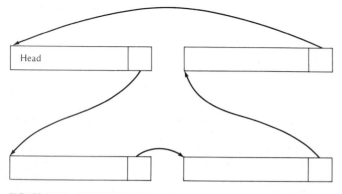

FIGURE 20-14   A SIMPLE RING STRUCTURE.

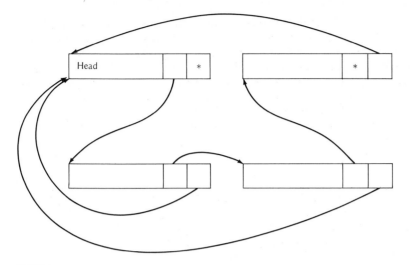

FIGURE 20-15   A TWO-POINTER RING STRUCTURE.

REVIEW

1   In terms of physical data structure, a data-item whose value indicates the storage location of some other record is called a _____.

pointer

2   In a simple list structure, if there is only one pointer per record, that pointer usually identifies the [preceding / succeeding] record.

succeeding

3   When a simple list structure is used, it [is / is not] necessary that the records in the file physically be in a logical order.

is not

4   The type of list chain structure in which one or more records in the chain point to the head record is called a _____.

ring

FILE INVERSION

It is often desirable to query a data base in the following fashion: retrieve all the employees who have a particular characteristic. If the file is ordered by that particular characteristic then the access to those records is easy. If, however, the file is ordered on some other basis then the entire file has to be read in order to retrieve all of the appropriate records. *File inversion* is a data structure which facilitates efficient data-base interrogation. Let us consider an example.

Figure 20-16 presents an ordinary flat file. Records are identified by EMPLOYEE-NO, the primary key. The file is (partially) inverted in Figure 20-17, where we have created two indexes. The first index is ordered by the DEPT-NO values and for each department it contains a pointer to the storage address of the EMPLOYEE-NO indicated. The second index is ordered according to JOB, and also contains a pointer to the storage address of the employee. The little arrow is included to show that the value stored there would be the storage address for the record of the employee-number shown, and *not* the employee-number as such. The department index indicates, for instance, that the records of employee 102 and 113 contain the department-number value of 10. Now look back at the Employee file. It consists of only three data items per record. The DEPARTMENT and JOB attributes have been eliminated on the assumption that the indexes suffice to provide this information. (We will return to this point shortly.)

Figure 20-17 is an example of partial inversion. A fully inverted file is one with an index for each attribute. In our example, full inversion would also include an index for NAME and an index for SALARY. Indexes created for inversion are called *secondary* indexes. The primary index is, of course, based on the record identifier (primary key).

In general, only partial inversion is necessary. In our example in Figure 20-17 the file is not inverted on NAME or SALARY. On close observation it will be seen that an index for either of these two attributes would be as long as the original file, since the values of SALARY and NAME are unique. For that reason we might pause before deciding to invert fully, and consider whether queries about salary or name are going to be frequent. If it is expected that queries about names or salaries are going to be frequent, then it would be preferable to invert the file on those two fields, as well. In the absence of inversion, if we were looking for a name in the file there would be no knowledge available as to where in the file that name is located. With inversion, however, the name index would be sorted and quick reference to a particular name would be possible.

One more observation is in order. In Figure 20-17 the Employee file does not contain data for DEPT-NO and JOB, which are the basis for the two secondary indexes. Suppose we ask the question: In what department is Employee 112 located? The required access path would be to search the Department Index in a serial fashion until we have satisfied the question. If we did want to have the ability to retrieve efficiently all the attributes of a given employee's record, then we could retain all the data in the

EMPLOYEE-NO	DEPARTMENT	NAME	JOB	SALARY
100	30	Doe	Plumber	17,600
102	10	Johnson	Carpenter	14,400
105	30	Taylor	Welder	13,000
112	20	Prentice	Carpenter	15,000
113	10	Brown	Plumber	14,800
122	20	Smith	Carpenter	11,900
125	30	Burger	Carpenter	12,000

FIGURE 20-16   A FLAT EMPLOYEE FILE.

EMPLOYEE FILE

EMPLOYEE-NO	NAME	SALARY
100	Doe	17,600
102	Johnson	14,400
105	Taylor	13,000
112	Prentice	15,000
113	Brown	14,800
122	Smith	11,900
125	Burger	12,000

DEPARTMENT INDEX

DEPT-NO	POINTER TO EMPLOYEE FILE		
10	102 ↑	113 ↑	
20	100 ↑	112 ↑	122 ↑
30	105 ↑	125 ↑	

JOB INDEX

JOB	POINTER TO EMPLOYEE FILE			
Carpenter	102	112	122 ↑	125 ↑
Plumber	100	113		
Welder	105			

FIGURE 20-17   AN ILLUSTRATION OF A PARTIALLY INVERTED FILE.

Employee file. But redundancy would thereby be introduced, since now the values for DEPARTMENT-NO and JOB would be stored both in the respective indexes and in the Employee file.

REVIEW

1   When a file is inverted, this means that one or more _____ are created to facilitate efficient data base interrogation.

indexes

2   When indexes are created for some but not all of the attributes in the records, the file is said to be _____. When indexes are available for all attributes, the file is said to be _____.

partially inverted; fully inverted

3   An objective underlying file inversion is to facilitate data base interrogation by [including / not including] redundancy in the file system.

not including

4   Consider a file which is ordered on the basis of PART-NO and has an index for CUSTOMER-NO. If a report is prepared according to CUSTOMER-NO, then the efficiency of processing for this report is [greater than / equal to / less than] it would be if the file were ordered according to CUSTOMER-NO.

less than

DATA BASE MANAGEMENT SYSTEMS

The conceptual design of a data base has to take into account the unique characteristics of each organization. However, the programming implementation need not be unique in the sense that file data definition and file processing as applied in different organizations are bound to include a great deal of common logic. Recognition of this fact has led to the development of a number of so-called data base management systems. These are software packages designed to minimize individual programming efforts in both the creation and use of data bases for report production. Presently, they are mainly available from software firms for a rental or purchase fee. Based on their degree of sophistication, the purchase price for such systems varies from about $10,000 to in excess of $100,000.

These generalized software packages represent extensive programming efforts. There are basically two types of data base management systems that have been developed: the host-language systems and the self-contained systems. The host-language systems are enhancements of procedure-oriented languages such as COBOL. Options within the language allow file management programming to be accomplished with a limited number of commands. The self-contained systems utilize their own language rules, and in this sense such a system can be thought of as a unique procedure-oriented language directed toward file management in data base systems. The Data Base Task Group (DBTG) appointed by the CODASYL Committee that oversees the development of COBOL has developed a set of specifications for incorporating data base management capabilities within the COBOL language. Therefore, it is likely that a COBOL feature for data management eventually will be adopted which will incorporate the standardization, self-documentation, and other features associated with COBOL.

As indicated above, from the user's standpoint the advantage of using a data base management system is that it minimizes the amount of individual program development on the part of the user. In more specific terms, the following advantages can be cited for using such a software package:

1   Allow the firm's programmer to work on complex tasks rather than on routine file maintenance and report generation.
2   Since the program statements in such systems are shorter than those in standard programming languages, reduce the amount of manual effort to create and transcribe programs.

3 Eliminate duplicate file design efforts through the availability of easily restructured file definitions.
4 Allow the execution of multiple tasks concurrently and the production of reports in many different sequences given one set of specifications.
5 Give the user the advantage of a debugged common program logic, thereby making the user's own debugging task less complex and less time-consuming.

The term *schema* is used to denote the logical description of the data base. Typically, there is a Data Base Administrator (DBA) in an organization whose main responsibility is to define and maintain the data base schema. Applications programmers need not be bound by the schema. Each applications program defines a *subschema,* which is a description of data from the viewpoint of this particular program. It will be recalled that one of the reasons for a data base is to have the capability to look at data from different perspectives for individual uses (subschema), while at the same time the overall relationships of data are maintained in the background (schema). Figure 20-18 presents the main elements in the operation of a data base system. The Data Base Management System (DBMS) is the central element. The DBMS interacts with the Operating System in controlling all aspects of data base operations. The schema describes the overall logical blueprint of the data base. The actual physical data base resides in direct access storage devices and it is stored and maintained there by the DBMS. Each subschema is used by the DBMS to access the physical data base

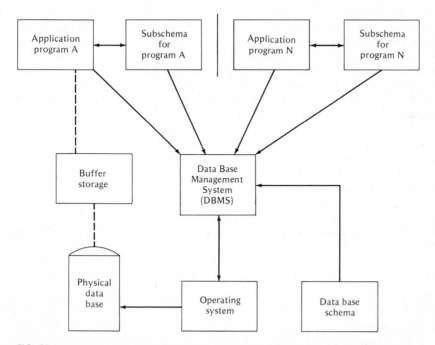

FIGURE 20-18   BASIC ELEMENTS OF A DATA BASE MANAGEMENT SYSTEM IN OPERATION.

and make it available through some buffer storage, which serves as the staging point for data access and manipulation.

In order to implement the functions required of a DBMS there are three types of languages needed. One is a language to enable the DBA to construct and maintain the schema. The CODASYL Data Base Task Group (DBTG) has proposed a Data Description Language (DDL) for such a purpose. A second language needed is one that can provide the interface between the applications programmer and the DBMS. The CODASYL proposed name is Data Manipulation Language (DML). In fact, the proposed CODASYL DML is an extension of COBOL and can be used by the COBOL programmer as part of the application program. For instance, the DML includes commands such as: CLOSE, DELETE, FIND, GET, INSERT, MODIFY, OPEN, ORDER, REMOVE, STORE.

The third type of language needed is one to describe data storage and retrieval at the physical level—a Device/Media Control Language (DMCL). This third type of language has to be oriented toward specific hardware, and therefore there is less of an agreement as to what such a language should be for general use. We might mention DL/I (Data Language I), an IBM product which can be used both for schema definition and for physical data description in that company's widely used IMS data base management system.

There are many data base software products available. These products vary in the conceptual basis for the data base and the features which are available, as well as the hardware for which they are programmed. Table 20-1 lists some of these products, but the list is by no means exhaustive. Even manufacturers of small computer systems are developing data base management systems. Choosing among these many and varied software offerings is not an easy task. Lack of accepted standardization makes the choice rather critical, since portability from one system to another is nonexistent. CODASYL has proposed a standard, but there exists wide controversy about this standard and, with a few exceptions such as IDMS, lack of implementation of the standard. It is therefore safe to predict that in the next few years organizations wishing to reap the benefits of the data base approach will continue making the committment to data base using nonstandard software. Then we may see the emergence of common

**TABLE 20-1 SOME WELL-KNOWN DATA BASE MANAGE-
MENT SYSTEMS**

VENDOR	DATA BASE SOFTWARE PRODUCTS
Burroughs	DMS II, Disk FORTE/2
CDC	CDCS, MARS VI
Honeywell	IDS
IBM	IMS, CICS
UNIVAC	DMS 1100
ICL	System 4 DBMS, 2900 DMS
Cullinane	IDMS
Informatics	MARK IV
Cincom	TOTAL
Software AG	ADABAS
MRI	System 2000

if not standard languages for data bases, at which point organizations will undergo major conversion efforts from the current multitude of varied software to a few common systems.

REVIEW

1 A data base management system is essentially a specialized type of _____ package.

software

2 Of the two types of data base management systems, the type for which the program statements used are similar to a procedure-oriented language such as COBOL is the [self-contained / host-language] system.

host-language

3 The main advantage associated with using a data base management system is that _____ .

it minimizes the amount of programming and debugging that has to be done for a particular system (etc.)

4 The overall logical description of the data base is included in the _____ for the data base, while each applications program defines a _____ for specific uses of the data.

schema; subschema

5 In the context of data base management systems, DBA stands for _____ _____ and DBMS stands for _____ .

Data Base Administrator; Data Base Management System

6 A language which enables the DBA to construct and maintain a schema is the DDL, or _____ .

Data Description Language

7 A language which serves to provide an interface between the applications programmer and the DBMS is the DML, or _____ .

Data Manipulation Language

8 At the current stage of development, it can be said that the software to be used to implement the data base approach [has / has not] been fairly well standardized.

has not

EXERCISES

1 Define the concept of a data base information system, and describe the data-oriented objectives associated with such a system.

2 Identify the principal advantages and disadvantages associated with the functional approach to information systems.

3 True or false: In order to eliminate the adverse consequences associated with the functional approach to information systems, organizations should be structured on some basis other than the functional approach. Discuss.

4 Differentiate the concepts of logical data structure and physical data structure in the design of a data base information system.

5 Give some examples of different logical data structures and describe some of the differences among these structures.

6 Various types of pointer structures provide the physical basis for implementing logical data relationships in computer storage. Describe some of the common pointer structures which are available.

7 What is the main objective associated with file inversion? Describe how this objective is achieved.

8 What are "data base management systems"? Describe the nature and availability of such systems at the present time, and the likely direction of future developments in this area.

ANSI COBOL
Reserved Words

ACCEPT	CHARACTER	DE
ACCESS	CHARACTERS	DEBUG-CONTENTS
ADD	CLOCK-UNITS	DEBUG-ITEM
ADVANCING	CLOSE	DEBUG-LINE
AFTER	COBOL	DEBUG-NAME
ALL	CODE	DEBUG-SUB-1
ALPHABETIC	CODE-SET	DEBUG-SUB-2
ALSO	COLLATING	DEBUG-SUB-3
ALTER	COLUMN	DEBUGGING
ALTERNATE	COMMA	DECIMAL-POINT
AND	COMMUNICATION	DECLARATIVES
ARE	COMP	DELETE
AREA	COMPUTATIONAL	DELIMITED
AREAS	COMPUTE	DELIMITER
ASCENDING	CONFIGURATION	DEPENDING
ASSIGN	CONTAINS	DESCENDING
AT	CONTROL	DESTINATION
AUTHOR	CONTROLS	DETAIL
BEFORE	COPY	DISABLE
BLANK	CORR	DISPLAY
BLOCK	CORRESPONDING	DIVIDE
BOTTOM	COUNT	DIVISION
BY	CURRENCY	DOWN
CALL	DATA	DUPLICATES
CANCEL	DATE	DYNAMIC
CD	DATE-COMPILED	EGI
CF	DATE-WRITTEN	ELSE
CH	DAY	EMI

ENABLE	KEY	PF
END	LABEL	PH
END-OF-PAGE	LAST	PIC
ENTER	LEADING	PICTURE
ENVIRONMENT	LEFT	PLUS
EOP	LENGTH	POINTER
EQUAL	LESS	POSITION
ERROR ESI	LIMIT	POSITIVE
EVERY	LIMITS	PRINTING
EXCEPTION	LINAGE	PROCEDURE
EXIT	LINAGE-COUNTER	PROCEDURES
EXTEND	LINE	PROCEED
FD	LINE-COUNTER	PROGRAM
FILE	LINES	PROGRAM-ID
FILE-CONTROL	LINKAGE	QUEUE
FILLER	LOCK	QUOTE
FINAL	LOW-VALUE	QUOTES
FIRST	LOW-VALUES	RANDOM
FOOTING	MEMORY	RD
FOR	MERGE	READ
FROM	MESSAGE	RECEIVE
GENERATE	MODE	RECORD
GIVING	MODULES	RECORDS
GO	MOVE	REDEFINES
GREATER	MULTIPLE	REEL
GROUP	MULTIPLY	REFERENCES
HEADING	NATIVE	RELATIVE
HIGH-VALUE	NEGATIVE	RELEASE
HIGH-VALUES	NEXT	REMAINDER
I-O	NO	REMOVAL
I-O-CONTROL	NOT	RENAMES
IDENTIFICATION	NUMBER	REPLACING
IF	NUMERIC	REPORT
IN	OBJECT-COMPUTER	REPORTING
INDEX	OCCURS	REPORTS
INDEXED	OF	RERUN
INDICATE	OFF	RESERVE
INITIAL	OMITTED	RESET
INITIATE	ON	RETURN
INPUT	OPEN	REVERSED
INPUT-OUTPUT	OPTIONAL	REWIND
INSPECT	OR	REWRITE
INSTALLATION	ORGANIZATION	RF
INTO	OUTPUT	RH
INVALID	OVERFLOW	RIGHT
IS	PAGE	ROUNDED
JUST	PAGE-COUNTER	RUN
JUSTIFIED	PERFORM	SAME

SD	STRING	UNSTRING
SEARCH	SUB-QUEUE-1	UNTIL
SECTION	SUB-QUEUE-2	UP
SECURITY	SUB-QUEUE-3	UPON
SEGMENT	SUBTRACT	USAGE
SEGMENT-LIMIT	SUM	USE
SELECT	SUPPRESS	USING
SEND	SYMBOLIC	VALUE
SENTENCE	SYNC	VALUES
SEPARATE	SYNCHRONIZED	VARYING
SEQUENCE	TABLE	WHEN
SEQUENTIAL	TALLYING	WITH
SET	TAPE	WORDS
SIGN	TERMINAL	WORKING-STORAGE
SIZE	TERMINATE	WRITE
SORT	TEXT	ZERO
SORT-MERGE	THAN	ZEROES
SOURCE	THROUGH	ZEROS
SOURCE-COMPUTER	THRU	+
SPACE	TIME	−
SPACES	TIMES	*
SPECIAL-NAMES	TO	/
STANDARD	TOP	**
STANDARD-1	TRAILING	>
START	TYPE	<
STATUS	UNIT	=
STOP		

ANSI COBOL

American National Standards Institute (ANSI) COBOL is defined in terms of a nucleus and 11 functional modules, as shown in Figure B-1. This structure contrasts with the fact that COBOL programs are structured in terms of four divisions: IDENTIFICATION, ENVIRONMENT, DATA, and PROCEDURE. The new structure is designed primarily for the guidance of compiler writers who may choose to implement the whole or one of many possible subsets of the language. Thus in learning the language, the structure of standard COBOL is of practically no importance. However, in using the language or in deciding on manufacturers and their compilers the level of language implemented becomes quite important.

In terms of the schematic diagram in Figure B-1, an implementation of ANSI COBOL can be represented by a combination of boxes, consisting of one box from each of the 12 vertical columns.

Full ANSI COBOL is composed of the highest level of the nucleus and of each of the functional processing modules.

A *subset* of ANSI COBOL is any combination of levels of the nucleus and of each of the functional processing modules other than full ANSI COBOL.

Minimum ANSI COBOL is composed of the lowest level of the nucleus and of each of the functional processing modules. (Because of the presence of null sets, the minimum standard consists of the low levels of the nucleus, table handling, and sequential I-O.)

Functional Processing Modules

Nucleus	Table handling	Sequential I-O	Relative I-O	Indexed I-O	Sort-merge	Report writer	Segmentation	Library	Debug	Inter-program communi-'cation	Communi-cation
Level 2	Level 2	Level 2	Level 2	Level 2	Level 2	Level 1	Level 2	Level 2	Level 2	Level 2	Level 2
Level 1	Level 1	Level 1	Level 1	Level 1	Level 1		Level 1	Level 1	Level 1	Level 1	Level 1
			Null	Null	Null	Null	Null	Null	Null	Null	Null

FIGURE B-1 STRUCTURE OF ANSI COBOL.

560

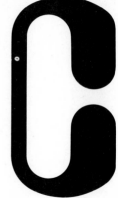

Complete
ANSI COBOL Language
Formats

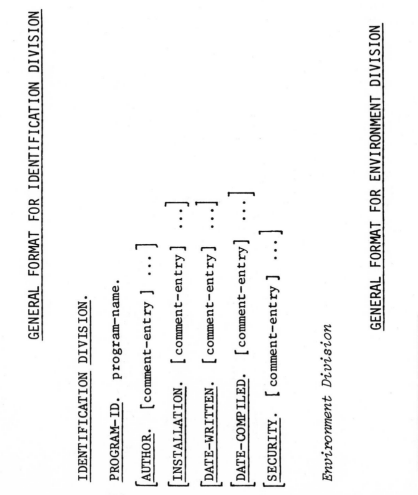

Identification Division

GENERAL FORMAT FOR IDENTIFICATION DIVISION

IDENTIFICATION DIVISION.

PROGRAM-ID. program-name.

[AUTHOR. [comment-entry] ...]

[INSTALLATION. [comment-entry] ...]

[DATE-WRITTEN. [comment-entry] ...]

[DATE-COMPILED. [comment-entry] ...]

[SECURITY. [comment-entry] ...]

Environment Division

GENERAL FORMAT FOR ENVIRONMENT DIVISION

ENVIRONMENT DIVISION.

GENERAL FORMAT FOR ENVIRONMENT DIVISION (CONT.)

CONFIGURATION SECTION.

SOURCE-COMPUTER. computer-name [WITH DEBUGGING MODE] .

OBJECT-COMPUTER. computer-name

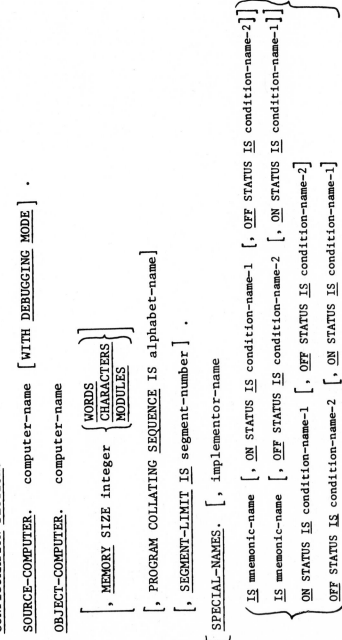

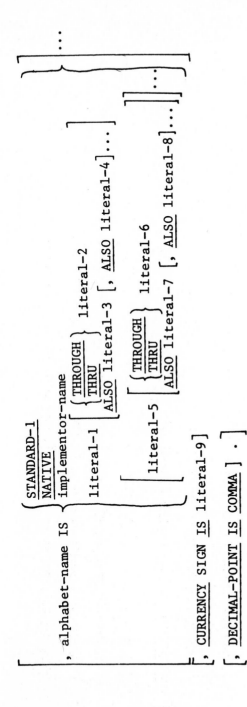

```
                                                                              ...
⎡                     ⎧ STANDARD-1       ⎫                                        ⎤
⎢                     ⎪ NATIVE           ⎪                                        ⎥
⎢ , alphabet-name IS  ⎨ implementor-name ⎬                                        ⎥
⎢                     ⎪          ⎡ ⎧ THROUGH ⎫ literal-2                   ⎤       ⎥ ...
⎢                     ⎪ literal-1 ⎢ ⎨ THRU    ⎬                            ⎥       ⎥
⎢                     ⎩          ⎣ ALSO literal-3 [, ALSO literal-4]...    ⎦       ⎥
⎢                               ⎡           ⎡ ⎧ THROUGH ⎫ literal-6        ⎤    ⎤  ⎥
⎢                               ⎢ literal-5 ⎢ ⎨ THRU    ⎬                  ⎥... ⎥  ⎥
⎣                               ⎣           ⎣ ALSO literal-7 [, ALSO literal-8]... ⎦ ⎦⎦

[ , CURRENCY SIGN IS literal-9 ]

[ , DECIMAL-POINT IS COMMA ] .
```

[INPUT-OUTPUT SECTION.

FILE-CONTROL.

{file-control-entry} ...

[I-O-CONTROL.

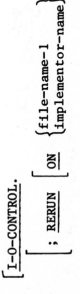

```
⎡            ⎡    ⎧ file-name-1      ⎫ ⎤
⎢ ; RERUN    ⎢ ON ⎨                  ⎬ ⎥
⎣            ⎣    ⎩ implementor-name ⎭ ⎦
```

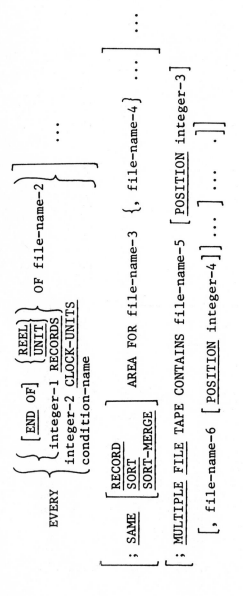

$$\text{EVERY} \left\{ \begin{array}{l} \left[\text{END OF}\right] \left\{ \begin{array}{l} \underline{\text{REEL}} \\ \underline{\text{UNIT}} \end{array} \right\} \\ \text{integer-1 RECORDS} \\ \text{integer-2 CLOCK-UNITS} \\ \text{condition-name} \end{array} \right\} \text{OF file-name-2} \quad \dots$$

$$; \underline{\text{SAME}} \left[\begin{array}{l} \text{RECORD} \\ \underline{\text{SORT}} \\ \underline{\text{SORT-MERGE}} \end{array} \right] \text{AREA FOR file-name-3} \left\{ \text{, file-name-4} \right\} \dots \quad \dots$$

$$; \underline{\text{MULTIPLE FILE}} \text{ TAPE CONTAINS file-name-5} \left[\underline{\text{POSITION}} \text{ integer-3} \right]$$
$$\left[\text{, file-name-6} \left[\underline{\text{POSITION}} \text{ integer-4} \right] \right] \dots \quad \dots \; .$$

Environment Division

GENERAL FORMAT FOR FILE CONTROL ENTRY

FORMAT 1:

<u>SELECT</u> [OPTIONAL] file-name

<u>ASSIGN</u> TO implementor-name-1 [, implementor-name-2] ...

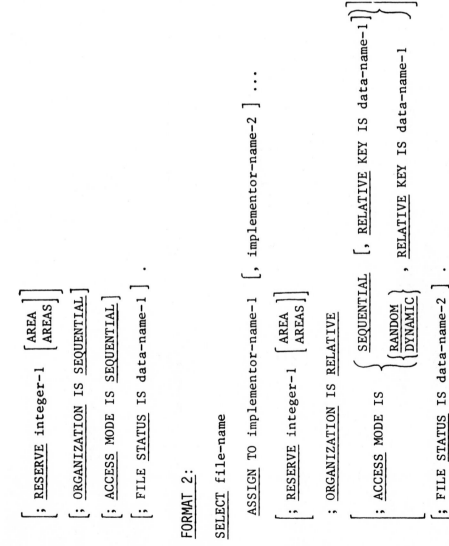

[; RESERVE integer-1 [AREA / AREAS]]

[; ORGANIZATION IS SEQUENTIAL]

[; ACCESS MODE IS SEQUENTIAL]

[; FILE STATUS IS data-name-1] .

FORMAT 2:

SELECT file-name

ASSIGN TO implementor-name-1 [, implementor-name-2] ...

[; RESERVE integer-1 [AREA / AREAS]]

; ORGANIZATION IS RELATIVE

[; ACCESS MODE IS { SEQUENTIAL [, RELATIVE KEY IS data-name-1] / {RANDOM / DYNAMIC} , RELATIVE KEY IS data-name-1 }]

[; FILE STATUS IS data-name-2] .

565

GENERAL FORMAT FOR FILE CONTROL ENTRY (CONT.)

FORMAT 3:

SELECT file-name

ASSIGN TO implementor-name-1 [, implementor-name-2] ...

[; RESERVE integer-1 [AREA
                        AREAS]]

; ORGANIZATION IS INDEXED

[; ACCESS MODE IS { SEQUENTIAL
                     RANDOM
                     DYNAMIC }]

; RECORD KEY IS data-name-1

[; ALTERNATE RECORD KEY IS data-name-2 [WITH DUPLICATES]] ...

[; FILE STATUS IS data-name-3] .

FORMAT 4:

SELECT file-name ASSIGN TO implementor-name-1 [, implementor-name-2] ...

Data Division

GENERAL FORMAT FOR DATA DIVISION

DATA DIVISION.

[FILE SECTION.

[FD file-name

$$\left[\text{; BLOCK CONTAINS } [\text{integer-1 } \underline{\text{TO}}] \text{ integer-2 } \left\{ \begin{array}{l} \underline{\text{RECORDS}} \\ \text{CHARACTERS} \end{array} \right\} \right]$$

$$\left[\text{; } \underline{\text{RECORD}} \text{ CONTAINS } [\text{integer-3 } \underline{\text{TO}}] \text{ integer-4 CHARACTERS} \right]$$

$$\left[\text{; } \underline{\text{LABEL}} \left\{ \begin{array}{l} \underline{\text{RECORD}} \text{ IS} \\ \underline{\text{RECORDS}} \text{ ARE} \end{array} \right\} \left\{ \begin{array}{l} \underline{\text{STANDARD}} \\ \underline{\text{OMITTED}} \end{array} \right\} \right.$$

$$\left[\text{; } \underline{\text{VALUE}} \underline{\text{OF}} \text{ implementor-name-1 IS } \left\{ \begin{array}{l} \text{data-name-1} \\ \text{literal-1} \end{array} \right\} \right.$$

GENERAL FORMAT FOR DATA DIVISION (CONT.)

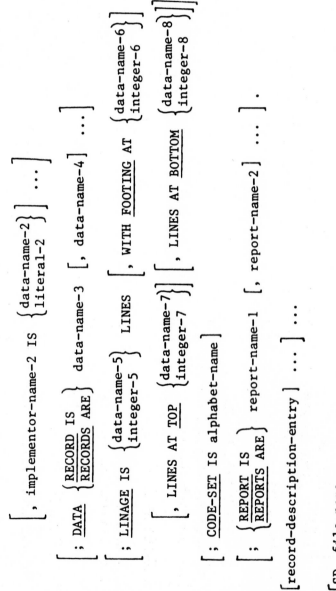

```
    [ , implementor-name-2 IS  { data-name-2  } ]  ...  ]
                               { literal-2    }

    [ ; DATA  { RECORD IS   }  data-name-3  [ , data-name-4 ]  ... ]
              { RECORDS ARE }

    [ ; LINAGE IS  { data-name-5 }  LINES  [ , WITH FOOTING AT  { data-name-6 } ]
                   { integer-5   }                              { integer-6   }

        [ , LINES AT TOP  { data-name-7 } ]  [ , LINES AT BOTTOM  { data-name-8 } ] ]
                          { integer-7   }                        { integer-8   }

    [ ; CODE-SET IS alphabet-name ]

    [ ; { REPORT IS   }  report-name-1  [ , report-name-2 ]  ... ] .
        { REPORTS ARE }

[ record-description-entry ]  ...  ]

[ SD file-name
```

```
     [ ; RECORD CONTAINS [integer-1 TO] integer-2 CHARACTERS ]

     [ ; DATA { RECORD IS   } data-name-1 [ , data-name-2 ] ... ] .
                { RECORDS ARE }

     {record-description-entry} ... ] ...


WORKING-STORAGE SECTION.

     [ 77-level-description-entry ] ...
       record-description-entry


LINKAGE SECTION.

     [ 77-level-description-entry ] ...
       record-description-entry


COMMUNICATION SECTION.

     [communication-description-entry

     [record-description-entry] ... ] ...


REPORT SECTION.

     [RD report-name
```

569

```
[; CODE literal-1]

    ⎧ CONTROL IS   ⎫  ⎧ ⎧ data-name-1 [, data-name-2] ...               ⎫ ⎤ ⎫
[;  ⎨             ⎬   ⎨ ⎨                                                ⎬ ⎥ ⎬
    ⎩ CONTROLS ARE ⎭  ⎩ ⎩ FINAL [, data-name-1 [, data-name-2] ...]     ⎭ ⎦ ⎭

         ⎡ LIMIT IS   ⎤            ⎡ LINE  ⎤
[; PAGE  ⎢            ⎥ integer-1  ⎢       ⎥ [, HEADING integer-2]
         ⎣ LIMITS ARE ⎦            ⎣ LINES ⎦

   [, FIRST DETAIL integer-3] [, LAST DETAIL integer-4]

   [, FOOTING integer-5] ] .

{report-group-description-entry} ... ]
```

Data Division

GENERAL FORMAT FOR DATA DESCRIPTION ENTRY

FORMAT 1:

```
                ⎧ data-name-1 ⎫
level-number    ⎨             ⎬
                ⎩ FILLER      ⎭

   [; REDEFINES data-name-2]
```

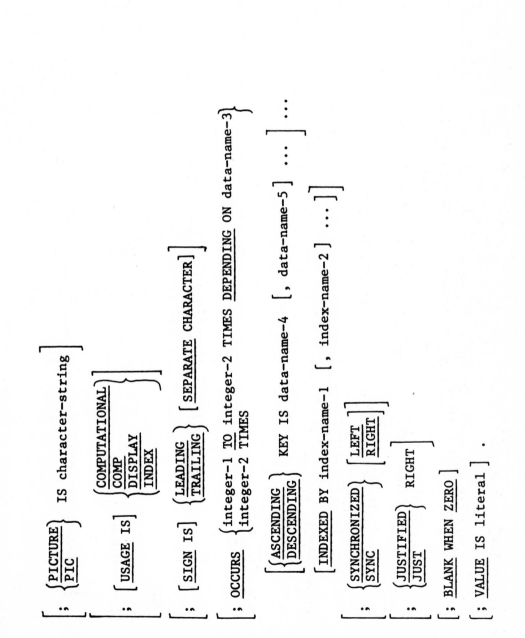

```
 ; {PICTURE} IS character-string
   {PIC    }

 ; [USAGE IS] {COMPUTATIONAL}
              {COMP         }
              {DISPLAY      }
              {INDEX        }

 ; [SIGN IS] {LEADING } [SEPARATE CHARACTER]
             {TRAILING}

 ; OCCURS {integer-1 TO integer-2 TIMES DEPENDING ON data-name-3}
          {integer-2 TIMES                                      }
     [{ASCENDING } KEY IS data-name-4 [, data-name-5] ... ] ...
      {DESCENDING}
     [INDEXED BY index-name-1 [, index-name-2] ...]

 ; {SYNCHRONIZED} [LEFT ]
   {SYNC        } [RIGHT]

 ; {JUSTIFIED} RIGHT
   {JUST     }

 ; BLANK WHEN ZERO

 ; VALUE IS literal .
```

FORMAT 2:

66 data-name-1; <u>RENAMES</u> data-name-2 $\left[\begin{Bmatrix} \underline{THROUGH} \\ \underline{THRU} \end{Bmatrix} \text{data-name-3}\right]$.

FORMAT 3:

88 condition-name; $\begin{Bmatrix} \underline{VALUE} \text{ IS} \\ \underline{VALUES} \text{ ARE} \end{Bmatrix}$ literal-1 $\left[\begin{Bmatrix} \underline{THROUGH} \\ \underline{THRU} \end{Bmatrix} \text{literal-2}\right]$

$\left[, \text{literal-3} \left[\begin{Bmatrix} \underline{THROUGH} \\ \underline{THRU} \end{Bmatrix} \text{literal-4}\right]\right]$ ... .

Data Division

<u>GENERAL FORMAT FOR COMMUNICATION DESCRIPTION ENTRY</u>

FORMAT 1:

<u>CD</u> cd-name;

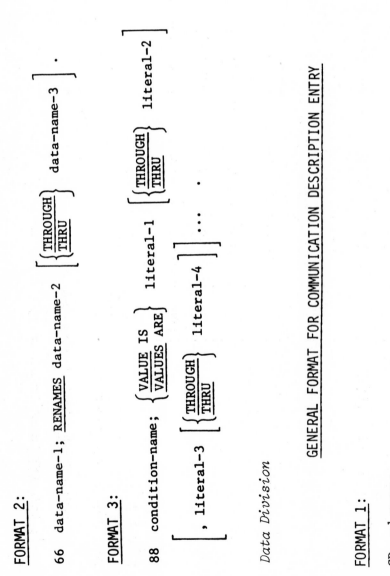

[[; SYMBOLIC <u>QUEUE</u> IS data-name-1]

[; SYMBOLIC <u>SUB-QUEUE-1</u> IS data-name-2]

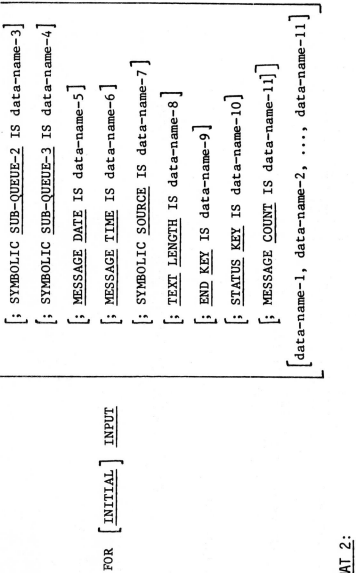

$$
\text{FOR } \left[\underline{\text{INITIAL}}\right] \quad \underline{\text{INPUT}}
$$

$$
\left[\begin{array}{l}
\text{; } \underline{\text{SYMBOLIC}} \ \underline{\text{SUB-QUEUE}}\text{-2 IS data-name-3} \\
\text{; } \underline{\text{SYMBOLIC}} \ \underline{\text{SUB-QUEUE}}\text{-3 IS data-name-4} \\
\text{; } \underline{\text{MESSAGE}} \ \underline{\text{DATE}} \text{ IS data-name-5} \\
\text{; } \underline{\text{MESSAGE}} \ \underline{\text{TIME}} \text{ IS data-name-6} \\
\text{; } \underline{\text{SYMBOLIC}} \ \underline{\text{SOURCE}} \text{ IS data-name-7} \\
\text{; } \underline{\text{TEXT}} \ \underline{\text{LENGTH}} \text{ IS data-name-8} \\
\text{; } \underline{\text{END}} \ \underline{\text{KEY}} \text{ IS data-name-9} \\
\text{; } \underline{\text{STATUS}} \ \underline{\text{KEY}} \text{ IS data-name-10} \\
\text{; } \underline{\text{MESSAGE}} \ \underline{\text{COUNT}} \text{ IS data-name-11}]
\end{array}\right.
$$

[data-name-1, data-name-2, ..., data-name-11]

FORMAT 2:

CD cd-name; FOR OUTPUT

$$
\left[\begin{array}{l}
\text{; } \underline{\text{DESTINATION}} \ \underline{\text{COUNT}} \text{ IS data-name-1} \\
\text{; } \underline{\text{TEXT}} \ \underline{\text{LENGTH}} \text{ IS data-name-2}
\end{array}\right.
$$

[; <u>STATUS KEY</u> IS data-name-3]

[; <u>DESTINATION TABLE</u> <u>OCCURS</u> integer-2 TIMES

    [; <u>INDEXED</u> BY index-name-1 [, index-name-2]...]]

[; <u>ERROR KEY</u> IS data-name-4]

[; <u>SYMBOLIC DESTINATION</u> IS data-name-5]

Data Division

<u>GENERAL FORMAT FOR REPORT GROUP DESCRIPTION ENTRY</u>

<u>FORMAT 1:</u>

01 [data-name-1]

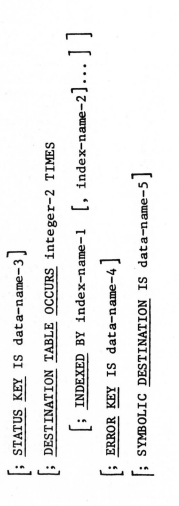

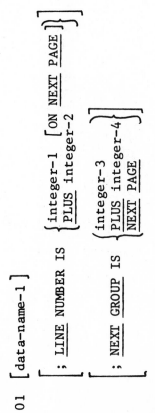

$$\left[\; \text{; } \underline{\text{LINE NUMBER}} \text{ IS } \left\{ \begin{array}{l} \text{integer-1 } [\text{ON } \underline{\text{NEXT PAGE}}] \\ \underline{\text{PLUS}} \text{ integer-2} \end{array} \right\} \right]$$

$$\left[\; \text{; } \underline{\text{NEXT GROUP}} \text{ IS } \left\{ \begin{array}{l} \text{integer-3} \\ \underline{\text{PLUS}} \text{ integer-4} \\ \underline{\text{NEXT PAGE}} \end{array} \right\} \right]$$

574

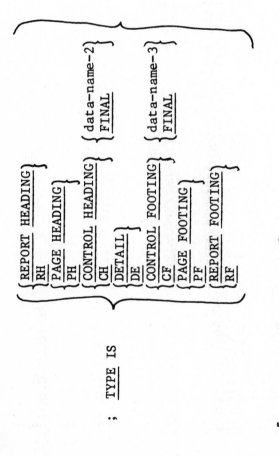

$$; \underline{\text{TYPE}} \text{ IS } \left\{ \begin{array}{l} \underline{\text{REPORT HEADING}} \\ \underline{\text{RH}} \\ \underline{\text{PAGE HEADING}} \\ \underline{\text{PH}} \\ \underline{\text{CONTROL HEADING}} \\ \underline{\text{CH}} \\ \underline{\text{DETAIL}} \\ \underline{\text{DE}} \\ \underline{\text{CONTROL FOOTING}} \\ \underline{\text{CF}} \\ \underline{\text{PAGE FOOTING}} \\ \underline{\text{PF}} \\ \underline{\text{REPORT FOOTING}} \\ \underline{\text{RF}} \end{array} \right\}$$

$$\left\{ \begin{array}{l} \text{data-name-2} \\ \underline{\text{FINAL}} \end{array} \right\} \quad \left\{ \begin{array}{l} \text{data-name-3} \\ \underline{\text{FINAL}} \end{array} \right\}$$

$$\left[; \left[\underline{\text{USAGE}} \text{ IS} \right] \quad \underline{\text{DISPLAY}} \right] .$$

FORMAT 2:

level-number [data-name-1]

$$\left[; \underline{\text{LINE NUMBER}} \text{ IS } \left\{ \begin{array}{l} \text{integer-1 } \left[\underline{\text{ON NEXT PAGE}} \right] \\ \underline{\text{PLUS}} \text{ integer-2} \end{array} \right\} \right]$$

$$\left[; \left[\underline{\text{USAGE}} \text{ IS} \right] \quad \underline{\text{DISPLAY}} \right] .$$

GENERAL FORMAT FOR REPORT GROUP DESCRIPTION ENTRY (CONT.)

FORMAT 3:

level-number [data-name-1]

[; BLANK WHEN ZERO]

[; GROUP INDICATE]

[; {JUSTIFIED / JUST} RIGHT]

[; LINE NUMBER IS {integer-1 [ON NEXT PAGE] / PLUS integer-2}]

[; COLUMN NUMBER IS integer-3]

[; {PICTURE / PIC} IS character-string

; SOURCE IS identifier-1

; VALUE IS literal]

$$\left\{ \begin{array}{l} ; \underline{\text{SUM}} \text{ identifier-2 } \left[, \text{ identifier-3} \right] \ldots \\[2mm] \left[\underline{\text{UPON}} \text{ data-name-2 } \left[, \text{ data-name-3} \right] \ldots \right] \ldots \\[2mm] \left[\underline{\text{RESET ON}} \left\{ \begin{array}{l} \text{data-name-4} \\ \underline{\text{FINAL}} \end{array} \right\} \right] \end{array} \right\}$$

$$\left[; \left[\underline{\text{USAGE IS}} \right] \underline{\text{DISPLAY}} \right] .$$

Procedure Division

GENERAL FORMAT FOR PROCEDURE DIVISION

FORMAT 1:

$\underline{\text{PROCEDURE DIVISION}} \left[\underline{\text{USING}} \text{ data-name-1 } \left[, \text{ data-name-2} \right] \ldots \right] .$

$\left[\underline{\text{DECLARATIVES}} . \right.$

$\left\{ \text{section-name } \underline{\text{SECTION}} \left[\text{segment-number} \right] . \quad \text{declarative-sentence} \right.$

$\left[\text{paragraph-name. } \left[\text{sentence} \right] \ldots \right] \ldots \right\} \ldots$

END DECLARATIVES.]

{section-name SECTION [segment-number] .

[paragraph-name. [sentence] ...] ... } ...

FORMAT 2:

PROCEDURE DIVISION [USING data-name-1 [, data-name-2] ...] .

{paragraph-name. [sentence] ... } ...

COBOL Verb Formats

GENERAL FORMAT FOR VERBS

ACCEPT identifier [FROM mnemonic-name]

ACCEPT identifier FROM {DATE / DAY / TIME}

ACCEPT cd-name MESSAGE COUNT

ADD $\left\{\begin{array}{l}\text{identifier-1}\\\text{literal-1}\end{array}\right\}$ $\left[\text{, }\begin{array}{l}\text{identifier-2}\\\text{literal-2}\end{array}\right]$ ... TO identifier-m [ROUNDED]

$\left[\text{, identifier-n [ROUNDED]}\right]$ ... [; ON SIZE ERROR imperative-statement]

ADD $\left\{\begin{array}{l}\text{identifier-1}\\\text{literal-1}\end{array}\right\}$, $\left\{\begin{array}{l}\text{identifier-2}\\\text{literal-2}\end{array}\right\}$ $\left[\text{, }\begin{array}{l}\text{identifier-3}\\\text{literal-3}\end{array}\right]$ ...

GIVING identifier-m [ROUNDED] $\left[\text{, identifier-n [ROUNDED]}\right]$ ...

[; ON SIZE ERROR imperative-statement]

ADD $\left\{\begin{array}{l}\underline{\text{CORRESPONDING}}\\\underline{\text{CORR}}\end{array}\right\}$ identifier-1 TO identifier-2 [ROUNDED]

[; ON SIZE ERROR imperative-statement]

ALTER procedure-name-1 TO [PROCEED TO] procedure-name-2

$\left[\text{, procedure-name-3 }\underline{\text{TO}}\text{ [}\underline{\text{PROCEED TO}}\text{] procedure-name-4}\right]$ ...

CALL $\left\{\begin{array}{l}\text{identifier-1}\\\text{literal-1}\end{array}\right\}$ $\left[\underline{\text{USING}}\text{ data-name-1 }\left[\text{, data-name-2}\right]\text{ ...}\right]$

[; ON OVERFLOW imperative-statement]

CANCEL $\left\{\begin{array}{l}\text{identifier-1}\\\text{literal-1}\end{array}\right\}$ $\left[\text{, }\begin{array}{l}\text{identifier-2}\\\text{literal-2}\end{array}\right]$ ...

GENERAL FORMAT FOR VERBS (CONT.)

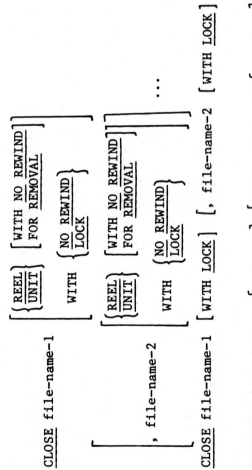

```
CLOSE file-name-1 [ {REEL} [WITH NO REWIND] ]
                    {UNIT} [FOR REMOVAL  ]
                          [WITH {NO REWIND}]
                                {LOCK     }

      [, file-name-2 [ {REEL} [WITH NO REWIND] ] ] ...
                       {UNIT} [FOR REMOVAL  ]
                             [WITH {NO REWIND}]
                                   {LOCK     }

CLOSE file-name-1 [WITH LOCK] [, file-name-2 [WITH LOCK] ] ...

COMPUTE identifier-1 [ROUNDED] [, identifier-2 [ROUNDED] ] ...
      = arithmetic-expression [; ON SIZE ERROR imperative-statement ]

DELETE file-name RECORD [; INVALID KEY imperative-statement]

DISABLE {INPUT [TERMINAL]} cd-name WITH KEY {identifier-1}
        {OUTPUT         }                   {literal-1    }
```

DISPLAY {identifier-1 / literal-1} [, identifier-2 / literal-2] ... [UPON mnemonic-name]

DIVIDE {identifier-1 / literal-1} INTO identifier-2 [ROUNDED]
[, identifier-3 [ROUNDED]] ... [; ON SIZE ERROR imperative-statement]

DIVIDE {identifier-1 / literal-1} INTO {identifier-2 / literal-2} GIVING identifier-3 [ROUNDED]
[, identifier-4 [ROUNDED]] ... [; ON SIZE ERROR imperative-statement]

DIVIDE {identifier-1 / literal-1} BY {identifier-2 / literal-2} GIVING identifier-3 [ROUNDED]
[, identifier-4 [ROUNDED]] ... [; ON SIZE ERROR imperative-statement]

DIVIDE {identifier-1 / literal-1} INTO {identifier-2 / literal-2} GIVING identifier-3 [ROUNDED]
REMAINDER identifier-4 [; ON SIZE ERROR imperative-statement]

DIVIDE {identifier-1 / literal-1} BY {identifier-2 / literal-2} GIVING identifier-3 [ROUNDED]
REMAINDER identifier-4 [; ON SIZE ERROR imperative-statement]

GENERAL FORMAT FOR VERBS (CONT.)

ENABLE $\left\{ \begin{array}{l} \underline{\text{INPUT}} \; [\underline{\text{TERMINAL}}] \\ \underline{\text{OUTPUT}} \end{array} \right\}$ cd-name WITH <u>KEY</u> $\left\{ \begin{array}{l} \text{identifier-1} \\ \text{literal-1} \end{array} \right\}$

<u>ENTER</u> language-name [routine-name] .

EXIT [<u>PROGRAM</u>] .

<u>GENERATE</u> $\left\{ \begin{array}{l} \text{data-name} \\ \text{report-name} \end{array} \right\}$

<u>GO</u> <u>TO</u> [procedure-name-1]

<u>GO</u> TO procedure-name-1 [, procedure-name-2] ... , procedure-name-n

<u>DEPENDING</u> <u>ON</u> identifier

<u>IF</u> condition; $\left\{ \begin{array}{l} \text{statement-1} \\ \underline{\text{NEXT}} \; \underline{\text{SENTENCE}} \end{array} \right\}$ $\left\{ \begin{array}{l} ; \; \underline{\text{ELSE}} \; \text{statement-2} \\ ; \; \underline{\text{ELSE}} \; \underline{\text{NEXT}} \; \underline{\text{SENTENCE}} \end{array} \right\}$

<u>INITIATE</u> report-name-1 [, report-name-2] ...

```
INSPECT identifier-1 TALLYING

   ⎧         ⎧ ⎧ ⎧ ALL     ⎫ ⎧ identifier-3 ⎫ ⎫ ⎡ ⎡ BEFORE ⎤         ⎧ identifier-4 ⎫ ⎤ ⎫
   ⎨ , identifier-2 FOR ⎨ ⎨ ⎨ LEADING ⎬ ⎨ literal-1    ⎬ ⎬ ⎢ ⎢ AFTER  ⎥ INITIAL ⎨ literal-2    ⎬ ⎥ ⎬ ...
   ⎩         ⎩ ⎩ ⎩ CHARACTERS        ⎭ ⎭ ⎣ ⎣        ⎦                ⎭ ⎦ ⎭
```

```
INSPECT identifier-1 REPLACING

   CHARACTERS BY ⎧ identifier-4 ⎫ ⎡ ⎡ BEFORE ⎤ INITIAL ⎧ identifier-7 ⎫ ⎤ ...
                 ⎨ literal-3    ⎬ ⎢ ⎢ AFTER  ⎥         ⎨ literal-5    ⎬ ⎥
                 ⎩              ⎭ ⎣ ⎣        ⎦          ⎩              ⎭ ⎦

   ⎧   ⎧ ALL     ⎫ ⎧ identifier-5 ⎫    ⎧ identifier-6 ⎫ ⎡ ⎡ BEFORE ⎤ INITIAL ⎧ identifier-7 ⎫ ⎤ ⎫
   ⎨ , ⎨ LEADING ⎬ ⎨ literal-3    ⎬ BY ⎨ literal-4    ⎬ ⎢ ⎢ AFTER  ⎥         ⎨ literal-5    ⎬ ⎥ ⎬ ...
   ⎩   ⎩ FIRST   ⎭ ⎩              ⎭    ⎩              ⎭ ⎣ ⎣        ⎦          ⎩              ⎭ ⎦ ⎭
```

```
INSPECT identifier-1 TALLYING

   ⎧         ⎧ ⎧ ⎧ ALL     ⎫ ⎧ identifier-3 ⎫ ⎫ ⎡ ⎡ BEFORE ⎤         ⎧ identifier-4 ⎫ ⎤ ⎫
   ⎨ , identifier-2 FOR ⎨ ⎨ ⎨ LEADING ⎬ ⎨ literal-1    ⎬ ⎬ ⎢ ⎢ AFTER  ⎥ INITIAL ⎨ literal-2    ⎬ ⎥ ⎬ ...
   ⎩         ⎩ ⎩ ⎩ CHARACTERS        ⎭ ⎭ ⎣ ⎣        ⎦                ⎭ ⎦ ⎭
```

```
REPLACING

   CHARACTERS BY ⎧ identifier-6 ⎫ ⎡ ⎡ BEFORE ⎤ INITIAL ⎧ identifier-7 ⎫ ⎤ ...
                 ⎨ literal-4    ⎬ ⎢ ⎢ AFTER  ⎥         ⎨ literal-5    ⎬ ⎥
                 ⎩              ⎭ ⎣ ⎣        ⎦          ⎩              ⎭ ⎦

   ⎧   ⎧ ALL     ⎫ ⎧ identifier-5 ⎫    ⎧ identifier-6 ⎫ ⎡ ⎡ BEFORE ⎤ INITIAL ⎧ identifier-7 ⎫ ⎤ ⎫
   ⎨ , ⎨ LEADING ⎬ ⎨ literal-3    ⎬ BY ⎨ literal-4    ⎬ ⎢ ⎢ AFTER  ⎥         ⎨ literal-5    ⎬ ⎥ ⎬ ...
   ⎩   ⎩ FIRST   ⎭ ⎩              ⎭    ⎩              ⎭ ⎣ ⎣        ⎦          ⎩              ⎭ ⎦ ⎭
```

<u>GENERAL FORMAT FOR VERBS</u> (CONT.)

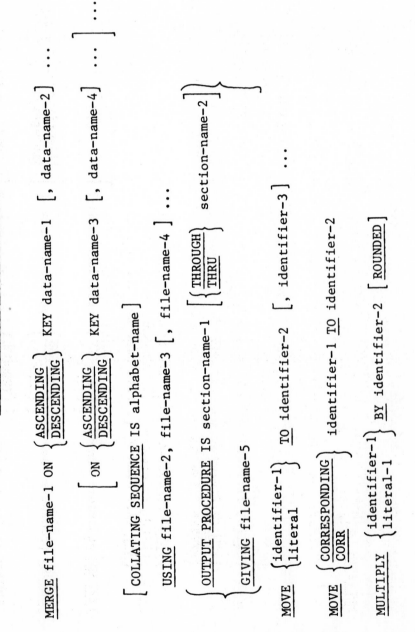

```
MERGE file-name-1 ON  {ASCENDING }  KEY data-name-1 [, data-name-2] ...
                      {DESCENDING}

              [ ON  {ASCENDING }  KEY data-name-3 [, data-name-4] ... ] ...
                    {DESCENDING}

   [ COLLATING SEQUENCE IS alphabet-name ]

   USING file-name-2, file-name-3 [, file-name-4 ] ...

   { OUTPUT PROCEDURE IS section-name-1 [ { THROUGH }  section-name-2 ] }
   {                                     { THRU    }                   }
   { GIVING file-name-5                                               }

MOVE {identifier-1}  TO identifier-2 [, identifier-3] ...
     {literal     }

MOVE {CORRESPONDING}  identifier-1 TO identifier-2
     {CORR         }

MULTIPLY {identifier-1}  BY identifier-2 [ ROUNDED ]
         {literal-1    }
```

```
[, identifier-3 [ROUNDED]] ... [; ON SIZE ERROR imperative-statement]

MULTIPLY {identifier-1 / literal-1} BY {identifier-2 / literal-2} GIVING identifier-3 [ROUNDED]

    [, identifier-4 [ROUNDED]] ... [; ON SIZE ERROR imperative-statement]

        INPUT file-name-1 [REVERSED / WITH NO REWIND] [, file-name-2 [REVERSED / WITH NO REWIND]] ...
OPEN    OUTPUT file-name-3 [WITH NO REWIND] [, file-name-4 [WITH NO REWIND]] ...
        I-O file-name-5 [, file-name-6] ...
        EXTEND file-name-7 [, file-name-8] ...

        { INPUT file-name-1 [, file-name-2] ... }
OPEN    { OUTPUT file-name-3 [, file-name-4] ... } ...
        { I-O file-name-5 [, file-name-6] ... }

PERFORM procedure-name-1 [{THROUGH / THRU} procedure-name-2]

PERFORM procedure-name-1 [{THROUGH / THRU} procedure-name-2] {identifier-1 / integer-1} TIMES

PERFORM procedure-name-1 [{THROUGH / THRU} procedure-name-2] UNTIL condition-1
```

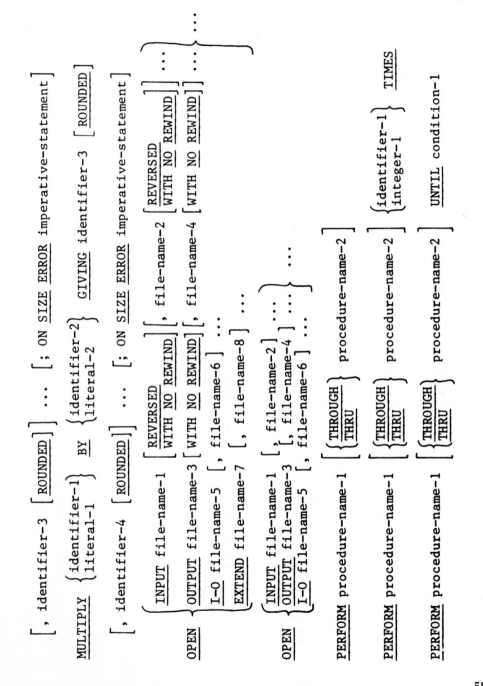

GENERAL FORMAT FOR VERBS (CONT.)

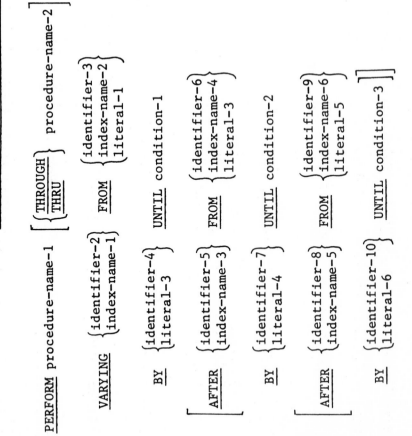

$$\underline{\text{PERFORM}} \text{ procedure-name-1} \left[\left\{ \frac{\text{THROUGH}}{\text{THRU}} \right\} \text{procedure-name-2} \right]$$

$$\underline{\text{VARYING}} \left\{ \begin{array}{l} \text{identifier-2} \\ \text{index-name-1} \end{array} \right\} \underline{\text{FROM}} \left\{ \begin{array}{l} \text{identifier-3} \\ \text{index-name-2} \\ \text{literal-1} \end{array} \right\}$$

$$\underline{\text{BY}} \left\{ \begin{array}{l} \text{identifier-4} \\ \text{literal-3} \end{array} \right\} \underline{\text{UNTIL}} \text{ condition-1}$$

$$\left[\underline{\text{AFTER}} \left\{ \begin{array}{l} \text{identifier-5} \\ \text{index-name-3} \end{array} \right\} \underline{\text{FROM}} \left\{ \begin{array}{l} \text{identifier-6} \\ \text{index-name-4} \\ \text{literal-3} \end{array} \right\} \right.$$

$$\underline{\text{BY}} \left\{ \begin{array}{l} \text{identifier-7} \\ \text{literal-4} \end{array} \right\} \underline{\text{UNTIL}} \text{ condition-2}$$

$$\left[\underline{\text{AFTER}} \left\{ \begin{array}{l} \text{identifier-8} \\ \text{index-name-5} \end{array} \right\} \underline{\text{FROM}} \left\{ \begin{array}{l} \text{identifier-9} \\ \text{index-name-6} \\ \text{literal-5} \end{array} \right\} \right.$$

$$\left. \left. \underline{\text{BY}} \left\{ \begin{array}{l} \text{identifier-10} \\ \text{literal-6} \end{array} \right\} \underline{\text{UNTIL}} \text{ condition-3} \right] \right]$$

READ file-name RECORD [INTO identifier] [; AT END imperative-statement]

READ file-name [NEXT] RECORD [INTO identifier]

[; AT END imperative-statement]

READ file-name RECORD [INTO identifier] [; INVALID KEY imperative-statement]

READ file-name RECORD [INTO identifier]

[; KEY IS data-name]

[; INVALID KEY imperative-statement]

RECEIVE cd-name {MESSAGE / SEGMENT} INTO identifier-1 [; NO DATA imperative-statement]

RELEASE record-name [FROM identifier]

RETURN file-name RECORD [INTO identifier] ; AT END imperative-statement

REWRITE record-name [FROM identifier]

REWRITE record-name [FROM identifier] [; INVALID KEY imperative-statement]

GENERAL FORMAT FOR VERBS (CONT.)

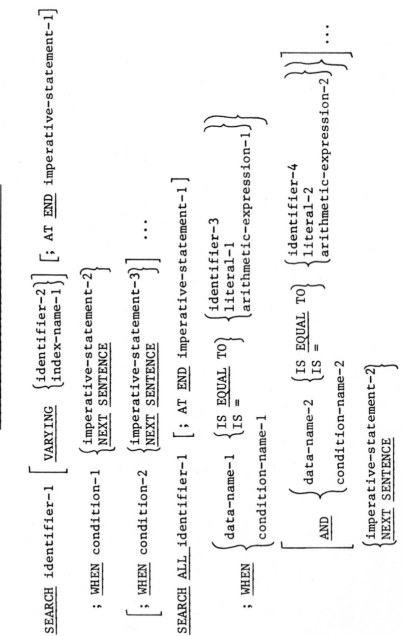

```
SEARCH identifier-1 [ VARYING { identifier-2  } ] [ ; AT END imperative-statement-1 ]
                               { index-name-1 }

; WHEN condition-1 { imperative-statement-2 }
                   { NEXT SENTENCE         }

[ ; WHEN condition-2 { imperative-statement-3 } ] ...
                     { NEXT SENTENCE         }


SEARCH ALL identifier-1 [ ; AT END imperative-statement-1 ]

; WHEN  { data-name-1 { IS EQUAL TO } { identifier-3             }        }
        {             { IS =        } { literal-1                }        }
        {                            { arithmetic-expression-1  }        }
        { condition-name-1                                                }
        {                                                                 }
        { [ AND { data-name-2 { IS EQUAL TO } { identifier-4            } ] ... }
        {       {             { IS =        } { literal-2               }       }
        {       {                            { arithmetic-expression-2 }       }
        {       { condition-name-2 }                                           }

    { imperative-statement-2 }
    { NEXT SENTENCE         }
```

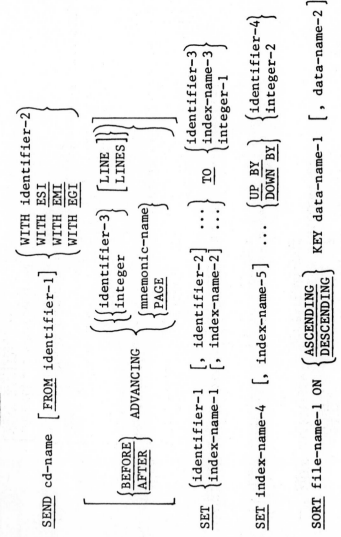

```
SEND cd-name FROM identifier-1

SEND cd-name [FROM identifier-1]
        ⎡              ⎧WITH identifier-2⎫⎤
        ⎢              ⎪WITH ESI         ⎪⎥
        ⎢              ⎨WITH EMI         ⎬⎥
        ⎣              ⎩WITH EGI         ⎭⎦
        ⎡⎧BEFORE⎫           ⎧⎧identifier-3⎫ [LINE ]⎫⎤
        ⎢⎨AFTER ⎬ ADVANCING ⎨⎨integer     ⎬ [LINES]⎬⎥
        ⎣⎩      ⎭           ⎩⎩mnemonic-name⎭       ⎭⎦
                                        ⎩  PAGE    ⎭

SET ⎧identifier-1 ⎫ ⎡, identifier-2 ⎤ ...    ⎧identifier-3 ⎫
    ⎨index-name-1 ⎬ ⎣, index-name-2 ⎦ ... TO ⎨index-name-3 ⎬
    ⎩             ⎭                           ⎩integer-1    ⎭

SET index-name-4 [, index-name-5] ... ⎧UP BY  ⎫ ⎧identifier-4⎫
                                      ⎨DOWN BY⎬ ⎨integer-2   ⎬
                                      ⎩       ⎭ ⎩            ⎭

SORT file-name-1 ON ⎧ASCENDING ⎫ KEY data-name-1 [, data-name-2] ...
                    ⎨DESCENDING⎬
                    ⎩          ⎭
```

GENERAL FORMAT FOR VERBS (CONT.)

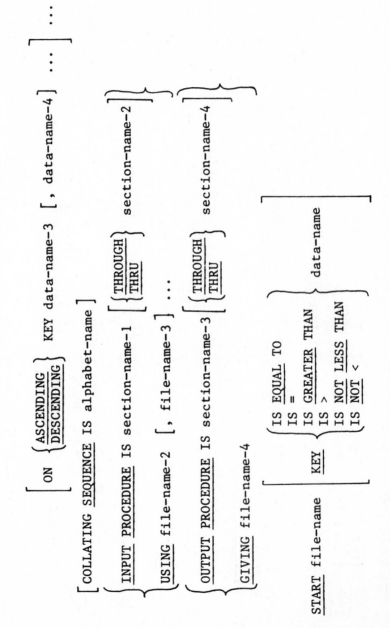

```
        ⎡    ⎧ ASCENDING  ⎫                            ⎤
        ⎢ ON ⎨ DESCENDING ⎬ KEY data-name-3 [, data-name-4]  ⎥ ...  ...
        ⎣    ⎩            ⎭                            ⎦

    [ COLLATING SEQUENCE IS alphabet-name ]

    ⎧                                    ⎧ THROUGH ⎫                ⎫
    ⎨ INPUT PROCEDURE IS section-name-1  ⎨         ⎬ section-name-2 ⎬ ...
    ⎩                                    ⎩ THRU    ⎭                ⎭

    USING file-name-2 [, file-name-3 ] ...

    ⎧                                     ⎧ THROUGH ⎫                ⎫
    ⎨ OUTPUT PROCEDURE IS section-name-3  ⎨         ⎬ section-name-4 ⎬
    ⎩                                     ⎩ THRU    ⎭                ⎭

    GIVING file-name-4


                ⎧ ⎧ IS EQUAL TO     ⎫           ⎫
                ⎪ ⎪ IS  =           ⎪           ⎪
    START file-name ⎨ KEY ⎨ IS GREATER THAN ⎬ data-name ⎬
                ⎪ ⎪ IS  >           ⎪           ⎪
                ⎪ ⎪ IS NOT LESS THAN⎪           ⎪
                ⎩ ⎩ IS NOT  <       ⎭           ⎭
```

[; INVALID KEY imperative-statement]

STOP { RUN / literal }

STRING { identifier-1 / literal-1 } [, identifier-2 / literal-2] ... DELIMITED BY { identifier-3 / literal-3 / SIZE }

[{ identifier-4 / literal-4 } [, identifier-5 / literal-5] ... DELIMITED BY { identifier-6 / literal-6 / SIZE }] ...

INTO identifier-7 [WITH POINTER identifier-8]

[; ON OVERFLOW imperative-statement]

SUBTRACT { identifier-1 / literal-1 } [, identifier-2 / literal-2] ... FROM identifier-m [ROUNDED]

[, identifier-n [ROUNDED]] ... [; ON SIZE ERROR imperative-statement]

SUBTRACT { identifier-1 / literal-1 } [, identifier-2 / literal-2] ... FROM { identifier-m / literal-m }

GIVING identifier-n [ROUNDED] [, identifier-o [ROUNDED]] ...

591

GENERAL FORMAT FOR VERBS (CONT.)

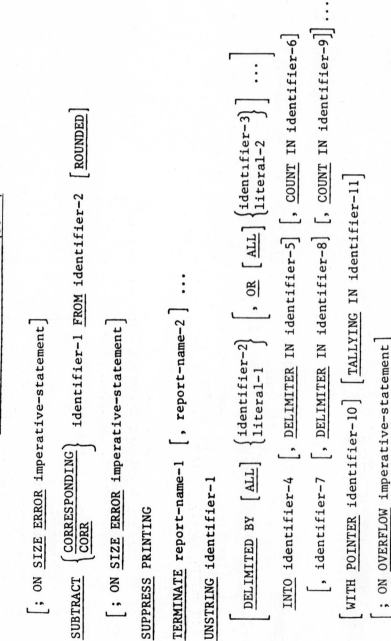

$\left[\text{; ON \underline{SIZE} ERROR imperative-statement}\right]$

$\underline{\text{SUBTRACT}} \left\{\begin{array}{l}\underline{\text{CORRESPONDING}}\\ \underline{\text{CORR}}\end{array}\right\} \text{identifier-1 FROM identifier-2} \left[\underline{\text{ROUNDED}}\right]$

$\left[\text{; ON \underline{SIZE} ERROR imperative-statement}\right]$

$\underline{\text{SUPPRESS}} \underline{\text{PRINTING}}$

$\underline{\text{TERMINATE}} \text{ report-name-1} \left[\text{, report-name-2}\right] \ldots$

$\underline{\text{UNSTRING}} \text{ identifier-1}$

$\left[\underline{\text{DELIMITED}} \underline{\text{BY}} \left[\underline{\text{ALL}}\right] \left\{\begin{array}{l}\text{identifier-2}\\ \text{literal-1}\end{array}\right\} \left[\text{, \underline{OR} } \left[\underline{\text{ALL}}\right] \left\{\begin{array}{l}\text{identifier-3}\\ \text{literal-2}\end{array}\right\} \right] \ldots \right]$

$\underline{\text{INTO}} \text{ identifier-4} \left[\text{, \underline{DELIMITER} IN identifier-5}\right] \left[\text{, \underline{COUNT} IN identifier-6}\right]$

$\left[\text{, identifier-7}\right] \left[\text{, \underline{DELIMITER} IN identifier-8}\right] \left[\text{, \underline{COUNT} IN identifier-9}\right] \ldots$

$\left[\underline{\text{WITH}} \underline{\text{POINTER}} \text{ identifier-10}\right] \left[\underline{\text{TALLYING}} \text{ IN identifier-11}\right]$

$\left[\text{; ON \underline{OVERFLOW} imperative-statement}\right]$

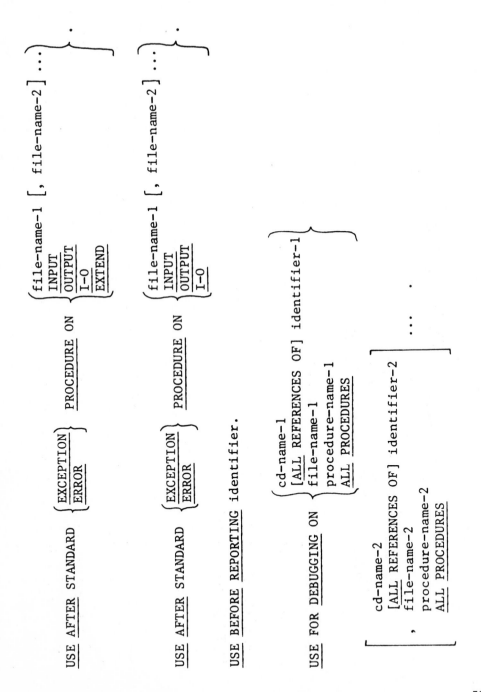

USE AFTER STANDARD $\left\{\begin{array}{l}\underline{\text{EXCEPTION}}\\ \underline{\text{ERROR}}\end{array}\right\}$ PROCEDURE ON $\left\{\begin{array}{l}\text{file-name-1 [, file-name-2]} \ldots\\ \underline{\text{INPUT}}\\ \underline{\text{OUTPUT}}\\ \underline{\text{I-O}}\\ \underline{\text{EXTEND}}\end{array}\right\}$.

USE AFTER STANDARD $\left\{\begin{array}{l}\underline{\text{EXCEPTION}}\\ \underline{\text{ERROR}}\end{array}\right\}$ PROCEDURE ON $\left\{\begin{array}{l}\text{file-name-1 [, file-name-2]} \ldots\\ \underline{\text{INPUT}}\\ \underline{\text{OUTPUT}}\\ \underline{\text{I-O}}\end{array}\right\}$.

USE BEFORE REPORTING identifier.

USE FOR DEBUGGING ON $\left\{\begin{array}{l}\text{cd-name-1}\\ \text{[ALL REFERENCES OF] identifier-1}\\ \text{file-name-1}\\ \text{procedure-name-1}\\ \underline{\text{ALL PROCEDURES}}\end{array}\right\}$ $\left[, \left\{\begin{array}{l}\text{cd-name-2}\\ \text{[ALL REFERENCES OF] identifier-2}\\ \text{file-name-2}\\ \text{procedure-name-2}\\ \underline{\text{ALL PROCEDURES}}\end{array}\right\} \right] \ldots$.

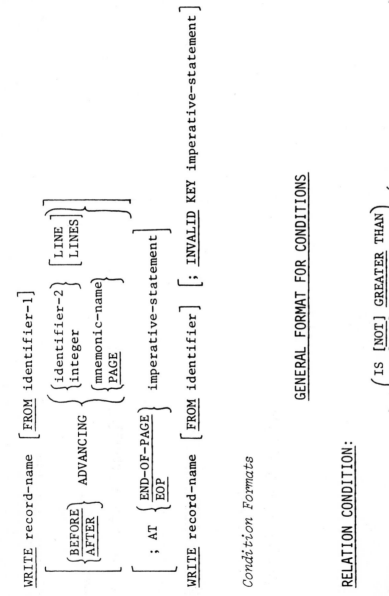

WRITE record-name [FROM identifier-1]

$$\left[\left\{\begin{array}{l}\underline{BEFORE}\\\underline{AFTER}\end{array}\right\}\ \underline{ADVANCING}\ \left\{\begin{array}{l}\left\{\begin{array}{l}identifier-2\\integer\end{array}\right\}\ \left[\begin{array}{l}LINE\\LINES\end{array}\right]\\\left\{\begin{array}{l}mnemonic-name\\\underline{PAGE}\end{array}\right\}\end{array}\right\}\right]$$

$$\left[;\ \underline{AT}\ \left\{\begin{array}{l}\underline{END-OF-PAGE}\\\underline{EOP}\end{array}\right\}\ imperative-statement\right]$$

WRITE record-name [FROM identifier] [; INVALID KEY imperative-statement]

Condition Formats

GENERAL FORMAT FOR CONDITIONS

RELATION CONDITION:

$$\left\{\begin{array}{l}identifier-1\\literal-1\\arithmetic-expression-1\\index-name-1\end{array}\right\}\ \left\{\begin{array}{ll}IS\ [\underline{NOT}]\ \underline{GREATER\ THAN}\\IS\ [\underline{NOT}]\ \underline{LESS\ THAN}\\IS\ [\underline{NOT}]\ \underline{EQUAL}\ \underline{TO}\\IS\ [\underline{NOT}]\ >\\IS\ [\underline{NOT}]\ <\\IS\ [\underline{NOT}]\ =\end{array}\right\}\ \left\{\begin{array}{l}identifier-2\\literal-2\\arithmetic-expression-2\\index-name-2\end{array}\right\}$$

CLASS CONDITION:

identifier IS [NOT] $\begin{Bmatrix} \underline{NUMERIC} \\ \underline{ALPHABETIC} \end{Bmatrix}$

SIGN CONDITION:

arithmetic-expression is [NOT] $\begin{Bmatrix} \underline{POSITIVE} \\ \underline{NEGATIVE} \\ \underline{ZERO} \end{Bmatrix}$

CONDITION-NAME CONDITION:

condition-name

SWITCH-STATUS CONDITION:

condition-name

NEGATED SIMPLE CONDITION:

NOT simple-condition

COMBINED CONDITION:

condition { {AND} / {OR} } condition ...

ABBREVIATED COMBINED RELATION CONDITION:

relation-condition { {AND} / {OR} } [NOT] [relational-operator] object ...

Miscellaneous Formats

MISCELLANEOUS FORMATS

QUALIFICATION:

{ data-name-1 / condition-name } [{OF} / {IN} data-name-2] ... [{OF} / {IN} section-name]

paragraph-name

text-name [{OF} / {IN} library-name]

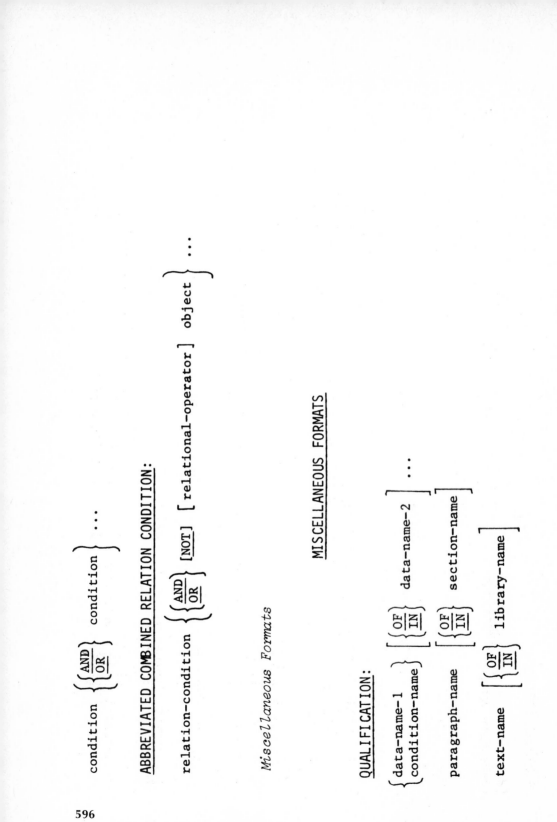

SUBSCRIPTING:

$$\left\{ \begin{array}{l} \text{data-name} \\ \text{condition-name} \end{array} \right\} \text{ (subscript-1 [, subscript-2 [, subscript-3]])}$$

INDEXING:

$$\left\{ \begin{array}{l} \text{data-name} \\ \text{condition-name} \end{array} \right\} \left(\left\{ \begin{array}{l} \text{index-name-1 [\{±\} literal-2]} \\ \text{literal-1} \end{array} \right\} \left[, \left\{ \begin{array}{l} \text{index-name-2 [\{±\} literal-4]} \\ \text{literal-3} \end{array} \right\} \left[, \left\{ \begin{array}{l} \text{index-name-3 [\{±\} literal-6]} \\ \text{literal-5} \end{array} \right\} \right] \right] \right)$$

IDENTIFIER: FORMAT 1

$$\text{data-name-1} \left[\left\{ \begin{array}{l} \underline{\text{OF}} \\ \underline{\text{IN}} \end{array} \right\} \text{data-name-2} \right] \cdots \left[\text{(subscript-1 [, subscript-2} \right.$$
$$\left[, \text{subscript-3]])} \right]$$

IDENTIFIER: FORMAT 2

$$\text{data-name-1} \left[\left\{ \begin{array}{l} \underline{\text{OF}} \\ \underline{\text{IN}} \end{array} \right\} \text{data-name-2} \right] \cdots \left[\left(\left\{ \begin{array}{l} \text{index-name-1 [\{±\} literal-2]} \\ \text{literal-1} \end{array} \right. \right.$$

597

COPY Statement

GENERAL FORMAT FOR COPY STATEMENT

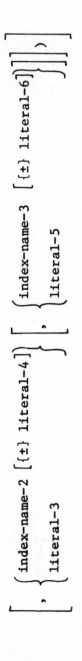

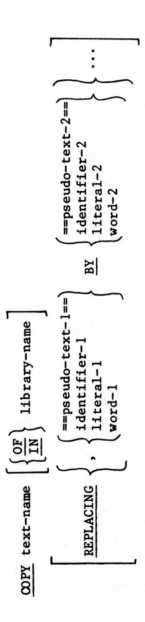

COPY text-name [{OF / IN} library-name]

[REPLACING { ==pseudo-text-1== / identifier-1 / literal-1 / word-1 } , BY { ==pseudo-text-2== / identifier-2 / literal-2 / word-2 } ...]

[, { index-name-2 [{±} literal-4] / literal-3 }] [, [{ index-name-3 [{±} literal-6] / literal-5 }]]

Index

Real Women, Real Leaders

Surviving and Succeeding in the Business World

Kathleen Hurley and
Priscilla Shumway
Editors

WILEY

Library of Congress Cataloging-in-Publication Data:

Real women, real leaders : surviving and succeeding in the business world /
Kathleen Hurley and Priscilla Shumway, editors.
    pages cm
  Includes index.
  ISBN 978-1-119-06138-0 (hardback); ISBN 978-1-119-09475-3 (pdf);
ISBN 978-1-119-06137-3 (epub)
  1. Women executives—Case studies.   2. Women in the professions—Case studies.
3. Leadership in women—Case studies.   4. Career development.   5. Success in business.
I. Hurley, Kathleen (Kathleen Mary)   II. Shumway, Priscilla.
  HD6054.3.R43 2015
  658.4'092082—dc23

                                                                    2015005236

Printed in the United States of America

V10007474_011019

CONTENTS

FOREWORD

I've generally steered away from books telling people how to do things that are mostly common sense, and books on "leadership" are no exception. Although just about every parent wants his or her children to be leaders, a parent could teach them to be Olympic athletes more easily.

There is no recipe for leadership, no book that tells you what you need to do to teach it or to be one, no school or apprenticeship that will give you the credential.

I've also avoided saying that women would be better leaders than men, because that generalization is unprovable. Women are as varied as men, their talents and behavior determined by their genes, their upbringing, their education, their environment, their hard work. But what I *can* say is that men have had a lot more opportunities to lead than women, especially in business and in government. So there is some work to be done.

I was lucky enough to get the chance to lead at two wonderful organizations: *The Economist* magazine and Pearson, plc. for a total of twenty-two years. I found in that time that the very best way to learn to lead is to meet leaders or read stories of their exploits. That is precisely what the authors of *Real Women, Real Leaders* have set out to offer us, and I hope you'll think they've succeeded.

If you know real stories—first-hand or second-hand—I predict that they'll leave you with what you really need: a few important personal mantras and a framework for how to make your decisions.

The simple mantras I carried around helped me enormously, although they were sparse: be brave, be imaginative, be decent. We adopted those goals for Pearson, and I thought they were pretty good guides for what a leader should be as well.

I was especially enamored with the word "decent," because it seemed to me that, in business, leaders sometimes thought that they had to be tough. To them, that meant that decisions had to be communicated without sympathy or compassion to be clear; and it meant that the company's role was not to help people get on in their lives.

My framework for how to make decisions was equally simple: be yourself—use your own voice; communicate; *if you are uncertain,* err on the side of generosity; strip everything down to its simplest elements. These were common sense, very common sense. But they served me well.

Women in work may be heartened or instructed by the stories in this book, but so also may girls from adolescence to college, all preparing to run the world (or some corner of it), too. And I hope that men, especially those who are in positions heading toward leadership, will gain some enlightenment as well. Let's not kid ourselves: it's important for women to help women, but it's also important for men to help women and, when needed, women to help men.

I have a wonderful friend who has made a great impact on the world she has lived in, and she attributes it all to Eleanor Roosevelt. In 1957 Mrs. Roosevelt was the commencement speaker at my friend's college, Sarah Lawrence. She made an inspirational speech. But what the girls remembered most was that, at the end, Mrs. Roosevelt stuck her fist in the air and exhorted them loudly and boldly: "Women. Go forth with courage." My friend said this shaped her life—her confidence, her sense of herself, the way she acted from then on. She's never forgotten it, and I've never forgotten the telling of it.

Courage, if you have nothing else, is enough to guide your way. But in the pages of this book I think you'll find many stories that may stir *you*, and I hope they will be the making of your leadership, probably a new kind of leadership!

Dame Marjorie Morris Scardino served as chief executive officer and as a member of the board of directors of Pearson plc, a publishing and education company, from 1997 to 2012. From 1985 to 1997, Ms. Scardino served in several roles at The Economist Group, a media company, including as chief executive officer. Ms. Scardino served on the board of directors of Nokia Corporation, a telecommunications company, from 2001 to April 2013. Ms. Scardino holds a B.A. in psychology from Baylor University and a J.D. from the University of San Francisco School of Law. In December 2013, she joined the board of Twitter as its first female director.

ACKNOWLEDGMENTS

"We learn best to listen to our own voices if we are listening at the same time to other women—whose stories, for all our differences, turn out, if we listen well, to be our stories also."

—Barbara Deming

One of the leadership competencies in which women leaders excel is collaboration and teamwork. This book is a testament to that skill. We are forever grateful to be surrounded by talented and competent women, and this book would not have been possible without the help of quite a few.

Our thanks to Cassandra Walker Harvey and Elizabeth Texeira; two recent graduates of the Harvard Graduate School of Education, who helped us with the research and writing. Their ability to capture the essence of the research and how it plays out in the essays was instrumental in bringing this collection of contributions together.

Ginny Kirkland, Mary McGoldrick, and Diane Rapley all played a part in keeping us on track; from gathering resources, to editing essays, these women have worked with us for many years, and will continue to be a part of our lives, both professionally and personally.

Our thanks go out to Carolyn Warner, who allowed us to use the quotes from her book, *Words of Extraordinary Women*.

Our hope is that you, dear reader, have surrounded yourself with strong teams with whom you can collaborate.

PREFACE

*R*eal *Women, Real Leaders* is a compilation of stories from some of the most successful women working today. We have identified women who are known to be transformational, exemplary leaders in their industries, everything spanning from business to politics, education to the arts. We have taken the opportunity to look at their stories, in their own words, and see how they have been able to find success across a wide range of industries in which women have traditionally been either excluded from or disempowered within. Through their eyes, we see stories of inspiration and strength, and we want to make sure that *every woman reading* has access to the role models and strategies that these women present.

To this end we have framed the book around the pivotal work of two extraordinary researchers, Dr. Jack Zenger and Dr. Joseph Folkman (full research article is reprinted in an appendix). Zenger and Folkman believe that a strengths-based leadership development model is the most effective way for businesses to amplify their organizational impact. Through this research, they defined sixteen key competencies that are crucial characteristics for inspirational leadership. "On twelve of sixteen competencies, females were rated more positively by the total of all respondents—manager, peers, direct reports, and others" (A Study in Leadership: Women Do It Better Than Men, *Harvard Business Review*).

As the data began to roll in, Zenger and Folkman started to notice a number of interesting trends that appeared along the lines of gender. They quickly decided to include additional facets to their research and began to analyze data that suggested that there were differences between men and women's leadership styles, and that women seemed to be surpassing the men. Jack Zenger, CEO and co-founder of Zenger Folkman, stated: "It is a well-known fact that women are underrepresented at senior levels of management. Yet the data suggests that by adding more women the overall effectiveness of the leadership team would go up."

Using this research as a catalyst to help organize these women's key strengths, the book *Real Women, Real Leaders* is able to balance between the worlds of academia and reality, showcasing real narrative with real data. We chose to group and organize the Real Women based on their professional industry, in the hopes that those reading would be able to draw connections between their own professional trajectories and those of our Real Women. We went even further, and each Real Woman has highlighted the competencies that she excels within in order to gain a working knowledge of each woman's incredible success.

Each chapter begins with a brief introductory section that includes a description of the top competencies that our Real Women have coalesced around, as defined by Zenger and Folkman. Next, each introductory section includes current day, actionable research and strategies on ways to develop each of these leadership competencies in the workplace. Each chapter then includes the personal narratives of a number of Real Women. It is our hope that, in addition to inspiration, each chapter will provide every reader with ideas, opportunities, and strategies to develop her personal leadership style. The Appendices of the book also includes a host of information, including research, a personal leadership assessment, and resources to further aid our readers in their personal growth and development.

Women are making changes and inspiring the world daily through their leadership. We believe that women everywhere can become the best possible versions of themselves and help make positive change in the world. This is our attempt to highlight but a few of those pioneers. Thank you for reading.

"So much of what it takes to be a leader has been historically defined by men. And while I was determined to be a leader, the last thing in the world I was going to do was to try to be like a man so that I could be taken seriously. I had to continue to be myself and create a leadership style that worked for me. I'm just not capable of being anyone other than who I am."

—LIBBY SARTAIN, YAHOO! INC.

A Note from Kathy Hurley

"In the future, there will be no female leaders. There will just be leaders."

  —Sheryl Sandberg, *Lean In: Women, Work, and the Will to Lead*

Sheryl Sandberg's quote from her recent book provides the answer to the question of why we chose to publish this book. Having been in the education industry for far longer than I care to admit (more than forty years), my own life has been a journey on a path to leadership and mentorship. My career began back in 1967 as a special education teacher. I spent five years in the classroom before moving to the private side of the industry to the publishing world. While most women dominated the teaching side of the education industry, it became clear, fairly quickly, that leadership in the publishing world was dominated by men. While there were many women in publishing, most were support roles and not leading divisions or making critical decisions. In a nutshell, at that time, we were the "worker bees." However, having been an educator, I found that knowing the language of the education world—a language that enabled me to relate to and converse with everyone, from a classroom teacher to a curriculum director to a large school district superintendent— gave me a unique perspective and set me apart from many of my male counterparts. Additionally, I learned that the skills I had been taught to lead a classroom full of students translated quite well to the private-sector side of the industry, and ultimately prepared me for leadership roles.

I should also add here that I am oldest of four children and was raised by two strong-willed and very determined parents. While some people may assume that the first-born child is a natural leader, I tend to agree with the Vince Lombardi quote that "leaders aren't born, they are made." While my parents each had his or her own approach to parenting, they both encouraged and nurtured leadership qualities in me. They encouraged me to be an independent risk-taker, and they supported my decision to leave the classroom (which was an encouraged "safe" profession for many young women in the 1960s) to join the private side of the education world. (You will find that this theme runs through the stories shared in this book. All of these women share that they had adult figures, early in their lives, who instilled confidence in them and encouraged them to pursue their ambitions.)

I have joked that, over the last forty years, so many of the companies I've worked for have been bought and sold that I've lost count. However, with each acquisition, transition, or change, I also found myself moving a little higher up the scale to a position of more influence in the industry. Yet, I could not have moved up had it not been for individual leaders taking an interest in me. In my early years, I sought out those leaders, those mentors, who had something to teach me. I observed them, listened to them, and did my best to emulate *their* successful qualities when the opportunities would present themselves. One of the most important things I learned from the many mentors I had is that people matter, networking matters, and that half of the battle is just showing up. I also learned that doing what you say you are going to do goes much further than being the person in the room with the best idea or the loudest voice.

Over the years, I came to realize that the leadership qualities that I had developed were a direct result of the mentors who had taken time to teach me the industry and to teach me the habits of a successful leader. I also came to realize that, in particular, many young women in our industry needed more women mentors to demonstrate quality leadership skills and help groom them to be leaders in the industry.

In the private side of the education industry, the world of print publishing dominated in the 1970s, but the 1980s ushered in the new world of software development and what we in the industry call "ed tech." Being ever ready to tackle new challenges, I jumped to the world of ed tech in the 1980s and worked as an executive at companies like IBM, SkillsBank, Grolier, and Mindscape before landing at The Learning Company. As an executive at those companies, I was also recruited to serve on the board of directors for industry associations and education non-profits. During that time, more and more women were entering ed tech and by nature, as women, we began networking with each other, seeking each other out at education conferences and collaborating as industry partners when possible. We also actively started mentoring each other and purposefully recommending our peers for executive leadership positions. Seeing a real need for this type of ongoing networking, a small group of us, led by Ellen Bialo, a true pioneer for women in the ed tech space, started an unofficial industry club in the 1990s called the DOLS—Dirty Old Ladies of Software. We would put together networking dinners at conferences—but the catch was you were encouraged to bring a younger woman from your organization or from the industry with you so that she could meet industry colleagues and begin to build those connections and provide opportunities for veteran women of the industry to serve as mentors to the newcomers. What started out as dinners of twenty to thirty women at these education industry events now easily tops 500 women—with a hundred or so attending at least one of the four or five dinners we host over the course of a year, all over the country.

In addition, in the 1990s, Deb deVries, who was then an executive at MECC, Pat Walkington, who was then an executive at The

Learning Company, and I, at SkillsBank, started a national awards program called Making IT Happen. Making IT Happen began as a way to recognize women who were leading the way to integrate technology into education, into classrooms around the country. More than 500 women have been recognized, and ultimately, we did find "a few good men" along the way who received recognition for their efforts as well. Making IT Happen has been such a success that it is now an awards program run by the largest education technology association in the world, the International Society for Technology in Education (ISTE). Women recognizing other women is important, and these are just a couple of examples of how, by working together, we can help and encourage one another.

Today, the education industry has many more women in leadership roles. A couple of years ago, Marjorie Scardino stepped down after fifteen years as the CEO of Pearson, plc. (In full disclosure, I worked for Pearson for ten years.) Marjorie was an exceptional leader in her fifteen years at Pearson. Until she was appointed CEO, Pearson had always been led by a man. During her tenure, she transformed the company from one of the "Big Three" educational print publishing companies to the largest education technology company in the world, providing educational services and products to ages Pre-K through adult in more than sixty countries around the globe. During her time at Pearson, Marjorie always had one rule that she emphasized and would reference time and again: when presented with various options, as a company or as an individual, you should "always, always err on the side of generosity." In other words, compassion from the top goes a long way to instill trust in others and make them want to follow you.

Knowing my commitment to Pearson and my interest in leadership, Marjorie recommended me for the Advanced Leadership Initiative (ALI) at Harvard University, which concluded in November 2014. During my time at ALI, my sister-in-law, Priscilla Shumway, who is an executive trainer and coach, was reading a report that had been featured in the March edition of the 2012 *Harvard Business Review*, "The Results Are In: Women Are Better Leaders." The report was by Dr. Jack Zenger and Dr. Joe Folkman. They had identified sixteen competencies that made an individual an outstanding leader. The results showed that women out-scored men in twelve of the sixteen competencies. Priscilla and I were pleasantly surprised and wondered how many other women would be surprised by the findings. Better yet, we thought, wouldn't it be great to show how successful women use these competencies as leaders in their chosen career fields?

It was also during my time at Harvard that I began researching my own way to provide a path to leadership and civic engagement for adolescent girls and young women around the world who traditionally do not have access to education and training. With the help of my good friend and business colleague, Deb deVries, and two recent graduates of Harvard's Graduate School of Education, Cass Walker and Liz Texeira, we founded Girls Thinking Global (GTG). Our mission is to create a global network of organizations that are serving girls and women to leverage resources to ensure that every possible dollar and resource is used to improve the quality of life for adolescent girls worldwide. To support our mission and to ensure that I am doing everything I can to create pathways to leadership for young women, I will be donating a portion of the proceeds from this book to Girls Thinking Global.

In the end, in this book we strive to share the stories of each contributor in a personal, meaningful way—in a way that will inspire girls and women to not only pursue their dreams but also leverage the skills that they have to be leaders, influencers, and role models in their chosen professions. Priscilla and I personally know all the women in this book. They have diverse backgrounds and experiences and are excited to share their journeys to success. And, in the end, we hope the words of Sheryl Sandberg will ring true and that you will not view them as female leaders, but rather as leaders who model successful habits for everyone around them, male or female, to emulate.

1 Leadership Journey: Skill or Personal Mission?

Priscilla Shumway

"Leadership is simply having something left over, after taking care of yourself, to care for someone or something else."

—John Ertha, Founder of Homestead

John Ertha died at the age of eighty-two after a life dedicated to education, theater, and leadership development for children and teens. He taught them to "work hard with others to achieve a common goal and to expect great things from themselves. Most importantly, they learned to value and respect the differences between people and understand that everyone has a contribution to make if allowed to participate" (*Portland Press Herald*, Oct. 18, 2009).

What wonderful lessons on leadership for children and teens—and what wonderful lessons for leadership in the world of work!

Leaders can be found in all walks of life, of all ages, races, creeds, and nations. Leadership demands much from us, despite our motivations to lead, the challenges we face, or the various opportunities

7

presented to us. As Carolyn Warner points out in her book, *Words of Extraordinary Women:*

> "The Japanese word for teacher is sensei, which means far more than just someone who instructs. The literal meaning of the word is honored leader. A sensei is a guide, a mentor, giver and sharer not just of information, but of knowledge. And when I think of the greatest leaders that I know, or have studied, they combine all of these qualities."

In *Real Women, Real Leaders*, our authors share stories about their mentors and guides, the various "sensei" in their lives, and how they have been impacted. In exploring those who have impacted them, they also share how they, themselves, have now taken on this role for others in their lives. The essays in this book show how these diverse authors view leadership and their personal journeys to becoming leaders. Their stories point out that leadership is not just a skill to be mastered, but also a mission, a value, a way to live.

For many of our authors, their earliest mentors or guides were their mothers, fathers, or grandmothers. Lessons learned in childhood supported them throughout life. In an article by Sorcher and Brant from the *Harvard Business Review* on the hardwiring of leadership, they concluded, " Our experience has led us to believe that much of leadership talent is hardwired in people before they reach their early or mid 20s. That means, as far as leadership is concerned, people are reasonably complete packages by the time they arrive at the corporate doorstep. Their ability to lead has already been shaped by a multitude of factors and experiences that took root early in their lives" (Are You Picking the Right Leaders? Melvin Sorcher and James Brandt, *Harvard Business Review,* February 2002).

Sorcher and Brant's conclusion holds true for the stories found in *Real Women* as the authors share how early experiences in their lives built their leadership qualities and propelled them to success.

My own personal journey to leadership also began as a young child. Presented with an opportunity, I was always willing to step up to the plate at school, Girl Scouts, or even planning a neighborhood talent show to raise money for charity. I loved the sense of control that leadership can bring. But the downside of that was that I often took it too far and alienated my friends. When three of my best friends in fourth grade formed an "I hate Priscilla" club, I was shocked, angry, and sad. I had not included them in the planning of our Girl Scout bicycle trip. But in fourth grade those issues usually flame out quickly and, thankfully, they did and within a week we were best friends again. Lessons learned? The art of humility coupled with the ability to include, inspire, and motivate others in tasks goes a long way toward persuading others to follow you. These are lessons I continue to teach myself every day!

In fact, in a 2012 Girl Scout study of eight- to seventeen-year-olds, one-third of the girls said they did not want to be leaders because they feared being disliked by their peers. The study goes on to state:

> "Leadership qualities girls would very much like to have as
> adults include:
> • Standing up for their beliefs and values (84 percent)
> • Trying to change the world for the better (68 percent)
> • Bringing people together to get things done (64 percent)"[1]

These qualities correspond to the leadership competencies from the Zenger Folkman study:

• Displays high integrity and honesty

• Champions change

• Collaboration and teamwork

---

[1]ToGetHer There: Girls' Insights on Leadership, Girl Scouts of the USA; January 2012

So Why This Book? Why Now?

When Kathy asked me to work with her on this book, I jumped at the chance. Kathy has been a leading mentor in my life. As a sister-in-law (full disclosure here! I am married to her only brother), we have worked together at various companies since 1991. She has supported me, pushed me, and exposed me to many professional opportunities. She has always believed in me and talked positively about me in front of others. Don't we all want praise, recognition, and encouragement? Do we do that enough for our co-workers, our children, our spouses? Kathy has definitely been instrumental in reminding me that giving credit where it's due is a strong, essential leadership quality.

While women have made great strides in leadership, and many of those stories have been documented, the truth is that today women represent only 5 percent of chief executives in Fortune 1000 companies (*Catalyst*, November 7, 2014, "Women CEOs of the Fortune 1000").

Knowing the tremendous stories of women that we encounter every day, Kathy and I felt it was time to gather these stories together, stories of other women, like us, who have been, and still are, on the journeys to leadership. And, as importantly, we wanted to include women who represent fields inside and outside of the corporate world—women who are impacting government, industry associations, non-profits, sports, and yes, the business world. So many books have been written about the topic of leadership, but *Real Women, Real Leaders* aims to tell a different story; in fact, twenty-four different stories, all bound together by the leadership competencies as described in the 2012 research by Zenger and Folkman. (The entire Zenger/Folkman research study, along with their sixteen identified leadership competencies, can be found in the Appendix of this book.) More than 7,300 leaders were studied, and it was discovered that, of the sixteen leadership competencies, women out-scored men on twelve, including:

- Taking initiative
- Inspiring and motivating others

- Driving for results
- Building relationships
- Collaboration and team work

Not surprisingly, when asked to list their top five competencies, our authors chose these as well.

As a corporate trainer who specializes in participant-centered instruction, training design, presentation skills, meeting facilitation, and adult learning theory, I often find myself observing and identifying leaders as I conduct group sessions. While I am fascinated by different leadership styles, it is equally fascinating to check off the list of competencies in action and to see first-hand how women differ from men in their leadership styles—most notably in communication, collaboration, and motivation. In my role as a consultant over the past twenty-four years, I have not been in a traditional leadership role: one where I manage other people or report to one organization. But in my role working with a wide variety of clients with diverse needs, my leadership role has been to communicate prolifically, exhibit expertise, motivate and inspire others, and model collaboration and teamwork. To make a lasting impact on people's lives, whether it be in a professional development workshop, in a community volunteer opportunity, at church or at work, leadership is a value and a mission that real leaders live on a daily basis.

In Discovering Your Authentic Leadership, a research report for the *Harvard Business Review* by George, Sims, McLean, and Mayer (2007), the researchers found that leadership emerged from life stories. After interviewing 125 leaders, they resolved: "The journey of authentic leadership begins with understanding the story of your life. Authentic leaders reframe life events to discover their passion to lead. Learning from life experiences is central to knowing who you are and your development and effectiveness as a leader."

The stories in our book explain the authors' personal vision of leadership, the obstacles they overcame, and the mentors and teachers they encountered along the way. Now is the time for their stories to be shared. As more and more women are taking on influential roles in our society, businesses, and the world, what are the lessons we can learn as we share our personal journeys? This book aims to encourage more mentors for young girls and young women as they enter and progress in the world of work. While it is especially important to have female role models, it is equally important that men support, mentor, and promote women at work.

With this book, we hope to help our readers to consider that leadership "is more than a science. It is an art—a condition of the heart rather than just a set of things to do. Leadership from the heart is what is required of the successful organization" (Max Dupree, *Leadership Is an Art,* 2004).

So please, open your hearts to these stories. Learn from the journeys of these women. Consider your leadership competencies. Reflect on how you can manifest them in your world of work, your family, your life. And consider making leadership your mission, rather than just a set of skills.

2 Inspires and Motivates Others

"When you are living the best version of yourself, you inspire others to live the best versions of themselves."

—Steve Maraboli

The ability to Inspire and Motivate Others is the quintessential characteristic that many people associate with transformational leadership. How to define it, however, is exceedingly difficult when inspiration can come in so many forms. When asked to provide examples of an excellent leader, many people choose the individuals who have inspired them, who have made them feel like anything was possible and that they could accomplish things of which they were not previously capable. This chapter shows the ways that our Real Women have been able to capitalize on this characteristic and have inspired millions to be the best versions of themselves through their own examples.

Author Kendra Cherry offers these suggestions in order to be a transformational leader who inspires and motivates:

- "be genuinely passionate about ideas or goals
- help followers feel included in the process
- offer recognition, praise and rewards for people's accomplishments"[1]

---

[1] www.about.com/psychology/od/leadership

These three distinct qualifications suggest that, in order to inspire and motivate others, leaders must not only inspire others with their own examples of excellence, but also must further convince others to expend additional effort, elevating themselves and their performance to a certain bar, idea, or notion. A number of applicable behavior traits epitomize this competency, including charisma, persuasion skills, and infectious enthusiasm.

Inspiring and motivating others, while a lofty order, can manifest itself in tangible, real-world ways. From inspiring others to be tidier at their desks through the visual example of a beautiful office space to motivating others to complete a work project in advance of a deadline through a rousing speech, this competency shows us that charismatic leadership can happen everywhere in every way.

Most notably this is a skill that is aspired to in the workplace; employees who are able to skillfully inspire and motivate others ensure that productivity—and morale—are high, and are able to maintain long-term engagement for the team.[2]

Our Real Women in this chapter were chosen in part because they present clear examples of inspiring leadership, and they have been able to rise to their current positions through their ability to inspire and motivate others in a particularly complex field, education. As this chapter details, the ability to inspire others was transformative to Kecia Ray as she entered into Tennessee's failing school system and became the assistant superintendent and remains critical as she executes on her role as the president of the board for the International Society for Technology in Education (ISTE).

It was essential to Lily Eckelston García as she learned what it would take to organize people, unionize, and fight for children with the National Education Association. An additional example of inspirational leadership, Deb Delisle, currently overseeing education at the

---

[2] www.about.com/psychology/od/leadership

national level in the role of assistant secretary of education, learned early in her career that motivating others was the way to achieve results, even at the national level. Eleanor Smalley had to inspire and motivate a team around the importance of STEM education before it was considered an essential component of a well-rounded education. And Julie Young knew the importance of inspiration as she insisted that her staff continue to learn and grow together and ensure that they were always putting their customers—students and families—first.

As you will read in this chapter, these five women were able to cultivate inspiration and motivate their networks. They participated in some of the key actions that made their employees happy, loyal, and more likely to stay in their jobs: achievement, recognition, understanding that the work itself is part of a larger purpose, responsibility, and advancement.

These women were able to take the tools of inspiration and motivation and apply them to the complex world of education in the United States of America, and in doing so, provide learning opportunities for all Real Women leaders, regardless of industry.

Kecia Ray

President of the Board, International Society for Technology in Education (ISTE)

"Cautious, careful people, always casting about to preserve their reputation and social standing, never can bring about reform."

—SUSAN B. ANTHONY

Grit, Fire, and Wisdom

All my life I dreamed of becoming an educator. My grandfather was an educator, my parents were educators, and all my aunts and uncles were educators. Teaching seemed to be a likely career path for me when I was young, but later I realized that it was more—education was my passion and my conviction. I dreamed of becoming a college professor or a school district administrator or of influencing the global education community.

But before I could pursue any of those dreams, I had to undergo mandatory career screening in high school so that my counselor could submit paperwork to the colleges I had selected. The outcome of the screening was bleak. It suggested I pursue a career in daycare centers. I have nothing against daycare centers, and I've worked in several in my lifetime, but my aspirations lay elsewhere. I was devastated but not defeated. I enrolled in my local university and took classes in early childhood, encouraged by two people who had never obtained a college degree, my grandmother, whom we called Nana, and my father.

Both of them continually told me that I could be whatever I dreamed of being. My father in particular did not want me to suffer in a man's world, so he armed me with the grit, fire, and wisdom to navigate complex male systems. He was my man spy! Nana reminded me that, in spite of my assertiveness and passion, I was a lady, and I needed to be committed to woman's rights, especially in education. In 1986, most administrators were male, and most teachers were female. Nana felt that the odds were overwhelming, and, although she supported my quest to become a leader in education, she worried about the challenges I would face along the way. She was right.

My Top Five Leadership Competencies

- Displays high integrity and honesty
- Takes initiative
- Builds relationships

- Inspires and motivates others
- Champions change

But when I obtained my first job as a teacher—a wonderful experience in an urban school district—I was fortunate to have an amazing female principal as my first professional role model. Dr. West was a tall, beautiful, resilient African-American woman who loved education as much as I did and was committed to her faculty. She advised me how to dress as a professional educator, how to manage time between home and work, and most of all, how to support students as they transitioned into adulthood. She was tough. I never thought of challenging her, and I believe she may have had to relinquish some of her femininity in order to obtain her position and function in the south Atlanta school district at that time. After Dr. West, I did not encounter another female principal for twelve years. This was a world dominated by men.

I taught in two other school districts in Georgia and Tennessee, and in 1995 I encountered my second female principal, Veronica Bender, another outstanding leader. She would usually insist that we called her Veronica, unlike Dr. West, who never allowed us to address her as Sarah. She was a petite, opinionated, robust African-American lady who could rip you to shreds if you crossed her—another tough woman in a man's world. She taught me how to be a leader and encouraged me to pursue my doctorate. She always told me I had potential, and I believed her because she believed in me.

When I finished my doctoral work, I was offered the opportunity to apply for a principal's position in one of the large high schools in the district, as well as a university position. After consulting with Veronica, I accepted the university position and left the school district. The high school had never had a female principal, and we agreed that I did not want to take on that role, even in 1998.

Takes Initiative

Being a college professor was invigorating, but the path to becoming an administrator, my goal, was full of challenges. Vanderbilt needed a few good science minds who loved technology, but, feeling that I would never achieve my goal of becoming a leader, I reached out to a male colleague and told him I was never able to get past being a helper to leaders. What more did I need to do? I had acquired all the necessary degrees and worked in a variety of settings, so what was the education industry looking for? He told me that I would make a wonderful consultant and advised me to consider consulting as a career option. I did not follow his recommendation at the time, but I did not forget it, and later consulting became a very rewarding experience for me.

I gave up on trying to become a tenured faculty member when the art museum asked me to design the technology in the new art center. I completed that project, and then I embarked on another pathway. I took a position at another private university in Nashville. I had high hopes, since I had been an adjunct professor there for more than ten years. I was invited to apply for the position of full-time faculty member because the university was going through an accreditation process and needed someone with a doctoral degree and technology expertise. It appeared to be a slam-dunk. But the university elected instead to send a male faculty member to graduate school, an all-expenses-paid graduate degree. As a woman, I continued to struggle to meet my career goals.

Finally, in 2007 I got my chance to become a public school district administrator. The State of Tennessee appointed me as an assistant superintendent to help address the failing status of Metropolitan Nashville Public Schools. Not the most positive way to enter my dream job—but two wonderful former administrators were appointed to support me. Ms. Ashcraft and Dr. Musgrove were always there for me, providing encouragement and enlightenment and an experience that changed my life. Today, I remain in the same school district as the executive director of learning technology.

I believe that over the course of my career, I had to always become tougher and more assertive to cope with the many challenges I faced. I never had children because I was so focused on becoming an administrator. I worked hard at being a great stepmom, but perhaps I could have done a better job if I wasn't trying so hard to be the best school administrator. I made many sacrifices along the way. My male colleagues faced fewer obstacles and were able to reach their goals much sooner than I, but I met the challenge of school leadership, and now I lead a nationally recognized team.

Throughout my career, I took the initiative to focus on my own self-development. I built the relationships I needed to be successful, and I focused on results. I always maintained my integrity and was honest with colleagues. And I have realized that I am a strategist. If I see something I want, I develop a strategy to help me get there. I now work with an amazing team of people, whom I encourage to take the same strategic view. I help them develop goals they feel are attainable and develop themselves so that they can reach their goals. I motivate and inspire people never to be satisfied with the status quo—to focus on their dreams and make it happen.

Kecia Ray

She began her career as a middle school science teacher in Georgia and Tennessee before becoming assistant superintendent in the Metropolitan Nashville Public Schools. She served as an assistant professor at Middle Tennessee State University. She went on to design technology-rich learning spaces for the Frist Center for the Visual Arts, and in 2000 she became the director of technology research in the Office of Science Outreach at the Vanderbilt University School of Medicine. She has

(continued)

consulted with school systems, universities, and museums on
designing learning networks and is the author of three books.
She currently serves as president of the board of directors for
the International Society for Technology in Education (ISTE).

Lily Eskelsen García

President, National Education Association

> *"Five promises anchor our efforts to help young people succeed in life:
> they need caring adults, safe places (homes or schools), a healthy start,
> effective education, and opportunities to help others."*

—ALMA POWELL

From School Lunch Lady to Union Leader

My father once told me, "When someone asks you to do something,
do more than they asked. Do it better than they expected." Over the
years, I've added to his advice. "Do it in a way that's not boring."
There are so many interesting things in the world, why would we
waste one instant being bored?

When my father retired from the Army, we moved to Brigham
City, Utah, and he opened a little gas station where we kids helped
him pump gas for our allowance. Business was often slow, so I'd ask
him to show me how to balance tires or change the oil. I got to be
pretty good, but more importantly, I got to spend time with my dad.
With a car up on the rack and grease in my hair, we talked politics
and religion, and he told me stories about growing up as a sharecrop-
per's son. Dirt under the fingernails, yes—bored, no.

I've had many jobs—gas station attendant, lunch lady,
kindergarten aide, secretary, teacher, union leader. I married right out
of school and found my first full-time job as the salad girl in a Head

Start preschool kitchen at the whopping minimum wage of $1.68 per hour. At home we needed a dining room table, but we had no money for such luxuries, so I made one in a shop class. Every morning I still sit at that table, covered by a big tablecloth to hide the mistakes I made, but still, I have never been bored.

My Top Five Leadership Competencies

- Takes initiative
- Inspires and motivates
- Solves problems and analyzes issues
- Communicates powerfully
- Develops strategic perspective

I started teaching in 1980 before standardized testing took a wrecking ball to teaching and learning. At Douglas T. Orchard Elementary, our reading textbooks bored me as much as they bored my fourth graders. But I sat around the lunch table with my wicked-smart colleagues, and we decided to put the boring books on the shelf and start a literature-based program. We wrote study guides and vocabulary lists for our favorite children's books—*Bridge to Terabithia, Old Yeller, Tuck Everlasting, Where the Red Fern Grows*. By the time I left Orchard ten years later, we had developed materials for more than 150 titles. Our students loved reading and complained when it was time to put the books down.

I wanted children to experience something real. Reading a paragraph and marking answers on a multiple-choice test is not real. Curling up on the couch and melting into the pages of a book is real. Learning about World War II from a senior pen pal is real. Organizing a blood drive is real. Talking about respecting gay friends and family when someone says, "That's so gay" is real. Asking the new Spanish-speaking student to be the Spanish teacher is real. Real is never boring.

Teaching is often still seen as supplementing the family income for women. Women teachers, especially young ones, who step out of that role to demand something different surprise some people. I volunteered to be on the bargaining team to negotiate the teachers' contract when I was thirty. I was elected president of the Utah Education Association when I was thirty-five. I was the Democratic nominee for U.S. Congress at age forty-two—I was the first Hispanic to run for Congress in Utah and earned 45 percent of the vote against the incumbent.

Communicates Powerfully

My friends always told me to wait, get more experience, and work my way up. It was good advice based on sound reasoning, and I never took it. If I wanted to do something, I thought about the pros and cons and made up my own mind. Once my mind was made up, there was no second-guessing. There was only forward, with an irrepressible—or annoying—positive attitude and a smile on my face.

This was not always easy for my family. My sons were school age and struggled for different reasons, and my husband suffered from depression, although we had little understanding of depression at the time. My children are now in their thirties, and both have survived drug issues. One is living the Utah lifestyle with his husband in the suburbs with an office job and a mortgage. His brother found work in the northern oil fields with a monster truck and a shared trailer in the man camps. My sweet husband, a victim of depression, took his own life a few years ago.

The purpose of my life as an educator was always clear. I was there to open children's minds to infinite possibilities. Students and parents appreciated my clear purpose, but politicians often did not. Teachers are still overwhelmingly women, and politicians are overwhelmingly men. No matter. I found the same teaching techniques I used with twelve-year-olds worked with legislators, and I mean no disrespect to twelve-year-olds. People of any age or gender respond to confidence and positive energy and a compelling reason to move forward.

I felt odd at first when I was called a role model. I am Latina, and I have a special sense of family within my heritage, as do the members of most ethnic and racial groups. I am often given the stage so that students and families can hear the story of one of their own, the daughter of an immigrant who moved past where the demographics placed her. I was reluctant at first, but friends reminded me that I had benefitted from many role models, and today I feel honored and humbled to think that a bit of my story means something in the unfolding lives of young Latina girls and families. It makes me cry.

Inspires and Motivates

I cry easily. Accepting what I cannot change, I have become one with the quivering lip. As president of the National Education Association, I give a hundred speeches a year. I cry as I make the case for public schools, telling stories that have touched me—a child showing compassion to another child, a dreamer who wants to call the U.S. home, a teacher who nurtures the humanity of her students through community service. I've learned to make a little joke about the medication not kicking in this morning, but passion spilling over into a few tears is anything but a sign of weakness. There is nothing stronger.

I am asked to give speeches across the country about No Child Left Untested, politics, and the future of our public schools. No one asks me to give speeches on how to balance work and family, but maybe they should. I would tell them the hard truth. That it's difficult, complicated, and lonely, for men as well as women. I give women the same advice I give to men—life is short, so don't be less than you can be, and don't give less than you can give.

I also tell them that there are precious few "either-or" situations in life. You might not be able to have it all, but you can almost always find the "and." That doesn't mean everything is easy. The purpose of life is not and should not be to find what's easy. At times I'm asked to talk about the need to help students be "globally competitive" and to restrict myself to just the facts—just the percentages and the statistically significant samples. But how boring. Instead, I do more than I'm asked. I do it better than they expected. I look for the "and."

I talk about the research, *and* I tell the stories. I show passion for the cause I believe in *and* the plan to achieve the goal. I organize inside the National Education Association so that educators stand strong for the whole child, *and* I support others outside the NEA to fight for the right of every child to receive an education that develops the creative mind, the healthy body, and the compassionate character. I speak, *and* I listen. I honor what brought me here, *and* I move forward. *And* I will never be bored.

Lily Eskelsen García

Lily Eskelsen García earned a B.A. in elementary education and a master's degree in instructional technology from the University of Utah. She began her career as a school lunch lady and a kindergarten aide before working her way through college. She was named Utah Teacher of the Year for her work as an elementary teacher and has served as president of the Utah Education Association, the Utah State Retirement System, and the Children at Risk Foundation. She is one of the highest-ranking labor leaders in the country and was named by President Obama to serve as a commissioner on the White House Commission on Education Excellence for Hispanics. She currently serves as president of the over three-million-member National Education Association. (Blog: Lilysblackboard.org)

Deborah S. Delisle

Assistant Secretary for Elementary and Secondary Education, U.S. Department of Education

"If your success is not on your own terms, if it looks good to the world but does not feel good in your heart, it is not success at all."

—ANNA QUINDLEN

Caring Enough to Try

When I was about five years old, my dad took me to a park near our home in Connecticut to teach me to catch a football. Granted it was a miniature version, but its significance was not lost on me even at that age—having an older sister meant that I was filling in for the son my dad did not have. As the day dragged on and I failed to catch the ball, I finally sat down in the dirt with tears streaming down my face.

Ever patient, dad waited a few minutes before he walked over, and the trajectory of my life changed at that moment, although I didn't realize it until many years later. Dad looked into my tear-filled eyes and said quietly, "You can do anything you want as long as you care enough. You just have to care enough to try. But don't do it for me. Do it for yourself. Do it because it feels right." Little did I know that my father was giving me a star by which to steer my life, a reason to keep going when faced with obstacles and challenges that can seem overwhelming.

Many years later, when I became the superintendent of a large urban school district in Ohio, I found myself reflecting on that moment in the park. My dad's words had become a mantra of sorts to me, without his ever realizing it. He had planted the seeds of courageous leadership deep in my heart, and I consider his words to be the best advice I have ever been given.

My Top Five Leadership Competencies

- Takes initiative
- Drives for results
- Inspires and motivates others
- Builds relationships
- Champions change

As a baby boomer, I often feel that I was born a bit too early to benefit from all the increased opportunities for women we have seen in our society in recent years. In high school and college, I saw no possibilities beyond the then stereotypical female roles of nurse or teacher. Although my teachers and professors said I had great potential, they never explained what that meant, and to this day I worry about what guidance is given to bright girls, especially those from underserved populations.

As a first-generation college student, I had to rely on my instincts and my passion to excel. While others can point to important mentors early on, that gift was lacking in my life when I was young. I started out in a traditional female role as a teacher, in Connecticut, not realizing that this typical path would lead me to amazing opportunities. However, one of my greatest moments of self-discovery came when I took a position as a middle school teacher in a suburb of Cleveland. The principal, a strong female leader, took me under her wing and also partnered me with a male colleague—a double gift for my leadership development. Both relationships have served as significant catalysts in my development.

These two colleagues were my first mentors, and they played such an important role in my life that I often wonder whether I would have become the leader I am without them. They modeled for me the importance of inspiring and motivating others and demonstrated that positive results come from collaboration and teamwork. They helped me to increase my confidence and fundamentally changed my self-image—from participant to leader. I learned that my ability to inspire others to attain better results is the energy that fuels me.

Inspires and Motivates Others

As I reflect on my career, I am struck by the number of times I've been in the minority as a female leader. I would like to believe that I did not act differently because I'm a woman, but the truth is that I've often found myself speaking louder, pushing harder, working longer hours, and producing more than my male counterparts. My decision to do so was not always a conscious one, but I usually felt the need to leave no one in doubt about my ability to handle leadership responsibilities. I came to understand that being a champion of change is essential, even when others believe that such actions may not yield greater results.

As a woman, I have often been in situations that made me cringe while the men in the room were perfectly comfortable, but sometimes the men spoke up. I remember once sitting around a conference table with a group of men planning a retirement celebration for a male colleague, when the leader suggested that we collect money for the party and insisted that I bake the cake. One of my male colleagues actually objected to the sexism of this remark—one of the first times a male colleague of mine spoke publicly about gender bias. Thereafter, I became much more vocal about comments and situations where I felt that gender bias was operating.

In my early years, I generally discounted the idea that leadership differences are based on gender; rather, I tended to view the differences in terms of personality. However, experiences have changed my view, and I now believe that males and females often do lead differently. One is not better than the other—just different. Rather, I know now that it is essential to be aware of how different perspectives and priorities influence leadership styles, and I need to respond accordingly.

My experience has led me to recognize that women leaders prioritize relationships. We women intuitively understand the importance of relationships, work to develop them early, and maintain them throughout our careers and private lives. As a woman leader, it is important to me to develop relationships that harness people's talents and then support them to become productive team players with a strong vision and valuable strategic skills that enhance the organization's effectiveness.

Builds Relationships

I have been given so many opportunities to exercise leadership and learn about leadership; however, if someone had told me when I first stepped into the classroom as a second-grade teacher that one day I would oversee education at the national level, I would have laughed. I could never see that far in front of me. From very humble beginnings to meetings at the White House, I have been entrusted with great opportunities by caring and supportive colleagues, and I am deeply grateful.

I have always believed that I should take any job I would wonder about later if I had not taken it—nothing scientific in this premise, but it's worked for me! All my professional roles have brought me much fulfillment and yielded great successes. Most importantly, they have brought me a network of colleagues and friends who have enriched my life in countless ways and supported the fragile transition from accepting myself as a leader to being recognized as one.

The people in my network always remind me that our choices must be thoughtful and feel right, in the words of my dad, as I strive to advance the possibilities. While I'm sorry that my dad never had the chance to see me in my most senior leadership roles, my heart still carries his lessons about courageous leadership from all those years ago. His wisdom lives on through my life and my work. Sometimes our best mentors and teachers are just a heartbeat away.

Deborah Delisle

Deborah Delisle earned an M.ED. from Kent State University in 1986. After beginning her career as an elementary teacher, she served in different roles at the school district level in Ohio and became the associate superintendent and then the superintendent of the Cleveland Heights-University Heights City School District and, from 2008 to 2011, the state superintendent of public instruction for the Ohio Department of Education. She has served on several education boards, including the Council of Chief State School Officers, and was a senior fellow with the International Center for Leadership in Education. In 2012 she became the assistant secretary for elementary and secondary education at the U.S. Department of Education, where she serves as the principal adviser to the Secretary of Education on all matters related to pre-k, elementary, and secondary education and directs programs that help state and local agencies improve the achievement of students.

Eleanor Smalley
COO and Executive Vice President, JASON Learning

"Some people see education in America as the little red schoolhouse, when the skies were not cloudy all day and nobody ever heard of smog. They are practicing selective amnesia. The truth of the matter is that education in America is what makes dreams come true for all students, able-bodied or not, rich or poor, whether their skin is white, yellow, or

black or brown or any shade of the rainbow. Education allows children
to enter into the richness of the experience of the mind."

—Shirley Hufstedler

Superwoman's View

Superheroes have always held a great attraction for me. The idea that you can be more than you appear to be has empowered and motivated me. When I was young, I always wanted to be a leader with x-ray vision, able to see through obstacles on the journey toward reaching my goals. I felt that leaders like Superwoman could break down barriers in pursuit of a vision—as John F. Kennedy did, so that we landed a man on the moon, as Martin Luther King, Jr., did, so that all races in America enjoy equal civil rights, and as Clara Barton did, so that today we have the Red Cross. These superheroes provided the leadership lessons that have most influenced my life.

My Top Five Leadership Competencies

- Takes initiative
- Displays high integrity
- Drives for results
- Inspires and motivates
- Collaboration and teamwork

I began teaching high school English at the age of twenty-two in a suburb outside of Richmond, Virginia, where I learned an important lesson. One of my students, a junior, was visually impaired but had chosen not to be classified as disabled, because he believed that this classification would make others respect him less. He was a dedicated student, but another teacher refused to give him extra time on tests.

I tried to resolve the issue by meeting with the teacher, guidance counselor, and principal, only to be told that there was no way around the rule. Finally, his parents requested that he be classified as disabled, but I still remember how angry he was with me for treating him disrespectfully by labeling him. He said he would have preferred to fail. The lesson I learned was this—school leaders do not always recognize that student learning is more important than labels.

At that point, I decided to become a school leader, in order to pursue a more progressive school model. I earned my master's degree and principalship endorsement, and at the age of twenty-eight I became the assistant principal in Fluvanna County High School in Virginia. I was the first female secondary administrator at that school, fortunate to work with an amazing mentor, Mr. Ervin McQuaige, the principal of the school.

The school was very diverse at that time—around 50 percent African-American and 50 percent white students, with 60 percent free and reduced lunch. There were no programs for academically challenged students, so many had failed multiple grades. The school was often a hotbed of emotion and anger, and most students came from households in which neither parent had a college education. But many students were amazing athletes, and the school needed a cultural shift to show students that they could succeed by becoming scholar athletes.

Mr. McQuaige taught me many lessons about dignity—how to change the system and create a culture of success by focusing on the concept of respect. Together we taught students, families, and educators that they could succeed if they treated each other with respect, and we found role models who could inspire students to translate their amazing physical prowess into academic success.

We worked long days, often starting at 6:30 a.m. and ending at 11:00 p.m. because of the large number of extracurricular activities. Student success became my passion, and I learned about the concept of flow—the idea that I could become completely involved in an activity for its own sake, so that time flew by, with every activity and thought flowing out of the previous one. The long days and hard work were highly positive because the flow constantly reinforced my passion for the vision and the mission.

After working in other positions and earning my doctorate, my sense of mission broadened, and I knew I could experience the same success at the district level. I became the assistant superintendent in Clarke County, Virginia, where I met Dennis Kellison, the superintendent, another mentor and colleague who shared my beliefs. We agreed that educators, like doctors, should take an oath to do no harm, that all children can learn, and that the job of schools is to adapt to the needs of students.

We began a journey of transforming the district into a community where all children could become successful learners because they were viewed as successful learners. Probably the two most important lessons I learned from Mr. Kellison were to engage all stakeholders in establishing the vision and to track the data, because metrics matter on the journey to fulfilling a vision.

Drives for Results

I became the superintendent in Clarke County at the age of thirty-nine and remained in that position for twelve years. We continually refined our vision statements and moved from a bell-curve thinking model to J-curve thinking. Our dropout rate fell to under 1 percent, we ranked in the top fifty for several consecutive years on the *Newsweek* Challenge Index, and we won multiple athletic titles that gave us three straight successes in the Wachovia Cup. When we connected extracurricular motivation to in-school learning, our students produced strong academic work and began to believe in their ability to learn.

The vision that all children can learn works—when students have access to a quality education, the time they need to complete their work, and motivation that is both extrinsic and intrinsic. To achieve success, a group of like-minded individuals came together to focus on the vision of all children learning at high levels of achievement. We modified systems to provide access to all students, linked motivational activities to learning, and provided extra time based on individual needs. The group efforts of smart, dedicated people who were focused on student learning made the difference.

Collaboration and Teamwork

The leadership lessons were clear. When there is a strong vision, when creative, strategic, and committed people work together toward the mission, the results can be amazing. Not everyone will share the vision, and those who do not may work hard to change it. They may create obstacles and erect walls, which can impede your progress if you let them. But with Superwoman's view and x-ray vision, it is possible to see right through those walls and continue along the path toward your goals.

My success came from working hard and being connected to critical people in my organization and community. I continually evaluated what I was doing to make sure it was working, and I fixed whatever needed to be fixed. I was offered a number of learning opportunities and much support, but, most importantly, my faith in my vision propelled me forward past every obstacle.

Now I have the opportunity to translate my success as a superintendent into student success on a national scale with my work at JASON Learning. The lessons that I learned in public education apply here. Employees are passionate about this organization, so there is a culture of flexibility and innovation, and as the team grows, we continue to attract smart, dedicated, and innovative people who work together toward a shared vision. Because we are a small team, it is easy to evaluate progress by capturing metrics and adapting our organization in light of what works.

We know we need other leaders who share our mission to change school cultures. We work every day to create partnerships with superintendents who share the belief that every student can learn and succeed. They spread the vision within their school districts, and we provide the access to high-quality online STEM (science, technology, engineering, and math) content that students use in school and at home. Our mission in this organization is to be leaders in transforming the driving force of education from literacy to scientific literacy, and we are pursuing our mission with x-ray vision.

Eleanor Smalley

Dr. Smalley holds a master's degree and doctorate in education leadership from the University of Virginia. She has served as an adjunct professor for the Curry School of Education for twelve years. She served for thirty years in public education, and her focus on early childhood programs was recognized as a model for the state of Virginia. She has co-authored *District Case Studies and Individual Lessons in Leadership* with Dr. Daniel Duke, consulted with Glenville State College in West Virginia on the twenty-one-district Hidden Promise Consortium, and designed a master's program in teaching science. She currently leads JASON Learning, a non-profit organization specializing in STEM (science, technology, engineering, and mathematics) programs used by over 2.7 million students across the globe (www.jason.org).

Julie Young

President, Julie Young Education, LLC; Founding President and Former CEO Florida Virtual School

"Education is for improving the lives of others and for leaving your community and world better than you found it."

—MARIAN WRIGHT EDELMAN

Living and Breathing the Vision

My parents were my first mentors, and my mom was my best teacher. She taught me grace, the meaning of family, and to challenge myself and never give up. My dad began his career in the mailroom of one of the largest banks in Lexington, Kentucky, and finished his career as the CEO of the bank. He passed on to me his gift for making people feel special, treating everyone with respect, and never putting himself above others.

The road to my current position began with a love of teaching and learning that goes back to my childhood. I went from playing school as a child to playing school as an adult. My work has always been my play, and I am fortunate to have a job that I love and one in which I am able to inspire others. Following my dream, I started my career as a sixth grade teacher in Palm Beach County, Florida. For the next thirteen years, I taught in elementary schools in Kentucky and Florida and held a variety of leadership roles. Teachers are the CEOs of their classrooms, and my humble beginnings in the classroom were the perfect training for the leadership position I hold today.

My Top Five Leadership Competencies

- Innovates
- Displays high integrity and honesty
- Champions change
- Inspires and motivates others
- Drives for results

In 1989, I became a curriculum technology specialist, where I was charged with developing technology-related strategies and training for schools. I worked closely with IBM, the provider for our school, and in 1991, I was hired by IBM as an education instructional specialist.

My passion became helping teachers to integrate technology into their classrooms and understand the impact of technology on student learning—well before the days of Internet access and cell phones. However, I always looked forward to the day when I could apply to education the business techniques and principles I was learning at IBM, and time would tell that those years were in fact very influential on my future career.

Innovates

When I moved to Orlando in 1996, I was thinking of staying in the corporate world, and I interviewed with a wonderful woman who was both an education relationship manager for a major telecom and a member of the Orange County School Board. After a three-hour lunch, my new friend looked at me and said, "You don't belong here. You belong in the schools." She was right! My résumé—with all the right technology words and a good word from my new friend—led to a call from the district office. The next thing I knew, Orange County Public Schools asked me to head up a $200,000 Break the Mold grant from the Florida Department of Education to develop an online high school for the state. I remember being very grateful for the power of networking and the wonderful gift of women helping women.

Florida Virtual Schools® was created in 1997. It became the nation's first Internet-based public high school—allowing students to learn any time, any place, any path, and any pace. Today, it is the nation's largest, statewide, online public school district and the model for distance learning initiatives around the world. I lead a staff of more than 1,700 teachers, curriculum developers, web designers, and information technology personnel. By designing a school around student needs instead of adult schedules, we developed a disruptive innovation that transformed education as we knew it.

Champions Change

In my transition from elementary to secondary education, I encountered some gender struggles, although they were generally minor. I often found myself in meetings with groups of male high school principals who were not overly excited to meet "that online lady who's trying to steal my students." I was the new kid on the block who stuck out like a sore thumb—young and green and out of my comfort zone. When I faced challenges, I often thought that the dialogue might be different if I were six feet tall and male. But I took one day at a time and was determined to prove myself, knowing that these experiences would prepare me for more difficult challenges ahead.

I have had the opportunity to watch, listen, and learn from some of the best and brightest around the globe, many working in education or technology. I try to live the leadership principles of John Maxwell, and I am a student of Jim Collins, who believes that no matter what stage a person is in—professional or personal—every challenge should be viewed as an opportunity to go from good to great. One of the most rewarding things I do is identify and grow future leaders, developing individuals regardless of gender. I am proud to do that for others and always humbled by the opportunity to impact someone's career.

I lead our organization by asking questions to leverage the thoughts of others who are smarter than I am and better positioned to problem solve. I listen to those who want to provide input and defer to those who are ready to bring concepts to life. I find that if I surround myself with people who have diverse perspectives and mutual trust, the debate is always healthy, and the ending is generally happy.

Every June, I send all staff members a letter requesting that they take time to reflect with their families about their work and the demands of their jobs. I ask them to intentionally commit to return to our school, its culture, and the beliefs we hold dear about students and learning. I engage in the same reflection myself, since one day I may have other commitments that lead me in another direction. By fostering reflection, I have seen leaders grow all around me.

I also insist that my staff read together. We have to be different from the century-old school model. We have to engage students and families and make them want to come to us. We have to have stellar service and treat students and parents as valued customers. So we read everything we can about organizational culture, from *Who Moved My Cheese* to *Good to Great* to *Customer Satisfaction Is Worthless*. We look for what makes sense in the context of teaching students, and we take the risk to try other ideas that may not seem to make sense at first. It's a privilege to lead when others are willing to take risks in the best interests of children, and it makes every day an adventure.

I have always lived by the philosophy that we are leaders not because of titles but because people choose to follow us. I hold myself and my teams accountable, and accountability is an important part of our culture. I have always been willing to make the hard decisions and own them. I explain the "why behind the what" so that everyone understands the decisions, and I lead Florida Virtual Schools® as I would like to be led. We all spend more waking hours at work than we spend with our families, so I believe that work should be a happy place filled with laughter, love, and respect.

I continue to create a culture that is different from the culture of traditional schools. Our goal has always been student performance—our success is measured by a student's mastery of a concept, not by the amount of time in a seat—and my team keeps students at the center of every decision. Because I live and breathe our vision, it becomes a reality every day, and embracing the vision is a cultural requirement for every employee.

Julie Young

Julie Young earned a B.A. in elementary education from the University of Kentucky and a master's degree in administration and supervision from the University of South Florida. After teaching elementary school for several years, she served as a teacher trainer for a partnership between her district and IBM and later joined IBM. In 1997, she joined Florida Virtual Schools®. She serves on several boards, including the United States Distance Learning Association, the International Association for K-12 Online Learning, Florida Learning Alliance, Florida Sterling Council, K-12 Blackboard Advisory Council, and Microsoft K-12 Advisory Council. She was recognized by *Technology & Learning Magazine* as one of the Top 30 influencers in ed tech, along with Bill Gates and Steve Jobs (www.flvs.net).

3 Takes Initiative

"There are three types of people in this world: those who make things happen, those who watch things happen, and those who wonder what happened."

—Mary Kay Ash

As one of the competencies with the largest differences between men and women, taking initiative seems to be at the core of many women's encounters with leadership and success. This chapter explores how our Real Women have taken initiative in all areas of their lives, innovating and seeking opportunities that will facilitate success.

Taking initiative can be defined in a variety of ways:

- "taking prompt action to accomplish objectives,
- self-starting,
- taking action to achieve goals beyond what is required,
- being proactive,
- thinking on your own feet,
- taking advantage of opportunities,
- taking charge,
- getting things done on your own."[1]

---

[1] http://campusservices.harvard.edu/system/files/documents/1865/harvard_competency_dictionary_complete.pdf

Taking initiative is demonstrated in actions as small as becoming captain of your high school cheerleading team, or as large as founding your own international non-profit. It can manifest through a philosophy of hard work, or knowing what you want and looking for opportunities to make that happen. In the everyday workplace, taking initiative is an act that takes place in a range of different styles and formats. The main actions involved in taking initiative are "responding quickly, taking independent action, and going above and beyond."[2]

People who are adept at taking initiative are generally sought after within an organization, as they are the people who will go beyond their responsibilities and need less direction or direct management than others. By continually looking for ways to solve problems, and more importantly, acting on these ideas, leaders who take initiative quickly prove themselves. According to Connie Jackson, chief executive of St. Bartholomew's & the Royal London Charitable Foundation: "As a leader, there are times you need to risk going in a direction that no one else has taken before. You just have to step out there and follow the path you think is right." Perhaps you see an opportunity to improve a strategy at work and take steps toward that change. Or perhaps you see the need to speak up and take charge of a task that has fallen by the wayside. Regardless of the opportunity, acting upon it defines this competency.

Bruttel and Fischbacher (2013) show how taking initiative in life is associated with leadership and suggest that, for initiative to take place, creativity or innovation is required. To become a leader who takes initiative, there are concrete mindsets, attitudes, and behaviors that one can take. Suggestions include "displaying a 'can do' attitude, even in difficult situations, going the extra mile and subsequently being noticed for your work, using initiative to act

[2]http://campusservices.harvard.edu/system/files/documents/1865/harvard_competency_dictionary_complete.pdf

on opportunities, showing enthusiasm, and taking ownership of problems."[3]

The essays in this chapter show real-life examples of all of these traits and illustrate how women can take initiative to become successful female leaders.

Searching the *Leadership Now* leading quotes wall on Initiative,[4] you will find few that originate from a woman. However, virtually all of our Real Women demonstrate the essential competency of taking initiative, showing clearly how this has enabled them to climb to their success. The world of business is a hard world, and those not willing to take initiative and prove themselves often are left behind.

Our Real Women show how they were able to think on their feet and be proactive in the workplace to ensure success. This competency can manifest at an early age, as Shannon Peters, former vice president of operations at J.P. Morgan Chase, demonstrates through her story of how, as an eight-year-old, she began to take initiative by learning how the family business ran. Taking initiative as a competency can also clearly be learned and perfected, as seen through Judith LaBelle, who describes how, despite her lack of role models at a young age, she grasped at every opportunity she was given in order to succeed in her career, eventually becoming the founding president of Glynwood. Making proactive decisions in order to open up new opportunities is a clear theme in the story of Susan Hall, founder and president of the 95 Percent Group, who discusses how her decision to leave the Fortune 500 world behind because of the limits placed on her shaped her career path. Building on this theme, Eileen Lento, K-12 strategist at Intel Corporation, describes how, when her opportunities were limited because of her sex, she searched for different paths to take her to success. Finally, Marguerite Kondracke, former CEO of America's Promise, discusses the difference between luck, risk taking, and initiative when seizing opportunities.

---

[3] www.kent.ac.uk/careers/sk/leadership.htm
[4] www.leadershipnow.com

Through these clear examples of initiative, you will learn how, even despite all odds, women are creating impact and leading change in the world. To help you practice this competency, a blog posting from *Forbes* magazine suggests five concrete steps on how to take more initiative and take on more responsibility at work:

1. Talk to your boss
   - What skills or knowledge do you want to develop to achieve your career goals? Write down some ideas and talk to your supervisor about extra projects you can work on to help you develop them.

2. Look for busy, stressed out co-workers
   - Find out who needs help, and offer your services. Just make sure you can take on extra tasks while completing your own.

3. Be proactive
   - If you see a task that needs doing, be proactive and do it. People will be grateful and respect you for your initiative.

4. Start with the fun stuff
   - Show your leadership skills through sports or extracurricular work activities. This will build community spirit and show people you are capable in a different environment.

5. Become an expert
   - Set up a "Google Alert" for topics relevant to your area of desired expertise. If you find something worth sharing, send it to your team. Make sure you know about the article you are sending, because if people think you are an expert, they will ask you questions![5]

Although sometimes hard, it is important to remember to have the confidence and drive to take initiative when you see an opportunity—and to encourage others to do the same.

---

[5] www.forbes.com/sites/prettyyoungprofessional/2011/04/19/5-ways-to-take-on-more-responsibility-at-work/

Shannon Peters

Former Vice President of Operations, J.P. Morgan Chase

"Women in leadership roles can help restore balance and wholeness to our communities."

—WILMA MANKILLER

Controlling the Checkbook

When I was eight years old, I used to pretend I was running the family business, a construction company in upstate New York, with the help of a fake checkbook. I was always trying to help out and run things, and my fake checkbook went everywhere with me—until one day I was crushed to learn that I needed to deposit some money into the bank first! After I picked myself up off the floor, I decided I was going to be a serious businesswoman and someday run the family business.

Both my parents were instrumental in my choice of career, and I never saw any role differences or power struggles between them. My mother ran the back office, and my stepfather never did anything without talking to her. I did end up working in the family business and then running it, and, between the ages of eleven and seventeen, I learned all the business fundamentals I thought I needed to know. But I couldn't have been more wrong. I didn't know that opting for a career in finance and operations would land me smack dab in the middle of a man's world. But I was right about one thing. In my career I have always managed a checkbook.

My Top Five Leadership Competencies

- Takes initiative
- Drives for results

(continued)

- Collaboration and teamwork
- Solves problems and analyzes issues
- Technical or professional expertise

I began my career as the business office manager for a partnership that owned and developed nursing homes and senior care facilities, where I worked with a wonderful woman who was the chief financial officer. We became good friends and, little by little, she began to mentor me. I was fascinated by what she knew and how she controlled everything in the company—because she controlled the checkbook. As we became closer, she gave me more financial and operational responsibilities and taught me the tricks of the trade. She exuded integrity and strength. She was everything I wanted to be and do.

Eventually, I ventured out on my own, first into the commercial real estate industry, working with one of the biggest companies in the world as the business operations manager for their New Jersey–based operations. *Star Wars* fans will understand that it was time for the young Padawan to put to use what she had learned from her master. After a few months, I was in charge of the operations and the sales team—all men—and loving it, although I was working long hours for what seemed like little pay. I soon realized that all the men around me were making millions of dollars in commissions, and almost all the women were business operations managers at my level. Hmmm. At that point, I began to wonder whether we were just glorified secretaries acting as mothers to the guys. However, I was making decent money and being noticed as a smart business person by the corporate top dogs. I loved my job.

Then the unthinkable happened. I stumbled into a situation I doubt that many employees, let alone women, have to endure. I learned of an affair in the workplace that impacted me. My boss's boss was having an affair with my assistant, who was no longer supporting our operational plan and actually intending to take over my job, which the big boss had promised her. When he found out that I knew, he threatened to fire me if I revealed anything. Does this happen to men? I don't know, but it happened to me.

I come from tough stock, and I had worked with a lot of tough guys in the construction industry, so when someone threatened my job it did not sit well with me. I was not the roll-over-and-take-it kind of gal. But most of the corporate personnel were male, so I knew this was going to be difficult. I decided the best strategy was to leave for a better job with more money and a bigger checkbook, but before I left I collected all the evidence. During my exit interview, with a man, I explained that lack of integrity was my main reason for leaving. Of course, they told me they would handle the situation, but my mind was made up, and I left on good terms.

Drives for Results

In my new job, I was the director of operations for one of the world's largest banks and brokerages in New York City. This led to a vice president position where I was responsible for managing a large team and millions of dollars of the U.S. Small Business Administration loan portfolio. That's a big checkbook. Now I was in the thick of the man's world of finance and banking—and loving it. I played all the corporate games, sometimes used my feminine wiles to get ahead, and worked long hours to prove my value. But I learned through a human resources department leak that the male vice presidents in similar roles were making over $50,000 a year more than me. Ouch!

Just as I was beginning to wonder whether it was worth all the sacrifice, 9/11 happened, right across the street from my office. It took me some time to recover from the trauma, and in the process, I realized I was not happy with my career. I did not want to play any more games, and I wanted more out of life. I resigned, and we moved to Seattle, where my husband's company had a satellite office. Five months later, I was pregnant and happily unemployed.

After our son was born, I got the business itch again. I wanted to put my experience to good use and earn the money I felt I was worth. I started a finance and operations consulting company, had lots of clients, and really liked being my own boss. One day, a client asked me to stay on as the full-time vice president of finance. I took a chance and said yes, and what I thought would be a short-lived experience turned out to be the best job I've ever had. Twelve years later, I am that same company's chief financial officer, working remotely and combining my knowledge of traditional banking and manufacturing processes with online business acumen.

Technical or Professional Expertise

I have become the Jedi Master of my craft. I've learned that the size of the checkbook is not as important as the quality of the work and the integrity of the people. I've also learned that, although I have reached the C level in business, the BS factor is always alive and well, and that it's up to every individual to stand up for her ideals and rights.

I'm not sure whether I have been treated differently from my male peers during my career—probably I have, in a few situations—but I am sure that I earned less than they did for the same if not more work. However, I don't look at myself as a minority or feel as though I have to respond differently to different genders. My emotions, ideals, and integrity are intact as I do the work dance every day, while maintaining a house and personal finances, raising a growing boy, and supporting an executive husband.

I was fortunate to have been taught by my parents to be myself, to be honest, to work hard and play hard, and that family always comes first. I have stuck to these rules, and I am doing just fine.

I thank God every day that I am a strong and healthy woman with the best family in the world. And I hope that my family-first attitude will help define society's view of a career-minded woman in the 21st century.

Shannon Peters

Shannon Peters attended Penn State University. She served for more than fifteen years in executive-level positions in organizations such as J.P. Morgan Chase, Grubb & Ellis, and Pall Trinity. Since 2005, she has worked remotely as the controller and chief financial officer of Bucky.com, a luxury pillow and travel accessories company, helping to define a new view of the successful female executive (www.bucky.com)

Judith LaBelle
Founding President, Glynwood

"We need leaders once again who can tap into that special blend of American confidence and optimism that has enabled generations before us to meet our toughest challenges. Leaders who can help us show ourselves and the world that with our ingenuity, creativity, and innovative spirit, there are no limits to what is possible in America."

—HILLARY RODHAM CLINTON

From a Small Farm to the Wider World

I recall as a young girl reading myself to sleep with *Kon-Tiki*, Thor Heyerdahl's book about his expedition to Easter Island, and dreaming about the mysteries of the world. Some nights I would look out across

the flat Wisconsin fields and wonder whether I might see the lights of
one of the UFOs that were in the news at the time. Maybe one would
even come and take me away, but to where?

Growing up on a small dairy farm right after the Second World
War, my parents gave me a solid set of values that have served me
well. But the environment I grew up in was also limiting. When I left
for college, the only professional women I had met were the elementary school principal, teachers, and nurses. I had met one lawyer, one
doctor, one dentist, and a few veterinarians—all men. So I had no
role models to introduce me to the wider world I knew was out there
somewhere.

My Top Five Leadership Competencies

- Takes initiative
- Displays high integrity
- Solves problems
- Communicates powerfully
- Connects the group

Meanwhile, I did my best with whatever opportunities I had. I
became captain of the cheerleading team, president of the student
body, and valedictorian, and all this caught the attention of a recruiter
from a small liberal arts college about 100 miles away from home,
which provided a scholarship. I have often been asked why I didn't
attend one of the elite schools in the Northeast. The answer is simple.
I did not know that they existed, and if I had, I would have thought
they were beyond my reach.

I minored in education, since I always assumed I would need to
make a living, but I took every opportunity to explore the world beyond
campus. I majored in political science, spent a semester on a special

program in Washington, D.C., where I also interned with my congressman and volunteered for a literacy action program in a poor neighborhood in Atlanta. These experiences sparked my interest in public service.

Fortunately, my congressman's chief of staff took an interest in my career, recommending me to the graduate program in practical politics at Rutgers, from which I received my master's degree. My education credentials led to an interesting job with the Wisconsin legislature that, unfortunately, fell victim to budget cuts the week before I was scheduled to start. To make ends meet, I found a temporary job at a non-profit. Soon I began spending nights and weekends volunteering for New York City Mayor John Lindsay's 1972 presidential campaign. The day after he lost the Wisconsin primary and dropped out of the race, the McGovern campaign asked me to work in California, where I ran the Get Out the Vote operation in Orange County in both the primary and general elections.

In spite of the disappointment of the election, the experience was pivotal for me. I was given the opportunity to work with senior officials from all levels of the campaign, play an integral role in developing and executing strategy, and manage a diverse array of colleagues and volunteers. Afterward, a colleague urged me to seek a job in the Lindsay Administration in New York, and I leapt at the chance to experience the Big Apple. I accepted a position in the department of parks and recreation and cultural affairs, where my boss and many other senior officials were attorneys. I also moonlighted as the campaign manager for a New York State legislature candidate who was an attorney, as were many of his supporters. I soon recognized that legal credentials and skills would help me advance if I wanted to stay in public administration and would also open up a world of other opportunities.

Communicates Powerfully

Fortunately, I was selected as a Root-Tilden Scholar at the New York University School of Law. This unusual program, designed

to encourage public interest law, helped confirm my commitment
to earn my living in a way aligned with my values. One law firm
in particular intrigued me. It was a small New York City firm that
combined a commercial practice with a deep commitment to public
interest law and the environment. It was highly regarded, and its hiring was very competitive, but during the campaign two years earlier
I had met several lawyers with the firm. I secured an interview and,
ultimately, the coveted position of associate. Again, work outside of
my day job had provided the contacts I needed to move forward.

I soon realized the obvious—lawyers need clients. I also realized
that my colleagues had tremendous networks as a result of having
gone to elite colleges and law schools in the Northeast, while my
undergraduate education in Wisconsin had provided nothing in this
regard. I was the first woman to become a member of this law firm
and the first partner who had not attended Harvard as an undergraduate or law student. I felt that I was starting nearly from scratch, so
I set about trying to expand my universe again. My partners encouraged me to build a practice that combined the commercial work that
paid the bills with a pro bono practice that related to my interest in
the environment and land use.

Solves Problems

As my reputation grew, I was invited to join the boards of non-
profit organizations, where I was able to meet a wide range of other
civic-minded people who shared my values around land conservation, parks and open space, environmental quality, and historic
preservation. They helped me create the network I needed to develop
my practice and career. Of course, we are all creatures of our time,
and I had the interesting experience of being a lawyer at a time when
the practice of law was evolving from a profession to a business, and
environmental law was evolving into another branch of commercial
practice. The values in my profession and my specialty were changing,

and I felt increasingly out of place. So I left the private practice of law and began a new journey.

I became the deputy director and counsel to a state commission on the Adirondacks, an effort to update the land use regulations covering approximately six million acres of upstate New York, then a Loeb Fellow at the Graduate School of Design at Harvard University, a mid-career program in advanced environmental studies, then the corporate counsel for the National Audubon Society, and finally the founding president of Glynwood, a non-profit located in the Hudson River Valley.

I served as president of Glynwood for nearly seventeen years. This position gave me a tremendous opportunity to be creative and proactive in the emerging field of sustainable food and farming. In late 2012, I became president emeritus and senior fellow. Freed from daily management responsibilities, I now have the luxury of time to think and write and continue to support Glynwood and the advancement of sustainable food and farming.

Given my life's journey away from a small farm, it may seem ironic that at Glynwood we encourage the next generation of farmers, the young people who will be the leaders in developing more resilient food systems. But living on a small farm today is not the isolated experience it was when I was growing up. Communications technology and new approaches to farming have changed everything, opening new vistas and opportunities for this generation and their children.

Although there was no clear design to my career path, several bright threads stand out for me now. First, I always sought to integrate my core values into my work. Second, I believed in the importance of activities outside of a standard job. Third, I made contacts that proved helpful as I navigated the many transitions in my career. And finally, I relied on family, friends, and my supportive husband as I tried to negotiate the life-work balance. I still haven't seen Easter Island or a UFO, but I have created a career that has allowed me to do meaningful work and have an interesting life beyond what I could ever have imagined back on the farm.

Judith LaBelle

Judith LaBelle earned a B.A. in political science from Carroll College, a Master's in Practical Politics from Rutgers University, and a law degree from New York University School of Law. She was a member of the firm of Berle, Kass & Case in New York City and served as corporate counsel to the National Audubon Society and deputy director and counsel to the New York State Commission on the Adirondacks in the Twenty-First Century. In 1990, the Graduate School of Design at Harvard named her a Loeb Fellow in advanced environmental studies. She has devoted her career to issues that link the environment, agriculture, and community and is recognized as a leader in the movement for regional food systems and sustainable agriculture (www.glynwood.org).

Susan L. Hall, Ed.D.
Founder and President, 95 Percent Group

"You can achieve great things by being willing to learn new things, being able to assimilate new information quickly, and being able to get along with and work with other people."

—SALLY RIDE

Life After the Fortune 500

I recently attended two events that confirmed my belief that women in my generation faced career obstacles just because of their gender—obstacles our male colleagues did not face—and that gender discrimination of women in business still exists today. The first was my Harvard Business School thirty-five-year reunion, where I listened to my male and female classmates talk about their careers. The second was the Harvard Business School W50 Summit, attended by more than 850 women graduates returning to Boston from all over the world to commemorate the fifty-year anniversary of women being admitted and consider the history of women at the school. Some things have improved, but much is still amiss.

I wonder how much progress society has forfeited over the years because women could not assume key leadership roles in corporations. Is it possible to analyze the lost opportunities? They are probably significant. But did many women sidestep the traditional leadership path because they found the corporate world unwelcoming, and did they make different, yet significant, contributions? That is certainly my story. I changed my path, and perhaps my contribution to society has been more meaningful as a result.

My Top Five Leadership Competencies

- Displays high integrity and honesty
- Communicates powerfully and prolifically
- Drives for results
- Builds relationships
- Technical or professional expertise

Two major events shaped my path, and gender discrimination in corporate America was one of them. I left the Fortune 500 world behind five years into my career because I was aware that the glass ceiling limited my opportunities, and I did not want to wait forever for significant responsibility. I joined a small executive education business that I grew from $100K to $3 million in two years while hiring and managing fifteen people.

Drives for Results

The other major event was the birth of my children. When my oldest child experienced reading difficulties, a whole new path opened up for me because I wanted to provide him and other children like him with the kind of help that was not available at the time. So my career is unusual because of its mixture of business and education experience. I spent the first third of my career in the traditional corporate world and the second two-thirds in the education world, where there is far less gender discrimination than in many other industries.

During the early part of my career, I wanted a finance leadership position. I attended Harvard Business School directly after completing my undergraduate liberal arts degree; this was in the thirteenth year women were admitted, when we made up only 11 percent of the students. Although I was the youngest woman in my section and felt completely unprepared, my discipline and determination got me through. After graduation I did not follow the well-worn path to a job in investment banking or consulting, but instead elected to pursue operating experience in a large corporation.

Two memories stand out from the years I spent in the corporate world. In my first job, I was transferred to an oilfield operating division in Houston after a year at headquarters. One day, as I was attending an important meeting in place of my boss, the general manager belted out a string of profanities. When he noticed me, he excused his language by telling the others that I was a "good ole girl." I guess I was supposed to feel included and accepted, but I just felt different. A few years later, after moving back to Chicago to get away from the oilfield business, I took a position in the treasury department of another Fortune 500 company. I worked long hours together with my immediate boss, also a woman, to complete a major financing. However we were both excluded from the closing celebration lunch because it was held at a private dining club where women were not allowed.

But probably the most important turning point in my life took place when my oldest child struggled in learning to read in first grade. I'll never forget the evening when he looked at us and asked why he was in the top math group but the bottom reading group. That turn of events brought me to a career that is far more satisfying than my original path. Our son is now twenty-six years old and is just finishing his master's degree in architecture—not bad for a kid who, according to the educational psychologist who tested him when he was six years old, would never attend college because of his severe dyslexia.

The anger I felt when that educational psychologist projected our son's lack of prospects propelled me into action. I began researching reading development and reading difficulties, and, in the process, I discovered my passionate feelings about children learning to read. I saw a huge need to bridge research and practice and to bring information and materials to teachers, not just for children who are dyslexic, but for all children who struggle with reading. Fast forward twenty years, and after completing a doctorate in education, volunteering to teach struggling readers, teaching thousands of teachers in workshops, I formed a company with my husband that is now in its ninth year.

Technical or Professional Expertise

Several of my business skills enabled me to bring something unique to the education field. My financial analysis skills helped me to look at student assessment data and see the patterns of errors. My presentation skills helped me figure out how to train teachers in complex concepts. Now my passion and profession are totally united, and I'm incredibly lucky to be able to spend every day doing something meaningful and where the difference we are making is evident.

When I was asked to identify my top five leadership competencies for this book, there was no doubt in my mind that high integrity and honesty was number one on the list. My Midwestern middle-class family background has served me well, and I believe that the authenticity of my passion for our mission is a defining differentiator. I believe in our tagline—that 95 percent or more of students reading at grade level is an achievable goal. I work alongside my husband, who joined me to manage the finance, technology, and legal departments so that I can focus on content and clients. I am very driven, willing to roll up my sleeves and do whatever is needed to get the job done and meet our goal—to provide better training for teachers and earlier intervention for struggling readers. I am a straight shooter who cares deeply about employees and family.

I love to write and have authored or co-authored seven books. Writing is a skill I learned after business school, and I have discovered that it is a specialty. I love to clarify technical information so that teachers can understand what the research means for their everyday practice so they can be more effective in the classroom. I feel fortunate that my business skills have helped me to run our organization successfully, but even more fortunate that I was able to leave the corporate world behind and embark on a life that I find more meaningful and fulfilling.

Susan L. Hall

Susan L. Hall earned her B.A. from Lawrence University, her M.B.A. from Harvard Business School, and her Ed.D. from National-Louis University. Her company, 95 Percent Group, works with hundreds of schools across the United States to improve reading achievement. She has developed proprietary analytical tools to help teachers interpret student data. She is the co-author, with Louisa C. Moats, of three books, including *Straight Talk About Reading* and *Parenting a Struggling Reader*. Dr. Hall is author of four additional books, including *I've DIBEL'd, Now What?* and *Implementing Response to Intervention*. She was named by the U.S. Department of Education as a member of the Reading First Review Panel. She serves on several boards, including an appointment to the Dean's Leadership Council at the Harvard Graduate School of Education. She is a frequent speaker and lecturer (www.95percentgroup.com).

Eileen Lento

K-12 Strategist, Intel Corporation

"If particular care is not paid to the ladies, we are determined to foment a rebellion, and will not hold ourselves bound by any laws in which we have no voice, no representation."

ABIGAIL ADAMS

From the Military to High Tech

My career trajectory has taken me through three fields dominated by men—the military, academia, and the high-tech industry. I spent twenty years in the U.S. Air Force, and when I look back on that time, my emotions are mixed. The Air Force provided me, as an officer, with rich resources and opportunities and cultivated my management and leadership skills, instilling in me a deep sense of accountability, discipline, and meritocracy that has proven highly valuable throughout my career.

However, access to certain limited and coveted opportunities, such as a slot in flight training or advanced in-residence leadership training, was limited for me and for other women. Historically, the highest leadership roles in the Air Force were held by aviators who were combat-cleared, and since women were not permitted in combat career fields, this factor alone significantly inhibited our ability to move up the chain of command. Only a few flying slots were available to us, so the competition was intense, and the women who did earn a slot were extremely qualified.

In the late 1970s and early 1980s, restrictions were eased, first when women were allowed into flight school for non-combat roles and then much later for all aircraft, including fighters. Our access to opportunity increased slightly, but our completion and advancement rates remained significantly below those of men.

My Top Five Leadership Competencies

- Drives for results
- Technical or professional expertise
- Solves problems and analyzes issues
- Communicates powerfully and prolifically
- Collaboration and teamwork

Additional duties are an important factor in military career advancement, and during my time in the Air Force women were typically assigned duties such as esprit-de-corps or social officer, while men were assigned the meatier duties that prepared them for career advancement. Even more distressing is the pattern of sexual assaults that has plagued the military. I personally saw inappropriate behavior go unchecked or covered up by senior male officers, and I am relieved that Senator Gillibrand is proactively drawing attention to the dominance of male voices in military decision making and the resulting gaps in justice.

The Air Force certainly taught me many valuable lessons. I learned to understand formal as well as informal power structures, recognize that an understanding of the culture and the rules of engagement is empowering. I learned to seek out male and female mentors, and realized that people who get stuff done are always valued, and develop strategies to increase visibility, for example, look for additional duties that provided the right kind of networks for advancement.

Collaboration and Teamwork

Although the situation has improved for women in the military, and today we can point to some inspiring examples of women who rose to the top, I believe it will take a critical mass of support, both in the military and in society as a whole, to meaningfully influence the dominant culture so that the military will turn the proverbial corner and begin to embrace real women as real leaders.

After the Air Force, I went to work in academia for ten years and then for a small, privately held, education technology company, and I had children in between. Then I joined Intel, where the strong, well-articulated, institutional culture felt comfortable, a bit like coming home, reminiscent of my time in the Air Force. One expression of the solid culture established by Intel's founders is that the company gives each employee a badge that specifies Intel's six values, with explicit indicators for each value. Another is that the writings of Andy Grove have significantly influenced me, in how I manage my career as well as in how I lead and manage others. In particular, I have been inspired by Andy's belief that "the output of a manager is the combined output of [her] subordinates."

However, although Intel has mindfully approached the issue of increasing the number of women in senior positions, the conceptions of leadership, from where I sit, remain predominantly masculine. Success, in terms of moving up in the company, requires that employees fit into the prevailing norms, even though much progress has been made and today the president, chief marketing officer, and chief information officer are all women.

The prevailing norms include business drivers, company values, and cultural expectations, and they drive the way Intel employees approach their work, interact with each other, and inform the culture. This culture in turn impacts work practices, how achievement and success are perceived and measured, and the expectation of how many hours employees must work and the experience they must accrue in order to progress in their careers and become leaders.

Drives for Results

Women working to advance their careers still face many cultural challenges at Intel. The results-oriented culture favors and rewards assertive, confident, and ambitious behavior, strategic relationship building with mentors, and political skills, rather than the collaboration and community building at which women excel. The culture officially acknowledges that collaboration is key to success, although in practice this effort is still a work in progress. There is a 24/7 work ethic, and hours worked are a de facto indicator of commitment. With each work day book-ended by early and late meetings, the implied expectation is that successful employees will put work before family.

During my first eight years at Intel, we had one CEO, but recently a new CEO has ascended from the ranks, and a woman has been appointed president. Change is in the air, and I am learning and adapting. Over the years, I have had the great good fortune to meet several wise and generous mentors who have come in and out of my career journey and influenced my path, and I still believe in Andy Grove's words on good management. Undoubtedly, hard work matters.

However, although many recent research studies show a strong positive correlation between a critical mass of women leaders and outstanding business performance, the message of those studies is only just starting to get through. Clearly, the price of ignoring gender diversity is high—as measured by lost potential, lost opportunity, and lost credibility—but in my experience, cultural norms underpin and drive the persistent tendency to ignore the potential of women. As the old saying goes, "it all depends on where you're sitting when you look."

My thinking about the condition of women in a man's world has become more mature and nuanced over time. And I am optimistic that with more women, not just at the top of organizations but at every level, organizational culture will shift to a broader view of leadership that will tangibly reward the important skills of women and lead to better business results. As companies increasingly recognize that women contribute to success, my hope is that that the tide will continue to turn.

Eileen Lento

Dr. Eileen Lento holds a B.S. from the University of Massachusetts, Amherst, along with an M.S. and Ph.D. from Northwestern University, Evanston, Illinois. She served twenty years as an officer in the U.S. Air Force and retired as a Major. She then taught and conducted research at Northwestern throughout the 1990s. Next, she served as the chief education officer at PASCO Scientific; then joined Intel in 2005. Eileen is currently the world wide director of marketing and advocacy for Intel Education. She designed Intel's K-12 Computing Blueprint and has served on a number of boards, including the International Society for Technology in Education (ISTE), the Software and Information Industry Association (SIIA), iEarn, and the One-to-One Institute. She also served as host for the annual Intel Education Visionary Conference.

Marguerite Kondracke

Former President and CEO, America's Promise Alliance

"Hope begins in the dark, the stubborn hope that if you just show up and try to do the right thing, the dawn will come. You wait and watch and work; you don't give up."

—ANNE LAMOTT

Good and Bad Luck on the Road to Leadership

I was impatient with the status quo and the injustice in the world I grew up in, the segregated South. But dissatisfaction with the status quo is often a catalyst for leadership, and so it was with me. My life has been shaped by luck—good and bad—and the ability to see opportunity where others saw obstacles. Luck played an important part in my career, but so did my initiative, my willingness to take risks, and my efforts to make a difference.

I was a restless little girl, never quite fitting in. I begged to quit ballet lessons, and I would rather play office than house. Instead of playing in the backyard, I wanted to ride the bus home with our black housekeeper, fascinated by her neighborhood. My mother allowed this without telling my father, who would not have approved. My parents, both alcoholics, divorced when I was still in school—one of the first times I experienced bad luck. But I was lucky that they sent me away to a summer camp where I could escape the tension at home. I was homesick, but I developed a sense of self-reliance that would serve me well for the rest of my life. Later, when I learned that leadership can be lonely and anxiety-ridden, self-reliance and inner peace came in handy.

My Top Five Leadership Competencies

- Displays high integrity and honesty
- Drives for results

- Inspires and motivates others
- Collaboration and teamwork
- Communicates powerfully and prolifically

My grandmother did not share my concern about racial injustice, but she did make it possible for me to go to a terrific girls' school where all the leaders were girls—more good luck. I thrived in various leadership roles and found that inspiring others to rally for a common cause was exciting. I went to Duke, then still very much a Southern university, but I discovered that quite a few other Southern girls were ready for change. We devoured the writings of Betty Friedan and Gloria Steinem, and I became a charter subscriber to *Ms.* and *Mother Jones*. We protested the Viet Nam war, and we cared deeply about the burgeoning civil rights movement.

In 1968, I went to Memphis to join the striking sanitation workers who were gathering to hear Dr. Martin Luther King, Jr., speak. History changed that day, for our country and for me. After Dr. King was shot, we were rounded up by the police, who were joined by the National Guard, and held in a vacant lot behind a chain-link fence at gunpoint. I was scared to death, and I learned what it means to be a victim of prejudice and at the mercy of others. From that day on, I dedicated myself to working for the vulnerable and disenfranchised. I wanted big ideas, big change, and meaningful disruption—I knew we had to change the system if we expected change to last.

Champions Change

After college, I married, but I wanted a career. I had studied computer science in college, and I tried to get into the IBM management training program. But I was rejected because I was married, and the assumption was I would soon quit to have children—more bad luck. I ended up working for a small data processing service and experienced the excitement of entrepreneurship—good luck again.

While I was putting my husband through medical school, I volunteered at an inner city maternal and child health clinic and was dismayed to see how many children were born into desperate situations. Later, I co-founded a Planned Parenthood affiliate, believing that young women should be able to plan their families and that every child deserves to be born wanted and loved.

Then my husband left me for a nurse. But this bad luck became an opportunity instead of a defeat. As a single mom, I had to focus on my career, and the real adventures began. I went to work for the state government in Tennessee, managing the family planning program. At that time, there were great opportunities for talented women in government because most of the talented men were in the private sector.

In Appalachian health clinics, I saw abject poverty and children with little or no future, and soon I designed a four-year statewide Healthy Children Initiative, led by the First Lady, Honey Alexander. We set stretch goals—prenatal care for every mom, a medical home for every child, better childcare, and before- and after-school programs in every district. We were successful beyond anyone's dreams, and so began a lifelong friendship with Honey and Lamar Alexander. Later I was named to Governor Alexander's cabinet as the Commissioner of Human Services.

After he left office, I thought I would be reappointed by his successor, but I was not. That was bad luck—I needed a job, I was a single mom, and I was panicked. But good luck came back around when Governor Alexander suggested we start a company together based on providing quality childcare for working mothers. I knew that the best businesses are built around unmet needs, and I had already experienced the excitement of entrepreneurial enterprises. This opportunity changed my life.

I relied on the advice of my mentors, read business books, developed a strategic plan and budget, and set stretch goals that still boggle my mind. I have never worked harder nor felt a greater sense of reward. The most important elements of our success were commitment to our vision, the support of key mentors, belief in the importance of our work, and attention to execution. We set out to invent a concept—employer-sponsored childcare—and to be the highest quality childcare provider in the country. And we did it.

After going public, we merged with our best competitor to build an even more successful company. I believe that being a woman helped me manage this courtship and successful merger of equals, because women have unique relationship skills and are more willing to set aside ego and focus on what's best for the enterprise. Today, the merger is listed on the NYSE with a market cap of almost $3 billion. The bad luck of being a single mom inspired the good luck of starting a company to fill an unmet need for better childcare for working moms.

Then a group of private equity investors asked me to lead a "roll up," acquiring small businesses to create a larger company. More good luck, but the bad luck was that we started this effort during a major national recession. Although I worked tirelessly, I learned that failure is sometimes inevitable. I told my investors that we needed to pull the plug and sell off the assets before we had gone too deep into their equity commitment. I can at least say that those investors remain friends and colleagues today.

Collaboration and Teamwork

I stepped away from that tough situation into another when I was recruited to run a "turnaround." I ran head on into a group of bully investors, who I'm sure would have treated me very differently had I been a man. I believed in stretch goals and results, but this was mission impossible. After two rounds of bad luck, another great piece of good fortune came my way. Lamar Alexander was elected to the U.S. Senate and asked me to join his staff in Washington. I was now a widow and an empty nester, so I agreed.

Setting goals and driving for results are not always compatible with life in the U.S. Senate, and I was often frustrated and not as effective as I wanted to be. But I worked with Senator Alexander to strengthen the quality of Head Start programs, improve the prospects for foster children, highlight the needs of military children, save the AmeriCorps program, and champion the beginnings of education reform. I was impatient with the pace of change and thought I was unlucky to have landed in Washington, D.C., but good luck was just around the corner again.

I was asked to be a candidate for CEO of America's Promise, the youth advocacy organization founded by Colin and Alma Powell. Everything in my life had prepared me for this opportunity. America's Promise needed new crispness and focus, metrics, the discipline that comes with private sector experience, and the ability to motivate other groups to work together. Most exciting for me was the opportunity to become a champion of at-risk young people.

Colin and Alma Powell became mentors and friends and inspired me to make the organization a leading voice for vulnerable children. I persuaded the presidents of 400 national organizations to join our alliance, and we found common purpose by focusing on the just-being-discovered high school dropout crisis. We created a big tent for shared work by partner organizations such as the U.S. Chamber of Commerce, the United Way, the National League of Cities, the Boys and Girls Clubs, La Raza, National Governors' Association, AFTA, and NEA. I am proud to say that America's graduation rate is now rising, and almost two-thirds of the states are on track to achieve a 90 percent graduation rate within our ten-year target.

Now in my retirement years, I'm still working to improve the prospects of at-risk children as a board member and advisor in the private and non-profit sectors. When I mentor young women, I always remind them that bad luck is inevitable but can open up new paths and leadership opportunities. Working through and with others has created my greatest successes, a quiet source of pride.

To me, "servant leadership" best describes the management style of most women leaders, a style that can make all the difference.

Marguerite Kondracke

Marguerite Kondracke earned a B.A. degree in computer science from Duke University, where she also served for eight years as a trustee. During her forty-year career, she has been both an entrepreneur and a public servant. She co-founded and was CEO of Bright Horizons Family Solutions and served in the cabinet of Tennessee Governor Lamar Alexander as commissioner of human services and as staff director of the Senate Subcommittee for Children and Families. As the president and CEO of America's Promise Alliance, she led a ten-year campaign, Grad Nation, to end the high-school dropout crisis. She was named by President Obama to the board of the Corporation for National and Community Service and today serves as an advisor and board member for several organizations seeking to make a difference for children and families.

4 Displays High Integrity and Honesty

"Real integrity is doing the right thing, knowing that nobody's going to know whether you did it or not."

—Oprah Winfrey

The Zenger and Folkman competency with the second-highest difference between women and men is *Displays High Integrity and Honesty*. This chapter discusses how our Real Women demonstrate this competency and how they have shown integrity, honesty, and trustworthiness in their decisions and lives, leading to their current successes. Our Real Women describe real-life examples of occasions in which it was hard to stay true to their values, but through integrity and persistence they overcame these challenges and developed into the leaders they are today.

We all know what it means to tell the truth. Integrity and honesty, however, can be somewhat more complex, especially in the workplace. The competency of displaying high integrity and honesty is defined as having strong moral principles, uprightness, and fairness. In leadership this manifests itself through consistency between words and actions.

Through integrity and honesty, leaders are able to create a culture of trust, which in turn leads to successful teams and organizations.

To display these characteristics, one must be willing to stay true to what he or she believes in and stand up for it, even if presented with opposition. How do we know whether someone is trustworthy and has integrity? Trustworthiness is thought to have four major qualities: integrity, honesty, promise-keeping, and loyalty. Integrity, involves personal convictions, stated values, operational values, and ethical principles.[1]

Leading with integrity and honesty is often portrayed as one of the most desirable skills in a leader, and is seen as the top essential trait for women leaders.[2] It has long been demonstrated as one of the most important leadership characteristics—one that differs between those who lead and those who don't. While women tend to have an advantage in this sphere, with a natural inclination to be more value-driven, there is also a warning against self-righteousness, which can lead to loss of respect as a leader.[3] Honesty and integrity seem like such obvious traits, so why is it sometimes so hard to achieve in the workplace? Staying true to your values when everyone else is opposed to your point of view is not easy, especially if you are new to your role or perhaps in the minority. However, as research shows, this is one of the most important competencies to master, and worth standing your ground for.

Demonstrating what can be achieved with the competencies of high integrity and honesty are the Real Women, who share that even in the most challenging of circumstances they have maintained fidelity to their beliefs, and this, in turn, has positively affected their careers. This can be seen clearly in the non-profit world, which often requires difficult and challenging decisions, and often means questioning judgment and values in the face of opportunities or

---

[1] http://josephsoninstitute.org/business/blog/2011/01/trustworthiness-and-integrity-what-it-takes-and-why-it%E2%80%99s-so-hard/

[2] www.turknett.com/wp-content/uploads/2013/07/WorldWIT7_05TenEssentialTraits.pdf

[3] www.turknett.com/wp-content/uploads/2013/07/WorldWIT7_05TenEssentialTraits.pdf

resources. We hear from Susan Stroud, executive director of Innovations in Civic Participation, who begins her essay with the discussion of Nelson Mandela—a person of extraordinary integrity. Stroud also discusses how trustworthiness leads to integrity as she tells us of her journey as a young woman in a position of high power at Brown University, in charge of creating a national coalition of university presidents. Stroud talks about how others trusted in her and the importance of empowering the young people around her to develop their leadership skills and integrity.

High integrity often translates to high achievement, and while this can be true, Natasha Porter, vice president of Leadership Ambassador Programs at People to People, talks about how you do not need to have all of the answers to succeed. You should trust your gut; you will make mistakes, but the most important part is to keep your integrity and audacity. Jennifer Corriero, executive director of TakingITGlobal, continues to develop this theme by example. As a nineteen-year-old founder, integrity and honesty were crucial tools for her.

High integrity and honesty are vital skill sets for women leaders not only in the non-profit world. This is starkly shown through Darline Robles' journey of becoming the first woman, and first woman of color, superintendent of three educational agencies. When faced with the challenging position of superintendent in the Montebello Unified School District, Robles faced a choice and describes how staying true to her principles and speaking up, even when it was hard, allowed her to make the right decisions. A mentor once advised her, "*The only thing a superintendent has is his or her integrity*," and this line has clearly guided Robles throughout her career.

How do we take the lessons learned by these Real Women and apply them in our own lives? Perhaps one of the more difficult and challenging competencies to display, it can be helpful to have some principles to guide our behavior as we strive to lead. Business Coaching Worldwide suggests five characteristics that demonstrate integrity, with some suggestions of how to improve and achieve these behaviors.

1. Behave honestly and practice ethical behavior in your interactions.

- Be consistent and clear about your ethical standards.
- Speak up, even when it is hard or risky to do so.

2. Ensure the highest standards for ethical behavior are practiced throughout your organization.

- If you have concerns about ethical behavior at work, raise and review them with your staff and management.
- Give open, honest feedback to your co-workers.

3. Avoid political and self-serving behavior.

- Be a team player.
- Share recognition, and don't accept undue credit.

4. Courageously stand up for what you believe in.

- Work to gain support and cooperation from key people in your organization.
- Encourage and support others to speak up and voice their opinions and viewpoints.

5. Be a role model for living your organization's values.

- Walk the talk! Live the example of what you would like your employees to be.
- Acknowledge the unique knowledge and talents of others.[4]

As you will see from the Real Women's essays, developing these competencies does not happen immediately. It takes time, practice, dedication, and motivation. Starting to incorporate small actions, such as those mentioned above, each day will improve your leadership, the leadership of others, and ultimately drive your organization to high integrity.[5]

---

[4]www.wabccoaches.com/bcw/2008_v4_i2/coaching-great-leaders.html
[5]www.icicp.org/

Susan E. Stroud

Executive Director, Innovations in Civic Participation

*"We never know how high we are Till we are called on to rise:
And then, if we are true to plan, Our statures touch the skies."*

—Emily Dickinson

Making the World a Better Place

The recent passing of Nelson Mandela has provided people around the world with an opportunity to reflect on the characteristics of his extraordinary leadership. Mandela set himself apart through his courage, extraordinary integrity, discipline, determination, high expectations, and ability to inspire others to pursue social justice—along with his humor and his famous concern for the personal lives of others. Mandela provides a role model for men and women across the globe who aspire to make the world a better place.

Like many leaders, I had strong role models in my family, especially my mother. She married a career army officer and moved her four children every two years to a different part of the country or the world. As a child, I thought this was a normal life for women —setting up a new household every two years, enrolling four children in new schools, meeting new people, and volunteering wherever we lived. Later in life I realized that leadership requires the qualities demonstrated by my mother—adaptability, resilience, and stamina.

My Top Five Leadership Competencies

- Displays high integrity and honesty
- Drives for results

(continued)

- Develops others
- Builds relationships
- Innovates

I was also extremely fortunate to have good teachers, especially in high school, who had high expectations for intellectual performance and personal behavior. No one who had Ms. Keene for English could fail to enjoy lively discussions and wrestling with ideas. "No sloppy thinking in my class" was her continual refrain. Like others who have worked with young people, she knew that it's all about high expectations and helping people to achieve beyond what they think they are capable of. So many great teachers are women to whom fall the job of creating high expectations for children and young people.

After graduate school and a five-year teaching job in a low-income community to pay off my student loans, I landed a job at Brown University, running a program that helped students at eight New England colleges take time off to gain work experience that would help guide their academic decisions. I met extraordinary leaders during my fifteen years at Brown who were extremely important to my professional development.

In the 1980s, higher education was led by a generation of public-spirited college presidents for whom John Gardner was a hero and role model. They were definitely of the Kennedy generation, drawn to public service, and believers that public service should be a key goal of higher education. Presidents like Howard Swearer, Frank Newman, Don Kennedy, and Tom Ehrlich fought back against the prevailing mantra from President Reagan that "doing well is doing good."

All these leaders had worked in government and had led universities. They were public intellectuals and believed that tackling large local, national, and global issues was part of their job descriptions. Together with other university presidents, their goal was to bring about a sea change in higher education, emphasizing that the ultimate purpose of education is to improve the public good, and not for private gain.

I worked closely with these four men, and I was also fortunate to work with many extraordinary women leaders in higher education like Adele Simmons, Johnnetta Cole, Margaret McKenna, and Judith Ramaley, all of whom transformed the universities they led and lent their voices to highlight the need for public service. These leaders, women and men, challenged the prevailing norms, always maintained an orientation to service, and understood the importance of building relationships and networks to accomplish goals.

At Brown I was tasked with creating the Center for Public Service and the Campus Compact, a national coalition of university presidents with a commitment to public service that has now expanded to include 1,100 universities across the United States. I was young and inexperienced, but President Swearer and others trusted me, and their expectations motivated me to accomplish what was needed. I have always tried to invest the same level of trust in the talented and hardworking young people I have been fortunate to work with.

Innovates

My work at Brown included advocating for a national service program that would engage young people in working in low-income communities in the United States while assisting them with the cost of higher education. In President Bill Clinton's 1992 presidential campaign, he became increasingly committed to establishing this kind of national service program. After he was elected, Eli Segal was appointed to head the Office of National Service in the White House, and I was asked to join a small team at the White House to design the program and push the legislation through Congress in record time. President Clinton took office in January 1993, and the AmeriCorps legislation was signed into law in September of the same year. Launched in

1994, AmeriCorps is a national service program in the tradition of the Civilian Conservation Corps, the Peace Corps, and VISTA.

Eli was a Pied Piper leader for whom all of us would have walked on nails. His total commitment to getting the job done was inspiring, and he made everyone on the team feel that he or she was making a critical contribution. Shirley Sagawa made it all happen. Mrs. Clinton's domestic policy advisor and Senator Ted Kennedy's point person on the first national service bill in the Bush Administration, Shirley was loaned to our office by the First Lady, herself a very strong advocate for national service. Shirley was one of the authors of the national service legislation and became the COO of the Corporation for National Service after the legislation was passed. Without her leadership, I really believe we would not have an AmeriCorps program.

The first 20,000 AmeriCorps members hit the streets in 1994. Today there are approximately 80,000 AmeriCorps members annually and waiting lists of many more thousands. From the beginning, some of the strongest programs were developed by women leaders. Dorothy Stoneman created YouthBuild, Wendy Kopp created Teach for America, Vanessa Kirsch created Public Allies, and many other women created non-profit organizations that have provided thousands of opportunities for young people from a wide range of backgrounds to grow personally and professionally through serving others. Women continue to provide leadership in the service field, both in the United States and overseas. Their leadership is characterized by creativity, risk taking, and teamwork in order to accomplish goals that are larger than their own interests.

The legislation that created AmeriCorps also created a new federal agency to administer AmeriCorps and two other programs—Senior Corps, which enlists 500,000 older people in service each year, and Learn and Serve America, which supported schools, universities, and youth-serving community organizations to develop high-quality service-learning programs. I was the first director of Learn and Serve America and also helped develop partnerships between AmeriCorps and other federal agencies.

I now direct a non-profit organization called Innovations in Civic Participation (ICP), which I founded in 2001 to work on national youth service programs and policies and youth civic engagement in educational and community settings around the world. ICP was made possible by multi-year funding from the Ford Foundation, where I worked for several years on youth civic engagement overseas after leaving the Clinton Administration. ICP also serves as the Secretariat for the International Association for National Youth Service (IANYS). Currently, we are working with universities in Pakistan, Japan, and the Arab world, examining the links between national youth service programs and employability in sub-Saharan Africa and scaling up a summer youth service program for low-income middle school students in the United States.

Builds Relationships

Although the projects are varied, the common thread is our commitment to giving young people the opportunity to make a positive difference in their communities. We are more convinced each year that young people all over the world are eager to tackle the social, political, and environmental issues they see in their communities, but often lack the opportunity to address.

In 2005, I co-founded the Talloires Network, an international version of the Campus Compact, which now includes more than 300 universities in more than seventy countries. Here I benefited from the examples of exceptional women leaders in higher education around the world, such as Brenda Gourley and Monica Jimenez de la Gara, who led universities in South Africa and Chile with nerves of steel during difficult and dangerous political times. Bravery and decisiveness are the qualities of leadership I admire most in these extraordinary women.

Vision, charisma, and the ability to motivate others are often mentioned as strong leadership characteristics of both men and women. I am not certain that the leadership styles of men and women differ radically, but I believe that some characteristics are more commonly found in women. These include character, resilience, care for others, the ability to listen and observe body language, communication skills that build knowledge and trust, and a focus on developing the capacity and leadership abilities of others.

I am fortunate to have worked with exemplary leaders throughout my career, and I have tried to be conscious of nurturing the leadership potential of many young women, adhering to the motto, "Each One Teach One." The world needs strong leadership if we have any hope of achieving social justice, and each of us must do his or her part.

Susan Stroud

Susan Stroud earned a B.A. degree in English from Duke University and an M.A. in Modern English and American Literature from Leicester University in the UK. She served at Brown University as assistant to the president and founding director of the Swearer Center for Public Service and Campus Compact, as the senior advisor to the director of the White House Office of National Service during the Clinton Administration, and as senior advisor to the CEO of the Corporation for National Service and director of Learn and Serve America and the Office of Federal Partnerships. She later joined the Ford Foundation to lead an initiative to support youth civic engagement overseas. She co-founded the Talloires Network, a global coalition of universities committed to education for civic engagement, and she is the founder and executive director of Innovations in Civic Participation, which supports the development of national youth service programs and civic engagement (www.icicp.org/).

Natasha Porter

Vice President of Leadership Ambassador Programs, People to People Ambassador Programs

"People are uncertain because they don't have the self-confidence to make decisions."

—Julia Child

Leadership Journey

When I reflected on my personal leadership journey for this book, I realized that I don't remember ever not being a leader. I grew up in Ukraine when it was still a part of the Soviet Union, and I was a leader in the Young Pioneers club—similar to the Girl Scouts, Boy Scouts, and student councils combined. But even before that, I was always trying to organize the kids in my class to do something.

One day I thought our school playground looked worn out, and I got the other first-graders to ask their parents to donate unused paint so that we could paint it. We showed up with an array of paint supplies—evidently a little too much initiative for my teacher, and I was disciplined for not asking permission. I learned an important leadership lesson that day—pre-sell your idea to your stakeholders and have your boss's backing before commandeering resources that don't belong to you. We weren't allowed to paint the school playground, but we used the supplies to paint the playground near our apartment complex. Later the facilities manager said he couldn't allow small children like us to paint the playground but then added with a wink, "It looks nice—good thing you didn't ask." Another important lesson—sometimes it's better to ask for forgiveness than permission. I think that my willingness to take the initiative is the single most important trait that has defined my leadership experience.

Takes Initiative

Fortunately, most of the time when I stuck my neck out, I had great support from my teachers and mentors. I went to a different school for second grade, and my new teacher thought my desire to organize the kids was something to encourage. She asked me to help with the first-graders in the after-school program, and so I had my first job as a teaching assistant. I went on to become school president and president of the student council for the city's middle schools by the time I finished sixth grade.

My Top Five Leadership Competencies

- Takes initiative
- Drive for results
- Practice self-development
- Build relationships
- Develop others

In my first real job, as a faculty member at Kokshetau Teacher Training University in Kazakhstan, I was fortunate to have great mentors who all happened to be women. I was teaching students just a year or two younger than I was. In the beginning, I needed all the confidence I could muster to face my students, but with lots of encouragement from my mentors I quickly thrived. To this day, I think of it as one of the most rewarding jobs I've ever had. My student group consisted of ten young women, to whom I taught English, linguistics, and English literature. We spent hours together every day, and it was incredibly rewarding to see these young women, self-conscious at first, blossom into capable, confident, and eloquent young women—and to know that I played a small part in that.

Another mentor of mine was a professor in my MBA program, who was also the director of global operations at a U.S. telecommunications company looking to expand its operations in

Europe, who hired me to lead that effort. I found a contract manufacturer in Poland, and within three months we were manufacturing our products in Europe. We put together a plan to acquire this company, but my manager soon left to start his own business. After my initial panic at the idea of doing it alone, I partnered with our CFO to finish the acquisition, and I went on to manage the integration of the newly acquired company, which involved me leading a team of senior managers who worked on this project with me. I was only twenty-five and with no real business experience, let alone in the international arena. But I had confidence in spades, I was a fast learner, and I was so passionate about the project that people wanted to help. Since then, I have not been afraid of big challenges—I thrive on them. I think these early work experiences that tested and stretched me built the confidence that has helped me succeed in business as a woman.

Through this experience, I also learned that in business, as in life, you don't have to have all the answers. It's more important to have audacity, conviction in your vision, and a rough plan of how to get there. Certainly, solid analysis and preparation are important. Use data to guide you 80 percent of the way, but be prepared to trust the remaining 20 percent to your gut—and then act. Some managers analyze important decisions ad nauseam and don't act because they are afraid of making a mistake, or because they don't have complete control over the outcome—a real killer of morale and innovation. In contrast, effective leaders believe in themselves and their teams and allow their people to plot the course to the goal. Many successful women leaders I admire have an amazing ability to make sound decisions intuitively, and they choose action over politics.

Drives for Results

I also firmly believe that one of the strengths a leader can have is emotional intelligence (EQ)—the ability to understand and manage emotion in positive ways in order to communicate effectively through

stress, defuse conflict, and build relationships. This self-awareness
and awareness of others are all critical workplace skills, important
for everyone, and highly developed in women. They build high-
performance teams and create an environment in which people like to
work, and therefore perform at their best.

In contrast to EQ, a high level of emotionality—being readily
affected by one's emotions—can be detrimental to a woman's chances
of advancement. I'm not talking about crying at work, because everyone can have a bad day once in a while. But mood swings that affect
others—or breakdowns at every setback or criticism—don't work. An
even temperament and the ability to keep cool under pressure send
a clear message about who can be trusted to lead in tough situations.
Women who have mastered it are good at managing through crises
and are called upon when there are opportunities for advancement.

Another leadership quality that my colleagues have pointed out in me
and I've seen in other women leaders is the ability to operate on both the
strategic and the tactical level. Women are often able to see things more
holistically than men and can quickly translate the vision into a tangible
plan, provide clear direction to teams, and remove complexity. However,
this skill can also have a downside. I sometimes find it difficult to distance
myself from operations and remain at the strategic level where I can have
the most impact, so I have to be mindful about balancing the two.

The other challenge for me, as for many women in business, is
balancing work and personal life. I travel a lot, and I work long hours
by most people's standards. Although I often tell myself that I need
to do a better job at the elusive work-life balance, in reality, I'm not
wired that way. I take pride in what I do, and I enjoy a challenge. I
like to be accessible for my team, and I have to have time to think
and strategize, which I do best when the office quiets down, and that
can mean long hours. Over the years, I've learned to carve out the
time to think and to know when it's time to recharge.

I am also blessed to have a husband who understands and supports me 100 percent. He has the same work ethics, and that's partly

what brought us together. We both work hard but make time to enjoy life—whether enjoying the beautiful outdoors at home, traveling abroad, or spending time with our two granddaughters, whom we adore. I most certainly would not be where I am today without him. I'm not talking just about my career or financial rewards, but how fulfilled I feel in my life. In my book, that's the true measure of success.

Natasha Porter

Natasha Porter graduated from Kokshetau University in Kazakhstan in 1994 with a bachelor's degree in teaching English as a second language and a master's degree in international management from Whitworth University in Spokane, Washington, in 1998. In her eighteen-year career, Natasha has been responsible for the development of new business and partnerships in Europe and Asia, and most recently expanding People to People Ambassador Programs' global partner network in Asia and Latin America. As the vice president of leadership ambassador programs, she is responsible for product development, marketing, student recruitment, teacher relations, and delivery of educational travel programs designed to educate and prepare youth from across the United States and around the world to be global-ready leaders.

Jennifer Corriero
Executive Director, TakingITGlobal

"We don't accomplish anything in this world alone, and whatever happens is the result of the whole tapestry of one's life and all the weaving of individual threads from one to another that create something."

—SANDRA DAY O'CONNOR

Mentoring by Others and for Others

My first mentors were my parents. They modeled confidence, diplomacy, and a sense of fairness right from the start. When my kindergarten teacher complained to my mother that I was bossy because I organized games in the schoolyard, my mother praised me for my leadership. She confronted a double standard and created a teachable moment to affirm who I was. I am my mother's daughter—full of ideas and enthusiasm and ready to lead.

Similarly, my father has always modeled fairness toward everyone, regardless of gender. He believes women can have a professional life and a family along with personal health and wellness. My self-confidence and determination are rooted in the faith my parents have always had in me—a privilege I am increasingly grateful for—and in my experience as a mentor and role model for my sister and brother.

My Top Five Leadership Competencies

- Takes initiative
- Practices self-development
- Displays high integrity and honesty
- Develops others
- Inspires and motivates others

I co-founded TakingITGlobal in 1999, when I was nineteen years old. As TakingITGlobal has grown, I have had the opportunity to be mentored by many leaders, both men and women, from the corporate world and the world of NGOs and non-profits, and I have become a mentor myself and recently a mother. These experiences have led me to identify six different types of mentors who have played a role in my life over the years.

Practices Self-Development

Deep listeners are important mentors who have helped me think through the most daunting challenges and develop a more strategic view. Currently, Beverlee Rasmussen spends an hour with me each week as an executive business coach, helping me to "transform frustrations into systems," as she puts it. As a deep listener, she can spot many things I might not have figured out on my own and generate new insights on future directions.

Enablers are another group of mentors who have played a huge role in my life, giving me access to resources as well as support and encouragement along the way. Kim Samuel enabled my participation in the World Economic Forum as a Young Global Leader and our work with the Youth Task Force. And Vivianna Guzman, CFO of the American Management Centre, has given me and my team access to many professional development learning opportunities over the years.

Then there are the shining light mentors, who provide inspiration even though they may be in a very different line of work. Madame Jean, the former governor general of Canada, is a shining light for me. She included me in her state visit to Brazil to showcase the ways that our work contributes to strengthening civil society.

I have been fortunate to meet a number of mentors I call "mama CEOs," many of them women leaders of non-profit organizations, who have taught me how to manage responsibilities at home and in the office. One example is Nancy Lublin at Do Something, who has given me tremendous insights and words of inspiration.

Collaborators from other organizations can also be wonderful mentors, offering many different opportunities to share and learn. Debra Kagan with the Pearson Foundation and Yvonne Thomas with Microsoft Corporate Citizenship and Public Affairs have both provided me with thought leadership on the new social innovation programs that we have launched together.

Finally, there are the inner circle mentors. My conversations with close friends and family—as well as with my team of staff, interns, and alumni—focus on mutual support and helping each other become the best we can be. As we express our concerns and hopes, share major life experiences, and overcome challenges together, we weave a social fabric that brings beauty into my life every day.

Now I spend a lot of time mentoring our interns, many of them young women who are either still in school or recent graduates and looking to build their portfolio of experiences, and I am continually growing into each of the mentoring roles that have been so meaningful for me. I am always looking for ways to help young people contribute meaningfully, develop their skills, and recognize the power of their talents and goals.

Develops Others

I draw on my own experiences. One of the challenges I faced as a young woman and a new social entrepreneur was being taken seriously. For example, I once attended an important networking event where the first person who approached me thought I was a waitress. I was sometimes dismissed as "cute," I had to learn to control my emotions when necessary, and I had to learn to ask for what I want.

Thanks to the example and input of my mentors, now I know how to communicate my message powerfully with conviction and delight. I confidently embrace my personal style while adapting to different environments. I know the difference between how I feel, what I think, why I have a point of view, and how I express it in a high pressure situation. I have learned that relationships are built on trust, that communication must be handled with care and kindness, and that situations must be viewed from multiple perspectives. Today I'm not afraid to pitch my ideas, and I welcome the input and collaboration of others. These are all lessons I try to share with younger people.

I really turned to the mentors in my life when my son was born in 2012. The midwife and the mama CEOs, among others, taught me that I cannot expect to always have control over everything, that I need to make the best of things, and that I have to ask for what I need. The discussion in our society about balancing work and family often implies that these are two disconnected worlds, but I like to think of life as having multiple dimensions that provide strength through interconnection. I am a stronger mother because of the work I do in the world and because I am doing what I love, and I am stronger in the workplace because of my experiences with my family. Also, the contributions I make professionally will strengthen the future opportunities for my son and the other members of his generation.

I have been finding a path where parenting and work co-exist and complement each other, thanks in part to my first mentors, my parents, who let me know I did not have to choose between work and family. Today, I meet many other young parents who are doing the same. Because we support and learn from each other, we are collectively building a better workplace culture around gender, one that respects the richness of life within and beyond the workplace.

Jennifer Corriero

Jennifer Corriero earned a master's degree in environmental studies from York University in Toronto, where she now serves

(continued)

as an adjunct professor in the faculty of health. In 2005, she
was named a Young Global Leader by the World Economic
Forum and in 2007 one of Canada's Top 100 Most Powerful
Women by the Women's Executive Network. She has developed youth engagement and technology-based education
programs supported by many major foundations and presented
at events in more than thirty countries, including the U.N.
High Level Meeting on Youth, the World Urban Forum, and
the International AIDS Conference. Jennifer is the co-founder
and executive director of TakingITGlobal, a non-profit social
network that empowers youth to act on the world's greatest
challenges and create a more peaceful, inclusive, and sustainable world (www.tigweb.org/about/).

Darline P. Robles

Professor of Clinical Education, Rossier School of Education, University of Southern California

"Don't compromise yourself. You're all you've got."

—JANIS JOPLIN

Initiative and Integrity as a Woman of Color

I was fortunate early on to be mentored by strong women—and
men—in my family and among my friends and colleagues and to
learn to persevere despite the barriers I encountered. In the process,
I learned a lot about the lack of equity, although at a young age I did
not know the word, but I did observe that people were treated differently based on income, color, family status, and gender. I grew up
during a time of major social change—the civil rights movement and
the women's rights movement—and my personal experiences during

this time gave me the strength to move forward. Two experiences in particular stand out.

My Top Five Leadership Competencies

- Displays high integrity and honesty
- Drives for results
- Builds relationships
- Innovates
- Solves problems and analyzes issues

I began my career as a middle school teacher in Montebello, California, not intending to become a leader but wanting to be the best teacher I could be. The principal at my school asked me to provide professional development to other teachers, and after word spread to the district office that I was an effective trainer, a district administrator, Dr. Mary Mend, asked me to join her team full time. When I was offered this leadership role, I faced unexpected barriers, but the barriers helped me learn the hard way that I needed to take the initiative to be in charge of my own career choices, especially when dealing with men in influential positions.

I was nervous, but I accepted Dr. Mend's offer. Because she needed to obtain a release from my principal to allow me to leave mid-year, we worked out a plan to find a good replacement for me and ensure a smooth transition with my help. A week later, the principal came to my classroom and told me he would not agree to release me, either that year or the following year. I was stunned. But this experience taught me that I would have to be in a leadership role in order to avoid being at the mercy of others in making my career choices. I have carried this lesson throughout my career and passed it on to many young women and men. Dr. Mend was eventually able to secure the transfer, and she became my mentor. I appreciated her guidance as a woman leader in my field and learned many lessons from her—take the initiative and don't wait for someone to hand opportunities to you, and don't take no for an answer if you are looking for the best for yourself and your organization.

Subsequently, I faced many more obstacles in my career, but none like the one I encountered as the superintendent in the Montebello Unified School District. We were dealing with a severe financial crisis at the time, and we were on the verge of being taken over by the state. When the board of education gave me two specific goals—ensure the financial viability of the district and maintain the academic achievement of our students—I hired a new business manager and a new business team. With their support and the support of our management team, the unions, and the board of education, within eighteen months we were financially solid, but in the process we, unfortunately, had to cut over 30 percent of our staff and reduce many student programs.

Drives for Results

Three years later, we were starting to heal, and we began to reinstate positions and programs and rebuild positive relationships with our employee groups. I was busy hiring new principals and including different stakeholders in the selection process. The committees sent me lists of candidates, and I was setting appointments for the final interviews when I received a call from a board member who wanted to discuss the process. At the end of our conversation, I was shocked to hear that he and two other board members wanted me to offer a position to a certain candidate because they had made a promise to the candidate's father in exchange for his support during the election. I told the board member that this candidate had, in fact, placed last on each committee list.

I could not accept this directive. But before sharing the incident with my board of education, I called my mentor, Dr. Mend, since

I was a fairly new superintendent with only about three years of experience. Dr. Mend suggested I speak to another superintendent who had found himself in a similar situation, Dr. Ray Cortines, chancellor of New York City Schools. I will always be grateful to Ray for taking my call, and he was clearly indifferent to my gender in his desire to help me out. I did not know him personally, but his return call told me a lot about him. Ray always finds time to mentor and assist others. When I described the situation to him, he reassured me that the only thing a superintendent has is his or her integrity. I decided I could not continue to work for this board and began to look for another position. I eventually decided to leave a district that had been my professional home for more than twenty-five years and a community where I had grown up and raised my family.

Displays High Integrity and Honesty

But if I was going to make a change, I wanted a big change. I was fortunate that during this period I was approached by a search firm that had been hired by the Salt Lake City School District to recruit a new superintendent. I applied, met with the Salt Lake City Board of Education, and accepted the position. I was following my earlier lesson, not allowing others to dictate my professional choices and taking the initiative to move forward.

These two experiences have guided me throughout my career and to this day. It is important to have mentors for guidance through difficult situations, but everyone must take the initiative to take control of his or her professional growth, and integrity must always be at the forefront of decision making. For women and women of color, this may be particularly true, since historically men have tended to assume that their goals will always be more important than those of women. But when women and diversity are valued, we all benefit from the increased capacity and strength that accrues in our schools, our communities, and our country from the talents and contributions of many. Very importantly, we inspire other women to become leaders. As John Quincy Adams said, "If your actions inspire others to dream more, learn more, do more, and become more; you are a leader."

As an educational leader for more than thirty years, people often remind me that I was the first woman or the first woman of color to lead certain organizations. It always surprises me to learn that I can still be the first woman or the first woman of color to do anything, but that is the case. We women need to keep up the good work, so that women leaders and women leaders of color one day will no longer be an anomaly.

Darline P. Robles

Dr. Darline P. Robles holds a B.A. from California State University at Los Angeles, an M.A. from Claremont Graduate School, and a Ph.D. from the University of Southern California. She has served as district coordinator for bilingual education at the Montebello Unified School District and then as superintendent, as the first Latina superintendent of the Los Angeles County Office of Education, and as the superintendent of the Salt Lake City School District. In 2009 and 2011 she was named a Top 100 Influential Hispanic American, and she is a member of the President's Commission on Educational Excellence for Hispanics. She is currently a professor of clinical education at the Rossier School of Education, University of Southern California, where she coordinates a new national hybrid master's degree program in school leadership.

5 Builds Relationships

"You can take my factories, burn up my buildings, but give me my people and I'll build the business right back again."

—Henry Ford

Building relationships is a competency at which many of our Real Women, Real Leaders excel. An empathetic trait, the ability to build coalitions, strengthen ties, and foster mutual respect and understanding has served our leaders well. This chapter shows how the ability to connect with people across demarcation lines has been one of the most important aspects of authentic leadership for women in positions of power.

Building a strategic network within and outside of an organization is also referred to as "building social capital." Women are strong in building supportive and strategic relationships. In a white paper on leadership by Shambaugh Leadership LLC, they state: "Think of a strategic network as a connected web of relationships versus a traditional organization chart. This web should be broad, deep, and diverse. This includes direct reports, peers, and executives in the organization, as well as people outside the organization who can give us the right advice and support our needs throughout our careers."

These traits are often ascribed to female leaders, but their importance for all leaders is highlighted in research. Many individuals in positions of power tend to shy away from these critical behaviors, but building an emotional connection is the foundation upon which many of the other competencies rely, and they can be fostered through simple actions.

In a study by Caliper, a global consulting firm, women leaders had a more inclusive style of building relationships, problem solving, and decision making. Women leaders also were found to be more empathic and flexible, as well as stronger in interpersonal skills than their male counterparts. "These qualities combine to create a leadership style that is inclusive, open, consensus building, collaborative and collegial," according to Herb Greenberg, president and chief executive officer of Caliper (*The Qualities That Distinguish Women Leaders*, 2005). Typical behaviors and skills that epitomize this characteristic include empathetic listening, friendliness, and mediation.

While these characteristics seem self-explanatory, they can be difficult to execute in real-world settings, with real-world personalities. Tina Mainar, a well-respected organizational blogger, outlines concrete, tangible steps that can be taken to not only build relationships, but create effective ones as well. Some of these tactics include:

- **Come with solutions.** Always try to share a few thoughtful, possible solutions when addressing problems with organizational staff.
- **Praise loudly.** Share credit for accomplishments and deadlines whenever possible, and continuously express gratitude for work done well.
- **But chastise softly.** Determine individuals involved in organizational problems and address them privately, with a goal of improvement; never blindside individuals in public.
- **Be aware of your nonverbal communication.** Ensure that you are consistently addressing co-workers and staff with positivity, and try to avoid sarcasm.

- **Keep your commitments and help others find their greatness.**
  Encourage a culture of respect and follow through with your
  example, and continuously empower your staff to be the best
  possible versions of themselves.[1]

Through the examples in this chapter, we see how this erroneously
labeled "feminine" characteristic has led to non-typical professional
and personal success. Allison Ray, former coach of Canada's Olympic
Men's Rowing Team, credits her entire career to building relationships
with experts in her male-dominated industry who were able to help
and guide her. Carol Waugh, an internationally renowned artist, saw
firsthand how important relationships were when she had to quickly
grow a professional network in order to succeed after being repeatedly
ignored in her professional roles. Kimberley Brock-Brown, an executive chef, believes that she learned to become a true chef and manager when she made the active decision to accept mentors along her
professional trajectory.

Building relationships was not seen as a feminine trait to these
women, but building a coalition was viewed as a highly effective tool
to develop skills, mindsets, and networks essential to professional success. Regardless of industry, these women have shown that building
relationships is a critical characteristic of true leadership, perhaps even
more important when considering a nontraditional path.

Allison Ray
Former Coach, Canadian Men's Olympic Rowing Team

"Champions keep playing until they get it right."

—BILLIE JEAN KING

---

[1] http://springboard.resourcefulhr.com/tips-for-creating-effective-relationships-
in-the-workplace/

Me and a Bunch of Men—Now What?!

Recently, to get a little exercise and meet people, I've started going to spin classes in my neighborhood. It's fun, and the person who leads the class is a dear friend of mine. She does everything so well—loud music, motivational sayings, a cool headset. And it occurred to me that this must be what people think I do. But the truth couldn't be more different.

In 2012, I coached the heavyweight men on the Canadian team at the Olympic Games in London. Instead of being on a platform with a headset and spandex, I was on a boat, in a parka, in the middle of a lake, for three practices a day, six days a week. I was working with two male coaches and up to twenty-five male athletes at every session. It wasn't really until after the Olympic Games that I realized I'm one of the few women to coach men at that level in rowing or any other sport. Even though it seems unremarkable to me, perhaps other women can learn some lessons from my experience.

My Top Five Leadership Competencies

- Takes initiative
- Practices self-development
- Inspires and motivates others
- Builds relationships
- Communicates powerfully and prolifically

The Canadian men's national team trains on Elk Lake in Victoria, B.C., where I coached for five years. I knew I wanted to coach the national team, but I had no idea the job would come with a boatload of testosterone, body hair, and egos. However, once I was in it, I loved it—the competition, the high performance environment, the leadership, the interpersonal dynamics, the massive personalities, the egos, the politics, the traveling, the technology, and the endless personal development. So that's the first lesson I learned—to follow something you love.

When I started coaching in 1999 I was just looking to make a buck. I needed to make some extra money while I finished my degree. I had been a rower myself, and when I gave up rowing, coaching seemed like a natural progression and a fun thing to do. Rowing is beautiful in every way. It involves effortlessness, flow, rhythm, and unison and is the ultimate team sport. It's technical and physically demanding and requires unwavering commitment, focus, and countless hours of practice.

For the first couple of years, I taught a wide range of people how to row. I coached thirteen-year-olds and sixty-year-olds and everyone in between. I enjoyed the challenge of getting nine people into a boat and figuring out how to teach each person to make the boat move and to do it together. Most people have seen rowing in the Olympic Games or on a lake or river, but when they show up for their first session, they often have no idea why they are there or whether they will stay. I learned that I had a skill for reading people. Understanding quickly why they were there and what they wanted to gain from the experience helped me connect with people to build programs I have managed, teams I have led, and coaches I have worked with. Another lesson—I had skills I didn't know I had.

Builds Relationships

When I was starting out, I was willing to trust my sense of people and to let things unfold. But I was lucky to be hired by someone who would become my mentor and friend for the next eight years. Craig Pond had unwavering confidence in me from the start. Without an open mind, I wouldn't have met him, and I wouldn't have achieved anything. He was the first in a line of great coaches and people who helped me on my way. He gave me those first few experiences because he believed I could be a good coach. Another lesson—always keep an open mind.

My first competitive coaching experience was with the Simon Fraser University Rowing Club in Burnaby, B.C., where I spent six years building a competitive program with six athletes who would go on to compete on the Canadian national team. The program enjoyed great results over time, and I had found a place to practice my skills and develop a vision of my own coaching and leadership style, training philosophy, and career goals.

When I was coaching women, I developed Operation Barbie. I wanted to help the women become independent, strong, and beautiful—capable of squats, dead lifts, sweating, grunting, and achieving their goals beautifully. It was all very tongue in cheek, but I wanted a training environment in which women supported each another, felt good about being women, and motivated each another to achieve their goals through healthy competition. Operation Barbie provided a humorous way to get at being powerful and beautiful women without the soapbox. The support of the athletes there gave me the confidence to commit to my goal of coaching on the national team. Another lesson—I learned to get my confidence and direction from everyone I met, including the people I was supposed to be leading.

Inspires and Motivates Others

I did not row for Canada. I worried that would prevent me from coaching the national team. I began setting goals that would let me experience coaching at every level of competition, and I attained a leadership role at each level—regional, provincial, national, and international. During that time I applied and was accepted to the National Coaching Institute, where I attained my Level 4 coaching certification. Along the way I met Terry Paul, a long-time men's national team coach and a gold medalist from the 1992 Olympics. Terry worked hard to develop coaches and athletes. Fortunately, he respected and supported the goals I had set for myself and the performances of the crews I had coached. I attended talks he gave, took notes, and was inspired by how devoted he was to the athletes he coached. He viewed me as a developing coach who was motivated to learn.

With his support, I was nominated to attend national development camps as an assistant coach. I coached a team selected to compete at World University Rowing Championships, and in 2007 was the head coach for the Canadian National Team at the Pan American Games. I coached men's crews at all of these camps and competitions. Another lesson—I learned that the shortcomings might be in my own mind, and I needed to let others believe in me.

In 2007 in Munich, I stood on the bike path that ran alongside the rowing course at the World Championships and watched the Canadian men's eight win a gold medal. I was there with Terry and the head coach of the men's team, Mike Spracklen. Mike has coached crews that medaled in every one of the nine Olympics Games since 1976, as well as at twenty-six World Championship events. Mike is a big deal. I was there because I had been asked to continue coaching the men's pair that had won gold at the Pan American Games and coach them while they competed at the World Championships in Germany. I was scared and felt out of my depth. But Mike supported me without question. I had spent time riding in his launch that year when I traveled to Victoria from Vancouver to learn from him. Sitting for hours beside him in his launch was often very quiet, but never without meaning. Another lesson—even legends will take time for you, so make the most of it.

Of course, I have also experienced failure. At the World Championships in 2007, the men's pair I coached failed to qualify for the 2008 Olympics, and a men's quad also failed to qualify. But both of those experiences were filled with successes and failures along the way, and I had to think about a lot of things we might have done differently. A final lesson—it's okay to make mistakes, just don't make the same one twice.

Allison Ray

Allison Ray worked as assistant rowing coach at the Victoria Training Centre in Canada from May 2007 to September 2012, after working with Rowing Canada Aviron in summer contract positions since 2003. Allison graduated from Simon Fraser University with a bachelor of arts degree. Allison has coached crews that competed at CANAMMEX, multiple provincial championships, the Commonwealth Regatta, the World University Championships, the Pan American Games, five world championship teams, and the 2012 Olympics. At the 2010 World Championships, she coached Canada's single sculler, Malcolm Howard, a two-time Olympic medalist in the men's 8+. She has twice received the Petro-Canada Coaching Excellence Award for a bronze and gold medal in the coxed pair. In 2012, she was named *Women in Sport* Coach of the Year. Currently, Allison coaches at the California Rowing Club in Oakland, California (www.californiarowingclub.com/).

Carol Ann Waugh

Artist and Gallery Owner

> "It's worth taking risks because failure isn't a bad thing as long as you learn from it and use it as a step toward eventual success."
>
> —Maria Shriver

Reinventing Myself

I just celebrated my sixty-fifth birthday, and I'm busier and happier than I've ever been in my life. I spend most of my day creating

art and teaching fiber art techniques to others. But at the beginning
of my career I had no idea that this would be my final destination.
Many twists and turns in the road have led me to this point, including theater, publishing, and marketing, with many lessons learned
along the way in a world ruled largely by men.

My Top Five Leadership Competencies

- Champions change
- Builds relationships
- Inspires and motivates others
- Communicates powerfully and prolifically
- Technical/professional expertise

I was lucky to have parents who always told me I could do anything I wanted in life, and my grandmother was known for her oft-
repeated phrase, "If you want it, get it!"

The first thing I decided I wanted was to be a famous musical
comedy star on Broadway, so I earned a degree in educational theater,
which unfortunately turned out to be useless since I could not get a
job teaching theater at a K-12 school without a degree in English or
speech. I did perform in one off-Broadway play, and then set about
finding a real job.

In those days, women had three career choices—nurse, secretary,
and teacher. I fainted at the sight of blood. I didn't type. I didn't have
the credentials to teach. I knew that I did not want to spend my life
transcribing the words of a male boss who was the vice president of
something, so I took a job as a senior clerk in the marketing and fulfillment department of a trade association.

The first obstacle I encountered was from my female supervisor. I
always finished my work ahead of time and wanted more interesting

projects, but she felt I was overstepping my boundaries. I made friends with people in other departments, away from her control, and started volunteering to do work for other people because I was bored. This was when I first learned that networking is a good thing.

Builds Relationships

When my boss became pregnant, which in those days meant that she had to quit, I went to the personnel department to apply for her job. That was an eye-opener about how things worked in corporate America! The head of personnel immediately called my boss, who told me in no uncertain terms that I would only get her job over her dead body. So I realized that my career path in this company was limited and the only way to progress was to leave. I had learned two lessons about the business world—don't let anyone convince you that you have any limits, and goal setting is essential to success. After some soul searching, I decided that what I wanted was to become the youngest woman vice president of a Fortune 500 company. I was twenty-four at the time.

So I went job hunting.

I had two criteria. I wanted a higher salary and a better job title. I thought that if I continued to follow my career-building strategy and changed jobs every two years, in ten years I would have climbed the ladder and be a highly paid vice president of marketing in a Fortune 500 company. This strategy turned out to be successful, and when I was thirty-two I became the vice president of the educational division of Butterick Publishing, a division of American Can, a Fortune 500 company.

When Butterick Publishing was sold, I was offered a new job as vice president of the database publisher that purchased some of its assets, and I found myself on an executive team where I was the only woman. The men excluded me from the monthly executive meetings, so I was completely out of the loop. I decided to leave again, but this time I was smarter, and I stayed long enough to learn everything I needed to know about database publishing. Then I crafted a plan of divisional consolidation that would show them how to get rid of me. I was able to negotiate an entire year's salary as my buyout, and in 1982 I started my own database publishing company with a couple of friends. We published the first directory of the emerging microcomputer industry, an industry that I thought would change the world—a prediction that came true!

Champions Change

Because I was single, the world of self-employment was frightening. But I bought myself a little time to make it happen. The next lesson I learned was to never be afraid to take risks—to develop the courage to go my own way in life. I ran my publishing company for two years, but no bank would lend me the money I needed for expansion, and I knew that, without new products and expanded marketing, the company would not survive. I reviewed my alternatives and decided to sell the company. I received the best offer from R.R. Bowker, where, because of my knowledge of the microcomputer industry, I was offered the job of vice president of marketing. I took it and helped develop and market the first viable CD-ROM product sold to libraries, *Books in Print*.

Then R.R. Bowker was sold to a company with no women executives. They fired my boss and brought in someone who didn't know anything about reference publishing and asked me to train him. I refused, resigned, and again needed to re-think my future.

When a friend called to see whether I would help with a strategic marketing plan for her company, I agreed, and I became a self-employed marketing consultant. For the next twenty-five years, I earned a living by advising clients on how to develop and sell educational materials to the K-12 market. This experience taught me perhaps the most valuable lesson of all—I didn't have to work for a company in order to make a living. Being able to generate my own income was a real eye-opener.

Technical and Professional Expertise

As the educational publishing industry consolidated, I knew my career as a consultant was coming to an end, and I had to find another career. I decided to go back to my creative roots and began creating fiber art. I started by developing a strong body of work (product development), rented a studio in an artist's building where I went to work every day (overhead), and began showing my work in art shows and galleries (marketing). It took me three years to make my first sale, but my investment in myself paid off handsomely. Now, I am an internationally known artist and making a good living selling my art, teaching, lecturing, and writing books.

When I started my career as an artist, I brought with me all the lessons I had learned in the business world. I learned many lessons about being successful in fields ruled by men, and those lessons have translated into the art world, which is also dominated by male artists, curators, critics, and gallerists.

Besides being a successful artist, my other passion in life is to help new and emerging artists connect with the art-buying community so that they can make a career out of making art, as I have. I opened a contemporary art gallery in Denver in 2013, where I showcase five or six artists a year. I have learned that life is not all about overcoming obstacles. It's also about mentoring others and passing on your knowledge from person to person and from generation to generation. This has given my life meaning and purpose, and I've changed my grandmother's mantra to, "If you want it, get it. Once you get it, share it!"

I believe that life keeps getting better as long as you are pushing yourself to do new things, learn new skills, and set new goals. I will never formally retire, and I hope to be still developing new ideas when I bite the dust.

Carol Waugh

Carol Waugh earned a B.S. from New York University and an M.A. in business administration from Pace University. After serving at the executive level for large database and educational multimedia publishers, she started and sold two publishing companies. Since 2007, her art has been included in more than fifty national and international exhibitions. She is the author of five books on quilt-making and fiber art, including *Stupendous Stitching*. Her art has been featured in books, magazines, and TV programs and has been purchased by major corporations and private collectors such as the City of Denver, Kaiser Permanente, Grand Hyatt Hotels, IMA, and Beaver Run Resort. Carol teaches online classes at Craftsy.com and is the owner of aBuzz Gallery in the RiNo art district of Denver (www.CarolAnnWaugh.com, www .aBuzzGallery.com).

Kimberly Brock-Brown

Executive Chef and Motivational Speaker

"Challenges make you discover things about yourself that you never really knew. They're what make the instrument stretch—what makes you go beyond the norm."

—CICELY TYSON

Overcoming Obstacles and Giving Back

In my career, I often felt that there were three strikes against me—being female, African-American, and a pastry chef, three minority categories. However, growing up in Chicago, I was used to seeing strong, independent women in leadership positions. My mom and her two sisters were heads of households with children and careers, and at our church all the ministers were women.

Sports also taught me about leadership after mom transferred me to a private school for seventh and eighth grades, where I had a choice of basketball, softball, volleyball, and track and field. I believe that individual and team sports helped me build the determination to get it done, both for myself and for the team.

My Top Five Leadership Competencies

- Practices self-development
- Collaboration and teamwork
- Develops others
- Builds relationships
- Inspires and motivates others

As a chef's apprentice with the American Culinary Federation (ACF), I was given menial tasks and had to earn my way up to the coveted positions and duties, but of course I was able to develop my skills in the process. I can only imagine where my knife skills would be today if I had not had to finely julienne so many buckets of dill pickles for the Stroganoff garnish. Or how my time management would have improved without the garde manger chef screaming at me to chop nine cases of romaine and head lettuce in forty-five minutes. Or how I would have learned to get water from the banquet coffee urns because tap water isn't hot enough when you have to scoop 300 glasses of ice cream in a below-zero-degree freezer.

But I rarely considered the chefs I worked with to be mentors. This term was foreign to me for a long time. Only a few chefs allowed me to work alongside them or invited me to come in early or stay late to see the finished results. However, when I was occasionally asked to do something outside of my job description, I jumped at the opportunity. This was a win-win for me. Not only would I earn over-time, but I was able to see something new and different and maybe even get my hands on it.

I was taken aback when one chef asked me what my intentions were after I graduated. He clearly did not want to waste his time teaching me if all I was going to do was get married and have babies. I was twenty-one years old, and having babies was still far off in the future for me. I have often wondered whether he asked the male apprentices the same question. When I did get married and became a mother, in my thirties, I gradually learned to develop my entrepreneurial side so that I could spend more time at home with my family, although I still missed many family events because of my work schedule. I knew from the start that my career would be determined not only by my skills but also by my ability to work long hours, weekends, and holidays.

Practices Self-Development

The chefs I worked with did not try to help me succeed because I was a woman, but they did, for the most part, help me obtain the training and skills I needed to improve. Along the way, I had learned to survive in some demanding situations. The bake shop was the last stop on my three-year culinary apprenticeship. The pastry chef who was there before I arrived had great culinary skills but no people skills, and temper tantrums were part of his daily routine. He cursed, spit, and threw pots, spoons, and food if you dared to do something he did not like. I am glad he left the company before I came into the shop!

But pastry chefs Whitney, Brian, and David were instrumental in my pastry skill development, and Momma Fay taught me how to run a pastry shop for optimum production. I stayed in the pastry shop because of these four people. They showed me the kind of manager I wanted to be, and they took the time to teach me the ins and outs of the bake shop. From them, I learned to collaborate with colleagues and be receptive to the ideas of co-workers, to be open to trying something new, and to always innovate, all while working fifteen hours a day.

Many people still believe that a woman's place is in the kitchen, and most men still don't cook at home. There is a strange double standard operating here. In high school, boys are teased about taking a culinary class, despite the large number of male celebrity chefs on TV. There are a great many women in culinary schools and restaurant kitchens nationwide, but men are generally elevated to the top spots, and women are left behind in subordinate positions that pay less. Even in a field that is widely considered to belong to women, men are often still considered superior.

But I hope that my example and that of other successful women chefs is helping to turn this situation around. I used to be the one asking the questions whenever I attended a conference or went to a culinary competition or food show, but somewhere along the way, students have started asking me. I have become a "senior" experienced chef in their eyes, and I am happy to help.

I am active in the ACF, where I have gained a network of friends and supporters. My three culinary certifications and the fact that I am the only African-American female fellow inducted into the honor society have opened many doors for me. And when I heard about a women chefs' initiative starting in WACS (World Association of Chefs Society), I set my sights on becoming part of it.

Develops Others

I was contacted by the president of Women in WACS, Joanna Ochniak of Poland, and featured on their website and in their magazine. I started to spread the word to other female chefs about this great group that supports women and provides networking help. Eventually, I was asked to become the North American Continental Director to help keep the momentum going and grow the organization. We are dedicated to seeking out women chefs, featuring them on a global platform, connecting them with others for support and mentoring, and facilitating the exchange of ideas, recipes, and photos. Now, helping women chefs succeed and seeing the gains they make is the best part of my work day.

Kimberly Brock-Brown

Kimberly Brock-Brown graduated as a chef's apprentice from El Centro Junior College in 1984. She has cooked in the kitchens of many large hotels in the South and at the James Beard House in New York City. She is currently the only African-American female chef ever inducted into the American Academy of Chefs and the only African-American female certified pastry chef in South Carolina. She has also served as a culinary arts adjunct teacher at Johnson and Wales University and the Culinary Institute of Charleston at Trident Technical College, and she is a participating chef in First Lady Michelle Obama's Chefs Move to Schools program. She regularly speaks to groups of young women interested in careers in the culinary arts (www.kimberlybrockbrown.net/).

6 Collaboration and Teamwork

"Never doubt that a small group of thoughtful, committed citizens can change the world. Indeed, it is the only thing that ever has."

—Margaret Mead

To most, it seems obvious that collaboration and teamwork are essential in the workplace. Working together seems so straightforward; however, in reality, with gender, race, culture, and many other elements coming into play, it is far from easy. This chapter explores how these Real Women have successfully used this vital competency to further their careers and increase their personal and professional successes.

Collaboration and teamwork are defined as "developing and using collaborative relationships to facilitate the accomplishment of work goals."[1] As Jesse Lyn Stoner from the Seapoint Center for Collaborative Leadership explains; "Collaboration is working together to create something new in support of a shared vision. The key points are that it is not through individual effort, something new is created, and that the glue is the shared vision."

---

[1]http://campusservices.harvard.edu/system/files/documents/1865/harvard_competency_dictionary_complete.pdf

How can you recognize good team players? Generally, they know how to do the following things:

• Seek out opportunities,
• Clarify the current situation,
• Develop others' and their own ideas,
• Facilitate agreement, and
• Use effective interpersonal skills.[2]

To lead while demonstrating teamwork and collaboration is a challenge for both men and women. In order to do this, four main functions and roles must be fulfilled within a team: vision, organization, relationship/team process, and connecting to the larger system. When a team has a sense of vision and purpose, is organized in how they will achieve their goals, is able to respect and manage relationships within teams, and can provide external perspectives, it will be more likely to achieve successful outcomes.[3]

If a leader is able to negotiate these roles and recognize when he or she should fulfill each need, that adaptability is likely to lend itself to successful teamwork and collaboration.

So where do women fall on the skill set of collaboration and teamwork? Presented as one of the top five most undervalued leadership traits in women, *being purposeful and taking meaningful actions* results in a collaborative leadership style, which is definitely undervalued in women.[4]

Women are traditionally thought of as team players, more so than men, and it has been thought and proven that women are more empathetic and have greater interpersonal skills. These skills are widely thought

[2]http://campusservices.harvard.edu/system/files/documents/1865/harvard_competency_dictionary_complete.pdf
[3]www.womenleadingtheway.com/womens-leadership-resources-teams.html
[4]www.forbes.com/sites/glennllopis/2014/02/03/the-most-undervalued-leadership-traits-of-women/

to be needed for collaboration and teamwork, meaning that, logically, women should outperform men in this regard. Research has also shown that women generally value personal relationships and perceptions of their behavior more, and often strive to improve in these areas.[5]

True to this, Real Women were indeed shown to outperform men on Zenger and Folkman's Collaboration and Teamwork competency, proving that women definitely possess the skills to become great leaders.

The following essays show how collaboration and teamwork were essential qualities that enabled these Real Women to make their journeys to success. When working in government and politics, collaboration and teamwork are vital skills to create change. Beverly Perdue discussed her role as the Governor of North Carolina and the journey of leadership that led her to this position. Stating Collaboration and Teamwork as one of her top five competencies, her skills in this area are clearly demonstrated in a variety of ways, from building coalitions of military personnel in order to defend North Carolina's military bases, to her clear belief in listening to stakeholders when making education legislation.

This belief in stakeholder involvement and collaboration is shared by Barbara Nielson, former state superintendent of schools in South Carolina, who discusses how this philosophy was put to the test when she received pressure from district superintendents to accept their word as rule. Describing successful leaders as having *"high expectations, communicating clear goals, and creating an environment of shared values while respecting and trusting themselves and others,"* Nielson is the epitome of how far collaboration and teamwork can take you in your career. Similarly, Linda McCulloch, Montana's Secretary of State, discusses how empathy and flexibility, two key qualities necessary for successful collaboration and teamwork, have enabled her to win against her male opponents.

---

[5]www.ccl.org/leadership/programs/WLPOverview.aspx

So how do we as women improve our collaboration and teamwork competencies? Learning by example is certainly a powerful tool, and as you read the following essays it will be clear that the Real Women, Real Leaders have many lessons to share. To share some concrete action items, Lynda Gratton and Tamara Erickson in the *Harvard Business Review* suggest Eight Ways to Build a Collaborative Team.[6]

1. *Investing in signature relationship practices*, e.g., investing in physical areas that will encourage collaboration, such as open plan offices or spaces for teamwork.

2. *Modeling collaborative behavior.* Practice what you preach!

3. *Creating a "gift culture."* This can be done through mentoring and coaching, enabling necessary networks to be built.

4. *Ensuring the requisite skills.* Professional development that focuses on building relationships, communicating well, and resolving conflicts will help people in the workplace develop the skills they need for collaboration and teamwork.

5. *Supporting a strong sense of community.* Building community builds collaborative practice.

6. *Assigning team leaders who are both task- and relationship-oriented.* Both are key to being a successful team leader!

7. *Building on heritage relationships.* People feel more comfortable when they know each other, so build on this and put at least some people who know each other on the same team.

8. *Understanding role clarity and task ambiguity.* Understanding roles and responsibilities is key, and essential for functional cooperation.

Using the lessons from our Real Women and the resources provided in this book, women can build on the competency of collaboration and teamwork in the workplace, becoming stronger leaders for both ourselves and the generations that follow us.

---

[6]https://hbr.org/2007/11/eight-ways-to-build-collaborative-teams/

Beverly Perdue

Governor of North Carolina, 2009–2013

"Men fear women's strength."

—ANAIS NIN

Working Harder Than Anyone Else

When I take the time to step back and reflect on my career, it seems to fall somewhere between *Coal Miner's Daughter* and *The Little Engine That Could*. I'm not sure whether leaders are born, but I was born into a family where a strong work ethic defined who you were and where you were going. My mother and my father, a former coal miner in Grundy, Virginia, who became a coal company executive, are responsible for my hard-working genes.

In the small Southern town where I was raised, the equation for success was straightforward—hard work + a good education = anything you want to be. However, that equation is not always as simple as it seems. Tough times, roadblocks, and life-changing challenges intervene, and how we overcome the challenges defines us as people and leaders. For me, it always came down to working harder than anyone else—a trait I relied on to survive in politics in the American South, to get past or break down barriers, and to achieve my goals.

My Top Five Leadership Competencies

- Takes initiative
- Drives for results
- Inspires and motivates others
- Collaboration and teamwork
- Champions change

When I moved to a conservative small town in North Carolina, I had three degrees and no job. I wanted to work, and I wanted to be involved in the community, so I found a job with a government council and then with the local hospital, developing long-term care programs for older citizens, a topic close to my Ph.D. dissertation. I soon learned about a committee of 100—all men—that helped direct business and civic decisions in the town and county. I knew a member of the committee and worked hard to convince him that I could contribute, and when I decided to run for the North Carolina House of Representatives in 1986, I relied on the support of many of the committee members. I won, the first woman to be elected for that district. Hard work!

That election began a series of firsts for women politicians in North Carolina. In 1990 I was the first woman from my district elected to the State Senate, in 1995 I was appointed the first woman chair of the powerful appropriations committee, in 2000 I was elected the first woman lieutenant governor, and in 2009 I became the first woman governor. I was only the third woman governor in the conservative South who did not follow her husband into office.

My political career has mirrored the changes that have affected American women over the last forty to fifty years. The modern women's movement grew out of the civil rights revolution of the 1960s and has gathered force ever since. For example, although there have been thirty-six women governors in U.S. history, thirty-one were elected since 1975, according to the Center for American Women and Politics at Rutgers University. Ironically, my own success as a woman in politics started not long after the North Carolina legislature voted in 1971 to ratify the 19th Amendment that allowed women to vote, which had been the law of the land since 1920.

How does a woman succeed in such a workplace? My success was made possible by the many mentors I sought and attracted—both men and women—who taught me how to negotiate, compromise, and hold firm on core principles. I listened to women friends—political realists who told me not to blink when an aging Southern committee chairman called me "sweetie." I studied legislation, talked to the people who knew the details, and prepared for committee meetings. So when leaders were asked about an issue such as education, they would say, "Go talk to Perdue." Hard work!

Women have supported me all along. Women's groups such as Lillian's List and Emily's List were among the first to support my campaign. Even women who were not always inspired by my politics joined in to elect a first woman governor. Women taught me—sometimes with blunt words—how to be a CEO in politics. In the 2008 election, the Women for Perdue network brought out crowds at my public appearances across the state. It may sound simple, but this kind of political activity requires intense collaboration, scheduling, communication, and, from the candidate and chairman, commitment to the supporters. And hard work.

Collaboration and Teamwork

I loved campaigning, and it came easy to me, but accomplishing something meaningful in office was often another story. When I was lieutenant governor, I quickly realized that this was the appendix office of politics, so I looked for opportunities to advance my own agenda while improving the life of our citizens. One such opportunity was preventing children from smoking—a goal that was not without political risks in the largest tobacco-producing state in the nation, where the tobacco industry had long held sway in the legislature.

But I knew the public was ahead of the politicians on smoking issues, and I persuaded Governor Mike Easley, a fellow Democrat who had fought the tobacco companies as attorney general, to appoint me chair of the Health and Wellness Trust Fund. I took the initiative to ask the fund to finance a successful anti-smoking campaign aimed at young people, and by 2012 teen smoking had declined by 55 percent in middle schools and by 43 percent in high schools, according to the North Carolina Department of Health and Human Services.

Takes Initiative

Another opportunity I took up was preventing the closure or downsizing of the state's military bases by the federal government. In 2005, I worked to build community coalitions of support and collaborated with many generals and other high-ranking military personnel to make the case for our state. As a result, the military presence in North Carolina was expanded, not reduced, with the addition of the U.S. Army Forces Command and the headquarters for the U.S. Army Reserve Command. North Carolina's military economy grew from $17.5 billion in 2004 to more than $23 billion in 2012 and approximately $27 billion in 2013.

Similarly, I listened to educators who believed in the value of expanding early childhood education. When I became governor at the start of the great recession in 2009, I asked the legislature to approve a one-cent sales tax increase to protect our schools, universities, and pre-K programs. It was unpopular, and I paid for it in the polls. Subsequently, the Republican legislature slashed education budgets, including the pre-K funding, cutting off thousands of poor children from a better start in life. So I determined that the cuts were unlawful and found other money to fund and expand the program.

One of my final acts as governor was to pardon the Wilmington 10 civil rights activists. Their sentences had been commuted by Governor Jim Hunt, but new facts had surfaced in 2012 about their trial. I read all the documents, changed my mind, pardoned them on my last day in office at the end of 2012, and issued a statement saying, "These convictions were tainted by naked racism and represent an ugly stain on North Carolina's criminal justice system that cannot be allowed to stand any longer."

For young women and men reading my story for lessons on leadership, my advice is to start with work that you like. Then set goals and be ambitious. Listen to others, but be willing to lead when action is required. Communicate continually with other people, whether they're on your executive team or sitting on the sidelines. And work hard every step of the way.

Beverly Perdue

Beverly Perdue earned a B.A. degree in history in 1969 from the University of Kentucky, as well as a M.Ed. degree in community college administration in 1974 and a Ph.D. degree in education administration in 1976 from the University of Florida. She worked as a public school teacher and as the director of geriatric services at a community hospital. Starting in the 1980s, she served in the North Carolina House of Representatives and State Senate before she was elected as the 32nd lieutenant governor in 2000 and the 73rd governor in 2008. In 2013, she became a resident fellow at the Harvard Institute of Politics and a distinguished visiting fellow at Duke University's Sanford School of Public Policy. She founded and currently chairs DigiLEARN, a non-profit organization that focuses on accelerating digital education for all learners.

Barbara Stock Nielsen

Former State Superintendent of Schools, South Carolina

"Because of their age-long training in human relations—for that is what feminine intuition really is—women have a special contribution to make to any group enterprise."

—MARGARET MEAD

The Courage to Make a Difference

Recently, I was asked to deliver the keynote speech for a twenty-year celebration of STEM (science, technology, engineering, and math) education in South Carolina. The group was honoring me for my leadership in making STEM an important part of my administration's efforts when I was the state superintendent. They asked me to reflect on what we were thinking as we worked our way through many systemic reforms and how leadership was a key ingredient in this journey.

It was an interesting process. I have always believed that leadership functions on many levels, that all stakeholders must be included, and that it takes everyone working together to bring about the desired results. My personal philosophy is that leadership is all about stepping forward and having the courage, passion, and commitment to make a difference. In retrospect, I cannot remember a time in my life when this was not the case.

My Top Five Leadership Competencies

- Drives for results
- Inspires and motivates others
- Builds relationships
- Collaboration and teamwork
- Champions change

As the oldest of seven children, I was used to taking charge and helping out. My mother taught me to be independent, respect others, work hard, be true to a set of core principles, have a strong faith, and help others, and I have tried to follow her advice. I was the first in my family to go to college, encouraged by my mother, grandmother, and great-aunt. They wanted opportunities for me that were not available to them. But none of us dreamed that I would serve as the first woman state superintendent of schools in South Carolina and only the second woman to serve as a Constitutional officer.

In my early career as an educator, I did not really encounter obstacles, or perhaps I did not think that being a woman could hold me back. I have never looked at myself as a minority, even though the literature said I was. For me, it was all about a commitment to do my best, build strong relationships, and learn from others around me. I was fortunate to be involved in jobs and projects that I believed in; I had the opportunity to practice leadership at many levels; and I do believe that we practice these skills and grow throughout our careers.

My major professor, Dr. Fran Thieman, helped me realize that change was the way of the future and taught me that every piece of the education system needs to be considered and aligned when making decisions or implementing new things, because one change always impacts the whole. He was a genius at finance, which was of great benefit to me, since this was traditionally an area where women leaders did not have a lot of experience. In my doctoral work, he opened up my world by arranging a very non-traditional program with one-third of my work in curriculum/administration, one-third in the school of business, and one-third in community development.

I was also fortunate to do an internship with the Prichard Committee, the education reform group in Kentucky that was looking forward, developing change, and bringing in full accountability for the state. A lesson I have always carried with me from that time was the mantra I heard over and over: "Don't say that something can't be done, because we're only going to talk about solutions."

I discovered early on that I had to be in a leadership position to get things done. Perhaps that was why I agreed to run for state superintendent of schools for South Carolina. Business leaders I knew and

worked with approached me to run, challenging me to prove what
I was saying about a better way to run education in the state. Never
having run for public office, I had no idea what a challenge it would
be. I was in a statewide race, running against a twenty-two-year
incumbent backed by a strong core of good old boys who did not feel
that women should be in leadership positions. Welcome to the real
world!

Several days after I assumed office, a delegation of district superintendents came to visit me with the clear message that they were the
ones running education in the state. They offered me the "queen on
the throne" position if I agreed to do as they said. I smiled, thanked
them, told them I valued their input, but explained that my leadership style was to be inclusive of all stakeholders. After a period of
culture shock, we gradually came to understand each other—a good
lesson in patience and resilience, for most of us. I served two terms
and lived to write about the experience.

Builds Relationships

Change will always be with us in education. Leaders must recognize
that they cannot be so vested in the system that they forget to look
ahead and use common sense, especially in this information age. As
we transition from a world of schooling to a world of learning, we
need a shared vision and a strong commitment to ensuring quality learning for all children. Strong leaders do not fear change. They
have a healthy respect for it, always look forward, set goals, focus on
results, and review, refine, and reinvent.

Champions Change

When I look back, I feel that to be a successful leader is to be a successful person—for both men and women. We can learn from both
sexes. And successful leaders must be committed to bringing others

along. Today I am sometimes disappointed to see that some women leaders do not help other women advance and move into leadership positions.

Successful leaders have high expectations, communicate clear goals, and create an environment of shared values while respecting and trusting themselves and others. They recognize the need to surround themselves with strong people. Weak leaders hire weak people, and strong leaders hire strong people. I was fortunate to have a wonderful team of strong leaders who have gone on to top positions of leadership in education and the corporate world.

My generation often felt we had to do it all—to be a wife, mother, leader, and community volunteer. For me, it was a delicate balance, helped along by my supportive husband. I tell women today that they can be all those things but never to lose sight of who they are. Today, the culture has changed to provide many opportunities for women to be themselves, to work and have a family.

My husband, who is also an educator, researcher, and evaluator, greatly influenced my thinking on testing, evaluation, and data analysis. I am a believer that data should be used for both accountability and instructional feedback. In my decision-making style, I have always tried to be inclusive by listening, bringing in divergent thinking, weighing all options, and reflecting on how they impact the whole. No one ever does it alone. But I recognized that being popular does not always make for good leadership. Sometimes you just have to do the right thing. It takes courage to lead.

Every night when I look in the mirror, I feel proud of the effort and commitment I made. Above all, I can say I did make a difference for the children of South Carolina. I've always loved the message of *The Little Engine That Could*, because I do believe that if we think we can, we will. And in the story, the engine that finally stopped to help was a she.

Barbara Nielsen

Barbara Nielsen earned a bachelor's degree in education from the University of Dayton, an M.Ed. in curriculum and instruction and an Ed.D. in educational administration from the University of Louisville. She served for forty-nine years as a teacher, administrator, and consultant. Dr Nielsen spent seventeen years in the Jefferson County Schools, Louisville, Kentucky, and she worked in the Beaufort County School System, South Carolina, as a curriculum specialist and school business partnership coordinator. She was elected South Carolina State Superintendent from 1990 to 1998 and has served as a member of the steering committee of the Education Commission of the States, a board member of the Council of Chief State School Officers, and on numerous other boards, including the South Carolina Public Charter School State-wide District Board. She also served as a senior scholar for the Strom Thurmond Institute at Clemson University. She was honored by the Network of Effective Schools as Eminent Educator of 1993, and in 1996 she received the State Elected Official Award from the White House Counsel on Library and Information Services.

Linda McCulloch

Montana Secretary of State

"Leadership is a communal responsibility with a concern for the welfare of the people or tribe and then sharing the work that needs to be done based on skills and abilities. Leadership is shared responsibility and promoting people's well-being."

—LaDonna Harris

The Power of Self-Belief

My interest in politics began in the seventh grade when I volunteered on my first campaign. My older sister worked for a man who was running for county commissioner, and he asked us to silkscreen his yard signs. I knew the project would take a lot of time, so I made an appointment to interview him—one of the first times I took the initiative to do something that I thought was right and that would help me do a good job! If I was going to give up my weekends for this man, I had to believe in him. I grilled him for an hour and a half on the issues—he later said it was the most rigorous interview he had ever had!

I knew that getting an education would drive my future success. I grew up in a lower class union family and dedicated myself to becoming the first on my father's side to graduate high school and the first on my mom's side to start and finish college. Talk about a journey! It took me almost ten years to earn my degree in four colleges and universities across three states, but I worked my way through and couldn't wait to begin my career as an elementary school teacher. Most public school teachers are women, and in twenty years of teaching I never experienced gender bias. It wasn't until I mustered up the courage to run my first political campaign that I faced the issue of being a woman in a male-dominated profession.

My Top Five Leadership Competencies

- Takes initiative
- Displays high integrity and honesty
- Inspires and motivates others
- Collaboration and teamwork
- Solves problems and analyzes issues

Have you ever secretly wanted something but were afraid if you said it out loud, it would sound foolish? That's how I felt about becoming an elected official. I had volunteered on a number of campaigns, and I knew what it took to be successful, but I was afraid to become a candidate. "I'm not smart enough," I replied when I was asked to run for the Montana State Legislature. Despite my ambition, I thought everyone in the legislature was an attorney who could quote the law from memory.

But I wanted to see for myself. I decided to take two days off work to observe the Montana Legislature in action. I sat through committee hearings, visited floor sessions, and talked to lawmakers about my ideas for improving education in the state. By the time I left the State Capitol, I knew I was smart enough to run. I even convinced myself that I was going to win. The fact that I was a woman did not influence my decision. Montana women were voting and serving in elected positions years before the 19th Amendment was passed. Montana was the first state to send a woman to Congress, when Jeannette Rankin was elected to the House of Representatives in 1914, and we had two women serving in the state legislature by 1917. By the time I ran for office, about thirty women were serving in the state House and Senate, and I soon learned that, in fact, fewer than ten of the 150 legislators were attorneys!

I was running as a Democrat against an incumbent in a district that had long been Republican. I had no name recognition, no experience as a candidate, and no money in the bank. But I hit the ground running. I knocked on doors seven days a week, exhausted my phone line with fundraising calls, and used my gender to my advantage, since women answered most of the doors and phone calls. Women told me they were surprised to find a woman running for office in their district, and that they would vote for me. Some even put up my sign on the other side of the lawn from my opponent's sign, set up by their husbands. I won by forty-six votes, and I'm sure that being a woman helped get me elected!

Collaboration and Teamwork

People often ask me what it's like being a woman in a man's world, but I don't see it that way. I've always been outspoken, and my honest opinions, problem-solving skills, and willingness to tackle the issues have regularly overshadowed my gender. As a first-time legislator, I quickly earned the respect of my colleagues for my collaboration and communication skills, and I solidified my leadership potential in three sessions by passing all but one of my bills with bipartisan support. As a woman, I was able to inspire others to come together to address important issues.

Inspires and Motivates Others

I believe that being a woman in politics is a strength, not a weakness. My ability to be more flexible and empathetic than my male counterparts has led to seven consecutive wins in twenty years. Sometimes people have tried to use my gender against me, but I have always been able to overcome the negativity by keeping my emotions at bay and focusing on the task at hand, because when it comes to emotions, being a woman in politics can be tricky. If a woman cries while giving a speech about women's rights, she can be labeled feeble or sensitive, whereas a man who cries might be seen as brave for letting his emotions show. On the other hand, a woman who never shows any emotion is considered cold, while an uncompromising man is considered efficient. However, I learned early in my career that leaders can't worry too much about labels. Getting work done is the priority!

I firmly believe in the need to increase participation in all levels of government. The earlier someone votes or becomes involved in government, the more likely he or she is to become an engaged and active citizen for life. I will never forget the first time I voted. The 26th amendment had recently passed, which meant I could vote at age eighteen! My parents and friends all had their opinions and choices, which seemed fine until I walked into the voting booth. I looked down at the ballot and felt like someone had punched me in the stomach! I realized I had the power to change the world with my vote. And after I won my first race by only forty-six votes, I became convinced that every vote mattered.

Women are a major force at the ballot box. Nationally, the number of female voters has exceeded the number of male voters in every presidential election since 1964. Yet, women account for less than 24 percent of elected federal and statewide officeholders. Men dominate the political landscape, and as a result, women are missing critical opportunities to advance their perspective. Raising the value of women begins with raising our participation in politics. Women are an unstoppable force on election day, but we can't vote for a woman unless she's a candidate!

Keeping silent about my youthful aspirations to run for office was foolish. I'm embarrassed now to admit that I ever believed I wasn't smart enough. I hope that by sharing some of my story, more women will be convinced to run for office and know that they can win. My life changed for the better the moment I stopped trying to convince others to believe in me and started believing in myself.

Linda McCulloch

Linda McCulloch holds B.A. and M.A. degrees in elementary education from the University of Montana, with an emphasis on supervision of library media programs. She taught in Montana for twenty years before she served three terms in the Montana House of Representatives, from 1995 to 2001. In 1999, she served as the minority caucus leader and vice-chair of the House Education Committee, and from 1995 to 2000, she was a faculty affiliate at the University of Montana. She served two terms as the Montana superintendent of public instruction and was elected Montana's first woman secretary of state in November 2008. Linda looks forward to retiring from politics after her second four-year term as Montana secretary of state and empowering women and girls by sharing her experiences as an elected official over twenty-two years.

7 Drive for Results

"We are what we repeatedly do. Excellence then, is not an act, but a habit."

—Aristotle

One of the primary ways that many of our Real Women have been able to distinguish themselves as exemplary in a man's world is through their ability to drive for results. This chapter shows the myriad ways in which our women have been able to push forward, elevating themselves, their careers, their families, and their lives through their outstanding work ethic and ability to get the job done, whatever it may be.

A tangible way to showcase impact, driving for results is the ability to accomplish tasks with excellence, regardless of obstacles present. A concrete competency, leaders who drive for results have the ability to "consistently focus themselves and others on achieving specific outcomes. They understand how and are able to align the appropriate level of human, physical and technical resources to achieve organizational goals and customer expectations" (Excelis Inc. Talent Competencies Drive for Results).

We can see through this classification that truly exemplary leaders not only meet existing goals, but they utilize all resources necessary to complete essential tasks and, even more, go above and beyond, ensuring that the task has been completed with excellence. Some of the classic behavior traits associated with this competency include timeliness, professionalism, perseverance, and follow-through.

Driving for results can manifest itself in concrete tasks, such as creating a home schedule that balances the needs of every family member and executing it daily, or in larger tasks such as the ideation and execution of a large-scale, multi-stakeholder project. Complexity of task is not an essential component to this competency; a leader's ability to execute every task with dedication, regardless of difficulty, is the hallmark of this proficiency.

The ability to drive for results in a world that responds to measurable progress and impact, but is rife with myriad distractions, is especially important for our Real Women. This quality results in leaders who are able to set appropriate benchmarks, surpass them, and inspire others to do the same. The level of dedication required to be single-minded in purpose, consistently and expertly ensuring that goals are met, is a quality that has served our Real Women across industry and experience.

Diane Durkin from *Baseline* magazine outlines six tangible strategies to help positively drive results in the workplace; unsurprisingly these strategies rely on the ability to manage a team:

- Engage employees in discussion, many minds are better than one.
- Create focus and shared vision; help people feel a part of the movement.
- Communicate constantly; if everyone is on the same page, results happen faster.
- Ask, listen, and empower employees; developing real loyalty is a sure way to advance your business.
- Recognize and praise staff, and work to promote a culture of respect.[1]

Harriet Sanford, president and CEO of the NEA Foundation, was taught to drive for results at an early age by her parents, an

---

[1] www.baselinemag.com/c/a/Project-Management/Leadership-Practices-That-Drive-Results-872165/

interracial couple who decided to marry despite the fact that it was widely illegal in the United States at that time. Although an extreme example, the message of completing a task despite popular opinion or an overwhelming obstacle was one that has served Harriet well as she has risen through the ranks to be a leader who drives for results by giving her staff an opportunity to excel.

Vicki Phillips, the current director of education for The Bill and Melinda Gates Foundation, has a similar personal story that exemplifies the essence of driving for results. As a teenager, Vicki made the difficult decision to pursue a college education in the face of her family's dissent; she not only went on to earn her doctorate, but also now works to ensure that all children have access to an education that was almost denied to her.

Karen Avery, the senior director of institutional giving at the PBS Foundation, drives for results in the manner in which she engages with the world. She understands that, in order to be a successful leader, one must also feel that he or she can "choreograph" the activities of life effectively.

With these specific examples of driving for results, we can see that Real Women leaders have found a way to focus on what needs to be done in their personal lives, their professional lives, and in all of the ways that they have chosen to lead. These women are showcasing their talents in the workplace and, further, amplifying impact across all sectors and truly driving for results.

Harriet Sanford

President and CEO, NEA Foundation

"Kids learn more from example than from anything you say. I'm convinced they learn very early not to hear anything you say, but to watch what you do."

—JANE PAULEY

The Lesson of My Father

As a child, I used to wait in the garden on warm August afternoons for my dad, for the precious moments he spent at home between his two jobs. With only a few minutes for dinner before heading to his evening job, I knew he'd go straight to the garden to check on his vegetables. Surrounded by tomatoes, greens, beets, and an assortment of other crops, I would help him weed and select items for supper.

My dad was hugely influential on my development as a leader. My parents' decision to marry when interracial marriage was still illegal in most states—and often provoked violent reaction—taught us kids to stand strong regardless of public opinion. Dad had successfully navigated many daunting challenges, including the Indiana Ku Klux Klan of his youth, racial bias in the military, and sometimes illegal treatment at the hands of others. It was clear to me that if he had succeeded and created a thriving family despite such challenges, whatever problems I faced would be small in comparison.

When dad was growing up, his family grew produce for themselves and for others, one of the early practices that formed his life-long habit of self-sufficiency and community service. He believed that each of us is in control of our own destiny, and so we kids learned to share that belief. My parents' expectations for us reflected their idea of equal opportunity, with equal standards regardless of gender or age. They taught us to use our talents in service to ourselves and to the community, even if the community was not always entirely welcoming.

My Top Five Leadership Competencies

- Practices self-development
- Develops others
- Collaboration and teamwork

- Inspires and motivate others
- Solves problems and analyzes issues

Dad stressed to us the concept of the Golden Rule—to do unto others as we would have them do unto us. He taught us empathy. We donated our allowances to those with less than we had and organized food and clothing drives. Helping others had a powerful effect on how we saw ourselves and ultimately molded my leadership style. We matured in a household built around the novel concept of service to others, and Dad taught us to put ourselves in the place of others to better understand their needs and perspectives.

Leadership for me is grounded in this ability to understand what motivates other people. I may be naïvely optimistic, but I believe that everyone wants to make the most of his or her gifts. The leadership challenge is about eliminating fear, tapping into positive energy, and sparking a sense of self-determination and confidence in others to help them excel in any chosen field.

Inspires and Motivates Others

My early notions of leadership were not limited by my color, gender, or intellectual boundaries. I was certain that all I had to do was give my best effort and the rest would take care of itself. Although I was technically a child of the sixties, women's lib existed in another solar system for me. I could not grasp why it was important, nor did I feel part of the discussion. My world was smaller and concerned with immediate issues, such as getting into college on a shoestring and living up to the understated but clear expectations of my father. Above average grades were never celebrated, they were expected, so I just worked harder. But I later learned to understand that the challenges of women were not unlike those faced by my father.

Another major role model for me was Atlanta Mayor Maynard Jackson. His work ethic was impeccable, with the same determined diligence as my dad. He required that any proposal describe at least three possible scenarios—one idea was never enough. Memos with even a single typographical error were returned for correction. I was grateful to my dad for preparing me with his equally high expectations, and I learned that leaders do not make or accept excuses.

I was also influenced by Fulton County Commissioner Michael Lomax, who was a shrewd negotiator. He did his best work away from the cameras, and the region benefited from his civic and cultural contributions. His habit of working without calling undue attention to himself helped to shape the kind of work environment I like to create, and I learned to prefer a low light, rather than a neon approach.

All these influences have led me to create a work environment in my organization that is based on trust, participation, and celebrating success. I believe that leaders need to create a safe place for others to learn from mistakes, where everyone understands that they play a critical role—from interns to chief financial officers—and where accomplishments are recognized to build morale and confidence.

Develops Others

Early in my career, I was not able to balance work and family demands very successfully, and as a result I have become an ardent advocate for work-family balance. I believe in policies that recognize the demands of family life, and I'm a passionate advocate for people who need time more than almost any other benefit. When my daughter asked me to volunteer at her middle school, although her classmates were telling their parents to stay away, it was clear that my involvement would reassure her she was as important as my job, and as a leader I try to make these opportunities available to others.

Finally, I believe that leaders must constantly mentor young women and men to work toward a better future. One of my former employees, Ayanna Hudson, still consults with me on big ideas. I have been proud to watch her move up from the local level to the national level at a national arts organization. I enjoy helping young people find their strength by learning to manage complex tasks, since I believe that problem solving is an art that must be nurtured. As I watch my colleagues and employees navigate the professional waters, I take pride in creating a safe environment for conversation and contributing to their success.

Dad's lessons on leadership, passed on largely by example rather than discourse, have guided my development as an executive and as a parent. I find that as a leader I am largely motivated to create the right conditions for people to grow—much as the gardens of my father created the right conditions for his beloved vegetables.

Harriet Sanford

Harriet Sanford holds an honorary doctor of humane letters degree and a B.A. in education from New England College, as well as an M.P.A. from the University of Connecticut. She began her career as a public school classroom teacher, which led to a senior executive career spanning more than twenty-eight years, with twenty-two years as the president and chief executive officer of non-profit organizations, including the Arts and Science Council in Charlotte, North Carolina, and the Fulton County Arts Council in Georgia. She has led the initiatives of the NEA Foundation since 2005, building on the foundation's commitment to supporting the collaborative efforts of public school educators, their unions, school districts, and communities to focus on learning conditions that improve student performance.

Vicki Phillips

Director of Education, College Ready, The Bill and Melinda Gates Foundation

> *"Each of us has the right and the responsibility to assess the roads which lie ahead and, if the future road looms ominous or unpromising, then we need to gather our resolve and step off, into another direction."*
>
> —MAYA ANGELOU

A Poor Kid Who Caught a Lucky Break

My path to leadership started on a dirt road in rural Kentucky in Falls of Rough, a town that sounds right out of an American version of a Charles Dickens novel. It was a place where we raised most of what we ate, often hunted for our supper, and had outhouses in the backyard. But it was also a place where you always knew you could count on your neighbor—if someone was sick, if your tire was flat, or if the shed fell down and you needed to build a new one. People knew me and looked out for me everywhere in the community, and I would not have traded that sense of community for anything.

But Falls of Rough was low on expectations, and not much was expected of me. I worked hard around the house and the farm, and I worked relatively hard in school, graduating near the top of my class. But no one expected me to do much more than graduate high school and settle down in the community. It wasn't until a friend from the affluent end of the county encouraged me to apply to college that I started to think about a different future and question whether where we grow up should determine where we end up.

My Top Five Leadership Competencies

- Practices self-development
- Drives for results

- Inspires and motivates others
- Collaboration and teamwork
- Champions change

When I was accepted into Western Kentucky University and finally told my parents about my plans, it was a blow to them, and in a curious way, a betrayal. College was only ninety miles from home, but for my family and me, it might as well have been 9,000 miles away. None of us had a frame of reference for college. My stepfather, who raised me and whom I thought of as my dad, was dead-set against it. He even told me not to come back if I decided to go off to college. When I left home, he was not speaking to me, and my mom was in tears. Happily, he later reached out and brought me back into the fold.

Practices Self-Development

But when I look back, these experiences shaped and strengthened me in two powerful ways. First, I was forced to weigh my aspirations against the genuine fears and concerns of others and make a life-altering choice. I had to follow the voice inside me that said, "You're not too poor to succeed. People shouldn't expect less of you or the kids down the road. It's okay to want a different future than what others envision for you." In many ways, I think this is an important first step for all women—we have to embrace our drive and vision for ourselves. Sometimes this requires a great deal of courage, especially if it involves redefining the status quo. Although it was not easy, my decision to go to college was pivotal. It set me on a professional and personal course and prepared me for the decisions I would later face as a leader.

Second, I learned the power of high expectations early on, starting when I went off to college and continuing to this day. At Western

Kentucky University, my professors challenged me to relearn how to learn after largely memorizing my way through high school. From then on, much has been expected of me, and I've experienced firsthand the difference between high expectations and low expectations. One prepares people and creates opportunities, and the other accepts limitations on what is possible. Through my own personal experience and as an educator, I've seen firsthand what happens when we expect more from kids. And, as an organization and community leader, I've seen time and again that when the bar is set high for adults, they reach for it and catch it.

As I've moved through my career, I've come to realize the value of a leader's commitment to learning, and there are many writers on leadership whose research sheds important light on this work. The work of Lee Bolman and Terry Deal stands out. In the early 1990s, I came across *Reframing Organizations: Artistry, Choice, and Leadership*, which breaks down the work of leaders into four categories—structural, human resources, political, and symbolic. The authors argue that effective leaders are able to set a vision, address the challenges, and work successfully within all four categories. Their framework helped me identify the categories where I was strong, those that came naturally, and those where I needed to invest time and work. Twenty years later, I am still using this framework to self-reflect and sharpen my skills.

Equally important for me is to intentionally connect leadership research to what I learn day in and day out from whatever position I'm in. Since my first teaching job, I've been privileged to work with a number of people, both men and women, who have exemplified effective leadership. I've learned a great deal by listening and by watching how they set a vision, engage staff and constituents, institute changes, and address challenges.

Champions Change

Early in my career, I worked for the Kentucky Commissioner of Education, Tom Boysen, on the Kentucky Education Reform Act at a time when the state had the lowest student achievement rate in the country. Redefining an education system at the state and district level was challenging, messy, and daunting work, filled with obstacles over which we often had no control. Through his skilled leadership, Mr. Boysen taught me how to navigate obstacles and find a viable solution if it was the right thing to do. He taught me that taking the opposing argument and seeing all sides of a challenge has merit, and that bureaucracy doesn't always have to win. He built a leadership team in which people did not share the same perspective, and I've emulated his approach in my own hiring and management practices.

Another role model for me in the Kentucky Department of Education was the director of instruction, Betty Steffy. Betty artfully managed Bolman and Deal's human resources and symbolic areas of leadership. During the most trying parts of the education reform efforts, she sent daily emails to the more than 300 members of her department to recap the events of the day, so that everyone heard the same information and benefited from the same insights. She ended her emails with a personal comment—whether it was letting people know she was going home to work in her garden or walk her dog or reminding them to take time to enjoy their children. These daily emails resonate with me to this day. They kept staff "in the know," reduced rumors, mitigated tensions, and allowed people to share the personal side of their work. They were small but authentic acts that made a large difference in the change process.

I was lucky. Many leaders stepped up to actively mentor me and open doors for me. They took a chance on me when I was young. They let me make mistakes and gave me strategies for addressing those mistakes. And it all helped shape me into the person I am today. I've never forgotten those gifts, nor where I came from. One of the beliefs I hold most dear is a commitment to pay it forward—to create support systems for other women as they prepare for and enter leadership roles and to emulate the mentors who have had such a profound influence in my life. I am truly excited to watch the next generation of women leaders emerge.

Develops Others

I've been a district superintendent, a state schools chief, a non-profit leader, and a teacher. But before I was any of these things, I was a poor girl from Kentucky who had the opportunity to bridge the gap between what I was expected to do and what I was capable of doing. I was a poor kid who caught a lucky break. My life changed because of a chance friendship with someone who was unwilling to accept the inequities between us. Today I work in education with a passion born from that experience—in a job where I get to give back and do my part to make sure that every child in America gets the opportunity I almost didn't have.

Vicki Phillips

Vicki Phillips earned a B.A. in elementary and special education and an M.A. in school psychology from Western Kentucky University, as well as a doctorate in educational leadership and management from the University of Lincoln in England. She began her career as a teacher and went on to serve at the state level in Kentucky. She has worked with the U.S. Department of Education, as Pennsylvania's Secretary of Education and Chief State School Officer, and as the superintendent of schools in Lancaster, Pennsylvania, and Portland, Oregon. She has trained school leaders in the U.K. and Australia, served on the governing council for England's National College for School Leadership, and co-founded the Global Education Leaders Program. In her work with The Bill and Melinda Gates Foundation, her goal is to ensure that high school students graduate ready for success in college and the workplace (www.gatesfoundation.org).

Karen Avery

Senior Director of Institutional Giving, PBS Foundation

"A mother is not a person to lean on, but a person to make leaning unnecessary."

—Dorothy Canfield Fisher

My Secret Leadership Sauce

Despite a long career in leadership roles, I found it somewhat daunting to reflect on my own leadership skills for this book. I asked myself whether it's really possible for me to see myself as a leader and wondered whether recognizing my own leadership skills might not be akin to hearing the proverbial tree fall in the forest. I rarely see myself as a leader, since I tend to view myself first and foremost as a mother—and one who is loud, laughing, and tired—rather than in standard leadership terms such as strong, forthright, bold, and energized. Yet, as I started to over-think it, I realized that the way I identify myself—in personal terms—precisely matches my perception and experience of strong leadership. My personal attributes are the ingredients in my secret leadership sauce!

My Top Five Leadership Competencies

- Takes initiative
- Inspires and motivates others
- Builds relationships
- Collaboration and teamwork
- Develops strategic perspective

In my early leadership roles, I was not a mother, yet today I cannot write about my leadership style without referring to motherhood.

I am the mother of two wonderful human beings, my daughter, who is fourteen at the time of this writing, and my son, who just turned twelve. Being a mother changed my life in many ways—glorious, painful, fulfilling, and deeply meaningful. Today it is my children who move me to stand strong and work hard to try to make a difference. Before they arrived, I used to believe that inner motivation was driving me to become involved and take a leadership role. But was that really the whole story? Did my capacity to lead come from me alone? I think not. Even though my maternal self would not surface for another twenty-six years, something external was driving me, and that was my own mother.

My mother moved me to be a leader very early on. She loved me beyond belief, routinely boosted me up, instilled in me a firm sense of self-confidence, and always burst with pride at my accomplishments. She was my biggest fan and toughest critic. In fact, far fewer copies of this book will move off the shelves now that she is no longer living. I believe that my mother planted the seeds of leadership within me and nurtured and protected those seeds to help me grow into the leader I am today. Her spirit lives on in me—sometimes when I catch myself acting just like her and saying the same things to my kids that she said to me, but most of all when I feel her guiding me to lead.

I am loud. People frequently tell me they hear me coming from a long way off. That's a good thing, right? My voice—loud and, I like to think, melodious—must cheer up so many people as I approach. Perhaps not. But one thing I've discovered about being loud is that it definitely gets you noticed. I tend not to wait at a crowded bar too long before I get the bartender's attention, and in college, when I was president of the house council, I never needed a microphone to make an announcement in the dining hall.

I'm sure you're familiar with that uncomfortable silence when the speaker asks the audience for questions at the end of a presentation. I'm one of those people who won't let the silence last too long. I always speak up. Being loud usually means being heard, and it can be very authoritative. But I've also learned to make sure that loud doesn't become obnoxious and to recognize whether I'm being listened to. Being loud and clear captures people's attention, but getting them to listen is what spurs them to action and leads to success.

I laugh a lot. Mainly because I think life—despite all its craziness, routine, and challenges—is really very funny. I smile a lot, and I feel fortunate to consider myself a very happy person. I believe that a sense of humor and the ability to laugh at oneself are essential for anyone in a leadership position in order to have an impact on others. But when we think of leaders in our lives or in history, we generally don't think about laughter and humor at all. Why is this? Is leadership always a serious business? Can't one lead and be funny? I believe one can.

Laughter makes people feel good. In times of crisis and pain, it can help to lift their spirits and move the healing process along. Leaders who take themselves too seriously run the risk of alienating those they are trying to move forward. Instead of jumping on the bandwagon, people may become resentful, bitter, or obstructive. Employees and volunteers may start talking behind the back of the leader they work for, and they'll be doing the laughing. We all know it's better to be laughed with rather than at, so leaders should recognize how to apply humor and promote laughter in order to achieve meaningful outcomes.

Inspires and Motivates Others

Je suis tres fatigue! Many years ago I convinced myself that sleep was overrated and that I could get by just fine on a handful of hours a night. I essentially run on fumes during the day. I maintain a fast-paced, jam-packed schedule, and I often don't give myself time to slow down and relax. I'm afraid I may have completely forgotten how! But come to think of it, I've never met a well-rested leader. Being tired, exhausted, and stressed out are all badges of successful leadership.

In recent years, one factor that has added to my perpetual fatigue is balancing the demands of career and family, or "choreographing" my life, as I like to call it. Some of my dances are designed for the big stage, but many are performed in the privacy of my own home. Juggling work and family remains a major challenge for women leaders because many workplace structures and environments fail to accommodate family commitments. However, I have been very fortunate to work with organizations that have been supportive of tired women trying to balance their professional and personal lives. But sadly, this is still the exception and not the rule.

In looking at the bigger picture beyond my own story, I believe we need to focus on certain priorities in order to reap the benefits of the leadership skills of women. From the courtroom to the boardroom, women are leading the way in government, business, nonprofit, and legal circles more than ever before, but they often feel the need to do more than men, prove themselves more than men, and create some sort of magic. In order to truly bring equality into leadership opportunities and leadership expectations, we must commit to developing more women leaders to allow women leaders to become the norm.

Builds Relationships

We must continuously reinforce their abilities, acknowledge their skills, and boost their self-confidence, so that they can achieve their full potential, starting with girls at a very young age. Women often learn how to deal with the setbacks of life through personal interaction, mentoring, and networking—skills that they possess in abundance. We can support the development of girls and women by helping them develop these skills along with additional strategies to help them compete on an equal footing in a complex world.

My mother used to say to me: "You can help make them better than they thought they could be." That kind of support helped me to be a leader. I'm now proud to be able to pass on that advice to my own daughter, to help her and the next generation of women leaders get real and lead on, while tirelessly laughing out loud.

Karen Avery

Karen Avery received her A.B. from Harvard University in psychology and social relations and her M.Ed. from the Harvard Graduate School of Education with a concentration in administration, planning, and social policy. She has served as a senior admissions officer for Harvard and Radcliffe Colleges, assistant dean of Harvard College, and the director of the Ann Radcliffe Trust, a women's initiative for Harvard undergraduates. She also spent seven years as director of foundation relations at the Smithsonian Institution. Karen joined PBS as senior director of institutional giving of the PBS Foundation in January 2011. She currently serves on the Wolf Trap Foundation associates board of directors and is especially proud to be closely connected with America's only national park for the performing arts (www.pbs.org).

8 Develops Strategic Perspective

"However beautiful the strategy, you should occasionally look at the results."

—Sir Winston Churchill

The stories from our Real Women show real-life examples of how leadership competencies manifest in the world of work. From business to education, from politics to the non-profit world, there are myriad lessons we can derive from the Real Women. However, while these women have taken paths to success, finding these paths can be difficult. In order to succeed in our quest to be transformational leaders, we must also talk about the competencies at which, according to the research, women do not naturally excel.

While women outperform men in almost all of the Zenger and Folkman competencies, it is also important to note the competencies in which we do not excel. Develops Strategic Perspective is the one competency on which males rated significantly higher than women (*A Study in Leadership: Women Do It Better Than Men*, by Zenger Folkman). In an attempt to address not only our strengths, but also our weaknesses, we discuss below what the competency entails and how you can improve your strategic perspective.

Strategic Perspective can be described and interpreted in a variety of ways. For this purpose, the competency is defined by Andrea Moore, senior consulting manager at FlashPoint as:

- Understand the current context
  - ◆ Assess current strategy/approach and results you are getting
- Develop high performance strategy
  - ◆ What's keeping you from realizing your vision and what it is that you want?
- Develop a plan to execute on the strategy
  - ◆ Develop roles and responsibilities, set goals, and develop action plans[1]

Marina Go, general manager of Hearst-Buaer, suggests that because women are typically great problem solvers, they overlook the bigger picture and vision in order to provide solutions to problems at hand.[2]

The question remains, however, how do we use our skills, but also develop the key leadership competencies necessary to succeed?

As you read through *Real Women, Real Leaders*, you found a variety of resources and action points, which we hope will help you find your inner leader and assist you in the development of your leadership qualities. As women, we must use the existing data to our advantage; understanding that, as a gender, we struggle to display strategic perspective, which allows us to actively plan for development of the competency.

In 1987, Mintzberg developed the 5Ps of Strategy. Almost thirty years later, these 5Ps continue to provide a useful tool to think about

---

[1] www.womensagenda.com.au/talking-about/the-daily-juggle/what-it-means-to-develop-a-strategic-perspective/201310062998#.VHTvSVfF9m0
[2] www.womensagenda.com.au/talking-about/the-daily-juggle/what-it-means-to-develop-a-strategic-perspective/201310062998#.VHTvSVfF9m0

how we approach strategic perspective and how to develop this as a competency in a concrete, tangible way, divided here into logical steps.

1. Plan

   a. Think about your mission, vision, and long-term goals.

   b. Use tools such as PEST (Political, Economic, Social, and Technological) analysis, SWOT (Strengths, Weaknesses, Opportunities, and Threats) analysis, or brainstorming to help you in the planning process.

2. Ploy

   a. Think about competitors, the market, allies, and where your organization fits into this picture.

   b. Use tools such as Impact Analysis or Scenario Analysis to help you think about this. Also consider reading up on Game Theory for some extra tools for competitive analysis.

3. Pattern

   a. Think about organizational behavior and how this affects overall strategy. Notice the behavior patterns you see in your team and organization, and analyze how these patterns affect your strategic perspective.

   b. Use tools such as core competency analysis to assess the resources you are working with.

4. Position

   a. Think about where you position yourself as an organization in the relevant environment. You need to understand where your organization fits into the bigger picture.

5. Perspective

   a. Think about your organization's culture. Does it encourage risk taking and innovation? Or does it rely purely on data? Understanding this will help you further develop your strategic perspective.

Finally, remember to focus on the "WHAT" and the "WHY" rather than the "HOW."[3]

From all of the women behind this book, we hope that our life lessons serve to inspire, teach, and coach future women leaders. As you have seen, the competencies discussed can manifest themselves in a range of different professions and styles, and focusing on developing the competencies you believe will lead you to success in your career is essential. We hope that the action points and tools we have provided in this book, along with the resources at the end of the book, will serve as a launching pad for each and every one of you to become a Real Woman, and Real Leader of your own.

[3]www.women-unlimited.com/blog/tag/female-business-leaders/

Leadership Self-Assessment

Self-reflection is an important component of developing leadership qualities. This self assessment is designed to help leaders determine which leadership skills they may need to develop. It focuses on eight components dealing with (1) *providing direction*, (2) *leading courageously*, (3) *fostering teamwork*, (4) *championing change*, (5) *coaching people*, (6) *motivating others*, (7) *building relationships*, and (8) *acting with integrity*. A set of five statements reflect various attributes of and skills for each component.

Instructions

Please read each statement carefully. Then rate yourself in terms of how well you think you possess the attribute or perform the leadership skill by circling the statement that best reflects your view. This is not a test; there are no right or wrong answers.

The rating scale provides three choices:

1 = I do not possess this attribute or do this skill well at all.

2 = I seldom possess this attribute or do this skill somewhat well.

3 = I possess this attribute or do this skill very well.

Circle your chosen response for each statement

Please respond to every statement. In selecting your response, be realistic about your assessment. Do not answer in terms of how you would *like* to see yourself, in terms of what you *should* be doing, or in terms of how you think *others view you*. Again, the purpose of this assessment is to help you focus on growth objectives that will stretch you in meaningful ways. Once the averages for each component are calculated, use the questions on pages 160 through 163 to enhance your assessment.

As I reflect on my leadership over the past twelve months, I can make the following assessment of my own leadership behavior:

	Do not do well	Do somewhat well	Do well
Providing Direction			
1. I articulate my organization's vision and mission to others.	1	2	3
2. I foster the fulfillment of a common vision.	1	2	3
3. I clarify roles and responsibilities.	1	2	3
4. I define priorities for our organization.	1	2	3
5. I make planning strategically a high priority.	1	2	3

Total Score of items circled, divided by 5. The resulting number is your average score for this area.

	Do not do well	Do somewhat well	Do well
Leading Courageously			
1. I take a stand for my values.	1	2	3
2. I understand the ethical responsibility that comes with leadership and act accordingly.	1	2	3
3. I deal with issues and concerns promptly.	1	2	3
4. I challenge others to make right choices.	1	2	3
5. I make tough decisions regardless of people's approval or rejection.	1	2	3

Total Score of items circled divided by 5. The resulting number is your average score for this area.

	Do not do well	Do somewhat well	Do well
Fostering Teamwork			
1. I prefer to work on tasks with a team versus individually.	1	2	3
2. I regularly build team spirit and morale and get results.	1	2	3
3. I encourage interaction and collaboration among team members.	1	2	3
4. I lead the celebration of team accomplishments.	1	2	3
5. To garner diverse perspectives, I solicit input from my team members.	1	2	3

Total Score of items circled divided by 5. The resulting number is your average score for this area.

	Do not do well	Do somewhat well	Do well
Championing Change			
1. I recognize the value of leading change.	1	2	3
2. I actively involve others in the change process.	1	2	3
3. I motivate others to embrace change.	1	2	3
4. I assess readiness and resistance to change.	1	2	3
5. I provide the energy that propels people along the change process, no matter how great the difficulties.	1	2	3

Total Score of items circled divided by 5. The resulting number is your average score for this area.

	Do not do well	Do somewhat well	Do well
Coaching and Developing People			
1. I identify and seek to tap people's potential.	1	2	3
2. I consider and offer developmental challenges.	1	2	3
3. I develop leaders at all levels of our organization.	1	2	3
4. I find ways to support and encourage others.	1	2	3
5. I invest in people development in my organization.	1	2	3

Total Score of items circled divided by 5. The resulting number is your average score for this area.

Motivating Others

1.	I inspire and provoke others to excel.	1	2	3
2.	I trust in people's competence.	1	2	3
3.	I establish high performance standards.	1	2	3
4.	I lead by setting a positive example that inspires others.	1	2	3
5.	I reward performance and provide constructive feedback.	1	2	3

Total Score of items circled divided by 5. The resulting number is your average score for this area.

Building Relationships

1.	I initiate relationships with others	1	2	3
2.	I work effectively with others who are different from me.	1	2	3
3.	I prioritize successful resolution of conflict with others.	1	2	3
4.	I leverage networks of people to resource and strengthen my tasks.	1	2	3
5.	I keep others informed about what I'm doing if it affects them.	1	2	3

Total Score of items circled divided by 5. The resulting number is your average score for this area.

Acting with Integrity

1.	I understand that leading begins with leading from the heart (with compassion, sensitivity, and integrity).	1	2	3
2.	I value the heart, character, and integrity of myself and others.	1	2	3
3.	I follow through on the promises and commitments that I make.	1	2	3
4.	I am open to making significant changes in my behavior when necessary.	1	2	3
5.	I am able to exert self-discipline when needed.	1	2	3

Total Score of items circled divided by 5. The resulting number is your average score for this area.

Scoring the Leadership Self-Assessment

Add the circled responses within each section and divide the total by 5. The result is your average score for each leadership component.

Using the Leadership Self Assessment

The results of your assessment are to help you think about how to address the varied skills and attributes of effective leadership. This assessment is also intended to help you think about how important these attributes and skills are to you and whether or not you wish to grow and develop them more.

The following questions are intended to assist you in analyzing your responses.

PROVIDING DIRECTION

Which **Providing Direction** skills/attributes do you do well?

     1._____ 2. _____

     3._____ 4. _____

Which **Providing Direction** skills/attributes do you not do well?

     1._____ 2. _____

     3._____ 4. _____

Which **Providing Direction** skills/attributes do you have the most interest in developing?

     1._____ 2. _____

LEADING COURAGEOUSLY

Which **Leading Courageously** skills/attributes do you do well?

     1._____ 2. _____

     3._____ 4. _____

Which **Leading Courageously** skills/attributes do you not do well?

1. _____ 2. _____

3. _____ 4. _____

Which **Leading Courageously** skills/attributes do you have the most interest in developing?

1. _____ 2. _____

FOSTERING TEAMWORK

Which **Fostering Teamwork** skills/attributes do you do well?

1. _____ 2. _____

3. _____ 4. _____

Which **Fostering Teamwork** skills/attributes do you not do well?

1. _____ 2. _____

3. _____ 4. _____

Which **Fostering Teamwork** skills/attributes do you have the most interest in developing?

1. _____ 2. _____

CHAMPIONING CHANGE

Which **Championing Change** skills/attributes do you do well?

1. _____ 2. _____

3. _____ 4. _____

Which **Championing Change** skills/attributes do you not do well?

1. _____ 2. _____

3. _____ 4. _____

Which **Championing Change** skills/attributes do you have the most interest in developing?

1. _____ 2. _____

COACHING AND DEVELOPING PEOPLE

Which **Coaching and Developing People** skills/attributes do you do well?

1. _____ 2. _____
3. _____ 4. _____

Which **Coaching and Developing People** skills/attributes do you not do well?

1. _____ 2. _____
3. _____ 4. _____

Which **Coaching and Developing People** skills/attributes do you have the most interest in developing?

1. _____ 2. _____

MOTIVATING OTHERS

Which **Motivating Others** skills/attributes do you do well?

1. _____ 2. _____
3. _____ 4. _____

Which **Motivating Others** skills/attributes do you not do well?

1. _____ 2. _____
3. _____ 4. _____

Which **Motivating Others** skills/attributes do you have the most interest in developing?

1. _____ 2. _____

BUILDING RELATIONSHIPS

Which **Building Relationships** skills/attributes do you do well?

    1. _____ 2. _____

    3. _____ 4. _____

Which **Building Relationships** skills/attributes do you not do well?

    1. _____ 2. _____

    3. _____ 4. _____

Which **Building Relationships** skills/attributes do you have the most interest in developing?

    1. _____ 2. _____

ACTING WITH INTEGRITY

Which **Acting with Integrity** skills/attributes do you do well?

    1. _____ 2. _____

    3. _____ 4. _____

Which **Acting with Integrity** skills/attributes do you not do well?

    1. _____ 2. _____

    3. _____ 4. _____

Which **Acting with Integrity** skills/attributes do you have the most interest in developing?

    1. _____ 2. _____

Note: This is only a preliminary self-assessment intended to promote personal reflection and further evaluation. It is not a statistically validated assessment.

Reprinted with Permission: Hill Consulting Group
1518 Elderberry Rd., Suffolk, Virginia 23435
757.686.5339
www.hillconsultinggroup.com

A Study in Leadership: Women Do It Better Than Men

Zenger Folkman

Which gender supplies better leaders for organizations? Based on research conducted by Zenger Folkman, the authority in strengths-based leadership development, the answer is rather clear and quite shocking. As far as the sixteen researched differentiating leadership competencies are concerned, women excelled in a majority of areas.

Below is the research of a sample of 7,280 leaders who had their leadership effectiveness evaluated in 2011. Sixty-four percent of our data set was male (4,651) and 36 percent was female (2,629). The data represents managers and executives who completed our Extraordinary Leader 360 assessment in 2011. Our clients tend to be progressive, successful companies that have a strong belief in leadership development. This is not a global random sample of leaders, but rather a sampling of male and female leaders from high performing companies. Perhaps the differences are more pronounced in this data because the organizations supported the development of their leaders. It is also interesting because 64 percent of the data comes from managers and executives in the United States, and the remainder from countries scattered all over the world. Many of the countries in the data showed the same trends between men and women.

Males tended to have a higher percent of leaders in top management and reports to top management positions.

Position	Male	Female
Top Management, Executive, Senior Team Members	78%	22%
Reports to Top Management, Supervises Middle Managers	67%	32%
Middle Manager	60%	39%
Supervisor, Front Line Manager, Foreman	61%	39%
Individual Contributor	45%	55%
Other	47%	53%

Overall Leadership Effectiveness by Gender by Position (*Percentile Scores)

Position	Male	Female
Top Management, Executive, Senior Team Members	52	61
Reports to Top Management, Supervises Middle Managers	47	53
Middle Manager	47	53
Supervisor, Front Line Manager, Foreman	52	51
Individual Contributor	51	52
Other	50	51

* Percentile scores were calculated by comparing the results of the 7,280 males and females to each other.

Overall Leadership Effectiveness by Gender by Function (Percentile Scores)

Of the fifteen functions listed, females were rated more positively in twelve. Some of the largest gaps were in functions that tended to be male dominated, such as sales, product development, legal, engineering, IT, and research and development. The percentage of women leaders represented in these functions ranged from 13 percent to 33 percent.

Function	Male	Female
Sales	55.9	62.6
Marketing	45.7	52.4
Customer Service	52.4	50.6
Operations	50.4	53.8
HR, Training	48.7	50.6
General Management	49.6	55.0
Finance and Accounting	46.2	50.6
Product Development	42.0	49.0
Legal	54.7	59.4
Engineering	41.1	44.5
Information Technology	42.0	52.1
Research and Development	47.4	52.2
Facilities Management, Maintenance	49.8	37.8
Quality Management	48.5	49.5
Administrative, Clerical	48.8	43.2

Differences in Overall Leadership Effectiveness

On an overall leadership effectiveness index, females were rated more positively than males. The overall leadership effectiveness index is a forty-nine-item index. The forty-nine items were found to be the most differentiating items separating the best versus the worst leaders. The items are associated with sixteen differentiating competencies. The overall index is the average rating from an aggregate of manager, peer, direct report, and other ratings.

	Male	Female	T Value	Sig. (2-tailed)
Overall Leadership Effectiveness (Average of Forty-Nine Leadership Items)	49	53	–6.17	0.00

Differences in Competencies

On twelve of sixteen competencies, females were rated more positively by the total of all respondents—manager, peers, direct reports, and others. On average, 12.7 raters evaluated males, 13.1 raters evaluated females.

The bias of most people is that females would be better at nurturing competencies, such as developing others and relationship building. While this is true, the competencies with the largest differences between males and females were taking initiative, practicing self-development, integrity/honesty, and driving for results.

	Male	Female	t	Sig. (2-tailed)
Takes Initiative	48	56	−11.58	0.00
Practices Self-Development	48	55	−9.45	0.00
Displays High Integrity and Honesty	48	55	−9.28	0.00
Drives for Results	48	54	−8.84	0.00
Develops Others	48	54	−7.94	0.00
Inspires and Motivates Others	49	54	−7.53	0.00
Builds Relationships	49	54	−7.15	0.00
Collaboration and Teamwork	49	53	−6.14	0.00
Establishes Stretch Goals	49	53	−5.41	0.00
Champions Change	49	53	−4.48	0.00
Solves Problems and Analyzes Issues	50	52	−2.53	0.01
Communicates Powerfully and Prolifically	50	52	−2.47	0.01
Connects the Group to the Outside World	50	51	−0.78	0.43
Innovates	50	51	−0.76	0.45
Technical or Professional Expertise	50	51	−0.11	0.91
Develops Strategic Perspective	51	49	2.79	0.01

Males were rated more significantly positively on one competency (Develops Strategic Perspective).

Survey Items

For thirty-six of forty-nine items, females scored significantly more positive. Men scored significantly positive in only two survey items. The rest of the survey items were neutral.

Below is a small sample of some of the items:

	Male	Female	t	Sig. (2-tailed)
22. Follow through on commitments.	47	56	−12.00	0.00
3. Honor commitments and keep promises.	48	56	−11.79	0.00
23. Willingly goes above and beyond.	48	56	−11.66	0.00
13. Improves based on feedback from others.	48	55	−10.89	0.00
41. Has a clear perspective between the over-all picture and the details.	51	49	2.29	0.02
42. Has a perspective beyond the day-to-day.	52	48	5.43	0.00

What does this mean for women in the workplace? Well, the implications of this research are quite profound. Jack Zenger, CEO and co-founder of Zenger Folkman, stated: "It is a well-known fact that women are underrepresented at senior levels of management. Yet the data suggests that by adding more women the overall effectiveness of the leadership team would go up." Organizations go outside to recruit effective leaders when in many cases they may well have internal people who could rise to fill the position that is vacant.

Joe Folkman, president of Zenger Folkman, noted that "while men excel in the technical and strategic arenas, women clearly have the advantage in the extremely important areas of people relationships and communication. They also surpass their male counterparts in driving for results. This we know is counterintuitive to many men."

Resources

Printed Books

Cronin, Lynn. *Damned If She Does, Damned If She Doesn't: Rethinking the Rules of the Game That Keep Women from Succeeding.* Amherst, MA: Prometheus Books, 2010.

Eagly, Alice H., and Linda L. Carli. *Through the Labyrinth: The Truth About How Women Become Leaders* (Center for Public Leadership). Boston, MA: Harvard Business Review Press, 2007.

Feldt, Gloria. *No Excuses: Nine Ways Women Can Change How We Think About Power.* Berkeley, CA: Seal Press, 2012.

Fletcher, Molly. *The Business of Being the Best: Inside the World of Go-Getters and Game Changers.* Hoboken, NJ: John Wiley & Sons, 2011.

Gerzema, John, and Michael D'Antonio. *The Athena Doctrine: How Women (and the Men Who Think Like Them) Will Rule the Future.* Hoboken, NJ: John Wiley & Sons, 2013.

Jones, Tamara Bertrand, LeKita Scott Dawkins, Marguerite McClinton, and Melanie Hayden Glover (Eds.). *Pathways to Higher Education Administration for African American Women.* Sterling, WV: Stylus, 2012.

Marquet, L. David. *Turn the Ship Around! A True Story of Turning Followers into Leaders.* New York, NY: Portfolio, 2013.

Reid, Jan. *Let the People In: The Life and Times of Ann Richards.* Austin, TX: University of Texas Press, 2013.

Rosin, Hanna. *The End of Men and the Rise of Women.* New York, NY: Penguin Group, 2012.

Sandberg, Sheryl. *Lean In: Women, Work, and the Will to Lead*. New York, NY: Alfred A. Knopf, 2013.

Shepherd, Molly D., Jane K. Stimmler, and Peter J. Dean. *Breaking into the Boys' Club: 8 Ways for Women to Get Ahead in Business*. Boulder, CO: M. Evans & Company, 2009.

Soupios, M.A., and Panos Mourdoukoutas. *The Ten Golden Rules of Leadership: Classical Wisdom for Modern Leaders*. New York, NY: AMACOM, 2014.

Warner, Carolyn. *The Last Word, A Treasury of Women's Quotes*. Upper Saddle River, NJ: Prentice Hall, 1992.

White, Kate. *I Shouldn't Be Telling You This*. New York, NY: HarperBusiness, 2012.

Wolf, Alison. *The XX Factor: How the Rise of Working Women Has Created a Far Less Equal World*. New York, NY: Crown, 2013.

Wolf, Jeff. *Seven Disciplines of a Leader*. Hoboken, NJ: John Wiley & Sons, 2014.

Young, Valerie. *The Secret Thoughts of Successful Women: Why Capable People Suffer from the Impostor Syndrome and How to Thrive in Spite of It*. New York, NY: Crown Business, 2011.

Newsletters, Blogs, and Papers

Coaching Tip: The Leadership Blog

www.coachingtip.com/women/

Coach John G. Agno is your own cultural attaché; keeping you abreast of what's effective in leadership. People learn better and are positively motivated when supported by regular coaching.

Center for Creative Leadership

www.ccl.org/Leadership/enewsletter/current.aspx

CCL's *Leading Effectively* e-newsletter delivers practical articles on leadership and management to help you tackle the daily challenges of leading.

Eblin Group

http://eblingroup.com/blog

The Eblin Group is a leadership development and strategy firm that helps executives, senior managers, and emerging leaders develop the presence they need to deliver game-changing results.

Executive Leadership

www.execleadership.com/newsletter.html

Executive Leadership is a monthly subscription newsletter published by Business Management Daily, a division of Capitol Information Group, Inc.

Huffington Post Women's Leadership

www.huffingtonpost.com/news/womens-leadership/

Articles on women's leadership.

Jon Gordon

www.jongordon.com/blog/

Writes about developing positive leaders, organizations, and teams.

Leader Values

www.leader-values.com/

LeaderValues provides students, researchers, and practitioners of leadership with one of the best meeting places on leadership, innovation, organization design, change, coaching, and value systems. Wide collection of free resources on leadership.

Leadership Now

www.leadershipnow.com

Providing articles, features, books, multi-media, and other resources on leadership.

Mark Sanborn

www.marksanborn.com/blog/

Writes on leadership development, customer service, team building, and personal development.

Michael Hyatt

http://michaelhyatt.com/

It is focused on intentional leadership. My mission is to help leaders leverage their influence. As a result, I write on personal development, leadership, productivity, platform, and publishing.

The Center for Association Leadership

www.asaecenter.org/Advocacy/contentASAEOnly.
cfm?ItemNumber=46583

ASAE represents more than 21,000 association executives and industry partners representing more than 9,300 organizations. They offer Sustainable Leadership newsletters.

The Global Citizen Daily

http://globalcitizendaily.com/

Part of People to People Ambassador Programs. Provides an engaging and diverse forum for discussion and ideas to support People to People Ambassador Program's mission of global understanding through student travel.

The Lead Change Group

http://leadchangegroup.com/blog/

Non-profit dedicated to instigating a leadership revolution.

The Skimm

www.theskimm.com/

Started by two former NBC producers, the Skimm is the daily e-mail newsletter that gives you everything you need to start your day. We do the reading for you—across subject lines and party lines—and break it down with fresh editorial content.

ToGetHerThere: Girls' Insights on Leadership

http://marketing.gfkamerica.com/Roper_Report_Girls_Scouts_ToGetHerThere.pdf

Report for Girls Scouts on young girls' thoughts on leadership.

Organizations

AASA: The School Superintendents Association

http://aasa.org/LeadershipDevelopment.aspx

Leadership Development department was established to address the leadership needs of school leaders.

American Business Women's Association

www.abwa.org

The mission of the American Business Women's Association is to bring together business women of diverse occupations and to provide opportunities for them to help themselves and others grow personally and professionally through leadership, education, networking support, and national recognition.

Athena International

www.athenainternational.org

Founded in 1982 by Martha Mayhood Mertz, ATHENA International is a non-profit organization that seeks to support, develop, and honor women leaders through programs that we administer in partnership with "host organizations" from local communities. These programs inspire women to reach their full potential and strive to create balance in leadership worldwide.

Catalyst

www.catalyst.org

Catalyst is the leading nonprofit organization with a mission to expand opportunities for women and business.

DOLS

http://thedols.net/

An informal professional organization for women who work in the business of education. Founded in the early 1990s, it serves as a networking and support group for women who share both a career in and a passion for improving education.

Center for Creative Leadership

www.ccl.org/Leadership/index.aspx

CCL® is a top-ranked, global provider of leadership development. By leveraging the power of leadership to drive results that matter most to clients, CCL transforms individual leaders, teams, organizations, and society.

Elevate (formerly 85 Broads)

www.ellevatenetwork.com/

We believe the research is clear that companies and the economy perform better when they fully engage women. We believe women are still an under-tapped resource in the business world and in society at large—and that it's time to change that. We believe that networking and lifelong learning are keys to business success. And we believe that by providing these capabilities, by working with companies and investors to help them see the opportunity, and by truly investing in women, we can be an active and positive part of that change. Elevate is a global professional women's network dedicated to these beliefs and to the economic engagement of women worldwide.

Girls Innovate!

http://girlsinnovate.org/

Girls Innovate! brings women and girls together to gain leadership in creating learning opportunities for the community. These learning opportunities revolve around bridging the disconnect between what is possible and required for extraordinary leadership in the modern world and the tools given at a young age to nurture that potential.

Girls Thinking Global

www.girlsthinkingglobal.org

Girls Thinking Global is creating a global network of organizations committed to educating and empowering girls and women by creating a collaborative space for best practices, sharing resources, recognizing and highlighting success stories, and leading the global movement for girls' empowerment and education.

Hill Consulting Group

www.hillconsultinggroup

Hill Consulting Group provides leadership consulting to non-profits and emerging leaders.

Institute for Women's Leadership

http://womensleadership.com

The Institute for Women's Leadership innovates in the area of women's leadership by focusing on gender partnership in addition to growing and developing women.

International Leadership Association

www.ila-net.org

The International Leadership Association (ILA) is the global network for all those who practice, study, and teach leadership. The ILA promotes a deeper understanding of leadership knowledge and practices for the greater good of individuals and communities worldwide.

ISTE Making IT Happen

www.iste.org/lead/awards/making-it-happen-award

The Making IT Happen award honors outstanding educators and leaders who demonstrate extraordinary commitment, leadership, courage, and persistence in improving digital learning opportunities for students. Since its inception in 1995, more than 500 educators from around the world have received the award.

Live Your Dream.org

www.liveyourdream.org/

A community that connects people online to do volunteer work offline that helps women and girls to live their dreams. When you join the Live Your Dream community, you join a group of like-minded individuals who dream of making the world a better place for women and girls.

National Association of Professional Women

www.napw.com/

NAPW's mission is to provide an exclusive, highly advanced networking forum to successful women executives, professionals, and entrepreneurs, where they can aspire, connect, and achieve. Through innovative resources, unique tools, and progressive benefits, professional women interact, exchange ideas, advance their knowledge, and empower each other.

National Girls Collaborative Project

www.ngcproject.org/

The vision of the NGCP is to bring together organizations throughout the United States that are committed to informing and encouraging girls to pursue careers in science, technology, engineering, and mathematics (STEM).

Network of Executive Women

www.newonline.org/

The Network of Executive Women inspires leaders, transforms organizations, and builds business through learning, best practices, research, leadership development, and more than 100 events each year.

Strong Women Strong Girls

http://swsg.org/

SWSG fosters leadership skills, a sense of female community, and a commitment to service among three generations: elementary school girls, undergraduate women, and professional women. The program spans the East Coast, serving women and girls in Boston, Massachusetts, and Pittsburgh, Pennsylvania.

The Bridgespan Group

www.bridgespan.org/

Collaborates with social sector leaders to help scale impact, build leadership, advance philanthropic effectiveness, and accelerate learning.

WIT (Women in Technology)

www.womenintechnology.org/

The premier professional association for women in the technology industry.

Women's Leadership Coaching

http://womensleadershipcoaching.com/

Women's Leadership Coaching, Inc., is dedicated to helping emerging women leaders advance into management and leadership positions.

WOMEN Unlimited Inc.

www.women-unlimited.com/home/

WOMEN Unlimited, Inc., is a world-renowned organization focusing on developing women leaders in major corporations.

Zenger/Folkman

www.zengerfolkman.com

The foremost authority in strengths-based leadership development, Zenger/Folkman helps organizations develop extraordinary leaders who achieve positive business results.

Education

Babson College–Center for Women's Entrepreneurial Leadership

www.babson.edu/Academics/centers/cwel/Pages/home.aspx

The Center for Women's Entrepreneurial Leadership (CWEL) at Babson College educates, inspires, and empowers women entrepreneurial leaders to reach their full potential to create economic and social value for themselves, their organizations, and society.

Barnard College Young Women's Leadership Institute

http://barnard.edu/precollege/summer-in-the-city/programs/ywli

The Young Women's Leadership Institute takes the complex relationship between gender and leadership as its focus. Students will develop action-oriented leadership plans during the session.

Bryn Mawr Nonprofit Executive Leadership Institute

www.brynmawr.edu/neli/

The Nonprofit Executive Leadership Institute offers nonprofit executives and ascending leaders the tools and time they need to examine and refine their leadership and management skills, while learning new theories and core competencies about nonprofit management.

Dale Carnegie Training

www.dalecarnegie.com/events/leadership-management-training-programs/

Leadership training for managers.

Dave Ramsey Entre Leadership

www.daveramsey.com/entreleadership/events/?ectid=gaw.entre-events1&gclid=CL6jkozkmcICFbBm7AodohAAmQ

Practical wisdom on winning in business.

Degree Directory

http://degreedirectory.org/

World's largest education and career help desk.

Eisenhower Fellowships Women's Leadership Program

https://efworld.org/our-programs/2015-women-leadership-program

The Women's Leadership Program (WLP) will promote women in leadership roles across all industries and sectors by providing strong networking and professional development opportunities. WLP participants will make a commitment to mentor and empower women in their countries and regions to advance the next generation of emerging women leaders.

Harvard Advanced Leadership Initiative

http://advancedleadership.harvard.edu/

The Advanced Leadership Initiative is designed to enhance and leverage the skills of highly accomplished, experienced leaders who want to apply their talents to solve significant social problems, including those affecting health and welfare, children and the environment, and focus on community and public service in the next phase of their careers.

Harvard Kennedy School Center for Public Leadership

www.centerforpublicleadership.org/

The Center for Public Leadership (CPL) at Harvard Kennedy School is dedicated to excellence in leadership education and research. It is equally committed to bridging the gap between leadership theory and practice.

Harvard Business School Women's Leadership Forum

www.exed.hbs.edu/programs/wlf/Pages/default.aspx

This intensive program is designed to advance your management and leadership skills.

Mount Holyoke Weissman Center for Leadership

https://www.mtholyoke.edu/wcl

The Weissman Center for Leadership supports students who aspire to become inspiring and effective agents of change in their chosen professions and communities.

Mount St. Mary's College

www.msmc.la.edu/student-life/leadership/office-of-womens-leadership.asp

Developing confident and conscientious leaders dedicated to making a difference. A leadership experience for women.

Network of Executive Women Leadership Summits

www.newonline.org/

The Network of Executive Women is a learning and leadership community with more than 8,000 members, and one of the largest event producers in the retail and consumer goods industry. We host two national conferences, webinars, and more than 100 regional learning events and mixers each year. These learning and networking events attract more than 20,000 emerging, mid-level, and senior leaders annually from Toronto to Tampa, Boston to L.A.

Omega

www.eomega.org/donate/major-projects/programs-and-conferences-at-omega

Each year Omega welcomes more than 23,000 people to workshops, conferences, and retreats at its Rhinebeck, New York, campus, as well as urban centers and exceptional locations around the world. Our more than 350 programs, taught by more than 500 leading teachers, are grouped into six learning paths: Body, Mind & Spirit; Health & Healing; Creative Expression; Relationships & Family; Leadership & Work; and Sustainable Living.

SHAMBAUGH Women's Leadership

www.shambaughleadership.com/our_programs/womens_leadership/

Developed to further the advancement of women leaders, SHAMBAUGH offers the following services and programs: customized in-house programs and solutions; Women in Leadership and Learning (WILL) Program; Women in Professional Services Leadership Program; Sponsorship Programs; Engaging Men; and Learning Circles.

Simmons Leadership Conferences

www.simmons.edu/leadership/

Considered to be the premier women's leadership conference in the world, the Simmons Leadership Conference attracts more than 3,000 middle- and senior-level women from companies and organizations across the country and around the globe.

Smith College Phoebe Reese Lewis Leadership Program

www.smith.edu/leadership/

The Phoebe Reese Lewis Leadership Program is a highly acclaimed, innovative program that provides undergraduate women with hands-on learning experiences and training in practical leadership skills.

Wellesley College Leadership Development Program

www.wellesley.edu/hr/empdev/leadership

Over the past two years, the College has successfully offered a Leadership Development Program for emerging leaders. While there remains a strong desire to continue this program in the future, for the 2014–2015 academic year, the leadership development program will focus on supporting the department heads at Wellesley College.

Wharton University of Pennsylvania Women's Executive Leadership: Business Strategies for Success

http://executiveeducation.wharton.upenn.edu/for-individuals/ all-programs/womens-executive-leadership-business-strategies- for-success?utm_campaign=wexl15&utm_medium=cpc&utm_

source=google&utm_content=General&utm_
term=leadership%20programs%20for%20
women&mkwid=sDWIq68CD_dc&pcrid=61857655153&p
mt=e&pkw=leadership%20programs%20for%20women

The week-long Women's Executive Leadership: Business Strategies for Success program is designed specifically for today's female executives and those who aspire to leadership roles. It covers new ground, as revealed by the latest Wharton faculty research in work motivation and engagement, career development, internal coaching, emotional intelligence, and women in leadership roles.

Women's College Coalition

http://womenscolleges.org

The Women's College Coalition (WCC) is the association and voice for women's colleges in the United States and Canada.

Women's Empowerment Network (WEN) Conference

The Women's Empowerment Network is a three-day leadership conference that features daily keynote speakers, general session trainings, panel discussions, and break-out sessions. WEN's progressive group of panelists consists of a diverse group of nationally recognized leaders with proven track records in finance, business, and personal development.

ABOUT THE EDITORS

Kathleen Hurley formerly served as executive vice president, Education Alliances, for the Pearson Foundation, a position she held since 2009. She is a forty-year veteran of the education industry, based in Washington, D.C., where she works closely with education associations and serves on several industry and education advisory boards, including the Partnership for 21st Century Skills, the National Coalition for Technology in Education and Training, the Software and Information Industry Association, the Association of Educational Publishers, and the Consortium for School Networking. Kathy is the recipient of many awards, including the prestigious SIIA Ed Tech Impact Award, the first ever Outstanding Private Sector Achievement Award from the Consortium for School Networking, a citation from State of Massachusetts Representative Cory Atkins for her mentoring of leaders in education, and special recognition of her twenty-five years of service to the Software and Information Industry Association. In 2003, she was inducted into the Association of Educational Publishers Hall of Fame for her service to the educational publishing industry. Kathy is a fellow from the Harvard Advance Leadership Initiative, which is designed to prepare experienced leaders to take on new challenges in the social sector, where they potentially can make an even greater societal impact than they did in their careers. In 2014, Kathy co-founded an international non-profit called Girls Thinking Global to empower girls and young women by creating a collaborative space for best practices, the sharing of resources, and the recognition of success stories. A portion of the proceeds from this book will be donated to Girls Thinking Global. Kathy is a contributing author to *The Experts' Guide to the K-12 School Market* (SIIA, 2008).

Priscilla Shumway is president and principal of New Learning Presentation Systems, a consulting company specializing in learning and development. As a senior national trainer for The Bob Pike Group since 1996, she has trained thousands of people nationally and internationally. An award-winning presenter, Priscilla has worked in a number of industries and has had many opportunities to observe the challenges and opportunities facing women in business. Priscilla is a contributing author to *The Experts' Guide to the K-12 School Market* (SIIA, 2008), *S.C.O.R.E III*, *SCORE for Technical Trainers*, and *SCORE for One on One Training*, 2013 and 2014.

INDEX